11th International Conference on Body Area Networks (BODYNETS 2016)

AA005633

Turin, Italy
15 - 16 December 2016

ISBN: 978-1-5108-4179-6

Printed from e-media with permission by:

Curran Associates, Inc.
57 Morehouse Lane
Red Hook, NY 12571

Some format issues inherent in the e-media version may also appear in this print version.

Copyright© (2016) by The Institute for Computer Sciences,
Social Informatics and Telecommunications Engineering (ICST)
All rights reserved.

Printed by Curran Associates, Inc. (2017)

For permission requests, please contact European Alliance for Innovation (EAI)
at the address below.

European Alliance for Innovation (EAI)
c/o Volha Shaparava , Dr
Publications
Via alla Cascata 56/D - 38123 Povo,
Trento - Italy

publications@eai.eu

Additional copies of this publication are available from:

Curran Associates, Inc.
57 Morehouse Lane
Red Hook, NY 12571 USA
Phone: 845-758-0400
Fax: 845-758-2633
Email: curran@proceedings.com
Web: www.proceedings.com

TABLE OF CONTENTS

Congestion Control for Biological Nanoscale Cyber-Physical Systems

Invited Paper

Luca Felicetti, Mauro Femminella and Gianluca Reali
Dept. of Engineering, University of Perugia, CNIT RU
via G. Duranti 93, 06125 Perugia, Italy
ing.luca.felicetti@gmail.com, mauro.femminella@unipg.it, gianluca.reali@unipg.it

ABSTRACT

Cyberphysical systems (CPSs) are a new class of engineered systems that offer close interaction between cyber and physical components, by integrating three main components: communications, control, and computing. When these systems are brought to the nanoscale, some design and implementation issues arise. A further level of complexity is due to the use of biological components in a CPS, such as engineered cells, which may play the role of sensors, actuators, or even controller. In this paper we study the effectiveness of control solutions implemented through the usage of molecular communications in a biological nanoscale cyber-physical system (BioNanoCPS), where a biological nanomachine plays the role of actuator, that releases drug molecules, and another has the role of both sensor and controller. The goal of the proposal is to control the release rate, so that target cells can receive the desired amount of drug in a given time, by limiting potential side effects. Basically, we aim to limit congestion, which can arise when large amounts of molecules are released towards a target. To this aim, we propose a simple congestion detection scheme, and compare different rate control algorithms used to throttle the molecules release rate at the transmitter upon the reception of a feedback signal sent by the receiver. We validate the proposed techniques against delivery efficiency and delivery time of molecules by means of an extensive simulation campaign.

Categories and Subject Descriptors

I.6.3 [**Simulation and Modeling**]: Model Validation and Analysis

Keywords

Congestion detection, congestion control, feedback-based rate control, diffusion-based molecular communications.

1. INTRODUCTION

Cyber-physical systems (CPSs) are a new class of engineered systems that include close interaction between cyber and physical components, by integrating three main components: communications, control, and computing [1]. CPSs are expected to play a major role in the research, design, and implementation of future technologies. When these systems involve devices at the nanoscale, some design and implementation issues arise. A further level of complexity is brought by the use of biological components in a CPS, such as engineered cells, which may play the role of sensors, actuators, or even controllers in living bodies. Such systems are emerging as natural exploitation of the field of molecular communications [2–4], in which artificial nanomachines and/or engineered cells communicate by means of the exchange of molecules, by mimicking the natural cell signaling. Molecular communication is a novel paradigm of communication happening between biological nanomachines (specifically bio-nanomachines) over short ranges, within aqueous environments. In this model, a transmitter nanomachine emits molecules, which act as communication signals, and are received by receiver nanomachines. The reception process usually consists of a chemical reaction between signal molecules (ligand) and compliant receptors present on the receiver surface. Given the intrinsic bio-compatibility of these systems, they could allow implementing closed loop systems (which make them CPS), which offer the possibility to tightly monitor and control biological processes. These features are expected to give birth to really disruptive applications in the fields of medicine, food production, and so on.

In this paper, we propose to use a biological, nanoscale cyber-physical system (BioNanoCPS) to control the process of drug delivery/tissue engineering [5–7] directly *in situ*. We assume that a number of biological nanomachines (bio-nanomachines) play the role of actuators, that are able to release drug molecules, and another bio-nanomachine has the role of both sensor and controller. When the controller detects the proximity of a given target (e.g. a tumor), it triggers the release of drugs from actuators through a command sent by using molecular communications. However, since the distance between actuators and and target is not known in advance, the release rate has to be adjusted in order to avoid wasting of molecules. Thus, the first tasks of the controller is to monitor the drug absorption rate (sensor function), by absorbing the emitted drugs as if it were the receiver. The second one is to control the drug release rate. The goals of this second function are both to allow target cells receiving the desired amount of drug in a given time and, at the same time, to avoid releasing an amount of drugs that cannot be absorbed by the target, which could likely produce undesired side effects and drug waste. Even the messages used to control the release rate are sent by using molecular communications.

In this paper, we focus on the effectiveness of the control solutions implemented through the usage of molecular communications in a BioNanoCPS. In more detail, we aim to limit the phenomenon of congestion due to accumulation of drug molecules, already in-

Permission to make digital or hard copies of all or part of this work for personal or classroom use is granted without fee provided that copies are not made or distributed for profit or commercial advantage and that copies bear this notice and the full citation on the first page. To copy otherwise, to republish, to post on servers or to redistribute to lists, requires prior specific permission and/or a fee.
BODYNETS 2016, December 15-16, Turin, Italy

troduced in [8] and further elaborated in [9], which can arise when a large amount of molecules are released towards a target. To this aim, we propose both a simple congestion detection scheme (first contribution), which can be implemented in a bio-nanomachine, and four different rate control algorithms (second contribution), all based on the negative feedback concept [10]. We compare these different rate control algorithms used to throttle the molecules release rate at the transmitter upon the reception of a feedback signal sent by the receiver. Some of them inspire to control mechanisms implemented in the TCP protocol, mentioned in [11]. Without any loss of generality, we use the communication protocols already defined in [11], which allows focusing only on the effectiveness of control algorithms. We have assessed the performance of the proposed techniques against delivery efficiency and delivery time of molecules. Performance have been estimated by means of an extensive simulation campaign, implemented by using the BiNS2 simulator [12, 13].

The paper is organized as follows. In section 2, we illustrate the related work in the field. Section 3 presents the system model. In section 4, we illustrate our congestion detection scheme. Section 5 shows our proposal for control actions to be implemented in the TX node, and the relevant decision logic to be implemented in the RX node. The results of the simulation campaign, used to validate the proposed mechanisms and to analyze the trade-off between throughput and communication efficiency, are presented in Section 6. Finally, we draw our conclusions in Section 7.

2. BACKGROUND AND RELATED WORKS

Major efforts in the area of molecular communications are focused on the physical layer issues of various types of molecular communication media. Information capacity and physical features (e.g., delay, signal attenuation, amplification, and energy requirements) of molecular communications are typically studied by using random walk models [14–16], random walk models with drift [17, 18], diffusion-reaction-based models [19, 20], active transport models [14, 21], collision-based models [22], and diffusion-based models [23–27], which is used in this paper.

Most of results have been obtained by assuming that a sufficiently high density of receptors are deployed on the receiver surface, so that all the available molecules coming in contact with the receiver surface come also in contact with the receptors and are absorbed (absorbing receiver assumption, [28]). A more refined model, which makes use of a finite number of receptors with a specific size, is presented in [29]. Although this model is more realistic, it assumes that each time a ligand molecule comes in contact with a compliant receptor, it is immediately absorbed (absorbing receptor assumption). Hence, the stochastic nature of ligand-receptor binding is not considered. Differently, a finite bonding duration is analyzed in [30], and further investigated in [31], which takes also into account the trafficking time [32], which can be essentially regarded as the molecule reception time. Specifically, it is defined as the time duration since the formation of the bond between a ligand molecule and a compliant receptor to the time instant in which, after the complex ligand-receptor has been internalized, the receiver is able to expose another free receptor on its surface. A reversible receiver model, which does not explicitly model receptors but rather their macroscopic behavior by means of a reaction constant, is presented in [33].

Finally, the papers [8, 9] analyze the congestion phenomenon in molecular communications, and provide theoretical models to predict it when a continuous stream of drugs are released towards a target. In this work, starting from these results, we develop a detection scheme able to early identify congestion conditions when a flow of molecules is released towards a target with variable rate and unknown release distance.

3. THE SYSTEM MODEL

The considered communication scenario consists of two fixed bio-nanomachines at a distance d: one acting as receiver and control node (RX), and the other as transmitting node (TX). Both TX and RX are assumed to be spherical nanomachines, with radius r_{TX} and r_{RX}, respectively. This is a simplified model, since it does not explicitly consider the effect of the target (e.g. tumor cells) on the sensing process carried out by the RX. However, an estimation of the presence of additional receivers (i.e. target cells) can be obtained by using the results presented in [34]. The communication happens by using two different types of molecules, which propagate by diffusion, modeled as Brownian motion [35]. The molecules transmitted by the TX node, and representing the signal to be delivered, are labeled as S, and those transmitted by the control node RX, to encode the control messages, are labeled R. The Brownian motion is characterized by the diffusion coefficient, given by $D = \frac{K_b T}{6\pi\eta r_c}$. K_b is the Boltzmann constant, T denotes the temperature expressed in Kelvins, η is the viscosity of the medium, and r_c is the radius of the considered molecules, i.e. $r_{c,rx}$ for type R molecules and $r_{c,tx}$ for type S molecules.

When a ligand molecule hits a free, compliant receptor with radius r_r, a bond is established. The bonding duration (or trafficking time) is modeled with an exponential random variable [32], with average value T_{traff}. A number R of receptors (R_{TX} on the TX for R molecules and R_{RX} on the RX for S ones) is distributed over the surface of each nanomachine.

Without any loss of generality, we use the protocol defined in [11], where the control signals are encoded in different patterns of bursts, with size B_{RX} of R molecules, by using the OOK modulation, and symbol duration T_S. The defined control messages are: START, encoded as 110, CONTROL, encoded as 10, and STOP, encoded as 111. For decoding the control bursts, the TX node adopts a threshold mechanism, with value ζ_S. Motivations about the design choices of the control protocol can be found in [11], whereas values used for carrying out simulations are reported in Table 1. We stress that any other connection-oriented protocol can be used to the goal of this paper, and that the choice of adopting the one presented in [11] as underlying communication framework is due to the fact that, to the best of the authors' knowledge, it is the only one currently proposed in literature.

In realistic condition, since the distance between RX and TX is unknown, the TX "probes" the channel with an increasing rate of S molecules in order to find the most suitable carrier release rate. This process is controlled by the RX, which sends throttling (CONTROL) messages when congestion is detected. Specifically, the TX nodes starts with a burst $B_{TX} = B_{0,TX}$ of S molecules and continues increasing the transmission burst B_{TX} by $B_{0,TX}$ S molecules each time interval Δt. Thus, the TX increases the release rate with a linear slope, until it receives either a STOP or a CONTROL message from the controller RX. Different reaction strategies to CONTROL messages at the TX node are presented in section 5.

At the RX site, connections are successfully established when ζ_{RTT} S molecules are received by a suitable time and, at the same time, also the round time time (RTT) of the communication path is estimated. The instant when the RTT is estimated and the connection is set up is denoted $t_{\zeta_{RTT}}$. The estimation of the RTT is equal to the time elapsed since the transmission of the final burst of the START signal from the RX to the time instant $t_{\zeta_{RTT}}$. Since $t_{\zeta_{RTT}}$, the RX starts monitoring the total amount of received S molecules

$N(t)$, updated with a period equal to T_w. The reception rate of the S molecules is denoted $\lambda_a(t)$, thus $N(t) = \int_0^t \lambda_a(t)$. However, when a molecule hits a compliant receptor already busy in another bond, it cannot establish a bond with it and we say that it is "rejected", as in an already full queuing system [8,9]. The rate of such rejections is denoted $\lambda_r(t)$. When a rejection happens, the ligand molecule is bounced back as a result of a partially inelastic collision. In [33], an alternative model to re-position a detached molecule that breaks a bond is presented.

The transmission is ended by the RX by sending a STOP message when either it estimates that the target amount of absorbed molecules ζ_{stop} has been already reached (i.e. $N(t) \geq \zeta_{stop}$) or it will be reached in the next few seconds by issuing a STOP message (i.e. $N_{stop}(t) \geq \zeta_{stop}$).

4. DETECTION OF CONGESTION

Intuitively, the RX can estimate that congestion conditions around the target are arising if the estimated absorption rate deviates from its expected behavior. Since the law used by the TX to transmit the signal is known by the RX (i.e. a linear increase by $B_{0,TX}$ of the burst size B_{TX} each Δt seconds), it is also known the expected assimilation profile at the RX, since the concentration of molecules around the RX linearly depends on the number transmitted ones. In addition, the authors of [29] have proved that upon transmitting a burst of Q molecules, the number of received molecules for large times is well approximated by

$$A_{RX}(R_{RX}, d, Q) = \frac{r_{RX}}{d} \frac{R_{RX} r_{r,rx}}{R_{RX} r_{r,rx} + \pi r_{RX}}. \quad (1)$$

We stress that any other transmission law would work. The only requirement is that the receiver has to be aware of it. Since molecular communications are characterized by high latency and high response times, we keep the linear increase, as in [11], to cope with slow reaction rates. The idea is to estimate the assimilation curve at run-time, and to detect congestion when a significant decrease with respect to the expected value is observed. Such a decrease has to be large enough to avoid taking natural fluctuations as congestion due to noise sources [30,36], and enough small to be early in detecting the phenomenon. In addition, since in general the estimation of a rate value is often noisy, we prefer to take our decisions on the overall number of assimilations (i.e. the overall stimulus received, which is the integral of the rate profile), which we will expect quadratic. Thus, the number of assimilations can be expressed as

$$N(t) = N_0 + a(t - t_0)^2, \quad (2)$$

where N_0 and t_0 are the initial offset values in terms of number of S molecules and relevant time. In our algorithm, initially $N_0 = \zeta_{RTT}$ and $t_0 = t_{\zeta_{RTT}}$. What is missing is the estimate of the parameter a of the assimilation curve, which may depend on different factors, such as trafficking time, number of receptors, distance between TX and RX, unexpected attenuation phenomena, or presence of noise sources. We propose a least squares estimate of a, that in the considered case turns out to be quite simple:

$$a = \frac{\sum_{j=1}^{N_s} (N(t) - N_0)\left(t - t_{\zeta_{RTT}}\right)^2}{\sum_{j=1}^{N_s} \left(t - t_{\zeta_{RTT}}\right)^4}, \quad (3)$$

where the number of the samples is equal to $N_s = \lfloor pRTT/T_w \rfloor$, and p is the fraction of the initial RTT duration used to carry out the estimation. We selected a variable duration of the estimation time, since it is more adaptive to the working context. In particular, binding it to the RTT value allows taking into account the distance among the TX and RX. We have verified numerically that, up to RTT seconds after RTT estimation, congestion has still not occurred. The overall machinery, including all operations carried out by the RX, is illustrated in Fig. 1. As shown in the figure, the RX takes a number of samples of a, to implement (3), and only when a is estimated it starts detecting possible congestion conditions.

As for this last point, we make use of two different functions, $N_{exp}(t)$ and $N_{stop}(t)$, to determine congestion and stop conditions. The first is equal to

$$N_{exp}(t) = N_0 + \beta a(t - t_0)^2, \quad (4)$$

where β is the tolerance coefficient used to discriminate between congestion condition and random fluctuation of absorbed molecules, whereas the offset values depend on the selected throttling rate algorithm. They are function of the values N_c, t_{prev}, and t_c estimated as shown in Fig. 1, and will be illustrated in the next section. As for the stop condition, the relevant function is equal to

$$N_{stop}(t) = N(t) + 2a(t - t_0)((\|STOP\| - 1)T_S + RTT), \quad (5)$$

which represents a linearization of the estimated curve (2) at time t, in order to take into account possible overload conditions occurring during the transmission of the STOP signal. The quantity $\|\cdot\|$ represents the number of symbols of a given sequence. The interval $t_{lock} - t$ represents the time needed to transmit the CONTROL message. During this interval all control operations at RX are frozen, since it cannot transmit anything until the control sequence has ended.

We remark that the law used here has the objective of an *early* congestion detection, differently from the one sketched in [11], which is less robust and designed to detect only heavy overload conditions. A further remark is that, even choosing an optimal rate in advance and keeping it constant for all the transmission time is tricky, since the actual distance among nanomachines is difficult to estimate precisely. Also the number of receptors is hardly known in advance, especially in bio-hybrid nodes [2], since it may be increased or decreased at runtime depending on the internal processing of the received stimulus, a process known as upregulation and downregulation, respectively [37]. Finally, the presence of inhibitory molecules in the surrounding environment [38] or of any other absorbing nodes [39] would alter the expected number of assimilated particles as well. Instead, the proposed adaptive approach learns the assimilation curve blindly with respect to all those parameters, thus largely simplifying the system design.

5. CONGESTION CONTROL SCHEME

In this section, we review four rate control algorithms, which can be triggered by the reception of a negative feedback (CONTROL message) sent by the RX. For each of them, we illustrate the new value of the rate upon feedback decoding, and also all the operation carried out at the RX in order to re-align with the new, expected assimilation profile.

5.1 Algorithm "Restart"

This algorithm is inspired by TCP Tahoe. However, since the slow-start method of the TCP would be to unfeasible in this scenario due to the absence of positive feedbacks, we will start directly with a scheme recalling the congestion avoidance. Specifically, when the CONTROL message is received, the transmission burst is reset to 1 molecule, that is $B_{TX} = B_{0,TX}$. At the RX side, this implies that the parabolic estimation restarts from the minimum of the parabola. In more detail, the effect of the control message will

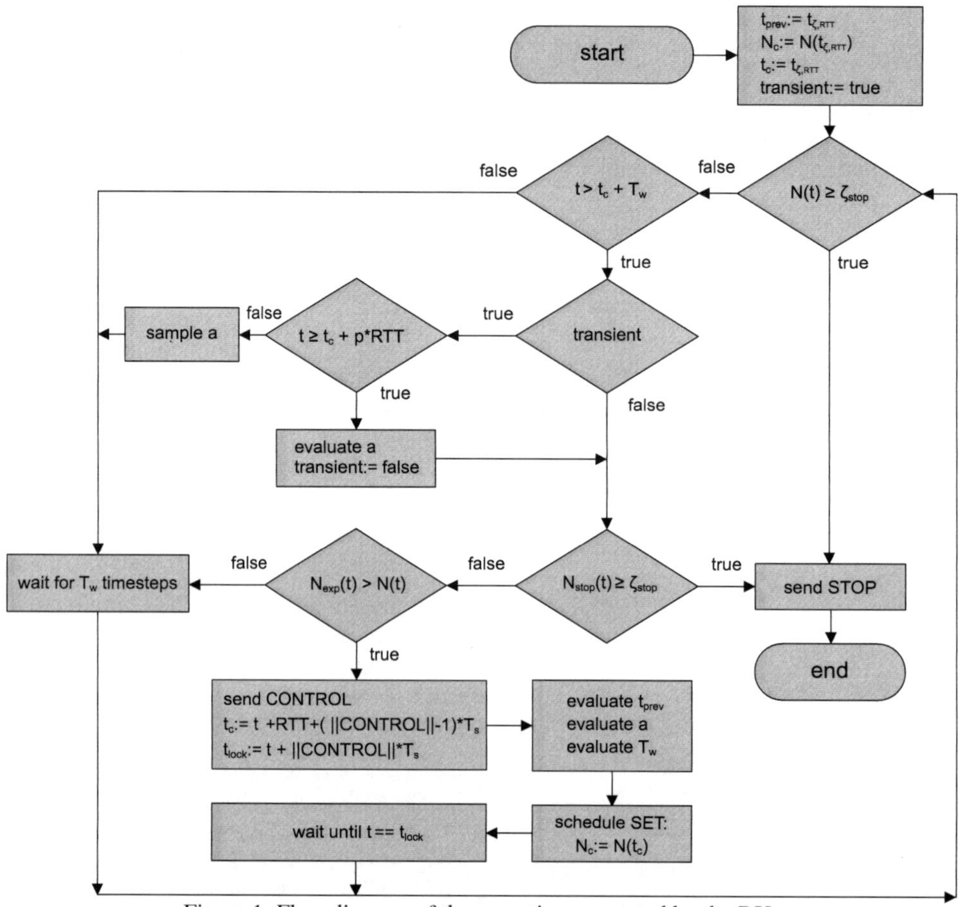

Figure 1: Flow diagram of the operations executed by the RX.

be visible at the RX at time $t_c = t + (\|CONTROL\| - 1)T_S + RTT$ defined in Fig. 1 and thus $t_0 = t_c$. The new offset will be estimated as the number of absorbed molecules at that time, that is $N_0 = N_c = N(t_c)$. The value of t_c takes into account the duration of transmission of control message, and the RTT time (see definition in section 3). Note that t_{prev} in Fig. 1 is not used here. The rationale of this algorithm is to allow decongesting the RX, by restarting transmission from the beginning.

5.2 Algorithm "Restart - Double"

This variant, in addition to performing the same operation of the algorithm "Restart", it doubles the transmission time $\Delta t \leftarrow 2 \times \Delta t$. As a consequence, we also double the observation time $T_w \leftarrow 2 \times T_w$ at the receiver, which has to be larger than the transmission time in order to correctly estimate the parabolic profile. The values of N_0 and t_0 are updated as in the previous case, but doubling the transmission time has an additional effect on the parameter a, which has to be updated accordingly. In particular, if in a time interval T the number of transmission bursts are $n_T = T/\Delta t$, starting from $B_{0,TX}$, then the number of transmitted molecules is simply $N_T = n_T(n_T+1)/2$. When the value of Δt is doubled the number of transmitted molecules in the same interval are approximately decreased by a factor 4, since

$$N_T = \sum_{i=1}^{n_T/2} i = \frac{n_T}{2}\frac{(n_T/2+1)}{2} = \frac{1}{4}\frac{n_T(n_T+2)}{2} \approx \frac{N_T}{4}. \qquad (6)$$

Clearly, this translates into updating $a \leftarrow a/4$. The rationale of this algorithm is to allow a complete decongestion of the RX, not only restarting the transmission process, but also by slowing the increase of the transmission rate.

5.3 Algorithm "Halve"

This algorithm is presented in [11], and inspired by TCP Reno. In this algorithm, the transmission window at the TX is halved, and not restarted from 1 molecule. Let us consider the time t_c at which the effect of this action is visible at RX. Since the transmission period has not changed, the values of a and T_w will remain unchanged. As for the time shift t_0, since the rate is perceived as halved at t_c and the previous starting point was estimated at $t_0 = t_{prev} = t_{\zeta_{RTT}}$, then it is shifted to

$$t_0 = \frac{t_c + t_{prev}}{2}, \qquad (7)$$

and then the new value of t_{prev} is set to $t_{prev} = t_0$. As for $N_{exp}(t)$, the value of N_c summarizes not only the number of assimilations before the control action, but also the initial $(t_c - t_0)$ seconds of the new parabola, as seen above. This means that

$$N_{exp}(t) = N_c - (t_c - t_0)^2 + \beta a (t - t_0)^2, \qquad (8)$$

and thus $N_0 = N_c - (t_c - t_0)^2$.

5.4 Algorithm "Halve - Double"

This last scheme is a variant of the "Halve" one, in which, similarly to "Restart - Double", upon receiving the CONTROL message, the TX node doubles the transmission period Δt. This implies that $\Delta t \leftarrow 2 \times \Delta t$, $T_w \leftarrow 2 \times T_w$, and $a \leftarrow a/4$. As for t_0, the same

Table 1: Simulation parameters

Symbol	Description	Value
dt	Simulation time step	20 μs
T	Temperature	310 K
e	Coefficient of restitution (partially inelastic collisions)	0.9
η	Viscosity	0.0011 $Kg \times (ms)^{-1}$
β	Tolerance factor	0.95
T_S	Symbol time	10 s [11]
r_{RX}	Radius node RX	2.5 μm
r_{TX}	Radius node TX	2.5 μm
R_{RX}	Amount of surface receptors (node RX)	10000
R_{TX}	Amount of surface receptors (node TX)	10000
$r_{c,rx}$	Radius emitted molecules (type R)	3.5 nm
$r_{c,tx}$	Radius emitted molecules (type S)	1.75 nm
$r_{r,rx}$	Receptor radius (RX), type S	4 nm
$r_{r,tx}$	Receptor radius (TX), type R	8 nm
T_{traff}	Trafficking time	4 s
ζ_S	Assimilation threshold (TX)	100 R molecules
Δt	Emission time (TX)	60 ms
ζ_{stop}	Assimilation threshold for STOP signal (RX)	100000 molecules
$START$	Signal pattern: START	110
$CONTROL$	Signal pattern: CONTROL	10
$STOP$	Signal pattern: STOP	111
d	Simulated distance	26.5 μm
B_{RX}	Burst for control signals (RX)	2000 R molecules
$B_{0,TX}$	Initial burst (TX)	1 S molecule
ζ_{RTT}	Threshold for RTT estimation (RX)	5 S molecules
T_w	Observation window default value (RX)	200 ms
p	Fraction of RTT used for a estimation	0.5

considerations done for the case "Halve" hold, but, in addition, we have to consider that the transmission rate increase is halved. Thus, according to the new transmission profile, in the time interval $(t_c - t_0)$, the TX would have transmitted exactly *half* the number of bursts with respect to the previous configuration, and thus it simply results that t_0 remain unchanged ($t_0 = t_{\zeta_{RTT}}$). As for $N_{exp}(t)$, it has the same value of (8), but with the updated a value.

6. PERFORMANCE EVALUATION

The performance evaluation of the system has been carried out by using the BiNS2 simulator. The main simulation parameters, together with their descriptions and values, are reported in Table 1.

We first performed a joint preliminary analysis in order to select the values of p parameters that allows obtaining a reliable estimation of a. For space limitations, we do not show it in details. We found that, for very low values of the parameter p, the estimation of a is quite unreliable, due to the low number of samples. As the value of p approaches 0.5, the estimation gets stable, and the decrease rate with p becomes less significant. Thus, in order to get a reliable estimation, values in the order of 0.5-1 are recommended. In addition, we evaluated also the impact of different T_{traff} and d values on the estimation of a. We found that binding the estimation of a to the value of RTT by means of p is reasonable since, when the distance increases, the S molecules concentration decreases, thus larger observation times due to larger RTT values do not lead to congestion. Note that the value selected for the trafficking times is realistic, since [32] reports also larger ones, in the order of many tens of seconds. In this paper, we used p=0.5.

Now, let us consider the system performance in terms of delivery efficiency and delivery time. We show some figure reporting time varying quantities, all for the case $T_{traff} = 4s$ and $p = 0.5$

Fig. 2 shows, for the four proposed algorithms, the values of assimilation (λ_a) and rejection (λ_r) rates, as a function of the simulation time. For all the schemes, it can be easily identified the time instant when λ_a begins deviating from the linear increase, and thus congestion is detected.In any case, the values of the first peak for λ_a are comparable, which are close to 1000 molecules/s, although some deviations occur due to the random nature of the assimilation process. In fact, the initial trigger of control messages is not uniform over time, since it depends on the initial, noisy estimation

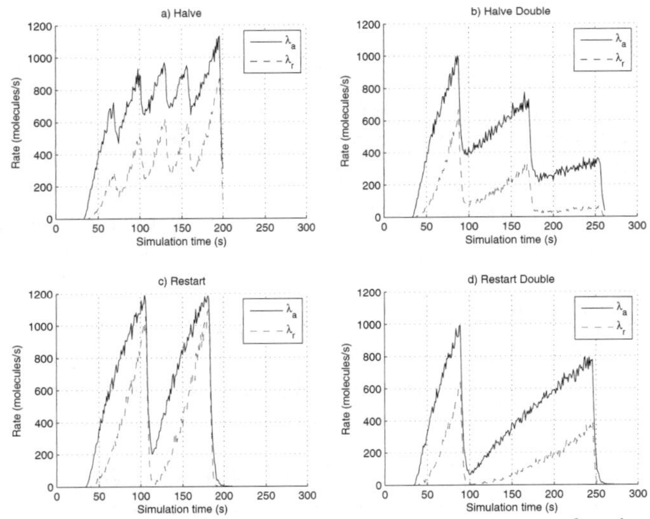

Figure 2: Assimilation (λ_a) and rejection (λ_r) rates as a function of time. Algorithms: a) Halve, b) Halve Double, c) Restat, and d) Restart Double.

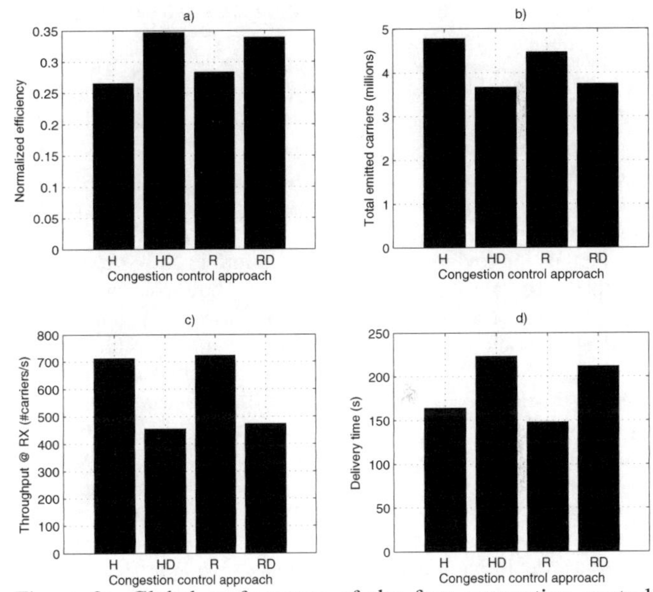

Figure 3: Global performance of the four congestion control schemes as a function of T_{traff} and p: a) delivery efficiency, b) total number of emitted carriers, c) receiver throughput, and d) delivery time. H means Halve, HD means Halve Double, R means Restart, and RD means Restart Double.

of a, and on the specific realization of the random arrival process. As for the Halve scheme (Fig. 2.a), it is evident a behavior which recalls the well known pattern of the TCP Reno. It is the control scheme that needs the transmission of the highest number of control messages. In the shown simulation, 4 control messages are sent. The net effect is that its assimilation rate, beyond an initial part which is clearly linear, evolves with a decreasing slope at the first t_c. In addition, this "continuous" transmission of control messages, in the specific simulation shown in the figure, causes some inefficiencies in meeting the target of ζ_{stop}, due to the lock effect of these transmissions on other possible actions (see also Fig. 1).

Instead, in the Restart one (Fig. 2.c), it is evident a behavior similar to the TCP Tahoe, without the initial slow start effect. It is characterized by two aspects: the number of control messages is just one, since it is able to completely decongest the RX node, thanks to a complete re-initialization of the transmission burst B_{TX}, and the full shape of the linear absorption rate is well recognizable.

A common comment to the Double schemes is that, due to the increase (doubling) transmission intervals Δt, when the congestion is detected, the absolute values of the assimilation rate reaches always smaller peaks. In fact, the number of transmission bursts occurring during the time necessary to transmit, to propagate, and to decode the CONTROL message decreases. Thus, congestion is not exacerbated. This has a positive impact on the delivery efficiency. In addition, for the Restart Double scheme the same comments done for the Restart hold.

Finally, a common point to Halve and Restart schemes is that, thanks to a constant transmission interval Δt, they are able to complete the transmission in a shorter time.

Fig. 3 shows a number of performance metrics. Fig 3.a shows the delivery efficiency, defined as $\zeta_{stop}/A_{RX}(R_{RX}, d, N_T)$, where N_T is the total number of emitted molecules by TX, as in (6), and A_{RX}, defined in (1), is the maximum number of molecules that RX is able to assimilate in absence of congestion upon a transmission of N_T molecules and with absorbing receptors (i.e. it is an upper bound). First, we observe that the efficiency values are always below 50%. In particular, it ranges from 0.25 for the Halve scheme, to about 0.35 for Halve Double and Restart Double.

Now, let us delve into comparison between congestion control algorithms. The Halve approach is the worst performing one in terms of efficiency, since it is the most aggressive, and forces the system to be continuously on the edge of congestion. On the other hand, Double-based approaches are the most efficient, since, by relaxing the transmission rate, they allows completely decongesting the RX, and thus improving its capability of absorbing the surrounding molecules. The number of emitted carriers, shown in Fig. 3.b, is the dual metric of the efficiency. Thus, the worst performing control solution is the Halve, which wastes a lot of molecules since it maintains the RX always close to saturation. Instead, Double-based approaches have similar behavior, with the best performance. Fig. 3.c show the throughput at the receiver, and Fig. 3.d its dual counterpart, i.e. the delivery time. Clearly, the Halve approach is the best performing one, having the highest throughput and, consequently, the lowest delivery time. Obviously, Double-based approach is the worst performing ones with respect to throughput and delivery time. In particular, the Restart Double approach, which is slightly less aggressive than the Halve Double approach, has the lowest throughput and, consequently, the highest delivery time. Summarizing, if all the performance metrics are equally important we can conclude that the best trade-off is the Restart approach, which exhibits good values in all metrics, by balancing efficiency and throughput. However, in the simulation presented, the Restart approach has been tested in a favorable condition, since it reaches the target ζ_{stop} with the peak rate (see Fig. 2.c). Thus, in more general conditions, it could have slightly less good performance. The less convenient approach is instead the Restart Double, which has performance similar to Halve Double in terms of high efficiency, but worst performance in terms of throughput and delivery time.

7. CONCLUSION

In this paper, we have analyzed do methods for handling congestion in diffusion-based molecular communications. We have first proposed a simple yet effective algorithm to detect congestion in its early stages. The proposed algorithm can be easily implemented in a device with limited memory and computing capabilities, and thus fits the requirements of nanomachines. In addition, it needs minimal configuration, since it estimates at run-time the system behavior and adapts accordingly. Then, we have proposed and compared four different control actions, triggered by the negative feedback sent by the receiver nanomachine and implemented in the transmitter nanomachine. From our results, obtained by considering realistic large trafficking times, it emerges that the best control scheme is the so-called Restart one, which couples the ability to decongesting the receiver with the capacity to quickly recover towards sustained bit rates. An interesting option could be also an hybrid approach, able to relax the transmission rate by means of the so-called "Halve - Double" scheme until the need of control actions is not frequent, and then using again the "Halve" control algorithm to maintain an high throughput. Clearly, in order to implement such an hybrid scheme, it is necessary to reconsider the message encoding adopted here and previously proposed in [11], by augmenting the number of symbols and thus the round trip latency of control actions, or resorting to molecule shift keying modulation (MoSK [40]) and using two types of molecules when switching from "Halve - Double" to "Halve".

Our ongoing and future work includes the extension of the congestion control strategy in a multi-access environment, which includes multiple TX and RX nodes, the commands of which may interfere each other. Another issues worth of investigation is the introduction of moving nanomachines. In this case, the estimation of the assimilation profile should be repeated upon movement detection, which could be implemented by periodically repeating the estimation of the RTT with off-band signaling, which translates into the usage of an additional, different types of control molecules.

8. ACKNOWLEDGMENTS

This work is supported by the EU project H2020 FET Open CIRCLE (project No. 665564) and by the MolML project funded by University of Perugia.

9. REFERENCES

[1] S. K. Khaitan and J. D. McCalley. Design techniques and applications of cyberphysical systems: A survey. *IEEE Systems Journal*, 9(2):350–365, June 2015.

[2] Ian F. Akyildiz, Fernando Brunetti, and Cristina Blázquez. Nanonetworks: A new communication paradigm. *Comput. Netw.*, 52(12):2260–2279, August 2008.

[3] T. Nakano, M.J. Moore, Fang Wei, A.V. Vasilakos, and Jianwei Shuai. Molecular communication and networking: Opportunities and challenges. *IEEE Transactions on NanoBioscience*, 11(2):135–148, 2012.

[4] V. Loscri, C. Marchal, N. Mitton, G. Fortino, and AV. Vasilakos. Security and privacy in molecular communication and networking: Opportunities and challenges. *NanoBioscience, IEEE Transactions on*, 13(3):198–207, Sept 2014.

[5] L. Felicetti, M. Femminella, G. Reali, and P. Lio. Applications of molecular communications to medicine: A survey. *Nano Communication Networks*, 7:27 – 45, 2016.

[6] I. F. Akyildiz, M. Pierobon, S. Balasubramaniam, and Y. Koucheryavy. The internet of bio-nano things. *IEEE Communications Magazine*, 53(3):32–40, March 2015.

[7] U.A. Chude-Okonkwo et al. Molecular communication model for targeted drug delivery in multiple disease sites with diversely expressed enzymes. *IEEE Trans. on NanoBioscience*, 15(3):230–245, April 2016.

[8] M. Femminella, G. Reali, and A. V. Vasilakos. A molecular communications model for drug delivery. *IEEE Transactions*

on NanoBioscience, 14(8):935–945, Dec 2015.

[9] Luca Felicetti, Mauro Femminella, and Gianluca Reali. A simple and scalable receiver model in molecular communication systems. In *Proceedings of the 3rd ACM International Conference on Nanoscale Computing and Communication*, NANOCOM'16, pages 39:1–39:2, New York, NY, USA, 2016. ACM.

[10] Tadashi Nakano, Yutaka Okaie, and Athanasios V. Vasilakos. Transmission rate control for molecular communication among biological nanomachines. *IEEE Journal on Selected Areas in Communications*, 31(12, supplement), 2013.

[11] L. Felicetti, M. Femminella, G. Reali, T. Nakano, and Athanasion V. Vasilakos. TCP-like molecular communications. *Selected Areas in Communications, IEEE Journal on*, Dec. 2014.

[12] Luca Felicetti, Mauro Femminella, and Gianluca Reali. A simulation tool for nanoscale biological networks. *Nano Communication Networks*, 3(1):2–18, 2012.

[13] Luca Felicetti, Mauro Femminella, Gianluca Reali, Paolo Gresele, and Marco Malvestiti. Simulating an in vitro experiment on nanoscale communications by using bins2. *Nano Communication Networks*, 4(4):172 – 180, 2013.

[14] M.J. Moore, T. Suda, and K. Oiwa. Molecular communication: Modeling noise effects on information rate. *IEEE Transactions on NanoBioscience*, 8(2):169–180, 2009.

[15] T. Nakano, Y. Okaie, and Jian-Qin Liu. Channel model and capacity analysis of molecular communication with brownian motion. *Communications Letters, IEEE*, 16(6):797–800, 2012.

[16] M. S. Kuran, H. B. Yilmaz, T. Tugcu, and B. Ozerman. Energy model for communication via diffusion in nanonetworks. *Nano Communication Networks*, 1(2):86 – 95, 2010.

[17] S. Kadloor, R.S. Adve, and A.W. Eckford. Molecular communication using brownian motion with drift. *IEEE Transactions on NanoBioscience*, 11(2):89–99, June 2012.

[18] K. V. Srinivas, A.W. Eckford, and R.S. Adve. Molecular communication in fluid media: The additive inverse gaussian noise channel. *IEEE Transactions on Information Theory*, 58(7):4678–4692, 2012.

[19] T. Nakano and Jian-Qin Liu. Design and analysis of molecular relay channels: An information theoretic approach. *IEEE Transactions on NanoBioscience*, 9(3):213–221, 2010.

[20] T. Nakano and Jianwei Shuai. Repeater design and modeling for molecular communication networks. In *IEEE INFOCOM Workshop*, pages 501–506, 2011.

[21] N. Farsad, A.W. Eckford, and S. Hiyama. A markov chain channel model for active transport molecular communication. *Signal Processing, IEEE Transactions on*, 62(9):2424–2436, May 2014.

[22] A. Guney, B. Atakan, and O.B. Akan. Mobile ad hoc nanonetworks with collision-based molecular communication. *IEEE Transactions on Mobile Computing*, 11(3):353–366, March 2012.

[23] Baris Atakan and Ozgur B. Akan. On molecular multiple-access, broadcast, and relay channels in nanonetworks. In *ICST BIONETICS 2010*, 2010.

[24] Baris Atakan and Ozgur B. Akan. Deterministic capacity of information flow in molecular nanonetworks. *Nano Communication Networks*, 1(1):31 – 42, 2010.

[25] Mohammad Upal Mahfuz, Dimitrios Makrakis, and Hussein T. Mouftah. On the characterization of binary concentration-encoded molecular communication in nanonetworks. *Nano Communication Networks*, 1(4):289 – 300, 2010.

[26] M. Pierobon and I.F. Akyildiz. A physical end-to-end model for molecular communication in nanonetworks. *IEEE Journal on Selected Areas in Communications*, 28(4):602–611, 2010.

[27] M. Pierobon and I.F. Akyildiz. Diffusion-based noise analysis for molecular communication in nanonetworks. *IEEE Transactions on Signal Processing*, 59(6):2532–2547, 2011.

[28] H.B. Yilmaz, A.C. Heren, T. Tugcu, and Chan-Byoung Chae. Three-dimensional channel characteristics for molecular communications with an absorbing receiver. *Communications Letters, IEEE*, 18(6):929–932, June 2014.

[29] A. Akkaya, H.B. Yilmaz, C. Chae, and T. Tugcu. Effect of receptor density and size on signal reception in molecular communication via diffusion with an absorbing receiver. *Communications Letters, IEEE*, 19(2):155–158, Feb 2015.

[30] M. Pierobon and I.F. Akyildiz. Noise analysis in ligand-binding reception for molecular communication in nanonetworks. *IEEE Transactions on Signal Processing*, 59(9):4168 –4182, September 2011.

[31] L. Felicetti, M. Femminella, G. Reali, J.N. Daigle, M. Malvestiti, and P. Gresele. Modeling CD40-based molecular communications in blood vessels. *IEEE Transactions on NanoBioscience*, 13(3):230–243, 2014.

[32] D.A. Lauffenburger and J.J. Linderman. *Receptors: Models for Binding, Trafficking, and Signalling,*. Oxford University Press, 1996.

[33] Y. Deng, A. Noel, M. Elkashlan, A. Nallanathan, and K. C. Cheung. Modeling and simulation of molecular communication systems with a reversible adsorption receiver. *IEEE Transactions on Molecular, Biological and Multi-Scale Communications*, 1(4):347–362, Dec 2015.

[34] Y. Lu, M. D. Higgins, A. Noel, M. S. Leeson, and Y. Chen. The effect of two receivers on broadcast molecular communication systems. *IEEE Transactions on NanoBioscience*, 2016.

[35] J. Philibert. One and a half century of diffusion: Fick, einstein, before and beyond. *Diffusion Fundamamentals*, 4:6.1–6.19, 2006.

[36] M. Pierobon and I.F. Akyildiz. Capacity of a Diffusion-Based Molecular Communication System With Channel Memory and Molecular Noise . *IEEE Transactions on Information Theory*, 59(2):942–954, February 2013.

[37] Joseph Feher. *Quantitative Human Physiology, An Introduction*. Academic Press, Boston, 2012.

[38] A Noel, K.C. Cheung, and R. Schober. Improving receiver performance of diffusive molecular communication with enzymes. *NanoBioscience, IEEE Transactions on*, 13(1):31–43, March 2014.

[39] Y. Okaie, T. Nakano, T. Hara, and S. Nishio. Distributing nanomachines for minimizing mean residence time of molecular signals in bionanosensor networks. *Sensors Journal, IEEE*, 14(1):218–227, Jan 2014.

[40] Hoda ShahMohammadian, Geoffrey G. Messier, and Sebastian Magierowski. Optimum receiver for molecule shift keying modulation in diffusion-based molecular communication channels. *Nano Communication Networks*, 3:183–195, 2012.

Networked Human Motion Capture System Based on Quaternion Navigation *

Jie Li
School of Control Science and Engineering
Dalian University of Technology
Dalian, China
1165530693@mail.dlut.edu.cn

Zhe-long Wang †
School of Control Science and Engineering
Dalian University of Technology
Dalian, China
wangzl@dlut.edu.cn

Hongyu Zhao ‡
School of Control Science and Engineering
Dalian University of Technology
Dalian, China
zhy.lucy@hotmail.com

Raffaele Gravina §
Department of Informatics, Modeling, Electronics and Systems
University of Calabria
Rende, Italy
r.gravina@dimes.unical.it

Giancarlo Fortino
Department of Informatics, Modeling, Electronics and Systems
University of Calabria
Rende, Italy
g.fortino@unical.it

Yongmei Jiang
The Second Affiliated Hospital of Dalian Medical University
Dalian, China

Kai Tang
The First Affiliated Hospital of Dalian Medical University
Dalian, China

ABSTRACT

In this paper, from the perspective of human ergonomics, we analyze the movement of the joints in the process of human body movements, and we establish a dynamic model according to the human skeleton structure. On this basis, from the rigid body dynamics point of view, combined with the principle of inertial navigation, a body sensor network based on MEMS inertial sensors is built to capture human body motion in real time. On the basis of space trajectory of human body movement and traditional human motion solution strategy, a human motion solution strategy based on particle filter fusion solution is proposed to realize the prediction of human motion analysis. Therefore, we evaluate the performance of the designed system by comparing with the real motion. Finally, in order to verify the human motion data, the motion capture data verification platforms are established. Experimental results show that the proposed joint attitude solution algorithm can achieve a relatively smooth tracking effect and provides a certain reference value.

Keywords

motion capture; inertial navigation; particle filter; body sensor network

*This work was supported by National Natural Science Foundation of China under Grant No.61473058, Fundamental Research Funds for the Central Universities (DUT15ZD114), and National Natural Science Foundation of China under Grant No.61174027.

†Corresponding author: wangzl@dlut.edu.cn.

‡School of Control Science and Engineering, Dalian University of Technology, Dalian, China, 116024

§Department of Informatics, Modeling, Electronics and Systems (DIMES), University of Calabria Via P. Bucci, cubo 41C, 87036 Rende (CS), Italy(email: g.fortino@unical.it)

Permission to make digital or hard copies of all or part of this work for personal or classroom use is granted without fee provided that copies are not made or distributed for profit or commercial advantage and that copies bear this notice and the full citation on the first page. Copyrights for components of this work owned by others than ACM must be honored. Abstracting with credit is permitted. To copy otherwise, or republish, to post on servers or to redistribute to lists, requires prior specific permission and/or a fee. Request permissions from permissions@acm.org.

1. INTRODUCTION

The behavior of all kinds of human actions are the embodiment of their physiological reaction mechanism and thinking consciousness. If it is possible to capture the process of human motion and physiological signals without the constraints of time and space, then according to captured results of human action, we can record, simulate and scale the human action process to analyze the details of the behavior of action process, simulate or reconstruct human action process, and evaluate the physiological function of target object. Therefore, according to captured results, we can make real-time identification for various types of behavior, understand the intention of the behavior about objects, get their behavior habits, and realize natural interaction between human and machine [1]. Throughout the applicability of human motion capture, it has a wide range of practical applications, such as human-computer interaction [2], film and television production [3], interactive game [4], sports training [5], and medical rehabilitation [6].

At present, human motion capture is mainly realized by optical principle. The history of motion capture began in the Chinese Warring States period with the traditional "shadow" theatre which represents the earliest optical motion capture technology. It uses light projection to project the motion of model onto a translucent screen, thus forming a lifelike character image [7]. State-of-the-art optical motion capture method has high precision and real-time performance, but its cost is too high and it is inconvenient to carry. Furthermore, it is easily influenced by light conditions, perspective, shadow, occlusion, scene and other factors [8].

With the development of micro-electromechanical systems, wireless communication and sensor network technology, wireless body sensor network (BSN) [9] [10] - a kind of wireless sensor network (WSN) - are becoming more and more popular. A BSN is composed of multiple sensor nodes (each capable of data acquisition, processing and communication) placed on different parts of human body. BSNs are being gradually applied in the human body motion capture field and inertial motion capture has become a new research hotspot [11]. The inertial motion capture technology is not affected by occlusions and illumination effects, and can be used both indoors and outdoors, so it is easier to achieve all-weather, unlimited motion capture [12]. However, it also has disadvantages; for example, number of sensors, layout and performance, and attitude solution algorithm can affect the accuracy, dynamic characteristics and stability of motion capture [13]. To overcome the limitations of current inertial motion capture, many domestic and foreign scholars have proposed different methods to solve these problems. For instance, Roetenberg et al. [14] proposed a compensation Kalman filter algorithm; Bachmann [15] proposed a Kalman filter algorithm based on quaternion, et al. But at present, the algorithms still have some limitations.

This paper aims at improving current state of the art methods. First, a microprocessor network intelligent motion capture node combined with an inertial sensor is designed. Furthermore, a motion sensing network composed of sensor nodes distributed on the human body is established to collect sensor data from different parts of the body. A particle filter fusion method is also proposed based on strap-down inertial navigation system by considering the complexity of the algorithm and interference effects. By using the parallel solution of each node, real-time performance of the attitude solving process is improved. With the aid of the high-speed wireless data channel, a kind of real-time wireless attitude data transmission protocol is established. Finally, according to the theory of computer graphics, we completed the real-time capture of human body motion attitude by using the captured attitude data to drive the human body model in host computer, and we built the MATLAB and Visual Studio attitude capture data verification platform to validate the motion captured data, which further improved the performance of our system.

2. METHODOLOGY

2.1 Human Body Model

Human body model is a kind of graphical description of human form by abstracting out the structure of the human body in the field of motion capture. Using the captured data obtained by tracking equipments, it is possible to simulate the movement of the human body mode.

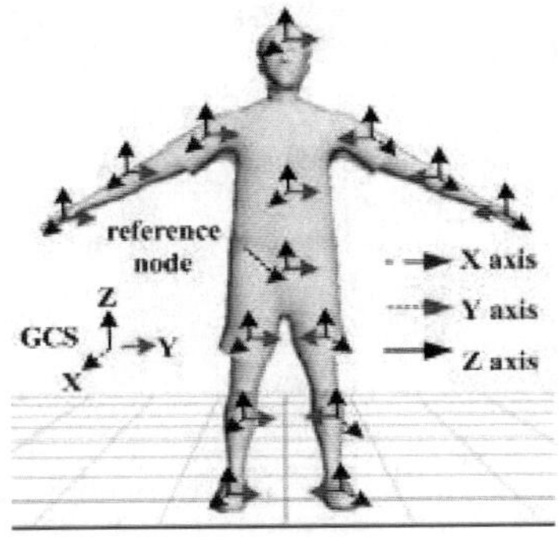

Figure 1: Definition of the human body coordinate system

In this paper, on the basis of human body biomechanics structure, referring to the idea of the surface model [16], the human body is divided into 15 major bone segments: pelvis, left thigh, right thigh, left calf, right calf, left foot, right foot, lumbar spine, the head, right arm, left arm, right elbow, left elbow, right hand, left hand respectively. The bones are connected through joints. Then, we set the pelvis as the reference node and traverse the skeleton structure by inverse kinematics principle. Finally, we define the human body coordinate system based on three-dimensional kinematic theory, as shown in Fig. 1. For convenience, we define Global Coordinate System GCS, Body Coordinate System BCS, and Sensor Coordinate System SCS.

Through the definition of the human body motion structure, in this paper, 3D human skeleton files based on the triangular mesh by 3Dmax are established, as shown in Fig. 2.

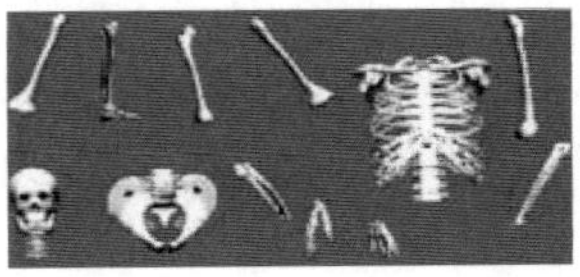

Figure 2: Scattered human skeleton model

In order to build a complete human model, we combine the Visual Studio integrated development environment with the OPENGL graphical program interface to load the skeleton files, so the scattered bones are finally assembled into a complete model of the human body by matrix operation. Fig. 3 depicts the 3D human body motion tracking platform constructed in this paper.

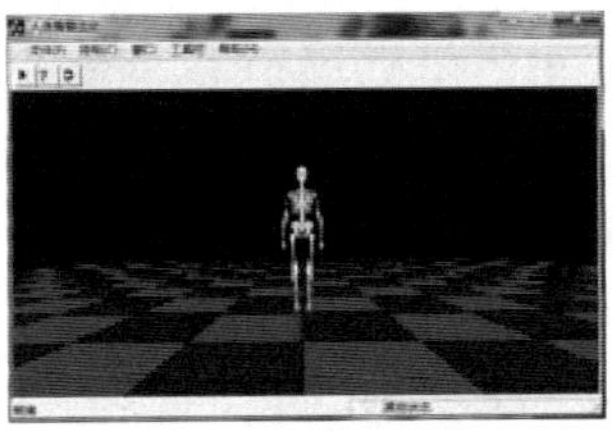

Figure 3: 3D human motion tracking platform

2.2 Design of the BSN-based motion capture system

In this paper, the network is composed of a sink node and multi-sensor nodes. Sensor nodes collect, deal with the attitude information in the process of human movement, and communicate with the sink node through high CAN bus. The sink node packages the whole data from the sensor nodes and passes them to the host computer through WiFi. The sensor network structure is shown in Fig. 4.

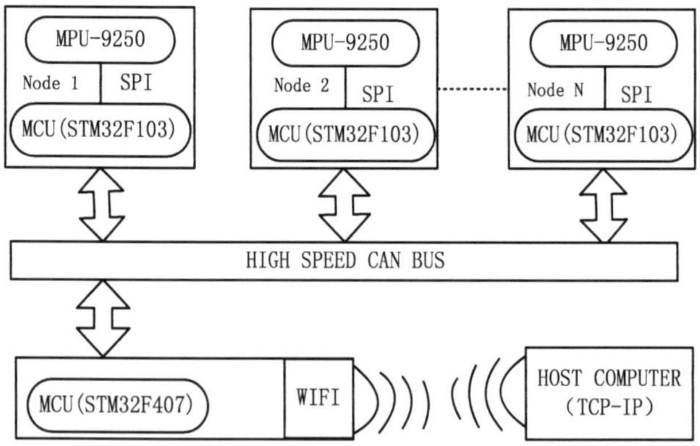

Figure 4: Structure of the BSN motion capture system

The sensor node, shown in Fig. 5, which is composed of a nine-axis inertial sensor (MPU9250) and a microprocessor (STM32F103T8U6). The inertial sensor integrates a three-axis accelerometer with a range of ±16 g, a three-axis gyroscope with a range of ±2000 dps, and a three-axis magnetometer with a range of ±12 gauss. SPI interface allows high-speed sampling rate up to ±18 MHZ. The main frequency of the microprocessor is up to 72 MHZ, which can achieve high-speed sensor data processing. Such design can reduce the physical dimension of the node and increase the processing speed. The sink node, shown in Fig. 5, is composed of 32 bit microcontroller (STM32F407) and MIXCHIP EMW3162 WiFi module. The sink node can receive the attitude data from sensor nodes in real time through high speed CAN bus and it forwards the packed data to the host computer by WiFi wireless data channel (TCP-IP).

Figure 5: Sensor node and Sink node

2.3 Body orientation estimation

According to the theory of spatial kinematics, the motion of human body can be expressed as a combined rotation from bone to space. In the present study of human navigation, we always use Euler angle, rotation matrix or quaternion to express the space movement of body. However, there is a singularity in the Euler angle during the rotation, which leads to the gimbal lock [17]; relatively speaking, the rotation matrix requires complex trigonometric function calculation, which takes a longer period of time. In order to improve the calculation efficiency, we use quaternion to express the space movement of body.

A quaternion is usually composed of a four-dimensional vector, which is in turn composed of an imaginary part $q_v = [q_x, q_y, q_z]^T$. and a real (scalar) part $q_w \in R$.

$$q = [q_w, q_v]^T = [q_w, q_x, q_y, q_z]^T \tag{1}$$

with $q_w^2 + q_x^2 + q_y^2 + q_z^2 = 1$. Any 3D rotation can be represented by a unit quaternion q. For example, given a point $p[x, y, z]$, we can build a quaternion $P[0, p]^T$. Given a unit vectorη , which is the desired axis, andθ , the desired angle of rotation, we build the quaternion $q = [q_w, q_v]$, where $q_w = \cos(\theta/2)$ and $q_v = \eta \sin(\theta/2)$. Then the process of this point revolves around the rotation axis of θ angle can be expressed as:

$$P_{rotate} = q * P * q^{-1} \tag{2}$$

Where $*$ represents quaternion multiplication and q^{-1} is the inverse quaternion of q. In order to smooth the motion between two frames, we need to interpolate the quaternions of frame t and t-1 using the Slerp function [18] by an amount $\lambda \in [0, 1]$.

$$Slerp(q_t, q_{t-1}, \lambda) = q_t \frac{\sin(1-\lambda)\varphi}{\sin\varphi} + q_{t-1} \frac{\sin(\lambda)\varphi}{\sin\varphi} \tag{3}$$

Where q_t and q_{t-1} are concatenated frames, furthermore, $\varphi = \cos^{-1}(q_t, q_{t-1})$. In order to express the segment kinematics of motion reconstruction, the relationship between the sensor attached to the segment and the corresponding joint of the segment needs to be established. Let us set the lower limbs as an example (see Fig. 6). Then, thigh and leg are expressed by F_i and F_{i-1} respectively, BCS r_{i-1}, r_i, r_{i+1} are calibrated on the 3 joints of the lower limbs. Sensor node are distributed on the surface of thigh, and calibrate SCS. For initialization, performers are required to perform a special gesture: the T-pose [19]. For frame t, we could estimate the sensors global orientation by fusing the sensor data with the fusion algorithm. However, q_t^{gs} cannot directly represent segment orientation as SCS and BCS are not exactly matched. We have to determine the global orientation of each bone segment q_t^{gr} by matching the orientation of the sensor q_t^{gs} with the transformation from SCS to BCS q_t^{rs} . As the relative relationship between SCS to BCS keeps constant during the movement, so q_t^{rs} is a fixed constant, and, so

$$q_t^{gr} = q_t^{gs} * (q_0^{rs})' \tag{4}$$

2.4 Motion Estimation by the Fusion of Sensor Data

In this paper, based on heterogeneous multi-sensor data fusion,such as complementary filter and kalman filter [17], [20], we design a quaternion attitude solution strategy based on particle filter. Algorithm execution flow chart is shown in Fig. 7. First, in the process of human motion, for each bone segment, we define a state variable x, the state variable contains two parameters: 1) the vector part of quaternion q^T 2) the gyro drift β^T, then the state vector x can be expressed as

$$x = [q^T \beta^T]^T \tag{5}$$

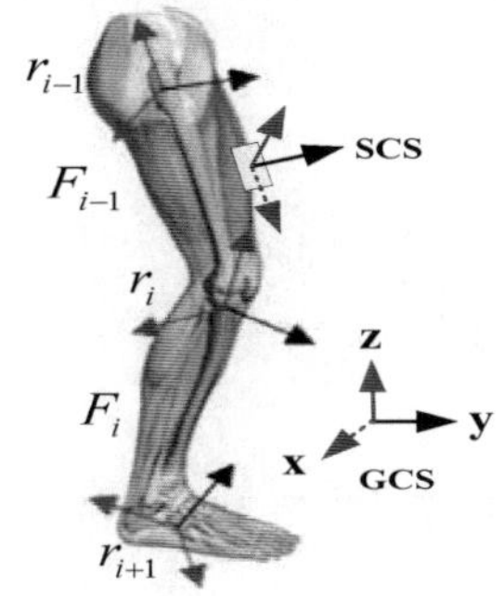

Figure 6: Definition of lower limb coordinates

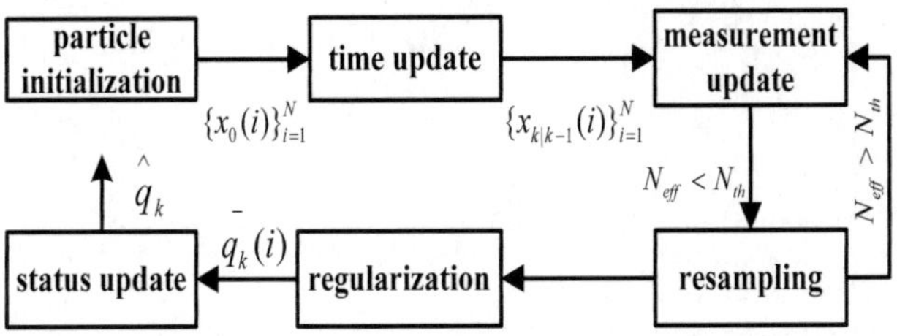

Figure 7: Algorithm execution flow chart

The quaternion q^T represents the quaternion vector from the GCS conversion to BCS, which can be calculated by combining the data of accelerometer and magnetometer on the basis of inertial navigation. Subsequently, we make filtering for quaternion, which can be mainly divided into the following six steps:

Step1 - particle initialization: when k = 0, we produce N particle points $x_0(i)_{i=1}^N$ from the vector x, which obeys the initial probability density $p(x_0)$, then we split these particles into quaternion part and gyro drift part, which can be expressed as:

$$x_0(i) = \begin{bmatrix} q_0(i) \\ \beta_0(i) \end{bmatrix} \tag{6}$$

Step2 - time update: at time K, we make sampling from the importance density function $x_k(i) \sim q(x_k|x_{0:k-1,z_{1:k}})$ to obtain the updated particle points $x_{k|k-1}(i)_{i=1}^N$,where $q(x_k|x_{0:k-1}, z_{1:k}) = p(x_k|x_{k-1})$,these particles can be divided into two parts which are called quaternion part and gyro drift part. The two parts can be expressed as:

$$x_{k|k-1}(i) = \begin{bmatrix} q_{k|k-1}(i) \\ \beta_{k|k-1}(i) \end{bmatrix} \tag{7}$$

Step3 - measurement update: when we get the measured values of $q_{s,k}$ at time K, the particle weight $\omega_k^*(i)$ can be updated through the likelihood probability density function$p(z_k|x_k)$:

$$\omega_k^*(i) = p_{z_k|q_k}(z_k|q_k(i))\omega_{k-1}^*(i) \tag{8}$$

Then, we normalize the weight of the particles, where:

$$\omega_k(i) = \frac{\omega_k^*(i)}{\sum_{i=1}^{N} \omega_k^*(i)} \tag{9}$$

At this point, we make state estimation for the quaternion [21]. State estimation and empirical covariance calculation can be expressed as

$$\hat{x_k} = \sum_{i=1}^{N} \omega_k(i) x_k(i) \tag{10}$$

$$S_k = \sum_{i=1}^{N} \omega_k(i)(x_k^i - \hat{x_k})(x_k^i - \hat{x_k^i})^T \tag{11}$$

Step4 - resampling: Before resampling, we need to judge the degradation of particles. The relationship can be evaluated as follows:

$$N_{eff} = \frac{N}{E_q[\omega_k^2]} < N \tag{12}$$

Where, the effective number of particles is defined as:

$$N_{eff} = \frac{N}{1/N \sum_{i=1}^{N} [\omega_k(i)]^2} \tag{13}$$

WhenN_{eff} is less than the predetermined threshold N_{th} , we make resampling.

Step5 - regularization: although the sampling process avoids the particle degeneracy phenomenon in a certain extent, it introduces the problem of particle dilution. To this end, we need to introduce a regularized resampling procedure [22]. After regularization, the regularized sampling quaternion is:

$$\bar{q_k}(i) = \delta q_k(i) \otimes q_k(i) \qquad i = 1, 2, \cdots, N \tag{14}$$

Where$\delta q_k(i) = [\delta\xi^T(i)1]^T$. $\delta\xi^T(i)$ is the vector of quaternion perturbation particle points [23].

Step6 - status update: After obtaining progeny particles by regularized sampling, in order to make the estimated particles more accurately, we re-compute the likelihood of posterior particles, which can be written as:

$$\hat{\omega}(i) = \frac{1}{N} p_{y_k|x_k}(z_k|\bar{q}(i)) \tag{15}$$

Finally, we can get the final estimated value of quaternion $\hat{q_k}$.

$$N\hat{q}_k = \lambda \hat{q}_k \tag{16}$$

Where the estimated quaternion $\hat{q_k}$ is the corresponding minimum characteristic vector of matrix N when cost function J is the smallest. The cost function J is discussed in detail in [23].

3. EXPERIMENTAL RESULTS

In view of the proposed algorithm model, three experiments are designed to verify its feasibility. Fig. 8 shows the sensor location on the body during the experiments. In experiment 1, we verify the superiority of quaternion relative to the Euler angle in the rotation by controlling the rotation of the rectangular. Experiment 2 shows the effect of the actual motion capture. In order to further verify the algorithm model, in experiment 3, we compared the real motion with the reductive motion.

Experiment 1 - The contrast of rotating effect between quaternion and the Euler angle: at first, in order to demonstrate the superiority of quaternion comparing to the Euler angle when represent rotation. We design an experiment with MATLAB. During the experiment, the calculated

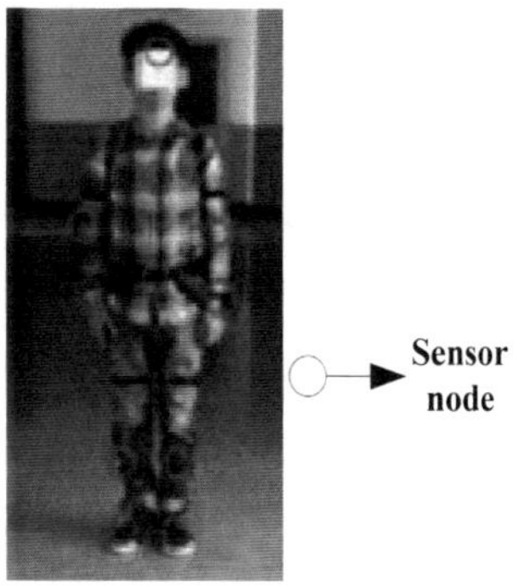

Figure 8: Sensor location on the body

quaternion and Euler angle by our algorithm are mapped to the center of a three-dimensional cuboid, which will be used to drive the cuboid rotation around the rotation center point. Fig. 9 shows the raw data, and Fig. 10, Fig. 11, Fig. 12 depict the comparison results.

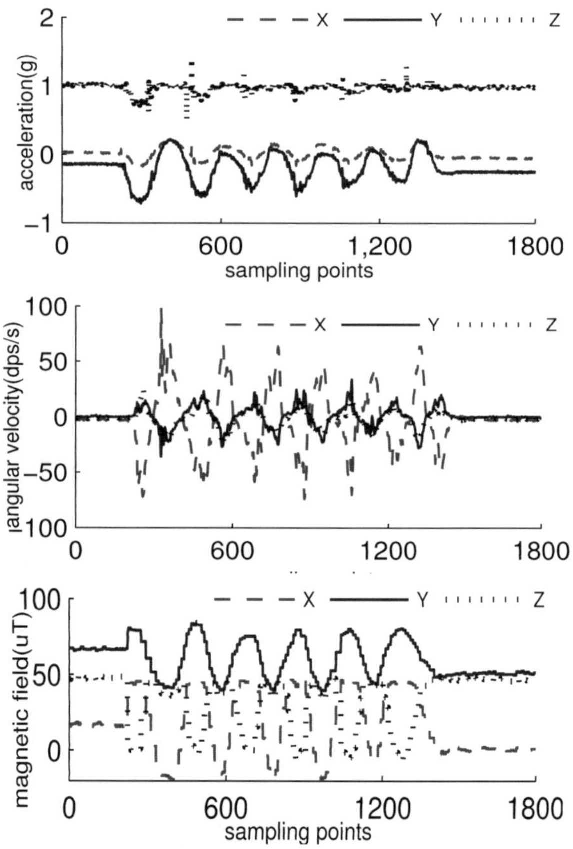

Figure 9: The RAW data of sensors

According to the results of experiment 1, when we use the quaternion and Euler angle to represent rotation, if the cuboid does not reach the rotation singularity, the two kinds of rotations can equally keep pace with each other. But when the cuboid reaches the rotation singularity, if we use Euler angle to represent the rotation, at this time, according to the scatter diagram, the particles will occur scattered

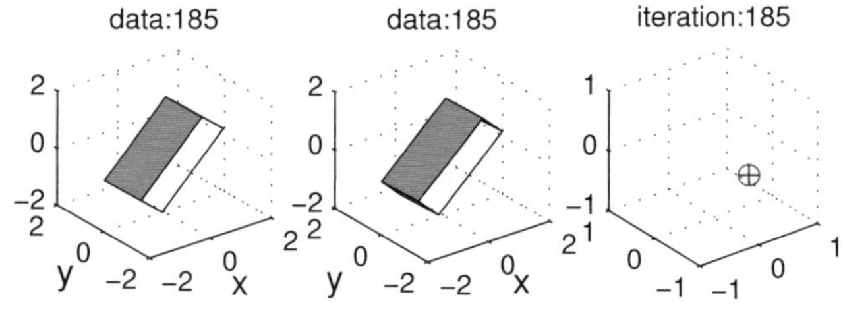

Figure 10: The object has not rotated to the singularity

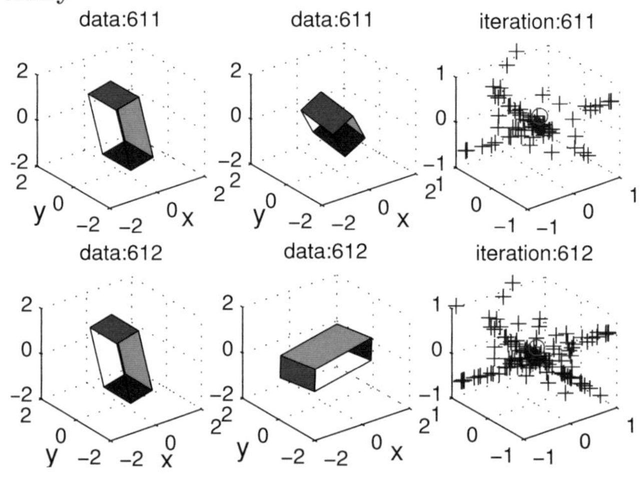

Figure 11: The object has rotated to the singularity

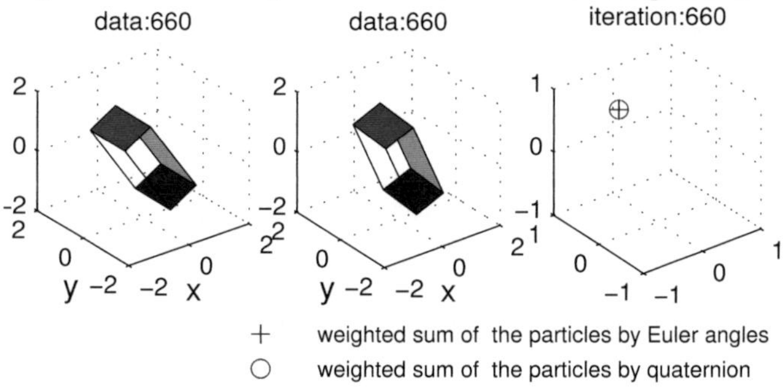

Figure 12: The object has returned from singularity

phenomenon, which will cause the disorder of rotation. The use of the quaternion can effectively avoid this issue. Thus, in the rotation process, quaternion is indeed better than the Euler angle. Fig. 13 shows the calculated quaternion by our method.

Experiment 2 - The evaluation of captured effect: this experiment has been carried out to evaluate the overall effect of the designed motion capture system. Taking the motion capture of full body as an example, Fig. 14 describes the whole motion capture effect of the system. By comparing the tracking effect of the 3D human model to the real human person, we can find that our designed system can effectively realize the task of human motion capture.

Experiment 3 - Validation of the data of motion: through the motion capture interface, we can get the corresponding Biovision Hierarchical Data (BVH) motion capture data in real time. The BVH data preserves the data of attitude

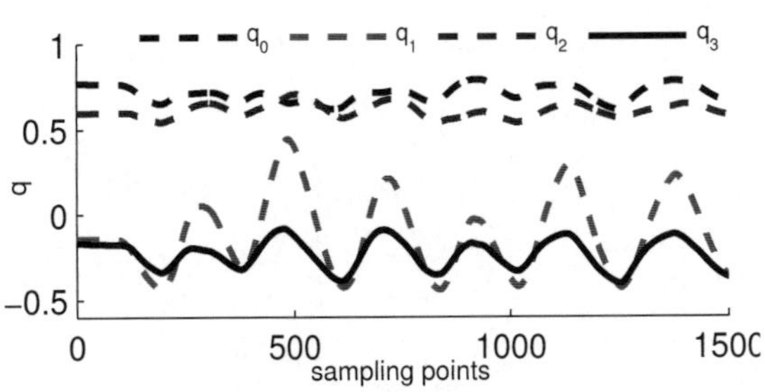

Figure 13: The calculated quaternion with our method

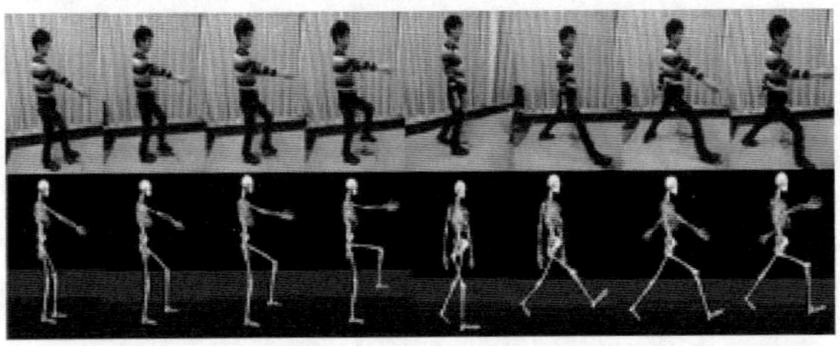

Figure 14: The effect of motion capture

corresponding to each node by frame format in the process of motion capture.

For the BVH format data, this paper establishes the motion capture data verification platform based on MATLAB and Visual Studio, which can realize analysis and reduction for the BVH motion capture data. Through comparison and verification, we can achieve a more accurate analysis of motion capture data flow.

In this paper, taking the walking and jumping movement as examples, the BVH data, which are exported by motion capture system, contain 713 frames walking data and 2980 frames jumping data, respectively. Fig. 15 and Fig. 16 show the comparison of the real action and the reductive action by BVH.

We find that the BVH data can basically rebuild the real motion through the reduction effect of motion, and the restored motion is very smooth. Thus, the preliminary results are promising and worth further investigation and quantitative evaluation.

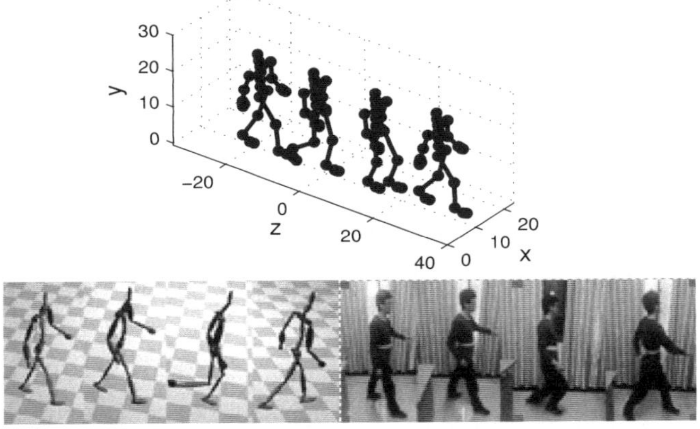

Figure 15: The reduction effect of walking

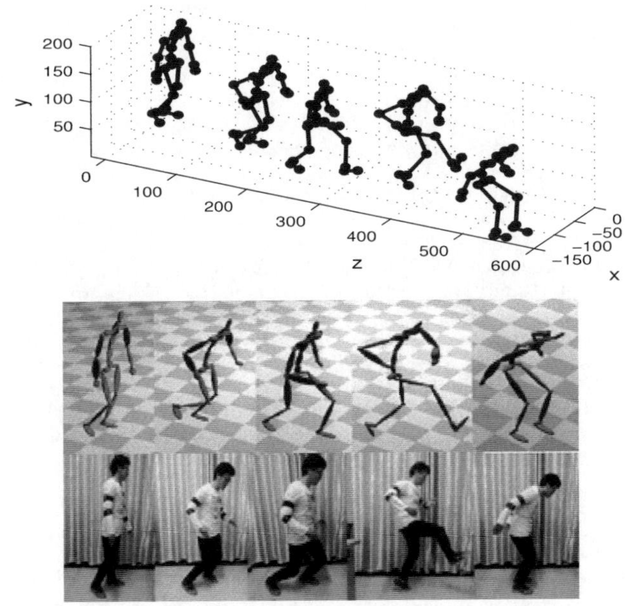

Figure 16: The reduction effect of jumping

4. CONCLUSIONS AND FUTURE WORKS

On the basis of distributed sensor motion capture system, the human motion capture based on quaternion navigation strategy has been designed. The paper then discussed the fusion optimization for the attitude quaternion by combining with the particle swarm filtering fusion algorithm. A geometric constraint model based on quaternion has been also established. All these make the human motion reconstruction more precise and smooth. Finally, we have compared the rotation effect between Euler angle and quaternion by empirical experimentation. In order to evaluate the performance of the system, we have also compared the capture effect of our system with real motion. At last, we validated the algorithm with MATLAB and Visual Studio motion capture platform. Ongoing works are devoted to improve the proposed method; for example we are improving its robustness against environmental noise, such as magnetic interference, which can currently degrade the acquired signal. The motion capture model also need further optimization, such as skinned mesh production.

Acknowledgments

This work was supported by National Natural Science Foundation of China under Grant No.61473058, Fundamental Research Funds for the Central Universities (DUT15ZD114), and National Natural Science Foundation of China under Grant No.61174027.

References

[1] C. M. N. Brigante, N. Abbate, A. Basile, et al., Towards Miniaturization of a MEMS Based Wearable Motion Capture System. IEEE Transactions on industrial electronics. 2011, 58(8), 3234-3241.

[2] W. Tan, W. Li, Y. Zheng, et al, A physical game based on wireless sensor networks.International Journal of Distributed Sensor Networks. 2009, 5(1):68.

[3] H. Wei, J. Zhao, Real-time control of 7R manipulator based

on motion capture. Journal of Mechanical Engineering, 2013, 23 (49):68-73.

[4] Z. Wang, S. Qiu, Z. Cao, et al., Quantiative assessment of dualgait analysis based on inertial sensors with body sensor networks. Sensor Review, 2013, 33(1):48-56.

[5] S. Wallace, J.E. Hubbel, J. Rogers, Driver shaft length influences on posture and swing tempo in skilled golfers. The Engineering of Sport, 2004, 1(5):216-223.

[6] Z. Wang, C. Zhao, S. Qiu, A system of human vital signs monitoring and activity recognition based on body sensor network. Sensor Review, 2014, 34(1):42-50.

[7] L-J. Gao, J-P. Cai, Analysis and implementation of features of character's action in shadow graph animation. Computer Engineering and Design. 2010, 31(10), 2335-2342.

[8] X-D. Li, M. Xiao, L, Zeng, Review on the Motion Capture Technologies. Science and Technology in Western China, 10(5):35-37, 2011.

[9] G.-Z. Yang (Ed), Body Sensor Networks, Springer, 2006.

[10] A. Augimeri, G. Fortino, S. Galzarano, R. Gravina, Collaborative Body Sensor Networks. Proc. of the International Conference IEEE Systems, Man and Cybertnetics (SMC2011), Oct. 9-12, Anchorage, Alaska, USA, 2011.

[11] X. Ling, L. Ren-fa, L. Juan, Recognition of Human Activity Based on Compressed Sensing in Body Sensor Networks. J. of Electronics and Information Technology. 2013, 35(1):119-125.

[12] K. D. Nguyen, I-M. Chen, Z. Luo, et al., A Wearing Sensing System for Tracking and Monitoring of Functional Arm Movement. IEEE/ASME Trans. On Mechatronics. 2011, 16(2):213-220.

[13] R. Zhi-neng, J. Wen-guang, L. Yi-xi, Design of wireless network on human motion capture. Journal of Zhejiang University, 2012, 46(7):1314-1319.

[14] D. Roetenberg, H. J. Luinge, C. T. M. Baten, et al., Compensation of magnetic disturbances improves inertial and magnetic sensing of human body segment orientation. IEEE Trans. on Neural System and Rehabilitation Engineering, 2005, 13(3):395-405.

[15] E. R. Bachmann, Inertial and magnetic tracking of limb segment orientation for inserting humans into synthetic environments Monterey, California,Naval Postgraduate School, 2000.

[16] G. Li, Z. Wu, X. Meng, et al., Modeling of Human Body for Animation by Micro-sensor Motion Capture. Second International Symposium on Knowledge Acquisition and Modeling, Nov.30- Dec.1, Wuhan, China, 2009.

[17] R. Gravina, P. Alinia, H. Ghasemzadeh, G. Fortino, Multi-Sensor Fusion in Body Sensor Networks: State-of-the-art and research challenges, Information Fusion, vol. 35, pp.68-80, 2017.

[18] J. B. Kuipers, Quaternions and rotation sequences, Princeton, NJ: Princeton Univ. Press, pp. 45-177, 2002.

[19] D. Roetenberg, I. Luinge, P. Slycke. Xsens MVN: Full 6DOF Human Motion Tracking Using Miniature Inertial Sensors. Xsens Technologies, pp.1-7, 2009.

[20] G. Fortino, S. Galzarano, R. Gravina, W. Li, A Framework for Collaborative Computing and Multi-Sensor Data Fusion in Body Sensor Networks. Information Fusion Journal, vol.22, pp. 50-70, Mar 2015.

[21] Q. Xiang-wei, Z. Wei-dong, Ji Yu-ren, Study on Aerial Vehicle Attitude Estimation Based on QuaternionParticle Filter Algorithm. Acta Armamentarii, 33(9):1070-1075, 2012.

[22] A. Doucet, N.D. Freitas, N. Gordon, Sequential Monte Carlo methods in practice. Springer, 2001.

[23] Q. Xiang-Wei, Attitude Determination Algorithm Based on Quaternion Nonlinear Filter for Spacecraft. PhD Dissertation, China, 2011.

Precise Detection and Treatment of Human Diseases Based on Nano Networking

Marc Stelzner[†], Florian-Lennert Lau[†], Katja Freundt[*], Florian Büther[†], Mai Linh Nguyen[†], Cordula Stamme[†*], Sebastian Ebers[†]

[†]University of Lübeck, Ratzeburger Allee 160, 23562 Lübeck, Germany
[*]Research Center Borstel, Parkallee 22, 23845 Borstel, Germany

{stelzner,lau,buether,nguyen,ebers}@itm.uni-luebeck.de
{kfreundt,cstamme}@fz-borstel.de

ABSTRACT

This paper presents an elaborate scenario to highlight and motivate interdisciplinary computer science involvement in nanotechnology for medical applications. Our scenario illustrates how nanotechnology can be employed to detect and potentially directly treat infectious diseases as a paradigm for human disorders associated with high morbidity and mortality. Thus, more precise techniques that monitor the presence and concentration of critical marker molecules (host- and pathogen-derived) may be applicable at an earlier stage of the disease. Moreover, since the concentration threshold varies from person to person, continuous and individualized monitoring of both diagnostic and therapeutic measures is required. To detect and treat diseases directly at the affected location, we propose the usage of an in-body nano network build by nano machines. To report findings and receive commands from outside of the body, the nano network is connected to a body area network via gateways. In this paper, we discuss the capabilities of nano machinery and presents the aforementioned network architecture.

CCS Concepts

•**Applied computing** → **Life and medical sciences;** Biological networks; •**Networks** → *Network protocols; Wireless access points, base stations and infrastructure;* Naming and addressing; Network simulations; Mobile networks; •**Hardware** → *Nanoelectromechanical systems;* Wireless devices; Biology-related information processing; Quantum dots and cellular automata;

Keywords

bacterial pneumonia; FCN; IoNT; molecular communication; tile-based self-assembly

Permission to make digital or hard copies of all or part of this work for personal or classroom use is granted without fee provided that copies are not made or distributed for profit or commercial advantage and that copies bear this notice and the full citation on the first page. Copyrights for components of this work owned by others than the author(s) must be honored. Abstracting with credit is permitted. To copy otherwise, or republish, to post on servers or to redistribute to lists, requires prior specific permission and/or a fee. Request permissions from permissions@acm.org.

BODYNETS 2016, December 25 - 16, 2016, Turin, Italy

1. INTRODUCTION

Diseases are an omnipresent topic in everyday life and of even greater interest in research. Scientists have analyzed new and old diseases in terms of origin, symptoms and their impact on biological—especially human—life for hundreds of years, constantly growing and updating the knowledge base. Researching diseases is of great importance, as virtually every human is confronted with different kinds of diseases throughout their life. To overcome diseases, people use traditional medicine, seek knowledge in (online) information sources, ask friends or use other resources from which they expect help. Usually only if the own or collective knowledge and treatments fail, a physician is consulted for diagnosis and treatment. Visiting a physician may not be an easy option. Often, a person needs to make an appointment, invest time for long waiting periods and eventually money.

However, time can be of the essence for some diseases that need to be diagnosed as soon as possible. For example, a tumor has to be detected before it starts metastasizing. Noticeable symptoms may appear too late or may be too indistinct to diagnose correctly right away. Different diseases have varying incubation times and progression speed. Persons with chronic diseases or conditions are even more endangered due to possible immunodeficiency. To be on the safe side, they would need constant monitoring, e.g., by daily medical appointments, which obviously is an unrealistic approach.

Therefore, it is desirable to (continuously) monitor the human body without the need for frequent examination in a hospital or clinic. To ease the load on physicians as well as potential patients, parts of the supervision and care may be outsourced to automated systems like implants. Some well-known types of implants (e.g., pace makers and insulin pumps) already function as a support for monitoring and treatment, but they are usually limited to a very specific use case.

An open research question of great interest is the reliable, local application of medical treatment, as opposed to systemic use. A systemic medicine application, e.g., an oral administration or an infusion, distributes medication within the whole body. The treatment thus not only acts on local symptoms or causes, but interacts with the non-affected, healthy body as well. For example, immunosuppressants globally inhibit the human immune system—the body's natural mechanism to maintain its own health status—which intervenes whenever necessary. Thus, the chance of new diseases to manifest themselves increases by systemic medical treatment. It is therefore desirable for a medical treatment to act as locally as possible in order to minimize any additional side effects.

We envision the use of nanotechnology, *body area networks* (BANs) and particularly nano communication as a locally deployable strategy for supervision and treatment inside the body without restricting individual mobility. BANs already offer many applications for sport, military, healthcare and more areas of interest [9,34,39]. Nanoscale devices allow these applications to be transferred to a much smaller and more accurate level. In the medical case, we expect in-body nano devices to provide continuous, precise and localized detection and possibly even treatment of diseases, while addressing the above-mentioned issues.

In the next section we explain the use of nanoscale technology based on a current medical research scenario. In Section 3, we explain the terminus and discuss the state of research in this area and define our own concept for achieving the scenario based vision in Section 4. We conclude the paper in Section 5 and pose upcoming challenges for our concept.

2. MEDICAL SCENARIO

Health care-associated bacterial pneumonias are a major cause of morbidity and mortality worldwide. Especially hospital-acquired pneumonia is associated with high mortality [6]. Currently, effective treatment of bacterial pneumonia is restricted by first, a dramatic increase of bacterial resistance to antibiotics [42] and second, by an altered patient clientele, i.e, elderly, immunosuppressed or chronically ill patients.

Moreover, all diagnostic strategies, i.e., clinical, radiologic, microbiologic, and molecular techniques have their intrinsic limitations.

Thus, antibiotic treatment is frequently performed based on clinical experience without prior detection of the specific pathogen. As an oral or intravenous application, these therapies always act systemically, thereby affecting the whole body. A systemic application of antibiotics without a defined pathogen aggravates and accelerates the problem of increasingly resistant bacteria [42]. Therefore, the development of new diagnostic and therapeutic measures is of great clinical relevance.

We envision a system to early, locally and specifically detect infections, estimate their relevance and check their severity. After consulting with an *analysis and control station* as shown in Figure 1, the proposed system responds to an infection in a suitable manner. This system comprises a (yet to be specified) number of nano machines, which act from within the human body as sensors or actuators. When equipped with communication capabilities, they form an in-body network to receive, send and forward messages. Additionally, implants or on-body microsystems form a BAN and serve as gateways between the nano machines and a control station. The control station (e.g., a smartphone) is located outside the human body, where it supplies appropriate computational power and memory to record and process the measurements taken by the nano machines and provides them to the patient or a physician. A control station with Internet access also allows to integrate external participants in the process, e.g., medical databases or physicians for additional analysis, monitoring or consultation. The whole system forms an *Internet of Nano Things* (IoNT).

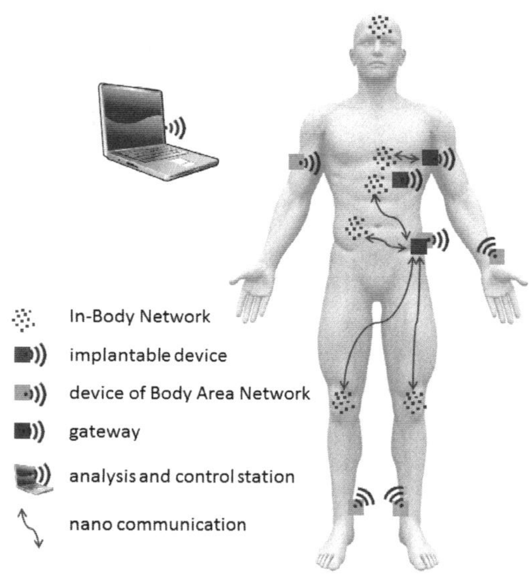

Figure 1: In-body and BAN Architecture [12]

In the presented scenario, one or more nano machines may aid in detecting a bacterial lung infection directly at the alveolar side, for example by detecting proinflammatory cytokines released by immune systems effector cells, or by detecting specific bacterial virulence factors, e.g., lipopolysaccharide, as a paradigm for the presence of Gram-negative bacteria. The machines communicate the measured concentration to the control station to decide whether the data constitutes sufficient evidence for a relevant and pathogenic infection. If appropriate, the nano machines can then be ordered to selectively release antibiotics and/or anti-inflammatory agents on spot.

3. NANOTECHNOLOGY IN MEDICINE

Nanotechnology is no new subject to medical research. It has various possible applications and promises to have a good chance of industrial and commercial success [28]. Current applications are therapeutical measures to fight cancer. For example, to remove malicious tissue, specifically designed magnetic nanoparticles may be deployed in the human body to attach themselves to a tumor. By heating these particles, the targeted tissue can be destroyed selectively [23].

While progress in nanomedicine and nanomaterials already leads to products being approved or reaching various stages of clinical studies [14], research on in-body communication between nano devices is still in a very early stage.

In this section, we explain termini as well as opportunities relevant for nano technology applied in medicine.

3.1 Characteristics of Nano Machines

Nano machines are devices with at most a few hundred nanometers in size. They aren't a mere further miniaturization of micro systems. At this magnitude, other physical laws do apply and quantum effects may disturb classical computational devices, forcing us to reconsider computation and communication at nanoscale [17]. There are currently three types of nano machines, i.e., biological, artificial and hybrid ones.

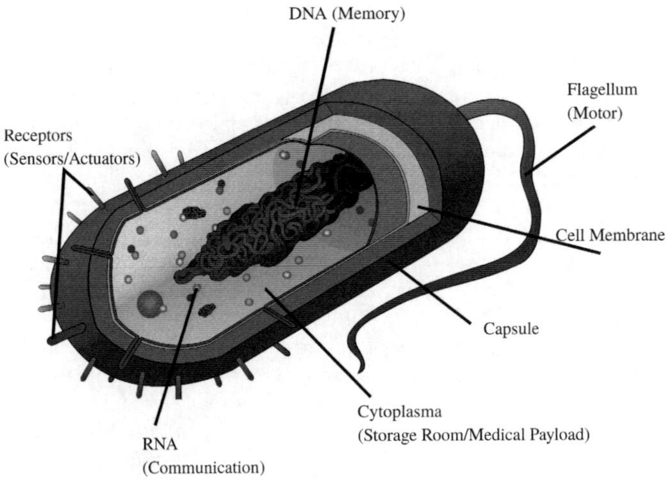

Figure 2: Structure and components of a prokaryote cell functioning as a nano machine.

As for the artificial nano machines, they can be seen as extremely resource constrained variants of micro system-devices known from the *Internet of Things* (IoT). Thus, we have to deal with constrained energy, memory and computation power. Solutions for the former involve zinc oxide high-density nano-wires as nano-sized batteries and piezoelectric energy harvesting techniques [24, 26] as well as heat engines the size of a single atom [37] as well as energy harvesting techniques. To solve the latter problem, many new concepts have been proposed, mostly involving carbon nanotubes (CNT), formed by one atom-thick sheets of graphene. The structural stability and conductivity of CNTs allow the construction of nanoscale field effect transistors (FET), but accurate manufacturing and placement are still open problems [21]. The physical integrity of a nano machine in the human body is another issue to be considered. Nano machines might be destroyed by chemical atom-sized reactions or carried away accidentally.

One key problem with the construction of nano machinery is the strictly limited size of the used components. Current CMOS-technology appears to malfunction due to quantum-effects at the nanoscale [17]. One approach to cope with the size-restrictions are alternative transistor-implementations that are robust to quantum-effects. CNTs have been suggested as a building block for future components.

Alternatively, nano machines can be biologically inspired constructs, for example cells (see Figure 2). All the challenges listed above do also apply here in a similar manner. The environment for a biological nano machine is the same and so are the problems. A cell may die or be destroyed and monitoring single cells is a difficult task. A cell requires cellular respiration to refill its ATP energy reserves that may be used for computational processes. Therefore, energy management facilities are required to regulate a modified cell's energy consumption. Otherwise, vital functionality may experience a lack of energy if other processes deplete the energy storage [25].

Additionally, bottom-up approaches may be used for the construction of nano machinery. In [43], Winfree suggests exploiting the process of DNA-self-assembly to construct arbitrary shapes out of artificially designed DNA-tiles. He also shows that his model is Turing-complete, while requiring vast amounts of space for those computations/constructions. DNA has also been suggested as a template for the construction of nano-electronics [8]. In this case, a self-assembled sheet of DNA is used to harbor a network of nanoscale computational- or memory-nodes. Depending on the implementation, this solution may be completely bio-inspired or a hybrid of DNA-scaffolding and artificially constructed nanoscale components.

3.2 Communication Types

Traditional means of communication use electromagnetic waves or wires. Radio communication in the range of megahertz radio waves using nanoscale antennas hasn't been possible yet [1]. CNT antennas [22] provide extremely good conductivity, while offering good stability. Given nanoscale size, the resulting wavelength of these antennas is in the terahertz band. At these high frequencies, atmospheric disturbances make communication distances exceeding 10 mm very susceptible to interferences [1].

Bio-inspired molecular communication is a completely alternative approach to traditional communication. It offers a range of different communication principles with varying properties in speed, accuracy, range, reliability and data capacity. For example, *pheromones* [33] can be used as a chemical long range communication option either through a fluid or aerial medium. The pheromones spread out via diffusion, a passive transportation process, where the direction of particle movement is not directly influenced by the source or messenger, but dependent on the surrounding environment. Although it provides a long range for organisms to communicate, the provided concentration for the diffused molecules has to be high enough to provide a sensible concentration at the target location. This may require a more potent source than a single nano machine can provide.

Furthermore, several new approaches exist: *calcium cell signaling* is a process of diffusion through calcium waves [31], the *optoacoustic effect* passes messages through optical excitation [38], *ultrasonic waves* feature a low frequency for reduced attenuation, i.e., increased range [15] and *neuronal communication* can make use of nerve tracts to transmit information by using electric surges [4].

3.3 Movement

It cannot be assumed that the position of a nano machine is static. As mentioned before, at least the environment has an impact on the position. Considering that nano machines in the human body are most likely be located in a fluid medium, this leads to different phenomena. In the bloodstream for example, the machines are driven by the flow velocity and direction, which is influenced by the proximity to the heart, general blood pressure, muscle contractions and gravitational acceleration. The devices are also exposed to effects that only exist at the nanoscale, like collisions with other moving atoms or molecules through Brownian motion. This constantly affects the direction of movement and thereby the relative position.

Means of targeted movement also exist in nature. Options inside the human body include *molecular motors* riding along rails like microfilaments or microtubules [3, 7]. Molecular motor proteins like Myosin and Kinesin harness ATP as chemical energy to power the movement process. They can also form a binding with other molecules and transport them along the rails. For railless locomotion some cells possess flagella [19]. A flagellum is a tentacle-like structure used to sense and to guide the cells movement process. These forms of biological movement can also be utilized as inter- and intracellular messages and therefore, as a means of communication.

Wang [41] provides a survey of recently developed ways of micro- and nanoscale locomotion advances, featuring Self-electrophoretic-, Bubble-, Electrical-, Magnetic- and Ultrasound Propulsion. For example, the hydrogen-bubble-propelled engine is a cone-shaped hollow rocket on the microscale [16]. It produces hydrogen from spontaneous chemical reaction at the inner zinc-coated inner layer. The resulting hydrogen is expelled through the wide end of the cone working as a bubble-propulsion. The engine does not need to carry additional fuel for movement, but requires an acidic environment.

The choice of locomotion closely relates to the structure of the nano machine and several self-directed motors have specific demands on the environment.

3.4 EHS and ELSI

When discussing nano machine deployment in human lifeforms, we cannot ignore the existence of environmental health and safety (EHS) risks as well as ethical, legal and social issues (ELSI).

When estimating the risks and safety issues of new technologies, the first approach often features an evolutionary analysis [11]. Substances (including particles) a species often experiences or interacts with are typically harmless [2]. Species adapt to the natural occurrence of particles and sometimes use them in their organisms as building blocks when suitable (food) while some of them become essential (vitamins/essential fats). Particles that are less common or less common in high quantities often impose a significant risk to a person's health or may at least trigger unpredictable consequences.

A suitable example are metal particles in the organism that might lead to metal intoxication once a certain threshold is met. Small quantities of iron are essential in the building process of red blood cells and zinc is required to build testosterone—too much might be lethal though. The filter-organs—liver, kidneys or spleen—never adapted to large quantities of rare or unknown particles and they naturally accumulate somewhere in the organism where it might be impossible to dispose of them.

Under these circumstances possible materials for in-body nano machines are harshly restricted—DNA appears to be a suitable building block tough. Even with DNA, safety issues might occur nevertheless. Chances are better that the liver or kidneys might be able to filter the resulting waste.

A precise estimation of the risks isn't possible for the above reasons, but a general direction may be derived. Clinical tests or animal studies are necessary to determine the true risk.

Environmental consequences are much harder to predict. For example, agricultural practices have shown that we aren't able to predict the effect pesticides like glyphosate have on the population of certain insects [18]. The effects of nano machinery in high quantities on the environment seems completely unpredictable[1] and thus are subject to laboratory tests. The advantages and possible future challenges render laboratory tests worthwhile, even despite risks.

Assuming that the proposed system may successfully complete the stages of simulation and in vitro testing from a scientific perspective, the ELSI still remain to place it on the market. International and national laws are still adapting to the upcoming nanotechnologies. In Germany, the system and its devices most likely are objective to the German *Medical Devices Act* [10] as it is a medical system to provide measurements, diagnosis and treatment. The Medical Devices Act is a legislation derived and implemented from the EU directives 93/42/EEC, 98/79/EEC and 90/385/EEC. In the process, an ethics commission and a federal authority need to approve the device before a clinical investigation is initiated for performance evaluation and exhibition. The devices will receive a classification to reflect its level of risk according to Annex IX from Directive 93/42/EEC. As nano machines are very invasive, may be long-living and may bear not yet completely investigated risks of impairing human health, the highest risk classification Class III is to be expected.

However, the ethics commission should not be the first group to think about ethical and social implications of new technologies for society. Public reception on the topic of invasive medical nanotechnology for monitoring and treatment has to be assessed and evaluated. If the technology is rejected by the society, it is less attractive to the market and more likely to be delayed. There has always been a co-influencing relationship between technology and society. New technology has the potential to heavily influence everyday life after integration, e.g. smartphones. Through change of society, new demands on technology arise, e.g. free high bandwidth access. The proposed system may change the frequency of how often medical examinations are applied or may change the job of a physician to be more remotely involved. But what are the consequences of continuous monitoring and maintenance of body functions? Will the personal freedom and range of possibilities increase, if medical treatment can be performed more independently from location and physician? To cope with this topic, Hunt and Mehta [20] investigated how nanotechnology is introduced, how it is perceived, which actors are involved—including governments—and how related sciences influence the framing.

4. CONCEPT

This section covers the concepts we envision as part of solutions for the medical scenario described in Section 2.

4.1 Function Centric Networking

In order to communicate in a network, message content needs to be delivered from one position to another. Since the possibilities of communication and machine types change drastically in the nanoscale environment, the protocols used in the Internet and IoT have to be analyzed for suitability.

Standard for traditional networks is the packet-switched Internet Protocol (IPv4/IPv6). This protocol requires at least addresses from sender and receiver. For resource constrained networks in the IoT lightweight solutions like 6LoWPAN [29], Zigbee or IEEE 802.15.4 [5] have been established to remove less relevant header information and therefore reduce communication overhead. These protocols may be viable approaches for an even more resource constrained WSN.

Nevertheless, even in conventional networks the IP-standard is questioned. IP is a host-centric architecture to connect

[1]Even *Grey Goo* apocalyptical scenarios seem possible.

endpoints with one another, while applications are typically focused on obtaining specific data and not on where the data is exactly located. E.g., *Named Data Networking* (NDN) [44] is a mature project for a data-centric architecture. Instead of addressing hosts, data is directly addressed in the NDN concept. An *Interest Packet*, carrying the name to identify the desired data, is emitted by the receiver to indicate interest. To match the interest a corresponding *Data Packet* has to be found. Routers in the network forward the interest by a lookup in the *Forward Interest Table* and leave a remark in a *Pending Interest Table* to remember interest and receiver. If the content is found at a host or router, it gets delivered backwards to the receiver and stored at *Content Stores* along the way.

A data-centric network is a useful approach in the medical IoNT as applications are not focused on communication with a specific nano machine itself but on receiving measurements and issuing treatments in defined body locations. We even have to reconsider the possibility or usefulness of addressing each nano machine individually. As depicted in Section 3.1, nano machines themselves are hard to monitor and may have a very short lifespan. Research is aimed at the production of self-assembling nano machines consisting of replaceable parts [7]. Additionally, a strong resource limit has to be expected, therefore stores and tables for routing and distribution—as used in NDN—will either have a very limited size or need to be discarded. On the other hand, information that is vital for the monitoring and treatment process for patients can be used in return. A nano machine needs to be aware of its sensory functions to provide semantically meaningful measurement data and its actor capabilities to correctly carry out requested actions. Hence we proposed the concept of *Function Centric Networking* (FCN) [40] to use the location[2] of a nano machine and its functional capabilities as part of the addressing scheme. This scheme does not allow to address a specific nano machine, but a group of nano machines fulfilling the same purpose in same position. For example, a message including the part 'Alice/LeftThumb/Sensor' addresses all nano machines in Alice's left thumb capable of any sensory action. Leaving function and/or location blank can be used like a broadcast, e.g., 'Alice/Leg/-' would address all nano machines in Alice's legs. Consequently, a nano machine can easily be replaced by another and multiple devices can handle requests. Applying this concept to a constantly mobile network of nano machines means that devices, which circle around in the human body irregularly, change their location and therefore their address. These machines only accept messages matching their current position. By this means, localized and precise treatment can be performed, e.g., releasing antibiotics on spot.

4.2 Nano Computation and Construction

Two key problems directly emerge from the presented vision. The first is the actual construction of nanoscale shapes, pattern or devices, while the second focuses on possible computer realizations that tolerate interfering quantum-effects. Various computational models haven been proposed to cope with the expected difficulties at the nanoscale. Nanoscale devices for in-body application have to fulfill special requirements in terms of bio-compatibility (see Subsection 3.4).

The discipline of DNA-computing features alternative models of computation on a biological basis. The process of self-assembly is often exploited to perform computations or grow arbitrary shapes using bottom-up principles.

Especially the DNA-self-assembly process is currently tested as a candidate for nanoscale circuit templates. Nano-electronics are often too small for conventional top-down construction. Self-assembly processes offer an alternative bottom-up approach. While DNA-self-assembly is capable of universal computation, it potentially requires vast amounts of space and differs fundamentally from elaborate approaches. The process seems to be better suited for the construction of scaffoldings or templates than computations.

An alternative computational model that theoretically enables computation at the nanoscale are quantum-dot cellular automata (QCA). QCA are a model of computation that exploits field-polarization to perform computations. Since it uses quantum-effects and electron-repulsion it is expected to function at the nanoscale and thereby offers an alternative to CMOS-technology. The automaton behavior may be exploited to form logical gates and compute boolean functions.

A combined approach of self-assembly systems and QCA may enable the construction of functioning nano machinery and thereby solve the most fundamental nanotechnology problem—from a computer science centric point of view. Once nano devices with capabilities comparable to current microchips are available, they may be applied to various medical problems.

We plan to explore the possibilities of the mentioned approach and establish a suitable mathematical model for simulations or general behavior prediction [27,35].

4.3 Nano Networking Simulation

Since we currently lack physical nano machines, we will investigate our previously presented concepts using simulations. For simulations, a model and simplified version of the original system, respectively, has to be created. However, aspects important for the investigation have to identified be modeled sufficiently precise to obtain accurate and useful results [32]. Thus, a simulation tool has to support domain-specific and up-to-date communication protocols as well as communication and mobility models. To find a suitable simulation tool, we investigated the current state of research in this field. We found, that *Nano-Sim* [36] is currently the most promising approach since it comes with models and protocol suites, especially developed to meet the complexity of communication at nanoscale. It supports communication based on electromagnetic waves and provides us a starting point for research in more advanced and efficient nano communication strategies. As a module of the ns-3 simulator[3], Nano-Sim can exploit models and protocols already available in ns-3. Also it lowers the hurdles for the research community to get in touch with nano communication as ns-3 is one of the most used network simulator. However, Nano-Sim does not cover all aspects needed for our evaluations like, e.g., a communication model for molecular communication in human bodies. The human body comprised many different types of fluids and tissues featuring their own characteristics which react differently on the various substances also present in the human body (cf. Section 2). These characteristics of the human body will influence the movement, communication

[2]Moore and Nakano [30] propose location-addressing using particle releasing beacons and chemotaxis navigation as some kind of biological triangulation.

[3]https://www.nsnam.org/

means and physical integrity of our nano machines. Thus, these aspects have to be modeled sufficiently precisely to get accurate results.

To the best of our knowledge, there is no simulation framework for nano networks providing appropriate communication models and protocols combined with means to model the human body's characteristics. Thus, we are currently developing a modular framework for simulating nano networks covering both aspects. The framework will comprise two modules, one will simulate communication, the other one human body characteristics. For simulating communication, we will build upon Nano-Sim and extend it where necessary. The architecture of our framework compares to the one used by *Veins*[4] which simulates vehicular networks by connecting a network simulator with a traffic simulator.

5. CONCLUSION AND FUTURE WORK

Nanotechnology on the described scale is still far from realizable, but also far from impossible and several scientific disciplines are currently creating the theoretical foundations—sometimes proving them in wet-lab experiments.

In this paper, we presented a medical scenario showing the benefit of employing nano technology for detecting and treating infectious diseases. However, the scenario can easily be adjusted to either detect or treat other diseases by modifying the sensors or actors to detect/treat accordingly.

We further presented an architecture comprising a combination of in-body nano network and body area network (BAN). The former consists of nano machines responsible serving as in-body sensors and actors. The sensed data is transmitted via gateways into the BAN to be analyzed by devices providing far more resources than the nano machines. If necessary, commands are issued from the BAN into the nano network, e.g., to directly and locally treat the detected diseases. We further presented concepts for addressing nano machines based on their location and functionality and discussed approaches for constructing nano machines and their computation capabilities. Additionally, we presented our requirements for a nano networking simulator and proposed elements of a suitable architecture based on the ns-3 simulator and its module Nano-Sim.

The FCN concept needs to be deployed as a protocol and defined in more detail. In this regard, safety and security [13] as well as routing of FCN messages will be explored as a next step.

Another goal of our research group it the design and evaluation of potential nano machine architectures. We aim at deriving a design template for possibly scalable, universal nano machines that fulfills the requirements of in-body environments. We currently research the limitations and possibilities of self-assembly processes at the nanoscale for the construction of nano machinery and explore if DNA-based self-assembly processes may be combined with quantum-dot cellular automata to form fully functional nano machinery with computational power comparable to current computers.

Furthermore, we are currently developing a simulation framework to be published in conjunction with the previously mentioned evaluation of current simulation tools.

[4]http://veins.car2x.org/

6. REFERENCES

[1] I. F. Akyildiz and J. M. Jornet. Electromagnetic wireless nanosensor networks. *Nano Communication Networks*, 1(1):3–19, Mar. 2010.

[2] D. Anderson, M. Sydor, F. P, and H. A. Nanotechnology: The risks and benefits for medical diagnosis and treatment. *Journal of Nanomedicine & Nanotechnology*, 7(4):1–2, 2016.

[3] B. Atakan, O. Akan, and S. Balasubramaniam. Body area nanonetworks with molecular communications in nanomedicine. *IEEE Communications Magazine*, 50(1):28–34, Jan. 2012.

[4] S. Balasubramaniam, N. T. Boyle, A. Della-Chiesa, F. Walsh, A. Mardinoglu, D. Botvich, and A. Prina-Mello. Development of artificial neuronal networks for molecular communication. *Nano Communication Networks*, 2(2):150–160, 2011.

[5] P. Baronti, P. Pillai, V. W. Chook, S. Chessa, A. Gotta, and Y. F. Hu. Wireless Sensor Networks: a Survey on the State of the Art and the 802.15.4 and ZigBee Standards. *Elsevier Computer Communications*, 30(7):1655–1695, May 2007.

[6] M. Bassetti, T. Welte, and R. G. Wunderink. Treatment of gram-negative pneumonia in the critical care setting: is the beta-lactam antibiotic backbone broken beyond repair? *Critical Care*, 20(1):1, 2016.

[7] S. F. Bush. *Nanoscale Communication Networks*. Artech House, 2010.

[8] V. Catania, A. Mineo, S. Monteleone, and D. Patti. A low-resource and scalable strategy for segment partitioning of many-core nano networks. In *Proceedings of International Workshop on Manycore Embedded Systems*, MES '14, pages 17:17–17:24, New York, NY, USA, 2014. ACM.

[9] M. Chen, S. Gonzalez, A. Vasilakos, H. Cao, and V. C. Leung. Body area networks: A survey. *Mobile networks and applications*, 16(2):171–193, 2011.

[10] S. W. Christian Johner, Matthias Hoelzer-Kluepfel. *Basiswissen Medizinische Software - Aus- und Weiterbildung zum Certified Professional for Medical Software*. dpunkt.verlag, 1 edition, 2011.

[11] T. Dobzhansky. Nothing in biology makes sense except in the light of evolution. *The american biology teacher*, 75(2):87–91, 2013.

[12] F. Dressler and S. Fischer. Connecting In-Body Nano Communication with Body Area Networks: Challenges and Opportunities of the Internet of Nano Things. *Elsevier Nano Communication Networks*, 6:29–38, June 2015.

[13] F. Dressler and F. Kargl. Towards security in nano-communication: Challenges and opportunities. *Elsevier Nano Communication Networks*, 3(3):151–160, September 2012.

[14] M. L. Etheridge, S. A. Campbell, A. G. Erdman, C. L. Haynes, S. M. Wolf, and J. McCullough. The big picture on nanomedicine: the state of investigational and approved nanomedicine products. *Nanomedicine: nanotechnology, biology and medicine*, 9(1):1–14, 2013.

[15] L. Galluccio, T. Melodia, S. Palazzo, and G. E. Santagati. Challenges and Implications of Using Ultrasonic Communications in Intra-body Area Networks. In *9th IEEE/IFIP Conference on Wireless*

On demand Network Systems and Services (WONS 2012), pages 182–189, Courmayeur, Italy, Jan. 2012. IEEE.

[16] W. Gao, A. Uygun, and J. Wang. Hydrogen-bubble-propelled zinc-based microrockets in strongly acidic media. *Journal of the American Chemical Society*, 134(2):897–900, 2011.

[17] N. Z. Haron and S. Hamdioui. Why is cmos scaling coming to an end? In *2008 3rd International Design and Test Workshop*, pages 98–103, Dec 2008.

[18] L. T. Herbert, D. E. Vázquez, A. Arenas, and W. M. Farina. Effects of field-realistic doses of glyphosate on honeybee appetitive behaviour. *Journal of Experimental Biology*, 217(19):3457–3464, 2014.

[19] H.-W. Huang, M. S. Sakar, A. J. Petruska, S. Pane, and B. J. Nelson. Soft micromachines with programmable motility and morphology. *Nat Commun*, 7, Jul 2016.

[20] G. Hunt and M. Mehta. *Nanotechnology:" Risk, Ethics and Law"*. Routledge, 2013.

[21] J. E. Jang, S. N. Cha, Y. J. Choi, D. J. Kang, T. P. Butler, D. G. Hasko, J. E. Jung, J. M. Kim, and G. A. J. Amaratunga. Nanoscale memory cell based on a nanoelectromechanical switched capacitor. *Nature Nanotechnology*, 3(1):26–30, Dec. 2007.

[22] K. Jensen, J. Weldon, H. Garcia, and A. Zettl. Nanotube radio. *Nano letters*, 7(11):3508–3511, 2007.

[23] A. Jordan, R. Scholz, P. Wust, H. Fähling, and R. Felix. Magnetic fluid hyperthermia (mfh): Cancer treatment with ac magnetic field induced excitation of biocompatible superparamagnetic nanoparticles. *Journal of Magnetism and Magnetic Materials*, 201(1):413–419, 1999.

[24] J. M. Jornet. A joint energy harvesting and consumption model for self-powered nano-devices in nanonetworks. In *IEEE International Conference on Communications (ICC 2012)*, Ottawa, Canada, June 2012. IEEE.

[25] M. Ş. Kuran, H. B. Yilmaz, T. Tugcu, and B. Özerman. Energy model for communication via diffusion in nanonetworks. *Nano Communication Networks*, 1(2):86–95, 2010.

[26] E. Lee, J. Park, M. Yim, Y. Kim, and G. Yoon. Characteristics of piezoelectric ZnO/AlN-stacked flexible nanogenerators for energy harvesting applications. *Applied Physics Letters*, 106(2):023901, Jan. 2015.

[27] C. S. Lent, P. D. Tougaw, W. Porod, and G. H. Bernstein. Quantum cellular automata. *Nanotechnology*, 4(1):49, 1993.

[28] L. Mazzola. Commercializing nanotechnology. *Nature biotechnology*, 21(10):1137–1143, 2003.

[29] G. Montenegro, N. Kushalnagar, J. Hui, and D. Culler. Transmission of IPv6 Packets over IEEE 802.15.4 Networks. RFC 4944, RFC Editor, Sept 2007.

[30] M. J. Moore and T. Nakano. Addressing by beacon distances using molecular communication. *Nano Communication Networks*, 2(2-3):161–173, June 2011.

[31] T. Nakano, T. Suda, M. Moore, R. Egashira, A. Enomoto, and K. Arima. Molecular Communication for Nanomachines Using Intercellular Calcium Signaling. In *5th IEEE Conference on Nanotechnology (NANO 2005)*, pages 478–481, Nagoya, Japan, July 2005. IEEE.

[32] B. Page. *Diskrete Simulation: Eine Einführung mit Modula-2*. Springer-Lehrbuch. Springer Berlin Heidelberg, 1991.

[33] L. Parcerisa Giné and I. F. Akyildiz. Molecular communication options for long range nanonetworks. *Computer Networks*, 53(16):2753–2766, Nov. 2009.

[34] M. Patel and J. Wang. Applications, challenges, and prospective in emerging body area networking technologies. *IEEE Wireless Communications Magazine*, 17(1):80–88, 2010.

[35] M. J. Patitz. An introduction to tile-based self-assembly and a survey of recent results. *Natural Computing*, 13(2):195–224, 2014.

[36] G. Piro, L. A. Grieco, G. Boggia, and P. Camarda. Nano-sim: Simulating electromagnetic-based nanonetworks in the network simulator 3. In *Proceedings of the 6th International ICST Conference on Simulation Tools and Techniques*, SimuTools '13, pages 203–210, ICST, Brussels, Belgium, Belgium, 2013. ICST (Institute for Computer Sciences, Social-Informatics and Telecommunications Engineering).

[37] J. Rossnagel, S. T. Dawkins, K. N. Tolazzi, O. Abah, E. Lutz, F. Schmidt-Kaler, and K. Singer. A single-atom heat engine. *Science*, 352(6283):325–329, 2016.

[38] G. E. Santagati and T. Melodia. Opto-ultrasonic communications in wireless body area nanonetworks. In *Asilomar Conference on Signals, Systems and Computers*. IEEE, Nov. 2013.

[39] R. Schmidt, T. Norgall, J. Mörsdorf, J. Bernhard, and T. von der Grün. Body area network ban–a key infrastructure element for patient-centered medical applications. *Biomedizinische Technik/Biomedical Engineering*, 47(s1a):365–368, 2002.

[40] M. Stelzner, F. Dressler, and S. Fischer. Function centric networking: an approach for addressing in In-Body nano networks. In *3rd ACM International Conference on Nanoscale Computing and Communication 2016 (ACM NanoCom'16)*, New York City, USA, Sept. 2016.

[41] J. Wang and W. Gao. Nano/microscale motors: biomedical opportunities and challenges. *ACS nano*, 6(7):5745–5751, 2012.

[42] WHO. 2014: Antimicrobial resistance global report on surveillance. 2014.

[43] E. Winfree, F. Liu, L. A. Wenzler, and N. C. Seeman. Design and self-assembly of two-dimensional dna crystals. *Nature*, 394(6693):539–544, 1998.

[44] L. Zhang, A. Afanasyev, J. Burke, V. Jacobson, k. claffy, P. Crowley, C. Papadopoulos, L. Wang, and B. Zhang. Named Data Networking. *ACM SIGCOMM Computer Communication Review*, 44(5):66–73, 2014.

Scalability of Kura-extended Gateways via MQTT-CoAP Integration and Hierarchical Optimizations

Paolo Bellavista
Dept. Computer Science and Engineering (DISI)
Alma Mater Studiorum – University of Bologna
Viale del Risorgimento, 2 – 40136 Bologna, Italy
paolo.bellavista@unibo.it

Alessandro Zanni
Dept. Computer Science and Engineering (DISI)
Alma Mater Studiorum – University of Bologna
Viale del Risorgimento, 2 – 40136 Bologna, Italy
alessandro.zanni3@unibo.it

ABSTRACT

The introduction of innovative Internet of Things (IoT) gateways, powered by efficient support protocols and tools, has the potential to boost IoT development and related opportunities. Some first open-source platforms and solutions have been developed along that direction, primarily with the goals of targeting device limitations in terms of available resources and of simplifying management operations in heterogeneous environments. This paper originally proposes a multi-protocol IoT gateway solution with the specific and main goals of enabling efficiency and scalability via proper MQTT-CoAP integration. To this purpose, we have extended the Kura framework, which exploits only MQTT for machine-to-machine communication, by implementing a significant CoAP support for scalable hierarchy-based coordination, capable of externally exposing any kind of resource with REST APIs. The paper also reports an extensive set of in-the-field measurements that show the scalability of the proposed prototype that, to achieve the desired performance, also exploits some original optimizations introduced by our work on both Kura and Californium frameworks.

CCS CONCEPTS

• **Computer systems organization** → **Architectures** → **Distributed Architectures** → n-tier *architectures*; • **Networks** → **Network types** → Cyber-physical networks → Sensor networks

KEYWORDS

Internet of Things (IoT), Scalability, Cloud-Sensor Interaction, IoT Gateways, Kura, Californium, MQTT, CoAP

1 INTRODUCTION

The Internet of Things (IoT) has rapidly become a tremendously growing research area of interest for both academia and industries. As many recent research activities have depicted, this exponential growth is expected to continue in the near future, towards a challenging mobile scenario where dynamicity and scalability are pushed to the extreme, thus posing very relevant and open technical challenges. This scenario also entails the relevance of middleware components, e.g., IoT gateways, able to reduce the complexities of IoT system deployment and application development, in particular to seamlessly support interoperability and scalability. Indeed, in the related literature IoT gateways are starting to demonstrate their potential in providing: i) scalability and data aggregations, working as dynamically identified data sinks; ii) interoperability at dynamically determined and most relevant network edges; iii) local support to resource-constrained devices (e.g., in the case of few remaining storage resources or energy power); iv) registration and discovery facilities, dynamically and efficiently, on behalf of their served devices.

Above all, we believe that IoT gateway scalability research is still in its infancy, with many open-source and industry-oriented platform initiatives still leaving open space to improve their scalability via specific optimizations. In particular, this paper proposes a significant scalability-oriented extension of the existing Kura industrial platform that allows hierarchical and efficient device/resource synchronization management in IoT scenarios. Our original solution is based on a dynamically managed tree structure [1] where, to provide scalability, we integrate the usage of standard MQTT (already included in the official Kura release) with the industry-widespread CoAP and the Californium framework.

By delving into finer details, on the one hand, we adopt a hierarchical tree solution to benefit from the topic-based publish/subscribe structure of MQTT that exploits hierarchical namespaces: we use MQTT to subscribe our IoT gateways and entities to multiple topics, to facilitate message management towards all the nodes of the hierarchy, and to add/remove IoT entities without changes in the whole topic hierarchy. On the other hand, MQTT has demonstrated some non-negligible limitations, in particular related to TCP usage and communications hold always open towards the employed brokers; for this reason, we have efficiently and scalably integrated MQTT in IoT Kura gateways with some purpose-specific CoAP usage (connection-less datagrams on top of UDP), especially on behalf of constrained devices, as detailed below. More specifically, we claim that our proposed solution is relevant and with good technical originality for multiple aspects:

- our solution is built on the top of a very promising and powerful open-source initiative, i.e., Kura, with mature ancillary frameworks, i.e., Guava and Kryo, and emerging open-standard protocols, i.e., MQTT and CoAP. In addition, SSL and DTLS integration is achieved for securing machine-to-machine communications;
- we have carefully evaluated MQTT and CoAP characteristics, in particular in terms of system performance and scalability, in order to combine them efficiently and to minimize their specific drawbacks;
- we propose an original IoT gateway extension, based on a dynamic and efficient tree structure to allow IoT resources on different devices to scalably interact even if deployed over a large-scale distributed area;
- we originally describe how we have specifically optimized both Kura MQTT and Californium CoAP supports to improve scalability performance when employed in our extended IoT gateways.

2 RELATED WORK

After seminal activities on scalability through replication and location-based optimizations [2, 3]Some research activities in the literature have recently proposed architectures to address IoT sensors/actuators federation, in particular within large-scale deployment scenarios, with particular focus on how to effectively and efficiently achieve scalability [2]. Even if they explored relevant solution guidelines and were someway inspiring for the community of researchers in the field, we claim that they only partially solved some aspects related to this hard technical challenge, thus leaving still open space for additional, especially industry-mature, solutions.

In particular, [4] proposes an architecture based on the RELOAD base protocol that provides a generic self-organized P2P overlay network service, by using CoAP as the transfer protocol to access RESTful services. Here CoAP is used as the common application layer protocol for heterogeneous and constrained devices, while RELOAD is employed primarily on proxy nodes with higher amount of resources. This work is also relevant to point out the relevance of open standard-based solutions for interoperability and the unsuitability of CoAP alone, e.g., because it is inappropriate to scalably aggregate IoT resources into a hierarchical organization.

[5] proposes a 3-layers architecture for cloud-integrated IoT services based on CoAP. The work proposes a Web integration platform that collects data from IoT devices and can outperform high-performance general-purpose Web servers that are not optimized for the IoT. [5] uses the Californium framework for CoAP integration, by showing its good throughput performance also in high-concurrency situations. Along with CoAP, the solution in [5] employs multi-threaded sockets, but shows that this implementation option is very resource-demanding while growing the number of clients, in particular in terms of memory.

Instead, [6, 7] mainly highlight successful examples of MQTT usage in some application domains. In particular, [6] proposes an architecture for adaptive periodic many-to-one communication in large-scale cyber-physical systems. The paper shows how MQTT can guarantee good flexibility in highly dynamic execution environments where publishers and subscribers can join/leave frequently. [7] reports the experience of a smart home management system where MQTT is used over a hierarchical architecture similar to ours, but with no integrated exploitation of CoAP.

3 AN ORIGINAL KURA EXTENSION FOR SCALABILITY THROUGH COAP

Our original Kura-extended IoT gateway exploits the integration and interworking between MQTT, already fully supported within Kura, and CoAP, with the main purpose of improving scalability in a resource-efficient way. In particular, we have organized IoT devices in a dynamic and hierarchical tree structure, where MQTT is primarily used for tree management and inter-node coordination/communication; instead, CoAP is primarily used for device discovery and external accessibility via REST. For the sake of briefness, we refer to [1] for the general description of our tree structure and for the description of the primary characteristics of the industry-widespread MQTT and CoAP protocols; in this paper, we originally focus on relevant design/implementation insights and performance results about our prototype.

By delving into finer details, we have decided to use MQTT for inter-node coordination/communication inside our tree organization to efficiently manage large-scale deployments via hierarchy- and locality-oriented optimizations. In particular, we exploit the MQTT publish/subscribe model for communications between CoAP servers to retrieve IoT device information and for tree management synchronization. Publishers and subscribers are well decoupled each other, thus also simplifying the dynamic variations in the tree structure via hierarchical topics: our nodes may subscribe to a topic and then observe their whole hierarchy by using wildcards. In addition, we exploit the useful MQTT characteristics of reliability and seamless NAT traversal in these cases.

Notwithstanding its many pros, it starts to be recognized that MQTT also presents some weaknesses for highly scalable IoT applications, such as, only to rapidly overview the two most relevant and recognized ones: i) TCP usage, more suitable for resource-full nodes than for constrained IoT devices; and ii) persistent (and expensive) node-broker TCP connections. Therefore, we believe that an MQTT-alone-based IoT gateway is inappropriate in large-scale scenarios and that CoAP is the right protocol to complement MQTT in IoT gateway implementations. In other words, the pervasive usage of MQTT introduces overhead for functions that are not crucial: using a less reliable but also less resource-demanding connection is often more suitable, especially if the sporadic loss of partial data is not critically impacting the overall system behavior. In particular, our original IoT gateway solution exploits CoAP i) to easily add new discoverable devices at runtime (accessible via REST API); and ii) for interactions where we need direct and very responsive lightweight communications, with low reliability constraints, such as for coordination and simple service interaction within single localities, where NAT drawbacks are ineffective and communication reliability is anyway adequate.

4 OUR KURA-EXTENDED IOT GATEWAY: IMPLEMENTATION INSIGHTS

This section presents our implementation work organized into i) internal node structure, replicated into all nodes, and ii) tree-based hierarchy management. The implemented prototype is based on widespread industry-mature solutions and frameworks, such as the MQTT and CoAP protocols, as well as the Kura [1] and Californium frameworks. Californium [8] is currently the most complete open-source implementation of CoAP, with the partial/complete support of many draft extensions. In particular, it provides implementations for: the observe draft [9] to enable CoAP clients to retrieve and update resource representations; the blockwise transfers draft [10] to support stateless behavior while handling transfer blocks separately; and the resource directory draft [11]. The Californium CoAP payload adopts the CoRE Link Format [12], uses the Datagram Transport Layer Security (DTLS) protocol [13], and exploits CoAP-HTTP cross-proxy support through HttpCore-NIO [14] and Guava [15].

4.1 Internal Node Structure

Our CoAP-based extension of the Kura IoT gateway is modularly and flexibly implemented via OSGi bundles, executed by the Kura framework on each IoT node. In addition, Kura allows to exploit a native MQTT support to select differentiated QoS levels: exactly-once semantics can be accessed via the so-called QoS2 mode and we use it for most relevant hierarchy management messages; MQTT QoS1, instead, offers at-least-once semantics that we adopt for more common inter-node communication, with overall performance benefits (see Section 5). For the sake of modularity and loose coupling, any node is structured into multiple components: CoAP server, Californium service, Resource Directory (RD), Remote Query Resource (RQ), and CoAP resource.

The CoAP server is the central component within a node, manages the properties of registered CoAP resources, and uses Californium to offer REST API operations. In particular, CoAP servers use the RD component as a data structure to store endpoints and to enable usual registry operations (e.g., register, maintain, lookup, remove endpoint and resource description) via REST requests. Each CoAP server leverages the RQ bundle for resource lookup inside the hierarchy, by interfacing CoAP server requests with the MQTT broker, with CoAPPublisher and CoAPSubscriber classes. The resource lookup is performed by a set of iterative requests towards other hierarchy nodes, starting from the parent node, that reply with the direct link to the resource or with a list of CoAP servers that may contain the resource for further search (see Figure 1). Finally, we provide the CoAP server implementation with the DTLS support extension, using the existing subproject Scandium [16] inside Californium.

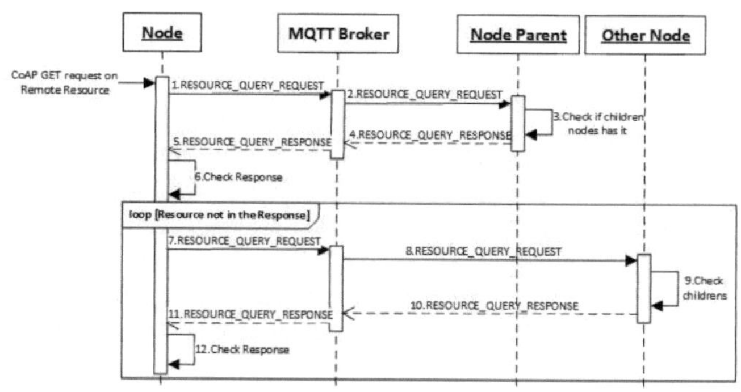

Figure 1: Resource lookup iterations.

4.2 Tree-based Hierarchy Management

Our IoT gateway dynamically joins a multi-layer hierarchy, structured into three levels, where each node specifies domain and group name used for identifying it. Level0 includes the root node and the CoAPTreeHandler (CTH), which enable inter-domain communication and manage the CoAP servers hierarchy, while level1 and level2 include all the nodes belonging, respectively, to a specific domain or domain/sub-group.

4.2.1 CoapTreeHandler. The CTH bundle dynamically manages the hierarchy and dispatch node requests: it provides hierarchy metadata to all nodes, returns the references to create a tree-structure organized with domains/groups; manages multiple node replications; and handles children nodes in case of parent disconnections. Internally, CTH consists of CTHListener and CTHCollections. CTHListener exposes an interface to interact with CTH, triggered by request from nodes that require actions on the hierarchy. The CTHCollections class stores information about the overall hierarchy and consists of two collections optimized for lookup and node substitutions: a Map-extension data structure to store node paths and properties; a data structure to map parent-children associations by using the Guava library in order to simplify collection updates, i.e., dynamic creation of one-to-many associations. To practically exemplify how the hierarchy management works, here we rapidly outline some common use cases:

- New root request. CTH returns the root reference and stores into CTHCollection the node address (root duplicates management). When root disconnects, CTHCollection contains references to suitable new root nodes to replace it and notify level1 nodes;
- Node addition (Figure 2). By providing its path, a node requests root information: if root is present, the node is notified with the root node reference (root_response); if root unavailable, the node is added as root (root_added) or updated (root_not_available). CTH checks the path provided: if new path, the node is added to the hierarchy; otherwise, the node becomes the child of the original node and will able to perform resource lookup or return a local resource;
- Node removal. i) If the node to be removed is the root, CTHCollection provides the reference to the new root, otherwise CTH searches a new root on level1. ii) If leaf, CTH only updates the hierarchy information. iii) Otherwise (Figure 3), children are associated to the root while CTH looks for a new parent, then children are restored;
- CTH failure. During CTH inaccessibility the root is not aware of hierarchy updates. Once CTH reconnects, an emergency MQTT topic (cth_online) triggers a stateless recovery with hierarchy node soft-reboot: i) parents remove all properties attached; ii) children remove parents and resend the request to join the hierarchy; iii) resource collections are sent to the parents and to CTH to be aligned again.

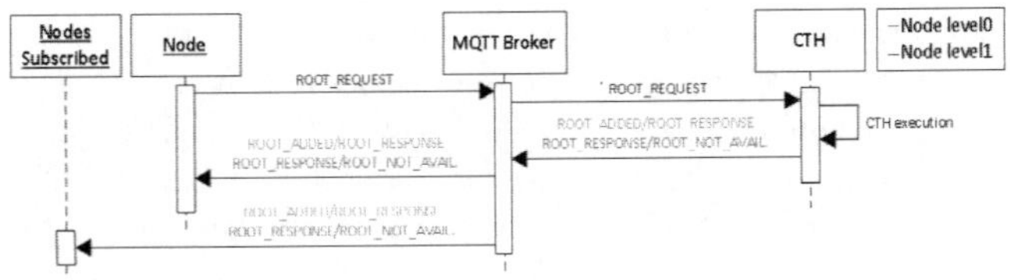

Figure 2: Node Connection iterations.

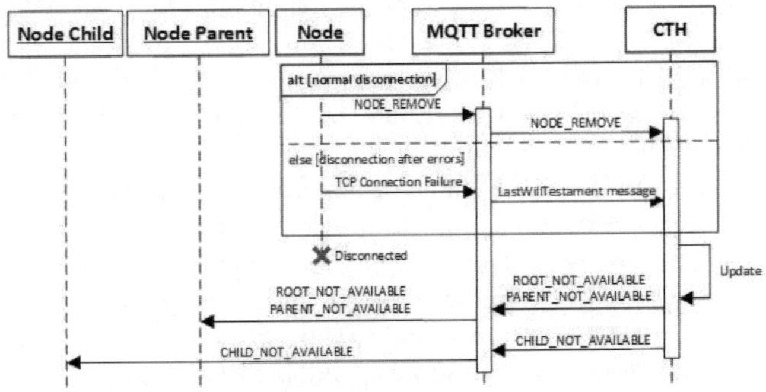

Figure 3: Node removal iterations.

4.3 Performance Optimizations

Although Kura and Californium are widespread and industry-mature frameworks, their default configurations have demonstrated to be not specifically optimized for our hierarchical IoT gateway organization. Thus, we introduce some non-negligible implementation/configuration improvements, focusing on the following primary critical scalability aspects: reducing the number of MQTT messages exchanged among levels and nodes; reducing the number of POST requests to RD.

4.3.1 Object Serialization (OS). MQTT is content-less and only support byte array as payload content. Thus, serialization is performed very often during regular operation: each CoAP message is serialized, then used into the Kura DataService class for MQTT communication, and de-serialized during responses. We have improved performance by integrating serialization based on the efficient Kryo framework. Kryo [17] is an open-source object graph serialization framework for Java.

4.3.2 Data Service (DS) and DataTransportService. The DataService class is the Kura component used to manage MQTT communication and offers several configuration options, delegating to the DataTransportService the implementation of the transport protocol to interact with the associated MQTT broker. When DataService receives a publish request, it stores the message into a DataStore and submits the message on the internal executor of DataTransportService. DataStore is a heavy storage structure that, in case of many messages published concurrently, may even cause unavailability of the device because of its high CPU consumption. Therefore, to reduce associated overhead, we have decided to exploit only the lower-level DataTransportService class, by removing the support to the features, irrelevant for our solution, of message priority management and message storage on behalf of temporarily disconnected devices. In addition, our DataTransportService performs event propagation by accessing methods and client listeners of the MQTT Paho implementation [18].

Our experimental work has pointed out that the default configuration of the Californium framework exhibits some performance drawbacks for highly scalable scenarios, in particular in terms of efficient message parsing. We have optimized the related aspects by providing original extensions for i) efficient data structures for CoAP payload parsing, ii) efficient support to most frequent regular expressions to identify message sections, and iii) exploitation of message setting patterns available into the CoRE Link Format.

4.3.3 RD Parsing (RP) and String Refactoring (SR). To optimize regular expression management and to speed up parsing, we have decided to represent any CoRE link with resource path in the first position of the RD attribute list (fixed static position). In addition, we adopt Guava libraries for efficient string management; for instance, we have replaced the Java Scanner class with the specialized Guava Splitter and used the optimized StringBuilder for string declaration.

4.3.4 Request Aggregation (RA). Since every node can send POST messages, it is likely that some nodes may send information about multiple resources. Thus, we optimize message management whenever possible (in absence of strict latency requirements) by aggregating multiple resources together into a single CoRE link format composition.

5 IN-THE-FIELD PERFORMANCE RESULTS

To quantitatively evaluate the scalability of our tree-based IoT gateway organization and the efficiency of our combined usage of MQTT and CoAP, we have extensively tested our solution in realistic application/deployment scenarios: the results reported in this section are average values over multiple runs and also compare the performance of MQTT and Californium default configurations with our original optimizations described above. In particular, in our tests we have used growing numbers of sequential MQTT requests and CoAP POST ones, distributed over a realistic testbed environment consisting of 10 nodes organized in a 4-layer tree, 20 service bundles per node, 2 devices per service bundle, and 10 sensors per device. Each regular (non-root) node is equipped with RaspberryPi 1 model B+, with Raspbian Whezzy, Kura version 1.1.1; Parallels VM, with 512 MB Ram, single core CPU, Xubuntu OS. The root node is 2.2 GHz Intel i7 CPU, 16 GB RAM, 1600 MHz DDR3. The integrated MQTT Broker is Mosquitto. Additional details about the exact setup of our testbed deployment and further performance results, e.g., on DTLS overhead, are not reported here for the sake of briefness and are available at our Web site http://lia.disi.unibo.it/research/MQTT_CoAP_Integration.

MQTT-related evaluation tests have started by sending a peak of 1000 concurrent requests between two RaspberryPi. Without any of our optimizations described above, our prototype is not able to handle them; exceptions related to too many messages stored and too many messages waiting the ACK are observed. Thanks to our object serialization optimization, we have observed a significant decrease of the total time needed to serve all the requests (around 49%), but anyway this is still insufficient to manage such a large peak with no exception occurrences. By adding also our DataService optimization, we have experienced another significant performance improvement, as well as the ability not to enter in exception situations due to overload.

After that preliminary experimentation, we have evaluated the behavior of our prototype while further increasing the number of MQTT exchanged messages. Table 1 reports the total time to complete MQTT transmissions in relation to the optimizations introduced. Note that, due to their limited capabilities and the high number of operations to perform, sometimes RaspberryPi nodes are affected by connection lost errors with the MQTT broker; this has shown to be prevalently due to the inability of sending MQTT heartbeat messages in time to keep the associated connection alive.

Table 1: MQTT Performance Results

Sender/ Receiver	Optimi zation	MQTT Req.	Time (s)	Errors
Raspberry/ Raspberry	-	1000	211	KuraStoreCapacityReached KuraTooManyInflight Messages
Raspberry/ Raspberry	OS	1000	109	KuraStoreCapacityReached KuraTooManyInflight Messages
Raspberry/ Raspberry	OS - DS	1000	14	-
VM/ Raspberry	OS - DS	1000	5	-
VM/VM	OS - DS	1000	1	-
Raspberry/ Raspberry	OS - DS	10000	120	Lost Connection

VM/ Raspberry	OS - DS	10000	60	-
VM/VM	OS - DS	10000	7	-
Raspberry/ Raspberry	OS - DS	60000	723	Lost Connection
VM/ Raspberry	OS - DS	60000	377	-
VM/VM	OS - DS	60000	34	-

By passing to some relevant results about RD (CoAP-centered) evaluation, we have started RD tests by sending 500 POST requests: already with this number of requests, the default Californium configuration has shown non-negligible performance issues; for instance, when working on top of a limited gateway such as the RaspberryPi one, this load peak may frequently generate errors. Therefore, we have applied our original RD optimizations, also in different partial subsets; Table 2 reports the related performance results in terms of total time to complete the POST requests on RD, with the different possible subsets of optimizations introduced.

Table 2: RD Performance Results

Sender/ Receiver	Optimization	POST Req.	Time (s)	Errors
Raspberry/ Raspberry	-	500	99	POST timeout
VM/ Raspberry	-	500	12	-
VM/VM	-	500	6	-
Raspberry/ Raspberry	RP	500	68	Possible POST timeout
VM/ Raspberry	RP	500	7	-
VM/VM	RP	500	4	-
Raspberry/ Raspberry	RP – RA	500	55	-
VM/ Raspberry	RP – RA	500	5	-
VM/VM	RP – RA	500	3	-
Raspberry/ Raspberry	RP – RA – SR	500	19	-
VM/ Raspberry	RP – RA – SR	500	4	-
VM/VM	RP – RA – SR	500	0.8	-
Raspberry/ Raspberry	RP – RA – SR	1000	51	-
VM/ Raspberry	RP – RA – SR	1000	11	-
VM/VM	RP – RA – SR	1000	1.8	-
Raspberry/ Raspberry	RP – RA – SR	5000	255	POST timeout, not responsive device, Californium server stops
VM/ Raspberry	RP – RA – SR	5000	54	-
VM/VM	RP – RA – SR	5000	3.3	-
Raspberry/ Raspberry	RP – RA – SR	10000	491	POST timeout, not responsive device, Californium server stops
VM/ Raspberry	RP – RA – SR	10000	104	-
VM/VM	RP – RA – SR	10000	6.9	-

In addition to the above results for communication performance, we have thoroughly investigated resource consumption on IoT gateways, which is crucial also to maintain full responsiveness of the participating nodes. CPU and RAM usage on RaspberryPi nodes, when 500 resources are registered (four description attributes each, on average) via POST REST invocations, is respectively 92% and 80%, with around 550 active threads. In fact, every time RD stores a resource, the Californium-based CoAP implementation associates a new thread to it in order to monitor its validity time and delete the registration once it expires. With a high amount of concurrent requests, this multi-threaded support is clearly not adequate. Therefore, we have decided to change the associated multi-threaded support via an optimized set of worker threads, each of them handling a partition of resources (the cardinality of the partition is dynamically determined and can change over time – self-adapting monitoring).

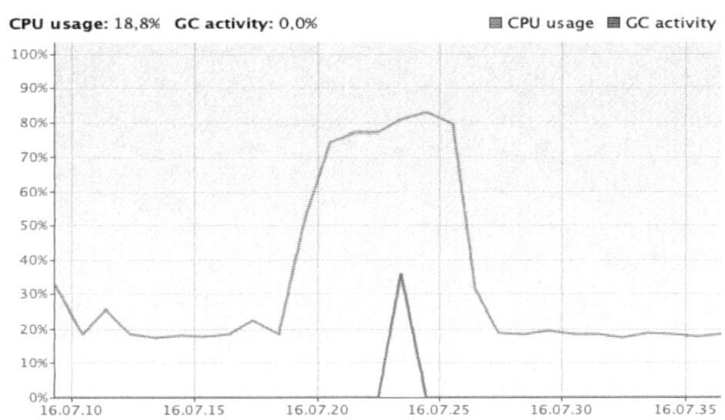

Figure 4: CPU usage

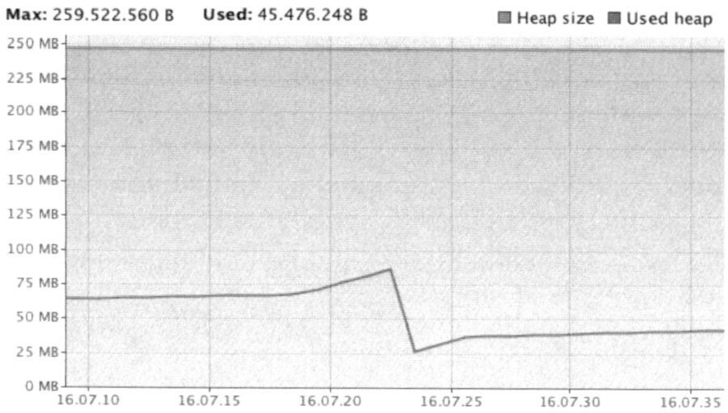

Figure 5: RAM usage

In particular, registration update periodicity may vary depending on desired responsiveness and available resources at gateways; consider also that in our application scenario, a false positive in resource registrations only generates the waste of a useless lightweight CoAP request that will not receive any response. Figures 4 and 5 show the performance results about resource consumption in the thread-optimized case (only 35 active threads on average).

6 CONCLUSIVE REMARKS

The paper has presented most significant implementation insights and in-the-field performance results about our CoAP-integrated Kura-extended IoT gateway. The reported results show that our solution can preserve scalability also in high-load scenarios, with overall latency that is proportional to the number of incoming requests and limited overhead. In addition, we have described some implementation/configuration optimizations that significantly improve the performance of both the standard Kura gateway and the exploited Californium framework for CoAP. Moreover, we were able to achieve good overall performance also with IoT devices with very strict resource constraints, like the used RaspberryPis.

ACKNOWLEDGMENTS

The Authors would like to take the opportunity to thank all the MSc students who participated to this project, with their extension and experimentation activities during course projects and MSc graduation works. A special thank goes to Gianvito Morena, whose contribution was substantial and essential for the results reported in this paper.

REFERENCES

[1] P. Bellavista, A. Zanni, "Towards Better Scalability for IoT-Cloud Interactions via Combined Exploitation of MQTT and CoAP", IEEE 2nd International Forum on Research and Technologies for Society and Industry (RTSI), 2016.
[2] P. Bellavista, A. Corradi, C. Giannelli. "Efficiently Managing Location Information with Privacy Requirements in Wi-Fi Networks: a Middleware Approach", 2nd Int. Symp. Wireless Communication Systems. IEEE, 2005.
[3] P. Bellavista, A. Corradi, E. Magistretti. "REDMAN: an Optimistic Replication Middleware for Read-only Resources in Dense MANETs", Elsevier Pervasive and Mobile Computing Journal, Vol. 1, No. 3, pp. 279-310, 2005.
[4] J. Mäenpää, J. Jiménez Bolonio, S. Loreto, "Using RELOAD and CoAP for Wide Area Sensor and Actuator Networking", Eurasip J. Wireless Communications and Networking, Vol. 121, pp. 1-22, 2012.
[5] M. Kovatsch, M. Lanter, Z. Shelby, "Californium: Scalable Cloud Services for the Internet of Things with CoAP", IEEE 4th International Conference on the Internet of Things, 2014.
[6] H. Jo, H. Jin, "Adaptive Periodic Communication over MQTT for Large-Scale Cyber-Physical Systems", IEEE 3rd Int. Conference on Cyber-Physical Systems, Networks, Applications, 2015.
[7] Y.T. Lee, et al., "An Integrated Cloud-Based Smart Home Management System with Community Hierarchy", IEEE Transactions on Consumer Electronics, vol. 62, issue 1, 2016.
[8] Californium. Available online at: https://eclipse.org/californium.
[9] K. Hartke, Observing Resources in CoAP, IETF Internet Draft, 2014. Available online at: https://tools.ietf.org/html/draft-ietf-core-observe-16.
[10] C. Bormann, "Block-wise transfers in CoAP draft-ietf-core-block-17", IETF Internet Draft, 2015. Available online at: https://tools.ietf.org/html/draft-ietf-core-block-17.
[11] Z. Shelby, C. Bormann, "CoRE Resource Directory draft-ietf-core-resource-directory-02", IETF Internet Draft, 2014. Available online at: http://tools.ietf.org/html/draft-ietf-core-resource-directory-02.
[12] Z. Shelby, "Constrained RESTful Environments (CoRE) Link Format", IETF Internet Draft, 2012. Available online at: https://tools.ietf.org/html/rfc6690.
[13] E. Rescorla, N. Modadugu, "Datagram Transport Layer Security Version 1.2", IETF Internet Draft, 2012. Available online at: https://tools.ietf.org/html/rfc6347.
[14] HttpCore-NIO. Available online at: http://hc.apache.org/httpcomponents-core-ga/index.html.
[15] K. Boumillion, J. Levy, "Guava: Google core libraries for Java 1.5+". Available online at: https://github.com/google/guava.
[16] Scandium. Available online at: https://github.com/eclipse/californium.scandium.
[17] Kryo. Available online at: https://github.com/EsotericSoftware/kryo.
[18] Paho. Available online at: https://eclipse.org/paho.

Multi-frame Transfer for Data Dissemination in LTE Device-to-Device Proximity Discovery

Paolo Bellavista
Dept. Computer Science and Engineering (DISI)
Alma Mater Studiorum – University of Bologna
Viale del Risorgimento, 2 – 40136 Bologna, Italy
paolo.bellavista@unibo.it

Jacopo De Benedetto
Dept. Computer Science and Engineering (DISI)
Alma Mater Studiorum – University of Bologna
Viale del Risorgimento, 2 – 40136 Bologna, Italy
jacopo.debenedetto@unibo.it

ABSTRACT

It starts to be widely recognized the growing and central relevance of Device-to-Device (D2D) interactions for future 5G networking and applications, also to stimulate opportunistic collaborations and efficient resource usage based on proximity. A crucial building block to enable such D2D collaboration is proximity discovery, hopefully with so limited network/energy overhead to have the opportunity to be "always-on". This paper proposes an original and efficient multi-frame transport protocol for disseminating data of any length over real industrial D2D solutions. In particular, even if of general applicability, we have originally implemented our protocol on top of the new LTE Direct proximity discovery, which has very strong limitations in the transmittable data for single discovery period. The paper not only describes our development experience with the brand new LTE Direct Qualcomm implementation, but also reports experimental results with the LTE Direct simulator included in the Qualcomm LTE Direct Trial SDK, which are relevant to tune our protocol and to robustly assess its validity.

CCS CONCEPTS

• **Computer systems organization** → **Architectures** → **Distributed Architectures** → n-tier *architectures*; • **Networks** → **Network types** → Cyber-physical networks → Sensor networks

KEYWORDS

Device-to-device Communications; Data Dissemination; Proximity; Discovery; LTE Direct.

1 INTRODUCTION

Device-to-Device (D2D) communications are expected to play a very relevant role in future smartphone generations and in several Internet-of-Things (IoT) application domains, also thanks to the associated opportunities of increasing spatial reuse of spectrum resources and of enabling low latency communication links [1-4]. The D2D paradigm has two fundamental building blocks: i) proximity discovery and ii) direct communication between proximate devices. While the latter one has already received considerable attention by research activities in the very last years, the former has only recently stimulated the first related and significant research efforts, in both industries and academia, in conjunction with the growing interest of its D2D-enabled IoT applications [5-11].

One of the main recognized challenges for the success of D2D proximity discovery is its ability to maintain the discovery functionality "always-on" and at the same time to keep its energy consumption at the lowest level. To this purpose, primary efforts are directed towards minimizing i) the power used in D2D data transmission/reception, and ii) the duration of the D2D active transmission/reception period. For instance, reducing transmission/reception power is often obtained by decreasing the number of channels used for D2D communication. In addition, reducing the active transmission/reception period is often pursued via the synchronization of advertise/scan periods between participating devices.

All the above requirements tend to lead, in D2D proximity discovery specifications for all major wireless connectivity technologies, as better detailed in Section 2, towards a strong limitation in the amount of data that can be sent/received at most in a single discovery period. This is sometimes reasonable and not too limiting for communications in some kind of Machine-to-Machine (M2M) applications, e.g., where a few predefined instructions/data can be expressed using only a very limited number of codification bytes and where the "polling" periods can be very frequent. However, this represents a too strong and limiting constraint when the opportunity of proximity discovery could be considered as a starting basis for:

- disseminating human-readable data in target proximity localities via geo-casting, e.g., for traffic monitoring/alert information to drivers;
- distributing larger amount of M2M data at less regular and less frequent time intervals, e.g., because of aggregating/batching actions over IoT gateways in order to improve network/energy efficiency;
- disseminating discovery data about extensive lists of available services in highly scalable deployment environments where large numbers of devices (and their offered facilities) may be present, in particular in dense urban environments.

Given the above impactful opportunities and the many application domains that can benefit from D2D proximity discovery-based data dissemination, we have decided to originally work on a simple but efficient protocol that allows the exchange of (theoretically) unlimited amount of data over any standard D2D proximity discovery solutions available in current wireless connectivity technologies (which are starting to support proximity discovery). Our original protocol splits data to be disseminated into chunks that, by using a dedicated header, can be transmitted independently the one from the other; the protocol is conceived to work in a relatively high-mobility scenario where the probability of losing some chunks is not negligible, also due to the intrinsic low-level characteristics of proximity discovery in all current wireless connectivity options.

In addition to the proposal of this multi-frame transfer protocol per se, which has its primary technical novelty in being suitable for D2D proximity discovery integration, we claim that this paper provides a significant contribution for the community of researchers in the field because it reports the experience and lessons learnt from the design/implementation of our protocol prototype on top of the brand new LTE Direct proximity discovery by Qualcomm. To the best of our knowledge, this is the first paper presenting an implementation (and related simulation work) of a multi-frame transfer protocol over LTE Direct, which is widespreadly considered a promising and potentially impactful technology advancement step if compared to "traditional" LTE, definitely of growing industrial interest for the years to come.

The remainder of the paper is structured as follows. Section 2 overviews the primary characteristics of D2D proximity discovery over the most relevant connectivity technologies where it starts to be standardly supported, i.e., Bluetooth Low Energy, Wi-Fi Aware, and LTE Direct; then, it focuses on the brand new LTE Direct specification on which our prototype works. Section 3 describes our multi-frame transfer protocol for high-mobility scenarios, along with its implementation over LTE Direct. Validation and assessment tests over the novel Qualcomm LTE Direct simulator, as well as conclusive remarks and directions of ongoing research work, end the paper.

2 TECHNOLOGIES AND PROTOCOLS FOR D2D DISCOVERY

For the sake of self-containment and for enabling the full understanding of the original proposal that follows, this section rapidly overviews the state-of-the-art about D2D proximity discovery technologies, by considering all the primary solutions of industrial interest nowadays, i.e., Bluetooth Low Energy (BLE), Wi-Fi Aware, and LTE Direct [12-23]. BLE, also indicated as Bluetooth Smart, is the "low power" and IoT-oriented version of Bluetooth, part of the Bluetooth 4.0 specification. Its power efficiency, mainly obtained principally via reduction of communication channels, well fits the energy requirements of devices that must run for long periods on limited power sources (e.g., coin cell batteries). Wi-Fi Aware, instead, is the new protocol for D2D proximity discovery proposed by the Wi-Fi Alliance, based on the concept of Neighbor Awareness Networking [15]. Wi-Fi Aware allows the always-on discovery functionality with a limited power consumption thanks to its low-duty-cycle Medium Access Control (MAC) and adaptive clustering. The low-duty-cycle MAC exploits an original mechanism to establish a common heartbeat for lightweight communication synchronization. LTE Direct, i.e., the evolution of the FlashLinQ project [3], is the D2D solution proposed by Qualcomm and standardized in the 3GPP Specification (Release 12) under the name ProSe (Proximity Services) [16]. Currently, only BLE is ready to be used in real deployment environments, while LTE Direct is still under development and Wi-Fi Aware is only a specification (not yet implemented), thus demonstrating the freshness of the proposals and the ongoing nature of the associated research and development activities.

2.1 LTE Direct

LTE Direct is an under-development technology for D2D communication by Qualcomm, very promising for D2D proximity discovery because it addresses internally all the related relevant issues, in particular security (authentication) and power consumption (timing). It utilizes licensed LTE spectrum for proximal discovery of devices/services. LTE Direct works seamlessly in collaboration with the regular LTE net-work: only a little amount of bandwidth (under 1%, exact quota depending on the implementation) is periodically assigned to LTE Direct for discovery actions (see the resource allocation example in Fig. 1). The "companion" LTE network is also used for the management of timing, resource allocation, and identification (Fig. 2). In fact, timing is a fundamental feature of LTE Direct, which allows reducing the active time of discovery: Qualcomm states that a device using LTE Direct can discover thousands of devices in approximately 75ms; to compare with existing competitor technologies, BLE devices can only discover hundreds of devices remaining active more than 1s, even with non-negligible battery consumption in such a long activity period [18].

In addition to regular LTE security mechanisms, LTE-Direct has some unique security-related features, the most relevant and original of them being the "expression" mechanism. In LTE-Direct, expressions are service layer identifiers and can represent an identity, a service, an interest, a location, etc. In the publish/subscribe paradigm, of central interest in D2D proximity discovery, an expression is what a publisher can broadcast (e.g., a device can broadcast an expression over the air for representing the information "we are a coffee shop").

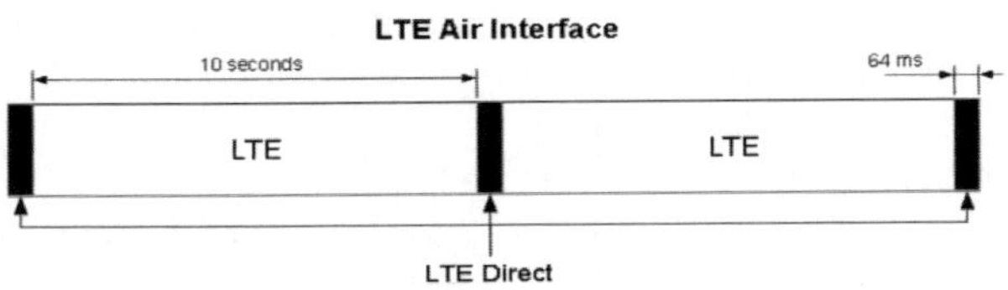

Figure 1: Example of resource allocation for LTE Direct: a period of 64ms for direct discovery is allocated every 10s of regular LTE communications.

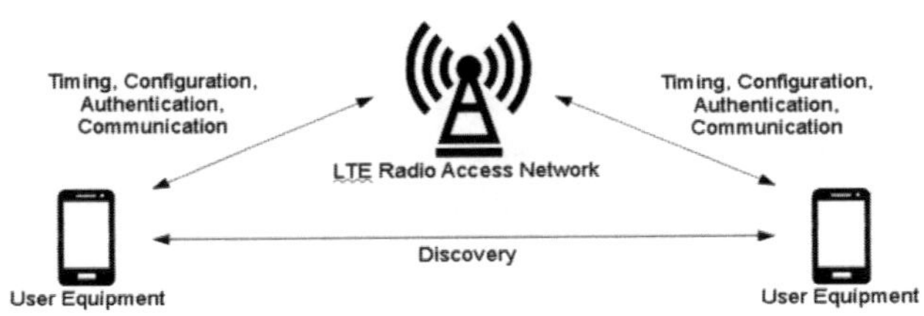

Figure 2: LTE Direct architecture.

An LTE-Direct expression consists of:

- name - an application-defined string used by the application layer;
- code - a shorter binary form of the name, used by the physical layer over the LTE Direct Over The Air (OTA) interface;
- metadata - extra data transmitted with the expression code over the OTA interface.

To receive this broadcast transmission, subscribers must not only be in "proximity" of the publisher, but must also have a key, called subscription key. Only the knowledge of that key allows receiving the related expressions. The subscription key is generated by the publisher with a one-way hash function starting from another key called publish key. This behavior assures that attempts like personification are not feasible: only the publisher (one or more) that owns the publish key can generate the correct OTA code that can be received with the specific subscription key. Note that an expression may have associated some metadata: if the expression code to be matched with the subscription key is typically used to represent the type of service offered by the publisher, the metadata can represent peculiar characteristic of that service (e.g., an expression associated with a shop discount advertise may have metadata describing the items in promotion and the related discount to apply). Another relevant point about the expression mechanism is that expressions are filtered at device level: applications are woken-up only when expressions matching their subscriptions are received, with positive effects on energy saving. In addition to simple subscriptions, LTE Direct also allows expressing filters (simple bitwise filters) on metadata; filters as well effectively work at the device level, thus enabling additional battery saving. Moreover, LTE Direct promotes a common framework to manage expressions, by making them application-agnostic: the framework is based on an entity called Expression Name Server (ENS) that maintains the mapping for the bits to text for an expression, thus supporting the length minimization of OTA messages. ENS is also used to store information about how to discover an expression: it is possible to "obtain" the subscription key of a given expression by sending a request to ENS with the name of the expression (already registered in the ENS). Those type of expressions are called public expressions, in contrast with private expressions that are application-specific and can be decoded/received only by devices that already own the associated subscription keys.

3 DESIGN AND IMPLEMENTATION OF OUR MULTI-FRAME TRANSFER PROTOCOL

In this section we present our original protocol for data dissemination over D2D proximity discovery. The main idea is to exploit discovery advertising messages for data dissemination to proximity listeners notwithstanding the length limitations that these messages usually have, typically for power saving motivations. Note that length restrictions in D2D proximity discovery messages are generating usage scenarios where participants share an a-priori and typically static common knowledge and where every transmitted bit has an application-specific meaning that can be understood only thanks to this static common knowledge. For example, BLE adopts the GATT (General ATTribute) specification for that, which includes already defined profiles such as for battery indicator and heart rate monitor data. Also LTE-Direct has a similar approach with Public Expressions: in this case the specification is maintained by a server and subscribers have direct access to the specification data to interpret "on the fly" the received bits. However, even when adopting these countermeasures, the amount of information that can be exchanged in a single discovery period remains small and the above work demonstrates the awareness of the associated limitation.

Differently from what already explored in the recent related literature, we have decided to originally investigate a multi-frame transfer protocol solution that clearly separates the transmission layer represented by the underlying D2D proximity discovery technology and the higher layer where possibly long messages are managed; in other words, in a transparent way from the perspective of the application layer, our protocol is able to broadcast data with no length limitations over multiple discovery periods in an effective and efficient way. The characteristics and features of the proposed protocol, moreover, are designed to fit the requirements of application domains of emerging relevance in the field, such as vehicular data dissemination and coordination. In particular, consider a scenario where there are several LTE Direct spots along the way, which periodically publish useful information for vehicles passing-by (e.g., traffic information or alerts in general). Our multi-frame transfer protocol can allow a vehicle to start receiving chunks (frames) of the information from one spot and continue receiving it from other spots, by seamlessly discarding duplicates and reconstructing the application-layer message even from multiple sources. In addition, it is possible to envision the usage of the vehicles themselves as frame repeaters (this type of interaction is currently not allowed in the standard LTE Direct specification), in order to maximize transfer rate and to virtually extend the spot transmission coverage.

3.1 Multi-frame Transfer Protocol for LTE Direct

Our protocol is developed on top of LTE Direct, but can be easily applied to every D2D proximity discovery solution adopting the publish-subscribe paradigm. It is also important to state that this protocol is particularly intended for scenarios where a de-vice (publisher) emits some information periodically and other devices (subscribers) can listen to it without any feedback to the sender. For instance, consider the case of a shop that advertises its promotional offerings to possible customers in proximity; in an "always-on" discovery scenario the advertising dissemination will be periodically repeated, also to cover different potential customers passing-by and dynamically changing.

In LTE Direct, an expression is the atomic unit of communication and generally maps a single information. An overall expression, by referring to 3GPP Release 12, consists of 184bits, a fraction of which are available for additional data apart from the expression code. This practically means that, in the case where a device is willing to send an arbitrary string inside an expression, its length will be limited to less than 20 characters (using an 8-bit character encoding). To overcome this limitation, our protocol splits the application-layer message data, if necessary, into frames included in multiple expressions, by adding some metadata to efficiently rebuild the application-layer message at the receiver. Our solution has been partially inspired by the well-known ISO-TP approach, which is a standard protocol for sending data packets over CAN bus, by allowing transmissions that exceed the maximum payload size of CAN frames [24]. In particular, our protocol defines four type of frames (see Table 1):

- SINGLE is a frame that contains all the info transmitted (payload + data length);
- FIRST is the first frame of a multi-frame transmission and contains the length of the entire data transmitted, as well as the first chunk of the information;
- CONSECUTIVE is one multi-frame transmission frame, different from the first one, and contains both its data chunk and an index to represent the chunk position in the overall multi-frame message;
- CONTROL is a frame for hash-based evaluation of message integrity.

Table 1. Frame structure in our multi-frame transfer protocol.

Byte Offset	0		1	2	3	4	...
Bit Offset	0-1	2-7	8-15	16-23	24-31	32-39	...
Single	0	size (max 64) in bytes	non-split data				
First	1	size (max 16384) in bytes		first part of the data			
Consecutive	2	index (max 16384) of the frame		I^{th} part of the data (where I is the index of the current frame)			
Control	3	total number of frames (max 16384)		Hash of the data (e.g.: crc32)			

Any frame contains a header that describes the frame itself, by specifying frame type and overall message length. In the case of a single-frame transmission, the first byte will be the header. The first two bits of the header represents the type of the frame, the remaining six bits contains a positive integer number that represents the length in bytes of the data transmitted. Using six bits to express data length imposes a limit of 64 bytes of data that can be transferred. This limitation is anyway compatible with most of the D2D proximity discovery technologies available or under specification and allows minimum header size. Anyway, we have designed the protocol so that it will be easy to extend the header size in the future. If message length exceeds the single frame, header included, the data will be prepared to be sent with multiple frames (see Fig. 3). The first step is to partition data according to the capacity of a single frame; if N is the number of parts in which the data is split, there will be N+1 frames to be sent by including also the CONTROL frame to for data integrity.

A relevant feature of the proposed protocol is that it can handle frame sending/receiving correctly independently from their order. This is particularly relevant in high-mobility scenarios where frames can be lost for many reasons (interference in communications, absence of direct connection, etc.) and a simple periodical retransmission of all the information by the publisher (or the set of collaborating publishers) allows the subscribers to retrieve the missing frames. The order irrelevance leads also to another advantage: the possibility to publish different pieces of the same data with different devices at the same time, for example to obtain improved transfer speed. Let us finally note that correctness is guaranteed even if the publisher starts transmitting a different message before the full reception of the previous message at some receivers thanks to the integrity check.

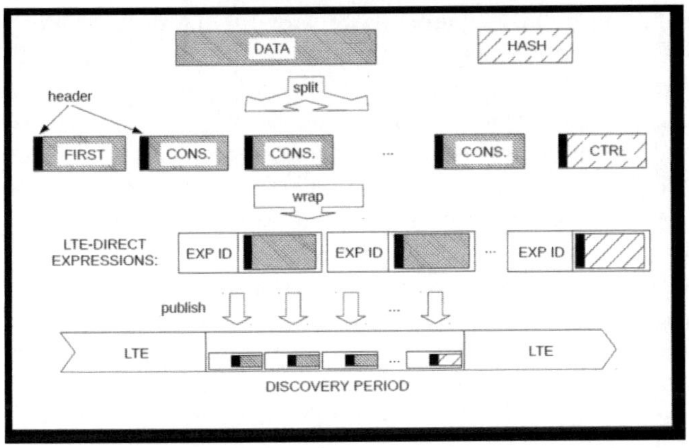

Figure 3. Multi-Frame protocol publish mechanism using LTE Direct expressions.

3.2 Implementation Insights

Our multi-frame protocol implementation code, together with additional implementation details omitted here for the sake of briefness, is available at http://lia.disi.unibo.it/research/MFTP_for_ProSe. To validate the protocol, we used the LTE Direct Trial SDK by Qualcomm Technologies [20], available for Android and iOS. This SDK allows developers accessing all the features to create, publish, subscribe, and manage LTE Direct expressions. In addition, the Android version of the SDK includes an LTE Direct simulator service that can emulate the presence of LTE Direct on the Android devices where the service runs on.

The first step in our validation work was to create a software module to manage the multi-frame transmission according to our protocol. In particular, this module allows specifying the size of a single frame that can be transmitted (this parameter is technology-dependent) and offers two functions:

- starting from the data length to be transmitted, it creates the corresponding frames based on the multi-frame protocol and the single frame dimension;
- rebuilds the original data bytes from the previous group of frames, by verifying their integrity via the hash described previously.

As depicted in Fig. 3, for the publish operation, our module simply splits the data bytes in the corresponding frames, builds the correct associated expressions, and publishes them on LTE Direct (in the case, frames are automatically distributed among different discovery periods).

The subscription part of the module works on receiving the expressions/frames and elaborating the included information. In particular, for each frame:

- if a frame of type FIRST is received, its payload is stored like the first part and in-formation is extracted about the size of the whole message. The reception of different type FIRST frames, before the completion of previous message reception, is supported and multiple messages can be received and processed concurrently;
- if a frame of type CONTROL is received, our module stores its payload (which rep-resents the hash of the entire data) apart;
- if a frame of CONSECUTIVE type is received, our module extracts the frame index from the header and uses it to store the payload in the correct position efficiently. If another CONSECUTIVE frame of the same message with the same index is received, we have decided that the new version overwrites the old one.

When all the frames are received, the original data is restored using the data length inside the FIRST frame header and the payload of all the frames received. If the re-stored data passes the integrity check, the data can be considered successfully received, otherwise the reception process for that message will start again.

4 EXPERIMENTAL VALIDATION

Our protocol implementation on top of the LTE Direct Trial SDK, originally presented for the first time in this paper, has been validated through different tests. First, we have verified the correctness of our multi-frame protocol when reconstructing messages with randomly generated frame repetitions.

Second, we have employed the LTE Direct simulator service for validation over real Android devices: the simulator service by default is configured to allow 32ms of direct discovery every 5s (this configuration is fixed and cannot be changed in the current version of the simulator service); LTE Direct allocates one sub-frame every 1ms; the LTE Direct simulator allows a device to publish one expression every sub-frame. In the first experiment we have used one only device to publish a message via our multi-frame protocol and two devices subscribed to it. Then, we tested a more articulated and challenging execution environment where two devices publish the same message concurrently: the associated peculiarity is that the entire message consists of more than 32 expressions, so it exceeds the number of expressions per device allowed for a single discovery period; this means that the entire information published by one device requires at least two successive discovery periods to be transmitted and correctly received. We have verified experimentally that the availability of two publisher devices allows overcoming this limitation: e.g., publishing the same frames, in the same time interval but not in the same order, by two devices allows subscribers to receive the entire set of frames even in only one discovery period in our tests. This points out and assesses another relevant feature of our protocol (see Fig. 4): using more than one publisher to transmit the same message can augment the perceived data rate at subscribers, of course within the boundaries of total traffic admitted by LTE in a proximity.

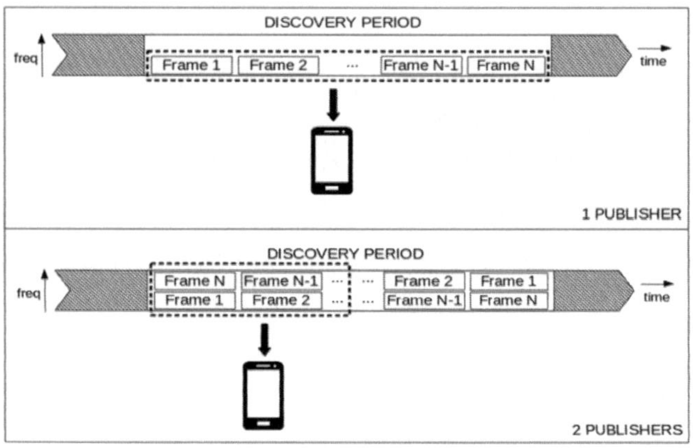

Figure 4. Validation tests with the LTE Direct simulator show the possibility to halve the reception time by using two publishers of the same information with frames in reverse order.

6 CONCLUSIVE REMARKS AND ONGOING RESEARCH WORK

This paper originally presents a protocol for D2D proximity discovery that allows to disseminate application-layer messages in proximity localities, even if the message length exceeds the single discovery transmission frame (as commonly occurs due to the strictly limited length imposed by standard D2D proximity discovery communication mechanisms). Even if a direct communication between devices would be possible using other technologies such BLE and Wi-Fi direct (and in the future also a specific feature for LTE Direct is expected), this protocol allows putting together the advantages of an always-on battery-efficient discovery solution, such as the one in LTE Direct, with the opportunity of broadcasting application-layer messages of reasonable length.

The presented protocol, although developed on top of the LTE Direct technology, is intended to be technology-agnostic and can be applied to all D2D proximity discovery scenarios. We have opted for the implementation of an LTE Direct prototype because we believe that LTE Direct is the most promising technology in this field at the moment; being still in its development stage, in this work we had only the opportunity to validate and assess our solution over the indicated SDK and simulator. However, initial experimentation tests by Qualcomm in collaboration with Deutsche Telekom and Huawei, recently presented in [22], confirm our performance observations based on simulations and the deriving expected behaviors.

Given the first encouraging results presented in this paper, we are pursuing two primary directions of related extension work: the former is oriented to experimentation in a real test-bed as soon as it will be available; the second relates to performance and robustness assessment while growing the probability of different types of interferences and disconnections (with consequent increase in frame loss probability).

ACKNOWLEDGMENTS

A special thank goes to Qualcomm and the supported LTE Direct initiative; without their development work and simulation tool, the results reported in this paper would not have been possible.

REFERENCES

[1] A. Arash, Q. Wang, V. Mancuso, "A Survey on Device-to-device Communication in Cellular Networks", IEEE Comm. Surveys and Tutorials, vol. 16, no. 4, pp. 1801--1819 (2014).
[2] K. J. Zou, et al., "Proximity Discovery for Device-to-device Communications over a Cellular Network", IEEE Commun. Mag., vol. 52, no. 6, pp. 98--107 (2014).
[3] X. Wu, et al., "FlashLinQ: a Synchronous Distributed Scheduler for Peer-to-peer Ad Hoc Network, "IEEE/ACM Trans. Networking, vol. 21, no. 4, pp. 1215--1228 (2013).
[4] P. Bellavista, A. Corradi, E. Magistretti. "REDMAN: an Optimistic Replication Middleware for Read-only Resources in Dense MANETs",

Elsevier Pervasive and Mobile Computing J., vol. 1, no. 3, pp. 279-310 (2005).
[5] S. Andreev, A. Pyattaev, K. Johnsson, O. Galinina, Y. Koucheryavy, "Cellular Traffic Offloading onto Network-assisted Device-to-device Connections", IEEE Commun. Mag., vol. 52, no. 4, pp. 20-31 (2014).
[6] P. Sartori, et al., "Design of a D2D Overlay for Next Generation LTE", IEEE 80th Vehicular Technology Conference (VTC), pp. 1-5 (2014).
[7] G. Fodor, et al., "Design Aspects of Network Assisted Device-to-device Communications", IEEE Commun. Mag., vol. 50, no. 3, pp. 170-177 (2012).
[8] S. Yasukawa, H. Harada, S. Nagata, Q. Zhao, "D2D Communications in LTE-Advanced Release 12", NTT DOCOMO Technical Journal, vol. 17, no. 2, pp. 56-64 (2015).
[9] X. Lin, J. Andrews, A. Ghosh, R. Ratasuk, "An Overview of 3GPP Device-to-device Proximity Services", IEEE Commun. Mag., vol. 52, pp. 40-48 (2014).
[10] A. Toninelli, et al., "Supporting Context Awareness in Smart Environments: a Scalable Approach to Information Interoperability", Int. Workshop Middleware for Pervasive Mobile and Embedded Computing. ACM (2009).
[11] P. Bellavista, A. Corradi, C. Giannelli. "Efficiently Managing Location Information with Privacy Requirements in Wi-Fi Networks: a Middleware Approach", 2nd Int. Symp. Wireless Communication Systems, IEEE (2005).
[12] Bluetooth SIG: Bluetooth Specification Version 4. https://www.bluetooth.org/docman/han-dlers/downloaddoc.ashx?doc_id=229737. Accessed May 2016.
[13] K. Mikhaylov, N. Plevritakis, J. Tervonen, "Performance Analysis and Comparison of Bluetooth Low Energy with IEEE 802.15.4 and SimpliciTT", J. Sens. Actuator Networks, vol. 2, no. 3, pp. 589-613 (2013).
[14] Apple, "Getting Started with iBeacon, version 1.0. https://developer.apple.com/ibeacon/Get-ting-Started-with-iBeacon.pdf. Accessed May 2016.
[15] Wi-Fi Alliance, "Neighbor Awareness Networking Technical Specification, version 1.0", https://www.wi-fi.org/file/neighbor-awareness-networking-technical-specification-v10-0. Accessed May 2016.
[16] 3GPP TS 23.303, "Proximity-based services (ProSe); stage 2", Tech. rep., http://www.3gpp.org/DynaReport/23303.htm (2014). Accessed 26 May 2016.
[17] Qualcomm, "LTE Direct Always-on Device-to-Device Proximal Discovery", https://www.qualcomm.com/media/documents/files/lte-direct-always-on-device-to-device-proximal-discovery.pdf (2014). Accessed 26 May 2016.
[18] Qualcomm, "LTE Direct Overview Presentation", https://www.qualcomm.com/documents/ creating-digital-6th-sense-lte-direct (2014). Accessed May 2016.
[19] LTE Direct Research Project, https://www.qualcomm.com/ invention/research/projects/lte-direct. Accessed May 2016.
[20] LTE Direct Developer Portal, https://ltedirect.qualcomm.com/
[21] Signals Research Group, "Expanding your Horizons with LTE Direct", Whitepaper, http://signalsresearch.com/ (2015). Accessed May 2016.
[22] Deutsche T., Huawei, Qualcomm, "LTE Direct Trial", Whitepaper, https://www.qualcomm. com/media/documents/files/lte-direct-trial-white-paper.pdf (2015). Accessed May 2016.
[23] Rohde & Schwarz, "Device to Device Communication in LTE", Whitepaper, https://www.rohde-schwarz.com/de/file/ 1MA264_0e_D2DComm.pdf (2015). Accessed May 2016.
[24] ISO 15765-2, "Road Vehicles - Diagnostic Communication over Controller Area Network (DoCAN) - Part 2", http://www.iso.org/iso/ catalogue_detail.htm?csnumber=54499 (2011). Accessed May 2016.

On The Optimum Data Carrier for Intra-body Communication Applications

Ahmed E. Khorshid, Ahmed M. Eltawil, Fadi Kurdahi
Electrical Engineering and Computer Science Department
University of California, Irvine.
{Khorshia, aeltawil, kurdahi} @uci.edu

ABSTRACT

This paper provides a comparative study between the different available mediums, to be used as data carriers, for intra-body communications. Properties of these data carriers experienced while propagating through the body tissues are calculated using sets of experimental data available in literature and then compared to show which carrier has higher potential to meet the intra-body communication requirements. A simple accurate model is then presented for the signal transmission through the body. Parameters studied are the attenuation and delay while factoring the effect of biological differences due to age, gender etc.

Categories and Subject Descriptors

• Networks~Wireless personal area networks; • Applied computing~Biological networks

Keywords

Body area networks; intra-body communications; channel modeling.

1. INTRODUCTION

Mobile health has recently expanded to include wearable devices as a part of the vision of a holistic approach to wellness in general and health care services in particular. Once wearables become ubiquitous, they can provide healthy users, patients and doctors with an accurate reflection of the state of their body. This information will ultimately lead to better preventative medical practices and a truly personalized medical approach. Driven by the vision of a cable-free biomedical monitoring system, new wireless technologies that focus on sensor applications have been promoted as the next biomedical revolution, promising a significant improvement in the quality of health-care services. However, a major barrier to adoption of wearable technologies is the size and power requirements of wireless sensors which are typically dominated by the RF section of the associated transceivers. This leads to centralized solutions that share a transceiver (e.g. smart watches) that are localized to one part of the body and hence cannot perform distributed measurements. Due to their centralized nature, these types of sensors are known to be highly inaccurate in collecting information about various vital signs such as temperature, perspiration, respiration rate, due to their confinement to a single location on the human body. There is a need to have a new class of devices that are wirelessly networked, small in area and exhibit ultra-low power consumption, thus having the ability to perform distributed monitoring in a seamless manner. An attractive solution to such emerging vision is the use of intra-body communication systems where data transmission is achieved through the *skin*, rather than through air. Sensors and actuators can then inter-communicate through skin and be relayed to a centralized wireless hub that could be a smart watch for instance. This technique would ultimately lead to body area networks (BANs) that operate at extremely low power, with minimal foot print by replacing expensive, power consuming Radio Frequency (RF) front ends, for each individual node with simpler interfaces. Furthermore, while the skin operates as an interference channel for the communicating nodes, it is relatively protected from the higher levels of interference expected when broadcasting via the air.

This paper presents a comparison of the main potential means of data carriers for intra-body communications, namely using electro-magnetic waves, ultrasonic waves and magnetic coupling. We discuss the pros and cons of each approach and quantitatively discuss the frequency response of different body tissues to these modalities. We then present a model for intra-body communications, using the galvanic coupling technique, in case electromagnetic waves are being adopted as the appropriate data carrier for this emerging technology. In the proposed model, biological parameters of the human body are accurately modeled, as well as assumed to be variable, taking into consideration the impact of important factors; such as age and weight, on these parameters and thus on the overall attenuation profile.

2. Body Area Networks Approach

The concept of communication through the human body was first introduced in late 1990s using near field coupling [1-2], where different approaches were investigated to study the use of data carriers that best suit the nature of the human body in a quest for minimizing power, size, system complexity and health hazards.

2.1 Electromagnetic (EM) Waves

The first and most traditional approach for data transmission is EM waves. Use of EM waves in intra-body communications can be categorized into two main types; capacitive coupling (near field coupling method) and galvanic coupling. In capacitive coupling, only the signal electrodes of the transmitter and the receiver are attached to the body while the ground (GND) electrodes are left floating in the air. The conductive body forms the forward path while the signal loop is closed through the capacitive return path between the transmitter and the receiver

GND electrodes. The second approach, which depends on the galvanic coupling principle, uses a pair of electrodes for both the transmitter and the receiver to propagate the electromagnetic wave. The signal is applied over two coupler electrodes and received by two detector electrodes. An attractive feature of the galvanic coupling approach is that the signal is totally confined to the body, unlike capacitive coupling where the signal return path is established through the air. Galvanic coupled signals experience minimal interference from other electronic devices, enabling robust and secure data exchanges.

2.2 Magnetic Human Body Communications

A new approach was recently proposed in [3] where resonant magnetic coupling was suggested to be used as an alternative physical layer for BAN. In this approach, coils wrapped around anatomy (arm, leg, head ...etc.) are used to generate and receive magnetic based signals. The main motivation is that the permeability of human tissues is similar to air which enables the magnetic fields to travel more freely through the human body. This approach suffers from some drawbacks. The fact that the permeability of human tissues are similar to air makes it more difficult to confine the signal within the human body, thus part of the signal will be lost in the air. Moreover, it is not possible to separate the electric and magnetic fields for an EM wave as long as the displacement current ratio to the conduction one is considerable. The ratio is plotted for different body tissues, as shown in Figure 1. , showing that in the Mega-Hertz frequency range it is not possible to assume that both fields are independent. Such results imply that data transmission cannot be attributed to the magnetic field only, but to the electric field as well since they cannot be separated at the frequencies of interest while propagating through human tissue. Moreover, the need to wrap a coil around the body wherever we need to setup a communication node limits the use of such approach, making it inconvenient especially if multiple nodes are considered.

2.3 Ultrasonic Waves

Acoustic waves are mostly used for underwater communications since they possess better propagation properties in water as compared to RF waves. Since more than 65% of the human body consists of water, ultrasonic waves (acoustic waves at the non-audible frequency range; above 20 KHz) was thought to have good potential as a means of communication for BAN. Research then followed [4-5] to investigate the efficiency of using ultrasonic waves in BANs, mainly to communicate between implantable devices, since ultrasonic waves propagate very poorly through air. This approach suffered from some drawbacks as well. A major drawback is the acoustic bio-effects, among which are heating and cavitation [6]. As ultrasonic waves propagate through the body tissues, a portion of the wave energy is absorbed and converted to heat, leading to an increase of these tissues' temperature, especially when wave intensity is increased, leading to undesirable biological effect. The other serious biological effect is cavitation. Ultrasonic waves are associated with pressure variations, causing bubbles in the propagation medium, body tissues in our case, to expand and contract. As this pressure variation activity increases, bubbles may collapse leading to tissue damage, a concern that has to be seriously considered when dealing with ultrasonic waves' propagation on a periodic, repeated manner. However, the impact of these two bio-effects can still be minimized through techniques of impulsive transmissions with low power and pressure levels, as ways of keeping the acoustic intensities to which the tissues are exposed to within the safety limits [7].

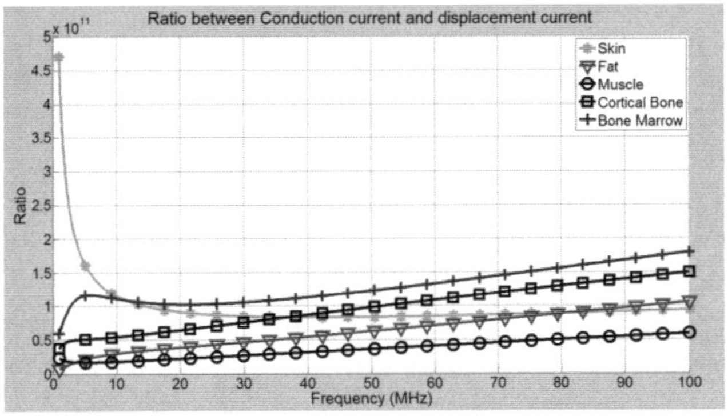

Figure 1. Ratio between displacement and conduction currents in different body tissues, showing that the displacement current values are large enough thus electric and magnetic fields cannot be assumed to be independent of each other in this frequency range.

3. Electromagnetic V.S. Ultrasonic Waves

From the discussion in previous section, it is concluded that electromagnetic waves and ultrasonic waves are more convenient as data carriers for BANs. In this section, more in depth comparison will be shown between the two mediums, taking into consideration the biological properties of the human body, within the frequency range for intra-body communications; from low KHz up to 100 MHz's. The main to consider, being key factors for any system design, are attenuation (gain) and the delay profiles

3.1 Attenuation

Human tissue is considered to be a lossy medium where ultrasonic waves are dissipated in the form of heat. Attenuation of acoustic waves is caused mainly due to the absorption of the pressure energy by the medium in which the wave is propagating. Such attenuation is dependent on the type of the tissue as well as the frequency of operation. In general, attenuation for acoustic waves follows the relation:

$$\alpha = af^{b} \qquad (1)$$

Where α is the attenuation in (Decibels/ (centimeter*Mega-hertz)), f is the frequency, a and b are constants that depend on the acoustic properties of each tissue.

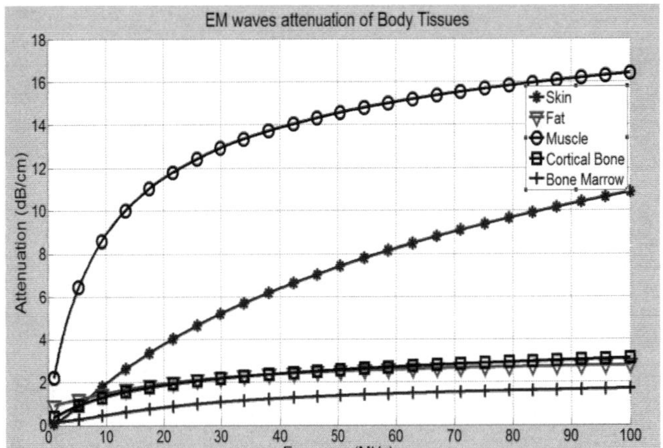

Figure 2. Attenuation that EM waves experience when propagating through each of the main five tissues of the human body.

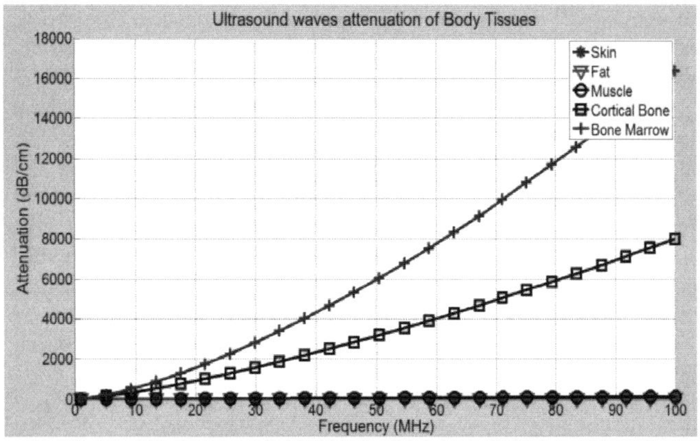

(a)

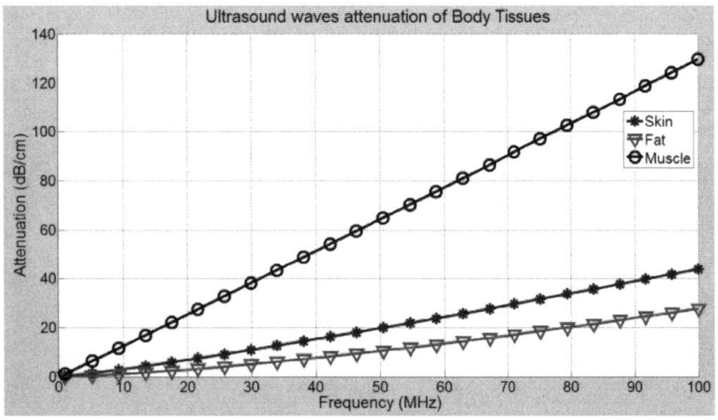

(b)

Figure 3. (a)Attenuation that Ultrasonic waves experience when propagating through each of the main five tissues of the human body, (b) zoomed in version to show attenuation for skin, fat and muscle tissues.

Figures 2 & 3 clarify the attenuation properties of the main human tissue types (skin, fat, muscle, cortical bone and bone marrow) to the propagation of both ultrasonic and EM waves. For ultrasound attenuation profiles versus frequency, the constants a and b are calculated from previous work in literature [8-10] using curve fitting techniques. As for EM attenuation, it was calculated according to the following equation:

$$\alpha = \frac{w}{2}\sqrt{\mu\ \varepsilon(w)}\ \tan\left(\delta(w)\right) \quad (2)$$

Where α is the attenuation (dB/cm), w frequency (rad/s), μ permeability, $\varepsilon(w)$ frequency dependant permittivity and $\tan(\delta(w))$ is the loss tangent, and these electrical properties were all calculated for each tissue [11]. It can be shown that according to the attenuation profiles for the human body tissues, ultrasonic waves experience more attenuation, in the form of heat dissipation, compared with EM waves within the targeted frequency range for BAN.

3.2 Delay

Another important aspect is the propagation delay, i.e. how fast these waves can travel through the body tissues. Ultrasonic waves are known to travel at very low speeds in the human body [12]; ranging between 1450 m/s in fat to 4080 m/s in bone. Such low speed introduces a significant delay at the receiver node which is directly translated into severe multi-path reflection problems. That drawback requires complicated system topologies and extra hardware at each node, leading to more complicated power hungry systems.

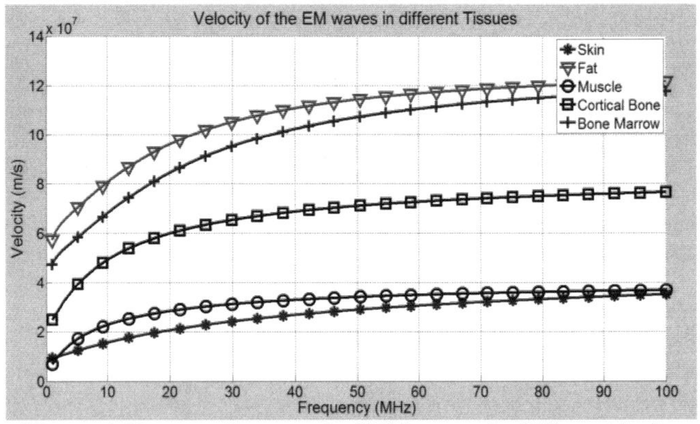

Figure 4. Propagation speed of EM waves in different body tissues.

Such a problem is much less pronounced in the case of EM waves' propagation. Velocity of EM waves' propagation within the different body tissues are shown in Figure 4. With such high propagation speeds, delay problems can be considered to be much less severe to deal with, especially with short distance communications as in the case of BANs, when EM waves are used as data carriers as opposed to Ultrasonic waves.

4. Channel Model

From the previous comparison, it was shown that EM waves are advantageous over other mediums for data transmission through the human body. Among the two available techniques, galvanic coupling is more attractive due to its immunity to interference and its potential for establishing a more secured closed loop network of sensors. To provide a reliable and flexible platform for smart bio-sensor networks, the intra-body channel model has to be well specified. Numerous research efforts exist that address modeling the body as a communication channel. Experimental trials were performed in [13-16]. Yet these models assumed constant parameters for the body's geometrical attributes. In our work [17], biological parameters are assumed to be variable, taking into consideration the impact of important factors; such as age and weight, on these parameters and thus on the overall attenuation profile. For the proof of concept, a model of the arm was considered, where simulation results are plotted and compared with published experimental results, showing high accuracy in identifying the optimum frequency for signal transmission for intra-body communications systems, as shown in Figure 5.

5. Conclusion

In this paper, possible mediums to be used as data carriers for intra-body communications were considered, namely; electromagnetic waves, pure magnetic waves and finally ultrasonic waves. Properties of each carrier were considered with respect to their propagation through the different body tissues. Then a more in depth comparison was shown between EM waves and ultrasonic waves concerning the attenuation and delay that each of them would experience when propagating through the human body, within the frequency range of interest for intra-body communications' applications. It was clearly shown that EM waves possess better properties, that can support BAN requirements, versus ultrasonic waves as EM waves experience much less attenuation and delay when traveling through the body. Such facts are crucial for system designers, as although ultrasonic circuits may appear simple in general, the hardware that would be required to compensate for the loss caused by ultrasonic waves' propagation in body tissues would add extra hardware and power compensation, making it a less attractive solution when compared

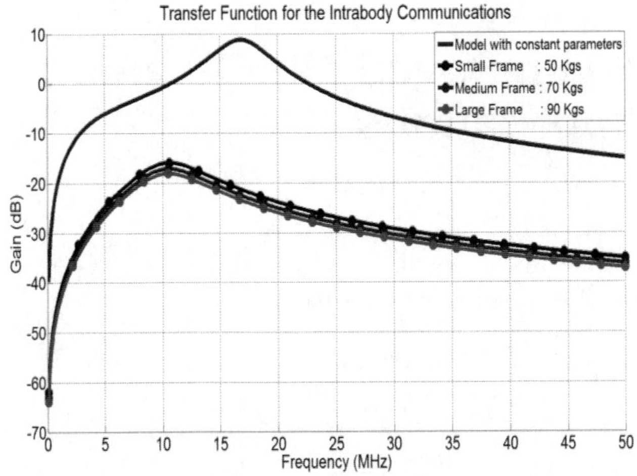

Figure 5. The proposed channel model frequency response, where simulation results show the gain in dB plotted from 100 KHz t0 50 MHz, considering different body frames; small, medium and large. The results from our model are compared to those obtained from circuit model in which the biological parameters are assumed to be constant. The proposed model succeeds in determining the optimum frequency -10.5 MHz- for data transmission.

with EM waves. Finally an accurate channel model for signal propagation (for EM waves using the galvanic techniques) is presented, showing the attenuation/gain profile for the human body over the frequency band of interest. Unlike in other intra-body communication research work where comparisons are shown between the main two techniques for EM signal transmission- capacitive and galvanic coupling, the novelty of this paper is that it takes one step back to provide a comparative study between the different data carriers that are used or proposed in the BAN field, where the electrical, acoustic and biological properties are discussed and thoroughly compared.

6. ACKNOWLEDGMENTS

The authors gratefully acknowledge that this work was supported by the National Institute of Justice (NIJ) grant number 2016-R2-CX-0014.

7. REFERENCES

[1] Zimmerman, T. G. 1995. Personal Area Network (PAN). M.S. thesis. MIT Press, Cambridge, MA.

[2] Handa, T., Shoji, S., Ike, S., Takeda, S., and Sekiguchi, T. 1997. A very low power consumption wireless ECG monitoring system using body as a signal transmission medium. *In Proc. Int. Conf. Transducers, Solid-State Sensors Actuators, 2* (June 1997), 1003-1006.

[3] Park, J. and Mercier, P.P. 2015. Magnetic human body communication. In *2015 37th Annual International Conference of the IEEE Engineering in Medicine and Biology Society (EMBC) (Aug. 2015),* 1841-1844.

[4] Galluccio, L., Melodia, T., Palazzo, S., & Santagati, G. E. 2012. Challenges and implications of using ultrasonic communications in intra-body area networks. In *9th Annual Conference Wireless On-demand Network Systems and Services (WONS), (Jan. 2012).* 182-189.

[5] Davilis, Y., Kalis, A., & Ifantis, A. 2010. On the use of ultrasonic waves as a communications medium in biosensor networks. *IEEE Transactions on Information Technology in Biomedicine,* 14(3), 650-656.

[6] Santagati, G.E. and Melodia, T. 2013. Opto-ultrasonic communications in wireless body area nanonetworks. In *2013 Asilomar Conference on Signals, Systems and Computers* (Nov. 2013), 1066-1070.

[7] Miller, D.L. 2008. Safety assurance in obstetrical ultrasound. In *Seminars in Ultrasound, CT and MRI*, 29, 2 (April 2008), 156-164. WB Saunders.

[8] Shore, D., Woods, M. O., & Miles, C. A. 1986. Attenuation of ultrasound in post rigor bovine skeletal muscle. *Ultrasonics*, *24*(2), 81-87.

[9] Pichardo, S., Sin, V. W., & Hynynen, K. 2011. Multi-frequency characterization of the speed of sound and attenuation coefficient for longitudinal transmission of freshly excised human skulls. *Physics in medicine and biology, 56, 1 (2011)*, 219.

[10] Moran, C. M., Bush, N. L. and Bamber, J. C. 1995. Ultrasonic propagation properties of excised human skin. *Ultrasound in medicine & biology* 21, no. 9 (1995), 1177-1190.

[11] Gabriely, S., Lau, R. W. and Gabriel, C. 1996. The dielectric properties of biological tissues: II. Measurements in the frequency range 10 Hz to 20 GHz. Phys. Med. Biol., 41, 11 (Nov. 1996), 2251–2269.

[12] Thurston, Robert, N., and Allan, D. Pierce, eds. 1999. *Ultrasonic Instruments and Devices I*. Academic Press.\

[13] Hachisuka, K., Terauchi, Y., Kishi, Y., Sasaki, K., Hirota, T., Hosaka, H., Fujii, K., Takahashi, M. and Ito, K., 2006. Simplified circuit modeling and fabrication of intrabody communication devices. In *Proc. IEEE Int. Conf. Solid-State Sens., Actuators, Microsyst.*(2005), 461–464.

[14] Fujii, K., Takahashi, M. and Ito, K. 2007. Electric field distributions of wearable devices using the human body as a transmission channel. *IEEE Trans. Antennas Propag., 55, 7* (Jul. 2007), 2080–2087.

[15] Wegmueller, M. S., Kuhn, A., Froehlich, J., Oberle, M., Felber, N., Kuster, N., and Fichtner, W. 2007. An attempt to model the human body as a communication channel," *IEEE Trans. Biomed.* Eng., 54, 10 (Oct. 2007), 1851–1857.

[16] Wegmueller, M.S., Oberle, M., Felber, N., Kuster, N. and Fichtner, W. 2010. Signal transmission by galvanic coupling through the human body. *IEEE Transactions on Instrumentation and Measurement*, *59*(4), 963-969.

[17] Khorshid, A.E., Eltawil, A.M. and Kurdahi, F. 2015. Intra-body communication model based on variable biological parameters. In *2015 49th Asilomar Conference on Signals, Systems and Computers (Nov. 2015)*, 948-951.

A Solar Energy Harvester with an Improved MPPT Circuit for Wearable IoT Applications

Taiyang Wu, Md Shamsul Arefin, Jean-Michel Redouté, and Mehmet Rasit Yuce

Department of Electrical and Computer Systems Engineering

Monash University, Melbourne, VIC-3800, Australia.

{taiyang.wu, md.arefin, jean-michel.redoute, mehmet.yuce}@monash.edu

ABSTRACT

One of the main issues of wearable IoT devices is the limited battery technology. Energy harvesting will be a key development for health and fitness oriented wearable devices that can measure signals continuously. In this paper, an analog maximum power point tracking (MPPT) circuit is presented to power a wearable pulse sensor with a Bluetooth low energy (BLE) module for transmission. The proposed MPPT algorithm uses only the output current to extract the maximum power from a flexible solar panel. The whole energy harvesting system was implemented and tested. Experiment results validate that the solar energy harvester has an overall efficiency of 66.5% and can provide sufficient power for the measurement of the pulse sensor and transmission with a BLE module.

Keywords

Energy harvesting; photovoltaic; MPPT; wearable sensor; Bluetooth low energy

1. INTRODUCTION

One of the key developments in wearable IoT applications is the energy harvesting technique [1], which provides solutions to extend the lifetime of batteries or directly supply energy for the wearable sensors in the IoT applications and deployments. Solar energy is one of the most favourable energy sources because it provides a higher power density than other sources, such as the piezoelectric, thermoelectric and radio frequency [2]. However, the power from a solar panel depends on its operating conditions. There exists a maximum power point of each solar panel, which changes with the environmental irradiance and temperature conditions. As a result, the maximum power point tracking (MPPT) circuits are essential in the solar energy harvesting systems.

There have been many researches on tracking the maximum power point of solar panels [3, 4]. Conventional MPPT algorithms, like perturb and observe (P&O) and incremental conductance (IC), require both the photovoltaic (PV) voltage and current to track the maximum power point [5, 6]. Though the open circuit voltage (OCV) algorithm or the short current circuit (SCC) algorithm needs only one parameter of the solar panel to operate, their tracking is "quasi" and cannot extract energy when the circuit is open or short [7, 8]. In this paper, an MPPT algorithm only based on the output current is proposed. Due to its analog design and only sensing the current at the output side, the implementation of this MPPT circuit is simplified and can be integrated with proper CMOS technology.

To validate the performance of the proposed MPPT algorithm, a pulse sensor circuit with wireless Bluetooth low energy (BLE) transmission is connected as a load for the real life application. The pulse sensor is implemented with an off-the-shelf piezo sensor [9]. With the BLE module, the sensor can transmit the pulse data to a terminal device (e.g. smartphones), which monitors user's health condition.

The rest of the paper is organised as follows. The next section presents the analysis and design of the proposed MPPT circuit. Section 3 introduces the implementation of the pulse sensor and BLE module. Experiment results of the whole energy harvesting system are demonstrated in Section 4 and Section 5 gives the conclusion of the paper.

2. SOLAR ENERGY HARVESTER

As the solar panel is a nonlinear device, it has an optimal working point at a certain irradiance and temperature condition. Usually a DC-DC converter is employed to regulate the output of the solar panel. The MPPT control circuit keeps adjusting the duty cycle (D) of the converter to track the maximum power point of the panel.

2.1 Proposed MPPT Algorithm

Figure 1 shows the block diagram of the proposed energy harvesting system, where a boost converter is used to connect the solar panel and the output load. The relationship of the voltage and current between the panel and load is:

$$V_{out} = \frac{1}{1-D} V_{PV}, \tag{1}$$

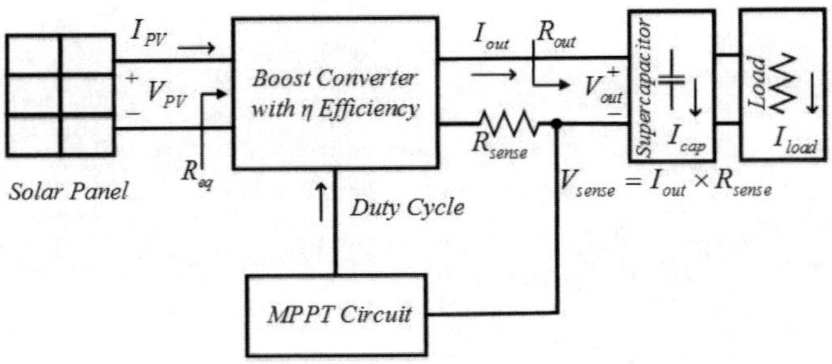

Figure 1: Block diagram of the solar energy harvesting system.

Table 1: Relationship of I_{out} and Duty Cycle

I_{out}	D	Next D
Increase (1)	Increase (1)	Increase (1)
Increase (1)	Decrease (0)	Decrease (0)
Decrease (0)	Increase (1)	Decrease (0)
Decrease (0)	Decrease (0)	Increase (1)

and

$$I_{out} = (1 - D)I_{PV} \tag{2}$$

Therefore the equivalent resistance seen by the solar panel through the converter is:

$$R_{eq} = (1 - D)^2 R_{out} \tag{3}$$

The MPPT control circuit will keep tuning the duty cycle of the converter until R_{eq} equals the load resistance of the solar panel at the maximum power point.

To calculate the maximum power, conventional MPPT algorithms (P&O and IC) need to multiply the sensed V_{PV} and I_{PV} at the input side of the converter. The proposed MPPT algorithm only measures the I_{out} at the output side without any multiplication [10]. If there is a fixed resistive load, the output power is:

$$P_{out} = I_{out}^2 R_{out} \tag{4}$$

For a boost converter with efficiency of η, the power from the solar panel will be:

$$P_{PV} = \frac{I_{out}^2 R_{out}}{\eta} \tag{5}$$

From (5) it can be seen the power from the solar panel is maximized when I_{out} is maximum. The MPPT control circuit changes D according to the comparison result between I_{out} and its previous value. If I_{out} increases, then change D in the same direction; otherwise change D in the opposite direction. The relationship of I_{out} and D is summarised in Table 1, which can be expressed by an "XNOR" logic.

For a varying resistive load or a supercapacitor, it can be approximated as a stair-case: the MPPT circuit will track the maximum power of the solar panel as the load is constant during a short period of time. As long as the change of the load does not exceed the convergence time of the MPPT circuit, the aforementioned analysis is still applicable.

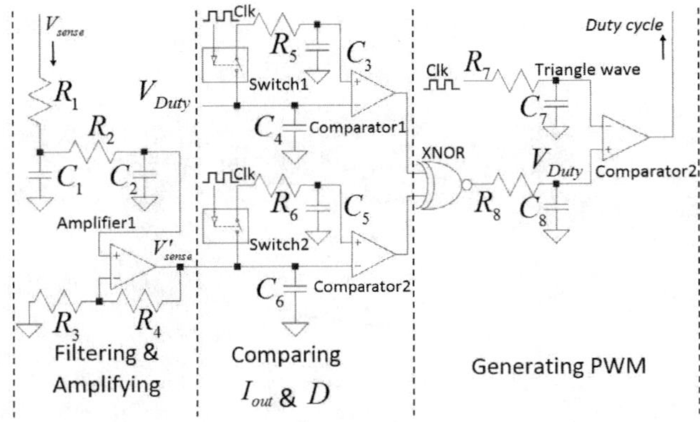

Figure 2: Schematic of the MPPT control circuit.

2.2 Design of the MPPT circuit

The implementation of the proposed output current based analog MPPT circuit is demonstrated in Figure 2. Firstly the V_{sense} ($I_{out} \times R_{sense}$) is filtered through a low-pass filter ($R_1, R_2, C_1\&C_2$) to remove high frequency noise. Since V_{sense} is really small it needs to be amplified to V'_{sense} by Amplifier1. V'_{sense} is then separated into two paths: one is directly connected to the inverting input of Comparator2; the other is connected to the noninverting input of Comparator2 through the clock-controlled Switch2 and delayed by an RC circuit ($R_6\&C_5$). This configuration compares the present value of V'_{sense} (inverting input) with the delayed value of V'_{sense} (noninverting input). The result of Comparator2 shows the changing trend of V'_{sense}, which represents the trend of I_{out}. The same topology applies to the measurement of the duty cycle (V_{Duty}) of the converter.

The results of Comparator1&2, representing the trend of D and I_{out} respectively, are fed into the XNOR gate, which determines whether to charge C_8 or not. The voltage of C_8 (representing the duty cycle value) is compared with a triangle wave (generated by R_7, C_7 and a clock), producing a variable duty cycle PWM signal to drive the boost converter. The duty cycle of the converter is changed continuously by the above process until the solar panel reaches the maximum power point. Then the duty cycle varies within a certain range, making the solar panel operates around the maximum power point with small oscillations.

3. WEARABLE PULSE SENSOR WITH BLE

3.1 Design of the Pulse Sensor

Figure 3 depicts a simple implementation of the pulse sensor, which consists of a piezoelectric transducer, an amplifier and an active low-pass filter. A commercial piezoelectric PVDF polymer, the LDT1-028K from Measurement Specialities®, is attached to the wrist to sense the pulse signal. The signal is then biased to a reference voltage (V_{ref}) by a large resistor R_1 and amplified by Amplifier1. The output of the pulse signal is:

$$V_{pulse} = V_{piezo}(1 + \frac{R_3}{R_2}) + V_{ref} \tag{6}$$

The right part of this schematic is a 2nd order active low-pass filter. Through this filter, the high frequency noise is

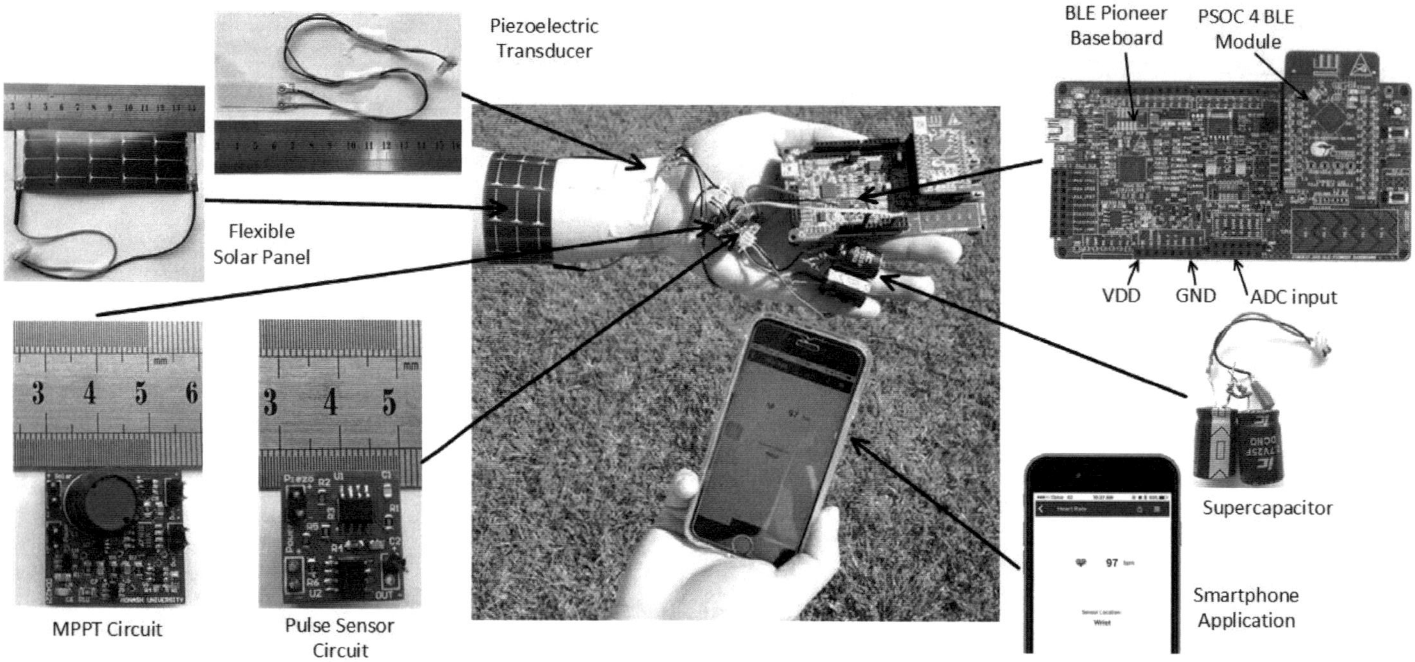

Figure 4: The setup of the solar energy harvesting system with a pulse sensor and BLE module.

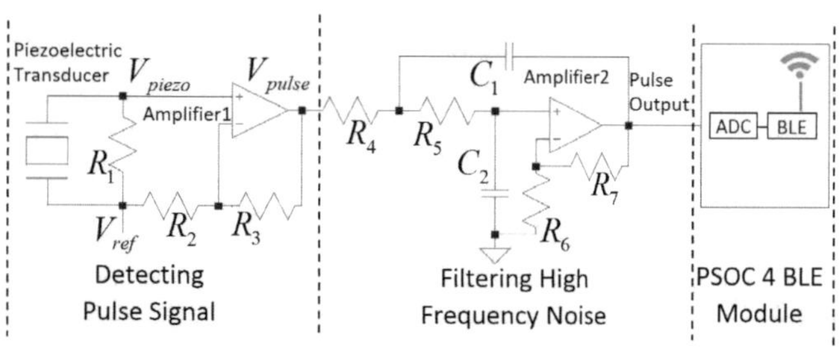

Figure 3: Schematic of the pulse sensor and BLE.

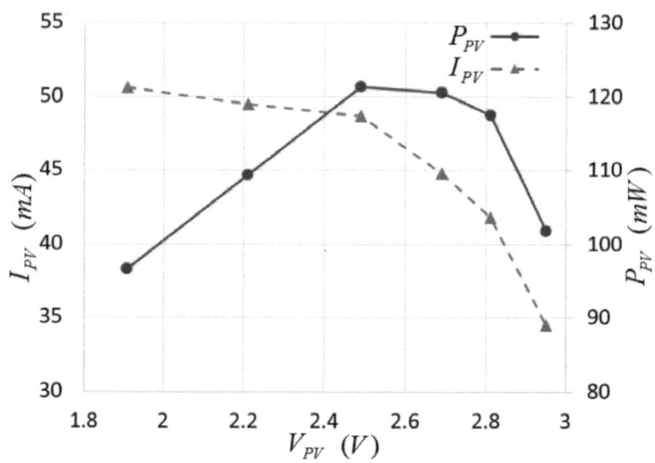

Figure 5: The I-V & P-V curves of the flexible solar panel under common sunlight.

eliminated. The pulse signal is then sent to the BLE module for wireless transmission.

3.2 Bluetooth Low Energy Transmission

Bluetooth low energy, also known as Bluetooth Smart, is an emerging wireless transmission technique developed by Bluetooth Special Interest Group [11]. Due to its extreme low power consumption and multiple applications, BLE is expected to be equipped into billions of electronic devices for use in wearable IoT devices in the next few years [12].

In this work, PSOC 4 BLE Module from Cypress® is chosen for the wireless data transmission. The BLE module along with the pioneer baseboard is shown in Figure 4. Its working voltage is 3.3-5 V with the transmitting current less than 15 mA. For this application, the BLE module is always active to transmit real time data. For lower power applications, it can be configured with sleep or deep-sleep mode, which consumes less than 3 mA or 15 μA, respectively. In this work, a smartphone application is designed for receiving the pulse signals from the sensor.

4. EXPERIMENTAL RESULTS

Figure 4 shows the setup of the proposed solar energy harvesting system and the pulse sensor with BLE. The MPPT circuit is fabricated and tested with a flexible solar panel, the MP3-37 from Sundance Solar®. Unlike conventional rigid solar panels, it can conform to the contour of a human body. Therefore the solar energy harvester is suitable for wearable devices. The MPPT circuit controls the flexible solar panel to operate at the maximum power point and supply energy to the pulse sensor and BLE module. It also charges a 12.5 F supercapacitor to store the backup energy for use without light. In the meantime, the pulse sensor detects the real time pulse signal and sends it to a smartphone APP through wireless BLE transmission.

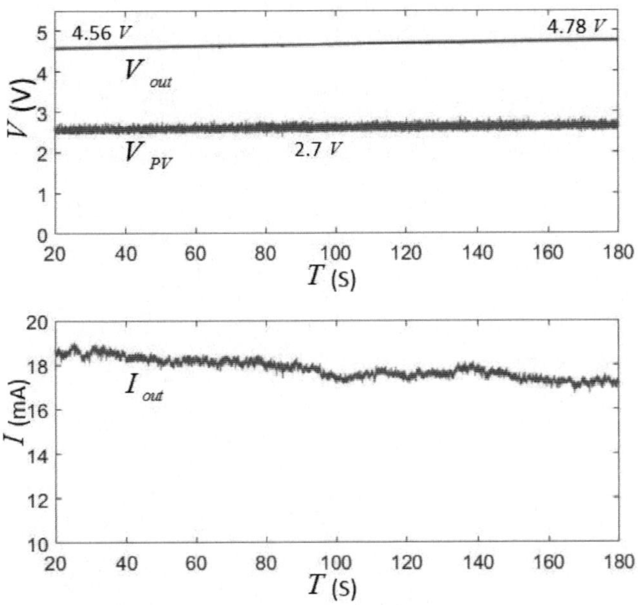

Figure 6: Experimental result of charging a 12.5 F supercapacitor with the MPPT circuit.

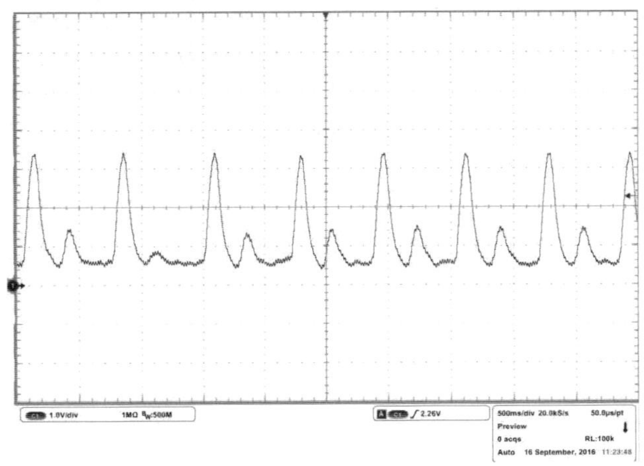

Figure 7: Experimental result of detecting the pulse signal with the pulse sensor.

4.1 Solar Energy Harvester

The first experiment was done outdoor testing the characteristic of the solar panel in the sunlight. Figure 5 depicts the I-V and P-V curves of the solar panel at the experimental condition. It can be seen the maximum power point of the panel is between 2.5 V and 2.7 V of the solar panel (the maximum power is 120.7 mW) at that condition.

Figure 6 shows the experiment result of charging a 12.5 F supercapacitor (two 25 F supercapacitor in series) with the proposed MPPT control circuit. The solar panel operated around 2.7 V while the supercapacitor was charged from 4.56 V to 4.78 V in 160 s. I_{out} is the output current to charge the supercapacitor. The output power from the solar panel is fixed at that irradiance condition, so I_{out} is decreasing with the increase of the supercapacitor's voltage. According to the analysis in Section 2, I_{out} is at its maximum value

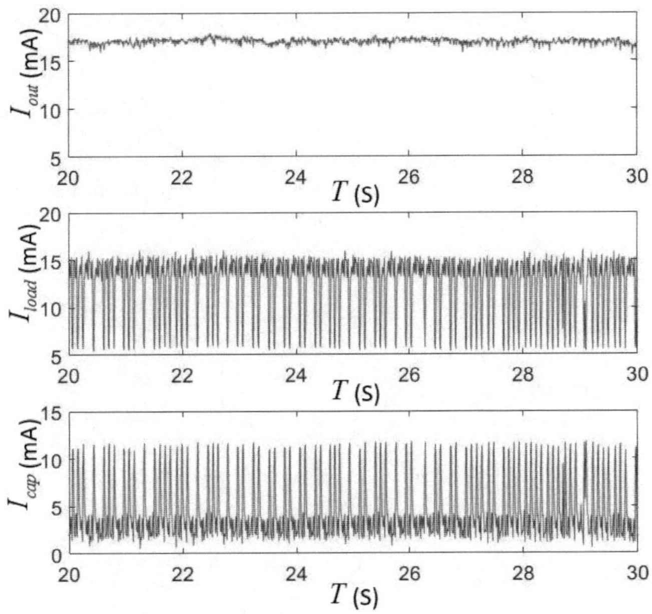

Figure 8: Experimental result of powering the pulse sensor and BLE while charging a supercapacitor.

for each constant supercapacitor's voltage during a short period of time. The charging power and overall efficiency of the solar energy harvesting system is 80.3 mW and 66.5%, respectively. The major power loss is due to the resistance of the inductor and voltage drop of the Zener diode used in the boost converter.

4.2 Self-powered Pulse Sensor with BLE Transmission

The pulse sensor was tested with the piezoelectric transducer attached to the wrist with the palm facing upwards. The experiment was performed without any wrist motion to get rid of artificial disturbances. Figure 7 shows that the sensor can successfully detect the pulse signal and eliminate high frequency noise. As the BLE module was active all the time for transmitting data, the overall power consumption of the pulse sensor and BLE was around 70 mW.

Figure 8 shows the experimental result of the MPPT circuit powering the pulse sensor and the BLE module from 20 s to 30 s. I_{out} is the overall output current through the converter, which consists of I_{load}, the current supplying the load (pulse sensor and BLE), and I_{cap}, the current charging the supercapacitor. During the experiment, the pulse sensor kept monitoring the pulse signal and transmitting it to a smartphone, while the supercapacitor was charged from 4.76 V to 4.79 V in 200 s. The charging power was around 8.9 mW, considering the power consumption of the pulse sensor and BLE module, it corresponded to the results of charging the supercapacitor alone.

5. CONCLUSIONS AND FUTURE WORK

This paper presents a solar energy harvesting system with an improved MPPT algorithm for wearable sensor applications. The proposed analog MPPT circuit needs only the output current for tracking the maximum power point, making the implementation of the circuit simpler. The experiment results demonstrate that the efficiency of the energy harvesting system is 66.5%. The MPPT circuit is applied to power a pulse sensor, which can transmit the real time pulse data to a smartphone through a wireless BLE module. The proposed system can be used to monitor people's health condition in daily life. The MPPT circuit with the flexible solar panel can also be applied to other wearable devices.

6. ACKNOWLEDGMENT

M. R. Yuce's work is supported by Australian Research Council Future Fellowships Grant FT130100430.

7. REFERENCES

[1] J. Gubbi, R. Buyya, S. Marusic, and M. Palaniswami. Internet of things (iot): A vision, architectural elements, and future directions. *Future Generation Computer Systems*, 29(7):1645-1660, Sept. 2013.

[2] Z.G. Wan, Y.K. Tan, and C. Yuen. Review on energy harvesting and energy management for sustainable wireless sensor networks. in *IEEE 13th Intl. Conf. on Communication Technology (ICCT)*, pp. 362-367, Sept. 2011.

[3] S.E. Babaa, M. Armstrong, and V. Pickert. Overview of maximum power point tracking control methods for pv systems. *Journal of Power and Energy Engineering*, 2(8):59-72, Aug. 2014.

[4] V. Salas, E. Olias, A. Barrado, and A. Lazaro. Review of the maximum power point tracking algorithms for stand-alone photovoltaic systems. *Solar Energy Materials and Solar Cells*, 90(11):1555-1578, Jul. 2006.

[5] M.A. Elgendy, B. Zahawi, and D.J. Atkinson. Assessment of perturb and observe MPPT algorithm implementation techniques for PV pumping applications. *IEEE Trans. sustainable energy*, 3(1): 21-33, Jan. 2012.

[6] J.H.Lee, H.S. Bae, and B.H. Cho. Advanced incremental conductance MPPT algorithm with a variable step size. in *Power Electronics and Motion Control Conf.*, pp. 603-607, Aug. 2006.

[7] R.Faranda and S.Leva. Energy comparison of MPPT techniques for PV Systems. *WSEAS transactions on power systems*, 3(6):446-455, Jun. 2008.

[8] T. Noguchi, S. Togashi, and R. Nakamoto, Short-current pulse-based maximum-power-point tracking method for multiple photovoltaic-and-converter module system, *IEEE Trans. Industrial Electronics*, 49(1):217-223, Feb. 2002.

[9] D. Buxi, J. Penders, and C. van Hoof. Early results on wrist based heart rate monitoring using mechanical transducers. in *Annual Intl. Conf. IEEE Eng. Med. and Biology (EMBC)*pp. 4407-4410, Aug. 2010.

[10] D. Shmilovitz. On the control of photovoltaic maximum power point tracker via output parameters. *IEE Proceedings - Electric Power Applications*, 152(2):239-248, Mar. 2005.

[11] B. Yu, L. Xu, and Y. Li. Bluetooth low energy (ble) based mobile electrocardiogram monitoring system. in *Intl. Conf. on Information and Automation (ICIA)*, pp. 763-767, Jun. 2012.

[12] C. Gomez, J. Oller, and J. Paradells. Overview and evaluation of bluetooth low energy: An emerging low-power wireless technology. *Sensors*, 12(9):11734-11753, Aug. 2012.

Step counting for slow and intermittent ambulation based on a smartwatch accelerometer

Vincenzo Genovese
The BioRobotics Institute,
Scuola Superiore Sant'Anna
Viale Rinaldo Piaggio, 34,
56025 Pontedera (Pisa)
Tel. +39050883410
vi.genovese@sssup.it

Andrea Mannini
The BioRobotics Institute,
Scuola Superiore Sant'Anna
Viale Rinaldo Piaggio, 34,
56025 Pontedera (Pisa)
Tel. +39050883410
a.mannini@sssup.it

Angelo Maria Sabatini
The BioRobotics Institute,
Scuola Superiore Sant'Anna
Viale Rinaldo Piaggio, 34,
56025 Pontedera (Pisa)
Tel. +39050883415
sabatini@sssup.it

ABSTRACT

The ambulatory monitoring of human movement can provide valuable information regarding the degree of functional ability and general level of activity of individuals. Since walking is a basic every day movement and an important element to introduce into one's daily routine, automatic step detection or step counting is very important in developing ambulatory monitoring systems. This paper is concerned with the development and the preliminary validation of a step counter (SC) that is especially designed for conditions of slow and intermittent ambulation. The SC was based on processing the accelerometer data measured by a Gear 2 smartwatch using a custom wearable app, named ADAM, running on the Gear 2. A dataset of 8 users, for a total of 80 trials, was used to tune ADAM. Finally, ADAM was compared with the native SC running in the Gear 2 smartwatch, and with the SC implemented in a waist-worn pedometer (Geonaute ONSTEP 400) (dataset of 8 users, for a total of 80 trials). The three SCs performed quite similarly in conditions of normal walking over long paths (1-3% of mean absolute relative error); ADAM outperformed the two other SCs in conditions of slow and intermittent ambulation; the error incurred by ADAM was limited to 5%, significantly lower than errors of 20-30% incurred by the two other SCs.

CCS Concepts

• **Human-centered computing → Ubiquitous and mobile computing**
• **Applied computing → Consumer health**

Keywords

step counting; accelerometer; smartwatch; pedometer; ambulation.

1. INTRODUCTION

Ageing of the population, especially in industrialized countries, and the concurrent increase of the number of people who spend a large part of their daily time in home, motivate the development of ambulatory monitoring systems that are capable to evaluate the level of physical activity, even in conditions of restrained mobility [1]. Because of the importance of walking for a healthy lifestyle, step detection and counting is thus one of the key problems for the understanding of the complex relationship between health and physical activity [2].

A large number of devices and applications have been developed for physical activity monitoring [3-5]. Accelerometry is the technology of choice for wearable devices to measure and assess physical activity. A pedometer – the device used for recording the number of steps taken – counts each step by detecting the motion of the person's arm or hip and it is considered a valid option for assessing physical activity in research and practice [6]. Differently from past switch-based devices, the recent pedometers are actually based on MEMS accelerometers whose data are processed by a dedicated algorithm that allows an accurate detection of steps. There are several factors that can limit the accuracy of pedometers, including placement site, intensity of walking, counting errors due to non-ambulatory activities [7-9]. The most common placement site of pedometers is the waist: devices are attached to the waistband or belt by means of a clip. Measuring the acceleration in all directions in the three-dimensional space relieves the wearer from the need to accurately position the device relative to an anatomical reference frame, which is important in the presence of body fat and clothing [7, 9]. User comfort and acceptability are generally high, since the freedom of movement is not restricted and donning-doffing is easy and convenient. Whereas counting errors due to non-ambulatory activities may not be critical to their performance, waist-worn pedometers are grossly inaccurate when the walking speed is low [1, 10].

Recent technological advances, in particular the development of mobile devices (namely, smartphones) that are endowed with inertial sensors, have motivated further research in the field. The problem with smartphone-based pedometers is that the mobile device is not necessarily taken in the same location at all times, and in the same position relative to the body (e.g., trouser pocket and bags) [11]. In contrast with waist-worn pedometers, smartphone-based pedometers are also more sensitive to the influence of non-ambulatory activities, although interesting results have been recently reported as for the recognition of activity and the estimation of spatial-temporal parameters of gait [12, 13]. Moreover, movements of the upper arm when the smartphone is carried in the hand are not necessarily correlated with walking, and can thus generate a lot of false positives. An interesting avenue of research concerns the creation of signal processing methods that can help reduce the sensitivity of step-counting algorithms to the issue of placement and non-ambulatory activities [11, 14, 15]. However, in a similar fashion to waist-worn pedometers, smartphone-based pedometers suffer from accuracy degradations when the walking speed is slow. In the attempt to improve the performance of smartphone-based pedometers, embedded MEMS gyroscopes have also been considered as an alternative to accelerometers [16].

The reluctance to accept and to routinely use new technologies is an important issue for the development of wearable sensor systems, such as activity monitors and pedometers. Lack of interest or motivation in using them is highly predictive of later refusal. In this regard, a new generation of mobile devices may imply a change of attitude. The compliance with the use of a device worn at the wrist (namely, a smartwatch) would be generally high, which is one reason for the increasing interest attached to this technology: recent works involving long-term monitoring in large cohorts of users highlighted that using wrist-worn sensor devices can grant longer wear times [17] [18]. Moreover, smartwatches provide unprecedented opportunity for collection of large datasets of continuous measurement of physiological parameters (e.g., heart rate, galvanic skin resistance and temperature), and activity-related data (e.g., built-in accelerometer recordings), which can be used for longitudinal monitoring of health status and for quantimetric self-tracking, as advocated by the Quantified Self movement [14, 19-22].

The problem of reliability of measurements is often cited as a major obstacle for wider use of wearable health monitoring devices such as smartwatches. For instance, processing the accelerometer data for activity recognition provides a challenge because of the wrist gesticulation and variability in movement, compared with placement sites such as waist or ankle [23]. The wrist may move differently during the same activity, depending on what is in the hand and what the hand is holding or stabilizing. It is expected that these difficulties may affect step counting using a wrist-worn pedometer, although arm movements are generally well correlated with leg movements during steady walking.

In the case of intermittent ambulation activities, a critical issue affecting the accuracy of existing pedometers is the number of missed steps that may occur due to the irregular signal patterns from the built-in accelerometer, regardless of placement site. For instance, consider the problem of estimating a few steps interspersed with frequent stops and restarts. In this scenario, acceleration peaks correlated with steps are expected to be distributed irregularly both in amplitude and in time; hence, any predictive mechanism embedded in the algorithm of step counting is likely to perform poorly, due to the difficulty to specify and match template patterns describing the events occurring during any single step. Another element of difficulty is that data windowing itself would be a critical process in conditions of slow and intermittent walking (low time-resolution issue) [9]. A wristwatch pedometer that would search for the periods inherent in the cyclical nature of walking would require indeed long signal windows for extracting, e.g., the frequency-domain features needed for step identification.

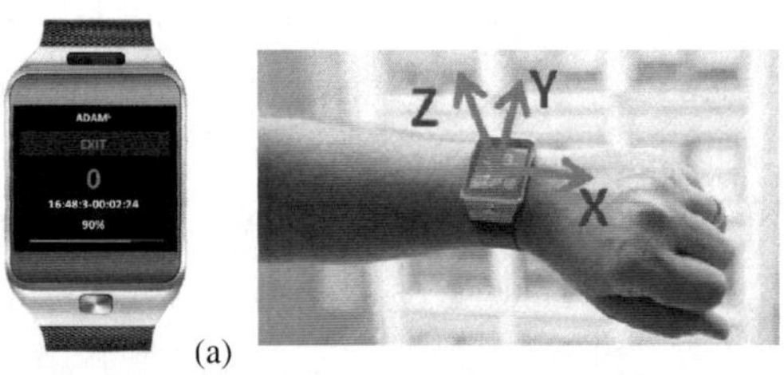

(a) (b)

Figure 1. (a) The Gear 2 smartwatch used for ADAM development; (b) The mobile reference frame aligned with the sensitivitv axes of the embedded accelerometer.

The literature existing on the application of wrist-worn accelerometry to the problem of step counting is still scarce, and scattered, especially in conditions of slow and intermittent ambulation. Few patents were also surveyed [24, 25]. This paper is an initial attempt to fill the gap. Previous research on smartphone pedometry showed that frequency-domain or correlation approaches did not accrue substantial benefits compared with windowed peak detect (WPD) methods for step counting in conditions of normal walking [9]; on the other hand, WPD methods are easier to implement and present reduced computational loads. Therefore, we developed an adaptive WPD algorithm for wrist pedometer step counting using the built-in accelerometer of a commercial smartwatch. We compared the performance of the proposed algorithm, the native app running in the smartwatch for step counting, and a waist-worn commercial pedometer. The experimental tests included steady walking at several speeds, jogging, non-ambulatory activities, and intermittent and slow ambulation.

2. EXPERIMENTAL SECTION

2.1 System Design and Implementation

The developed algorithm was implemented in a wearable app named ADAM (Advanced Daily Activity Monitor) running on a commercial Tizen smartwatch (Gear 2, Samsung Electronics Co., Ltd.), Fig. 1a. ADAM was written in HTML5 using the IDE Tizen SDK for Wearable (version 1.0.0). The smartwatch provided acceleration components a_x, a_y, a_z (normalized to the gravitational acceleration g, g = 9.81 m/s^2) relative to the mobile reference frame shown in Fig. 1b. The MP65M 6-axis chip manufactured by InvenSense, Inc., San Jose CA, USA serves as the inertial measurement unit within the smartwatch. The acceleration was measured by the embedded tri-axial accelerometer, internally sampled at the sampling frequency f_s = 25 Hz (sampling interval T_s = 40 ms). Additionally, a tri-axial gyroscope was available to measure the angular velocity at the rate of, approximately, one sample per second (feature not used in this work). Although it might be interesting to use the measured angular rate for step counting purposes, this sampling rate was believed too low for allowing any use in the present context..

2.2 Experimental Protocol

Two sets of experimental trials were performed, with the aim to build one dataset for tuning the parameters needed by the step counting algorithm (training dataset), and another dataset for assessing its performance (testing dataset). Two groups of healthy adult subjects participated in the experiments. All participants signed an informed consent before starting experimental sessions. Research procedures were in accordance with the Declaration of Helsinki. All subjects wore the Gear 2 smartwatch at the non-dominant hand wrist and a commercial pedometer (Geonaute ONSTEP 400), which was clipped to the waist belt at the right anterior iliac spine. During experimental sessions, subjects were free to wear their preferred shoes. Although the testing was not done in true naturalistic environments, we took care to minimize experimental biases, by asking subjects to move as naturally as they could. Moreover, they did not receive verbal or any other feedback information about their performance, only start and stop messages were issued to them. The subjects were instructed to walk at their preferred speed (free-selected speed), slower, or much slower, than normal and faster than normal, being free to interpret the speed at their own convenience. The set of activities considered for training ADAM and for testing ADAM, the Gear 2 and the Geonaute step counters (SCs), is given in Table 1. The experimenter observed the participants while performing activities and counted the number of steps walked in each trial, so as to compute the reference step count N_{ref} used for algorithm performance assessment.

Table 1. Activity types and description

Type	Description
Walk-turn-walk	Walk ten steps along a straight path, including a half-turn to walk ten steps in the opposite direction so as to return to the initial location (a rest of two seconds allowed before and after the half-turn). Repeat at four different speeds: slower than normal, normal (i.e., free-selected), faster than normal, jogging.
Slow and steady walk	Walk 500 steps at constant, slow speed (level walking); directional changes are allowed.
Variable-speed walk	Walk 500 steps at variable speed (level walking), with walking speed being freely changed (slower than normal, normal, faster than normal); directional changes and stops-starts are allowed.
Very slow walk	Walk 100 steps at very low speed (level walking), with minimal trunk and head oscillations; directional changes and stops-starts are allowed.
Jog	Jog 100 steps; directional changes and stops-starts are allowed.
Going up-and-down stairs	Climb a staircase of 11 steps (16-cm high), including a half-turn to the higher floor; walk downstairs along the same staircase, so as to return to the initial location.
In-home task	Subjects were asked to do a predefined sequence of actions in a structured room, walking at their own preferred speed (see figure 2): a) Take a box placed on the desk at point A and place it on the top of the shelf at point B (d = 7.8 m) b) Reach the coat rack at point C and pick up a bag (d = 3.6 m) c) Carry the bag on the top of a second shelf at point D using the smartwatch side arm (d = 8.4 m) d) Reach the shelf at point B and recoup the box (d = 7.2 m) e) Bring the box on the desk at point A (d = 7.8 m) f) Reach the shelf at point D and recoup the bag (d = 4.2 m) g) Carry the bag to the coat rack at point C using the left arm (d = 8.4 m) h) Reach the point A (d = 6.6 m) The distance walked in each section from a) to h) is denoted with d. Between each section, subjects were asked to rest for two seconds.

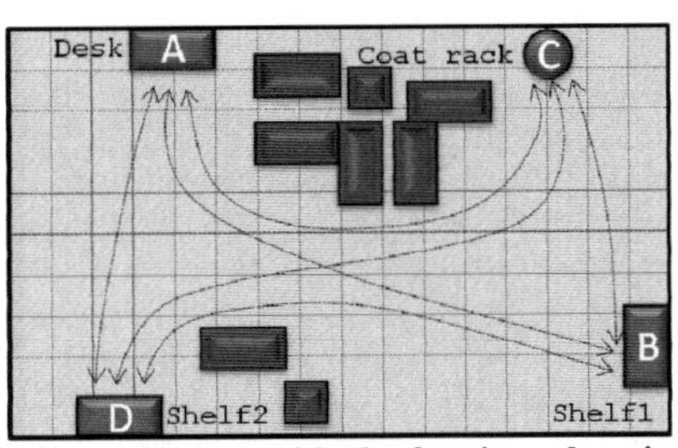

Figure 3. Room layout, with the furniture location for the *In-home task* activity. The red shapes are fixed obstacles to be avoided. The blue shapes are the target points. The grid size is 60 cm × 60 cm

The training dataset included the accelerometer data acquired from group 1-subjects asked to perform the *Walk-turn-walk* activity, with all variants indicated in Table 1. Eight subjects (5 males and 3 females) participated in the training phase. Age ranged from 28 to 55 years (38.5 ± 11.8 years) and height from 160 to 185 (172.8 ± 10.5 cm). The testing dataset included the accelerometer data acquired from group-2 subjects asked to perform all activities in Table 1. Eight subjects (3 males and 5 females) participated in the testing phase. Age ranged from 29 to 54 years (37.2 ± 9.7 years) and height from 158 to 187 (172.1 ± 9.5 cm).

2.3 The Step Counting Algorithm

A standard calibration procedure was employed to calibrate the built-in tri-axial accelerometer [24]. The computed values of offset and scale factor along the three sensitivity axes were used to compensate for calibration errors before processing the accelerometer measurements by ADAM.

The acceleration magnitude

$$A_m = \sqrt{a_x^2 + a_y^2 + a_z^2} \qquad (1)$$

was computed from the acceleration components. An 8-point moving average filter was applied to the acceleration magnitude, followed by a 3-point moving median filter, in the combined effort to remove the high-frequency noise and mitigate the effects of outlying measurements. If the absolute difference between the current sample and the previous sample at the output of the moving median filter was less than a small threshold (λ_M), the current sample was clipped to the previous sample, yielding A_{mL}. A high-pass filtered version of A_{mL} was obtained, namely A_{mH}, by subtracting an 8-point moving averaged version of A_{mL} from A_{mL} itself. On a separate conditioning line, the acceleration components a_x, a_y, a_z were filtered using a 16-point moving average filter, yielding a_{xL}, a_{yL}, a_{zL}.

2.3.1 Dynamic Thresholding

In accordance to previous studies, we hypothesize that local maxima of the acceleration magnitude correlate with foot contacts at the beginning of each gait step, provided that such peak values are high enough and are not determined by acceleration measurement noise [25]. Hence, each peak of A_{mL} whose value exceeds some threshold value λ_D *can* increase the step count by one unit, depending on the outcome of the step validation procedure described in the following. We propose to determine the threshold value on line (dynamic thresholding) by clipping A_{mL} to a minimum value (to reduce the effects of the pedometer vibrating very rapidly or very slowly from a cause other than walking), before being time-shifted by $\tau_d = K_d T_s$ units of time. The rationale for this choice is explained, first, by analyzing the shortcomings of a popular means to compute λ_D [25]:

$$\lambda_D = \frac{max\{A_{mL}\}_{\tau_w} + min\{A_{mL}\}_{\tau_w}}{2}. \qquad (2)$$

The adaptive threshold is computed as the arithmetic mean between the maximum and the minimum values of A_{mL}. These values are evaluated using a signal window of length τ_w extending from the current sample of A_{mL} backwards; the threshold is then clipped to a minimum value A_{min}. The peak is searched in the time interval from the positive crossing time (rising time), i.e., when A_{mL} crosses λ_D with positive slope to the negative crossing time, to the negative crossing time (falling time) i.e., when A_{mL} crosses λ_D with negative slope. In the example reported in Fig. 3, λ_D is computed over different time windows according to (2), and clipped to A_{min} (A_{min} = 1.033 g). In the time window over which

A_{mL} exeeds (or not) the dynamic threshold λ_D the step counter state is: armed (not armed).

In the example, it is noted that the step annotated as P4 is not detected when $\tau_w = 1$ s, yielding a false negative in the step detection process (Fig. 3a). This behavior is quite typical, especially when the peak values of A_{mL} differ markedly during consecutive steps, namely when left and right steps are not symmetric. Slight asymmetries are typical even of healthy gait as highlighted by analyzing data from waist-worn sensors [26] and they are likely to exist as far as the motion of the upper arm is considered; intermittent ambulation (e.g., frequent stops and starts, abrupt directional changes) thus further exacerbates the problem. In the effort to make the dynamic threshold adapting faster to the signal shape, τ_w can be reduced, as in Fig. 3b, where $\tau_w = 0.08$ s. The peak at P4 is correctly detected, however we observe a false positive occurring in the case of the peak at P0. It is also noted that the time function of the dynamic threshold λ_D tends to a delayed replica of A_{mL} as long as the window's length τ_w is reduced. Let us suppose that the time window is narrowed down to the point when $\tau_w = T_s$, in which case the dynamic threshold turns out to be A_{mL} delayed by one sample. Following the reasoning above, the algorithm would become highly responsive, with the consequence that several false positives might arise, especially when the (wrist) acceleration patterns are irregular. In our WPD implementation, we propose to design the dynamic threshold using a deliberate time-shift of A_{mL} by $K_d > 1$ samples,

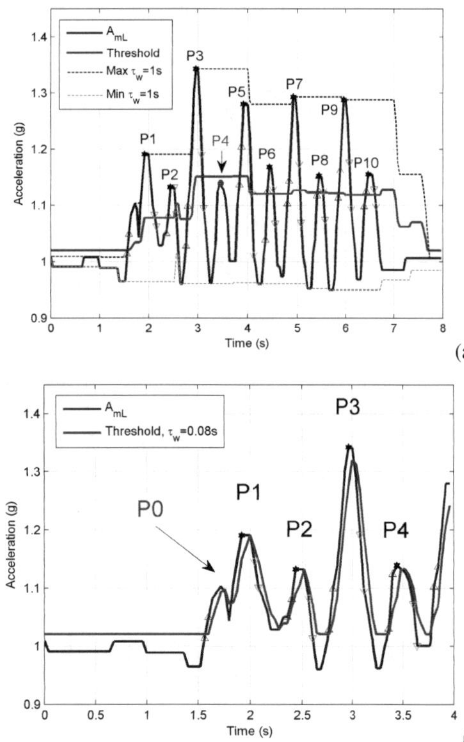

Figure 3. The time functions of A_{mL} (blue) and λ_D (red) are reported for a representative walking bout from activity *Walk-turn-walk*. (a) $\tau_w = 1$ s; (b) $\tau_w = 0.08$ s. Red and green triangular markers indicate the samples within which the dynamic threshold is crossed in rising and falling directions, respectively.

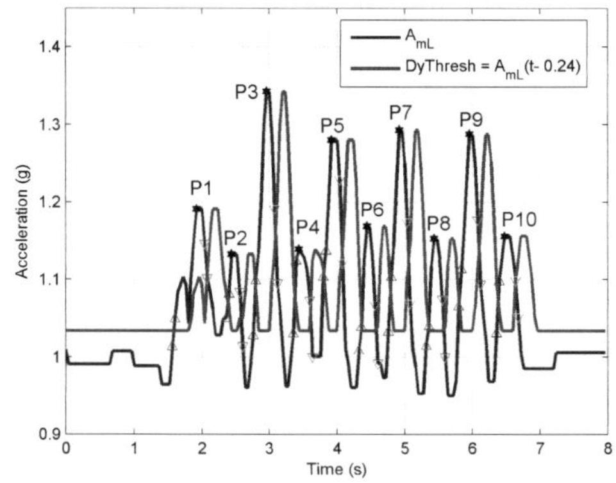

Figure 4. The time functions of A_{mL} (blue) and λ_D (red) are reported for the same walking bout from activity *Walk-turn-walk* in Fig. 3.

in the effort to avoid proliferation of false positives, whilst retaining good adaptation properties. Hence, λ_D is computed as the clipped (to $A_{\min}$) and time-shifted (by $\tau_d = K_d T_s$ units of time) replica of A_{mL}. We hypothesize that this approach may ensure fast adaptation to any change of the underlying signal shape. Figure 4 shows the results for the same example as in Fig. 3: λ_D is computed by delaying A_{mL} by four samples, and the result is then clipped to $A_{\min}$.

In this particular example, the peak at P4 is correctly detected, without introducing false positives in the step detection process. However, successful peak identification does not imply that the step count be increased necessarily by one unit; the detected step-related event must be further validated for achieving better robustness to false positives. In preparation for the step validation phase, the following quantities are computed. The step time, expressed in seconds, is computed as the difference between successive occurrences of A_{mL}-peaks that are identified by dynamic thresholding. The cadence, expressed in Hz, is computed by inverting the average step time, which is estimated from a specified number of step times. Finally, the Root Mean Square of A_{mH} (RMS_H) is calculated in a window of length τ_s extending from the current sample of A_{mH} backwards over the window τ_s.

2.3.2 Step Validation

The proposed procedure of step validation runs a set of rules that are applied at the time when a peak is detected and on a sample-by-sample basis. The SC status is determined by two values: the total number of steps counted so far (N_{step}) and the current number of consecutive peaks that are recognized as steps (ContStep).

The set of rules and the related parameters is illustrated in Table 2. Rule #1 is related to the assumption that a steady walking activity requires at least some consecutive steps to occur [25]. Rule #2 to rule #6 code the intuitive notion that a gait step cannot have abnormal durations (neither too long nor too short), and must be characterized by a significant acceleration footprint [27]. Rule #7 can detect sudden stops of walking (no additional steps have been counted in a given time interval). Rule #8 helps detecting situations when the wristwatch orientation in the three-dimensional space is likely to be inconsistent with the forearm orientation of a walker. Rule #9 helps detecting false positives that are likely to occur due to arm swinging during the last step before a walk stop.

2.4 Metric of Performance

The Count Error (*CE*) was defined as follows (*i*-th activity, *j*-th subject):

$$CE(i,j) = N_{\text{step}}(i,j) - N_{\text{ref}}(i,j),\ i = 1,\ldots,10;\ j = 1,\ldots,8. \quad (3)$$

The Mean Absolute Relative Error (*MARE*) was also considered as performance metric:

$$MARE(i) = 100 \cdot \frac{1}{8}\sum_{j=1}^{8}\left|\frac{CE(i,j)}{N_{\text{ref}}(i,j)}\right|, \qquad i = 1,\ldots,10. \quad (4)$$

CE and *MARE* are the metrics to investigate the accuracy of the three SCs. Henceforth, the term *complete failure* will be used to denote when one method was 100% inaccurate, in the sense that it could not register any valid step in a particular activity.

3. RESULTS AND DISCUSSION

ADAM was trained using the *CE*-statistics generated from the training dataset to handcraft the setting of the input parameters needed by the algorithm, Table 3.

The parameters λ_M, K_d, $A_{\min}$ and StMin were tuned by performing a grid search for determining their optimal value. Empirically, we verified that they were important in determining the algorithm performance, especially the time delay K_d, which turned out to be the essential element of the proposed WPD method. Compared with the case when $K_d = 4$, a too small value tended to increase the detection sensitivity at the expense of the specificity; conversely, a too high value (say, $K_d > 8$) tended to improve the detection specificity, at the expense of the sensitivity.

The parameters TstMin (minimum step time), TstMax (maximum step time), StfMax (maximum cadence), AccMax (maximum value of A_{mL}), AccMin (minimum value of A_{mL}), StRMS (maximum value of RMS_H), and TimeOverT (minimum duration of a step-related acceleration burst) were used to implement simple heuristics that helped improving performance by enforcing reasonable constraints of walking [27]. All other parameters that were grouped under the category Step validation in Table 3 (i.e., A_xMin, A_yMin, A_zMin, A_zMax) helped essentially to improve the capability of rejecting the many false positives that could be collected during activities of daily living involving hand movements that were not necessarily related with walking (rule #8). We performed several tests with the subjects wearing the smartwatch; they were asked to freely perform sedentary activities (i.e., answering phone calls, drinking, typing a keyboard, gesticulating while speaking) and exercise breaks (i.e., outstretching the arms in different spatial orientations) – total recording time: 30 min per subject. By careful analysis of the accelerometer data recorded during these tests, we were able to choose a parameter setting that turned into 100% specificity. It goes without saying that the native Samsung SC accumulated several counts in the same situation where ADAM was not affected by false positives.

Table 4 reports the data concerning the complete failures of each SC. Not surprisingly, the Geonaute SC performed worse in conditions when the number of consecutive steps walked before any stop was not high enough for step validation (*Walk-turn-walk* and *In-home task*); moreover, it suffered from some difficulties even during the activity *Very slow walk*. The explanation is that the factory calibration of the Geonaute SC was for conditions of continuous walking at not-too-low speeds. The Samsung SC

Table 2. Step validation rules

Rule	Description	State
1	Wait updating N_{step} until ContStep ≥ **StMin**	Falling
2	If step time ≤ **TstMin** or step time ≥ **TstMax**, then ContStep = 0	Falling
3	If cadence ≥ **StfMax**, then ContStep = 0 (cadence is computed from the last StMin steps)	Falling
4	If A_{mL}-peak ≥ **AccMax**, then ContStep = 0	Falling
5	If A_{mL}-peak ≤ **AccMin**, then ContStep = 0	Falling
6	If A_{mL} exceeds λ_D for a time less than **TimeOverT**, then ContStep = 0	Falling
7	If the time elapsed from last valid step (ElapsedTimeFromLastStep) exceeds **TstMax**, then ContStep = 0	Not armed
8	Suspend dynamic thresholding if ContStep ≥ 2 StMin, or the step counter is armed or one of the following four conditions is true: Workspace check: 1. a_{xL} ≥ **A_xMax** 2. a_{yL} ≤ **A_yMax** 3. a_{zL} ≥ **A_zMax** 4. a_{zL} ≤ **A_zMin**	Sample by sample
9	If the following conditions are true: 1. RMS_H ≥ **StRMS** 2. ElapsedTimeFromLastStep ≥ TstMax 3. ContStep ≥ StMin 4. $N_{\text{step}} > 0$ then $N_{\text{step}} = N_{\text{step}} - 1$, and ContStep = 0	Not armed

Table 3. Input parameters of ADAM.

Processing	
λ_M, g	0.017
Dynamic thresholding	
K_d	4.000
$A_{\min}$, g	1.033
Step validation	
StMin	6.000
TstMin, s	0.300
TstMax, s	1.500
StfMax, Hz	3.000
A_xMin, g	0.250
A_yMin, g	0.150
A_zMin, g	–0.360
A_zMax, g	0.800
AccMax, g	2.500
AccMin, g	1.040
TimeOverT, s	0.120
τ_s, s	3.000
StRMS, g	0.080

Table 4. Number of complete failures for each method.

Activity	ADAM	Samsung SC	Geonaute SC
Walk-turn-walk (slow)	0	3	8
Walk-turn-walk (normal)	0	3	8
Walk-turn-walk (fast)	0	6	8
Walk-turn-walk (jogging)	0	5	7
Slow and steady walk	0	0	0
Variable-speed walk	0	0	0
Very slow walk	0	4	2
Jog	0	0	0
Going up-and-down stairs	0	0	0
In-home task	0	0	5
Total	0/80	21/80	38/80

Table 5. Statistics of the performance metric *CE*.

Activity	ADAM				Gear SC				Geonaute SC			
	Mean	Max	Min	Std	Mean	Max	Min	Std	Mean	Max	Min	Std
Walk-turn-walk (slow)	0.7	4	−1	1.5	−3.0	−2	−4	1.0	NA	NA	NA	NA
Walk-turn-walk (normal)	0.6	3	−1	1.4	−1.8	1	−4	2.1	NA	NA	NA	NA
Walk-turn-walk (fast)	1.0	4	−2	2.0	−1.0	−1	−1	0.0	NA	NA	NA	NA
Walk-turn-walk (jogging)	2.7	7	−3	3.2	2.3	7	−7	8.1	4.0	4	4	0.0
Slow and steady walk	−4.9	3	−20	7.1	−4.5	0	−17	5.5	−4.8	3	−18	8.3
Variable-speed walk	−11.1	18	−84	30.9	−4.6	23	−50	20.8	4.4	36	−10	14.1
Very slow walk	−2.9	8	−17	7.1	−21.5	0	−76	36.4	−30.0	1	−82	38.5
Jog	0.0	5	−3	2.8	−5.5	15	−63	24.0	4.0	17	−4	6.4
Going up-and-down stairs	−0.1	3	−2	1.6	−1.3	1	−4	2.1	0.8	3	0	1.0
In-home task	−5.5	1	−26	9.0	−10.5	10	−42	19.0	−61.0	2	−103	55.6

performed better than the Geonaute SC in our experiments, but not for the activity *Very slow walk*. The same comment concerning the factory calibration is pertinent to explain the Samsung SC behavior.

Limiting the statistical analysis just to the trials when the methods did not undergo complete failure, Table 5 reports the *CE* statistics for each activity, averaged across subjects (mean value, standard deviation, minimum value, maximum value). The two commercial devices, particularly the Samsung SC, tended to undercount steps, especially when the walking conditions differed to some extent from those assumed for the factory calibration. Conversely, ADAM performed acceptably, although, due to an outlying subject performing the activity *Variable-speed walk*, namely one subject for which ADAM heavily undercounted steps, the mean error and the standard deviation were slightly greater than those achieved by the two other methods in the same conditions.

Finally, Table 6 reports the *MARE* values scored by the three SCs.

The three tested SCs performed similarly during the extended walks of *Slow and steady walk*, *Variable-speed walk* and during *Going up-and-down stairs*; conversely, ADAM outperformed the two other pedometers in all conditions when the movement was very slow (i.e., during *Very slow walk*) and more intermittent [*Walk-turn-walk* (except jogging) and *In-home task*]. *Walk-turn-walk (jogging)* was the only activity where the three methods performed poorly, although ADAM was better even in this case (no complete failures and lower MARE values).

The complete failures and the errors incurred by the three methods, and especially by the Geonaute SC, during the activity *Walk-turn-walk*, in all conditions of walking speed, can be partly explained as the consequence of the built-in assumption of registering a step only after that a certain number of consecutive steps have been observed. This assumption is common to all tested methods. In the absence of documented information about the behavior of the two commercial devices, we can only conjecture which value of the parameter StMin they have (StMin = 10, we believe). The approach we propose to dynamic thresholding allowed reducing StMin without substantial performance degradation, provided that the time delay K_d was suitably chosen.

From inspecting the performance data reported in Tables 4-6, the Samsung SC outperformed the Geonaute SC; ADAM outperformed both during *Walk-turn-walk* (in all variants) and *In-home task*. Moreover, the two wrist-worn SCs tended to perform better than the waist-worn SC when the walking speed was slower than normal, with the preference to be given to ADAM. We can conclude that the two customer SCs were not probably designed to perform accurate step counting in those situations (slow and

Table 6. Values of the performance metric MARE.

Activity	ADAM	Samsung SC	Geonaute SC
Walk-turn-walk (slow)	5	15	NA
Walk-turn-walk (normal)	6	11	NA
Walk-turn-walk (fast)	9	5	NA
Walk-turn-walk (jogging)	18	35	20
Slow and steady walk	1	1	1
Variable-speed walk	3	2	2
Very slow walk	5	21	30
Jog	2	12	5
Going up-and-down stairs	2	3	2
In-home task	6	17	61

intermittent walking) where ADAM suited better. The data reported in Table 6 indicate MARE values incurred by ADAM lower than 5% during continuous walking across a range of speeds, which increased to 5%-18% when short walking bouts were considered. We consider the results of this paper in connection with the results reported by Cheng et al [28], who analyzed step counts using a custom smartphone algorithm and a commercial waist-band pedometer when two healthy subjects walked 500 consecutive steps. The custom smartphone algorithm outperformed the waist-band pedometer, showing performance comparable to ours (activities *Slow and steady walk* and *Variable-speed walk*). However, they taped together the smartphone and the waist-band pedometer and fixed them at the L3 level (lower trunk). In these conditions, trunk accelerometry is widely regarded as a feasible technique to accurately measure spatio-temporal parameters of gait, including step time and cadence [29], [30]; however, serious concerns exist for its suitability when gait is pathologic, the gait speed is low, or both [31]. Cheng et al recognized This same difficulty was recognized in [28], in experiments involving COPD (Chronic Obstructive Pulmonary Disease) patients that performed the Six Minutes Walking Test (6MWT); see also [32], for a discussion of the trend of state-of-the-art pedometers to undercount steps in conditions of slow walking. We verified the same behavior of either the Samsung or the Geonaute SC, which sometimes also completely failed to count at slow walking speeds. On the other hand, the undercount bias of ADAM was generally small. We consider therefore the ADAM error rate, particularly during the activity *Very slow walk*, a very promising result.

It is noted that ADAM and the Samsung pedometer are two apps that run on the smartwatch, sharing the same raw accelerometer data. The ADAM step counting loop works at the rate of 25 samples per second; in the absence of any further information, we believe that the sampling rate is the same for the Samsung pedometer. In terms of power consumption, we verified that the time from full charge to complete discharge of the battery system is 72 hours (low-power screen-off mode) and 5 hours (screen-on mode), irrespective of whether the Samsung pedometer runs alone or ADAM works in conjunction with it (the Samsung pedometer is a permanent application that can never be aborted). The computational load of ADAM is therefore similar to that of the Samsung SC, and both apps drain only a limited amount of battery power, compared with the battery draining due to, e.g., the screen condition. Of course, any further consideration about the battery life must consider that smartwatches are devices that can be used for fulfilling many functions, including, e.g., telephony, e-mailing, Bluetooth connectivity, which all are known to be greedy of battery power. In this sense, the power requirements and the battery charging policies of a smartwatch would not be dissimilar from those of a smartphone.

4. Conclusions and Outlook

This paper was concerned with the development and the preliminary validation of a step counter that was designed for applications when ambulation can be slow and intermittent. The step counter was based on processing the accelerometer data measured by a commercial smartwatch using a custom wearable app (ADAM). Compared with either the native step counter running in the smartwatch or a waist-worn pedometer, ADAM exhibited similar accuracy levels in conditions of normal walking, and was superior in conditions of slow and intermittent ambulation. The WPD algorithm developed in this paper for step counting can be ported to any wrist-worn mobile device that embeds a tri-axial accelerometer to measure wrist acceleration. Our novel approach to dynamic thresholding might be useful even in the implementation of WPDs for step counting using other accelerometer placement sites, although we have not yet tested it. As for the wrist, the experimental results shown in the paper offer promise for a robust solution to the problem of step counting in difficult conditions of slow and intermittent walking.

5. ACKNOWLEDGMENTS

This work was partly supported by the EC funded project I-SUPPORT "ICT-Supported Bath Robots" (H2020 PHC-19 643666).

6. REFERENCES

[1] Storti, K. L., Pettee, K. K., Brach, J. S., Talkowski, J. B., Richardson, C. R. and Kriska, A. M. 2008. Gait speed and step-count monitor accuracy in community-dwelling older adults. *Medicine & Science in Sports & Exercise*, 40, 1 (2008), 59-64.

[2] Storm, F. A., Heller, B. W. and Mazzà, C. 2015. Step detection and activity recognition accuracy of seven physical activity monitors. *PloS one*, 10, 3 (2015), e0118723.

[3] Yang, C.-C. and Hsu, Y.-L. 2010. A review of accelerometry-based wearable motion detectors for physical activity monitoring. *Sensors*, 10, 8 (2010), 7772-7788.

[4] Fortino, G., Giannantonio, R., Gravina, R., Kuryloski, P. and Jafari, R. 2013. Enabling effective programming and flexible management of efficient body sensor network applications. *IEEE Trans Hum-Machine Syst*, 43, 1 (2013), 115-133.

[5] Fortino, G., Gravina, R., Li, W. and Ma, C. 2015.Using cloud-assisted body area networks to track people physical activity in mobility. *Proc. of the 10th EAI International Conference on Body Area Networks* (2015).

[6] Tudor-Locke, C., Williams, J. E., Reis, J. P. and Pluto, D. 2002. Utility of pedometers for assessing physical activity. *Sports Medicine*, 32, 12 (2002), 795-808.

[7] Duncan, S. J., Schofield, G., Duncan, E. K. and Hinckson, E. A. 2007. Effects of age, walking speed, and body composition on pedometer accuracy in children. *Research quarterly for exercise and sport*, 78, 5 (2007), 420-428.

[8] Horvath, S., Taylor, D. G., Marsh, J. P. and Kriellaars, D. J. 2007. The effect of pedometer position and normal gait asymmetry on step count accuracy. *Applied Physiology, Nutrition, and Metabolism*, 32, 3 (2007), 409-415.

[9] Melanson, E. L., Knoll, J. R., Bell, M. L., Donahoo, W. T., Hill, J., Nysse, L. J., Lanningham-Foster, L., Peters, J. C. and Levine, J. A. 2004. Commercially available pedometers: considerations for accurate step counting. *Preventive medicine*, 39, 2 (2004), 361-368.

[10]Dondzila, C. J., Swartz, A. M., Miller, N. E., Lenz, E. K. and Strath, S. J. 2012. Accuracy of uploadable pedometers in laboratory, overground, and free-living conditions in young and older adults. *International Journal of Behavioral Nutrition and Physical Activity*, 9, 1 (2012), 143.

[11]Brajdic, A. and Harle, R. 2013.Walk detection and step counting on unconstrained smartphones. *Proc. ACM Internat Joint Conf on Pervasive and ubiquitous computing*, 2013, 225-234.

[12]Susi, M., Renaudin, V. and Lachapelle, G. 2013. Motion mode recognition and step detection algorithms for mobile phone users. *Sensors*, 13, 2 (2013), 1539-1562.

[13]Renaudin, V., Susi, M. and Lachapelle, G. 2012. Step length estimation using handheld inertial sensors. *Sensors*, 12, 7 (2012), 8507-8525.

[14]Case, M. A., Burwick, H. A., Volpp, K. G. and Patel, M. S. 2015. Accuracy of smartphone applications and wearable devices for tracking physical activity data. *Jama*, 313, 6 (2015), 625-626.

[15]Mannini, A., Sabatini, A. M. and Intille, S. S. 2015. Accelerometry-based recognition of the placement sites of a wearable sensor. *Pervasive and Mobile Comput*, 21(2015), 62–74.

[16]Jayalath, S. and Abhayasinghe, N. 2013.A *gyroscopic data based pedometer algorithm*. Proc Internat Conf on Computer Science & Education, 2013, 551-555.

[17]UBC 2009. *UK Biobank Coordinating Centre. Category 2 enhanced phenotyping at baseline assessment visit in last 100-150,000 participants. Addendum to main study protocol*. Stockport Cheshire 2009.

[18]Troiano, R. and Mc Clain, J. 2012. *Objective measures of physical activity, sleep, and strength in U.S. National Health and Nutrition Examination Survey (NHANES) 2011-2014*. 8th Internat Conf on Diet and Activity Methods, Roma, Italy, 2012.

[19]Appelboom, G., Camacho, E., Abraham, M. E., Bruce, S. S., Dumont, E., Zacharia, B. E., D'Amico, R., Slomian, J., Reginster, J. Y. and Bruyère, O. 2014. Smart wearable body sensors for patient self-assessment and monitoring. *Archives of Public Health*, 72, 1 (2014), 28.

[20]Rawassizadeh, R., Price, B. A. and Petre, M. 2014. Wearables: has the age of smartwatches finally arrived? *Communications of the ACM*, 58, 1 (2014), 45-47.

[21]Mannini, A. and Sabatini, A. M. 2015. A smartphone-centered wearable sensor network for fall risk assessment in the elderly. *Proc. of the 10th EAI International Conference on Body Area Networks* (2015).

[22]Patel, M. S., Asch, D. A. and Volpp, K. G. 2015. Wearable devices as facilitators, not drivers, of health behavior change. *Jama*, 313, 5 (2015), 459-460.

[23]Mannini, A., Intille, S. S., Rosenberger, M., Sabatini, A. M. and Haskell, W. 2013. Activity recognition using a single accelerometer placed at the wrist or ankle. *Medicine & Science in Sports & Exercise*, 45, 11 (2013), 2193-2203.

[24]Rohit, M. Y. 2014. *Wrist Pedometer Step Detection* US Patent 2014/0140074431.

[25]Sourabh, R. 2013. *Adaptive step detection* US Patent 2013/0191069 A1.

Optimum Receiver Location for Ultra Wideband In-Body Communication Based on Channel Capacity Calculation

Jan-Christoph Brumm
jan.brumm@tuhh.de

Gerhard Bauch
bauch@tuhh.de

Hamburg University of Technology
Institute of Communications
21073 Hamburg, Germany

ABSTRACT

For the design of ultra wideband (UWB) in-body communication links, e.g. for capsule endoscopes, it is vital to know which maximum data rates are achievable. The channel capacity gives a tool to quantify this theoretic limit. Calculating the channel capacity in a frequency dependent environment requires the knowledge of the transfer function of the communication channel. For this reason, a new channel modeling approach based on a multi-layered dielectric approximation of the human body is presented. From this model, the transfer functions for in-body communication are derived. Based on the channel capacity, we then investigate the number of receive antennas required for reliable high data rate transmission and where to place the receivers on the abdominal surface for optimum reception. Results show that one antenna is not sufficient for in-body UWB communication. However, if the number of antennas is increased to five, the 10 %-outage channel capacity can be increased up to 1.55 Gbit/s.

CCS Concepts

•Networks → Wireless personal area networks; Network performance modeling; •Mathematics of computing → *Information theory;*

Keywords

In-body, channel modeling, ultra wideband, channel capacity, receiver diversity

1. INTRODUCTION

Capsule endoscopes are a popular application for wireless in-body communication as they provide an alternative for classical endoscopy. However, for the capsule endoscopy to work, a lot of images have to be transmitted from a small device with limited energy reservoir. Most implants available today use the Medical Implant Communication Service Band (MICS) from 402 MHz to 405 MHz [8]. However, due to restrictions on the allowed bandwidth (300 kHz) only a data rate of up to 455.4 kbit/s is standardized [7].

To allow for better and more confident diagnoses by the physician, higher resolution images are required. Today's capsule endoscopes use images of at most 320 × 320 pixels [8]. Increasing the size of the images requires higher data rates. If the bandwidth is kept constant, a higher data rate requires a higher modulation order. To achieve the same bit error rate with a higher modulation order, the transmit power needs to be increased. However, if the bandwidth is increased as well, the data rate can be increased without having to increase the transmit power. For this reason ultra wideband is very attractive for high data rate transmission in in-body communication although the attenuation is much higher for higher frequencies.

Ultra wideband communication is allowed in the range of 3.1 GHz to 10.6 GHz whereas narrowband communication standards for in-body communication use frequencies up to 2.4 GHz. For UWB communication an equivalent isotropically radiated power spectral density of −41.3 dBm/MHz is allowed as maximum [3]. Furthermore, much smaller and simpler transmitter can be build for ultra wideband technology compared to narrowband communication [10].

To develop reliable communication links a good channel model is needed to simulate the data transmission. Channel models for in-body UWB propagation in the abdominal region have been published in literature, e.g. in [11][12][14]. However, in none of them the channel capacity has been investigated. In most of the published studies finite-difference time-domain (FDTD) simulations were carried out to gain insight into the propagation behavior. Additionally, experimental studies were carried out in [1] and [4]. Most of the studies resulted in path loss models only. However, for the calculation of the channel capacity in a frequency dependent medium like the human body an impulse response or transfer function model is needed. The authors in [12] developed a statistical impulse response model. Unfortunately, this has some plausibility problems.

For this reason, a new channel modeling approach is presented in the following. The idea is to model the transmission of the electromagnetic wave inside the human body with the help of a multi-layered dielectric. This simplification has the advantage that results can be calculated analytically with results from transmission line theory. With this approach, scattering at tissue boundaries inside the body is neglected. In [13] the basic idea of this approach is presented and formulas for the transfer function of a plane electromagnetic wave passing through a multi-layered dielectric are derived. These formulas are then validated with experiments and show that the analytically calculated path loss coincides well with the experimental results.

In this paper the idea from [13] is extended. Using the formulas from [13] the transfer functions for multiple possible transmitter and receiver locations inside the body and on the body surface are calculated. From these transfer functions the channel capacity will be computed. Using the statistical distribution of the channel capacity, given a certain distance between transmitter and receiver, the optimum receiver locations for multiple antennas are determined. Multiple antennas are combined using a selection diversity scheme. The selection diversity scheme selects always the antenna with the highest received signal power as the receiving antenna.

An important simplification, besides the fact that only plane wave propagation is considered, is that antenna effects are not included in our calculations. However, as the channel capacity gives an upper bound on the data rate, these simplifications will still lead to an upper bound. Moreover, comparison to other path loss models available in literature shows that the difference in path loss is acceptable, as will be shown later in this work.

The remaining paper is structured as follows. In Section 2 the channel modeling approach is described in detail and formulas for the channel capacity are derived. Section 3 compares our proposed channel model to already existing path loss models and power delay profiles to validate the results. Furthermore, in Section 4 the optimum receiver locations for different number of antennas are presented together with the achievable channel capacity. Section 5 concludes the paper.

2. CHANNEL MODELING SETUP AND CAPACITY CALCULATION

2.1 Prerequisites and Assumptions

For the development of a channel model for in-body communication, a model of the human body is needed. In this paper the Visible Human body model provided by the Helmholtz Zentrum München is used [6]. The provided model consists of a 3D matrix indicating the position of the different human tissues inside the body. Each voxel element in this matrix has a resolution of 0.91 mm × 0.94 mm × 5 mm in (x, y, z) direction. Figure 1 shows one slice in the (x, y)-plane and the view from the right side onto the body.

To calculate transfer functions for the in-body communication channel, the following setup was used. At first 7405 possible transmitter locations inside the gastrointestinal tract have been randomly selected, such that the distance between each location is at least 4 mm. For each of these possible transmitter locations the tissue composition (thickness and type) is investigated along a straight line in the (x, y)-plane. In total 100 directions were analyzed per transmitter location, as indicated in Figure 1a for two examples. Thus, it is assumed for simplicity reasons that a receiver is always positioned at the same height z on the body surface as the transmitter inside the body. In total 740 500 communication links were investigated in terms of their tissue composition.

The tissue composition is then interpreted as a multi-layered dielectric consisting of the found tissue types. This

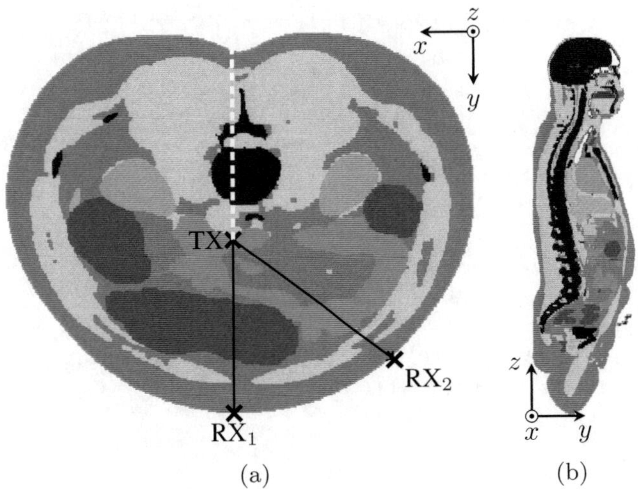

Figure 1: Visible Human voxel model. (a) View of one slice in the (x, y)-plane from top. (b) View from the right side. The ●-colored area is the small intestine and the ●-colored area is the colon. Two possible receiver locations are marked with RX and one possible transmitter location is marked with TX. The tissues along the dashed white line are used for the source impedance calculation of the link from TX to RX$_1$.

setup can be seen in Figure 2. In the following sections, the formulas to determine the transfer function of a plane electromagnetic wave traveling through a multi-layered dielectric are derived.

2.2 Dielectric Properties of Human Tissue

The tissue in the human body is essentially a frequency dependent lossy dielectric. Investigations from Gabriel *et al.* showed that the frequency dependent behavior of the relative permittivity can be modeled by the following Cole-Cole expression [5]:

$$\varepsilon_r(f) = \varepsilon_\infty + \sum_{n=1}^{4} \frac{\Delta\varepsilon_n}{1 + (j2\pi f \tau_n)^{1-\alpha_n}} + \frac{\sigma}{j2\pi f \varepsilon_0}, \quad (1)$$

where ε_∞ is the permittivity for $f \to \infty$, σ is the conductivity, ε_0 is the permittivity of free-space, f is the frequency, and $\Delta\varepsilon_n$, τ_n, α_n are tissue specific parameters. Details on the parameters can be found in [5]. The relative permeability of human tissue is assumed to be $\mu_r = 1$.

2.3 Transfer Function of a Multi-Layered Dielectric

The propagation of a plane wave through a multi-layered dielectric, as depicted in Figure 2, can be described by the transmission matrix $\mathbf{T}$ of the dielectric. The matrix $\mathbf{T}$ gives the relationship between the electric and the magnetic fields at the boundary i to the fields at the boundary $i + 1$

$$\begin{bmatrix} E_i \\ H_i \end{bmatrix} = \mathbf{T}_i \begin{bmatrix} E_{i+1} \\ H_{i+1} \end{bmatrix}. \quad (2)$$

For each layer i the transmission matrix $\mathbf{T}_i$ is defined as [13]

$$\mathbf{T}_i = \begin{bmatrix} A_i & B_i \\ C_i & D_i \end{bmatrix} = \begin{bmatrix} \cosh \gamma_i d_i & \eta_i \sinh \gamma_i d_i \\ \frac{1}{\eta_i} \sinh \gamma_i d_i & \cosh \gamma_i d_i \end{bmatrix}, \quad (3)$$

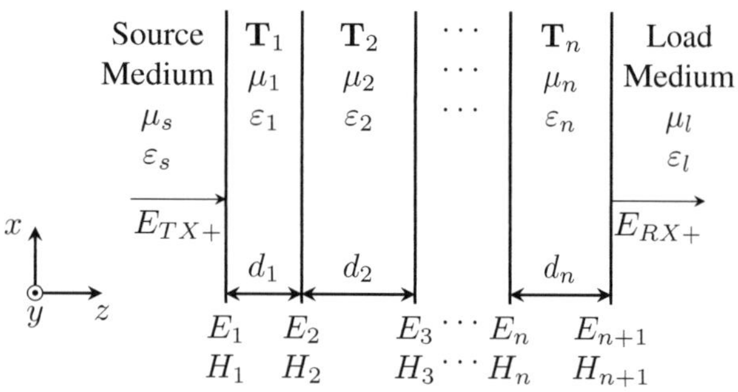

Figure 2: A plane wave E_{TX+} propagating through a multi-layered dielectric. The wave propagates along the positive z-direction.

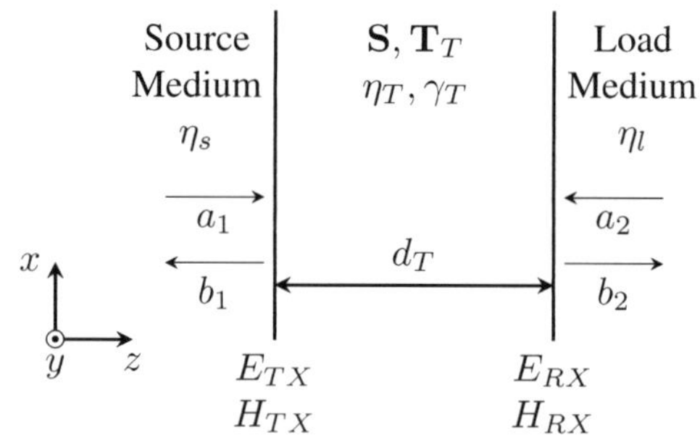

Figure 3: Equivalent dielectric of the total tissue composition for the computation of the S-parameters.

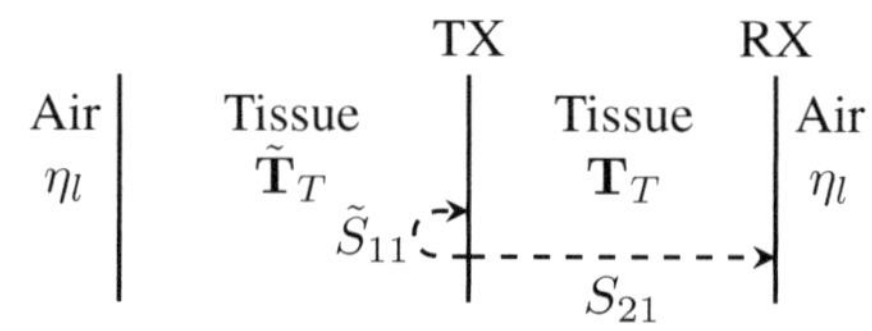

Figure 4: Calculation of the source impedance is based on the reflection coefficient $\tilde{S}_{11}$ at the transmitter.

where $\gamma_i = j2\pi f\sqrt{\mu_i\varepsilon_i}$ is the propagation constant, $\eta_i = \sqrt{\mu_i/\varepsilon_i}$ is the wave impedance and d_i is the thickness of the i-th medium. With these definitions the total composition of all n dielectrics can be described by $\mathbf{T}_T = \mathbf{T}_1 \cdot \mathbf{T}_2 \cdots \mathbf{T}_n$.

To calculate the transfer function $H_{CH}(f) = \frac{E_{RX+}}{E_{TX+}}$, a conversion of the $\mathbf{T}$-matrix into its scattering ($\mathbf{S}$-) parameters is needed. Note that the source and load impedances are not real. For this scenario Theilmann *et al.* derived the necessary conversion formulas in [13]. For a better understanding the derivation is summarized here. Refer to [13] for more details.

The matrix $\mathbf{T}_T$ is now converted into its $\mathbf{S}$-parameter representation with power parameters a_1, a_2, b_1, and b_2 as shown in Figure 3. The power parameters are defined as [13]:

$$a_1 = \sqrt{\Re(\eta_s)}H_{TX+} \qquad b_1 = \sqrt{\Re(\eta_s)}H_{TX-} \tag{4}$$

$$a_2 = \sqrt{\Re(\eta_l)}H_{RX-} \qquad b_2 = \sqrt{\Re(\eta_l)}H_{RX+}, \tag{5}$$

where η_s and η_l are the wave impedances of the source and load medium, respectively. The electric and magnetic field at the boundaries to the source and load medium have been split into a forward and a backward traveling wave $E_{TX} = E_{TX+} + E_{TX-}$ and $H_{TX} = H_{TX+} - H_{TX-}$, likewise for E_{RX} and H_{RX}. The subscripted $+$ indicates a wave traveling in positive z-direction and a $-$ indicates a wave traveling in negative z-direction. Moreover, the following relationship of electric and magnetic field of a plane wave holds[1]:

$$E_{TX+} = \eta_s H_{TX+} \qquad E_{TX-} = \eta_s H_{TX-} \tag{6}$$

$$E_{RX+} = \eta_l H_{RX+} \qquad E_{RX-} = \eta_l H_{RX-}. \tag{7}$$

Taking (4) to (7) the power parameters are defined in such a way that the squared magnitude of the scattering parameters give the ratio of incoming to outgoing power for each medium. The path loss is then

$$|S_{21}|^2 = \left|\frac{b_2}{a_1}\Big|_{a_2=0}\right|^2 = \frac{\frac{1}{2}\Re(\eta_s)\,|E_{RX+}|^2}{\frac{1}{2}\Re(\eta_l)\,|E_{TX+}|^2} = \frac{P_{RX+}}{P_{TX+}}, \tag{8}$$

where P_{TX+} is the time average power transmitted inside the dielectric from the source medium and P_{RX+} is the power received by a receiver inside the load medium. With these definitions, S_{21} can be expressed in terms of the entries of the $\mathbf{T}_T$-matrix as

$$S_{21} = \frac{\sqrt{\Re(\eta_l)}}{\sqrt{\Re(\eta_s)}} \frac{2\eta_s}{\eta_l A_T + B_T + \eta_l\eta_s C_T + \eta_s D_T}. \tag{9}$$

Combining (9) with (8), the channel transfer function $H_{CH}(f)$ can be derived in terms of S_{21} as

$$\begin{aligned} H_{CH}(f) = \frac{E_{RX+}}{E_{TX+}} &= \frac{\eta_l\sqrt{\Re(\eta_s)}}{\eta_s\sqrt{\Re(\eta_l)}} \cdot S_{21} \\ &= \frac{2\eta_l}{\eta_l A_T + B_T + \eta_l\eta_s C_T + \eta_s D_T}. \end{aligned} \tag{10}$$

As the source and load impedance are complex in this case, it has to be noted that in general $S_{21} \neq S_{12}$. This does not influence the electromagnetic reciprocity, only $\mathbf{S}$ is not necessarily symmetric [9].

2.4 Source and Load Impedance

The receiver is placed on the body surface, that means the wave impedance of the load medium is always set to the wave impedance of air $\eta_l = 376.73\,\Omega$. However, the transmitter is placed somewhere in the gastrointestinal tract and, thus, there are reflections occurring from parts of the wave that propagate away from the receiver. These reflection effects will be included in the source impedance. Consider the example depicted in Figure 1a. The tissue through which the wave passes on its way to the receiver lies along the black arrow connecting TX and RX_1. To include the reflections occurring at the transmitter, the tissues in the opposite of this direction are considered (indicated by the dashed white line in Figure 1a). This idealized setup is shown in Figure 4. The tissue composition along the opposite direction of the communication signal is denoted by the matrix $\tilde{\mathbf{T}}_T$. With this, the source impedance can be calculated from the

[1] Note: the conjugate complex that occurs at this point in [13] in equation (A2) should in our opinion not appear here.

reflection coefficient $\tilde{S}_{11}$ as [13]

$$\eta_s = \frac{\eta_l \tilde{A}_T + \tilde{B}_T}{\eta_l \tilde{C}_T + \tilde{D}_T} . \quad (11)$$

Where η_l is the impedance of air and $\tilde{A}_T, \tilde{B}_T, \tilde{C}_T$, and $\tilde{D}_T$ are the components of $\tilde{\mathbf{T}}_T$.

2.5 Channel Capacity in Frequency-Selective AWGN Channels

The channel capacity gives an upper limit on the data rate that may be transmitted over a communication channel. As long as the data rate is smaller than the capacity, there exist error correcting codes which theoretically enable communication with an arbitrarily low error rate. However, if the data rate is greater than the capacity, there exist no such codes.

For a real channel with additive white Gaussian noise limited to the frequency band B the channel capacity in bit/s can be calculated as [2]:

$$C = B \log_2 \left(1 + \frac{P_{TX+}}{N}\right) = B \log_2 \left(1 + \frac{2 \cdot E_s}{N_0}\right) . \quad (12)$$

Where P_{TX+} is the transmit power, N is the noise power, $E_s = \frac{P_{TX+}}{2B}$ the energy per transmit symbol, and $\frac{N_0}{2}$ the two-sided noise power spectral density.

In a frequency-selective channel the capacity can be defined for a small subband Δf around a center frequency f_i. If the channel transfer function $H_{CH}(f)$, the power spectral density of the transmit signal $S_{XX}(f)$, and the power spectral density of the noise $S_{NN}(f)$ are assumed to be constant in this subband, the resulting channel capacity is [2]

$$C(f_i) = \Delta f \log_2 \left(1 + \frac{2 \cdot S_{XX}(f_i) \left|H_{CH}(f_i)\right|^2}{S_{NN}(f_i)}\right) . \quad (13)$$

For $\Delta f \to 0$ the total capacity C of the channel yields

$$C = \int_0^\infty \log_2 \left(1 + \frac{2 \cdot S_{XX}(f) \left|H_{CH}(f)\right|^2}{S_{NN}(f)}\right) \mathrm{d}f . \quad (14)$$

As an AWGN channel is assumed, the noise power spectral density is $S_{NN} = \frac{N_0}{2} = \frac{kT}{2} = -156.93\,\text{dBm/Hz}$ ($T = 20\,°\text{C}$ and an additional 20 dB noise figure in the receiver).

3. COMPARISON TO EXISTING CHANNEL MODELS

To classify our results, the following section compares the presented model to other models available in literature. The comparison is limited to those studies which also investigate the propagation behavior in the abdominal region for ultra wideband transmission.

3.1 Path Loss Comparison

For better comparability we split the different available path loss models into two groups. The first resides in the frequency band of 1 GHz to 6 GHz and the second from 3.4 GHz to 4.8 GHz.

3.1.1 Path Loss for 1 GHz to 6 GHz

In [12] Støa *et al.* simulated a plane wave with the finite-difference time-domain (FDTD) method. This plane wave, excited by a Gaussian pulse, was sent onto the body surface.

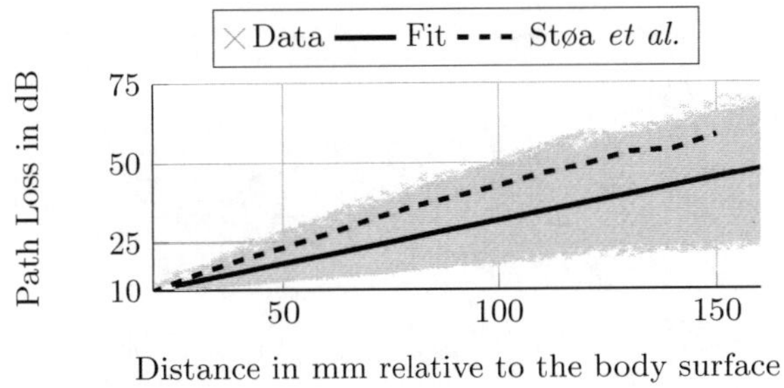

Figure 5: The path loss model from Støa *et al.* [12] compared to the data and the exponential fit determined from our proposed model. In both cases the transmission bandwidth was 1 GHz to 6 GHz.

The pulse had most of its energy in the frequency range of 1 GHz to 6 GHz. Their resulting path loss model is calculated from the received power inside the abdomen with several hundred ideal electric and magnetic field probes. Thus, their model excludes any antenna effects. However, as they did a FDTD simulation, scattering of the signal inside the body is included. The average path loss from the simulation in [12] is shown in Figure 5 with the dashed line.

In our proposed model antenna effects are excluded as well. However, also scattering inside the body is not taken into consideration, that means on average a lower path loss is expected. In Figure 5 the path loss of all the 740 500 communication links is depicted with gray crosses. This path loss was calculated from (9) in the range of 1 GHz to 6 GHz. An exponential fit through that data gives the average path loss, which can be expressed in dB as

$$P_{\text{dB}} = P_0 + \alpha \cdot d , \quad (15)$$

where $P_0 = 4.86\,\text{dB}$, $\alpha = 0.268\,\text{dB/mm}$ and d is the distance between transmitter and receiver in the interval from 21 mm to 335 mm. The average path loss is shown in Figure 5 with the solid black line. It can be seen that, as expected, the average path loss of the proposed model is smaller. However, the model from Støa *et al.* still lies inside the data range of our model.

3.1.2 Path Loss for 3.4 GHz to 4.8 GHz

For this frequency range three paper were found. Their path loss models are compared in Figure 6. Shi *et al.* did a FDTD simulation including transmit and receive antenna in the range of 3.4 GHz to 4.8 GHz. Thus, scattering inside the body was considered. Experimental results are reported in [4] from Floor *et al.* Using an anesthetized pig the authors measured the path loss with a vector network analyzer in the frequency range of 1 GHz to 6 GHz. Figure 6 shows the curve for 4 GHz. The two curves from Floor *et al.* and Shi *et al.* show a very similar behavior. However, the result from Thotahewa *et al.* does not fit to them. In [14] Thotahewa *et al.* did a FDTD simulation in the frequency range 3.5 GHz to 4.5 GHz also including antenna effects. Nevertheless, the results from Thotahewa *et al.* are approximately 10 dB above the results from the other two papers. The reason might be that different antennas were used.

The results from our model are again plotted with gray crosses and an exponential fit approximates the average path loss very good. The parameters for (15) are in this case

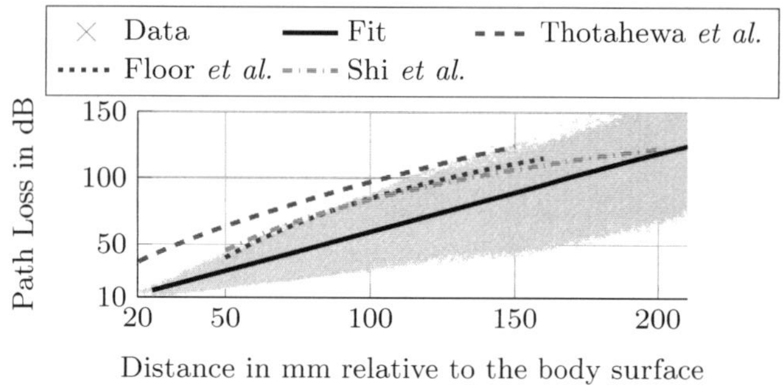

Figure 6: The path loss models from Thotahewa *et al.* [14], Floor *et al.* [4], and Shi *et al.* [11] compared with the data and exponential fit from our proposed model for a frequency range of 3.4 GHz to 4.8 GHz.

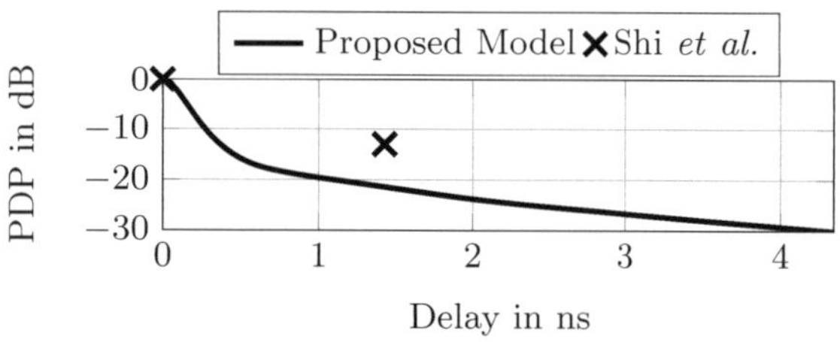

Figure 7: Power delay profile of the model from Shi *et al.* [11] and of the proposed model shown in dB relative to the first path.

$P_0 = 0.401\,\text{dB}$ and $\alpha = 0.592\,\text{dB/mm}$. The resulting curve is shown as a solid black line in Figure 6.

As in Figure 5, it can be seen from Figure 6 that all models from literature estimate a higher path loss than our model, due to the scattering inside the body that is included. Another fact that can be observed is that the shape of the curves is different whether antenna effects were included or not. All path loss models without any antenna effects have a more linear behavior in dB. Those models including antenna effects have a more logarithmic behavior.

3.2 Power Delay Profile Comparison

A common way to compare the channel models of multi-path propagation environments is the power delay profile. It is a measure of how the received power is spread in time. Of all the available channel models only the one of Shi *et al.* [11] lead to a reproducible power delay profile. In Figure 7 the power delay profile from Shi *et al.* is compared to the resulting power delay profile of our proposed model. The resulting RMS delay spread is $\tau_{\text{RMS}} = 0.58\,\text{ns}$ for our model and for the model from Shi *et al.* $\tau_{\text{RMS}} = 0.31\,\text{ns}$. Additionally, the difference between the two models at a delay of $\tau = 1.43\,\text{ns}$ is only 8 dB. Hence, the multi-path characteristics of the two models are very similar.

4. CHOICE OF THE OPTIMUM RECEIVER LOCATION

For the calculation of the channel capacity a transmission bandwidth of 3.1 GHz to 4.8 GHz was considered; this is the so-called UWB low band which is preferable due to its lower attenuation [11]. The transmit power was set to 21.5 mW and distributed equally in the transmission band. Simulations in [14] revealed that this is the maximum transmit power that can be used without violating the specific absorption rate limits set by the International Commission on Non-Ionizing Radiation Protection.

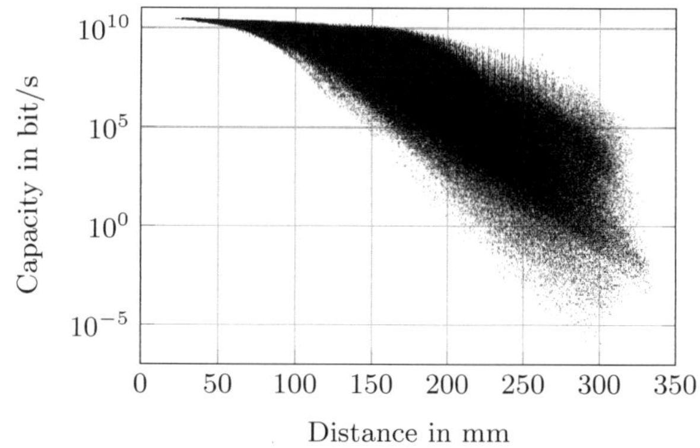

Figure 8: Scatter plot of the channel capacity over the distance between tansmitter and receiver.

4.1 Distance Dependency of the Channel Capacity

The channel capacity is calculated using (10) and (14) for each of the 740 500 communication links. In Figure 8 every dot represents the channel capacity of one communication link plotted against the distance between transmitter and receiver. It can be seen that as the distance increases the scattering of the channel capacity is increasing drastically. At a distance of 250 mm for example the channel capacity varies between 10^{-3} bit/s and 10^{7} bit/s. Starting from approximately 320 mm the capacity drops drastically. The largest distance occurring in the simulation is 335 mm.

Based on this capacity distribution the optimum position of the receive antennas is calculated. The distance d between transmitter and receiver is discretized in steps of 1 mm. From all capacity values that fall into one of these distance bins the probability distribution of the channel capacity C given a certain distance d $f_C(C|d)$ is calculated.

For the plot in Figure 8 it was assumed that the receiver is always placed on the same height as the transmitter. This was done to simplify the simulation and reduce the number of possible communication links to simulate. As the composition of the human body is highly heterogeneous, it should on average not make a significant difference if the signal is transmitted a certain distance in a strictly horizontal direction or the same distance in any inclined direction. For this reason the probability distribution $f_C(C|d)$ will be used as a model to calculate the channel capacity based on the distance d between any point on the body surface and a point in the gastrointestinal tract.

4.2 Optimum Receiver Location Based on the Maximum 10 %-Outage Channel Capacity

To determine the optimum receiver location, the abdominal surface was discretized in 181 patches, which were investigated as possible receive antenna location (these are the non-white patches in Figure 9). In Figure 9 the 10 %-outage capacity is shown for one antenna placed at each of the dis-

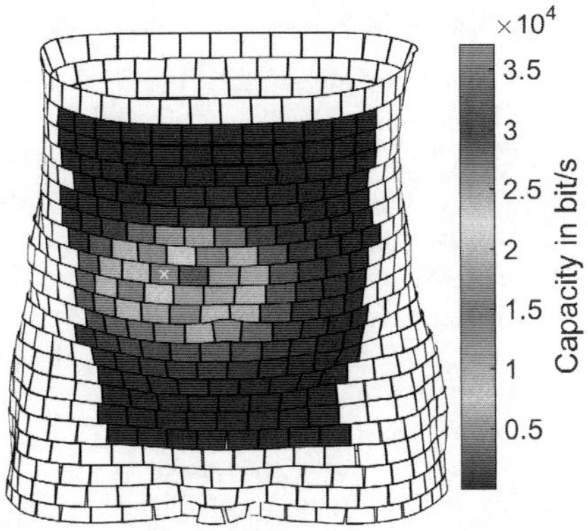

Figure 9: Distribution of the 10 %-outage capacity on the abdominal surface for one receive antenna. The optimum location is marked with a white X.

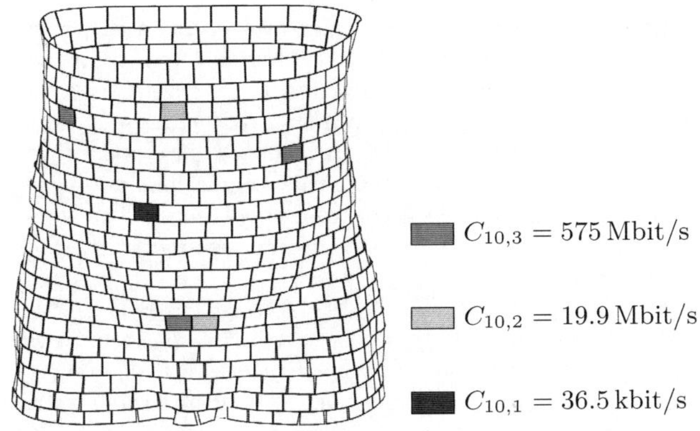

Figure 10: Optimum position in terms of maximum 10 %-outage channel capacity of up to three receive antennas operating in a selection diversity scheme.

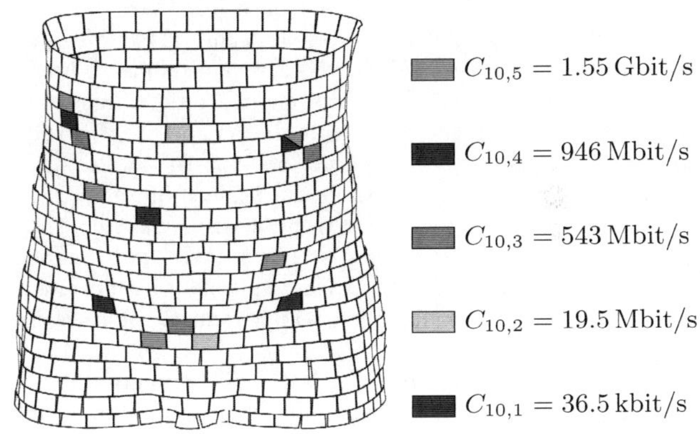

Figure 11: Optimum position determined based on the minimum 90th percentile of the distance of up to five receive antennas operating in a selection diversity scheme.

crete patches. For each patch i in Figure 9 the distances to all 7405 transmitter locations inside the body were determined, rounded to the nearest mm and stored in the vector $\mathbf{d}_i$. Distances larger than 335 mm were mapped to a distance of 335 mm as higher distances are not present in our model.

The probability distribution of the capacity $f_C(C|d)$ was then used to draw 100 samples of the capacity for each distance in $\mathbf{d}_i$. Finally, the statistical distribution of all capacity samples was used to calculate the 10 %-outage capacity. The 10 %-outage capacity is the capacity value which is achieved at least in 90 % of all realizations. Thus, it gives an indication of the reliability of the connection under the present channel conditions.

It can clearly be seen that there is only one area slightly above the navel where the capacity is greater than 5×10^3 bit/s. The location marked with the white X is the optimum position where a 10 %-outage capacity of 3.6×10^4 bit/s can be achieved.

Comparing this resulting capacity with the data rates specified for communication in MICS band in IEEE 802.15.6 [7] of 455.4 kbit/s it is clear that using only one antenna is not sufficient to improve the data rate.

Thus, it was investigated how the usage of multiple antennas can improve the channel capacity. The antennas were assumed to operate in a selection diversity scheme. Selection diversity is a non-optimal receiver diversity scheme in which the strongest received signal is selected. The diversity gain with other techniques as maximum-ratio combining might be higher, but this scheme requires more complex simulation and is out of the scope of this paper.

The approach to find the optimum position of multiple receive antennas on the abdominal surface is the same as for one antenna. However, the capacity samples are drawn for each receiver location separately. The samples are then compared for each realization and for each the maximum is picked. This resembles the selection diversity scheme, as the highest available channel capacity is related to the channel with the highest SNR. From this resulting vector of samples the 10 %-outage capacity is calculated. This calculation was repeated for all possible combinations of locations until the maximum was found.

In Figure 10 the results for one, two and three receive antennas are shown. For two antennas the locations indicated by the light red patches are optimum and yield a total 10 %-outage channel capacity of 19.9 Mbit/s. This is an improvement of nearly three orders of magnitude compared to one receive antenna. However, increasing the number of antennas to three does not lead to another increase in capacity of that amount. The capacity is 575 Mbit/s for three receive antennas placed at the orange patches in Figure 10.

The result for three antennas already indicates that there is potential for a high data rate transmission using UWB for in-body communication. Nevertheless, we were interested in the effect of even more receive antennas. Unfortunately, the computation time for the calculation of the optimum position based on the channel capacity is very high. However, it was observed that using only the minimum distance as a criterion for the optimization showed results that were near the ones shown in Figure 10.

4.3 Optimum Receiver Location Based on the Minimum Distance

To compute the optimum receiver locations based on the minimum distance, the distance vectors $\mathbf{d}_i$ were computed for each of the involved possible receiver locations i. The distance vectors were then compared directly. It was assumed that the link with the shortest distance results in the highest channel capacity, although it can be seen from Figure 8 that this is not necessarily the case. Thus, a vector with the minimum distance from each position inside the body to a receiver on the body results. From this vector the 90th percentile is computed. Hence, only 10 % of the communication links have a larger distance than this value. This value is computed for each possible combination of receiver locations on the body and from them the minimum is selected as the optimum.

For this optimum position the 10 %-outage capacity is calculated and shown in Figure 11. It can be seen that the optimum location for one antenna is the same as in Figure 10. For two and three antennas the optimum locations are slightly different by just one discrete patch. The resulting 10 %-outage channel capacity for these configurations is only slightly smaller than the results using optimization based on the channel capacity. Hence the optimum location for four and five antennas is calculated and indicated by the dark blue and light green patches in Figure 11, respectively. The resulting 10 %-outage capacity is 946 Mbit/s for four antennas and 1.55 Gbit/s for five antennas. These results show that the 10 %-outage capacity seems to increase by $\approx$ 500 Mbit/s per receive antenna that is added after the second antenna. However, this behavior has to saturate at some point, as the capacity cannot increase infinitely. For 181 antennas, each placed on one of the discrete patches, the 10 %-outage capacity converges to 10.2 Gbit/s. Due to time constraints it was not possible to evaluate more than five antennas. Thus, it is unclear for which number of receive antennas the saturation starts.

As can bee seen in Figure 11 it is for all numbers of antennas optimum to place the receive antennas in a circular shape around the navel. Moreover, it is important, if more than two antennas are positioned, to place one of the antennas in the upper most right corner of the abdominal surface for optimum reception.

5. CONCLUSION

In this paper a new approach for the modeling of ultra wideband in-body communication was presented. It is based on a multi-layered dielectric representation of each communication link. With this model the channel capacity can be calculated. A comparison to already existing path loss models showed that the difference in path loss is small, although antenna effects and scattering inside the body were neglected. Based on the probability density function of the channel capacity the optimum locations for one to three receive antennas, working in a selection diversity scheme, were determined. It has been shown that with three antennas in their optimum position a 10 %-outage channel capacity of 575 Mbit/s can be achieved. Furthermore, results for four and five antennas were computed based on the minimum of the 90th percentile of the distance. For five receive antennas the 10 %-outage channel capacity is 1.55 Gbit/s. This shows that an increase in data rate, to support higher resolution images for capsule endoscopy, is achievable with ultra wideband technology as long as enough receive antennas are placed on the abdomen. Furthermore, it can be seen from the results that by adding more antennas the 10 %-outage channel capacity increases approximately linear with the number of antennas.

6. REFERENCES

[1] D. Anzai *et al.* Experimental Evaluation of Implant UWB-IR Transmission With Living Animal for Body Area Networks. *IEEE Transactions on Microwave Theory and Techniques*, 62(1):183–192, Januar 2014.

[2] J. R. Barry *et al.* *Digital Communication.* Springer, 3rd edition, 2004.

[3] Federal Communications Commission. Revision of Part 15 of the Commission's Rules Regarding Ultra-Wideband TransmissionSystems.

[4] P.-A. Floor *et al.* In-Body to On-Body Ultra Wideband Propagation Model Derived from Measurements in Living Animals. *IEEE Journal of Biomedical and Health Informatics*, 19(3):938–948, 2015.

[5] S. Gabriel *et al.* The dielectric properties of biological tissues: III. Parametric models for the dielectric spectrum of tissues. *Physics in Medicine and Biology*, 41(11):2271–2293, 1996.

[6] Helmholtz Zentrum München Deutsches Forschungszentrum für Gesundheit und Umwelt. Virtual human database, 2016. [Online]. Available: http://www.helmholtz-muenchen.de/amsd/service/scientific-services/virtual-human-database/index.html

[7] IEEE Std 802.15.6-2012, IEEE Standard for Local and metropolitan area networks - Part 15.6: Wireless Body Area Networks, 2012.

[8] A. Kiourti *et al.* Implantable and Ingestible Medical Devices with Wireless Telemetry Functionalities: A Review of Current Status and Challenges. *Bioelectromagnetics*, 35(1):1–15, 2014.

[9] R. B. Marks and D. F. Williams. A General Waveguide Circuit Theory. *Journal of Research of the National Institute of Standards and Technology*, 97(5):533–562, 1992.

[10] A. F. Molisch. Introduction to UWB Signals and Systems. In B. Allen *et al.* , editor, *Ultra-Wideband: Antennas and Propagation for Communications, Radar and Imaging*, pages 1–17. John Wiley & Sons, Ltd, Chichester, UK, 2006.

[11] J. Shi *et al.* Channel Modeling and Performance Analysis of Diversity Reception for Implant UWB Wireless Link. *IEICE TRANSACTIONS on Communications*, E95-B(10):3197–3205, 2012.

[12] S. Støa *et al.* An Ultra Wideband Communication Channel Model for the Human Abdominal Region. In *IEEE Globecom Workshops*, pages 246–250, 2010.

[13] P. Theilmann *et al.* Computationally Efficient Model for UWB Signal Attenuation Due to Propagation in Tissue for Biomedical Implants. *Progress In Electromagnetics Research B*, 38:1–22, 2012.

[14] K. M. S. Thotahewa *et al.* Propagation, Power Absorption, and Temperature Analysis of UWB Wireless Capsule Endoscopy Devices Operating in the Human Body. *IEEE Transactions on Microwave Theory and Techniques*, 63(11):3823–3833, 2015.

Eigenwalk: a Novel Feature for Walk Classification and Fall Prediction

Masoud Hemmatpour, Renato Ferrero, Bartolomeo Montrucchio, Maurizio Rebaudengo
Dipartimento di Automatica e Informatica, Politecnico di Torino
{ masoud.hemmatpour, renato.ferrero, bartolomeo.montrucchio, maurizio.rebaudengo } @polito.it

ABSTRACT

Predicting a fall is one of the most promising approach to avoid it. Different studies strive to classify abnormal and normal walks in order to predict a fall before its occurrence. This study introduces *eigenwalk*, a novel feature based on the principal components of the accelerometer and gyroscope signals. This feature, in conjunction with a random forest classifier, is able to distinguish walk patterns and to estimate a fall risk. As the accelerometer and the gyroscope embedded in a smartphone are recognized to be precise enough for fall avoidance systems, they have been exploited in an experimental analysis in order to compare the proposed approach with the most recent ones. The results have shown that the new feature in combination with the random forest classification outperforms state-of-the-art approaches, by improving the accuracy up to 98.6%.

1. INTRODUCTION

Falls are a serious problem in both medical and social aspects. Unintentional falls are one of the causes of hospitalization that mostly increases health service costs [1]. Falls are particularly critical among elderly people. So, international organizations such as the United Nations advises improving health care systems and creating a supportive environment in order to decrease and control falls in the elderly community. Consequently, different fall avoidance systems have been developed. Generally speaking, fall avoidance systems can be categorized into two different types: fall prediction and detection systems. Fall prediction systems (FPSs) recognize abnormal walks and predict a fall occurrence [2]. Fall detection systems only notify an acquaintance of the user in case of fall occurrence [3, 4, 5, 6, 7]. Since the latter systems do not avoid a fall, they are less effective than FPSs. FPSs strive to avoid a fall with common sensors, such as accelerometer (for measuring the acceleration, i.e, rate of change of the velocity of an object) and gyroscope (for measuring the angular rate around one or more axes of the space). FPSs usually follow a unique procedure: firstly, data are collected from sensors, then, data are analyzed to compute an appropriate feature set. Finally, a classification algorithm recognizes abnormal walks based on the feature set. Most of FPSs usually analyze user's posture or gait variables to investigate the characteristics of the movement. This study investigates FPS considering in particular data acquired with gyroscope and accelerometer. In this study, a new feature, called *eigenwalk*, is proposed in combination with a random forest classifier. The eigenwalk feature is based on the analysis of the principal component of the data from accelerometer and gyroscope. Random forest is a classification method that creates a multitude of decision trees at training time, and then it makes predictions according to the majority rule [8].

The remainder of the paper is organized as follows. Relevant work in literature is reviewed in Section 2. The proposed feature is described in Section 3. Exploited classification methods in FPS are explained in Section 4. Evaluation criteria are explained in Section 5. Then, the experimental setup and the results are presented in Section 6. Finally, some conclusions are written in Section 7.

2. RELATED WORK

Several types of FPS have been developed over the past decade. FPSs usually regard tilt and acceleration changes, which are obtained by means of gyroscope and accelerometer.

When a user significantly tilts in a direction, he/she assumes an abnormal posture, which can lead to a fall. So, the user tilt can be a factor to assess the risk of a fall. User tilt can be estimated with the combination of gyroscope and accelerometer [9]. Data collected from the accelerometer and gyroscope of a smartphone are processed to classify the user's gait pattern. If the system monitors an abnormal gait pattern, it warns the user of a potential fall. The user's tilt is computed to predict the fall, as described in the following. In the formulas, $A(t)$ indicates the acceleration and $A_x(t)$, $A_y(t)$, $A_z(t)$ refer to its components along the 3 axes. Furthermore, A_{xi}, A_{yi} and A_{zi} are the discrete i-th acceleration samples in the 3 axes. Similarly, $G(t)$ indicates the gyroscope measure and $G_p(t)$, $G_r(t)$, $G_y(t)$ refer to the measure on pitch, roll, and yaw.

First, the average value of N instances in the acceleration vector is computed as:

$$\overrightarrow{B}(t) = \frac{1}{N}\Sigma_{t=1}^{N}\overrightarrow{A}_0(t)\ . \tag{1}$$

The tilt angles are defined as:

$$\theta_1 = \arctan\left(\frac{B_y}{B_z}\right) \tag{2}$$

$$\theta_2 = \arctan\left(\frac{B_x}{B_y\sin(\theta_1) + B_z\cos(\theta_1)}\right)\ . \tag{3}$$

The tilt acceleration is computed as follows:

$$\overrightarrow{A}_1(t) = \begin{bmatrix} \cos(\theta_2) & \sin(\theta_1)\sin(\theta_2) & -\cos(\theta_1)\sin(\theta_2) \\ 0 & \cos(\theta_1) & -\sin(\theta_1) \\ \sin(\theta_2) & \sin(\theta_1)\cos(\theta_2) & \cos(\theta_1)\cos(\theta_2) \end{bmatrix} \times \overrightarrow{A}_0(t)$$

The tilt gyroscope $\overrightarrow{G}_1(t)$ is computed similarly to $\overrightarrow{A}_1(t)$. Subsequently, the gravity vector is removed from the accelerometer data:

$$\overrightarrow{A}_2(t) = \left[\overrightarrow{A}_1x(t), \overrightarrow{A}_1y(t), \overrightarrow{A}_1z(t) - \frac{1}{N}\Sigma_{t=1}^{N}\overrightarrow{A}_1z(t)\right] \quad (4)$$

$$\overrightarrow{A_h}(t) = \sqrt{A_{2x}(t)^2 + A_{2y}(t)^2} \quad (5)$$

$$\overrightarrow{G_t}(t) = \sqrt{G_{1p}(t)^2 + G_{1r}(t)^2} \quad (6)$$

Finally, a general tilt vector is created by computing the magnitude of the horizontal acceleration and combining it with the measurement of the gyroscope. Afterwards, *Hjorth parameters* and *energy* are computed on the tilt vector.

Hjorth parameters are statistical measures of the signal, based on its variance $var(A(t))$ in the time domain [10]:

- $Hjorth\ activity = var(A(t))$ indicates the signal power
- $Hjorth\ mobility = \sqrt{\frac{var(A'(t))}{var(A(t))}}$ shows the smoothness of the signal curve
- $Hjorth\ complexity = \frac{mobility(A'(t))}{mobility(A(t))}$ measures the irregularities in the frequency domain.

The *energy* of the acceleration signal specifies the amount of activity in the vertical and horizontal directions. It estimates the strength of the contact with the floor, so it can be used to recognize abnormal walk pattern such as stumbling. The energy of the signal is computed as follows:

$$E_x = \int_{-\infty}^{\infty} |A(t)|^2 dt, \quad (7)$$

Other acceleration-derived parameters that can be good fall indicator are the *signal magnitude area* (SMA), *signal magnitude vector* (SMV), *derivative of the acceleration* and *peak* analysis [11].

SMA is used to classify the user activities. It is computed as:

$$SMA = \frac{1}{T}\left(\int_0^T |A_x(t)|dt + \int_0^T |A_y(t)|dt + \int_0^T |A_z(t)|dt\right) \quad (8)$$

where T is the monitored interval.

SMV specifies the degree of the movement intensity and the resultant of the acceleration signal:

$$SMV = \frac{1}{n}\Sigma_{i=1}^{n}\sqrt{A_{xi}^2 + A_{yi}^2 + A_{zi}^2} \quad (9)$$

where n is the number of samples.

The derivative $A'(t)$ of the acceleration indicates the vibration of the movement.

The peak and the peak-to-peak are simple and useful measurements of data changing over time. The peak is the maximum value of the signal over the period of time, and the peak-to-peak is the difference between minimum and maximum value of the signal.

Another features used in FPS relies on the relative frequency in the data distribution [12]. Firstly, the collected data are ordered in different intervals from the minimum to the maximum value. Then, a histogram based on the repetition of the values is computed as shown in Algorithm 1, where n specifies the number of intervals, Y is the set of input values and X is the sequence of endpoints of the intervals. After computing the relative frequency, the standard deviation of the relative frequency distribution is exploited to classify normal and abnormal walks.

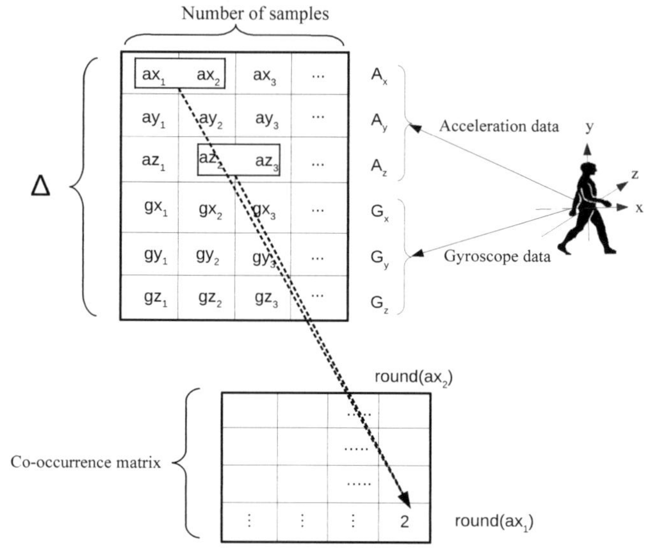

Figure 1: Computation of the co-occurrence matrix.

Algorithm 1: Computation of relative frequency

```
numIntervals = n;
intervalWidth = (max(Y) − min(Y)) / numIntervals;
x0 = min(Y);
for (i = 1; i < numIntervals; i ++)
    xi = xi−1 + intervalWidth;
ncount = histc(Y, X);
relativefreq = ncount / length(Y);
```

3. EIGENWALK

The principal component analysis is a mathematical procedure based on an orthogonal transformation of data. In this context, the input is the set of signals obtained from accelerometer and gyroscope, and the output of this transformation is a set of vectors called eigenvectors. Since the signals are obtained from users during walking, the eigenvectors are called $eigenwalks$. In this transformation, the first eigenwalk element presents the most dominant feature. To reduce the computation effort, the dimensionality of the original training set is usually reduced. In this study, the dimensionality is reduced by computing the eigenwalks on a characteristic list of the training set, based on a co-occurrence matrix.

A co-occurrence matrix shows the similarity of adjacent values at a given offset. It is usually exploited to process images [13], but its application in fall prediction has been recently investigated [12]. Fig. 1 shows an example of a co-occurrence matrix obtained from the accelerometer and gyroscope signals. Firstly, the acceleration and gyroscope data are stored in a matrix Δ: each column of the matrix presents a sample per instant. This matrix has 6 rows: at every instant, 3 values are obtained from the accelerometer and 3 from the gyroscope. The number of columns depends on the length of the monitoring interval, as one column is added at every instant. Firstly, each cell of the co-occurrence matrix is initialized to zero. Then, each couple of consecutive cells in Δ is analyzed to find similar patterns. Afterwards, the number of similar patterns is reported in the co-occurrence matrix at the coordinates given by the cell content. For example, if pairs (ax_1, ax_2) and (az_2, az_3) in Δ are equal, i.e., $ax_1 = az_2$ and $ax_2 = az_3$, the cell (round(ax_1), round(ax_2)) in the co-occurrence matrix is set to 2. Since the data obtained from accelerometer and gyroscope are float numbers and the indices of the co-occurrence matrix are integer, float numbers are rounded to the closest integer value. Moreover, the number of rows and columns of the co-occurrence matrix is equal to the max-

$$\Gamma = \begin{pmatrix} \text{Contrast}^1 & \cdots & \text{Contrast}^n \\ \text{Homogeneity}^1 & \cdots & \text{Homogeneity}^n \\ \text{Correlation}^1 & \cdots & \text{Correlation}^n \\ \text{Uniformity}^1 & \cdots & \text{Uniformity}^n \\ \text{Maximum probability}^1 & \cdots & \text{Maximum probability}^n \end{pmatrix}$$

Figure 2: Eigenwalk computation procedure.

imum value in Δ. For example, if round(ax_1) and round(ax_2) are the maximum values among the cells in Δ, the dimension of the co-occurrence matrix is equal to round(ax_1)×round(ax_2).

Let p_{ij} be the ratio of the $(i, j)th$ element of the co-occurrence matrix to the sum of all the elements. The co-occurrence matrix can be characterized as follows:

- *contrast* shows the intensity between a cell and its neighbors:

$$contrast = \sum_{i=1}^{K}\sum_{j=1}^{K}(i-j)^2 p_{ij} \tag{10}$$

- *homogeneity* measures the spatial closeness of the distribution of elements to the diagonal of the co-occurrence matrix:

$$homogeneity = \sum_{i=1}^{K}\sum_{j=1}^{K}\frac{p_{ij}}{1+|i-j|} \tag{11}$$

- *correlation* shows how a value is related to its neighbors:

$$correlation = \sum_{i=1}^{K}\sum_{j=1}^{K}\frac{(i-m_r)(j-m_c)p_{ij}}{\sigma_r\,\sigma_c} \tag{12}$$

where m_r, m_c, σ_r and σ_s are computed as follows:

$$m_r = \sum_{i=1}^{K}\sum_{j=1}^{K} i p_{ij},\; m_c = \sum_{j=1}^{K}\sum_{i=1}^{K} j p_{ij} \tag{13}$$

$$\sigma_r = \sum_{i=1}^{K}\sum_{j=1}^{K}(i-m_r)^2 p_{ij},\; \sigma_c = \sum_{j=1}^{K}\sum_{i=1}^{K}(i-m_c)^2 p_{ij}$$

- *uniformity* computes the sum of the squares of the elements:

$$uniformity = \sum_{i=1}^{K}\sum_{j=1}^{K} p_{ij}^2 \tag{14}$$

- *maximum probability* measures the highest value of the co-occurrence matrix. Simply, it can be computed by max(p_{ij}).

In order to compute the eigenwalks, firstly a new matrix Γ is created with the contrast, homogeneity, correlation, uniformity, and maximum probability of all samples, as shown in Fig. 2. For every row in Γ, the average value of the row is subtracted from all elements in the row, in order to build a new matrix Φ. Finally, the covariance matrix C is computed as $C = \Phi\Phi^T$. Then, the eigenvectors of C are computed. Generally speaking, given an $m \times m$ matrix K, the number λ is an eigenvalue of the matrix if there exists a non-zero vector v such that $Kv = \lambda v$. The vector v is called eigenvectors of K corresponding to the eigenvalue λ. Finally, the eigenvectors of the covariance matrix C are defined as eigenwalks because they present walking features.

4. CLASSIFICATION METHOD

In order to classify abnormal walks and normal daily activities, a classification algorithm should be performed on selected features. FPSs usually use the following classification methods:

1. Threshold-based algorithm
2. Decision tree (DT)
3. Support vector machine (SVM)
4. Multi-layer perceptron (MLP)
5. Random forest (RF)

A threshold-based algorithm utilizes a threshold to classify the feature set of the user gait. After being extracted from the input signals, the features are compared with pre-defined thresholds. Since the thresholds have an important effect on the performance of the algorithm, the biggest challenge of a threshold-based algorithm is determining the thresholds.

The decision tree is a directed tree with a root node without incoming edges, decision nodes with one incoming edge and possible outcoming edge; leaf nodes without outcoming edges. At the training stage, each internal node splits the instance space into two or more parts with the goal to optimize the performance of the classifier. Then, every path from the root to a leaf node forms a decision rule to determine which class a new instance belongs to [14].

A support vector machine is used for classifying separable classes of the observations. The SVM finds the best hyperplane with the maximum margin to separate two classes. The SVM can be defined as linear or non-linear according to the hyperplane function used for the classification.

The multi-layer perceptron is a neural network with different layers between input and output layers. The data flows in one direction from input to output layer.

Random forest is a large collection of decision trees. It consists of an arbitrary number of simple trees, which are used to determine the final outcome. For classification problems, the set of trees vote for the most popular class. The main idea in random forests is to reduce the correlation between the trees, without increasing the variance [8].

5. EVALUATION CRITERIA

Given a set with P positive instances and N negative instances, True Positive (TP) and True Negative (TN) are defined as correct identification of a true classification of positive and negative instance, respectively, while False Positive (FP) and False Negative (FN) misidentify a positive and negative instances. The most common criteria for evaluating classification algorithms in FPSs are:

1. *specificity* or *true negative rate (TNR)* measures the rate of negative instances that are correctly identified as negative:

$$specificity = \frac{\#TN}{\#TN + \#FP} \tag{15}$$

Moreover, $generality$ is computed as 1 - *specificity*.

2. *sensitivity* or *true positive rate (TPR)* measures the rate of positive instances that are correctly identified as positive:

$$sensitivity = \frac{\#TP}{\#TP + \#FN} \tag{16}$$

3. *accuracy* counts the number of samples correctly classified:

$$accuracy = \frac{\#TP + \#TN}{\#P + \#N} \quad (17)$$

4. *error rate* is the number of wrong classifications:

$$error\ rate = \frac{\#FP + \#FN}{\#P + \#N} \quad (18)$$

5. *precision* is the ratio of correctly classified samples as positive to the number of all samples classified as positive:

$$precision = \frac{\#TP}{\#TP + \#FP} \quad (19)$$

6. *recall* is the ratio of correctly classified samples as positive to all real positive samples:

$$recall = \frac{\#TP}{\#TP + \#FN} \quad (20)$$

In addition, the ROC curve is a graphical plot that illustrates the performance of a classifier [15]. The curve is drawn by sensitivity and generality. The generality and sensitivity are plotted on the x and y axes of the ROC plot, respectively. The best classifier is located at the top left corner of the ROC graph, which represents 100% sensitivity and 100% specificity. For example, Fig. 3 shows the ROC of four prediction instances. The further the result is from the diagonal in the above space, the better the accuracy is, so A has the best prediction. C is the worst among the four instances, because it is below and far from the diagonal line. B is a good classifier but not as much as A, because it is above but not far from the diagonal line. Moreover, since D is closer to the diagonal line, it is preferable than C.

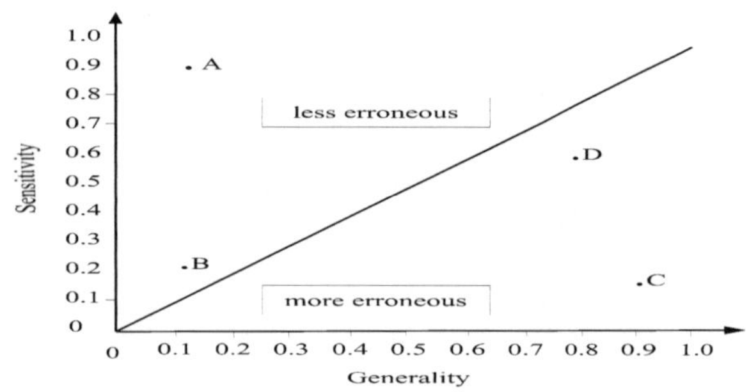

Figure 3: ROC plot.

6. EXPERIMENTAL ANALYSIS

A fall may be due to weakness, balance deficit, gait deficit, visual deficit and mobility limitation. Based on these fall factors, the methods used most frequently to simulate an abnormal walks are:

- walking with a straightened knee [9, 2, 16]
- walking with a leg length discrepancy [9, 2, 16]
- walking on a rough surface [17]
- walking through obstacles [11].

In the experiments, a flat area with different types of obstacle are prepared. Users are asked to walk through obstacles without looking them for 10 seconds, so they can lose their balance. This can

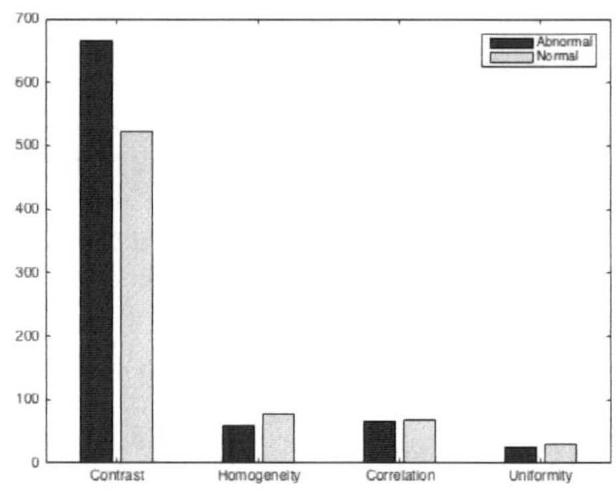

Figure 4: Normal VS abnormal walks.

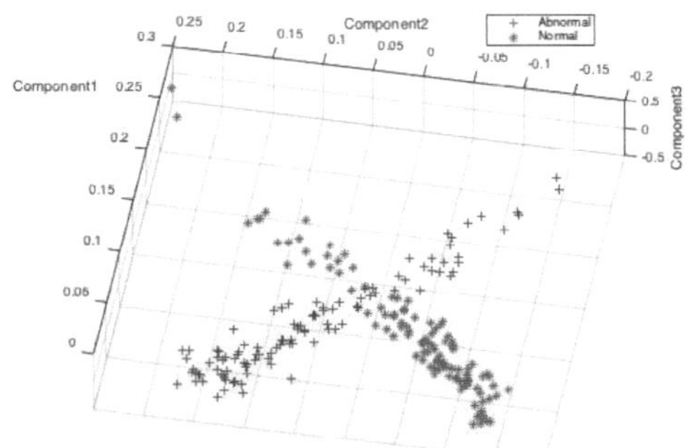

Figure 5: Normal VS abnormal eigenwalks.

be a good simulation of abnormal walks in real cases. The users in the experiments are 22 men with a weight in the range of 65-110 kg and height in the range of 160-185 cm, and 3 women with a weight in the range of 50-60 kg and height in the range of 157-165 cm. They are in the range of 18-35 years old. Since exploiting a middleware is a common approach to collect the user sensor data [18], MATLAB R2015b is used in this study. WEKA version 3.6.13[1], an open source tool for data mining, has been used to classify the data.

An iPhone 4S is adopted in the experiments, equipped with the STMicro STM33DH 3-axis accelerometer and the STIMicro AGDI 3-axis gyroscope. The smartphone is placed on the back trunk of the user to be closed to the center of the body.

Fig. 4 shows the average characterization of the co-occurrence matrix. Homogeneity, uniformity, maximum, and correlation in normal walks are higher than in abnormal walks. On the contrary, the contrast in abnormal walks is higher. However, these characterization need to be more precise to be effectively used for the walking classification. Therefore, the principal component analysis is computed. Fig. 5 shows the first three eigenwalks of the co-occurrence matrix. These eigenwalks are representative of normal and abnormal walks because they are located along two different directions in the plot.

Different state-of-the-art approaches are implemented [9, 11, 12]. Table 1 compares their performance with respect to the proposed method, by applying different classification methods. The accuracy is increased by more than 7%.

[1]http://www.cs.waikato.ac.nz/ ml/weka/

Measures	[9]	[11]	[12]	Proposed method
	DT	DT	MLP	RF
Accuracy	83.88	81.42	90.82	98.623
Error Rate	16.11	18.57	9.17	1.376
Sensitivity	0.88	0.78	0.87	0.991
Generality	0.21	0.15	0.06	0.018
Precision	0.81	0.83	0.93	0.981
Recall	0.88	0.78	0.87	0.991
F-Measure	0.84	0.82	0.90	0.986
ROC Area	0.86	0.82	0.96	0.999

Table 1: Result comparison.

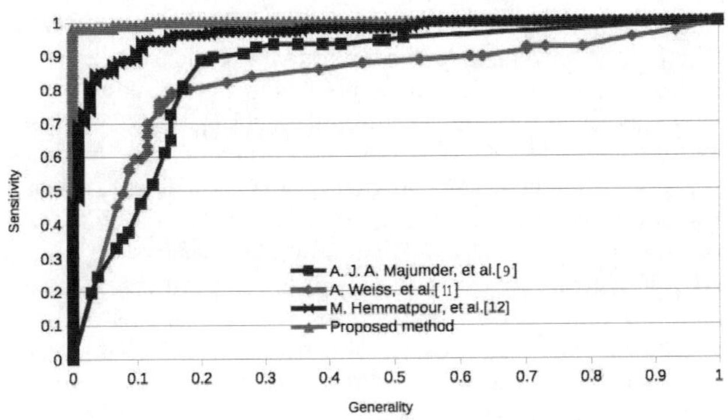

Figure 6: ROC curves of different approaches.

The best performance of the proposed method is confirmed by the ROC curves, as shown in Fig. 6: the area under the ROC curve of the proposed method is higher than for the other techniques.

7. CONCLUSIONS

This paper has analyzed various gait features based on data obtained from accelerometer and gyroscope. A new gait feature, called eigenwalk, has been proposed based on a co-occurrence matrix. Furthermore, the state-of-the-art fall prediction algorithms have been experimentally evaluated. Based on the presented results, the proposed feature in combination with a random forest classifier presents the best performance among the other fall prediction algorithms.

8. ACKNOWLEDGMENTS

This work was partially supported by the grant "Bando Smart Cities and Communities", OPLON project (OPportunities for active and healthy LONgevity) funded by the Italian Ministry for University.

9. REFERENCES

[1] Alexander, B. H., Rivara, F. P., and Wolf, M. E., "The cost and frequency of hospitalization for fall-related injuries in older adults." *American journal of public health*, vol. 82, no. 7, pp. 1020-1023, 1992.

[2] Majumder, A. J. A., Zerin, I., Uddin, M., Ahamed, S. I., and Smith, R. O., "Smartprediction: A real-time smartphone-based fall risk prediction and prevention system," in *Proceedings of the Research in Adaptive and Convergent Systems*, pp. 434-439, 2013.

[3] Shen, V. R., Lai, H., and Lai, A., "The implementation of a smartphone-based fall detection system using a high-level fuzzy Petri net." *Applied Soft Computing*, pp. 390-400, 2015.

[4] Li, Y. K., Ho, K. C., and Popescu, M., "A Microphone Array System for Automatic Fall Detection," in *IEEE Transactions on Biomedical Engineering*, vol. 59, no. 5, pp. 1291-1301, 2012.

[5] Zigel, Y., Litvak, D., and Gannot, I., "A Method for Automatic Fall Detection of Elderly People Using Floor Vibrations and Sound-Proof of Concept on Human Mimicking Doll Falls," in *IEEE Transactions on Biomedical Engineering*, vol. 56, no. 12, pp. 2858-2867, 2009.

[6] Bian, Z., Hou, J., Chau, L., and Magnenat-Thalmann, N., "Fall detection based on body part tracking using a depth camera" *IEEE Journal of Biomedical and Health Informatics*, vol. 19, no. 2, pp. 430-439, 2015.

[7] Fortino, G., and Gravina, R., "Fall-MobileGuard: a smart real-time fall detection system." in *Proceedings of the 10th EAI International Conference on Body Area Networks*, pp. 44-50, 2015.

[8] Friedman, J., Hastie, T., and Tibshirani, R.. "The elements of statistical learning second edition", Springer, 2001.

[9] Majumder, A. J. A., Rahman, F., Zerin, I., William, E. J., and Ahamed, S. I., "iPrevention: Towards a novel real-time smartphone-based fall prevention system," in *28th Proceedings of the ACM Symposium on Applied Computing*, pp. 513-518, 2013.

[10] Hjorth, B., "EEG analysis based on time domain properties," *Electroencephalography and clinical neurophysiology*, vol. 29, no. 3, pp. 306-310, 1970.

[11] Weiss, A., Shimkin I., Giladi N., and Hausdorff, J. M., "Automated detection of near falls: algorithm development and preliminary results," *BMC research notes*, vol. 3, no. 1, p. 1-8, 2010.

[12] Hemmatpour, M., Ferrero, R., Montrucchio, B., and Rebaudengo, M., "A neural network model based on co-occurrence matrix for fall prediction" In *Proceedings of the 6th EAI International Conference on Wireless Mobile Communication and Healthcare*, 2016.

[13] Gonzalez, R.C., and Richard, E. W., "Digital image processing", 2008.

[14] Dai, W., and Ji, W., "A mapreduce implementation of C4. 5 decision tree algorithm." In *International Journal of Database Theory and Application*, vol. 7, no. 1, pp. 49-60, 2014.

[15] Fawcett, T., "An introduction to ROC analysis." Pattern recognition letters, vol. 27, no. 8, pp. 861-874, 2006.

[16] Majumder, A. J. A., Zerin, I., Ahamed, S. I., and Smith, R. O., "A multi-sensor approach for fall risk prediction and prevention in elderly," in *ACM SIGAPP Applied Computing Review*, vol. 14, no. 1, pp. 41-52, 2014.

[17] Otis, M. J-D., and Menelas, B. A. J., "Toward an augmented shoe for preventing falls related to physical conditions of the soil." In *IEEE international conference on systems, man, and cybernetics*, pp. 3281-3285, 2012.

[18] Fortino, G., Giannantonio, R., Gravina, R., Kuryloski, P., and Jafari, R., "Enabling effective programming and flexible management of efficient body sensor network applications." in *IEEE Transactions on Human-Machine Systems*, vol. 43, no. 1, pp. 115-133, 2013.

A baseline walking dataset exploiting accelerometer and gyroscope for fall prediction and prevention systems

Masoud Hemmatpour, Renato Ferrero, Bartolomeo Montrucchio, Maurizio Rebaudengo
Dipartimento di Automatica e Informatica, Politecnico di Torino
{ masoud.hemmatpour, renato.ferrero, bartolomeo.montrucchio, maurizio.rebaudengo } @polito.it

ABSTRACT

Fall datasets usually record normal activities and transitions from one posture to another one with falls. Many fall detection datasets based on different sensors are adopted by researchers to improve their systems. Although fall avoidance are dramatically increasing, a public fall prediction and prevention dataset based on an accelerometer and gyroscope is absent. So, this study creates a dataset based on the state-of-the-art techniques in simulating a fall. Different techniques are evaluated to find the best fall simulation. Since accelerometer and gyroscope sensors embedded in a smartphone are recognized to be suited for fall avoidance systems, in this study, they are used to obtain data from users. At the end, some statistical analysis of the observed data are presented and a nonlinear regression model is proposed.

1. INTRODUCTION

Fall prediction and prevention systems usually have some steps in common: firstly, data are collected from sensors, then data are analyzed to compute the appropriate feature set. Finally, the risk of a possible fall is evaluated through some classification algorithms. Fall prediction systems only recognize the probability of a fall occurrence while fall prevention systems provide a solution for preventing it. This study considers the fall prediction step. Fall prediction and prevention studies are able to predict two types of falls: future and real-time falls. Future fall solutions evaluate the user to estimate the user fall risk in the future: if the user fall risk is high, there is a probable future fall which can be prevented through some exercises [1]. Real-time fall solutions predict a fall in real-time and avoid the fall through alerting the user [2, 3, 4, 5] or using an external aid such as walker or robot [6, 7]. This study covers both real-time and future fall prediction.

A fall dataset can facilitate evaluating and comparing different fall avoidance systems in a homogeneous environment. Although algorithms are slightly sensitive to the sampling frequency, the number of training samples in a dataset have an influence on the performance. Actually, a higher number of samples in a dataset makes it more valuable. Several datasets have been made publicly available to evaluate fall detection systems [8, 9, 10, 11, 12]. Although one of the most promising approaches of fall avoidance system is fall prediction and prevention, to the best of our knowledge, there is not a challenging baseline dataset for predicting and preventing a fall. Firstly, this paper investigates different abnormal walk simulation techniques in order to find the best one. Then, a preliminary test was taken to find the best simulation of an abnormal walk. Then, a dataset of different tests for fall prediction and prevention systems was created and published[1]. Since movement sensors are usually used to investigate the extrinsic parameters of a fall, this study exploits the accelerometer and gyroscope to create a dataset.

The remainder of the paper is organized as follows. In Section 2, parameters of a dataset are presented and several fall detection dataset have been reviewed. Sections 3 describes fall factors and experiments of future fall. Then, Section 4 describes real-time evaluation techniques. Section 5 describes the experiments. Section 6 presents primary analysis on the dataset. The proposed dataset is published, and researchers might have access to develop services which are specialized for fall prediction and prevention.

2. RELATED WORK

In order to evaluate a fall avoidance method, preparing a dataset with realistic parameters is essential. Datasets strive to record a scenario which resembles an actual fall incident as closely as possible. To reduce the gap between fall simulation dataset and real-life, several parameters have to be considered.

Realistic setup is one of the most important parameters. Datasets record the real life activity in comparison with fall incident or abnormal walk simulation. They attempt to cover the majority of daily activities such as normal walking, sitting, changing clothes, fall, etc., [13].

Different fall factors require *different sensors*. For example, some datasets use camera but, since visual sensors disturb users privacy, exploiting movement sensors is more preferable [13, 8].

The *number of samples* is a parameter that directly affects the performance of a fall avoidance system. In case of few samples more probably the classification algorithm faces either underfitting or overfitting. An algorithm underfits or overfits when the model is not able to classify properly the case under analysis. In other words, the model is not predictive (underfit) or only works with the presented training data (overfit).

Chronological and physiological parameters such as age, weight, and height are recorded in most of the datasets [9, 10, 11].

Table 1 shows different datasets and their parameters. The following notation is used: Accelerometer (Accl), Gyroscope (Gyr), Daily Activity (DA), Walking (W), Standing (S), Ascending (A) and Descending (D) stairs, Lie down (L), Sit down, Stand up (SS),

[1] http://ubi.polito.it/research/fall.htm

Dataset	DA	Sensor	NS	Age	Weight (kg)	Height (cm)
[8]	W, S, A, D, JO, JU	Accl/Gyr	57	20-47	55-120	161-193
[9]	W, S, A, D, JO, JU, SS	Accl/Gyr	11	22-36	50-102	160-189
[10]	W, L, SS	Accl/Gyr	NA	NA	NA	NA
[11]	S, W, L, SS	Accl/Gyr	42	18-30	50-82	162-177

Table 1: Comparison among online fall datasets.

Jumping (JU), and Jogging (JO).

MobiFall is an activity dataset for fall detection based on inertial sensor of a smartphone [8]. The dataset contains signals recorded from the accelerometer and gyroscope sensors. Moreover, a software-based orientation data which is derived from the accelerometer and the geomagnetic sensors are also recorded in the dataset.

Mobiact is a publicly available dataset which includes data from a smartphone with different types of activities and a range of falls [9]. It is based on the MobiFall dataset which was initially created with fall detection in mind.

Another dataset records falls and activities of daily life exploiting mobile phone integrated accelerometer and gyroscope sensor data [10]. It uses five different mobile phones to prepare the dataset. Dataset records the data of five martial artists in parallel.

The last dataset simulates four types of falls (forward, backward, lateral left and right) and daily activity [11]. In this study, forty-two volunteers are participated.

Actually, all presented datasets are used to evaluate fall detection systems, which only notify an acquaintance of the user in case of fall occurrence. The dataset proposed in this study can be used for fall prediction and prevention, which is one of the most promising approaches in fall avoidance systems.

3. FUTURE FALL

The relation between falls and lower muscle strength is studied in many contexts [14, 15, 16]. Decreased muscle strength of lower limbs is an important risk factor for falls in elderly people [17]. Because it reduced capacity to deal with a balance disturbance. There are various standard tests to estimate a future fall risk. In the Sit-To-Stand test (STS), firstly, a user sits in the middle of a chair, and he/she places his/her hands on the opposite shoulder crossed at the wrists. Then, he/she keeps feet flat on the floor. Afterwards, he/she rises to a full standing position and then he/she sits back down again. Eventually, this test counts the number of full stands that is completed in 30 seconds. Since slowing of postural movements can be an indicator of the weak lower limb, a low number of full stands shows a high risk of a fall. The statistical parameters of the postural transition duration in each step of the STS test is an indicator of the fall risk. Since the trunk tilt has an important role in the maintenance of the posture, it can be measured during the sit to stand phase to assess risk of a fall. Acceleration and angular rotation of the chest are used to extract the mentioned measures of the STS test. The first step to calculate the measurements is the signal segmentation according to the postural transition, either standing up or sitting down. Segmentation can be performed based on the repetitive patterns produced by the signals, which vary in line with the movement. An application exploits the mentioned features to automatically count and evaluate the user [18]. The output of the accelerometer and gyroscope sensors of the STS test are recorded in dataset.

The maintenance of posture and the mobility depend on orientation and balance. So, keeping balance is important to avoid a fall during the movement. The One Leg Stand (OLS) test is used in fall prediction and prevention system to evaluate the user's balance. A user stands with feet together and arms down. Then, he/she raises one leg, either leg, with the foot approximately six inches off the ground, keeping raised foot up for 30 seconds. He/she can sway side-to-side or back-and-forth while maintaining the one-leg stand position. If a user puts his/her foot down some times during the 30-second period, then he/she will fail the test. The OLS test measures the Center Of Mass (COM) displacement and speed of COM displacement. Displacement can be computed by the acceleration of the COM to evaluate balance.

4. REAL-TIME FALL

The best way to predict and prevent a fall in real-time is identifying abnormal and normal walks. A fall may happen due to the weakness, balance deficit, gait deficit, visual deficit and mobility limitation. The most frequently method which can lead to a fall are:

- Walking with straightened knee [2, 4, 3]
- Walking with leg length discrepancy [2, 4, 3]
- Walking on rough surface [19]
- Walking through obstacles [20].

In order to evaluate the different methods, accuracy and ROC area criteria are used as explained in the following. In all the presented formulas, P and N represent the total number of positive and negative instances while True Positive (TP) and True Negative (TN) are defined as correct identification of a true classification of positive and negative instance, respectively. False Positive (FP) and False Negative (FN) present misidentifying a positive and negative instances, respectively.

- Accuracy
  The accuracy of an algorithm demonstrates the number of samples correctly classified:

$$Accuracy = \frac{\#TP + \#TN}{\#P + \#N}. \quad (1)$$

- Specificity
  The specificity or True Negative Rate (TNR) measures the rate of negative instances that are correctly identified as negative. Moreover, generality is computed as 1 - specificity.

$$Specificity = \frac{\#TN}{\#TN + \#FP}. \quad (2)$$

- Sensitivity
  The sensitivity or True Positive Rate (TPR) measures the rate of positive instances that are correctly identified as positive:

$$Sensitivity = \frac{\#TP}{\#TP + \#FN}. \quad (3)$$

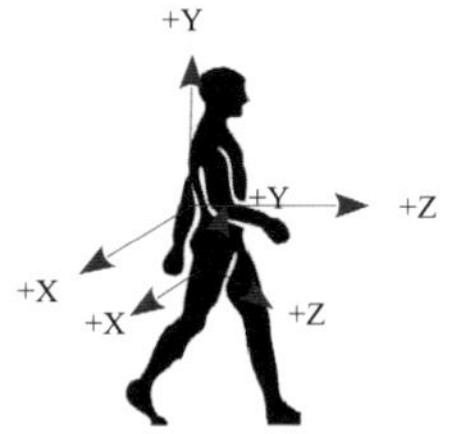

Figure 1: Sensors axes and positions.

The ROC curve is a graphical plot that illustrates the performance of a classifier [22]. The curve is drawn by sensitivity and generality. The generality and sensitivity are plotted on the x and y axes of the ROC plot, respectively. The best classifier is located at the top left corner of the ROC graph, which represents 100% sensitivity and 100% specificity. Moreover, A higher ROC area i.e, the area under the ROC curve indicates a better accuracy.

Since people with increased fall risk tend to walk slower, the actual fall risk can be quantified according to the gait speed [21]. In the act of motion, the acceleration varies according due to the body movements, it can be an indicator of the pre-fall state [20]. Moreover, when a user tilts in a direction more than normal, it shows an abnormal posture which can be led to a fall. So, the user tilt can be a factor to assess the risk of fall. User tilt is estimated with the combination of a gyroscope and accelerometer [3, 4, 2].

5. EXPERIMENT

There are many studies proving that sensors (accelerometer and gyroscope) present in a smartphone are precise enough to be used in fall avoidance systems [23, 21, 18]. Therefore, a smartphone is adopted in the experiments. Most of the developed applications exploit two main approaches to obtain and analyze the sensors signals: low-level programming and general-purpose middleware [24]. In this study, MATLAB R2015b is used as a middleware to obtain and analyze the data. Before creating the main dataset an experiment is done to find the best method in simulating an abnormal walk. Data is collected through an Iphone 4S which is equipped with the STMicro STM33DH 3-axis accelerometer and the STIMicro AGDI 3-axis gyroscope.

WEKA tool version 3.6.13, a powerful data mining toolkit, is used to classify the obtained data. Decision Tree (DT) and Support Vector Machine (SVM), two commonly used classification algorithm in fall prediction and prevention system, are used in WEKA to classify the input. In order to see the impact of the position of the sensor on the performance, the smartphone is used once on back trunk and once on the pocket of the participants. The directions of x, y, and z-axis of the accelerometer and yaw, pitch and roll of the gyroscope, and the body of the participant in both positions are illustrated in Fig. 1. In order to eliminate the initial condition, the participants walk from a standing start.

Table 2 shows the result of the experiment with different permutations of normal and abnormal walks. N-A is the abbreviation of the Normal versus Abnormal (with different kind of abnormal technique), N-O is the abbreviation of Normal versus walking through Obstacles, N-S means Normal versus walking with Straightened knee and N-L means Normal versus walking with Leg length discrepancy. As can be seen, in both position, Normal waking versus walking through obstacles with DT classification has the highest ROC area and accuracy. So, in the main experiments of the dataset, the participants walk through obstacles to simulate an abnormal walk. Moreover, as the result shows, back position is more appropriate for the sensor location in the body.

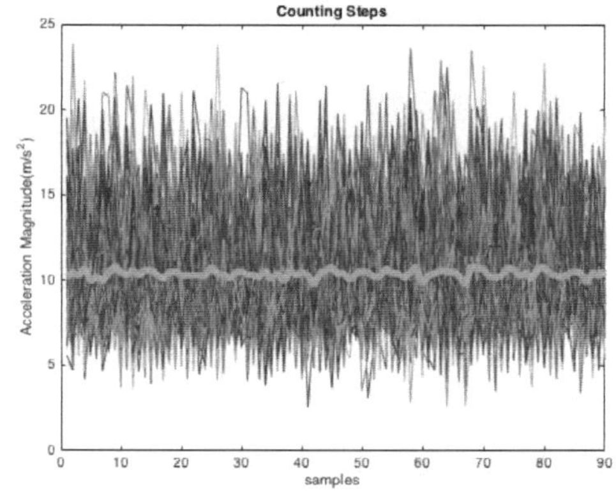

Figure 2: Normal walk.

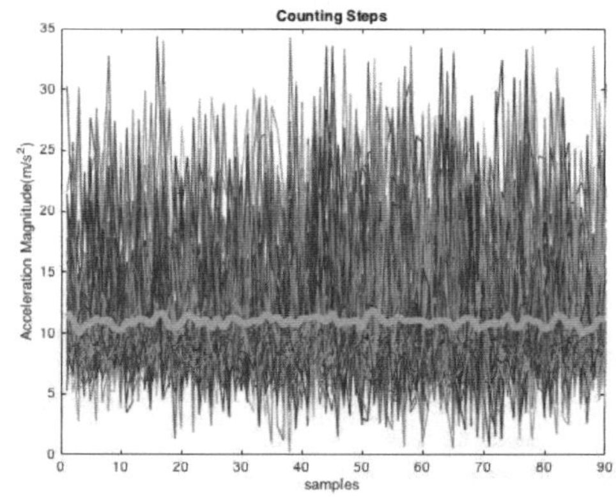

Figure 3: Abnormal walk.

The main experiments are designed according to the tests for future fall (STS and OLS) and real-time fall (normal and abnormal walks). 25 participants with age 18-35, weight 80±10 kg and height 160-185 cm are involved in the experiments. In order to do the STS and OLS tests, a smartphone is located on the chest of the participants to record the acceleration and gyroscope data. Since the experiments showed the back trunk position has higher accuracy in fall prediction and prevention system, a smartphone is located on the lower back trunk of the participants in real-time fall test. Participants are asked to walk normally, and also walk through the obstacles for 10 seconds. Finally, the collected data, three axes of accelerometer and gyroscope of each user, are stored in the dataset.

6. DATA ANALYSIS

To analyze a dataset a function model should be defined for data behaviour. Finding a suitable model to present the data is called curve fitting. The model can be linear, polynomial, nonlinear, etc.. Firstly, an average signal of all abnormal walks is computed. Then, a simple nonlinear regression model is developed according to the average signal. Fig. 2 and 3 show the normal and abnormal acceleration signal magnitude of the users. The average signals are plotted with thicker line. The average signal is a sinusoidal function so, firstly, a model function is defined as follows:

$$F(x, [a, b]) = asin(x) + cos(x) + b \tag{4}$$

	Back				Pocket			
	N-A	N-O	N-S	N-L	N-A	N-O	N-S	N-L
ROC Area	0.905	0.953	0.925	0.825	0.850	0.930	0.735	0.900
Accuracy	85%	97.5%	92.5%	82.5%	88.7%	95%	77.5%	92.5%
Classification	DT	DT	SVM	SVM	DT	DT	DT	DT

Table 2: Result of the experiment on different abnormal walks.

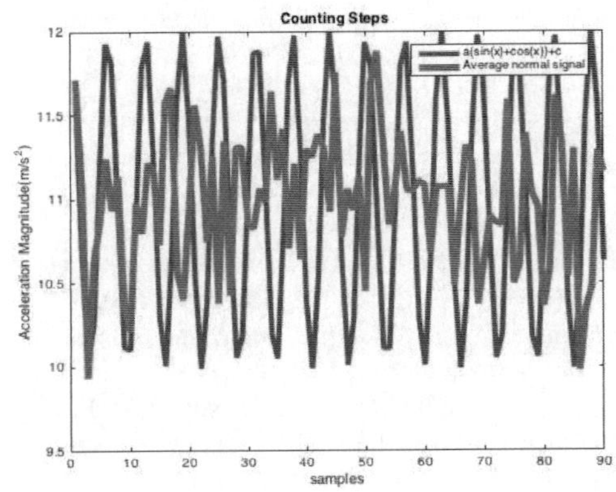

Figure 4: Comparison between normal walks and adopted model.

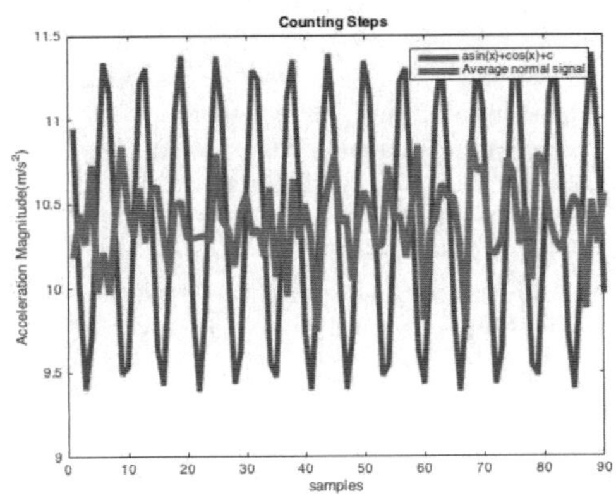

Figure 5: Comparison between abnormal walks and adopted model.

The important point is finding the best coefficients of the model function to be more representative as the dataset behaviour. There are different techniques which can solve the problem but in this study least-squares is exploited. Least-square strives to minimize the sum of squared difference between a value and the fitted value provided by a model. In other words, the main problem is solving the following optimization problem:

$$S = min \sum_{i=1}^{n} (F(x, [a, b]) - \bar{y}_i)^2 \quad (5)$$

where n presents number of data, and $\bar{y}$ is the given observed data. The goal is to find the best $F(x, [a, b])$ to reduce the error. Fig. 4 and 5 show the function model in comparison with normal and abnormal walk. This function model is appropriate for an abnormal walk. The coefficients in the presented functions are [0.0259, 10.3892] for abnormal and [0.0926, 10.9925] for normal walk. Another statistical analysis on the dataset is measuring the number of observations with value higher than average acceleration. As Fig. 6 shows, the number of observations in normal walk is much higher than in abnormal walk. Observations support the idea that high acceleration is not a feature of abnormal walk, since walking with lower speed may increase the risk of fall [21].

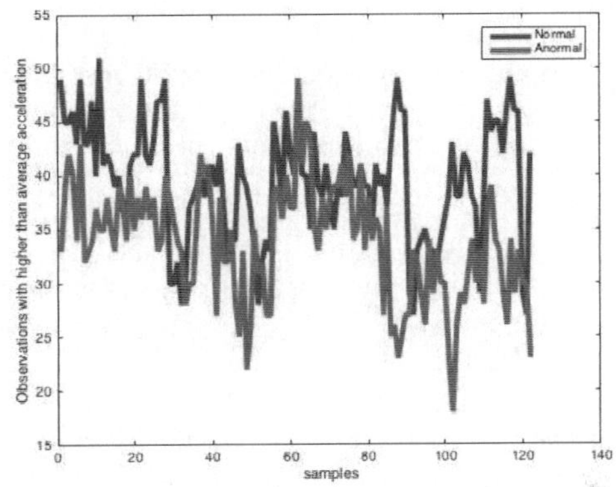

Figure 6: Average signal of abnormal and normal walks.

7. CONCLUSION

Evaluating a fall avoidance system requires a coherent dataset with realistic parameters. Actually, most of the existing dataset are used in fall detection systems. Since fall prediction and prevention systems are one of the most promising approaches to avoid a fall, this study evaluates different parameters to create a dataset based on the state-of-the-art fall prediction and prevention studies. 25 users participated in four different tests. One-Leg Stand and Sit-to-Stand tests were used to evaluate the risk of a fall in the future. Moreover, walking through obstacles has been proposed to simulate an abnormal walk and to evaluate the real-time fall risk. Furthermore, acceleration and gyroscope embedded in a smartphone were used to collect the data. All the recorded data are published to facilitate the access to the dataset.

8. ACKNOWLEDGMENT

This work was partially supported by the grant "Bando Smart Cities and Communities", OPLON Project (OPportunities for active and healthy LONgevity) funded by the Italian Ministry for University.

9. REFERENCES

[1] Ferreira, B.N., Guimaraes, V., and Sereno, H., "Smartphone based fall prevention exercises." In *15th IEEE International*

Conference on e-Health Networking, Applications & Services, pp. 643-647, 2013.

[2] Majumder, A.J.A., Rahman, F., Zerin, I., EbelJr, W., and Ahamed, S.I., "iPrevention: Towards a novel real-time smartphone-based fall prevention system." In *28th Proceedings of the ACM Symposium on Applied Computing*, pp. 513-518, 2013.

[3] Majumder, A.J.A., Zerin, I., Ahamed, S.I. and Smith, R.O., "A multi-sensor approach for fall risk prediction and prevention in elderly," in *ACM SIGAPP Applied Computing Review*, vol. 14, no. 1, pp. 41-52, 2014.

[4] Majumder, A.J.A., Zerin, I., Uddin, M., Ahamed, S.I. and Smith, R.O., "Smartprediction: A real-time smartphone-based fall risk prediction and prevention system." In *Proceedings of the Research in Adaptive and Convergent Systems*, pp. 434-439, 2013.

[5] Hemmatpour, M., Ferrero, R., Montrucchio, B., and Rebaudengo, M., "A neural network model based on co-occurrence matrix for fall prediction" In *Proceedings of the 6th EAI International Conference on Wireless Mobile Communication and Healthcare*, 2016.

[6] Hirata, Y., Asami, M., and Kazuhiro, K., "Motion control of intelligent passive-type walker for fall-prevention function based on estimation of user state." In *Proceedings IEEE International Conference on Robotics and Automation*, 2006.

[7] Di, P., Huang, J., Sekiyama, K., and Fukuda, T., "A novel fall prevention scheme for intelligent cane robot by using a motor driven universal joint." In *International Symposium on Micro-NanoMechatronics and Human Science (MHS)*, pp. 391-396, 2011.

[8] Vavoulas, G., Chatzaki, C., Malliotakis, T., Pediaditis, M. and Tsiknakis, M., "The MobiAct dataset: recognition of activities of daily living using smartphones."In *Proceedings of the International Conference on Information and Communication Technologies for Ageing Well and e-Health*, p. 143-151, 2016.

[9] George, V., Matthew, P., Emmanouil, G. S., Tsiknakis, M., "The MobiFall dataset: an initial evaluation of fall detection algorithms using smartphones". In *13th IEEE International Conference on Bioinformatics and Bioengineering (BIBE)*, 2013

[10] Wertner, A., Pammer, V., Czech, P., "Dataset for Mobile Phone Sensing Based Fall Detection". https://dx.doi.org/10.6084/m9.figshare.1444405.v1. Accessed: Oct 05, 2016

[11] Olukunle, O., Gaura, E., and Brusey, J., "Data set for fall events and daily activities from inertial sensors". In *Proceedings of the 6th ACM Multimedia Systems Conference*, p. 243-248, 2015.

[12] Fortino, G., and, Gravina, R., "Fall-MobileGuard: a smart real-time fall detection system." in *Proceedings of the 10th EAI International Conference on Body Area Networks*, pp. 44-50, 2015.

[13] UniversitÃă Politecnica Delle Marche, http://www.tlc.dii.univpm.it/blog/ databases4kinect, Accessed: 12-10-2016

[14] Fukagawa, N., Wolfson1, L., Judge, J., Whipple1, R., and King, M., "Strength is a major factor in balance, gait, and the occurrence of falls." *The Journals of Gerontology Series A: Biological Sciences and Medical Sciences* vol. 50, pp. 64-67, 1995.

[15] LaStayo, P.C., Ewy, G.A., Pierotti, D.D., Johns, R.K. and Lindstedt, S., "The positive effects of negative work: increased muscle strength and decreased fall risk in a frail elderly population." *The Journals of Gerontology Series A: Biological Sciences and Medical Sciences*, vol. 58 no. 5, pp. 419-424, 2003.

[16] Pijnappels, M., Reeves, N.D. and van DieÃńn, J.H., "Identification of elderly fallers by muscle strength measures.". *European journal of applied physiology* vol. 102 no. 5, pp.585-592, 2008.

[17] Eleni, S., Chris, K., Yvonne, H., and Varvara, L., "Leg strength improvement." In *elderly fallers and non fallers after eight week of isokinetic strengthening, Biology of Exercise*, vol. 8.1, 2012.

[18] Guimaraes, V., Ribeiro, D., and Rosado, L., "A smartphone-based fall risk assessment tool: Measuring one leg standing, sit to stand and falls efficacy scale." In *15th International Conference on e-Health Networking, Applications & Services*, pp. 529-533, 2013.

[19] Otis, M.J.D., and Menelas, B.A.J., "Toward an augmented shoe for preventing falls related to physical conditions of the soil," in *IEEE International Conference on Systems, Man, and Cybernetics (SMC)*, pp. 3281-3285, 2012.

[20] Weiss, A., Shimkin, I., Giladi, N., and Hausdorff, J.M., "Automated detection of near falls: algorithm development and preliminary results." In *BMC research notes*, vol. 3, no. 1, pp. 3-62, 2010.

[21] Guimaraes, V., Teixeira, P. M, Monteiro, P. M., and Elias, D., "Phone based fall risk prediction." In *Wireless Mobile Communication and Healthcare*, pp. 135-142, 2013.

[22] Fawcett, T., "An introduction to ROC analysis." Pattern recognition letters, vol. 27, no. 8, pp. 861-874, 2006.

[23] Ferrero, R., Gandino, F., Montrucchio, B., Rebaudengo, M., Velasco, A., Benkhelifa, I., "On gait recognition with smartphone accelerometer." In *4th Mediterranean Conference on Embedded Computing (MECO)*, IEEE, 2015.

[24] Fortino, G., Giannantonio, R., Gravina, R., Kuryloski, P., and Jafari, R., "Enabling effective programming and flexible management of efficient body sensor network applications." in *IEEE Transactions on Human-Machine Systems*, vol. 43, no. 1, pp. 115-133, 2013.

From Activity Recognition to Motion Assessment: Delimitate against the Other Class within a WBAN

Martin Seiffert
Dep. of Mathematics and Computer Science
Freie Universität Berlin
Takustraße 9, 14195 Berlin, Germany
seiffert@inf.fu-berlin.de

Flavio Holstein
Dep. of Computer Science
Technical University of Berlin
Straße des 17. Juni 135, 10623 Berlin, Germany
flavio.holstein@campus.tu-berlin.de

Jochen Schiller
Dep. of Mathematics and Computer Science
Freie Universität Berlin
Takustraße 9, 14195 Berlin, Germany
schiller@inf.fu-berlin.de

ABSTRACT

Wearable sensor nodes use activity recognition systems to identify human activities. However, several applications such as physical rehabilitation and professional sports coaching require not only the identification of motion but also quality assessment to provide appropriate feedback to the user. In this work, we present AAC, a generalized trainable process chain for the online assessment of periodic human activity within a WBAN. AAC evaluates the execution of separate movements of a prior trained activity on a fine-grained quality scale. We connect qualitative assessment with human knowledge by projecting the AAC on the hierarchical decomposition of motion performed by the human body as well as establishing the assessment on a kinematic evaluation of biomechanically distinct motion fragments. We evaluate AAC in a real-world setting and show that AAC delineates movements of correctly performed activity to faulty ones and provides detailed reasons for the activity assessment. Both are crucial for an appropriate feedback to the user.

CCS Concepts

•**Computer systems organization** → *Sensor networks;* •**Computing methodologies** → *Instance-based learning; Anomaly detection; Distributed artificial intelligence;*

Keywords

activity assessment chain; motion quality; wearable sensors;

1. INTRODUCTION

Driven by cheap to produce and easy to apply ubiquitous wireless sensor nodes (hereafter nodes) equipped with inertial sensors such as accelerometers and gyroscopes, activity recognition (AR) based on wearable nodes is a field broadly explored in recent research. Such AR systems typically utilize the data of multiple nodes attached to the limbs of the human body to recognize a predefined set of common activities. To achieve this goal, machine learning algorithms are used to train a model from prior labeled training data of the wireless body area network (WBAN). Subsequently the model is used to classify new data of the WBAN as one of the prior trained activities.

In [4] Bulling et al. give a tutorial to the typically used general-purpose framework called activity recognition chain (ARC). The ARC comprises raw data acquisition of multiple nodes, preprocessing of the data to remove noise and interfering artifacts, data segmentation, feature extraction and selection, and finally activity classification and decision fusion. Many of the current AR approaches are focused on improving the basic processes of the ARC. In [11] Khan et al. investigate optimal sampling rates for accelerometry based AR to reduce system requirements related to energy consumption or memory whilst retaining recognition accuracy. In [2] Banos et al. investigate signal segmentation and present a study that analyzes the effects of the windowing process on AR system performance. In [7] Ghasemzadeh et al. present a feature selection approach that considers classification accuracy as well as the energy consumption required for feature computation.

More complex approaches focusing on generic activity recognition use the concept of hierarchical decomposition of activities into time series sub patterns. These approaches in general utilize processes of the ARC to classify low level sub patterns of activities first, to identify higher level activities as sequential or concurrent combinations of sub patterns. These approaches contribute to real-world problems, for example: AR on streaming data to identify activities of interest among other activities [13, 15], recognition of concurrent and interleaved activities [17, 16], training of AR systems based on limited training data [19], or sharing AR Systems across platforms [20].
Beyond the classification of activities, a WBAN equipped with inertial sensors contains great potential for qualitative activity analysis [5]. Feedback relating to the quality of execution of an activity is a very interesting field in AR especially within the application domains of sports and healthcare. In sports training and physical rehabilitation, feedback regarding wrong body movements is crucial for learning and improvement of motor skills and physical fitness [21, 6].

Most approaches to quality evaluation of activities are straightforward and implement expert knowledge of a specialized application domain [18, 23, 14]. However, these assessment approaches are not designed to generalize well beyond the corresponding application domain. There are a number of approaches that handle activity assessment as a classification problem [25, 9, 1]. This research successfully demonstrates that AR can be used to detect erroneous activity executions, but the inherent requirement to train defective activities restricts these approaches to applications were this is affordable.

Research on more generalized activity assessment is very scarce. In [12] Khan et al. address the challenging problem of generality and propose a framework for skill assessment in the context of AR that enables automatic quality analysis of complex human activities without domain-specific knowledge as a part of the system. The framework utilizes a rule induction tree built on the symbolic abstraction of the raw sensor data of an accomplished activity. The quality measure is computed from features concerning the complexity of the rule tree as well as metrics of the induced transitions. The final rating of new activity samples is based on the ratings of prior trained activity samples in different quality levels. In [22] we introduce a trainable system architecture for complex online motion assessment that requires the training of the correctly executed activity only. The assessment is based on the classification of motion fragments as atomic parts of an intuitive description of a body movement. The system identifies and assesses movements of an activity by reference to the amount of correctly classified motion fragments. The presented approach states very good identification accuracy of motion fragments but lacks in definite differentiation between correct and faulty movements.

The contribution of this paper is three-fold: i) First we classify methods for quality quantification in AR what was not done before. We give reason for the method we use and show how semantic property's can be added. ii) We extend our work in [22] by investigating the delimitation of a trained activity against untrained activity as well as the detailed assessment of motion fragments. As a result, we present a generalized activity assessment chain (AAC) for the detailed assessment of cyclic activity, which is designed to work in a fully distributed fashion within a WBAN. iii) We implement AAC and evaluate the applicability and the practical value in a real-world case-study of indoor rowing.

2. ASSESSMENT METHOD

	DM	EML	IML
configuration effort	+	-	(+)
semantic properties	+	+	-
generalization ability	-	(+)	+

+ favourable (+) constrained - adverse

Figure 1: Comparison of assessment methods

For the assessment of activities, a reference for quality quantization is needed. We differentiate between three methods used in the related work to model this reference: domain modeling (DM), explicit machine learning (EML), and implicit machine learning (IML). As described below and depicted in Fig. 1, these methods differ in the effort necessary for the inertial system configuration (Configuration Effort), in the meaning of their computed assessment values (Semantic Properties) as well as in their ability to be transferred across multiple application domains (Generalization Ability).

Domain Model. The DM method relies on manually modelling domain specific features based on expert knowledge [23, 18, 14]. In [14] for example, the quality of climbing moves is determined based on features implemented specifically for rock climbing. These approaches have the advantage that, based on the semantic expert knowledge included in the implemented domain specific assessment model, feedback concerning the activity assessment can be easily connected to the knowledge of the user. In addition, after implementation, these approaches do not necessarily need an inertial training, neither of correctly nor of incorrectly conducted samples of the activity. Hence, no inertial configuration effort is necessary. However, domain specific modelling do not generalize well, as the implemented domain specific logic cannot be easily applied to other application domains.

Explicit Machine Learning. For the EML approach, an explicit model for any quality class which should be distinguished is learned by a supervised training of a classifier on appropriately conducted activity samples. Activity assessment is thus translated into a classification task as it is done in [25, 9, 1]. Subsequent new samples of the activity are assigned to one of the previously trained quality classes. As a result of the supervised training, the domain specific meaning of the different quality classes is known. Thus, an appropriate semantic feedback to the activity assessment is possible. Systems using this approach can be transferred to other application domains where an appropriate training of correctly as well as incorrectly conducted activity samples is possible. Depending on the intended granularity of the activity assessment, the inertial training of the quality classes can be expensive. Nevertheless, the training of all intended quality classes is not always possible. Especially in motor learning or physiotherapy applications, the accomplishment of the purposefully incorrectly performed activity is not recommended. In this case the approach is restricted to applications where historical data on incorrectly performed samples of the activity is available. Another drawback of the EML approach is that the resolution of the assessment is limited to the amount of explicit trained quality classes. [12] addresses this by assigning relative quality labels through pairwise comparison of explicit trained activity samples by a domain expert and thus providing a quality scale. New activity samples are assessed by ranking them within the prior trained quality scale.

Implicit Machine Learning. By IML we summarise approaches where a model is generated from ground truth data representing activity samples at the best affordable quality only [22, 3, 24, 8]. Upcoming activity samples are assessed by delimitation of the previously modelled ideal quality class against motion data which do not correspond to the trained activity. Hence, this approach makes use of algorithms known from the *null class* problem [4], also known as the problem of the *other class* [13] respectively. This can be seen as a form of implicit learning, in other words, learning about faulty conduction of the activity without knowing the faults in particular. In [3], for example, selected feature values, which were extracted from the raw data of a movement, are checked for predetermined thresholds. If a feature value exceeds the corresponding threshold, the movement is reported as faulty. As for the second approach, a supervised training is needed for generalization across application domains. But the training is limited to the correct conduction of samples of the intended activity only, which results in a reduced inertial configuration effort. As the supervised training did not comprise any faulty activity samples, this method did not include semantic knowledge corresponding to faulty conductions by default.

In our work, we focus on proving a generalized process chain for activity assessment. Hence, the IML method can be generalized across multiple application domains by an affordable need of inertial training we make use of this method. As a drawback, this approach lacks in semantic knowledge, included by design (e.g. what is the assessment composed of and what can be done to improve the performance). We address this gap by adding biomechanically modelled aspects to the processes chain. As in [22] we establish the activity assessment on biomechanically distinct motion fragments and aggregate the motion assessments on different abstraction layers concerning the hierarchical decomposition of a motion performed by the human body. Thus we add temporal and spatial context to the assessment. In contrast to [22] we realize the fragment assessment by detailed evaluation of the feature values which characterize a motion fragment. Therefore we implement a descriptive set of kinematic features that give intuitive reason to the assessment of a fragment.

3. DESIGN CONCEPT: AAC

For the implementation of the IML method by consideration of the mentioned semantic demands we propose the concept of AAC for generalized activity assessment within body area networks as depicted in Fig. 2a. The AAC consists of a sequential flow of processes which are assigned to abstraction layers related to the hierarchical decomposition of motion performed by the human body, namely: *raw data layer*, *fragment layer*, *body part layer*, and *body layer*. The AAC contains processes known from AR which are marked with a grey background. We distribute the work load within the WBAN by processing the motion data of a certain body part concerning the first three layers directly on a node which is attached to the respective limb. On the last layer, the data computed on the nodes attached to multiple body parts are exchanged and fused to achieve the whole picture of the body movement.

Each abstraction layer contains processes of three data flows which accomplish different functions within the AAC: *recognition*, *reasoning*, and *assessment*.

Recognition. The recognition flow involves processes aiming for the basic identification of the trained activity and implements a typical ARC. On the raw data layer, the *segmentation* process recognizes biomechanically distinct motion segments within the processed raw data stream that contain information about a potential activity. Typically, before segmentation, the raw data passes a *filter* process to reduce noise and interfering information on the raw data signal. On the fragment layer, recognized segments are identified and labelled by the *fragment classification* process based on features extracted by a *feature extraction* process. On the body part movement layer in the resulting temporal sequence of classified motion fragments, a *sequential pattern mining* process identifies accomplished body part movements of the conducted activity. On the body layer, several concurrently identified body part movements are collected and combined by the *concurrent pattern mining* process to obtain the body movement in its entirety.

Reasoning. In a real-world setting not all parts of a continuous data stream are relevant for the trained activity, e.g. when disrupting the trained activity with other activities. To avoid diffusing assessments, the reasoning flow discards motion data which do not correspond to the trained activity and thus handles the problem of the other class on multiple layers. On each abstraction layer, a *delimitation* process verifies the decision of the preceding recognition process and thus determines which motion data will be handled by the subsequent *assessment* process and which motion data will be discarded. Depending on the algorithm utilized for recognition, the delimitation process can be included in the preceding recognition process.

Assessment. The assessment of biomechanically distinct motion fragments passing the delimitation process on the motion fragment layer ensures that the assessment can be intuitively connected to natural parts of movements of an activity (see fig. 2 b)). The fragment quality (QF) can be derived on the detailed evaluations (QX) of the features extracted by the feature extraction process. The quality of recognized body part movements (QP) as well as the body quality (QB) can be aggregated from the assessments of the respective previous abstraction layer. Assessments on the fragment layer contain temporal semantic as they are connected to successive motion fragments. Assessments on the body part layer contain spatial semantic by their assignment to body parts.

WBAN. The AAC is designed to run online and completely distributed within a WBAN. Hence we respect the limited resources of wearable wireless nodes: computational power, memory, and energy. With the abstraction of the raw data by feature extraction and numerical classification early at the fragment layer, memory needed for the expensive raw data buffering is bounded to the size of a single motion fragment. Additionally, the complexity of the data processing at higher abstraction layers is reduced to save computational power at subsequent processes of the AAC. Up to the body part layer, no data had to be exchanged between the nodes. For the body layer, only a few data characterizing body part movements are exchanged between nodes to support recognition, reasoning, and assessment (e.g. time stamp, duration, and quality). Thus we respect the energy consumption needed for costly wireless communication.

4. IMPLEMENTATION: AAC

As almost all movements of the human body are made possible by the joints and are mainly rotational, we focus on angular motion data gathered from a three-axis gyroscope. We apply a Butterworth low-pass filter of second order with a cutoff frequency of 3 Hz for the reduction of noise and interfering information within the angular motion signal. For segmentation, we stick with the biomechanic segmentation algorithm in [22] as previous results demonstrate that this approach reliably produces segments of angular raw data based on kinematics of human motion.

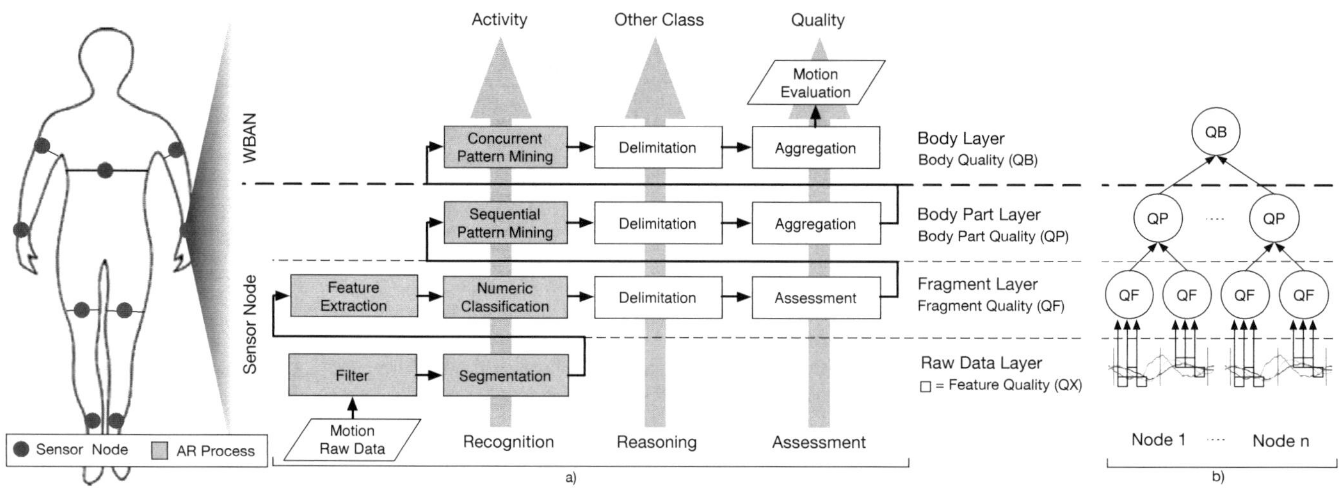

Figure 2: a) AAC b) Quality aggregation model

Fragment Layer. Within the feature extraction process on the fragment layer, we use four kinematic feature-types [21] applied separately to the three axis of the angular motion data obtained from the gyroscope. We measure *displacement* (DP), *maximum velocity* (MV), *average velocity* (AV), and *time-to-peak* (TTP). We compute DP straightforwardly by computing the integral from the angular velocity signal. It is worth mentioning that motion segments built by the utilized biomechanical segmentation algorithm in general comprise small data sequences of a few seconds. Thus, the error generated during integration is tolerable. By TTP we measure the time from the beginning of the motion fragment until the maximum of the velocity signal is reached and divide the value by the length of the motion fragment. In total, we compute a feature vector $x = (x_1, x_2, ..., x_n)$ composed of $n = 12$ feature values from the raw data of any motion segment.

For the classification of motion segments we implement a classical nearest prototype classifier [10] characterized by a set W of prototypes $w \in \mathbb{R}^n$, with w representing the feature vector and $c(w) \in \{1, ..., Z\}$ its assigned class label. The class of a feature vector x of a new segment is defined by Eq. 1.

$$c(x) := c(arg \min_{w \in W} \{d(w, x)\}) \tag{1}$$

We normalize x before classification and utilize the Euclidean distance measure as distance measure d. As in [22], we derive W by k-means cluster analysis of feature vectors extracted from motion fragments of movements that where performed while the training of the activity. The number of partitions k is provided by the number of motion fragments expected for a movement of the trained activity.

For delimitation we consider the minimum bounding hyper rectangle R_c^T covering the set V_c^T of feature vectors v, which represents all motion fragments observed during the training (T) for the classification $c(x)$, see Eq. 2.

$$R_c^T := \prod_{i=1}^{n} [v_{i\wedge}^{T,c}, v_{i\vee}^{T,c}] \; with \; \begin{cases} v_{i\wedge}^{T,c} := \min\limits_{v \in V_c^T} v_i \\ v_{i\vee}^{T,c} := \max\limits_{v \in V_c^T} v_i \end{cases} \tag{2}$$

The training contains only examples of the correctly performed activity. Hence we add a margin to the intervals of R_c^T so that motion fragments can pass the delimitation process even if they contain a limited error in their execution. This results in an extended (E) hyper rectangle R_c^E, see Eq. 3, $\delta > 0$.

$$R_c^E := \prod_{i=1}^{n} [v_{i\wedge}^{E,c}, v_{i\vee}^{E,c}] \; with \; \begin{cases} v_{i\wedge}^{E,c} := v_{i\wedge}^{T,c} - \delta * (\overline{v}_i^{T,c} - v_{i\wedge}^{T,c}) \\ v_{i\vee}^{E,c} := v_{i\vee}^{T,c} + \delta * (v_{i\vee}^{T,c} - \overline{v}_i^{T,c}) \\ \overline{v}_i^{T,c} = \operatorname{mean}\limits_{v \in V_c^T} v_i \end{cases} \tag{3}$$

We define that any feature vector x outside of R_c^E did not represent the classified motion fragment of the trained activity and belongs to the other class. Hence we relax the classification and reject x and the motion segment respectively. Any motion segment which passes the delimitation process is regarded as a fragment of a movement of the trained activity and assessed by focusing on the position of x in the decision space in detail. Depending on $c(x)$ we compute the quality q_c^X for each feature x_i by quantizing the error with a linear function crossing the value range between R_c^T and R_c^E, see Eq. 4, Fig. 3.

$$q_c^X(x_i) = \begin{cases} 1 - (v_{i\wedge}^{T,c} - x_i)/(v_{i\wedge}^{T,c} - v_{i\wedge}^{E,c}) & \text{if } x_i < v_{i\wedge}^{T,c} \\ 1 - (x_i - v_{i\vee}^{T,c})/(v_{i\vee}^{E,c} - v_{i\vee}^{T,c}) & \text{if } x_i > v_{i\vee}^{T,c} \\ 1 & \text{otherwise} \end{cases} \tag{4}$$

We determine the fragment quality q^F as the mean of the single feature qualities of x. The scaling parameter δ defines the tolerance of error accepted for the motion fragment layer as well as the value range for quality quantization.

Body Part Layer. On the body part layer in sequence recognized fragments are represented by $f = (c, t_s^F, t_e^F, q^F)$ where c represents the class label, t_s^F the start-time, t_e^F the end-time, and q^F the assigned fragment quality. The sequence of classifications is compared to a reference symbol sequence which represents the sequence of classifications determined for the trained activity at the dedicated body part

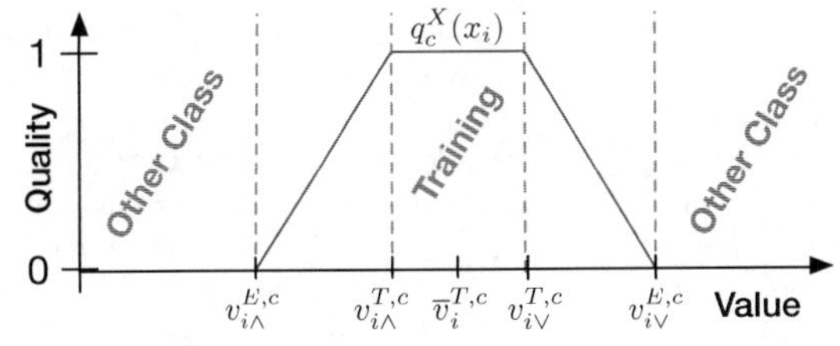

Figure 3: Quality Assessment Model

out of the training data, as in [22]. As distance measure we use the Levenshtein distance which is a well-known metric in AR [16, 17, 22]. If the measure is below a predefined threshold γ, a body part motion is recognized. A body part quality q^P is assigned by the mean of the qualities of the motion fragments which the body part motion consists of. Fragments which do not belong to any match are considered as motion of the other class and thus rejected.

Body Layer. On the body layer in parallel recognized body part movements of several nodes arrive, $m = (id, t_s^P, t_e^P, q^P)$, and are stored in a buffer M of size r, where r is determined by the number of nodes attached to the body, *id* is the node id, t_s^P the start time, and t_e^P the end time of the body part movement. For recognition of the overall body movement the relative temporal coverage $u(M)$ of buffered body part movements is determined by Eq. 5.

$$u(M) = (\min_{m \in M} t_e^P - \max_{m \in M} t_s^P)/(\max_{m \in M} t_e^P - \min_{m \in M} t_s^P) \quad (5)$$

Given a minimum coverage threshold p^T, a body movement is recognized if $u(M) \geq p^T$. p^T is defined by the minimum coverage determined for a movement of the training data $u_{min}^T * \epsilon, 0 < \epsilon \leq 1$. Incoming body part movements supersede the body part movement $m \in M$ which ends first. Body part motions which are not part of a recognized body movement are rejected. The body quality q^B for a recognized body movement is computed by the mean of the qualities of the respective body part movements.

The triple δ, γ, and ϵ controls the sensitivity of the reasoning flow of the AAC. A small δ, small γ, and big ϵ induce a sensitive delimitation on the abstractions layers closely to the trained activity. A bigger δ, bigger γ, and smaller ϵ induce more tolerance for error within the evaluated activity.

5. CASE STUDY: INDOOR ROWING

For evaluation, we chose the assessment of rowing activity on an indoor rowing machine. Rowing is a continuous motion comprising a sequence of strokes. The rowing cycle at an indoor rowing machine comprises two major phases: *drive* and *recovery*. Regarding this, two positions are relevant: *catch* and *finish*. The drive phase starts with the catch of the handle and is initiated with a push from the legs. After the legs are almost extended, the rower first begins to lean back and then the arms begin to draw the handle toward the body until the stroke is finished. The recovery phase begins at the finish and is initiated with the arms straightening followed by the trunk raising. If the arms are almost straight and the trunk reaches the upright position, the legs begin to flex until the shins are vertical and the catch position is reached again.

5.1 Setup

Driven by the needs of the application domain for distributed activity assessment within WBANs, we make use of the sensor board F4VI2 [26]. For the experiment we use the data of the three-axis gyroscope of the integrated nine degrees of freedom motion tracking device MPU9150 at a sampling frequency of 100Hz. For characterization of the rowing activity we use three F4VI2 nodes attached to the human body (see Fig. 4). We add one node to the right wrist (RW), one node to the upper back (UB), and one node to the upper right leg (RL). The rowing activity was performed on a concept 2® indoor rowing machine of type D. The nodes are synchronized by broadcast at the start-up sequence.

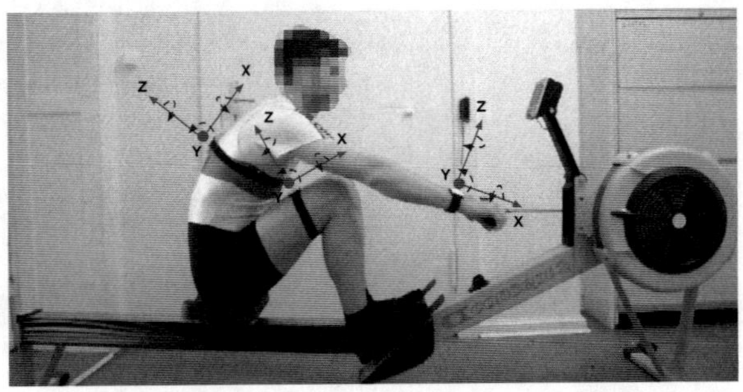

Figure 4: Setup and node placement

We record rowing activity of two rowing athletes $RA1$ and $RA2$ with several years of rowing experience. The rowing activity was supervised by an expert with more than ten years of rowing experience and documented by a video camera. All subjects are instructed by the expert to perform a continuous sequence of rowing activity in six different qualities C and $E1$-$E5$. C represents correctly performed rowing strokes while $E1$ to $E5$ include a certain technical error.

E1: At the finish the rower did not lean back far enough. The stroke did not reach the maximum power.
E2: The rower leaned back too far. The energy costs for leaning back too far are greater than the gain from rowing a longer stroke.
E3: The rower accelerated the handle too much at the finish. Instead of pulling the handle toward the body, he pulled himself forward toward the handle.
E4: The rower did not complete the pull of the handle toward the body and wasted a few centimeters of the stroke.
E5: The rower rushed down the slide during the recovery. He accelerated and wasted energy to stop the movement at the catch.

Every subject starts the rowing session with two sequences of 22 correctly performed strokes. Thereafter the subject performs five sequences of 22 technically incorrect strokes according to the quality classes $E1$-$E5$. In total, every subject performs 154 strokes. The recorded motion data contain periods of resting between rowing sequences as well as the period of attaching the nodes at the beginning of the session. In total, every rowing session resulted in a data set of about 17 minutes. We train the AAC for every subject separately on the first sequence of 22 correct performed strokes. We skip the first and the last stroke, as these are influenced by taking and putting back the handle respectively, and train the AAC on the remaining 20 strokes. Therefore we provide $k = 2$ equal to the number of phases of a rowing stroke: drive and recovery. For activity recognition and assessment, the rest of the session including 132 strokes is processed by the trained AAC. We provide $\delta = 50$, $\gamma = 0$, and $\epsilon = 0.6$, as this tolerance configuration recognizes correctly conducted as well as faulty strokes of the rowing activity while other motion is rejected very well.

5.2 Results

First we evaluate the recognition and delimitation flow of the AAC followed by focusing on the assessment of the rowing activity. In detail for RA1 and RA2 and all nodes together 2137 fragments are recognized on the fragment level. Through cooperation of the nodes, 31, 5% of these fragments are rejected on certain abstraction levels: 7, 7% on the fragment level, 13, 1% on body part level and 10, 7% on the body level. The AAC recognized 92, 4% of the 264 accomplished strokes on the body level. Every detected stroke belongs to a stroke sequence. The AAC missed 20 accomplished strokes as they differ too much from the trained strokes. Almost all belong to the start or the end of a stroke sequence. One stroke of RA2 within E5 could not be detected. The AAC is able to recognize correctly conducted strokes as well as faulty ones, while rejecting any motion belonging to the other class. These results constitute a very good recognition and delimitation accuracy and provide a strong basis for activity assessment.

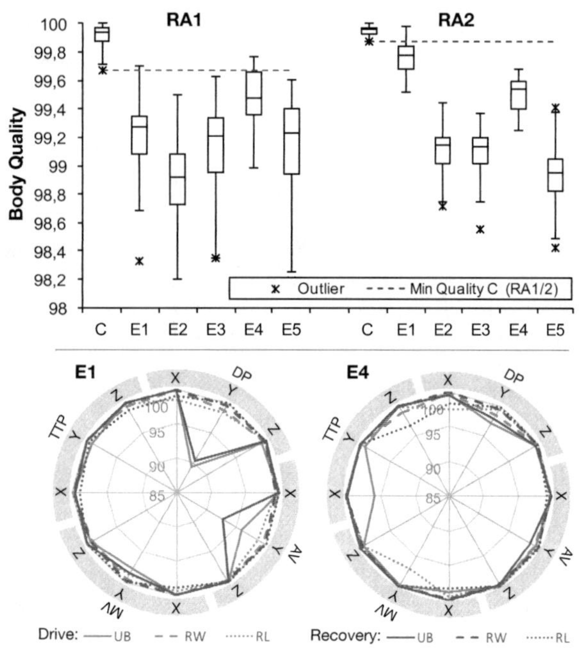

Figure 5: Body level assessment (top), detailed fragment level assessment (bottom)

Fig. 5 (top) depicts the final assessment of the 240 recognized rowing strokes on the body layer. The assessment shows a similar pattern of the ratings of the different quality classes of RA1 and RA2. As expected, the correctly performed strokes are rated with the highest quality and clearly stand out from the incorrectly performed strokes. 94, 5% of the incorrectly performed strokes are rated with a lower quality than the minimum quality reached by the respective correctly performed strokes. 6 strokes of E1 and 5 strokes of E4 are rated with a quality above the minimum quality of respective correctly performed strokes. The box plots for E1-E5 are comparatively tall, meaning a larger distribution of the assessments than for the correctly performed strokes.

The review of the video data, recorded while the rowing motion was carried out, states the distribution for E1-E5. Correct strokes are trained as usual for RA1 and RA2. Thus, rowing strokes at quality C at constant level is easier than the simulation of a certain technical error. In addition, the error in strokes of E1 and E4 includes only small deviations to strokes of respective quality C. The error of the back in E1 is estimated by the expert for RA2 in average to 6° and for RA1 in average to 14° compared to the back in the respective quality C. The error of the handle for RA1 in E4 amounts to $4cm$ in average to the respective quality C and thus causes only minimal deviations of the angular motion.

Furthermore we evaluate the temporal and spatial semantic in terms of which features of which motion fragment and which body part give reasons for the assessment. By reference to the aggregation model (Fig. 2b) we build 12-D spider plots for the visualization of the feature assessments. In Fig. 5 (bottom) the spider plots for E1 and E4 of RA1 are depicted. Therefore we compute the average of the feature assessments of E1 and E4 respectively. E1 is dominated by an error of DP-Y as well as AV-Y of the back within the drive and the recovery respectively. As E1 is defined by an angular error of the back at the finish and the rotation on the y-axis of UB correlates to the rotation of the back on the sagital plane of the human body, the assessment of E1 conducted by RA1 can be easily connected to the error description of E1. For E4, a correlation between the error description and the feature assessments is less evident. The worst rated features for E4 are TTP-X (95,9%) of UB followed by TTP-Z (96,8%) and MV-Y (97,0%) of RL. We expected to measure the worst error on RW because E4 is defined by an unfinished arm movement. The worst feature quality of RW is measured with DP-Y at the drive (98,6%).

The results of our case study demonstrate the practical value of the AAC as almost all strokes of the rowing activity are recognized, all motion of the other class is rejected and clear differentiation between rowing strokes in different qualities is possible. Furthermore, the AAC gives detailed insights concerning the reason of the activity assessment. For enough significant deviations of the conducted rowing activity from the trained activity, the AAC can provide a reasonable feedback which can be used to identify the cause of the error and improve the performance. The cause of error is not obvious for very small deviations.

6. CONCLUSION

In this paper we categorized the current solution space for quality quantification in AR. We found that most approaches are domain-specific and thus prevent re-use in different application scenarios. Hence we introduced and analyzed the concept of AAC, which is a generalized trainable activity assessment chain for distributed online evaluation of periodic activity within WBANs. Our activity assessment leverages the position of a characteristic set of kinematic features in the decision space to reject untrained motion and to achieve a fine-grained evaluation of distinct motion fragments. To include spatial and temporal semantics, AAC first decomposes the human motion and then aggregates multiple levels of the resulting hierarchical structure. Our case study shows that AAC can be applied with minor configuration effort to indoor rowing activity and is not only able to clearly distinguish rowing activity from other motion but also to provide a detailed reasonable assessment of rowing strokes in different qualities. Thus, an informational feedback to the user concerning the cause of the error becomes possible. In future work, we will compare AAC to additional scenarios. Furthermore, we will extend AAC by weighting feature assessments depending on the intensity of motion within the WBAN to work out the most relevant assessments.

7. REFERENCES

[1] R. Adelsberger and G. Troster. Experts lift differently: Classification of weight-lifting athletes. In *2013 IEEE International Conference on Body Sensor Networks (BSN)*, Cambridge, MA, USA, 2013.

[2] O. Banos, J.-M. Galvez, M. Damas, H. Pomares, and I. Rojas. Window Size Impact in Human Activity Recognition. *Sensors*, 14(4):6474–6499, 2014.

[3] G. Bleser, D. Steffen, M. Weber, G. Hendeby, D. Stricker, L. Fradet, F. Marin, N. Ville, and F. Carré. A personalized exercise trainer for the elderly. *Journal of ambient intelligence and smart environments*, 5(6):547–562, 2013.

[4] A. Bulling, U. Blanke, and B. Schiele. A tutorial on human activity recognition using body-worn inertial sensors. *ACM Comput. Surv. (CSUR)*, 46(3):33, 2014.

[5] A. I. Cuesta-Vargas, A. Galán-Mercant, and J. M. Williams. The use of inertial sensors system for human motion analysis. *Physical Therapy Reviews*, 15(6):462–473, 2010.

[6] A. I. Cuesta-Vargas and J. Williams. Inertial sensor real-time feedback enhances the learning of cervical spine manipulation: a prospective study. *BMC Medical Education*, 14:120, 2014.

[7] H. Ghasemzadeh, N. Amini, R. Saeedi, and M. Sarrafzadeh. Power-Aware Computing in Wearable Sensor Networks: An Optimal Feature Selection. *IEEE Transactions on Mobile Computing*, 14(4):800–812, 2015.

[8] H. Ghasemzadeh and R. Jafari. Coordination analysis of human movements with body sensor networks: A signal processing model to evaluate baseball swings. *IEEE Sensors Journal*, 11:603–610, 2011.

[9] H. Ghasemzadeh, V. Loseu, E. Guenterberg, and R. Jafari. Sport training using body sensor networks: A statistical approach to measure wrist rotation for golf swing. In *Fourth International Conference on Body Area Networks (BodyNets 09)*, 2009.

[10] A. B. Graf, O. Bousquet, G. Rätsch, and B. Schölkopf. Prototype classification: Insights from machine learning. *Neural computation*, 21(1):272–300, 2009.

[11] A. Khan, N. Hammerla, S. Mellor, and T. Plötz. Optimising sampling rates for accelerometer-based human activity recognition. *Pattern Recognition Letters*, 73:33–40, 2016.

[12] A. Khan, S. Mellor, E. Berlin, R. Thompson, R. McNaney, P. Olivier, and T. Plötz. Beyond activity recognition: skill assessment from accelerometer data. In *2015 ACM International Joint Conference on Pervasive and Ubiquitous Computing*, 2015.

[13] N. C. Krishnan and D. J. Cook. Activity recognition on streaming sensor data. *Pervasive and Mobile Computing*, 10:138–154, 2014.

[14] C. Ladha, N. Y. Hammerla, P. Olivier, and T. Plötz. ClimbAX: skill assessment for climbing enthusiasts. In *2013 ACM International Joint Conference on Pervasive and Ubiquitous Computing*, 2013.

[15] R. J. M. Lemmens, Y. J. M. Janssen-Potten, A. A. A. Timmermans, R. J. E. M. Smeets, and H. A. M. Seelen. Recognizing Complex Upper Extremity Activities Using Body Worn Sensors. *PLoS ONE*, 10(3):e0118642, 2015.

[16] L. Liu, Y. Peng, S. Wang, M. Liu, and Z. Huang. Complex activity recognition using time series pattern dictionary learned from ubiquitous sensors. *Information Sciences*, 340-341:41–57, 2016.

[17] Y. Liu, L. Nie, L. Liu, and D. S. Rosenblum. From action to activity: Sensor-based activity recognition. *Neurocomputing*, 181:108–115, 2016.

[18] R. Mooney, G. Corley, A. Godfrey, L. Quinlan, and G. ÓLaighin. Inertial sensor technology for elite swimming performance analysis: A aystematic review. *Sensors*, 16(1):18, 2015.

[19] L. T. Nguyen, M. Zeng, P. Tague, and J. Zhang. Recognizing new activities with limited training data. In *2015 ACM International Symposium on Wearable Computers*, 2015.

[20] D. Roggen, S. Magnenat, M. Waibel, and G. Tröster. Wearable Computing: Designing and Sharing Activity-Recognition Systems Across Platforms. *IEEE Robotics & Automation Magazine*, 18(2):83–95, 2011.

[21] D. J. Rose and R. W. Christina. *A multilevel approach to the study of motor control and learning.* Allyn and Bacon, Boston, 1997.

[22] M. Seiffert, N. Dziengel, M. Ziegert, R. Kerz, and J. Schiller. Towards motion characterization and assessment within a wireless body Area Network. In *8th International Conference on Internet and Distributed Computing Systems*, 2015.

[23] R. Thompson, I. Kyriazakis, A. Holden, P. Olivier, and T. Plötz. Dancing with horses: automated quality feedback for dressage riders. In *2015 ACM International Joint Conference on Pervasive and Ubiquitous Computing*, 2015.

[24] A. A. A. Timmermans, H. A. M. Seelen, R. P. J. Geers, P. K. Saini, S. Winter, J. te Vrugt, and H. Kingma. Sensor-Based Arm Skill Training in Chronic Stroke Patients: Results on Treatment Outcome, Patient Motivation, and System Usability. *IEEE Transactions on Neural Systems and Rehabilitation Engineering*, 18(3):284–292, 2010.

[25] A. Yurtman and B. Barshan. Automated evaluation of physical therapy exercises using multi-template dynamic time warping on wearable sensor signals. *Computer Methods and Programs in Biomedicine*, 117(2):189–207, 2014.

[26] M. Ziegert, N. Dziengel, M. Seiffert, S. Pfeiffer, and J. Schiller. A developer and a reference board for distributed motion evaluation in Wireless Sensor Networks. In *IEEE International Conference on Industrial Technology (ICIT '15)*, 2015.

Characteristics Comparison of Three Different WCE Implanted Antennas in UWB Low Band

Qiong Wang, Dirk Plettemeier
Chair for RF Engineering, Communication Laboratory
Dresden University of Technology, Dresden, Germany
+49 351 463-42387
qiong.wang@tu-dresden.de
dirk.plettemeier@tu-dresden.de

Carlos Andreu, Concepcion García-Pardo, Narcis Cardona
Institute of Telecommunications and Multimedia Applications (iTEAM)
Universitat Politècnica de València, Valencia, Spain
+34 963 877 007-88141
caranes@iteam.upv.es
cgpardo@iteam.upv.es
ncardona@iteam.upv.es

ABSTRACT

This paper proposes and compares three different kinds of implanted antenna designs operating in ultra-wide band (UWB) low band 3.1-4.8 GHz to meet the demand of deep implantation and larger bandwidth for medical wireless capsule endoscope (WCE) application. The proposed antennas can be accommodated in the capsule dome and are characterized by light weight, low profile, low cost, small size. Antenna characteristics are compared in terms of input impedance matching, impedance bandwidth, axial ratio, radiation power, front-to-back ratio, peak gain, as well as near-field E field. Measurement results will be shown in presentation also with different TX orientations and receiving antennas.

Keywords

Implanted antenna; dielectric resonator antenna (DRA); WCE; UWB.

1. INTRODUCTION

Wireless capsule endoscope (WCE) capsule can take pictures/videos and then transmit the real-time biological data from the inside of the gastrointestinal tract to exterior medical instruments. The current technical challenges for WCE communications lies in the demands of deep implantation and larger bandwidth for higher-resolution video transmission. RF frontend antennas of the TX/RX system play a critical role in the high performance of the high frequency and larger bandwidth for deep implantation communication. In the previous work, we have proposed a conformal trapezoid strip excited broadband hemispherical dielectric resonator antenna (DRA) design in ultra-wide band (UWB) low band 3.1-4.8 GHz [1]. In this paper, we propose other two designs for implanted WCE capsule and compare the antenna characteristics of all the three designs.

2. ANTENNA CHARACTERISTICS

Figure 1 summarizes the proposed three antenna types, which are all accommodated in half sphere of the capsule end with dimension 11x6mm. In UWB low band, the surrounding medium of the capsule antenna can be approximately determined as one homogeneous medium with average muscle tissue at 4GHz which has dielectric constant of 51.5 and average conductivity of 3.2 S/m [1]. Figure 2 shows the return loss comparison in average muscle tissue phantom. All of the three antennas can be tuned to have a good matching performance within UWB low band in spite of different impedance bandwidths.

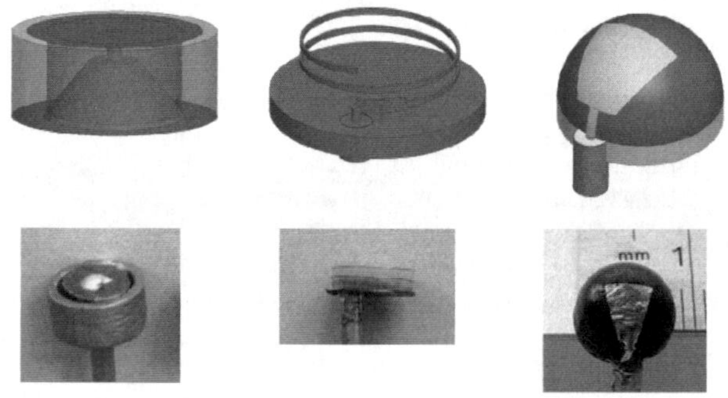

(a) discone (b) helix (c) DRA

Figure1. Three proposed antenna designs operating in UWB low band, (a) discone antenna with back cavity and shorting wall; (b) helix antenna with matching stub; (c) conformal trapezoid strip excited hemispherical DRA.

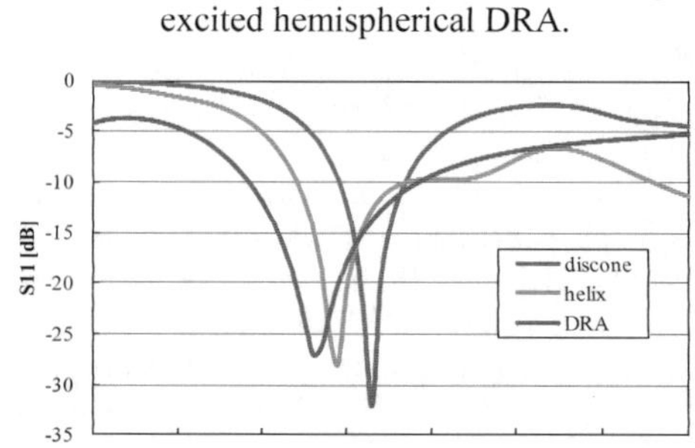

Figure 2. Comparison of the simulated return losses in tissue-simulating fluid phantom.

The conformal trapezoid strip excited broadband hemispherical DRA has been described in detail in [1]. The discone antenna can increase bandwidth with introduction of the back cavity and achieve good impedance matching with shorting wall between disc and cone. Figure 3 shows the impedance improvement and as expected [2] largely declined impedance of the implanted antenna has been enhanced and matched to 50 Ohm. The resonance frequency of the proposed discone antenna can be tuned easily via shorting wall position as well as the cone slope.

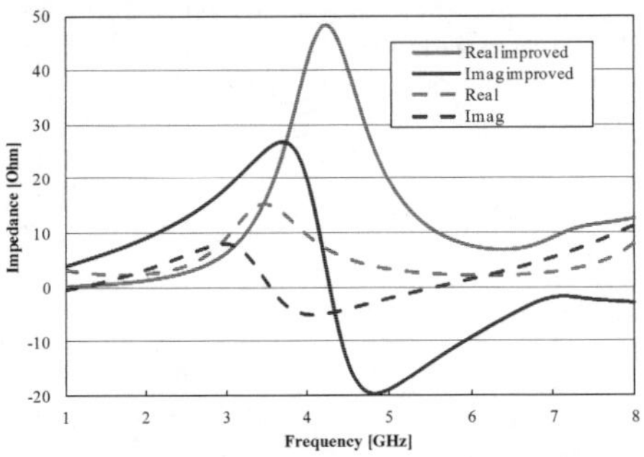

Figure 3. Impedance of discone antenna with back cavity; improved impedance matching with shorting wall.

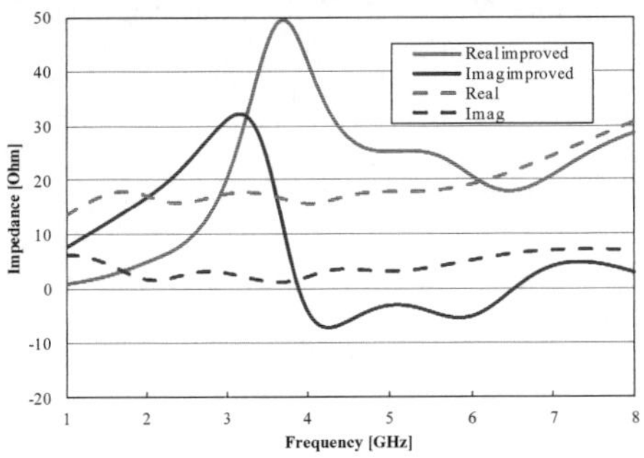

Figure 4. Impedance of helix antenna; improved impedance matching with short shunt stub and flattening feeding.

The proposed helix antenna operates in quasi-axial mode with fair cross-polarization ratio. The terminal impedance of a helix radiating in the axial mode in free space is nearly resistive with values 100–200 ohms. When the helix is implanted inside biological tissue, the impedance will be as expected largely reduced as shown in Figure 4 [2]. In order to provide a better matching inside biological tissue, a short stub between the first helix pitch and ground plane as well as a wider flat strip at the feeding start are employed. The improved impedances are shown in Figure 4, from around 20 ohm up to around 50 ohm. The resonance frequency of the helix antenna can be tuned easily changing the short stub distance from the coaxial transmission line as well as the feeding height.

Table 1 and Table 2 compare the far-field and near-field characteristics of the proposed three antennas respectively. DRA can cover the full UWB low band, nearly 3-5 GHz and bandwidth of the helix is 1.5 GHz, while discone has relatively narrow bandwidth, i.e., 0.8 GHz. Both DRA and discone antenna have relatively good linear polarization characteristics with high axial ratio. Helix antenna works in the axial mode and possesses elliptical polarization. The radiated power is integrated over a far-field sphere with 80 mm radius. In terms of the radiation ability, DRA exceeds helix and helix further exceeds discone. DRA explicitly shows higher power radiating outwards than the helix and discone antennas. This characteristic plays an important role in WCE

Table 1. Far-field characteristic comparison

	Discone	Helix	DRA
Bandwidth [GHz]	0.8	1.5	2.0
Axial ratio [dB]	50	6	48
Radiated power [dBW]	-88.8	-68.1	-59.1
Front-to-back ratio [dB]	2.33	3.9	6.2
Peak gain [dBi]	-79.6	-55.8	-49.3

Table 2. Near-field characteristic comparison

Max near field E field [V/m]	Discone	Helix	DRA
20mm Sphere	0.88	13.5	33.8
40mm Sphere	0.09	1.14	3.1

communications. On the other hand, obviously, due to the high lossy characteristics of the biological tissue in UWB, path loss is much larger than that in free space. That is why the radiated power seems relatively low. Front-to-back ratio can represent partly the directivity of the implanted antenna. DRA exceeds the other two in terms of the front-to-back ratio and transmitting power can be more directed. In fact, when the receiving antenna locates in the near-field region of the transmitting implanted antenna, the radiating/coupling front-to-back ration may be distance-dependent. About the gain at the maximum radiation direction, the peak gain of DRA also shows better performance than the other two antennas.

In the near-field comparisons, two near-field spheres with radius of 20 mm and 40 mm are set up to measure the maximum E field. The capsule antenna accommodation half sphere has a diameter around 11mm and the effective wavelength at 4 GHz inside biological torso tissue is around 10 mm. Therefore 20 mm and 40 mm sphere can be approximately regarded in near-field region of the implanted antenna in ideal case (with ideal transmitting source and same-aperture receiving antenna). The maximal near-field coupled E field of DRA is still higher than helix and discone.

In words, DRA can have good impedance bandwidth, good linear polarization, high radiated power and good directivity compared with the other two proposed helix and discone. In terms of communication with wearable receiving antenna, if the transmitting implanted antenna with strong linearized directivity, the wearable receiving antenna array will undertake more performance responsibilities, since the transmitting implanted antenna will randomly move inside the gastrointestinal tract. However, on the other hand, strong radiating/coupling capability will lead a dominant role rather than the other characteristics, such as circular polarization or omni-directional radiation characteristics.

3. ACKNOWLEDGMENTS

This research is supported by "WiBEC" (Wireless In-Body Environment) project which has received funding from the European Union's Horizon 2020 research and innovation programme under grant agreement No 675353.

4. REFERENCES

[1] Wang Q., Wolf K., and Plettemeier D. 2010. An UWB capsule endoscope antenna design for biomedical communications. In 3rd International Symposium on Applied Sciences in Biomedical and Communication Technologies (Rome, Italy, November 07-10, 2010), ISABEL.

[2] Fenwick R. and Weeks W. 1963. Sumberged antenna characteristics. IEEE Transactions on Antennas and Propagation Volume: 11, Issue: 3 Pages: 296 - 305, DOI: 10.1109/TAP.1963.1138035.

The identification of multiple U-turns in gait: comparison of four trunk IMU-based methods

M. Bertoli[1,2], A. Cereatti[1,3], D. Trojaniello[1,4], A. Ravaschio[5], U. Della Croce[1]
1 POLCOMING Department, University of Sassari, Sassari, Italy
2 DIAG Department, University of Rome "La Sapienza", Rome, Italy
3 DET Department, Polytechnic University of Turin, Turin, Italy
4 e-Services for Life and Health, San Raffaele Scientific Institute, Milan, Italy
5 DINOGM Department, University of Genoa, Genoa, Italy

mbertoli@uniss.it

ABSTRACT
The identification of turns during walking allows for the segmentation into straight and turn walking bouts. Several IMU-based methods were developed to this purpose, however many of them were tested on specific subject population. In this study, we tested four methods for the identification of turns in walking tasks with multiple U-turns that did not exploit any *a-priori* knowledge of the turn occurrences. We evaluated their robustness by recording IMU data on healthy and pathological subjects (healthy elderly, stroke survivors, patients with Parkinson disease and choreic patients) walking at two different speeds along a closed loop formed by straight bouts and U-turns. Overall, all methods identified correctly the totality of the U-turns when elderly and Parkinsonian patients were analyzed. When stroke survivors and choreic patients were analyzed, U-turns were either missed or erroneously detected in a limited number of cases. The only method using the magnetometer signals was the best performing, highlighting the usefulness of the magnetometer when turns are being investigated.

CCS Concepts
•General and reference~Measurement
•General and reference~Validation
•Hardware~Microelectromechanical systems

Keywords
Walking; Gait analysis; U-Turn; Inertial sensors; Gyroscopes; Accelerometers; Monitoring.

1. INTRODUCTION
Gait analysis is used in clinical contexts to quantitatively assess individuals with conditions affecting their ability to walk, with the goal of limiting motor impairments or rehabilitating from traumatic events [4]. Measurements are usually carried out using either stereo-photogrammetric systems or inertial measurement units (IMUs). As opposed to vision-based systems, wearable IMUs allow for the low-cost analysis of gait in both ambulatory and unsupervised settings.

SAMPLE: Permission to make digital or hard copies of all or part of this work for personal or classroom use is granted without fee provided that copies are not made or distributed for profit or commercial advantage and that copies bear this notice and the full citation on the first page. To copy otherwise, or republish, to post on servers or to redistribute to lists, requires prior specific permission and/or a fee.
Conference'10, Month 1–2, 2010, City, State, Country.
Copyright 2010 ACM 1-58113-000-0/00/0010 ...$15.00.
DOI: http://dx.doi.org/10.1145/12345.67890

Traditionally, gait analysis focuses on the study of straight walking. As a result, protocols and definitions for the estimate of spatio-temporal parameters (step and stride duration and length, etc.) are clearly defined and widely accepted when the analysis is carried out on bouts of straight walking [20]. However, the mentioned parameters lack of a standardized definition in some variants of gait such as those including stairs and/or turns [10].

Numerous clinical motor tests may include one or more turns between straight gait segments, either due to space constraints or to analyze the subject's motor ability under more challenging tasks. In fact, it has been observed that in pathologic subjects turning can pose more difficulties in goal-directed locomotion. For instance, functional turning is a common problem in people with Parkinson's disease (PD), who take more steps to turn than those without PD [12]. Similarly, hemiparetic post-stroke subjects tend to struggle with sensory and neuromotor organization and so with controlling movement: it has been demonstrated a relationships between physical impairments, locomotor capacities and frontal plane gait parameters [3].

Such difficulties can be revealed by a widely used clinical test: the Time-Up-and-Go (TUG), where a 180 degrees turn (U-turn) is expected approximately in the middle of the trial followed by a second one toward the end. U-turns were therefore chosen to be studied in this work, since they are commonly employed in such clinical examinations [5, 9, 16, 18, 22].

The correct U-turn identification is the primary step to segment a walking trial. The gait bout can thus be segmented into straight walks and turns, so that the standard gait parameters can be computed from the isolated portions of straight walk, and peculiar traits of the U-turns can be described.

Identifying turns during walking is of great interest also in remote monitoring applications aiming at describing activities during daily life, including straight walking and turns.

In the literature, two main approaches have been employed to identify and analyze turns in gait. One consists in segmenting the gait into steps, defining a direction of progression (DoP) for each step, and identifying as turns those steps whose DoP shows an angle with the previous one [11]. This methodology is mostly used in pedestrian navigation applications [1, 2]. The second approach identifies a turn from the analysis of the IMU signals characteristics, and works independently from step detection [6, 8, 13, 14].

The objective of the present study is to perform a comparative evaluation of four automated methods to be used in a clinical context during a walking trial to identify U-turns. The algorithms were designed to segment a gait bout into straights and turns without the preliminary determination of the gait cycles. Furthermore, the selected methods distinguish multiple U-turns without the a-priori knowledge of their number and timing in the walking bout, contrary to others [7, 17, 22].

The selected methods have shown satisfactory performance when applied to the specific pathological populations, however their applicability over a variety of different pathological gait conditions or different gait speeds has not been systematically explored.

2. MATERIALS AND METHODS

2.1 Experimental Setup

2.1.1 Instrumentation

Data were recorded by an IMU (Opal™, APDM, Inc,) positioned on the low back between L4 and S2 [19]. The performance of the IMU was tested according to the guidelines proposed by [15]. The IMU recorded linear accelerations, angular velocities and local magnetic field with respect to the axes of a local frame (LF: xyz, z pointing upwards) aligned to the edges of the unit housing. The IMU was positioned so that its reference axes were oriented approximately along the three anatomical directions. An estimate of the LF orientation with respect to the global frame (GF: XYZ, Z coinciding with the gravity direction) was provided by an on-board Kalman filter. The signals from the IMU were recorded at 128 Hz, streamed wirelessly to a laptop and stored for offline analysis. A gait pressure mat (GAITRite Electronic Walkway, CIR System Inc) acquiring at 120 Hz was used for validation purposes. The instrumented mat returned the timing of all foot contacts, in particular initial and final ones for every passage on it. The IMU and the instrumented mat were synchronized (±1 sample).

2.1.2 Subjects

Ten healthy elderly (ELD), ten PD subjects, ten stroke survivors (ST) and ten subjects with a choreic movement disorder (COR) were enrolled. Their sex and range age were 6F(4M), 61÷79 ELD; 5F(4M), 68÷79 PD; 2F(8M), 38÷76 ST; 5F(5M), 29÷79 COR. The ST group was equally divided into subjects with left or right most affected side. The Declaration of Helsinki was respected, all subjects provided informed written consent, and local ethic committee approval was obtained.

Table 1. Total number of actual U-turns analyzed

	ELD	PD	ST	COR
NW	48	41	30	47
FW	63	49	38	72

Figure 1. Experimental setup

2.1.3 Data acquisition Protocol

Subjects were asked to walk along a pre-designed loop made of two U-turns, as depicted in Figure 1. At the beginning of each acquisition, subjects were asked to stand still for a few seconds. Subjects wore their own shoes, and walking aids such as canes or tripods were allowed if used routinely. Subjects could rest in between acquisitions if requested.

Two gait conditions were recorded for each subject: self-selected, comfortable velocity (Normal Walk, NW) and higher velocity (Fast Walk, FW). Each data acquisition lasted about one minute. The total number of U-turns performed for each group for both walking speeds is reported in Table 1.

2.2 Methods Description

2.2.1 Method A

In the work of El-Gohary and colleagues, data were collected by an IMU positioned on the lumbar spine of 19 healthy subjects and 21 patients with PD [6]. As a first step, exploiting orientation estimates in the quaternion form, body frame sensor measurements were expressed in the GF. Angular velocity vertical component ωz was extracted and low pass filtered (Butterworth, 1.5 Hz cutoff frequency). Candidate turns were isolated for each ωz maximum higher than 15°/s, and their duration was set based on 5°/s threshold. Additional controls were performed to reduce false positives. First of all, candidate turns in the same direction separated by less than 50ms were merged. Then, turns lasting less than 0.5s or more than 10s were discarded. Finally, the relative turn angle was computed integrating ωz over the turn duration and, when resulting less than 45°, lead to the turn elimination. The remaining ones were detected as U-turns.

2.2.2 Method B

In the work of Nguyen and colleagues, data were collected from 16 ELD by IMUs mounted on a motion capture suit [13]. Among other sensors locations, they determined that the IMU on the back was the best suited for identifying turns. A band pass filter was first applied to the raw z-component of the angular velocity (zero-phase, second-order Butterworth filter, low and high cut off frequencies set at 0.0025 Hz and 0.7 Hz, respectively). The filtered signal was then de-trended and normalized for uniformity across subjects. A U-turn was detected for each peak higher than 0.6 (absolute value), as shown in Figure 2. In addition, in our implementation when the time distance between two or more peaks was less than four

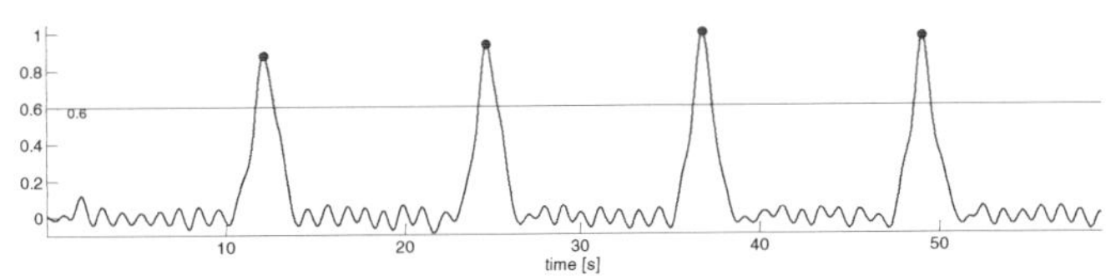

seconds, they were associated to a single turn.

Figure 2. Filtered, normalized angular velocity. Each red dot represents a detected U-turn

2.2.3 Method C

In the work of Novak and colleagues, data were collected by nine IMUs placed on the entire body of ten healthy subjects and one above-knee amputee [14]. Comparing different sensor locations, they found that using a sensor on the back yields the best results. Their work is based upon previous research by Mariani et al. and El-Gohary et al. ([6, 11]), and it combines the analysis of the orientation around the Z axis (Kalman filter output, angular displacement) and of the angular velocity (raw gyroscope output, ω_z). The U-turn is detected by optimizing parameters of empirically-defined rules. Orientation angles were derived directly from the quaternions (estimated by the sensor through the Kalman filter). In our implementation, the Z-angular displacement was then filtered (zero-phase, second-order Butterworth filter with high cut-off frequency set at 1 Hz) and smoothed by means of mobile average windows two seconds long. The ω_z was also filtered (zero-phase, second-order Butterworth filter, 1.5 Hz high cut-off frequency). A U-turn is detected when a heuristically determined threshold is exceeded in the Z-angular displacement (90° in 3 s), or in the ω_z (45°/s).

2.2.4 Method D

In the work of Fleury and colleagues, data were collected by a tri-axial magnetometer located on the upper trunk of eight healthy subjects [8]. They pre-processed the raw signal filtering in the bandwidth [0.5Hz; 2Hz] with a three order bandstop digital filter, and then low-pass filtering with a 4Hz cutoff frequency. "Activity windows" were then defined using the standard deviation computed on 2s windows. The turn was identified by measuring the change of the local magnetic field as measured in the magnetometer LF (plane xy). The Euclidean norm of the difference of the local magnetic field vector measured in two instants (2s apart) of the gait trial was computed over the entire signal. A U-turn is detected for each peak in the norm higher than empirically-fixed threshold.

2.3 Data Analysis

To facilitate the comparison between methods and avoid misinterpretation, those gait trials ending while the subject was performing a turn were truncated in order to eliminate the last turn.

2.3.1 Number of Missed and Extra U-turns

The number of actual U-turns was provided by the mat. The number of U-turns detected was determined for each tested method. From actual and detected U-turns, missed U-turns and extra U-turns could be determined for each tested method, group and walking speed [21].

3. RESULTS

All four methods showed neither extra nor missed U-turns in the ELD and PD groups at both speeds.

Method A was the only method to detect two extra U-turns in the NW trials of the COR group, and one in the FW.

Method B showed no missed U-turns in the NW trials for all groups. For the FW trials, one and two missed U-turns were observed in the ST and COR groups, respectively.

Method C missed only a single U-turn in the NW trials of ST group.

Method D showed neither extra nor missed U-turns.

4. DISCUSSION

The aim of the present study was to test different methods for the identification of U-turns on various pathological groups walking at different speeds. In the original works, all the tested methods, except for method A, were applied and tested on the gait of healthy subjects.

When applied to the ELD group, none of the methods missed any U-turns or detected any extra ones, thus confirming their adequacy as long as physiological gait is analyzed. Interestingly, the same consideration applies to the PD group.

The results obtained indicate that the tested methods are more likely to fail when applied to the gait of stroke survivors and the choreic subjects, which is characterized by irregular walking patterns.

Method A only failed when applied to the gait of choreic subjects (three extra U-turns out of 109 total actual U-turns), probably due to the increased variability of the gyroscopic signals associated to the jerky nature of choreic motion.

Method B missed a few U-turns at fast walking speed, probably because the thresholds, defined on the normalized signal recorded at comfortable speed, resulted to be too high (scaled peaks below threshold were missed).

Methods C and D were the best performing on our dataset. Method C may take advantage of the combined analysis of the angular velocity and orientation angle, possibly reducing the probability of detecting extra U-turns.

Method D is the only one based on magnetometer signals, and it appeared to be extremely robust with respect to the location of the IMU. In fact, while its original version requires the IMU to be placed on the upper chest, we obtained excellent results from signals recorded by an IMU placed on the lower back. A limitation of this method though is the intrinsic low reliability of the magnetometer due to possible ferromagnetic disturbances.

Additional work will be necessary to test methods that identify and characterize turns other than 180 degrees. In fact, the use of the magnetometer might not be as successful as it was shown for U-turns identification.

In this study, we have shown that a single IMU located on the low back can better identify U-turns. However, as shown by [20], gait events and all the derived spatio-temporal parameters can be best detected with IMUs attached to the lower limbs. As a consequence, three IMU configuration (two IMUs on the lower limbs and one on the lower back) may effectively describe crucial features of both straights and turns in both healthy and pathological gait at different walking speeds.

5. REFERENCES

[1] Alvarez, J.C., Alvarez, D., López, A. and González, R.C. 2012. Pedestrian Navigation Based on a Waist-Worn Inertial Sensor. *Sensors*. (2012), 10536–10549.

[2] Bebek, Ö., Suster, M.A., Rajgopal, S., Fu, M.J., Huang, X., Cavusoglu, M.C., Young, D.J., Mehregany, M., van den Bogert, A.J. and Mastrangelo, C.H. 2010. Personal Navigation via High-Resolution Gait-Corrected Inertial Measurement Units. *IEEE Transactions on Instrumentation and Measurement*. 59, 11 (Nov. 2010), 3018–3027.

[3] De Bujanda, E., Nadeau, S., Bourbonnais, D. and Dickstein, R. 2003. Associations between lower limb impairments, locomotor capacities and kinematic variables in the frontal plane during walking in adults with chronic stroke. *Journal of Rehabilitation Medicine*. 35, 6 (2003), 259–264.

[4] Cappozzo, A. 1984. Gait analysis methodology. *Human Movement Science*. 3, 1–2 (Mar. 1984), 27–50.

[5] Coulthard, J.T., Treen, T.T., Oates, A.R. and Lanovaz, J.L. 2015. Evaluation of an inertial sensor system for analysis of timed-up-and-go under dual-task demands. *Gait and Posture*. 41, 4 (2015), 882–887.

[6] El-Gohary, M., Pearson, S., McNames, J., Mancini, M.,

Horak, F., Mellone, S. and Chiari, L. 2013. Continuous Monitoring of Turning in Patients with Movement Disability. *Sensors*. 14, 1 (Dec. 2013), 356–369.

[7] Fino, P.C., Frames, C.W. and Lockhart, T.E. 2015. Classifying step and spin turns using wireless gyroscopes and implications for fall risk assessments. *Sensors (Switzerland)*. 15, 5 (2015), 10676–10685.

[8] Fleury, A., Noury, N. and Vuillerme, N. 2007. A fast algorithm to track changes of direction of a person using magnetometers. *Annual International Conference of the IEEE Engineering in Medicine and Biology - Proceedings*. (2007), 2311–2314.

[9] Higashi, Y., Yamakoshi, K., Fujimoto, T., Sekine, M. and Tamura, T. 2008. Quantitative evaluation of movement using the timed up-and-go test. *IEEE Engineering in Medicine and Biology Magazine*. 27, 4 (Jul. 2008), 38–46.

[10] Huxham, F., Gong, J., Baker, R., Morris, M. and Iansek, R. 2006. Defining spatial parameters for non-linear walking. *Gait & Posture*. 23, 2 (Feb. 2006), 159–163.

[11] Mariani, B., Hoskovec, C., Rochat, S., Büla, C., Penders, J. and Aminian, K. 2010. 3D gait assessment in young and elderly subjects using foot-worn inertial sensors. *Journal of Biomechanics*. 43, 15 (Nov. 2010), 2999–3006.

[12] Morris, M.E., Huxham, F., McGinley, J., Dodd, K. and Iansek, R. 2001. The biomechanics and motor control of gait in Parkinson disease. *Clinical Biomechanics*.

[13] Nguyen, H.P., Ayachi, F., Lavigne–Pelletier, C., Blamoutier, M., Rahimi, F., Boissy, P., Jog, M. and Duval, C. 2015. Auto detection and segmentation of physical activities during a Timed-Up-and-Go (TUG) task in healthy older adults using multiple inertial sensors. *Journal of NeuroEngineering and Rehabilitation*. 12, 1 (Dec. 2015), 36.

[14] Novak, D., Goršič, M., Podobnik, J. and Munih, M. 2014. Toward Real-Time Automated Detection of Turns during Gait Using Wearable Inertial Measurement Units. *Sensors*. 14, 10 (Oct. 2014), 18800–18822.

[15] Picerno, P., Cereatti, A. and Cappozzo, A. 2011. Gait & Posture A spot check for assessing static orientation consistency of inertial and magnetic sensing units. *Gait & Posture*. 33, 3 (2011), 373–378.

[16] Salarian, A., Horak, F.B., Zampieri, C., Carlson-Kuhta, P., Nutt, J.G. and Aminian, K. 2010. iTUG, a Sensitive and Reliable Measure of Mobility. *IEEE Transactions on Neural Systems and Rehabilitation Engineering*. 18, 3 (Jun. 2010), 303–310.

[17] Salarian, A., Zampieri, C., Horak, F.B., Carlson-Kuhta, P., Nutt, J.G. and Aminian, K. 2009. Analyzing 180° turns using an inertial system reveals early signs of progression of parkinson's disease. *2009 Annual International Conference of the IEEE Engineering in Medicine and Biology Society* (Sep. 2009), 224–227.

[18] Smith, E., Walsh, L., Doyle, J., Greene, B. and Blake, C. 2016. The reliability of the quantitative timed up and go test (QTUG) measured over five consecutive days under single and dual-task conditions in community dwelling older adults. *Gait and Posture*. 43, (2016), 239–244.

[19] Trojaniello, D., Cereatti, A. and Della Croce, U. 2014. Accuracy, sensitivity and robustness of five different methods for the estimation of gait temporal parameters using a single inertial sensor mounted on the lower trunk. *Gait & Posture*. 40, 4 (Sep. 2014), 487–492.

[20] Trojaniello, D., Cereatti, A., Pelosin, E., Avanzino, L., Mirelman, A., Hausdorff, J.M. and Della Croce, U. 2014. Estimation of step-by-step spatio-temporal parameters of normal and impaired gait using shank-mounted magneto-inertial sensors: application to elderly, hemiparetic, parkinsonian and choreic gait. *Journal of NeuroEngineering and Rehabilitation*. 11, 1 (2014), 152.

[21] Trojaniello, D., Ravaschio, A., Hausdorff, J.M. and Cereatti, A. 2015. Gait & Posture Comparative assessment of different methods for the estimation of gait temporal parameters using a single inertial sensor : application to elderly , post-stroke , Parkinson ' s disease and Huntington ' s disease subjects. *Gait & Posture*. (2015).

[22] Weiss, A., Herman, T., Plotnik, M., Brozgol, M., Giladi, N. and Hausdorff, J.M. 2011. An instrumented timed up and go: the added value of an accelerometer for identifying fall risk in idiopathic fallers. *Physiological Measurement*. 32, 12 (2011), 2003–2018.

Analytical Modelling of Near-Field Coupling Communication between Persons Equipped with Wearable Terminals through Handshaking

Ryo Takeuchi
Kyoto Institute of Technology
Matsugasaki Sakyo - ku
Kyoto, Japan

Shin Hasegwa
Kyoto Institute of Technology
Matsugasaki Sakyo - ku
Kyoto, Japan

Yuichi Kado
Kyoto Institute of Technology
Matsugasaki Sakyo - ku
Kyoto, Japan
kado@kit.ac.jp

Daiki Ayuzawa
Hosei University
3-7-2, Kajino-cho, Koganei-shi
Tokyo, Japan

Mitsuru Shinagawa
Hosei University
3-7-2, Kajino-cho, Koganei-shi
Tokyo, Japan
m.shina@hosei.ac.jp

Kyoji Ohashi
Nippon Signal Company
11-2, Hiraidekogyodanchi
Utsunomiya-shi, Tochigi, Japan

Daisuke Saito
Nippon Signal Company
11-2, Hiraidekogyodanchi
Utsunomiya-shi, Tochigi, Japan

ABSTRACT
Near-field coupling communication (NFCC) is a communication technology that treats the surface of the human body as a transmission path using a carrier frequency below 10 MHz. Because the radiation signal to a space is suppressed in NFCC, humans wearing an NFCC transceiver (TRX) can exchange personal information through handshaking without having to worry about information leakage. This work examines the mechanism of communication between wearable transceivers by NFCC through handshaking and the requirements for stable handshaking communication. The establishment of handshaking communication requires the signal propagation loss in the handshaking posture to be at least 10 dB smaller than in the standing posture. Signal propagation losses in the standing and handshaking postures were measured with an electrically isolated probe when TRXs were attached to the front of two human bodies standing face to face 600 mm apart. We investigated a simulation model of handshaking communication using a phantom we developed instead of a real human body by electromagnetic simulation and circuit simulation. On the basis of the simulation results, we proposed the signal propagation path for the realization of handshaking communication. When wearable TRXs are inserted into the soles of shoes, the signal propagation path is satisfied. In this case, we experimentally confirmed that the signal propagation loss in handshaking is smaller than that in the standing posture by 10.6dB.

Categories and Subject Descriptors
B.4.1 [**INPUT/OUTPUT AND DATA COMMUNICATIONS**]: Data Communications Devices – *Receivers, Transmitters.*
B.4.2 [**INPUT/OUTPUT AND DATA COMMUNICATIONS**]: Input / Output Devices -*Channels and controllers*

General Terms
Measurement, Design, Reliability, Experimentation, Security, Human Factors, Standardization

Keywords
Near-field coupling communication (NFCC), Electrically isolated measurement, Human equivalent phantom, Signal propagation loss, Electrical-to-optical and optical-to-electrical measurement (E/O and O/E measurement).

1. INTRODUCTION
Near-field coupling communication (NFCC) is a communication technology that uses the surface of the human body as a transmission path since the signal loss propagating through the conductor surface is less than the signal loss propagating through the space by using a carrier frequency below 10 MHz [1]. The main advantages of NFCC are the short radial distance and the establishment of a "touch and connect" intuitive form of communication. Figure 1 shows examples of NFCC application. A person can walk through a ticket gate without bringing out a card device, and two persons can exchange electronic business cards by handshaking. They are wearing NFCC devices that can exchange personal information through handshaking without any concern for leakage of information. Communication by handshaking with TRX installed on the soles of shoes has been reported [2]. However, the mechanism and requirements to establish stable communication by NFCC though handshaking have not yet been clarified. This work examines the feasibility of communication between wearable transceivers by NFCC through handshaking. We call such communication "handshaking

communication". Signal propagation losses in the standing posture and handshaking posture were measured with an electrically isolated probe when TRXs were attached to the front of two human bodies facing each other. We investigated the simulation model of handshaking communication using our developed phantom instead of a real human body by electromagnetic simulation and circuit simulation. On the basis of experimental and simulated results, we came up with the signal propagation path for the establishment of handshaking communication.

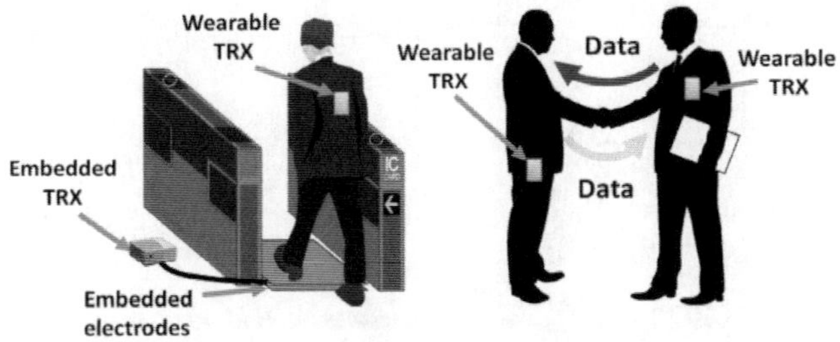

Figure 1. Hands-free ticket gate and handshaking communication systems using near-field coupling communication technology.

2. REQUIREMENTS FOR REALIZATION OF HANDSHAKING COMMUNICATION

Figure 2 shows a photograph of prototype TRX that we developed [3]. For realization of handshaking communication, signal propagation loss in the handshaking posture needs to be smaller than that in standing posture as shown in the Fig. 3. We need to consider the manufacturing variation of about 2 dB in TRX performance and the propagation loss variation of about 2 dB depending on human shape when we investigate the requirements for realization of handshaking communication. Since handshaking communication consist of two persons and two TRXs, we need to take into account the margin of 2 dB for the worst case when the performance variation between two TRXs is 4 dB (2 dB × 2 TRXs) and the signal propagation loss variation regarding the human factor is 4 dB (2 dB × 2 persons). Therefore, we set the first requirement as a value of 10 dB (the margin of 2 dB + 4 dB + 4 dB) for the signal propagation difference between standing and handshaking posture. Furthermore, we set the second requirement as a 20 dB or higher S/N ratio for the communication system in the handshaking posture when handshaking communication uses the prototype TRX that we developed. In this paper, we discussed first requirement.

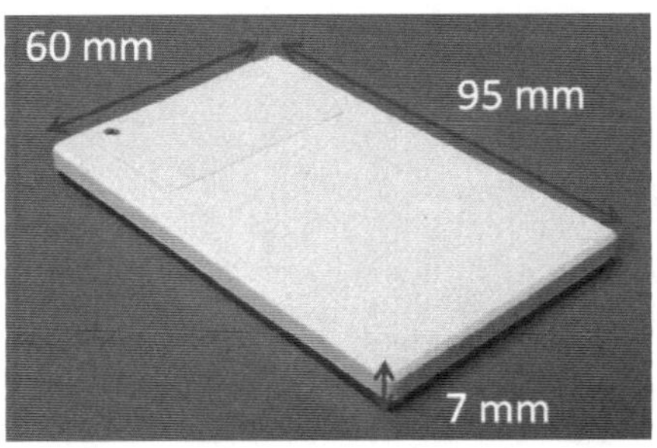

Figure 2. Photograph of prototype TRX.

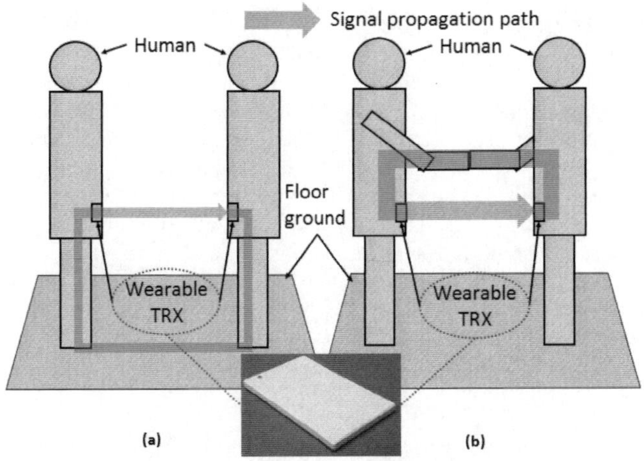

Figure 3. Signal propagation path in (a) standing posture and (b) handshaking posture.

3. MEASUREMENT TOOL

3.1 Battery-powered Transmitter

We developed a battery-powered transmitter (TX) to reduce the signal propagation path enhancement by electrically connecting to a signal generator [4, 5]. The battery-powered TX includes a direct digital synthesizer (DDS) oscillator. It generates a sinusoidal wave. Figure 4 (a), (b), and (c) shows the internal circuits, a block diagram of the TX, and the external shape. To eliminate the effect of voltage drop in a lithium ion battery, we connected the battery to a regulator. The frequency of the sinusoidal wave can be modified from 50 Hz to 20 MHz in 1 Hz increments. The dimensions of the TX were 85 × 62 × 10 mm. The electrodes in the TX were 70 × 50 mm each. The signal voltage of the TX changes from 1 to 2 $V_{p\text{-}p}$ when changing its frequency. The output impedance was 50 Ω.

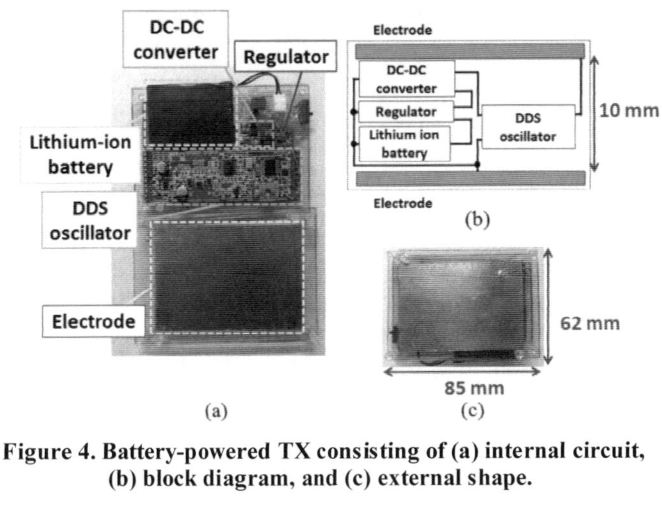

Figure 4. Battery-powered TX consisting of (a) internal circuit, (b) block diagram, and (c) external shape.

3.2 E/O-O/E Probe

Figure 5 (a) shows a photograph of the E/O-O/E probe. The probe has E/O and O/E conversion functions. A block diagram of the E/O probe is shown in Fig. 5 (b). The E/O converter consists of an E/O amplifier, peaking circuit, coupling capacitor, current source, and laser diode. The O/E converter consists of an O/E amplifier, peaking circuit, load resistor, and photodiode. The E/O converter receives the electrical signal, the E/O circuit converts the electrical signal into an optical signal, and the O/E circuit reconverts the optical signal into an electrical signal. These circuits enable the E/O converter to be electrically isolated from the measuring instrument. The circuit gain of the E/O-O/E probe is 71 dB at 6.75 MHz [6, 7].

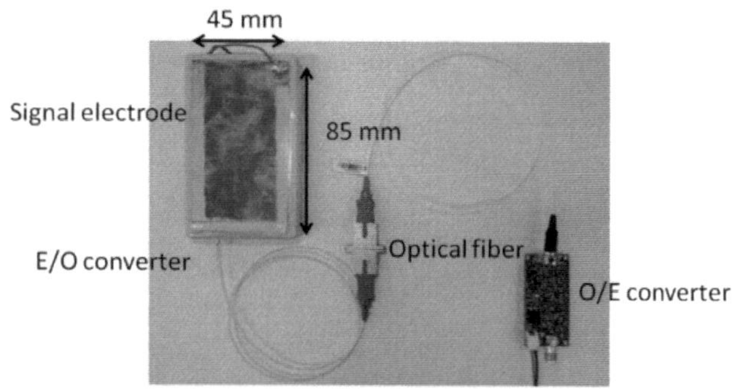

(a)

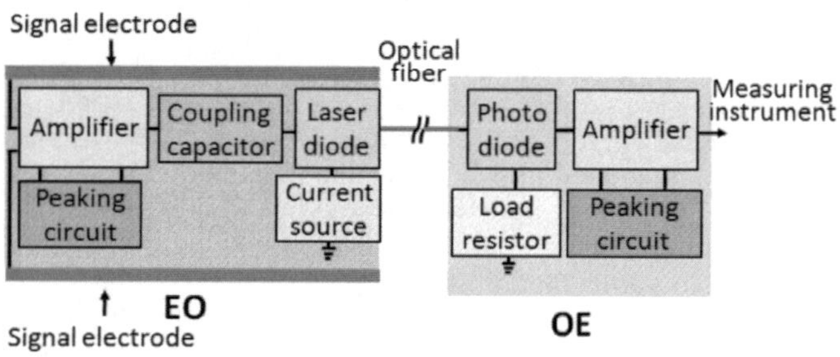

(b)

Figure 5. E/O-O/E probe: (a) external view and (b) block diagram.

4. MEASUREMENT SYSTEM AND RESULTS

We assumed a situation where two humans wearing a TRX stand face to face 600 mm apart and shake hands. The schematic of our experimental system is shown in Fig. 6. The height of the human was 170 cm. We used a battery-powered TX as a TX and an E/O-O/E probe as a receiver (RX). The battery-powered TX generates a sinusoidal wave at 6.75 MHz. The floor ground was measured to be 2000 × 3000 mm. The battery-powered TX and E/O-O/E probe were moved on the front of the human bodies. We measured the received voltage with the E/O-O/E probe while changing the distance between TRX and floor ground. We evaluated the signal propagation loss, which was represented by the ratio of the received voltage to the transmission voltage, defined as

$$\text{Signal propagation loss} = -20 \times \log_{10}\{\frac{\text{Received voltage}}{\text{Transmitted voltage}}\} \quad (1)$$

Figure 7 shows the signal propagation losses that were calculated from the experimental results. A signal propagation loss difference of more than 10 dB between standing posture and handshaking posture is required for the establishment of handshaking communication. When the distance between TRX and floor ground was from 100 mm to 600 mm, the signal propagation loss differences were very small. When the distance between TRX and floor ground was from 600 mm to 1400 mm, the signal propagation losses of the handshaking posture were bigger than those of the standing posture. These results indicate that it is difficult to establish a handshaking communication system when the wearable TRXs are placed on the front of a human body.

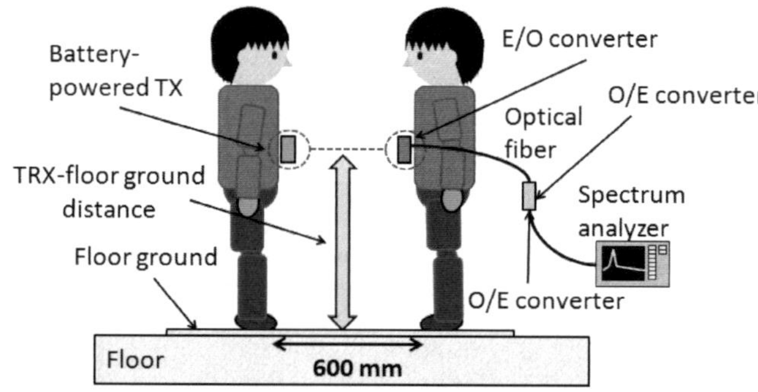

(a)

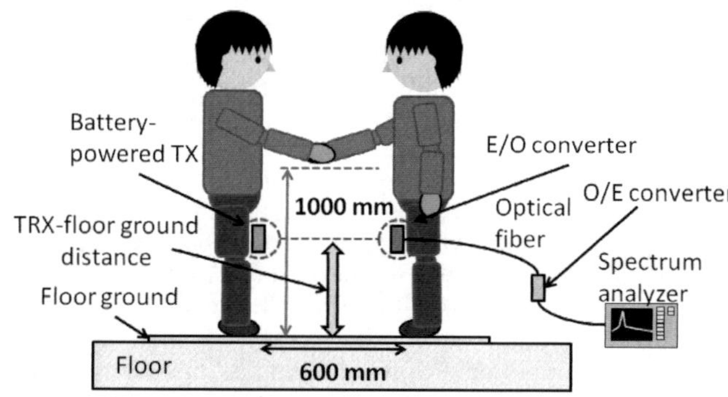

(b)

Figure 6. Measurement systems with (a) standing posture and (b) handshaking posture.

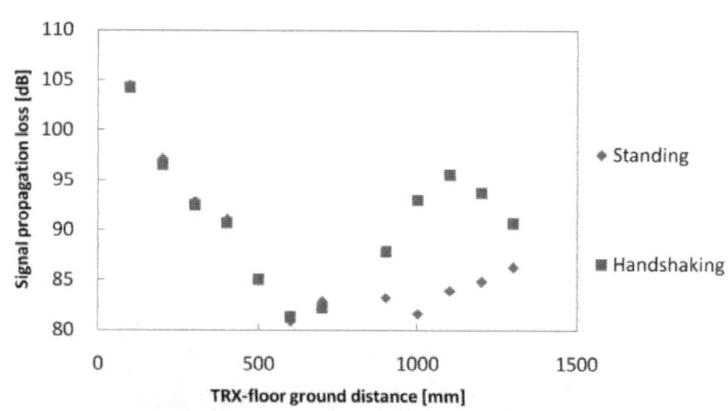

Figure 7. Dependence of signal propagation loss on distance between TRX and floor ground in experiment.

5. ANALYTICAL MODELLING OF NFCC

5.1 Model of Handshaking Communication Using Human Equivalent Phantom

We used phantoms having the same electrical characteristics as the human body in order to obtain reproductive results constantly [8]. Figure 8 shows a photograph of a phantom. Its outer shell is a polyvinyl chloride (PVC) pipe with a diameter of 250 mm, a thickness of 8 mm, and a height of 1800 mm. The pipe was filled with salt water, the conductivity of which was adjusted to 0.6 S/m at 6.75 MHz (human body: 0.6 S/m) [9]. The water level was 1500 mm. The relative permittivity of the water was 80.

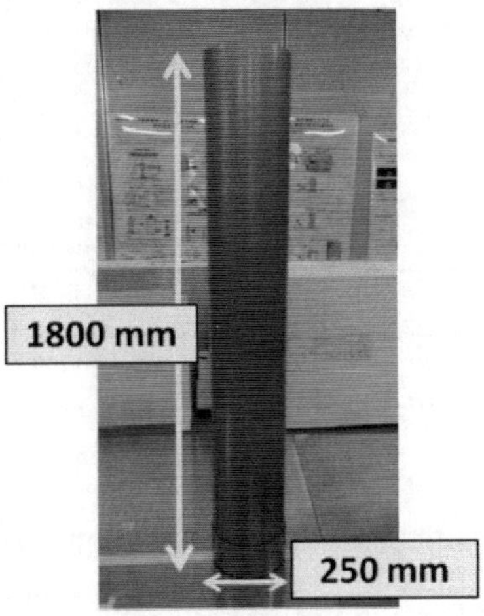

Figure 8. Photograph of human equivalent phantom.

The handshaking communication was modeled using the human body equivalent phantom in place of a real human body in the measurement system shown in Fig. 6 (a). We call this the "handshaking communication model". Figure 9 shows the handshaking communication model. The model was composed of seven conductors (phantom 1 (no. 1) and a signal electrode 1 of the wearable TX (no. 2), a signal ground electrode 1 of the wearable TX (no. 3), a signal ground electrode 2 of the wearable RX (no. 4), a signal electrode 2 of the wearable RX (no. 5), phantom 2 (no. 6), and a floor ground (no.7)), as shown in Fig. 9.

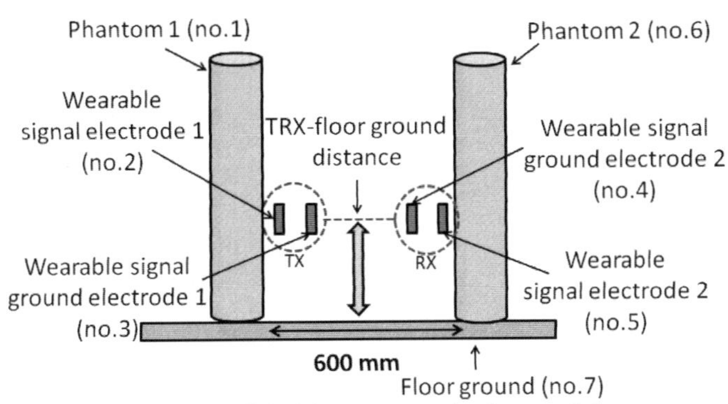

Figure 9. Handshaking communication model.

5.2 Equivalent Circuit Model of Handshaking Communication

An equivalent circuit of the handshaking communication model is represented by capacitances because conductors are capacitively coupled with each other in the NFCC system [10]-[12]. We calculated the capacitances between seven conductors with the 3D electromagnetic field simulator (Q3D Extractor) using a finite element method [13]. As shown in Fig. 10, these capacitances were applied to the lumped-parameter equivalent circuit for the handshaking communication model. The conductors shown in Fig. 9 are represented as nodes in the equivalent circuit. Figure 11 shows the simulation results of the capacitances as a function of the distance between TRX and floor ground in the standing postures. By substituting the capacitance in the equivalent circuit, signal propagation loss was calculated by a circuit simulator. Figure 12 shows the signal propagation loss of the handshaking communication model in the standing posture. The tendency of signal propagation loss by equivalent circuit was qualitatively similar to the tendency of the experimental results, which demonstrates that the handshaking communication model is valid.

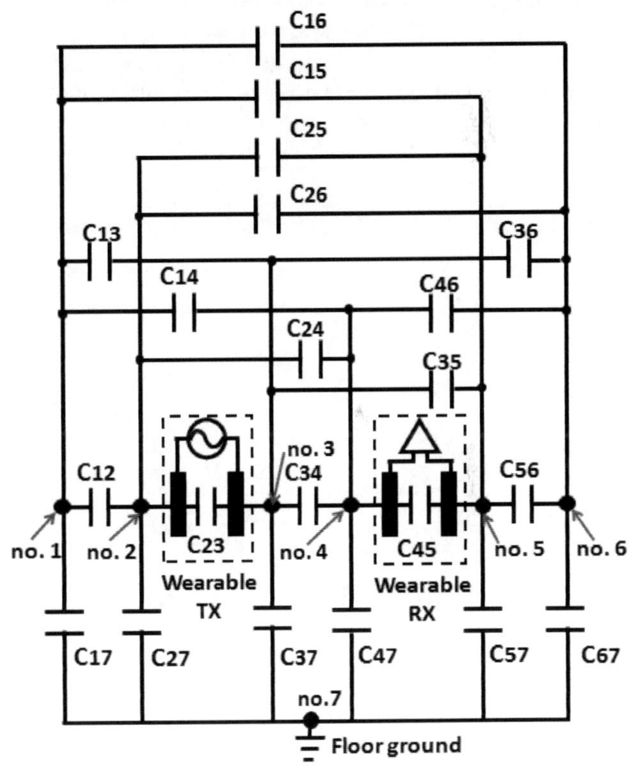

Figure 10. Lumped-parameter equivalent circuit.

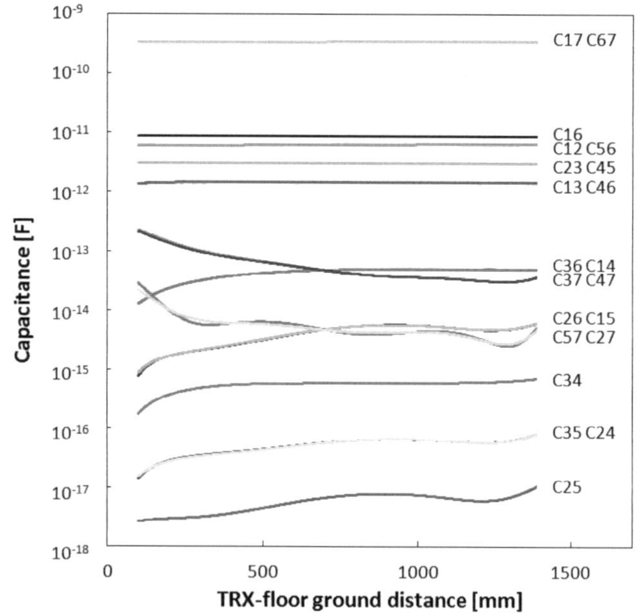

Figure 11. Dependence of capacitance values between seven conductors on the distance between TRX and floor ground in standing posture.

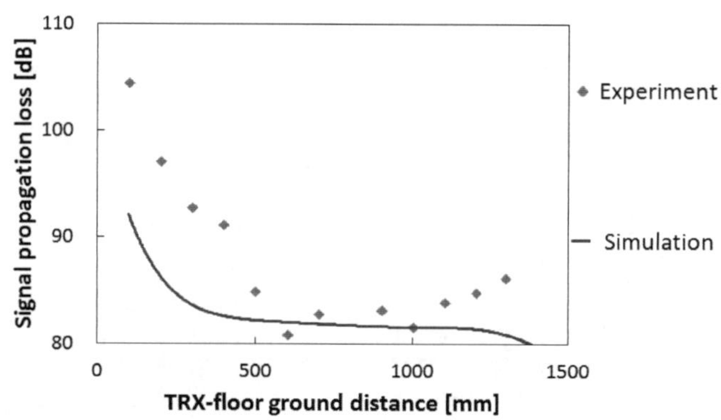

Figure 12. Signal propagation loss as a function of distance between TRX and floor ground in standing posture.

5.3 Handshaking Communication Mechanism

We discuss the signal propagation path from TX to RX to enable handshaking communication based on the equivalent circuit. The coupling force of the capacitive coupling C16 between phantom 1 (no. 1) and phantom 2 (no. 6) was strengthened by handshaking. In order to obtain the signal propagation loss difference between standing posture and handshaking posture, the C16 needs to be a component of the signal propagation path from TX to RX. The currents that flow each capacitance of the equivalent circuit are calculated by circuit simulation. Figure 13 shows the current direction in each capacitance of the equivalent circuit. Figure 14 shows the simulation results of the capacitances as a function of the distance between TRX and floor ground in the standing posture. We investigated the largest outflow currents from each conductor, as shown in Fig. 15. C12, C13, and C23 were components of the signal propagation path. However, because C45 was not a component, this was not a signal propagation path from TX to RX. We therefore proposed two signal propagation paths from TX to RX composed of C16, C23, and C45 by the largest outflow current from each conductor. If the coupling force of the capacitive coupling C34 was strengthened so as to be I34 > I13 and the coupling force of the capacitive coupling C16 was strengthened so as to be I16 > I67, the signal propagation path from the TX to RX follows the path indicted by the red line in Fig. 16. We call the red line signal propagation path 1. If the coupling force of the capacitive coupling C37 was strengthened so as to be I37 > I13 and the coupling force of the capacitive coupling C47 was strengthened so as to be I47 > I17, the signal propagation path from the TX to RX follows the path indicated by the green line. We call the green line signal propagation path 2. I67 is larger than I16 in the outflow current from the phantom 2 (no. 6), as shown in Fig. 15. However, I16 is the largest in outflow current from the phantom 2 (no. 6) because the direction of I67 was inverted when the coupling force of the capacitive coupling C37 and C47 was strengthened.

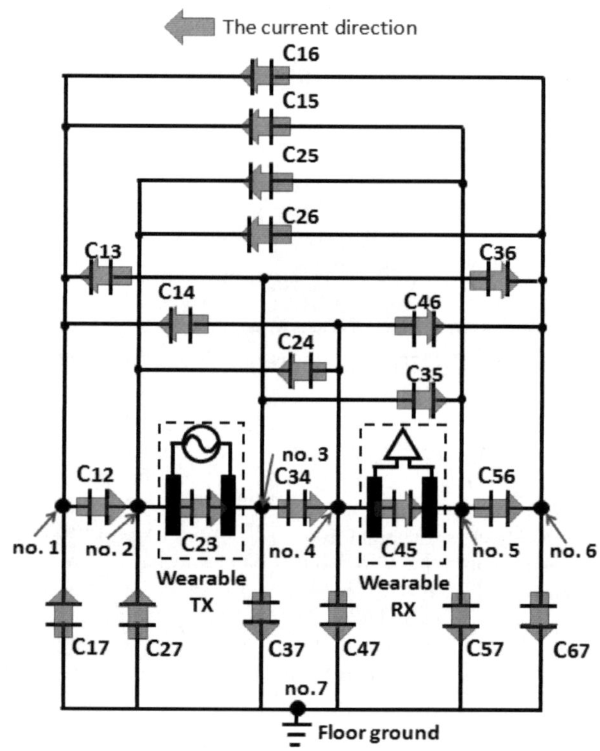

Figure 13. Current direction of the equivalent circuit.

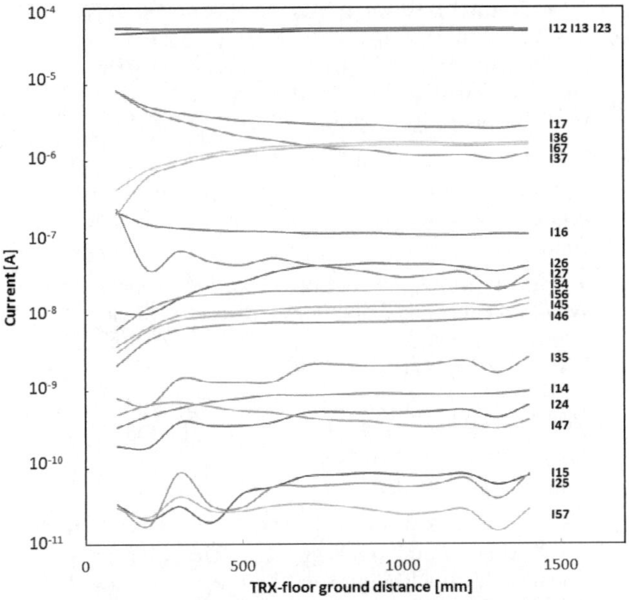

Figure 14. Dependence of current values between seven conductors on the distance between TRX and floor ground in standing posture.

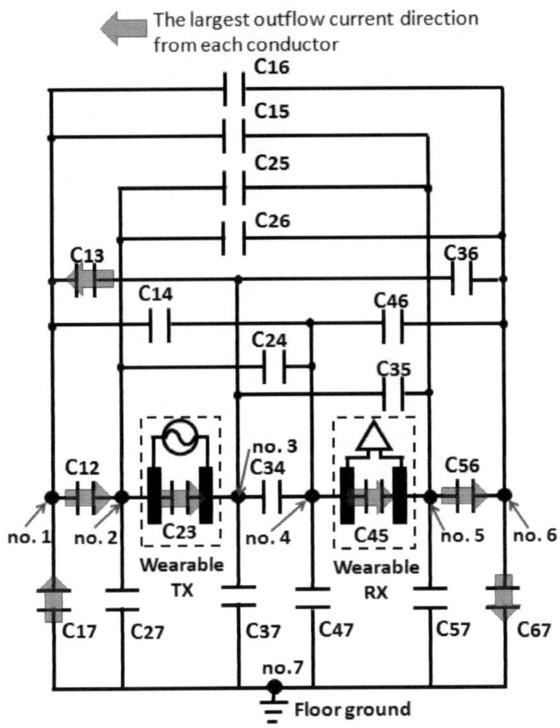

Figure 15. The largest outflow currents direction from each conductor.

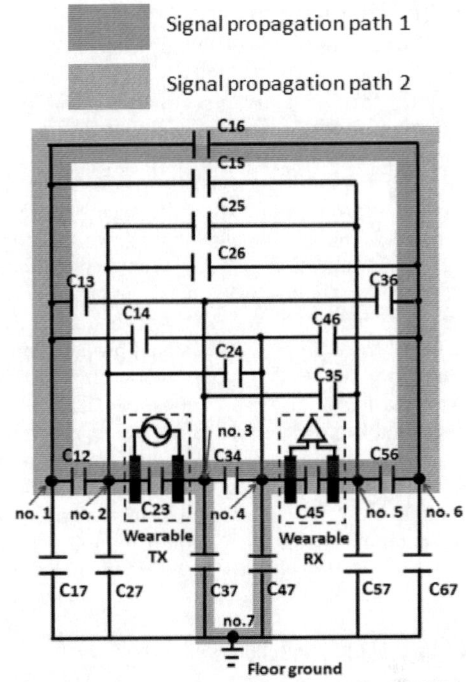

Figure 16. The signal propagation path from TX to RX.

In order to form signal propagation path 1, it is necessary to strengthen the coupling force of the capacitive coupling C34. However, to do so, it is necessary to have a short distance between TRXs and to change the size of TRX, as it is difficult to strengthen the coupling force of the capacitive coupling C34 using the prototype TRX. Handshaking communication does not form the signal propagation path 1. In order to form the signal propagation path 2, it is necessary to strengthen the coupling force of the capacitive coupling C37 and C47. When the distance between TRX and floor ground was short, the coupling force of the capacitive coupling C37 and C47 was strengthened. We propose wearable TRXs that are inserted into the soles of shoes. The schematic of our experimental system with the wearable TRXs in shoe soles is shown in Fig. 17. Also shown is the schematic of our experimental system using an E/O-O/E probe. In this case, we experimentally confirmed that the signal propagation loss in the handshaking posture was smaller than that in the standing posture by 10.6 dB.

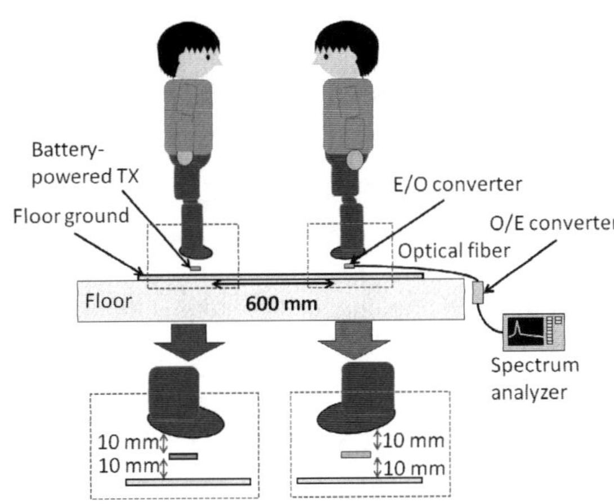

Figure 17. Measurement system when wearable TRXs are inserted into the soles of shoes.

6. CONCLUSION

We discussed the feasibility of handshaking communication between two humans wearing NFCC TRX using the carrier frequency of 6.75 MHz. Signal propagation losses in the standing posture and handshaking posture were measured with an electrically isolated E/O-O/E probe when TRXs were attached to the front of two humans facing each other. In order to clarify the cause of the signal propagation loss difference between the two postures revealed in the experimental results, we investigated the handshaking communication model with simulations using phantoms we developed in place of a real human body. The signal propagation path from TX to RX was revealed by circuit simulation. Finally, we proposed the signal propagation path for the establishment of handshaking communication. When wearable TRXs are inserted into the soles of shoes, the signal propagation path for the establishment of handshaking communication is satisfied. In this case, we experimentally confirmed that the signal propagation loss in handshaking is smaller than that in the standing posture by 10.6 dB, which demonstrates that handshaking communication using current NFCC TRXs can be realized.

ACKNOWLEDGMENTS

Part of this work was supported by a Grant-in-Aid for Scientific Research (A) 23246073 from the Ministry of Education, Culture, Sports, Science and Technology of Japan.

REFERENCES

[1] Y. Kado and M. Shinagawa. 2011. AC Electric Field Communication for Human-Area Networking. *IEICE Trans. Electron*, vol.E93-C, 234-243.

[2] T. G. Zimmerman. 1996. Personal Area Networks: Near-field intrabody communication. *IBM System.* J, 35(3/4) 609-617.

[3] Electric field communication system of the Nippon signal, "elefin" [http://www.signal.co.jp/products/elefin/] (accessed 2016- 10-7).

[4] M. Ishida, T. Nakamura, M. Nozawa, N. Watanabe, Y. Kado, and M. Shinagawa. 2014. MHz-Band RF Signal Propagation Characteristics on Human-Equivalent Phantom for Intra-body Communication. *EuCAP 2014*. 2284-2288.

[5] M. Ishida, T. Nakamura, M. Nozawa, N. Watanabe, Y. Kado, and M. Shinagawa. 2014. MHz-Band RF Signal Propagation Characteristics on Human Body for Intra-body communication. *I2MTC 2014*. 797-801.

[6] D. Ayuzawa, N. Sekine, M. Shinagawa, D. Saito, T. Yamada, and K. Oohashi. 2016. Wearable-to-Wearable Device Measurement for Intra-Body Communication Using Electro-Optic Technique. *International Symposium on Optical Memory 2016*. Tu-J-31.

[7] M. nozawa, T. Nakamura, H. Shimasaki, Y. Kado and M. Shinagawa. 2013. Signal Measurement System Using Electrically Isolated probe for MHz-Band Near-Field Coupling Communication. *IEEE International Instrumentation and Measurement Technology Conference 2013*. 37-40.

[8] S. Hasegawa, M. Ishida, I. Yokota; Y. Kado, K. Ohashi and D. Saito. 2016. Human body equivalent phantom for analyzing of surface and space propagation in MHz-band signal transmission, *EuCAP 2016*. DOI= http://dx.doi.org/10.1109/EuCAP.2016.7481823.

[9] S. Gabriel, R.W.Lau and C.Gabriel. 1996. The dielectric properties of biological tissues: II .Measurements in the frequency rage 10 Hz to 20 GHz. *Phys. Med. Biol.* 41, 2251-2269.

[10] N. Haga, K. Motojima, M. Shinagawa and Y. Kado. 2014. System of equations describing charges of multiple conductors immersed in electrostatic fields. *IEICE Electronics Express*. 11, no. 19.

[11] Y. Hayashida, R. Sugiyama, Y. Ido, A. Suzuki, Y. Takizawa, M. Shinagawa, Y. Kado, and N. Haga. 2014. Capacitance Model of Embedded Transceiver for Intra-body Communication. *BODYNETS 2014*. 222-228.

[12] S. Hasegawa, I. Yokota, M. Ishida, H. Shimasaki, Y. Kado and M. Shinagawa. 2015. Signal Interference Analysis Model in Near-Field Coupling Communication. *BODYNETS 2015*. 210-215.

[13] 3D electromagnetic field simulator, "ANSYS Q3D Extractor" [http://www.ansys.com/Products/Electronics/ANSYS-Q3D-Extractor] (accessed 2016- 11-18).

Reduction of the mutual coupling between implanted microstrip antennas on a cylindrical biocompatible metallic ground plane

Jie Huang
Department of Electronics and Telecommunications
Politecnico di Torino - Italy
+86 15236293747
janemeloo1314@gmail.com

Ildiko Peter
Department of Applied Science and Technology
Politecnico di Torino - Italy
+39 011 090 4670
ildiko.peter@polito.it

Ladislau Matekovits
Department of Electronics and Telecommunications
Politecnico di Torino - Italy
+39 011 090 4119
ladislau.matekovits@polito.it

ABSTRACT

The effect of mutual coupling between two antennas within a human body model is studied. The multilayer model includes highly lossy materials in which biocompatible metal implant is inserted, that in the present study serves as a ground plane of the conformal radiators. The effect of the mutual coupling between two antennas sharing the same ground plane is numerically studied and quantified. For its reduction a grounded microstrip line configuration is proposed, that can be easily inserted in the considered geometry. Its presence increases the directivity of the 2-element conformal array and reduces the level of the sidelobes.

CCS Concepts

• Hardware → Printed circuit boards → Electromagnetic interference and compatibility • Hardware → Communication hardware, interfaces and storage → Signal processing systems → Beamforming.

Keywords

Implanted antenna, mutual coupling reduction, In-body wireless electronic

1. INTRODUCTION

Medical telemetry - also called biotelemetry- involves the application of telemetry in medicine and other healthcare. It allows remotely monitoring various vital signals of ambulatory patients and it is exploited more and more in the today healthcare system. If adequately implemented, i.e., allowing real-time transmission of biological signals from the body - as the human temperature, blood pressure and to monitor of cardiac beat in sickrooms, etc., - in a plausible way to a far located medical center, it is possible to distantly monitor patient and for example to send medical team just if necessary. The use of such technologies can strongly reduce hospitalization time, and consequently associated costs, without affecting the efficiency of the service. On the other hand, having the possibility to continuously collect the biological data, algorithms to predict the evolution of the medical condition of the patients can also be developed, which again can reflect in a higher quality of the service, for example by considering recovery only when in fact necessary.

In some cases, on-body sensors can collect the signal of interest, but in other cases, the information has to be obtained from inside the body. In this case, the collected information should be transmitted outward from inside the body. Implanted antennas are the basic elements of any of such system, where communication between an implanted device in the human body with the outside receivers is required.

The location of the implanted antennas depends on the given application. Some of them, e.g., for a wireless RF powered brain machine interface applications are located in brain [1], [2]. In [1] it is shown that the position of the implanted antenna and electrical properties of insulating layer will also affect the RF power reception and the properties of the tissues surrounding the implanted antenna can influence the electrical characteristics of the antennas. In [2] a planar spiral antenna (PSA) is designed in the brain to detect the existence of tumor. In the presence of tumor, the resonant frequency of the PSA is larger than for healthy tissues. Other antennas are implanted in human arms. In [3], an implanted cavity slot antenna with H-shape slot is proposed and characterized. Few examples of antennas on the bone are in [4], [5]. In [4] an implanted antenna located between the two parts of a broken femur is considered. It consists of a conformal slot array that is part of a wireless battery system. In [5], the reason of using implanted antennas in bone rather than in the muscle and skin is discussed: a comparison between bone implanted antenna and muscle implanted antenna is presented.

Radiation performances of antennas can be increased, for example, by considering an array of radiators. This solution also presents some drawbacks, as the larger dimension of the antenna, and the effect of the mutual coupling between the radiators, that can, in turn, reduce the gain or increase the level of sidelobes. In the literature, different ways to reduce the effect of the mutual coupling have been proposed. In [6], parasitic tape on microstrip patch elements is experimented. This mechanism of mutual coupling reduction has been studied by observing the field distribution in the presence of the tape, and compare it with the initial case when the tape is not present. In [7], a solution consisting of the use of one pair of slit between two walls of a printed circuit board in air is studied aiming to improve the isolation of a pair of closely packed antenna elements. In [8], a suspended line that links 2 planar inverted-F antennas (PIFAs) is used to compensate the coupling.

By this way, an opposite coupling can be introduced that if properly designed will offset the unwanted interaction and in turn can increase the antenna efficiency. Similar solution is proposed in [9], where a connection between two ports is considered. Such a solution is convenient and easy to be implemented by suitably designing the dimension of the connection. However, the reduction of the coupling i.e., S_{21} parameter, is put side-by side by a shift of the resonant frequency. Another class of solutions for reducing the mutual coupling between radiators consist of using Electromagnetic Band-gap (EBG) structures. In [10], a periodic structure on a conformal ground plane, which exhibits EBG in the interested band, is used. In [11], a defected ground structure (DGS) with two H-shaped slots between the antennas are used which are placed very closely each to other (distance less than 0.3λ). With this structure, the mutual coupling reduces up to 50 dB without significant influence on the radiation pattern. In [12], a comparison between an EBG structure and DGS structure is performed. However, the study of the mutual coupling for implanted antennas is at the early stage, and at the best of the authors' knowledge, only few examples are reported in the literature.

Bearing in mind the classes of the implanted antennas, where space and material constrains are to be strongly considered in this paper, the reduction of the mutual coupling in the case of an implanted 2-element antenna array is investigated. The radiators are placed on a metallic cylinder (the implant) embedded in a polymer dielectric that acts as a substrate between the ground plane and radiators, all of them being conformal. For the reduction of the coupling, a narrow, grounded microstrip line is inserted between the antennas. Quantification of the coupling with and without the proposed shield is performed, and the amount of the reduction of the coupling is studied for different positions of the two radiators. In each cases, the grounded line is positioned midway between the radiators. The solution does not require any additional space, since the grounded line is located in the already available space halfway between the antennas.

2. THE BODY MODEL

In this paper a cylindrical body model is considered, that has dimensions similar to an adult leg. The different tissues are modeled as concentric cylinders characterized with different thicknesses and material parameters. A CAD model of the geometry under investigation is presented in Fig. 1.

The material parameters, i.e., relative dielectric constant and conductivity (S/m) are reported in Tab. 1. In all cases the magnetic properties of the different tissues and dielectric have been neglected, i.e. a relative magnetic permeability equal to 1 has been considered.

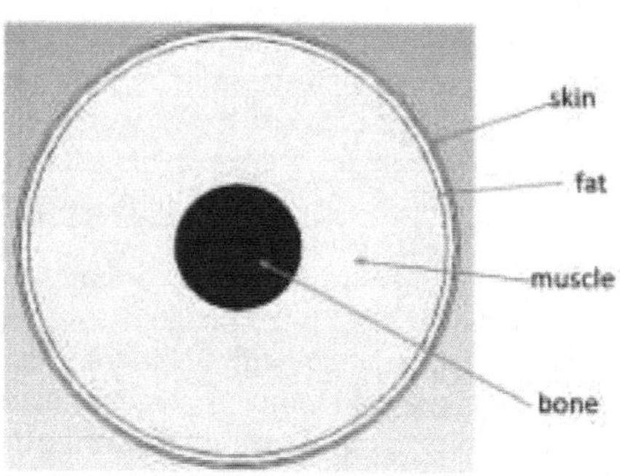

Figure 1. Cross section of the considered geometry.

Table. 1: Characteristics of the different tissues at f=2.45 GHz and metal (implant and antenna)

	muscle	fat	skin	PDMS layer	Bone (Titan)
Epsilon (relative)	57.1	5.6	46.7	2.667	Lossy metal
El.Cond. (S/m)	0.79	0.04	0.69	0.034	1e7

In the considered model, the central part of the geometry in Fig. 1, i.e., the bone, is replaced by an implant of the same dimensions made up by a biocompatible metal chosen between the most commonly used as stainless steels (maybe the cheapest solution), titanium and its alloys, cobalt and its modified compositions, etc.. However, because of their encouraging mechanical properties, high corrosion resistance and thanks to their exceptional biocompatibility Ti and its alloys are the foremost materials used in the orthopedic field. In particular, Ti–6Al–4V is used in a multiplicity of stress-bearing orthopedic applications, but some investigations [13, 14] have demonstrated that the release of Al and V ions can progressively determine well-being problems. Because of this, recently the attention is focalizing on the study of Al, V-free metallic alloys: starting from a basic Ti alloys composition and replacing the risky elements by Nb, Ta, Mo, Zr or a mixture of them, such release can be significantly reduced or even eliminated. Zr belongs to the same group as Ti and it shows an allotropic transformation similar to that of Ti. Both Ta and Nb are non-toxic elements and reveal very alike physical and chemical properties. Because of their good biocompatibility and high corrosion resistance, these metals have been employed as constituent elements of Ti alloys even for the applications under investigation in the present paper. Ta exhibits excellent chemical stability and good biocompatibility similar to that of Ti. In particular, porous Ta has been developed for bone in-growth applications, for example hip and knee arthroplasty. Besides, introduction of Ta in Ti-Ni shape memory alloy leads to a reduced happening of artifacts: the blood compatibility of Ta was supposed to be higher, compared to other metals [15-22]. These are just some aspects why Ti and its alloys are used for the considered investigation.

Such a large extension metallic part is used as ground plane for a conformal rectangular microstrip antenna as reported in the model in Fig. 2.

The antenna is separated from the metallic cylinder by a conformal substrate made up of Polydimethylsiloxane (PDMS). In the considered model, a second layer of PDMS is also present that acts

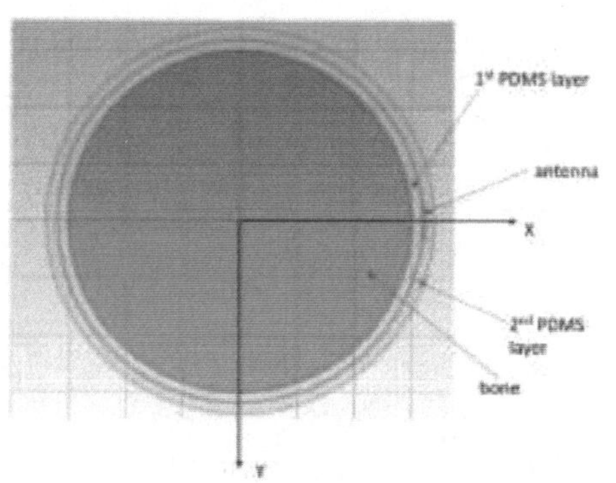

Figure 2. Position of the conformal antenna and PDMS substrate and superstrate with respect to the implant "bone".

as superstrate. In the numerical modelling, the thicknesses of the two PDMS layers, are considered equal. The other leading dimensions are reported in Tab. 2

Table. 2: The parameters of the model

Parameter	Description	Value (mm)
r_{bone}	The radius of the bone	30
l_{str}	The overall length of the structure	100
l_{PDMS}	The length of the PDMS layer	66
th_{PDMS}	The thickness of the PDMS layer	2
th_{muscle}	The thickness of the muscle	70
th_{met}	The thickness of the metal	0.5
th_{fat}	The thickness of the fat	4
th_{skin}	The thickness of the skin	2

3. DESIGN A SINGLE ANTENNA

In the first step of the analysis, a single antenna element has been designed. It is a rectangular microstrip patch antenna of length l_{ant} and width w_{ant}, fed by a probe on its symmetry axis, and at a distance l_z from one of the edges. The three aforementioned parameters have been used in an optimization process to minimize the reflection coefficient with respect to standard 50 Ω at the center of the 2.4 - 2.5 GHz Industrial, Scientific and Medical (ISM) radio band, i.e. at 2.45 GHz. The optimization process was necessary, since considering the body environment, no analytic formulas for the design are available. After the optimization by Genetic Algorithm, the dimensions of the antenna result to be l_{ant}=32 mm, w_{ant}=7 mm and l_z=0 mm, respectively. The corresponding reflection coefficient is reported in Fig. 3.

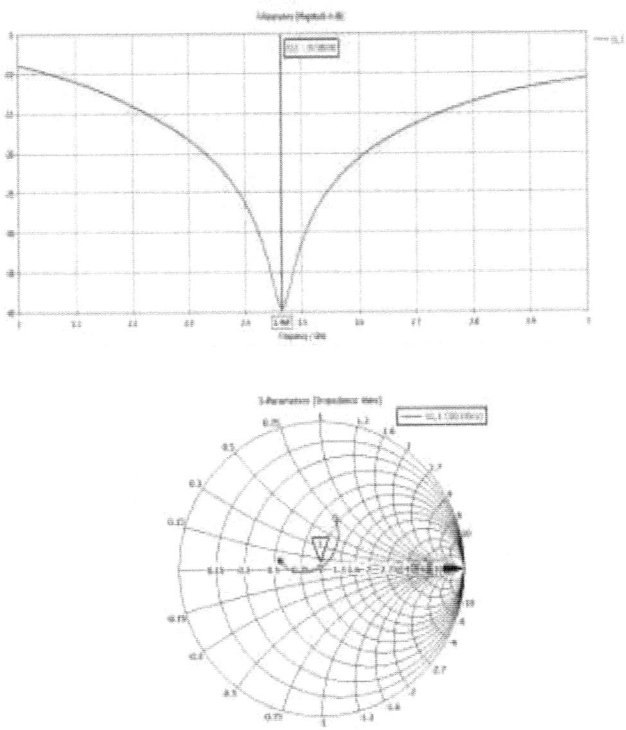

Figure 3. Impedance matching of the optimized antenna.

The resulting geometry exhibits a good matching at 2.464 GHz, which is close the center of the considered band, and a good bandwidth (also due to the losses considered in the simulation).

4. QUANTIFYING THE MUTUAL COUPLING

As mentioned above, our interest is the quantification of the coupling between two antennas. The corresponding scenario is presented in Fig. 4. Two identical antennas have been considered. The first one is considered in a fix position, and the second one is moved around the implant by an angle alpha.

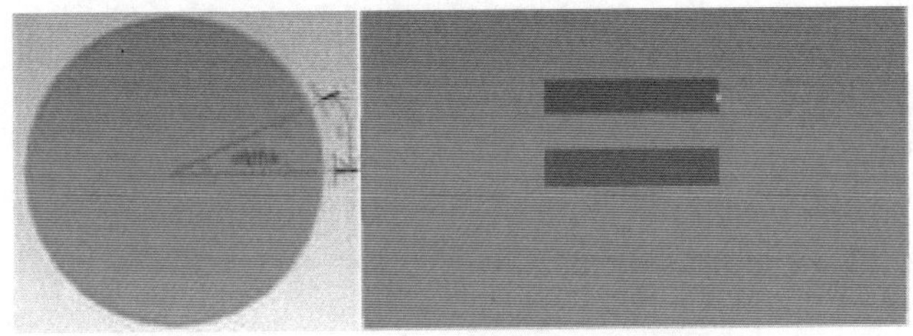

Figure 4. Model of the two parallel antennas around the cylindrical implant: front view (left), side view (right).

The complex scattering matrix has been computed and the mutual impedance Z_{21} evaluated for different rotation angles alpha, in the interval from 25° to 180° with a step of 5°. The corresponding results are reported in Fig. 5.

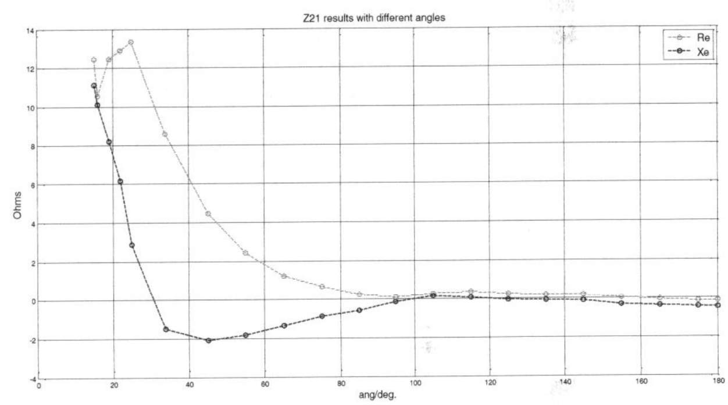

Figure 5. Real and imaginary part of the mutual impedance between the two dipoles for different rotation angles.

From the data in Fig. 5 it results that the coupling has an oscillatory behavior and presents a strong reduction while the distance between the antennas increases, similar to what happens for the planar case [23].

However, since the active input impedance Z_{inp} of the single element is influenced by the self-impedance of the two elements Z_{11} and Z_{22}, respectively, and by the mutual coupling Z_m according to

$$Z_{inp} = Z_{11} - \frac{Z_m^2}{Z_{22}}$$

for small angles the large coupling can have a significant effect. In order to reduce this influence, in the following section a solution for the reduction of the mutual coupling is proposed and analyzed.

5. REDUCTION OF THE MUTUAL COUPLING

A common practice to reduce mutual coupling between parallel lines (as our geometry can be approximated) is to introduce a grounded line between the two antennas. The corresponding model is shown in Fig. 6.

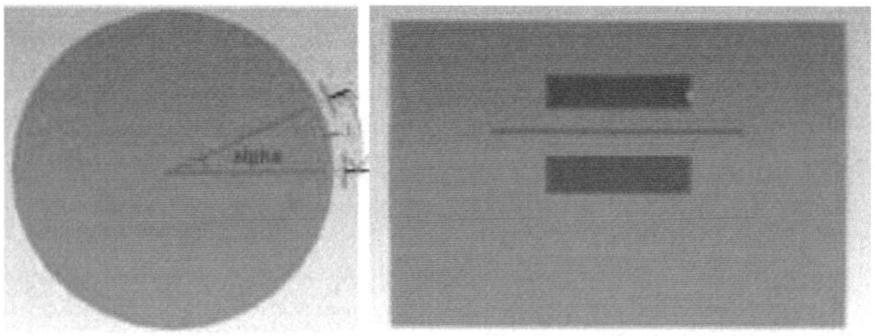

Figure 6. Model of the two parallel antennas around the cylindrical implant separated by a grounded narrow microstrip line: front view (left), side view (right).

The material of the line is the same as of the implant and antennas. Its width has been chosen to be equal to 0.4 mm. As concern its length, it has been chosen in such a way to avoid resonance; the value of 55 mm has been used in the following simulations performed in the angular interval of 25° to 90°. The two ends of the line are connected to the implant by two metallic cylinders. The values of the scattering matrix entries for the two analyzed cases, i.e. no line, and presence of the grounded line, respectively, are reported in Fig. 7.

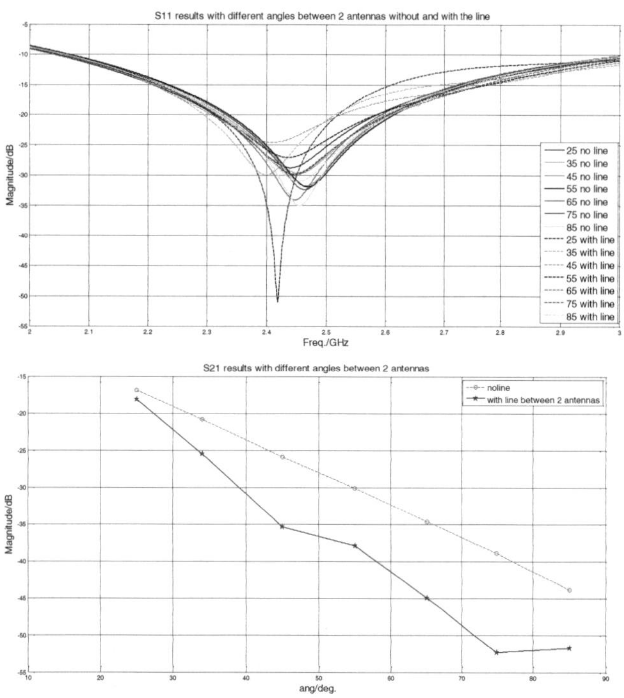

Figure 7. Reflection (top) for the initial (solid line) and proposed scheme (dotted line) and transmission coefficient (bottom) for the initial ("circle") and proposed scheme ("star").

As it can be observed, the presence of the grounded line between the antennas reduces the mutual coupling between them while their resonance frequencies are only marginally affected. It is significant that at 75°, the coupling is reaching the maximum reduction, and at 25°, the reduction is minimum.

In the following, the effects of the proposed scheme on the radiation performances is analyzed for the separation angles when the reduction of the coupling is minimum, namely for 25°. Moreover a broadside configuration has been considered, i.e., where the phase difference between the feeding signal of the two antennas is equal to zero. As results from the plots in Fig. 8, presence of the line reflects in a higher directivity that increases from 6.195 dBi to 6.59 dBi, i.e., about 0.4 dBi increment, and lower sidelobes, as expected. The scan of approximatively 12° is due to the fixed position of one of the antennas, while the second one is positioned at 25°, as mentioned above.

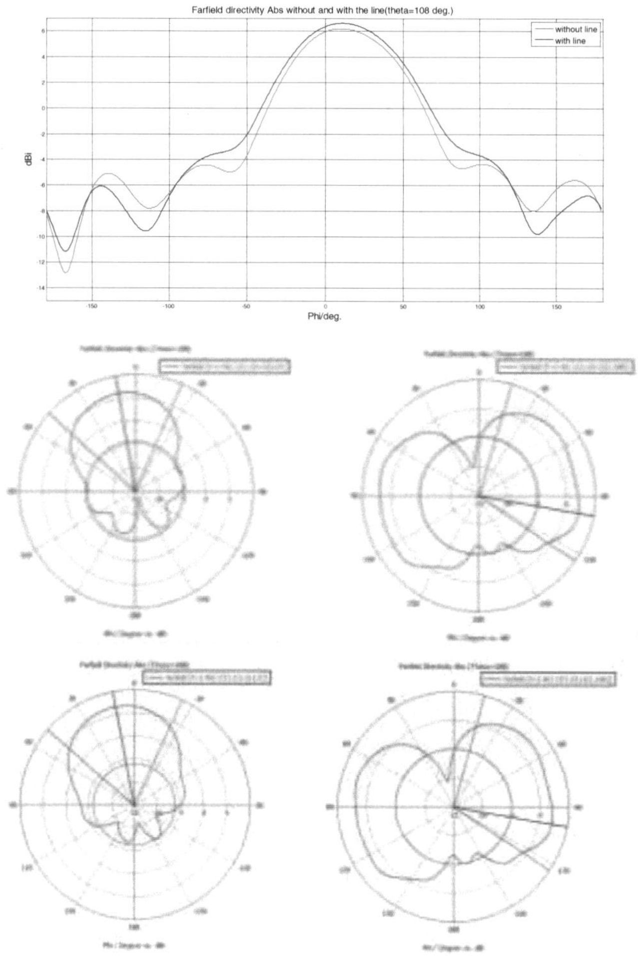

Figure 8. Directivity (top) and radiation patterns of the 2-element array for alpha=25°: initial case (middle) and with the proposed solution (bottom).

6. CONCLUSIONS

A simple method to reduce the coupling between two implanted microstrip antennas has been proposed. It consists of the insertion of a grounded, non-resonant narrow microstrip line halfway between the radiators. The effect of the coupling reduction has been quantified, and it was numerically verified that the reduced coupling manifests in a higher directivity and lower sidelobes of the antenna, as expected.

7. REFERENCES

[1] Zhao, Y., Rennaker, R., Hutchens, C., Ibrahim, T. S., Simulation of Implantable Miniaturized Antenna for Brain Machine Interface Applications.

[2] Shokry M.A., Allam A.M.M.A., Implanted Antenna in Brain ,*IEEE Antennas and Propagation Conference (LAPC), 2013 Loughborough*, DOI= http://dx.doi.org/10.1109/LAPC.2013.6711977

[3] Xia W., Saito K., Takahashi M., Ito K., "Performances of an Implanted Cavity Slot Antenna Embedded in the Human Arm", *IEEE Transactions on Antennas and Propagation*, Vol.57, No.4, April 2009. DOI= http://dx.doi.org/10.1109/TAP.2009.2014579

[4] Zakavi P., Karmakar N. C., Griggs I., Wireless Orthopedic Pin for Bone Healing and Growth: Antenna Development, *IEEE Transactions on Antennas and Propagations*, vol. 58, no. 12, pp. 4069 - 4074, December 2010. DOI= http://dx.doi.org/10.1109/TAP.2010.2078459

[5] Alrawashdeh R., Huang Y., Sajak A.A.B., A Flexible Loop Antenna for Biomedical Bone Implants, *8th European Conference on Antennas and Propagation (EUCAP)*, 2014. DOI= http://dx.doi.org/10.1109/EuCAP.2014.6901898

[6] Wang H., Fang D., Ge P., Mutual coupling reduction between two conformal microstrip patch antennas, *Proc. of 5th Asia-Pacific Conference on Environmental Electromagnetics, 2009. (CEEM 2009)*, 2009, pp. 176 –179. DOI= http://dx.doi.org/10.1109/CEEM.2009.5304778

[7] Neyestanak A. A. L., Jolani F., Dadgarpour M., Mutual coupling reduction between two microstrip patch antennas, *in Proc. of Electr. Comput. Eng.*, 2008, pp. 739–742. DOI= http://dx.doi.org/10.1109/CCECE.2008.4564633

[8] Diallo A., Luxey C., Thuc P. L., Staraj R., Kossiavas G., Study and reduction of the mutual coupling between two mobile phone PIFAs operating in the DCS1800 and UMTS bands, *IEEE Trans. Antennas Propag.*, vol. 54, no. 11, pp. 3063–3074, Nov. 2006. DOI= http://dx.doi.org/10.1109/APS.2008.4620064

[9] Ezzat M., Lee C.S., A simple optimization technique for reducing mutual coupling between two coupled antennas, *2015 IEEE International Symposium on Antennas and Propagation & USNC/URSI National Radio Science Meeting*, 2008, DOI= http://dx.doi.org/10.1109/CCECE.2008.4564633

[10] Kawakami, Y., Hori, T., Fujimoto, M., Yamaguchi, R., Cho, K., Mutual coupling reduction effects of EBG structure located on cylinder surface. *Antennas and Propagation Society International Symposium (APSURSI)*, 2010 IEEE, Page(s): 1 - 4. DOI= http://dx.doi.org/10.1109/APS.2010.5561160

[11] Acharjee J., Mandal K., Mandal S.K., Sarkar P.P., Mutual coupling reduction between microstrip patch antennas by using a string of H-shaped DGS, *2016 International Conference on Microelectronics, Computing and Communications (MicroCom)*, 23-25 Jan. 2016, DOI= http://dx.doi.org/10.1109/MicroCom.2016.7522477

[12] Mahmoud A. Abdalla, Ahmed M. Abdelreheem, Mohamed H. Abdegellel, Ali M. Ali, Surface Wave and Mutual Coupling Reduction Between Two Element Array MIMO Antenna, *Antennas and Propagation Society International Symposium (APSURSI), 2013 IEEE*, DOI= http://dx.doi.org/10.1109/APS.2013.6710750

[13] Cvijovic Alagic I., Gubeljak N, Rakin M, Cvijovic Z, Geric K., Microstructural morphology effects on fracture resistance and crack tip strain distribution in Ti–6Al–4V alloy for orthopedic implants. *Materials Design* 53 (2014) 870–80. DOI= http://dx.doi.org/10.1016/j.matdes.2013.07.097

[14] Wen M., Wen C., Hodgson P., Li Y., Fabrication of Ti–Nb–Ag alloy via powder metallurgy for biomedical applications, *Materials Design* 56 (2014) 629–634. DOI= http://dx.doi.org/10.1016/j.matdes.2013.11.066

[15] Zardiackas LD, Mitchell DW, Disegi JA., In: Brown SA, Lemons JE, editors. Medical applications of titanium and its alloys: the material and biological issues. West Conshohocken (PA): *ASTM International* (1996) 60-75.

[16] Kondo R, Nomura N, Suyalatu, Tsutsumi Y, Doi H, Hanawa T., Microstructure and mechanical properties of as-cast Zr–Nb alloys, *Acta Biomaterials* 7 (2011) 4278–4284. DOI= http://dx.doi.org/10.1016/j.actbio.2011.07.020

[16] Suyalatu, Kondo R, Tsutsumi Y, Doi H, Nomura N, Hanawa T., Effects of phase constitution on magnetic susceptibility and mechanical properties of Zr-rich Zr–Mo alloys, *Acta Biomaterial* 7 (2011) 4259–4266. DOI= http://dx.doi.org/10.1016/j.actbio.2011.07.005

[17] Ho WF, Chen WK, Wu SC, Hsu HC., Structure, mechanical properties and grindability of dental Ti-Zr alloys, *Journal of Material Science - Matererials Medicine* 19 (2008) 3179-8316. DOI= https://dx.doi.org/10.1007/s10856-008-3454-x

[19] Takahashi M., Kikuchi M., Okuno O., Grindability of dental cast Ti-Zr alloys, *Materials Transaction* 50 (2009) 859-863. DOI= http://dx.doi.org/10.2320/matertrans.MRA2008403

[20] I. Peter, M. Rosso, Study of Ti-enriched CoCrMo alloy for dental application, *IEEE Access*, Vol.3 (2015) 73-80. DOI= http://dx.doi.org/10.1109/ACCESS.2015.2398312

[21] Ho WF, Ju CP, Chern Lin JH., Structure and properties of cast binary Ti-Mo alloys, *Biomaterials* 20 (1999) 2115-2122. DOI= http://dx.doi.org/10.1016/S0142-9612(99)00114-3

[22] Ho WF., A comparison of tensile properties and corrosion behavior of cast Ti-7.5Mo with c.p. Ti, Ti-15Mo and Ti-6Al-4V alloys, *J Alloys Compounds* 464 (2008) 580-583. DOI= http://dx.doi.org/10.1016/j.jallcom.2007.10.054

[23] John D. Kraus, Antennas, New York: McGraw-Hill, 1950.

FaceDate: A Mobile Cloud Computing App for People Matching

Invited Paper

Pradyumna Neog
New Jersey Institute of Technology
University Heights
Newark, NJ 07102
pkn7@njit.edu

Hillol Debnath
New Jersey Institute of Technology
University Heights
Newark, NJ 07102
hd43@njit.edu

Jianchen Shan
New Jersey Institute of Technology
University Heights
Newark, NJ 07102
js622@njit.edu

Nafize R. Paiker
New Jersey Institute of Technology
University Heights
Newark, NJ 07102
nrp48@njit.edu

Narain Gehani
New Jersey Institute of Technology
University Heights
Newark, NJ 07102
gehani@njit.edu

Reza Curtmola
New Jersey Institute of Technology
University Heights
Newark, NJ 07102
reza.curtmola@njit.edu

Xiaoning Ding
New Jersey Institute of Technology
University Heights
Newark, NJ 07102
xiaoning.ding@njit.edu

Cristian Borcea
New Jersey Institute of Technology
University Heights
Newark, NJ 07102
borcea@njit.edu

Abstract

This paper presents FaceDate, a novel mobile app that matches persons based on their facial looks. Each FaceDate user uploads their profile face photo and trains the app with photos of faces they like. Upon user request, FaceDate detects other users located in the proximity of the requester and performs face matching in real-time. If a mutual match is found, the two users are notified and given the option to start communicating. FaceDate is implemented over our Moitree middleware for mobile distributed computing assisted by the cloud. The app is designed to scale with the number of users, as face recognition is done in parallel at different users. FaceDate can be configured for (i) higher performance, in which case the face recognition is done in the cloud or (ii) higher privacy, in which case the face recognition is done on the mobiles. The experimental results with Android-based phones demonstrate that FaceDate achieves promising performance.

CCS Concepts

•Human-centered computing →Mobile computing; •Computer systems organization →Cloud computing; •Software and its engineering →Middleware;

Keywords

Mobile cloud app, face matching

1 Introduction

Alice and Bob are sitting in nearby restaurants, and they do not know each other. Alice's favorite actor is Tom Cruise and would love to meet someone who looks like him. Bob, on the other hand, is keen on meeting someone like Shakira, and Alice resembles her. Bob also has facial similarity with Tom Cruise, and Alice might be interested in him. However, it is likely that they will never get a chance to meet. The outcome could be different if there was an app that could learn their face preferences and match them in real-time based on these preferences.

To the best of our knowledge, no current application can automatically solve this situation and suggest a location-based, *mutual match* in real-time to the two users. Many matching apps developed in the last decade [10, 16] use text-based profiles, which do not consider the face preferences of the users. Tinder [7], a newer and very successful app, provides options to filter out the results based on age-group, gender, and geographical proximity. In addition, it shows the photos of the matched users. However, it asks the user to decide if s/he likes the suggestions or not. This may be time consuming and, also, it does not ensure that the match is mutual. The work in [2] could be seen as an extension of Tinder, as the app trains on the user's photo choices over time. However, there is a high probability that the users will stop using the app if it does not provide any good recommendation in the initial stages. Also, showing user photos in situations where there is no mutual match could be considered a privacy problem.

This paper presents FaceDate, a mobile, location-based app that matches people based on their face preferences in real-time. The first novelty of FaceDate is that the users can train/re-train the app with photos of faces they like, and then the app can immediately provide good matches based on a face recognition algorithm. Unlike existing apps, FaceDate does not need potentially long time to learn the user preferences from the app usage. The second novelty of our app is that it can independently make a decision if two users satisfy each other's facial preferences and instantly inform them. FaceDate does not require manual input from the users during the match process. The third novelty is that, from a privacy point of view, FaceDate shares photos between users only if they mutually match. Therefore, user faces are not shown to people they do not like; thus, users can avoid potentially unpleasant interactions.

While our current design performs just face matching, FaceDate could be extended to use both face matching and traditional text-based profile matching.

We implemented a prototype of FaceDate on top of our Moitree [12] middleware for mobile distributed apps assited by the cloud. Moitree simplifies app development and provides cloud support for communication and computation offloading. In FaceDate, the users may choose to perform face recognition in the cloud for faster response time. If they have privacy concerns, they may choose to execute this operation on the mobile devices. In addition, Moitree provides support for dynamic group management, which allows FaceDate to adapt to users moving in and out of each other's proximity. For face recognition, FaceDate uses the Local Binary Patterns Histogram (LBPH) algorithm [11].

Experimental results over Android-based phones and Android-based virtual machines in the cloud demonstrate that FaceDate can provide good matches in a few seconds even when several users are searching for matches simultaneously in the same area. FaceDate scales with the number of users because the first phase of the face matching process, which involves potentially many users, is done in parallel at these users. This phase results in only a few good matches, and therefore, the sequential processing of the matches in the second phase (i.e., ensuring a mutual match) is bound by this low number of matches.

The rest of the paper is organized as follows. Section 2 provides an overview of FaceDate, followed by a brief description of Moitree, its supporting middleware, in Section 3. Section 4 presents FaceDate's design and implementation. Section 5 shows experimental results. Section 6 discusses related work, and the paper concludes in Section 7.

2 FaceDate Overview

The screenshots in Figure 1 show the steps taken by a FaceDate user to find a match. Figure 1a shows the "Profile Setup" screen. The user uploads a profile photo and provide basic information such as date of birth, gender, and a brief write-up about herself. Figure 1b shows the "Face Preference Setup" screen, where the user provides a set of preference photos. FaceDate will train itself automatically to perform matches on these photos. The "Search for Matches" screen, shown in Figure 1c, allows the user to start a search. FaceDate has a timeout (currently set to 5 seconds) to find a match; if a match request does not yield any result within this period, a *"No Match Found"* notification is displayed. If FaceDate is successful, the results are shown in the "Results" screen (Figure 1d). The user can then simply touch the photo, and the "Chat with Match" screen (Figure 1e) will appear.

Figure 2 provides an overview of the operation of FaceDate: the Querier starts the "Search" for a match; the two other users, Neighbor 1 and Neighbor 2, are in the neighborhood and participate in the search. The training of the app for each user happens before the search. When the search is activated, the Querier's device sends her profile photo to all FaceDate users in the neighborhood. The receiving devices execute a face recognition algorithm to try and match the received profile photo with their set of preference photos. In the figure, the Querier's profile photo matches only the preference photos of Neighbor 1. Thus, Neighbor 1 will respond with its profile photo, and the Querier will run the same face recognition algorithm on the response photo with respect to its preference photos. The profile photo of Neighbor 1 matches the preference photos of the Querier. Since it is a mutual match, FaceDate declares success and displays the profile photo of Neighbor 1 on the Querier's screen. The Querier then initiates a chat session with Neighbor 1.

While FaceDate has been designed to perform matching based only on facial features, it is straightforward to extend the app to work in conjunction with traditional text-based profile matching. The users could for example set a configuration parameter to choose between the two alternative matching processes.

Our implementation of FaceDate uses the Moitree [12] middleware that facilitates the execution of collaborative apps within groups of mobile users. Moitree has the following key features:

(1) High-level API for development of mobile collaborative apps assisted by the cloud.
(2) Seamless offloading and communication with app components in the cloud.
(3) Efficient user group management for location based apps, where the groups are dynamic over time and space.

These features are ideal for FaceDate since it is a collaborative location-based app and requires groups to be dynamically formed based on user location. The next section gives an overview of Moitree.

3 Moitree Overview

Avatar [8] is a mobile distributed platform which pairs each mobile device with a virtual machine (avatar) in the cloud. This setup supplements the limited resources available on the mobile with virtually unlimited resources in the cloud. However, it complicates the programming/execution of distributed apps, as they have to work over sets of mobile/avatar pairs.

Moitree is a middleware for the Avatar platform that facilitates the execution of collaborative apps within groups of mobile users. Each group is represented by a collection of mobile-avatar pairs. Groups can be context-aware, and Moitree takes care of their dynamic membership. For example, the group creation criteria can be based on location, time, and social ties.

Figure 3 shows a simple architectural view of Moitree. The middleware hides the low level details of the platform from programmers, and it provides a unified view of the mobile-avatar pairs by taking care of data synchronization, input abstraction, and computation and communication offloading. Moitree has APIs for managing groups and for abstract communication channels. All Moitree APIs are event-driven and callback-based. Moitree offloads user-to-user data communication to the cloud in order to save wireless bandwidth and improve latency. Its communication API provides four types of channels: ScatterGather, AnyCast, BroadCast, Point2Point to exchange data among group members.

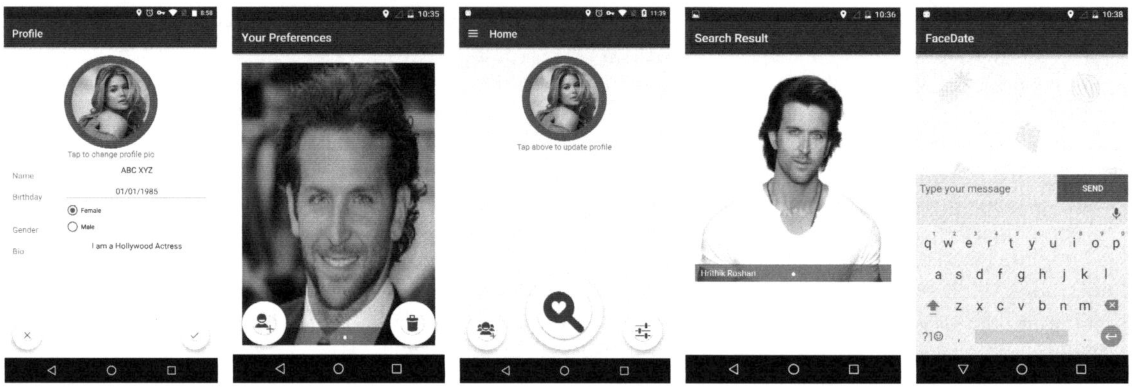

(a) (b) (c) (d) (e)

Figure 1: FaceDate Screen-shots: a)Profile Setup, b)Face Preference Setup, c)Search for Matches, d)Results, e) Chat with Match

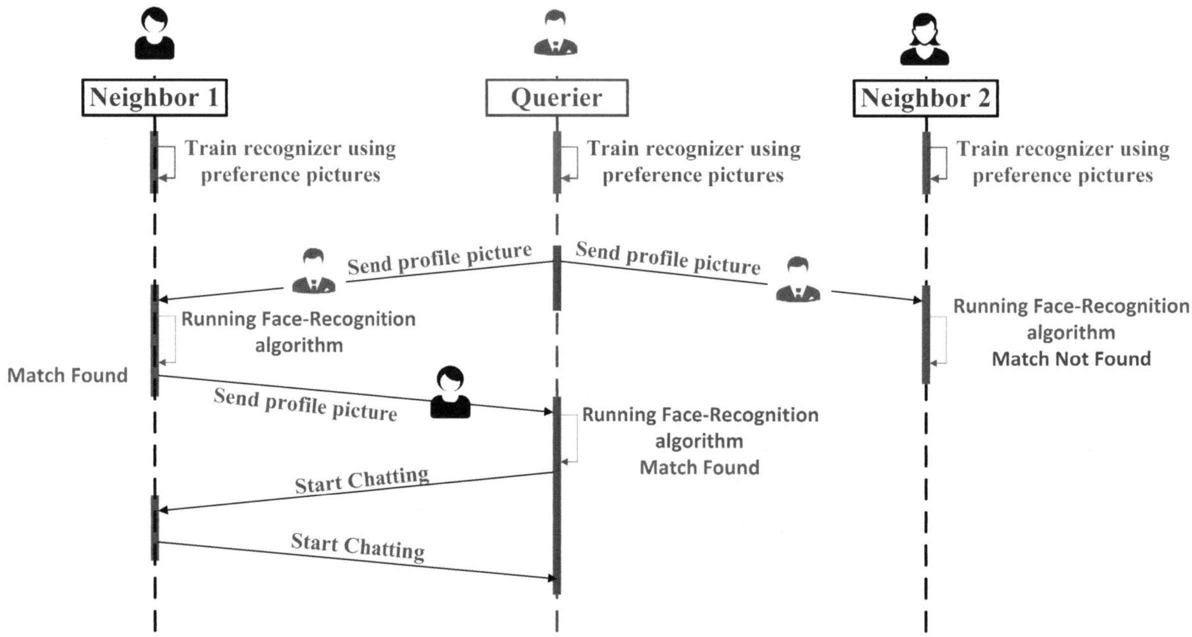

Figure 2: Overview of FaceDate Operation

4 Design and Implementation

Figure 4 shows the architecture of FaceDate. The *Search Manager* distributes the search requests from the user looking for a match to other users (i.e., to their FaceDate instances); it is also responsible for handling search requests from other users and delivering responses. The *Trainer* trains the app with preference photos of the user to facilitate face matching. The training results and the photos are stored in the *Photo Database.* The *Match Manager* matches photos by testing the similarity between the profile photos included in requests and the preference photos in the *Photo Database.* The *Search Manager* calls Moitree API functions to establish user groups for face matching and to enable communication among FaceDate instances at different user devices. Similarly, the *Chat Manager* uses the Moitree API for user-to-user communciation.

The pseudo-code in Algorithm 1 shows the workflow of matching in FaceDate, which consists of three major steps: (i) Location Updates, (ii) Profile and Preferences Setup, and (iii) Searching.

4.1 Location Updates

FaceDate needs to create location-based groups. Thus, it periodically updates the current location of the user by invoking the Google Location Services API [3] and notifies Moitree about location changes. The location is updated by a background thread initiated when the app is started (line 1 of Algorithm 1).

4.2 Profile and Preferences Setup

Before any search request can be handled, the user needs to setup her profile and add photos of her face preferences (lines 2 and 3). The app trains itself on the preference photos using the LBPH

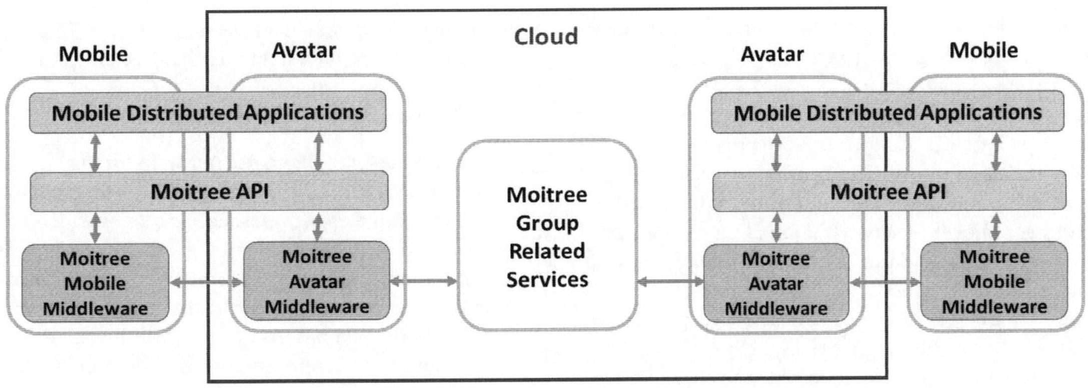

Figure 3: Architecture of Moitree Middleware

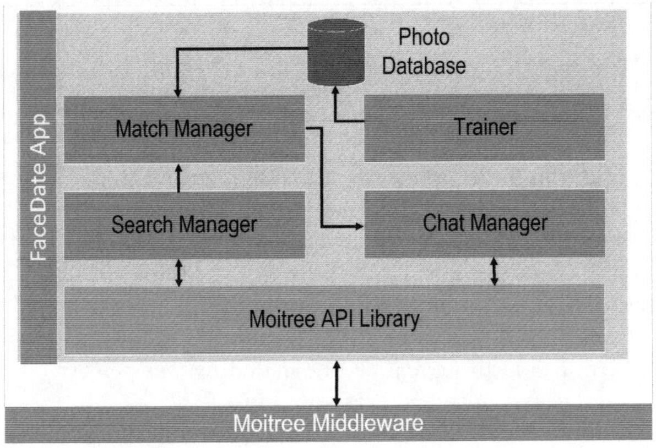

Figure 4: Architecture of FaceDate

algorithm provided by the JavaCV library [4], which is a wrapper to the OpenCV library [9].

FaceDate seeks similar looking faces rather than exact matches, within a user-specified threshold. To increase search accuracy, we have used three different settings of the LBPH algorithm: (1,8,8,8,60), (1,9,8,8,60) and (1,8,8,8,70). Each setting is a combination of radius, neighbors, grid x, grid y, and the threshold respectively. [1] We have also used a voting mechanism to reduce false positive results. For the same photo, if the results of at least two settings match, it is considered to match the preference photos.

4.3 Searching

In this step, FaceDate first calls the createGroup() method of Moitree to identify a *group* of users who are close to the geographical position of the querier. The search will be performed within the group. The invocation returns a "group" object in its callback method, as shown in line 4. Each member of the group (the querier and the participants) receives a group object as illustrated in lines 7 and 10. The callback methods dealing with the communication among the group members are setup earlier, as shown in line 5. The most important callback function handles query requests and responses, and it is defined in lines 13-32. For a participant, the receipt of the group object also triggers the getPersistentData() function of Moitree (line 11) to retrieve any available persistent data from the group; if any data is received as a response, the app can process these data to check for a match.

Algorithm 1 FaceDate Matching Pseudo-Code

```
1: runThreadForLocationUpdates()        ▷ Thread to send
   location updates to Moitree
2: setupProfile()
3: setupPreferencePictures()
4: setupGroupCallback()
5: setupCommunicationCallback()
6: if querier == true then
7:    Group group = createGroup(RADIUS)
8:    group.distribute(querierProfilePicture)
9: else if participant == true then
10:    Group group = joinGroup()  ▷ Moitree pushes the
   group object
11:    getPersistentData()
12: end if
13: group.callBack(data){
14: if participant == true then
15:    querierProfilePicture = data.getPhoto()
16:    runFaceMatch(querierProfilePicture)
17:    if match == true then
18:       group.reply(participantProfilePicture)
19:    else
20:       discard()
21:    end if
22: else if querier == true then
23:    participantProfilePicture = data.getPhoto()
24:    runFaceMatch(participantProfilePicture)
25:    if match == true then
26:       displayResult()
27:       startChatManager()  ▷ Prepares "Chat Manager"
   to handle chat
28:    else
29:       discard()
30:    end if
31: end if
32: }
```

Line 8 of Algorithm 1 describes how the querier uses the group object to forward the profile photo of the user to the other members of the group through the Scatter-Gather channel of Moitree. On receiving the profile photo, the participants run the face recognition algorithm to find a match as shown in lines 15-16. This process is

[1] LBPH is a widely used algorithm for face matching, which is beyond the scope of this paper. Readers can access external sources for the algorithm and its settings.

the same for the participants in the group, no matter whether they joined the group from the beginning or at a later stage. Let us note that Moitree seamlessly manages dynamic group joins and leaves.

If a match is found, the participant responds with its own profile photo using the same channel. Otherwise, it discards the message. This logic is shown in lines 17-21. The querier processes the response by running the face recognition algorithm to find a match with its own preference images. If a match is found on the querier's side as well, the profile photo in the response is then displayed to the querier as a "Match". Lines 22-31 cover the matching at the querier's side. The querier can select the photo displayed on the screen to start chatting with the other user (line 27). At this point, the *"Chat Manager"* is initialized to enable the chat through a Point2Point channel in Moitree.

5 Experimental Evaluation

This section evaluates the performance of the FaceDate prototype. The goals of the evaluation were to measure the time to train a dataset of preference photos, the time to match a photo against a trained dataset, and the end-to-end latency to perform matches.

We performed the experiments using multiple smart phones with different configurations: two Nexus 5, two Moto X, one Moto G3, and one Nexus 6. Each phone is paired with an avatar in an OpenStack-based cloud. The avatars are instantiated as Android 6.0 x86 VMs, configured with 4 virtual CPUs and 3GB memory. The Moitree group-related services are running on a Linux-based server in the cloud. The smart phones communicate with the avatars over the Internet, using WiFi.

FaceDate has two main phases:

- Training: This phase includes reading the preference photos, detecting and cropping faces, and training the LBPH recognizer for face recognition. The training phase is executed by all devices that run the FaceDate app.
- Matching: This phase includes sending the querier's profile photo, detecting and cropping the face from the profile photo received at participating devices, and performing face recognition using the LBPH recognizer.

We evaluated the performance of FaceDate when training and matching is done: (i) on the mobile devices, and (ii) at the avatar VMs. The first case corresponds to a setting in which users are concerned with privacy and store their profile photo and preference photos on their mobiles. The second case corresponds to a setting in which low latency is more important for users than privacy.

5.1 Performance of Training Phase

Figure 5(a) presents the total training time for each smart phone and the avatar as a function of an increasing training dataset. We varied the number of preference photos in the training dataset between 10 and 100. We used photos from several public datasets, and each photo was of a different individual. As expected, the training time on the avatar is substantially lower that the training times on the phones. We also observe significant differences between the smart phones, with the newer ones performing better. For all the phones and the avatar, the training time does not increase significantly up until 50 preference photos, but we notice a significant increase between 50 and 75 photos. We believe this is the result of Android's heap memory management mechanism used in the ART runtime: the increase in dataset size between 50 and 75 photos cause the ART VM to suddenly enlarge the heap to allocate more memory.

5.2 Performance of Matching Phase

Figure 5(b) presents the matching time for each smart phone and the avatar as a function of an increasing training dataset. As we increase the number of preference photos, the increase in matching time is substantially less steep than the increase in training time. When matching is performed on the avatar, the matching time remains almost constant. From the results, we can also see that there are some fluctuations in the matching time with the increase in the number of preference photos. We speculate that it is caused by the hardware and/or software optimization of the mobile devices rather than the matching operation.

The conclusion of these two experiments is that both phases should be performed at the avatars to achieve lower latency, if the users are not concerned about privacy. This alternative also saves energy on phones.

5.3 End-to-End Latency

In the following experiments, we measured the end-to-end latency for the FaceDate app. First, we used one querier and an increasing number of potential matching participants. The end-to-end latency is measured from the moment the querier starts the search until the querier finishes processing the received results. We configured this experiment such that, if there are n potential matching participants, all of them will return a match. The matching was performed on the phones to test the worst case scenario.

We used a Moto X phone as the querier and varied the number of participant phones. Figure 5(c) shows that the end-to-end latency increases almost linearly with the number of participants. On the other hand, the effect of increasing the number of preference photos is small. Several factors contribute to the increase in the end-to-end delay: (a) the slow response time on lower-end devices (such as the Moto G3 and Moto Nexus 5), and (b) the increasing number of matching operations on the querier device.

The next experiment investigated a more practical scenario where only one of the participants (among 5) will have a positive match result. This is to simulate a 20% positive match scenario, which is more reflective of FaceDate's performance in terms of real-life situations. Figure 5(d) shows that FaceDate is able to perform close to an ideal situation, where end-to-end latency does not vary almost at all. These results reflect the parallelism achieved by the app.

Finally, we evaluated the app to stress the system, where there is only one participant who responds positively and a varied number of queriers. Figure 5(e) shows the average latency for the queriers. In this experiment, each participant is a member of all the groups initiated by the queriers. The results for the "No Group Reuse" case show a significant increase in latency for each addition of a querier because a new group is created for each new query. To optimize on situations like this, when multiple users initiate the creation of different groups described by the same properties (e.g., location, time), Moitree can verify if a group with the same properties already exists and simply return a reference to this group. Thus, the overhead associated with group creation and management is

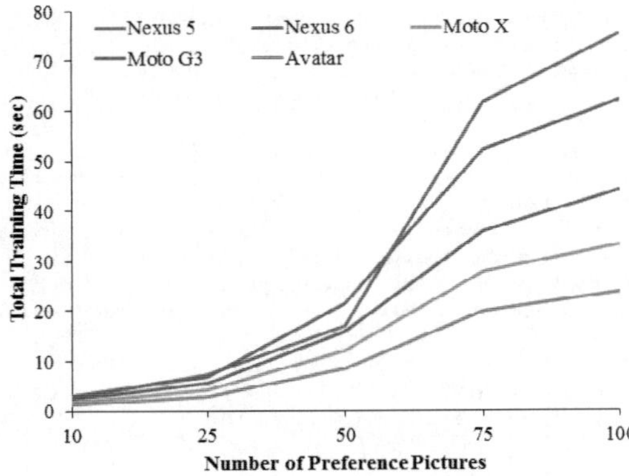

(a) Training time

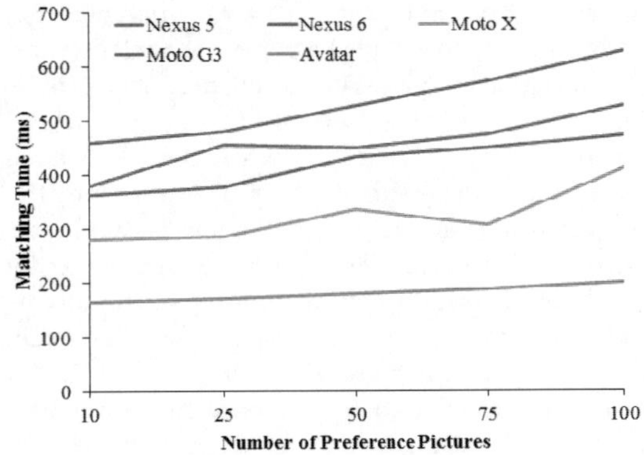

(b) Matching time

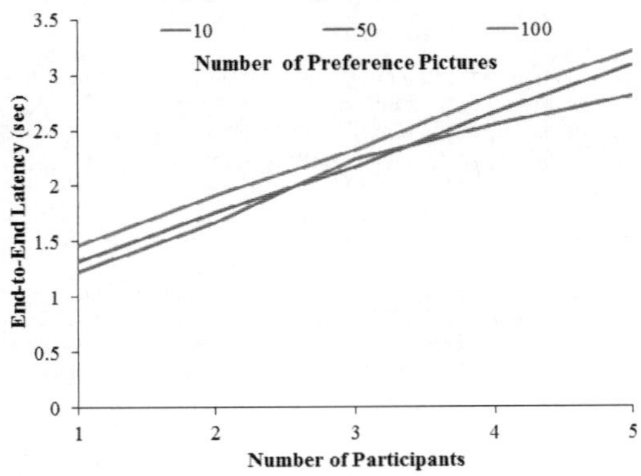

(c) End-to-end latency for one querier when all responses are positive

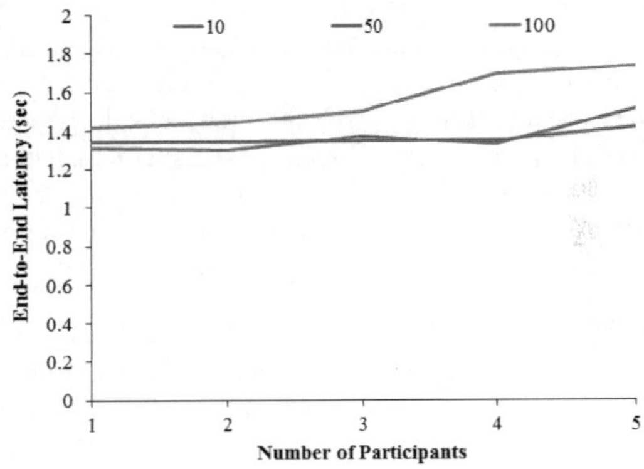

(d) End-to-end latency for one querier when only one response is positive

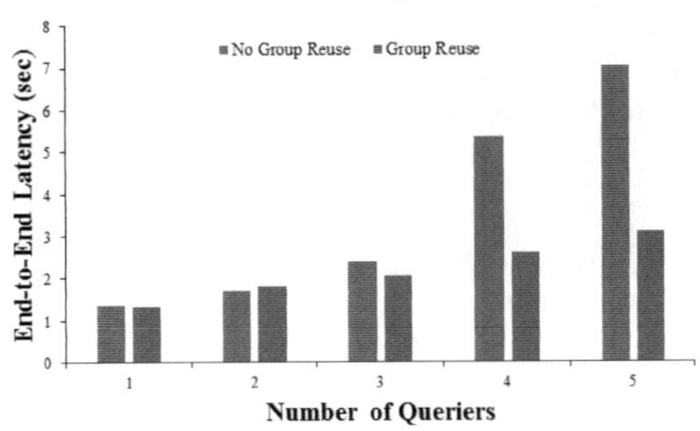

(e) End-to-end latency with an increasing number of queriers and one positive responder

Figure 5: FaceDate Performance

drastically reduced. Therefore, the latency for the "Group Reuse" case is substantially lower.

6 Related Work

Social Matching [17] has been studied for a long time. The authors in [13] explored a theoretical framework of social, personal, and relational context for social matching by using interview studies. The work in [14] studied the essence of being familiar among strangers. SocialNet [16] tried to find people with common interests using social networks and co-location information collected by RF-based mobile devices. Serendipidy [10] used Bluetooth to find people in the proximity and then employed a profile database to suggest face-to-face interactions. Although these works identified common location as one potential matching criteria, they are mainly reliant on complex text-based profile matching. Similarly, popular online matching platforms [1, 5, 6] are also dependent on user-provided profiles and answers to questionnaires. In comparison, FaceDate uses an automated face matching algorithm to find matches, under the assumption that appearance is generally the essential characteristic that makes people connect at the beginning of a relationship. Nevertheless, FaceDate could work in conjunction with profile-based matching.

Tinder [7] is another dating application, where the user can see the faces of all the nearby persons that match the filters set by the user. However, the results are not filtered on any facial characteristics. The user needs to manually select or discard images by browsing through all of them. In addition to being potentially tedious, this process does not guarantee that two people are mutually interested in each other. Furthermore, disclosing people's photos when they are not interested in each other could be viewed as a privacy-sensitive issue. FaceDate, on the other hand, provides only mutual matches to users; in this way, it simplifies user interaction and improves user privacy.

Similar to FaceDate, the work in [15] uses cloud and cloudlets to complete face recognition tasks faster. However, this solution works in an one-to-one scenario (mobile to cloud), without any collaborative computation. Photos taken by the mobile devices are pre-processed and sent to a centralized photo database for matching. In comparison, FaceDate works in a distributed manner, and the face recognition tasks can run on mobiles or be offloaded to the cloud depending on the user's privacy preferences.

7 Conclusion

This paper presented FaceDate, a mobile distributed app for location-based, real-time matching of people based on looks. FaceDate uses the Moitree middleware, which provides cloud support for the creation and maintenance of dynamic groups as well as abstract communication channels among mobile devices. The experimental results obtained using our Android-based prototype demonstrate end-to-end latency in the order of seconds and reasonable scalability. Therefore, FaceDate is practical in real-life scenarios. The app can be further improved through a hybrid search based on photos and profile text.

Acknowledgments

This research was supported by the National Science Foundation (NSF) under Grants No. CNS 1409523, SHF 1617749, CNS 1054754, DGE 1565478, and DUE 1241976, the National Security Agency (NSA) under Grant H98230-15-1-0274, and by the Defense Advanced Research Projects Agency (DARPA) and the Air Force Research Laboratory (AFRL) under Contract No. A8650-15-C-7521. Any opinions, findings, and conclusions or recommendations expressed in this material are those of the authors and do not necessarily reflect the views of NSF, NSA, DARPA, and AFRL. The United States Government is authorized to reproduce and distribute reprints notwithstanding any copyright notice herein.

References

[1] *eHarmony.* http://www.eharmony.com/.

[2] *Facedate.* https://angel.co/facedate.

[3] *Google Location Services.* https://developers.google.com/android/reference/com/google/android/gms/location/LocationServices.

[4] *JavaCV.* https://github.com/bytedeco/javacv.

[5] *Match.com.* http://www.match.com/.

[6] *okCupid.* https://www.okcupid.com/.

[7] *Tinder.* https://en.wikipedia.org/wiki/Tinder_(app).

[8] C. Borcea, X. Ding, N. Gehani, R. Curtmola, M. A. Khan, and H. Debnath. 2015. Avatar: Mobile Distributed Computing in the Cloud. In *2015 3rd IEEE International Conference on Mobile Cloud Computing, Services, and Engineering.* 151–156. DOI: http://dx.doi.org/10.1109/MobileCloud.2015.22

[9] I. Culjak, D. Abram, T. Pribanic, H. Dzapo, and M. Cifrek. 2012. A brief introduction to OpenCV. In *2012 Proceedings of the 35th International Convention MIPRO.* 1725–1730.

[10] N. Eagle and A. Pentland. 2005. Social serendipity: mobilizing social software. *IEEE Pervasive Computing* 4, 2 (Jan 2005), 28–34. DOI: http://dx.doi.org/10.1109/MPRV.2005.37

[11] K. Kadir, M. K. Kamaruddin, H. Nasir, S. I. Safie, and Z. A. K. Bakti. 2014. A comparative study between LBP and Haar-like features for Face Detection using OpenCV. In *2014 4th International Conference on Engineering Technology and Technopreneuship (ICE2T).* 335–339. DOI: http://dx.doi.org/10.1109/ICE2T.2014.7006273

[12] M. A. Khan, H. Debnath, N. R. Paiker, N. Gehani, X. Ding, R. Curtmola, and C. Borcea. 2016. Moitree: A Middleware for Cloud-Assisted Mobile Distributed Apps. In *2016 4th IEEE International Conference on Mobile Cloud Computing, Services, and Engineering (MobileCloud).* 21–30. DOI: http://dx.doi.org/10.1109/MobileCloud.2016.21

[13] Julia M. Mayer, Starr Roxanne Hiltz, and Quentin Jones. 2015. Making Social Matching Context-Aware: Design Concepts and Open Challenges. In *Proceedings of the 33rd Annual ACM Conference on Human Factors in Computing Systems (CHI '15).* ACM, New York, NY, USA, 545–554. DOI: http://dx.doi.org/10.1145/2702123.2702343

[14] Eric Paulos and Elizabeth Goodman. 2004. The Familiar Stranger: Anxiety, Comfort, and Play in Public Places. In *Proceedings of the SIGCHI Conference on Human Factors in Computing Systems (CHI '04).* ACM, New York, NY, USA, 223–230. DOI: http://dx.doi.org/10.1145/985692.985721

[15] T. Soyata, R. Muraleedharan, C. Funai, M. Kwon, and W. Heinzelman. 2012. Cloud-Vision: Real-time face recognition using a mobile-cloudlet-cloud acceleration architecture. In *2012 IEEE Symposium on Computers and Communications (ISCC).* 000059–000066. DOI: http://dx.doi.org/10.1109/ISCC.2012.6249269

[16] Michael Terry, Elizabeth D. Mynatt, Kathy Ryall, and Darren Leigh. 2002. Social Net: Using Patterns of Physical Proximity over Time to Infer Shared Interests. In *CHI '02 Extended Abstracts on Human Factors in Computing Systems (CHI EA '02).* ACM, New York, NY, USA, 816–817. DOI: http://dx.doi.org/10.1145/506443.506612

[17] Loren Terveen and David W. McDonald. 2005. Social Matching: A Framework and Research Agenda. *ACM Trans. Comput.-Hum. Interact.* 12, 3 (Sept. 2005), 401–434. DOI: http://dx.doi.org/10.1145/1096737.1096740

Recent Advances in Body Area NanoNetworks: Electromagnetic, Materials and Communications

Valeria Loscrí
INRIA
Fun Research Team - Lille
Nord Europe
Lille, France
valeria.loscri@inria.fr

Ladislau Matekovits
Department of Electronics and Telecommunications
Politecnico di Torino
10129 Torino, Italy
ladislau.matekovits@polito.it

Ildiko Peter
Department of Applied Science and Technology
Politecnico di Torino
10129 Torino, Italy
ildiko.peter@polito.it

Anna Maria Vegni
Department of Engineering
Roma Tre University
Rome, Italy
annamaria.vegni@uniroma3.it

ABSTRACT

In recent years, nanotechnology has emerged as a novel evolution in technology enabling the design of miniaturized devices (*i.e.*, nanodevices). At this scale, the behaviors and characteristics of nanodevices require a deep understanding and a revision of well-known features of devices at the macroscale level. Indeed, due to their specific nanoscale features, a fundamental requirement is to enable nanodevices to collaborate collectively to achieve a common objective. As a result, a set of nanodevices, sharing the same medium and collaborating for the same task, through communication and networking at the nanoscale, forms a nanonetwork.

Nanonetworks are expected expanding the capabilities of single nanodevice and enabling new nanotechnology applications including healthcare, biomedical, environmental, military, as well as industrial fields. In particular, through a nanoscale communication paradigm,as well a network of nanodevices can constitute a Body Area NanoNetwork (BANN), and new and revolutionary complex applications can be envisaged. This new context requires a deep analysis of the innovative technological solutions suitable for the specific features under consideration.

In this paper we aim to report the last advancements of the BANNs in a 360° vision, from three different perspectives, such as (*i*) electromagnetics, (*ii*) materials, and (*iii*) communications. We will also give a global vision of the three perspectives, by showing the glue elements of each other.

1. INTRODUCTION

Nanotechnology is a new research domain that is finding applications in several areas, from telecommunications to nanomedicine, from environmental to military and security, ust to mention some of the most common ones [3]. It is more and more gaining consensus in different fields, especially for (in)body applications, since the use of nanodevices, opportunistically functionalized, may improve the therapeutic index and increase their tolerability in the body, by drastically reducing the interferences at minimum.

In this context, a nanodevice is usually designed to perform a set of elementary actions, such as sensing and actuation. A dense wireless interconnection of nanodevices, could potentially accomplish novel and complex functionalities. Nanorobots distributed in or on top of the human body could enable pervasive and reactive continuous in-vivo monitoring.

The field of nanomedicine is a complex scenario, where the interaction of nanodevices is affected by the presence of the human body. This issue represents a very hot topic that only recently has started to be considered by researchers [28]. The interaction between the nanoparticulate system and the biological environment (*i.e.* the human body) is strictly correlated with the nanodevice material and the signaling considered for communication purpose.

From a "material" point of view, several types of nanoparticles can be exploited for body networks applications, constructed with a huge range of organic or inorganic materials, such as emulsions, Solid Lipid Nanoparticles (SLNs), gold nanoparticles, silver nanoparticles, titanium dioxide TiO_2 nanoparticles, dendrimers, Carbon Nano-Tubes (CNTs), etc. [24]. When these materials are opportunistically functionalized, it has been shown that can be used for localized Drug Delivery Systems (DDSs) and/or for diagnostic objectives.

Regarding the electromagnetic nanonetworks, the required downsize imposes the use of very high operating frequencies (several hundreds of Terahertz), thus limiting the feasibility of nanonetworks. In fact, according to the classical antenna theory, a one-micrometer-long antenna would radiate at approximately 150 THz with the assumption of a Perfect Electrical Conductor (PEC). Normally, at these higher frequencies, metallic materials are frequency-dependent and then far to be PEC material. Alternatively, nanomaterials (*e.g.* graphene or specific metamaterials (MMs)) enable the developments of nano-antennas that can operate at much

Permission to make digital or hard copies of all or part of this work for personal or classroom use is granted without fee provided that copies are not made or distributed for profit or commercial advantage and that copies bear this notice and the full citation on the first page. Copyrights for components of this work owned by others than ACM must be honored. Abstracting with credit is permitted. To copy otherwise, or republish, to post on servers or to redistribute to lists, requires prior specific permission and/or a fee. Request permissions from permissions@acm.org.
BodyNets '16 Torino, italy

lower frequencies. This type of considerations implies that there exists a very strict interrelation between the nature of the material constituting the antenna and the electromagnetic features.

Finally, from a communication point of view, different innovative communication paradigms have been proposed during the last few years, such as molecular and neural communications [13, 37], terahertz band communications [2], opto-ultrasonic communication [42], acoustic communication approaches [29].

The aim of this paper is to analyze the last advances of Body Area Nanonetworks from three different perspectives, such as (*i*) electromagnetics, (*ii*) (meta)materials, and (*iii*) communications. Furthermore, we try to identify the common points and the interdependencies of the three (sub)-domains.

The rest of the paper is organized as follows. In the Section 2 we report the recent advances in the context of electromagnetism applied to nanonetwork domain. The Section 3 will be devoted to the description of the last results in terms of material and meta-material for nanonetworks and body area nanonetworks. In Section 4 we will revise the major considerations that have been done on the interferences between the body networks with the human immune system. In the Section 5 we will report the most recent results in terms of communication paradigms for BANNs. Finally, conclusions are drawn at the end of the paper, together with some directions for future works.

2. RECENT ADVANCES IN ELECTROMAGNETIC NANONETWORKS

On-going research on graphene-based nano-transceivers [19, 41] and nano-antennas [21, 46] witness the Terahertz Band (0.1−10 THz) as the communication frequency band for nanodevices. The peculiar propagation properties of electrons in graphene [14, 15] enable the creation of compact miniaturized RF components, alleviating the energy constraints of nanodevices.

The Terahertz Band brings many opportunities for communication among nanodevices, mainly due to the huge amount of available unlicensed band. Although long-range Terahertz Band communications are drastically limited by the molecular absorption loss [40], for short distances below one meter [20] the THz band acts as a single transmission window almost 10-THz-wide. This very large band can theoretically support data transmissions at very high rates, and also enables new communication mechanisms to be adopted by nanodevices with very limited capabilities.

In this direction, novel channel models need to be designed since existing models used for lower frequencies are not suitable in the THz band context. One of the main channel models for THz band has been presented in [20], where the authors investigate the effects due to molecular absorption and free space loss. Other works [22, 38] investigate the scattering effect in realistic environments for THz communications, while in [16] the authors present a channel model based on multi ray approach that considers both reflected, scattered, and diffracted rays.

Recently, it has been shown that the chirality effect of specific materials (*i.e.*, metamaterials) strongly affects the performance of channel in THz band [49, 50]. Metamaterials exhibiting Giant Optical Activity in a specific range of THz band (*i.e.*, from 4 to 10 THz) affect the channel response, and then it is possible to tune the working frequency in order to enhance the channel performances.

Following novel results in channel modeling in THz band, novel communication schemes need to be figured out. Recently, a technique based on the transmission of one-hundred-femtosecond-long pulses spread in time known as TS-OOK has been proposed in [19]. This modulation takes into account the difficulty of generating high-power carrier signals at Terahertz Band frequencies from a nano-transceiver and leverages the state of the art in pulse-based nano-transceivers.

3. ADVANCED MATERIALS FOR BANNS

Noble metals, like silver and gold, polymer based materials, silica nanoparticles, carbon nanotubes, etc. are largely employed in the design of nanoparticles and can be exploited to accomplish different tasks, e.g. they can be used as carriers of medicament and/or bioactive molecules to a desired intracellular cells, host materials for bioimaging and biosensing agents [45, 48].

Colloidal silver has been used as an antibacterial agent able to weakening DNA replication. Gold-based nano components have been often utilized since the low toxicity versus biological systems [7, 54]. In particular, Ti, Mg, steel and their alloys are considered important metallic materials for both *bioengineering* and for human *implants*; as well, their porous metal interface can be exploited as a drug delivery plate and stimuli reactive material.

The central point and the success of the usage of these metallic materials for the purpose of interest are governed by their capacity to develop biocompatible carriers allowing high loading of drug molecules with no any early release of the load before getting the target.

In order to serve as an efficient drug delivery system, among other characteristics, the carrier material should be biocompatible and it has to show (*i*) high loading ability for the chosen drug particles, (*ii*) cell type or tissue specificity, (*iii*) controlled release of the molecules with an appropriate ratio of release [10, 18]. Complementarily, surface chemistry and morphology are considered as key features for determining the biological performance of bio-metallic implants, to support or stimulate the preferred host response [53].

Modification of the physical properties of nano- and micro-particles radically changes their biological functions, representing an important aspect when drug delivery system is under development for highly specific sensibleness, e.g. long circulation. The effects that size [12], shape [8, 34], surface charge [9, 52] and hydrophobicity [17, 52] have on the transfer capabilities of particles have been extensively investigated during the time.

According to [5], modulating the elasticity of nano- and micro-particles is a feasible approach to control some biological interactions. In-vitro studies pointed out that softer particles show lower internalization in immune cells which is supported by in-vivo studies that jointly demonstrate that softer particles circulate for longer periods as compared to their hard counterparts. Additionally, computational studies in detail described how hard particles have individual returns over their soft counterparts in cellular internalization. The transformation of the metal-based materials surface into a porous network obtained by different methods (surface anodization, plasma or laser treatments, chemical etching, ultrasonic technique, sol-gel route, etc.), as well as amplification of their biocompatibility, lead obtaining an intelligent metal surface (spongy like material). Such a bio-metal becomes more attractive for functional molecules (surface attached pills) in a complex biological system, where the strict control over the physical or chemical absorption of functional biomolecules and cells is encouraged. As for example, a textured bio-metal surface with a fully hydrophilic nature, determining a positive reaction of distinguished cells to the surface and their attachment(s) has been discussed in [6].

Development of a passive oxide layer on the bio-metallic implant surfaces is considered as one of the crucial element as concerns the protection of their surfaces and their biocompatibility: once the implant will be embedded, the biological environment will be in contact with the oxide layer and not with the metal themselves. Additionally, the developed oxide layer could guarantee the chemical attachment of functional molecules (pharmaceutical agents, drugs, etc.).

The modification of the metal surfaces can further prevent the introduction and release of toxic compounds from the surface of the bio-device [35], [36]. Supplementary, an intelligent metal surface is capable to control the behavior of the biomolecules during the time. The properties of such surfaces can be manipulated externally (humidity, temperature, pH change, presence of an electric or magnetic field, etc.) giving rise to different structures to be selectively used for particular applications [11], [43]. Appropriately modified metallic surfaces can present advanced features: e.g. Ti wires and nanotubes groups are considered innovative drug releasing structures with the additional benefit related to a localized approach, that reduces the toxic effect of drug to the healthy tissues and at the same time diminishes the severity of side effects [23].

As well, local treatment allows high drug concentration at the target site and prolonged pharmacological exposure. Ionic dissolution is strictly related to the specific surface area of the materials and affects the biocompatibility of the materials. Specific surface area increases as particle size decreases, and the chemical reactivity of the system is more evident.

In most cases, the interaction of materials with cells and tissue starts from ionic dissolution and is an expression of the materials toxicity, which is directly correlated to the corrosion resistance of the material [33]. Rise in specific surface area, typically counted as the nanosizing effect, origins the improvement of the chemical reactivity and toxicity for soluble materials. In the case of a non-soluble and biocompatible material, like Ti and TiO_2, when the particle size is 200 nm or minor, they are less stimulative and their identification by the body protection systems becomes weaker. They can arrive into the organism through the respiratory or the digestive apparatus and then spread out inside the whole body [51].

In the last a few years the research field of material science has a bit changed its primary focus, by shifting it for engineering materials with specific features instead of studying the properties and characteristics of the existing materials. This new field of research is well represented by the field of metamaterials. Metamaterials are complex materials with artificial structures and are particularly interesting, since they exhibit features that are not existing in nature, *e.g.* negative refraction index [4, 44]. These characteristics have attracted several researchers in several research areas [55]. One of the most prominent example of scientific and technical applications concerned with metamaterial is certainly nanotechnology. The typical feature of metamaterials construction is the possibility to achieve the user defined electromagnetic response at a precisely controlled target frequency and this represents a very interesting aspect in the context of photonic/phononic domain [47].

Normally, the parameters of an MM are established from the beginning and cannot be altered later (*e.g.* programmatically). On the other hand, the concept of reprogrammable metamaterial has been considered for the first time in [25], where the authors propose a new class of real-time reconfigurable MMs, named Software Defined Metamaterials (SDMs).

4. IMMUNE HUMAN SYSTEM CONSIDERATIONS

One of the most important considerations that need to be done related to the context of BANNs is about the impact that the Immune Human System (IHS) can exert on the nanoparticulate system performance, as well as how this latter stimulates a response of IHS. Of course, the desirable effect would be to have as minimum interference as possible.

Despite the great importance of this research topic, it has only recently started to be investigated by the researchers [26, 31]. The main difficulty in this context, is to identify a "right" model that can capture the necessary features of the IHS in a way that the interferences can be correctly modeled by keeping the system as "tractable" as possible (*i.e.* not too much complex). In [32], the authors review the different effects of nanoparticles on the specific immune cells (*i.e.*, dendritic cells, neutrophils, mast cells, T cells, B cells, etc.). The authors distinguish two types of immune response such as (*i*) innate, and (*ii*) adaptive immunity. Innate response is the non specific and first response of the immune system, and plays a very important role in the early recognition and proinflammatory response. The adaptive immune response of the IHS is antigen specific and reacts with the organism that induced the response. Normally, nanoparticles are identified as "foreign" entities and then are eliminated by the IHS, as it has also already mentioned in the previous paragraph.

However, the human body can also identify the foreign elements but does not consider them as a threat. In this case the IHS will tolerate the nanoparticles. The response of the immune system to the presence of the nanoparticles has to be considered when developing a nanomaterial for in-vivo applications. As outlined in [32] a different perspective is given by a different application, such as nanoparticles targeting immune cells that have to manipulate or control immunological diseases. In this case, the material of nanodevices has to be designed to opportunistically modify the immune response.

In any case, the conclusion is that a deep and accurate knowledge of a nanoparticulate system with the IHS is fundamental. This purpose has been pursued by the researchers in [30] and [31], where the authors introduced a mathematical model to effectively represent the IHS and to be able to also incorporate both time and spatial correlations with an external system composed of nanoparticles.

5. COMMUNICATION PARADIGMS FOR BANNS

One key factor of BANN technology is represented by data communications, and specifically the need for short-range data communications. Several new communication paradigms in the context of BANNs have been proposed in the last few years. Among them, electromagnetic communications in the terahertz band [2], neural communications [13], chemical communication or molecular communications [37], opto-ultrasonic [42], and phonon-based [27] communication techniques have been proposed.

In particular, in [39], the authors investigate electromagnetic propagation and communication in human tissues, by demonstrating the challenges that characterize a similar environment as transmitting medium. A terahertz channel characterization inside the human skin has been derived in [1], where the authors propose a novel radio channel model inside the human skin and compare the model with terahertz time-domain spectroscopy based measurement of skin sample.

Chemical and molecular communications represent a kind of straightforward and natural way to communicate at this size, since molecules and cells naturally communicate in living beings. The counter side of this type of communications is based from one side by the high communication latency that generally characterize this type of communication, and from another side the still scarce control on molecules. In fact, targeting specific actions at this level is not at all trivial, and *synthetic biology* is still in its infancy.

A different point of view in terms of BANN communications is represented by the approach considered in [42]. The authors exploit the optoacoustic effects enabling the generation of high-frequency acoustic waves when the medium is irradiated with electromagnetic energy at the optical frequency. In [27], the authors argue that quantum phenomena may represent a natural direction for developing nanotechnology. A specific type of nanoparticles is considered, namely phonons, and by considering them as specific information carriers, it is possible to compute the theoretical capacity in a body network context.

6. CONCLUSIONS

Based on the recent advancements on electromagnetism, (meta)material for nanodevices and nanocommunication approaches, it is clear a very strict interrelation existing among these three fundamentals aspects of BANNs. In particular, electromagnetic communication seems a viable solution for BANN if innovative materials with specific properties are considered, such as graphene, carbon nanotubes or metamaterial with specific features. On the other hand, the type of communication is strictly dependent on the specific technology selected that depends on the characteristics of the material used as transmission means. Most important, in biological contexts not only the transmission features matters but also fundamental aspects such as bio-compatibility and low impact in terms of immune systems have to be taken into consideration.

From one side it is clear that a global and multi-disciplinary approach has to be considered in order to investigate novel and revolutionary solutions in the context of BANNs that takes into considerations the different aspects we have envisaged in this position paper. On the other hand, we realize that a convergence of different disciplines is always a complex process and is more complicated in this case where all the research domains (*i.e.* electromagnetism, material and communications) for BANNs are still in infancy.

7. REFERENCES

[1] Q. Abbasi, H. E. Sallabi, N. Chopra, K. Yang, K. A. Qaraqe, and A. Alomainy. Terahertz channel characterization inside the human skin for nano-scale body-centric networks. *IEEE Transactions on Terahertz Science and Technology*, 6(3):427–434, 2016.

[2] I. F. Akyildiz and J. M. Jornet. Electromagnetic wireless nanosensor networks. *Nano Communication Networks*, 1(1):3–19, 2010.

[3] I. F. Akyildiz, J. M. Jornet, and M. Pierobon. Nanonetworks: A new frontier in communications. *Commun. ACM*, 54(11):84–89, Nov. 2011.

[4] A. Alú, N. Engheta, A. Erentok, and R. W. Ziolkowski. Single-negative, double-negative and low-index metamaterials and their electromegnetic applications. *IEEE Antennas Propag. Mag.*, 49(1):423–436, 2007.

[5] A. C. Anselmo and S. Mitragotri. Impact of particle elasticity on particle-based drug delivery systems. *Advanced Drug Delivery Reviews*, 2007.

[6] M. Bereznai, I. PelsĄ0Ń2czi, Z. TÍőth, K. TurzÍő, M. Radnai, Z. Bor, and A. Fazekas. Surface modifications induced by ns and sub-ps excimer laser pulses on titanium implant material. *Biomaterials*, 24(23):4197–4203, 2003.

[7] D. Bhumkar, H. J. andM. Sastry, and V. Pokharkar. Chitosan reduced gold nanoparticles as novle carriers for transmucosal delivery of insulin. *Pharmaceutical Research*, 24, 2007.

[8] J. Champion, Y. Katare, and S.Mitragotri. Particle shape: a newdesign parameter for micro-and nanoscale drug delivery carriers. *J. Control. Release*, 121:3–9, 2007.

[9] S. charge of gold nanoparticles mediates mechanism of toxicity. Particle shape: a newdesign parameter for micro-and nanoscale drug delivery carriers. *Nanoscale*, 3:410–420, 2011.

[10] C. X. Chen, L. Liu, and C. Jiang. Charge-reversal nanoparticles: novel targeted drug delivery carriers. *Review Article Acta Pharmaceutica Sinica B*, 6(4):261–267, 2016.

[11] T. L. Deans, D. W. Grainger, and M. Fussenegger. Synthetic biology: Innovative approaches for pharmaceutics and drug delivery. *Advanced Drug Delivery Reviews*, 105:1–2, 2016.

[12] P. Decuzzi, B. Godin, T. Tanaka, S.-Y. Lee, C. Chiappini, X. Liu, and M. Ferrari. Size and shape effects in the biodistribution of intravascularly injected particles. *J. Control. Release*, 141:320–327, 2010.

[13] L. Galluccio, S. Palazzo, and G. E. Santagati. Characterization of molecular communications among implantable biomedical neuro-inspired nanodevices. *Nano Communication Networks*, 4(2):53–64, 2013.

[14] A. K. Geim and K. S. Novoselov. The rise of graphene. *Nature Materials*, 6(3):183–191, 2007.

[15] V. P. Gusynin, S. G. Sharapov, and J. P. Carbotte. Ac conductivity of graphene: from tight-binding model to

2+1-dimensional quantum electrodynamics. *International Journal of Modern Physics B*, 21(4611), 2007.

[16] C. Han, A. Bicen, and I. Akyildiz. Multi-ray channel modeling and wideband characterization for wireless communications in the terahertz band. *IEEE Trans. Wireless Commun.*, 14(5):2402Ď1d'72412, 2015.

[17] D. O. III and N. Peppas. Opsonization, biodistribution, and pharmacokinetics of polymeric nanoparticles. *Int. J. Pharm.*, 307:93–102, 2006.

[18] D. M. Jarosz, A. Pawlik, M. Szuwarzyĺ¡ski, and G. D. S. M. JaskuĄ0Š0a. Nanoporous anodic titanium dioxide layers as potential drug delivery systems: Drug release kinetics and mechanism. *Colloids and Surfaces B: Biointerfaces*, 143:447–454, 2016.

[19] J. Jornet and I. Akyildiz. Graphene-based plasmonic nano-transceiver for terahertz band communication. In *In Proceedings of European Conference on Antennas and Propagation (EuCAP)*, 2014.

[20] J. M. Jornet and I. F. Akyildiz. Channel modeling and capacity analysis of electromagnetic wireless nanonetworks in the terahertz band. *IEEE Transactions on Wireless Communications*, 10(10):3211–3221, 2011.

[21] J. M. Jornet and I. F. Akyildiz. Graphene-based plasmonic nano-antenna for terahertz band communication in nanonetworks. *IEEE JSAC, Special Issue on Emerging Technologies for Communications*, 12(12):685–694, 2013.

[22] J. Kokkoniemi, J. Lehtomaki, K. Umebayashi, and M. Juntti. Frequency and time domain channel models for nanonetworks in terahertz band. *IEEE Trans. Antennas and Propagation*, 63(11):678Ď1d'7691, 2015.

[23] K. Krukiewicz and J. K. Zak. Biomaterial-based regional chemotherapy: Local anticancer drug delivery to enhance chemotherapy and minimize its side-effects. *Materials Science and Engineering C*, 62:927–942, 2016.

[24] N. Kumar. Handbook of particulate drug delivery. *A.S. Publishers*, 2008.

[25] C. Liaskos, A. Tsioliaridou, A. Pitsillides, I. Akyildiz, N. Kantartzis, A. Lalas, X. Dimitropoulos, S. Ioannidis, M. Kafesaki, and C. Soukoulis. Design and development of software defined metamaterials for nanonetworks. *IEEE Circuits and Systems Magazine*, 15(4):12–25, 2015.

[26] V. Loscrí, L. Matekovits, I. Peter, and A. Vegni. Modeling and experimental analysis of an in-body area nanonetwork. In *In Proc. of BodyNets*, 2015.

[27] V. Loscrí and A. Vegni. Channel modeling in a phonon-based quantum network for nano-communications. In *In Proc. of ACM NanoCom*, 2016.

[28] V. Loscrí, A. Vegni, and G. Fortino. On the interaction between a nanoparticulate system and the human body in body area nanonetworks. *Micromachines, Special Issue ""Sensors and Systems for Medical Applications and Personal Health Monitoring*, 6(9):1213–1235, 2015.

[29] V. Loscrí and A. M. Vegni. An acoustic communication technique of nanorobot swarms for nanomedicine applications. *IEEE Trans. NanoBioscience*, 14(6):598–607, 2015.

[30] V. Loscrí, A. M. Vegni, and G. Fortino. On the interaction betwen a nanoparticulate system and the human body in body area nanonetworks. *Micromachines, Special Issue âĂĪSensors and Systems for Medical Applications and Personal Health MonitoringâĂİ*, 6(9):1213–1235, 2016.

[31] V. Loscrií and A. Vegni. On the affection of the human immune system on a nanoparticulate nanomedicine system. In *In Proc. of BodyNets*, 2014.

[32] Y. H. Luo, L. W. Chang, and P. Lin. Metal-based nanoparticles and the immune system: Activation, inflammation, and potential applications. *Hindawi BioMed Research International*, 14(6):1–12, 2015.

[33] H. Matsuno, A. Yokoyama, F. Watari, M. Uo, and T. Kawasaki. Biocompatibility and osteogenesis of refractory metal implants, titanium, hafnium, niobium, tantalum and rhenium. *Biomaterials*, 22(11):1253–1262, 2001.

[34] S. Mitragotri. In drug delivery, shape does matter. *Pharm. Res.*, 26:233–234, 2009.

[35] M. Niinomi, M. Nakai, and J. Hieda. Development of new metallic alloys for biomedical applications. *Acta Biomaterialia*, 8:3888–3903, 2012.

[36] I. Peter and M. Rosso. Study of ti-enriched cocrmo alloy for dental application. *IEEE Access*, 3:73–80, 2015.

[37] M. Pierobon and I. Akyildiz. A physical end-to-end model for molecular communication in nanonetworks. *IEEE Journal on Selected Areas in Communications*, 28(4):602–611, 2010.

[38] R. Piesiewicz, C. Jansen, D. Mittleman, T. Kleine-Ostmann, and T. K. M. Koch. Scattering analysis for the modeling of thz communication systems. *IEEE Trans. Antennas and Propagation*, 55(11):3002Ď1d'73009, 2007.

[39] G. Piro, K. Yang, G. Boggia, N. Chopra, L. A. Grieco, and A. Alomainy. Terahertz communications in human tissues at the nanoscale for healthcare applications. *IEEE Transactions on Nanotechnology*, 14(3):404–406, 2015.

[40] S. Priebe, C. Jastrow, M. Jacob, T. Kleine-Ostmann, T. Schrader, and T. Kurner. Channel and propagation measurements at 300 ghz. *IEEE Transactions on Antennas and Propagation*, 59(5):1688–1698, 2011.

[41] V. Ryzhii, M. Ryzhii, V. Mitin, and T. Otsuji. Toward the creation of terahertz graphene injection laser. *Journal of Applied Physics*, 110(9), 2011.

[42] G. E. Santagati and T. Melodia. Opto-ultrasonic communications in wireless body area nanonetworks. In *In Proc. of IEEE Asilomar Conf. on Signals, Systems, and Computers*, 2013.

[43] D. Schmaljohann. Thermo- and ph-responsive polymers in drug delivery. *Advanced Drug Delivery Reviews*, 58:1655–1670, 2006.

[44] V. Shalaev. Optical negative-index metamaterials. *Nature Photon.*, 1(1):41–48, 2007.

[45] B. I. I. Slowing, J. L. Vivero-Escoto, and V. S.-Y. L. C.W. Wu. Mesoporous silica nanoparticles as controlled release drug delivery and gene transfection carriers. *Advanced Drug Delivery Reviews*,

60(11):1278–1288, 2008.

[46] M. Tamagnone, J. S. Gomez-Diaz, J. R. Mosig, and J. Perruisseau-Carrier. Reconfigurable terahertz plasmonic antenna concept using a graphene stack. *Applied Physics Letters*, 101(21), 2012.

[47] B. Tao, J. J. Strikwerda, A. Fan, D. Kaplan, X. Zhang, R. Averitt, and F. Omenetto. Metamaterial silk composites at terahertz frequencies. *Adv. Mater.*, pages 3527–3531–406, 2010.

[48] C. Tsai, J. L. Vivero-Escoto, I. I. Slowing, B. G. T. I.J. Fang, and V. S. Y. Lin. Surfactant-assisted controlled release of hydrophobic drugs using anionic surfactant templated mesoporous silica nanoparticles. *Biomaterials*, 32:6234–6244, 2011.

[49] A. M. Vegni and V. Loscrí. Characterization and performance analysis of a chiral-metamaterial channel with giant optical activity for terahertz communications. *Nano Communication Networks*, 9:28 – 35, 2016.

[50] A. M. Vegni and V. Loscrí. Chirality effects on channel modeling for thz-band wireless communications in los/nlos propagation. *Nano Communication Networks*, pages –, 2016.

[51] F. Watari, N. Takashi, A. Yokoyama, M. Uo, T. Akasaka, Y. Sato, S. Abe, Y. Totsuka, and K. Tohji. Material nanosizing effect on living organisms: non-specific, biointeractive, physical size effects. *J. R. Soc Interface*, 6:371–388, 2009.

[52] J. Yoo, E. Chambers, and S. Mitragotri. Factors that control the circulation time of nanoparticles in blood: challenges, solutions and future prospects. *Curr. Pharm. Des.*, 16:2298–2307, 2010.

[53] E. X. Zhao, G. Wang, H. Zheng, Z. Lu, X. Zhong, X. Cheng, and H. Zreiqat. Delicate refinement of surface nanotopography by adjusting tio2coating chemical composition for enhanced interfacial biocompatibility. *ACS Appl. Mater.Interfaces*, 5:8203–8209, 2013.

[54] Y. Zhou, Y. Kong, S. Kundu, J. Cirillo, and H. Liang. Dantibacterial activities of glod and silver nanoparticles against escherichia coli and bacillus calmette-guérin. *Journal of Nanotechnology*, 10, 2012.

[55] S. Zouhdi, A. Sihvola, and A. Vinogradov. Metamaterials and plasmonics: Fundamentals, modelling, applications. In *In Proceedings of the NATO Advanced Research Workshop on Metamaterials for Secure Information and Communication Technologies*, 2008.

Towards Interoperability of IoT-based Health Care platforms: the INTER-Health use case

Pasquale Pace
DIMES - University of Calabria
Rende - ITALY
ppace@dimes.unical.it

Gianluca Aloi
DIMES - University of Calabria
Rende - ITALY
aloi@dimes.unical.it

Raffaele Gravina
DIMES - University of Calabria
Rende - ITALY
rgravina@dimes.unical.it

Giancarlo Fortino
DIMES - University of Calabria
Rende - ITALY
g.fortino@unical.it

Giovanna Larini
TIM - Telecom Italia
Turin - ITALY
g.larini@telecomitalia.it

Margherita Gulino
Azienda Sanitaria Locale TO5
Turin - ITALY
gulino.m@aslto5.piemonte.it

ABSTRACT

The paper proposes a novel approach to support interoperability between different IoT platforms with a particular focus on the healthcare context and applications.

A novel IoT-based healthcare platform, supporting decentralized and mobile monitoring of assisted livings in highly heterogeneous contexts, can be obtained by integrating two already existing heterogeneous, non-interoperable IoT platforms (BodyCloud and e-Care) according to the strategy proposed in the ongoing INTER-IoT (Horizon 2020) European project.

A specific lifestyle monitoring use case, named INTER-Health, will be used to guide and validate such integration process in order to show the potential of the presented solution in terms of faster detection and correction of wrong lifestyles or critical healthcare situations.

CCS Concepts

•Human-centered computing → Ubiquitous and mobile devices; Smartphones; •Applied computing → Health care information systems; Health informatics;

Keywords

Computing systems; Wearable devices; Healthcare platforms.

1. INTRODUCTION

E-health and m-Health have captured huge attention in the last decade due to their promise to more effectively support health care of assisted livings at hospitals, homes and everywhere [1]. Most of the commercial or non commercial e-health platforms aim to achieve similar goals such as *i)* to improve the quality of life of patients that can be monitored directly from their home without having to go to a clinic or hospital, *ii)* to offer physicians the information in order to have the situation under control of the measurements performed by the patient in real time, without having to spend time on a dedicated visit, *iii)* to support the hospital and home care through the use of ICT and biomedical technologies that facilitate the monitoring of the patient and his relationship with the most appropriate clinician referent (doctor and / or medical specialist, nurse, carer), and *iv)* to help in costs reduction because a patient can be adequately monitored, de-hospitalized in advance and can make use of targeted drug therapy changes. However, specific problems were often addressed with specific solutions that were not interoperable. This has led to the development of many IoT-based health care systems that may constitute an added-value if we were able to integrate them thus supporting decentralized and mobile monitoring of assisted livings in highly heterogeneous contexts.
Every year in the world 2.8 million people die for obesity or overweight; 2.6 million people die for high cholesterol levels; 7.5 million people die for hypertension; 3.2 million people die for physical inactivity [2]. The growing increase of these statistics justifies the interest in designing new platforms to monitor physical activity, lifestyle and health of people in their daily activities.

The IoT paradigm [3] can boost the health care industry by enabling an easier interconnection of wireless sensors and mobile or embedded devices. A broad state of the art in this field is given in [1]. In this work, authors survey advances in IoT-based health care technologies and reviews the state-of-the-art of architectures and platforms. Many examples could be made, however, here we will introduce only a few emblematic example. In [4] authors propose a smart hospital system for patient monitoring and management of emergency. The system allows also automotive monitoring and tracking of patients, personal and biomedical devices within hospitals and nursing institutes.

A personalized IoT healthcare platform in smart homes environment is introduced in [5]. The system supports the monitoring and processing of several physical parameters and exposes RESTful web services to the consumers. Finally, a review of the existing wearable sensors for human activity monitoring is discussed in [6]. The work motivates the important role of wearable devices system to support the continuous monitoring of physiological parameters especially of the elderly or chronic patients.

The plethora of existing solutions highlights the evident lack of interoperability and fragmentation of existing IoT healthcare platforms. Accordingly, this paper describes the potential of the under development INTER-IoT [10] framework to support the interoperability in a reference m-health use case based on two already developed and widely used IoT healthcare platforms presenting distinctive features.

The rest of the paper is organized as follows. In section 2 we point out the motivations of the proposed study. In section 3 we describe the characteristics of different IoT-based healthcare platforms highlighting the main issues related to lack of interoperability between them. In the same section we discuss about the requirements, the methods and the benefits coming from platforms integration. Section 4 proposes and describes a specific use case called INTER-Health to demonstrate the usefulness of the IoT platforms integration also explaining the next steps towards the realization of the real pilot test. Finally, section 5 concludes the paper presenting future research directions.

2. MOTIVATIONS

Many different IoT platforms already exist [7], [8],[9] providing specific solutions for different application scenarios such as healthcare, logistics, home automation, etc... however, the quick integration and interoperability of those heterogeneous IoT platforms, allowing heterogeneous elements to cooperate seamlessly to share data, infrastructures and services as in a homogeneous scenario, is still a challenging issue.

It is worth noting that, when we consider any IoT platform, the complexity of technologies used to build up the platform further arises as each defined layer (device, networking, middleware, application service, data and semantics) exploits specific heterogeneous IoT technological solutions that need to be holistically adapted to form the final platform without providing any (or even limited) interoperability. Thus, it is critical to provide bottom-up "*voluntary*" approaches able to integrate, interconnect, merge, heterogeneous IoT platforms to build up extreme-scale interoperable ecosystems on top of which large-scale applications can be designed, implemented, executed and managed.

A possible solution to the interoperability issue is being developing within the ongoing INTER-IoT project [10] whose main ambition is the design of a framework for interoperability, interconnection and integration between two or more heterogeneous IoT platforms. INTER-IoT will provide the first full-fledged methodological and technological suite to completely address the fundamental issue of "voluntary interoperability". The suite will be composed of three main building blocks: (i) Layer-oriented infrastructures (INTER-LAYER) to adapt heterogeneous peer layers (device-to-device, networking-to-networking, middleware-to-middleware, application services-to-application services, data and semantics-to-data and semantics); (ii) Interoperable open framework (INTER-FW) to program and manage integrated IoT platforms; (iii) engineering methodology and tools (INTER-METH) to drive the integration process of heterogeneous IoT platforms. Figure 1 shows the proposed INTER-IoT framework to make interoperable different IoT platforms.

The INTER-IoT project will address IoT platform heterogeneity by granting interoperability through the methodology-driven integration and ensuring open accessibility to the integrated IoT platforms through distributed management software. To ensure this (i) the INTER-LAYER tools will provide techniques and technology allowing interoperability and integration between the layers of heterogeneous IoT platforms, (ii) the INTER-FW tool will offer programming library, service APIs and reference architecture to manage integrated IoT platforms and (iii) INTER-METH will be a full-fledged methodology and a tool that will drive the integration performing of heterogeneous IoT platforms. The main aim of this work is to demonstrate the usefulness of the INTER-LAYER tools to support the interoperability in a reference m-health use case based on two already developed IoT platforms presenting distinctive features.

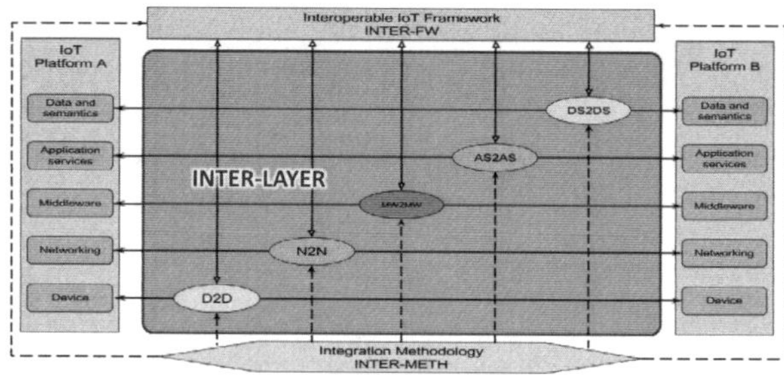

Figure 1: INTER-IoT architecture.

The use of the INTER-LAYER allow the integration of IoT heterogeneous throughout a suitable layered approach:

- at the device level (D2D), it is allowed a fast growth of smart objects ecosystems, seamless inclusion of novel IoT devices and their interoperation with already existing, even heterogeneous ones;
- at the networking level (N2N), is allowed the design and implementation of fully connected ecosystems, seamless support for smart objects mobility and information routing;
- at the middleware level (MW2MW), it is allowed a global exploitation of smart objects in large (even extreme) scale (multi-platform) IoT systems, seamless service discovery and management system for smart objects and their basic services;
- at the application service level (AS2AS), it is allowed the reuse and exchange (import/export) of heterogeneous services between different IoT platforms;
- at the data and semantics level (DS2DS), it is allowed a common interpretation of data and information based on global shared ontology in order to achieve semantic interoperability between heterogeneous data sources.

3. INTEROPERABILITY OF IOT-BASED HEALTHCARE PLATFORMS

In this section we describe two representative IoT healthcare platforms (BodyCloud and e-Care), well suited for e-health contexts, that will be integrated to obtain an INTER-Health IoT use case.

3.1 Bodycloud

BodyCloud is a software as a service (SaaS) architecture that supports the storage and management of body sensor data streams and the processing (online and offline analysis) of the stored data using software services hosted in the Cloud [11]. Figure 2 shows an high-level BodyCloud architecture to support several cross-disciplinary applications and specialized processing tasks. It enables large-scale data sharing and collaborations among users and applications in the Cloud, and delivers Cloud services via sensor-rich mobile devices. BodyCloud also offers decision support services to take further actions based on the analyzed BSN data.

Bodycloud has been used to support research prototypes in diversified application domains including physical rehabilitation [12], activity monitoring of healthy subjects [13],[14] and community-scale cardiac monitoring [15].

The BodyCloud approach is centered around four main decentralized components (or sides): Body, Cloud, Viewer, Analyst:

- The Body-side is the component, currently based on SPINE Android [19],[20] that monitors an assisted living through wearable sensors and stores the collected data in the Cloud by means of a mobile device.

- The Cloud-side is the component, currently implemented atop Google App Engine, that provides fully support for specific applications through data collection, processing, analysis and visualization.

- The Viewer-side is the Web browser-enabled component able to visualize the output of data analysis through advanced graphical reporting.

- The Analyst-side is the component that supports the development of BodyCloud applications.

The core of the BodyCloud architecture is the Cloud-side that offers high-level Web-based programming abstractions for the rapid prototyping of Cloud-assisted BSN applications: group, modality, workflow, and view. A group formalizes a specific application which manipulates a specific BSN data source. A modality formalizes a specific interaction between the Body-, Cloud- and Viewer-sides within a group. It specifies the input data, the actions to be performed on the input data, and the output data. A workflow formalizes an analysis process, producing output data from input data; it is specifically composed of one or more nodes (organized in an acyclic graph) representing specific algorithms. A view formalizes the graphical visualization of output data for the Viewer-side. The proposed SaaS approach is, to the best of our knowledge, the first general-purpose software engineering approach for Cloud-assisted community BSNs. It notably allows for rapid prototyping of Cloud-assisted BSN applications, customizability of the architectural components through Web standards-based procedures, and scalability due to the employed Google App Engine PaaS infrastructure.

3.2 e-Care

The e-Care platform is a cloud based platform and an evolution of the commercial service *"Nuvola It Home Doctor"* [7], the distance monitoring system, developed for the prevention and cure environment. The platform has been developed within the SmartHealth 2.0 research prohject [16] experimenting an innovative technological infrastructure and

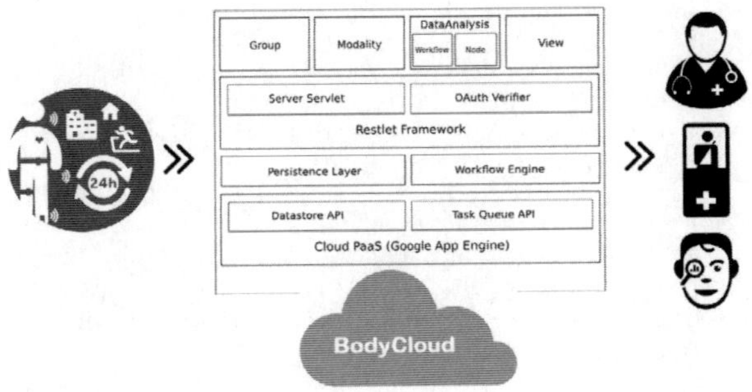

Figure 2: High-level BodyCloud architecture.

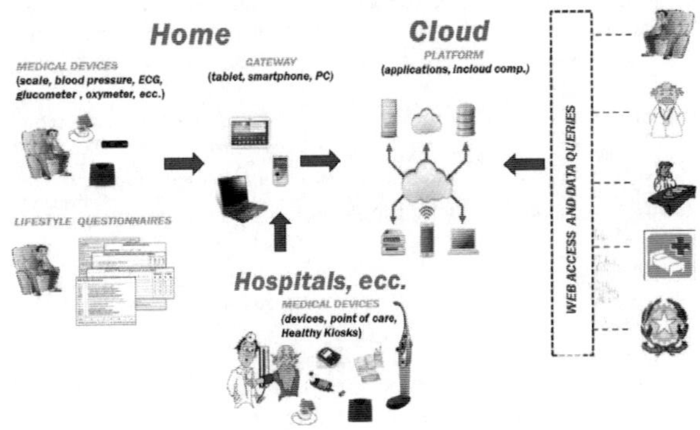

Figure 3: e-Care IoT Platform.

services in the area of health and well-being: telemonitoring heart failure, children and adult prevention of elderly people with risk of cognitive impairment [18]. This platform allows to collect objective measures (such as blood pressure, weight) and subjective informations (by questionnaires); these measures are gathered by gateways (on smartphones, tablet and PC), sent and stored in cloud to the platform and released to different stakeholders (patients, physicians and caregivers) by different channels (mail, web portals, sms and so on).

The doctor performs the clinical interpretation of the received parameters, monitors the data trend and activates any corrective action (*e.g.*, change in therapy, frequency of measures, etc.).

The doctors of the health care facility can be automatically notified to the occurrence of some particular situations (*e.g.*, parameters exceeding certain threshold values) and in case of need can interact directly with the patient himself.

Patients can receive messages reminding them to take measurements or to take the drugs as prescribed by protocol set by the doctors.

Figure 3 synthesizes the generic actors and entities involved into the e-Care Platform that can support different application scenarios such as in the hospital, hospital at home, continuity of care, chronic diseases, remote assistance of vulnerable people, emergency, wellness and prevention. Moreover, depending on the specific needs of the healthcare facility, the service can be adapted to other scenarios, with different level customizations actors, roles, responsibilities and protocols of care. In particular, the platform enables three modes of operation:

- *Home telemonitoring on their own* - Indicated for patients with a high degree of autonomy and empowerment, prevention, chronic diseases, patients which should be kept under observation.
- *Home telemonitoring with Tutor* - The Sanitary Operator goes to patient's homes in order to control their physiological parameters. This model is indicated in order to de-congest the hospital activities and for patients inserted in house assistance programs.
- *Telemonitoring in surgery* - Indicated when the logistical situation is unfavorable for direct access to the hospital and primary care are made available to the territory (small islands, mountain communities, remote locations). Also useful for screening campaigns and prevention.
- *Electronic Medical Report* - To allow citizens or patients to easily access to sanitary and social information services on mobile terminals. Electronic Health Records (EHR) and Personal Health Records (PHR) of patients are stored in Service Center equipped with physical and logical application modules. EHRs are managed by institutions (*e.g.,* hospital, health care provider) while PHRs are maintained by the patients but also accessible to authorized health operators.

Moreover, many different measures are supported such as Weight, Systolic and Diastolic Pressure, Heart rate, Glycemia, Oximetry (minimum, average, maximum, 6 minute walking test, nocturnal oximetry), Spirometry, Electrocardiogram (7/12 leads), Prothrombin time expressed as INR (International Normalized Ratio), Temperature, Height, Body fat, Blood analysis by selecting the specific devices.

3.3 Platforms integration: requirements, methods and benefits

As highlighted in previous sections, the two platforms e-Care and BodyCloud share some high-level characteristics while differs in objectives and technology. Specifically, they are both e-Health platforms, based on Bluetooth technology to interact with measurement devices, and based on Cloud infrastructures to enable data storing, off-line analysis, and data visualization. However, the two platforms have different specific objectives and are not interoperable from a technological point of view. Their specific objectives are complementary: e-Care is focused on non-mobile remote monitoring based on non-wearable measurement devices, whereas BodyCloud provides monitoring of subjects in mobility through wearable devices organized as body sensor networks (BSN). Thus, their integration would produce a full-fledged m-Health platform atop of which multitudes of m-Health services could be developed and furnished.

3.3.1 Integration requirements

In the following we define the main integration requirements, at the global IoT platform management level and at the different IoT platform layers, to integrate and make interoperable e-Care and BodyCloud. At global level, the integrated platform needs to be accessed by users and managed by administrators from a unified interface; in this context several non functional requirements need to be satisfied:

- *Security* to not allow third parties to take over control of a private system that is working over an IoT-based health care platform.
- *Privacy* to provide protection for accessing information about physical devices, services or whole connected platforms. Privacy protection needs to be supported during data transmission, aggregation, storage, mining and processing and it should not set a barrier to data source authentication.
- *Reliability* between devices belonging to different platforms, usually expressed as the allowable time between failures, or the total allowable failure rate.
- *Dependability* of the global platform consisting of two dependable platforms. In this case, even if the two distinctive platforms are dependable, the new interoperable platform could be not dependable; thus, a special attention should be devoted to guarantee the dependability of the global platform avoiding mistakes, detecting and removing errors and limiting damage caused by failure.

By looking the integration from the layer-oriented perspective, the requirements to be satisfied can be summarized as follows:

- DS2DS - Collected data need to be stored according to the same format and semantics (*e.g.,* in relation to measures of weight, the format between kilograms and pounds or the interpretation of GPS tuples (latitidine, longitude) needs to be standardized);
- AS2AS - Application services should be furnished in an integrated fashion and activated contextually (*e.g.,* at the healthcare center, at home and in mobility);
- MW2MW - Middleware services such as user identification and location, and device and service discovery and management should interoperate;
- N2N - At networking level, devices belonging to different platforms have to be seen as belonging to a single network so accessible, addressable and configurable
- D2D - As measurement devices do not interact directly with each other, but only transmit measures to the central local smart coordinator (according to a master-slave paradigm), it should be guaranteed only interoperability at the communication level between the measurement devices (medical devices and wearable sensors) and the smart coordinator (PC, laptop, tablet, smartphone) based on some widely available communication standards.

Table 1 resumes the main characteristics of the two IoT-based health care platforms by following the described layer-oriented approach.

3.3.2 Methods

The new IoT platform coming from the integration of e-Care and BodyCloud will be obtained through a customized implementation of the INTER-LAYER component depicted in figure 1 in which both N2N and MW2MW layers are not considered. This choice is motivated by the analysis

Table 1: Layer-oriented comparison.

Layer	BodyCloud	e-Care
D2D	Mobile Gateway	Mobile Gateway
N2N	Not Available	Not Available
MW2MW	SPINE[19]	Proprietary (Closed)
AS2AS	REST/XML	REST/XML
DS2DS	Proprietary	Proprietary

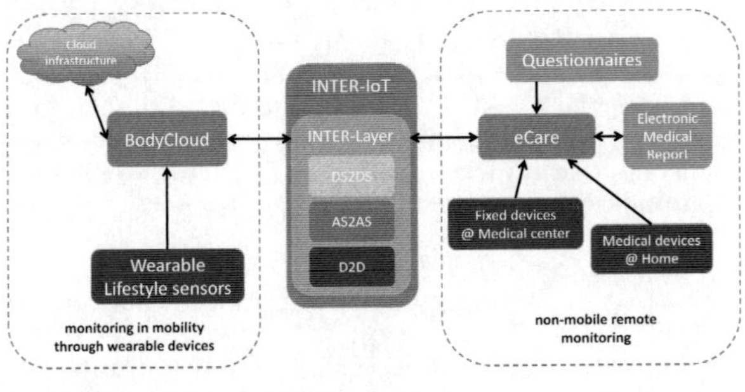

Figure 4: INTER-Health: BodyCloud and e-Care integration.

presented in table 1 in which it is clear that, the N2N layer is not available in any of the platforms and the MW2MW layer is based on a proprietary and closed solution for the e-Care platform that does not allow the possibility of any integration a this layer.

In particular, the INTER-LAYER approach will provide a set of tools to allow the data access, communication and integration at different layers: *i)* at device layer (D2D) the new IoT platform will be able to communicate with the wearable devices supported by the BodyCloud and with the non-mobile and non-wearable measurement devices installed at the medical center or at home; *ii)* at the application services layer (AS2AS), the specific reports of the patients provided by the e-Care platform will be integrated and enriched with data coming from the BodyCloud platform to complement the analysis; *iii)* at the data and semantics layer (DS2DS) all the acquired information will be made consistent according to a common data format. Figure 4 shows the integration of the two IoT platforms by using the INTER-LAYER approach.

3.3.3 Benefits

INTER-IoT project aims to guarantee an effective and efficient interoperability between heterogeneous IoT platforms such as the two described e-Health IoT Platforms (i.e., e-Care Platform and BodyCloud). Thanks to the proposed interoperable approach new cross-platform services can be developed. Thus, the main benefit of the proposed integration and interoperability consists into the availability of a more powerful IoT healthcare platform for lifestyle monitoring to support new application services that individual platforms were not able to support.

Finally, by exploiting the novel fully integrated IoT environment, the aforementioned monitoring process can be decentralized from the healthcare center to the monitored subjects' homes, and supported in mobility by using on-body physical activity monitors; this approach, allows to reduce both the transfer costs of patients at medical centers and the waiting times, also obtaining constantly updated results to make the necessary adjustments in a faster and precise manner.

4. INTER-HEALTH USE CASE

The proposed use case, based on the integration of the described IoT platforms, aims to develop an integrated IoT system for monitoring humans' lifestyle in a decentralized mobile way to prevent health issues resulting from food and physical activity disorders. The aforementioned monitoring process can be decentralized from the healthcare center to the monitored subjects' homes, and supported in mobility by using on-body physical activity monitors.

It is worth noting that, the strategic importance of such complete use case, is largely motivated by the fact that wrong lifestyles such as improper and hypercaloric diet and, in particular, the lack of physical activity, are at the base of main chronic diseases [2].

During the use case experimentation, the effectiveness, in terms of lifestyle improvement indices, of the novel system will be evaluated with respect to the current "manual" monitoring performed by conventional Healthcare Centers.

4.1 Lifestyle monitor: Medical Perspective

According to the reference standard medical protocol for the global prevention and management of obesity [21], [22] written by World Health Organization, in order to assess the health status (underweight, normal weight, overweight, obesity) of the subject (of a given age) during the visit at the healthcare center, objective (weight, height, body mass index, blood pressure, waist circumference) and subjective (eating habits and the practice of physical activity) measurements should be collected (and/or computed) by a healthcare team (doctor, biologist nutritionist, dietitian, etc).

For these reasons, the objective of this use case consists of monitoring humans' lifestyle in a decentralized way and in mobility, to prevent health issues mainly resulting from food and physical activity disorders.

In particular, the use case needs to take into account the following state of health indicators:

- *The Body mass index (BMI)* - it is an objective measure, calculated with formula: $weight/height^2$, that allows to assess the health status (underweight, normal weight, overweight, first level obesity, second level obesity and 3rd level obesity) of subjects, also allowing to make the diagnosis of overweight and obesity.
- *The waist circumference* - it is an objective measure used to diagnose overweight and obesity; values greater than 94 cm in men and 80 cm in women are considered pathological.
- *The physical activity practice* - it is a subjective measure that detect the amount (hours / daily and hours / week) and the type of physical activity (no activity; light, moderate and intense activity). This measure is used to detect a wrong lifestyle with physical inactivity.
- *The eating habits* - it is a subjective measure that detect the quality and quantity of food consumed daily and weekly. This measure is used to detect a wrong lifestyle due to improper diet and high-calories.

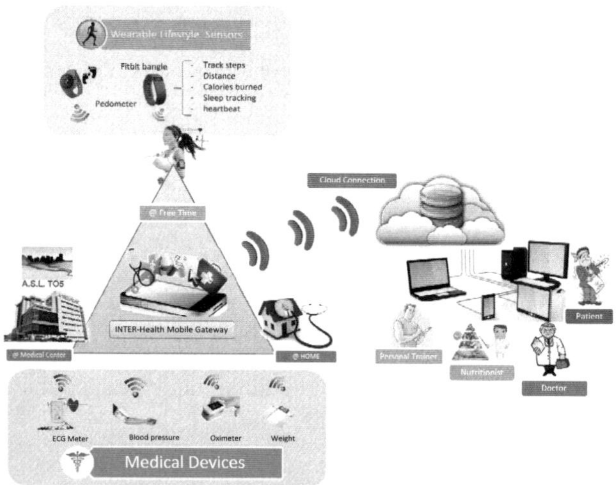

Figure 5: INTER-Health full-fledged IoT platform.

The defined use case would be fully deployable atop the integration of e-Care and BodyCloud as the automated monitoring at the healthcare center and the decentralization of the monitoring at the patients' homes would be supported by the e-Care remote services, while the physical activity monitoring in mobility would be enabled by the BodyCloud mobile BSN services.

4.2 INTER-Health technical functionalities

The main functionalities of the integrated and interoperable IoT platform are the followings:

- collection of objective (weight, height, body mass index, blood pressure or waist circumference) and subjective (questionnaires concerning the eating habits and the practice of physical activity) measures during the visits at the healthcare center (based on e-Care);

- telemonitoring at the healthcare center of subjective (questionnaires) and objective (weight, blood pressure, etc...) measures sent by the patients at home (based on e-Care platform);

- telemonitoring at the healthcare center of the physical activities performed by patient at home with wearable devices (based on BodyCloud platform) report and visualization of all the measurements collected for analysis and interaction on treatments.

4.3 Pilot deployment

The INTER-Health pilot allows the conduction of an experimental nutritional consulting the aim of which is to reduce health risk factors, at the basis of major chronic diseases, such as incorrect lifestyles which are typically characterized by both high-caloric diet and the lack of an adequate physical activity. In such a way, the pilot involves a group of about 200 patients who want a medical support to improve their lifestyle.

Patients will be involved in the pilot for a whole year during which they will be constantly monitored through a set of wireless wearable devices such as bangles, pedometers and heart rate monitors communicating through standard communication technologies (*i.e.*, Bluetooth for medical devices and Bluetooth or IEEE 802.15.4 for wearable sensor nodes).

Patients will equipped with smartphones, acting as interoperable gateways[23] toward a cloud repository that will be accessed by experts in the specific field, such as doctors, nutritionists and personal trainers, in order to constantly monitor the user behaviours. Figure 5 shows the new integrated and interoperable IoT platform.

The study, non-invasive and without risk to health, is conducted by the Nutritional Unit (NU) of the Department of Prevention of the Complex Structure of Food, Hygiene and Nutrition of the fifth Local Health Unit of the Italian department of Turin (ASL TO5). The pilot is an observational study that involves subjects divided into two groups: a group called the Control Group (CG), represented by the patients involved only in the traditional nutritional consulting, and an Experimental Group (EG), represented by the patients that will be involved in the experimental nutritional consulting.

During nutritional consulting, the NU will collect and monitor a set of patients data: anthropometric (*i.e.*, weight, height, body mass index, blood pressure, waist circumference), clinical and dietary history (*i.e.*, eating habits and physical activity). All these data will be collected by the researcher and stored in the EHRs of patients. After the first clinical visit, the CG health status will be checked every three months, while the EG will be constantly monitored trough the INTER-Health technological platform. For the EG, there are planned also two overhaul physical visit in the 6th and 12th month of the pilot.

In particular, the INTER-Health pilot of experimental nutritional consulting will allow:

- the recording at home, with weekly frequency, of patient weight by using electro-medical devices (*i.e.*, smart balance) provided by ASL TO5 during the study period;

- the recording at home, with daily frequency, of patient blood pressure by using electro-medical devices (*i.e.*, smart blood pressure meter) provided by ASL TO5 during the study period;

- the continuous live recording of daily physical activity, burned calories and the duration of aerobic activity performed, by using wearable mobile devices (*i.e.*, smartphone and electronic bracelet) provided by ASL TO5 during the study period;

- the weakly recording of eating habits by filling in online questionnaires made available both via web and via smartphone's apps.

It is worth noting that the proposed INTER-Health pilot presents the following expected and relevant medical results:

1. Overcome the traditional methods in the relationship between doctor and patient making easier the interaction;

2. Improve the system's efficiency increasing the number of patients that can be assisted;

3. Provide quality advantages originating from a higher number of objective measures, that are more effective and appropriate;

4. Obtain new standards for the management of nutritional units, supporting more efficient and responsive nutritional advice services;
5. Achieve the same or better health goals using new technologies, that are more efficient, allowing the extension of preventive action to a larger population, without greater outlays.

5. CONCLUSIONS

This work presented a novel approach to support the integration and interoperability between different and already developed IoT-based healthcare platforms by using the so called INTER-LAYER component. The conducted analysis has been focused to design a specific INTER-Health use case through which it is possible to obtain, with reduced effort, new application services that the specific healthcare platforms were not designed for. The performance testing of the integrated platform, in terms of efficiency and reliability, is in progress at this time and the results will presented and detailed in future works.

6. ACKNOWLEDGMENTS

This work has been carried out under the framework of INTER-IoT, Research and Innovation action - Horizon 2020 European Project, Grant Agreement #687283, financed by the European Union.

The authors would thank Claudio Maggi, Anna Costa, Monica Minutolo, Marina Mortara, Ilaria De Luca, Angelina Della Torre, Domenica Pata, Bartolomeo Avataneo, Anna Aldrighetti, Carlo Aldera, Fabio D'Ercoli and Alberto Delpiano for their valuable support.

7. REFERENCES

[1] S.M.R. Islam, D. Kwak, M.H. Kabir, M. Hossain, K. Kwak "The Internet of Things for Health Care: A Comprehensive Survey", *IEEE Access*, Vol. 3, pp. 678-708, 2015.

[2] World Health Organization. "Global status report on non communicable diseases", 2010.

[3] G. Fortino, P. Trunfio "Internet of Things Based on Smart Objects, Technology, Middleware and Applications", Springer 2014, ISBN 978-3-319-00490-7.

[4] L. Catarinucci, D. de Donno, L. Mainetti, L. Palano, L. Patrono, M.L. Stefanizzi, L. Tarricone, "An IoT-Aware Architecture for Smart Healthcare Systems", *IEEE Internet of Things Journal*, vol. 2, no. 6, pp. 515-526, Dec. 2015.

[5] S.K. Datta, C. Bonnet, A. Gyrard, R.P. Ferreira da Costa, K. Boudaoud "Applying Internet of Things for personalized healthcare in smart homes", WOCC, pp. 164-169, 2015.

[6] S.C. Mukhopadhyay, "Wearable Sensors for Human Activity Monitoring: A Review", *IEEE Sensors Journal*, Vol. 15, Issue 3, pp. 1321-1330, 2015.

[7] Nuvola It Home Doctor, *https://tmed.telecomitalia.it/en/home*

[8] Kaa IoT Platform, *http://www.kaaproject.org/overview/*

[9] Jasper - Control Center for Security & Home Automation *http://www.jasper.com/security-home-automation*

[10] INTER-IoT European project, Research and Innovation action - Horizon 2020 - available on line at *http://www.inter-iot-project.eu/*

[11] "BodyCloud: A Cloud-assisted Software Platform for Pervasive and Continuous Monitoring of Assisted Livings using Wearable and Mobile Devices", *http://bodycloud.dimes.unical.it*

[12] G. Fortino, R. Gravina "A Cloud-Assisted Wearable System for Physical Rehabilitation", In ICTs for Improving Patients Rehabilitation Research Techniques, Vol. 515, pp. 168-182, Nov 2015.

[13] R. Gravina, C. Ma, P. Pace, G. Aloi, W. Russo, W. Li, G. Fortino "Cloud-based Activity-aaService cyberphysical framework for human activity monitoring in mobility", *Future Generation Computer Systems*, Available online 22 September 2016, DOI: 10.1016/j.future.2016.09.006

[14] G. Fortino, R. Gravina, W. Li, C. Ma "Using Cloud-assisted Body Area Networks to Track People Physical Activity in Mobility", In Proc. of the International Conference on Body Area Networks (BodyNets 2015), pp. 85-91, Australia, Sep 2015.

[15] G. Fortino, R. Gravina, A. Guerrieri, G. Di Fatta "Engineering Large-Scale Body Area Networks Applications", In Proc. of the International Conference on Body Area Networks (BodyNets 2013), Boston, United States, ACM press, pp. 363-369, 2013.

[16] SmarthHealth 2.0, *http://www.smarthealth2.com/eng/*

[17] V. C. Gungor, P. Pace, E. Natalizio "AR-TP: An adaptive and responsive transport protocol for wireless mesh networks", IEEE International Conference on Communications, ICC 2007, pp. 3740-3745, doi:10.1109/ICC.2007.616

[18] A. Ricauda, N. G. Isaia, V. Tibaldi, G. Bestente, A. Frisiello, A. Sciarappa, S. Cavallo, M. Ghezzi, G. Larini " Telecare and Telemedicine in Home Care Practice: Field Trial Results", *Distributed Diagnosis and Home Healthcare (D2H2)*, American Scientific Publishers (ASP), Vol. 2, pp. 281-303, 2011.

[19] G. Fortino, S. Galzarano, R. Gravina, W. Li "A framework for collaborative computing and multi-sensor data fusion in body sensor networks", *Information Fusion*, Vol, 22, pp. 50-70, 2015.

[20] F. Bellifemine, G. Fortino, A. Guerrieri, R. Giannantonio "Platform-independent development of collaborative Wireless Body Sensor Network applications: SPINE2", IEEE International Conference on SMC, pp. 3144-3150, 2009.

[21] Obesity: Preventing and Managing the Global Epidemic. WHO Obesity Technical Report Series 894. Geneva, Switzerland: World Health Organization, 2000.

[22] Physical Status: The Use and Interpretation of Anthropometry. Technical Report Series 854. Geneva, Switzerland: World Health Organization, 1995.

[23] G. Aloi, G. Caliciuri, G. Fortino, R. Gravina, P. Pace, W. Russo, C. Savaglio "Enabling IoT interoperability through opportunistic smartphone-based mobile gateways", *Journal of Network and Computer Applications*, Available 20 October 2016, DOI: 10.1016/j.jnca.2016.10.013.

Impact of Random Body Movements on 60-GHz Doppler Radar for Real-Time Monitoring of Vital Signs

Ting Zhang
UPMC Univ Paris 06, UR2, L2E
Sorbonne Universités, F-75005
Paris, France
ting.zhang@upmc.fr

Guido Valerio
UPMC Univ Paris 06, UR2, L2E
Sorbonne Universités, F-75005
Paris, France
guido.valerio@upmc.fr

Julien Sarrazin
UPMC Univ Paris 06, UR2, L2E
Sorbonne Universités, F-75005
Paris, France
julien.sarrazin@upmc.fr

Dan Istrate
CNRS, UMR 7338, Biomechanics and Bioengineering (BMBI)
Université de Technologie de Compiègne
Compiègne, France
mircea-dan.istrate@utc.fr

ABSTRACT

We show the impact of random body movements when contactless detection of vital signs is performed with a 60-GHz Doppler radar. Since the monitoring should reveal dangerous events in real-time home-care scenarios, constraints is present on the durations of the observation windows. Body movements of different duration are here considered in connection with such a short-time signal observation.

Keywords

Non–contact vital–sign monitoring, Doppler radar, Optimization algorithm, 60 GHz

1. INTRODUCTION

Population aging is a major factor motivating the development of home-care services to reduce costs and improve the quality of life of patients [1], and the need for more reliable technical instrumentation for medical monitoring and diagnosis. Specifically, real-time estimation of vital signs is required to detect dangers and act accordingly.

In this framework, the use of continuous wave Doppler radar for non-contact monitoring of vital signs, namely heartbeat (HB) and respiration rates (RR), is a recently established technique. It is based on the detection of the Doppler frequency shift of a wireless signal scattered by the patient. While several applications are envisaged around 5 GHz [2], working at millimeter waves (i.e., around 60 GHz) provide a more robust estimation of the weaker HB signal [3].

On the other hand, current solutions do not specifically aim at reducing the duration of the observation window. When this duration becomes small (of the order of a few seconds compared with several tens of seconds often used in the existing literature), the estimation is more difficult and dependent on random body movements (RBM), which are not effectively averaged as in the long-duration window.

In this work, RBM of different durations are added to the usual chest movements, and the impact of these movements on the estimation of the vital signs of interest is studied with reference to reasonable accuracies required in this kind of applications.

Permission to make digital or hard copies of all or part of this work for personal or classroom use is granted without fee provided that copies are not made or distributed for profit or commercial advantage and that copies bear this notice and the full citation on the first page. Copyrights for components of this work owned by others than ACM must be honored. Abstracting with credit is permitted. To copy otherwise, or republish, to post on servers or to redistribute to lists, requires prior specific permission and/or a fee. Request permissions from permissions@acm.org.

2. FORMULATION OF THE PROBLEM

In CW Doppler radar presented here, a sinusoidal signal (here with frequency $f = 60$ GHz) is transmitted towards a person's chest, at an average distance d_0 (see Fig. 1). The reflected signal is phase-modulated by the signal $x(t)+x_{\mathrm{d}}(t) = x_{\mathrm{h}}(t) + x_{\mathrm{r}}(t) + x_{\mathrm{d}}(t)$, the sum of the heartbeat $x_{\mathrm{h}}(t)$, the breathing $x_{\mathrm{r}}(t)$, and a possible RBM $x_{\mathrm{d}}(t)$. Each vital signal is a simple sinusoid: $x_{\mathrm{h}}(t) = m_{\mathrm{h}}\sin(2\pi f_{\mathrm{h}}t + \phi_{\mathrm{h}})$, and $x_{\mathrm{r}}(t) = m_{\mathrm{r}}\sin(2\pi f_{\mathrm{r}}t + \phi_{\mathrm{r}})$, whose amplitudes ($m_{\mathrm{r}}$ and m_{h}), frequencies (f_{r} and f_{h}), and initial phases (ϕ_{r} and ϕ_{h}) are unknown. The RBM is here a random signal with a prescribed maximum amplitude and time duration. The received signal is demodulated by an IQ quadrature receiver. The two baseband signals $\mathrm{B_I}$ and $\mathrm{B_Q}$ are of the form

$$B_{\mathrm{I/Q}}(t) = \begin{matrix}\cos\\ \sin\end{matrix}\left[\frac{4\pi x(t)}{\lambda} + \frac{4\pi x_{\mathrm{d}}(t)}{\lambda} + \frac{4\pi d_0}{\lambda}\right] + n_{\mathrm{I/Q}}(t), \quad (1)$$

λ being the wavelength at f. $n_{\mathrm{I/Q}}(t)$ represent the Gaussian noise in the system. A complex demodulation is performed on the received signals, where the final baseband signal is $\mathrm{B_C}(t) = \mathrm{B_I}(t) + j\mathrm{B_Q}(t)$.

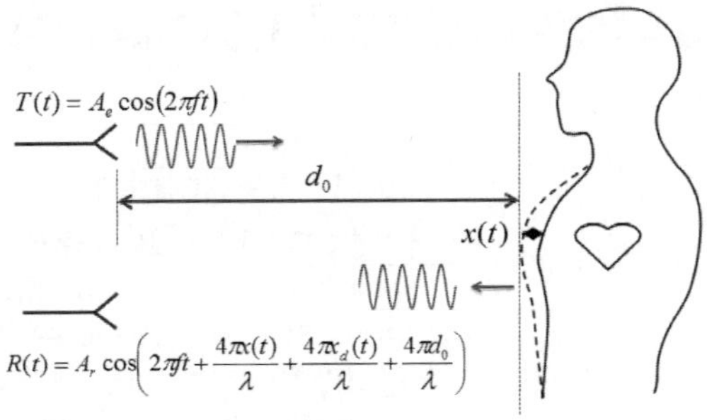

Figure 1: Representation of CW Doppler radar system for vital signs monitoring.

To achieve an accurate frequency estimation, we solve an optimization problem, consisting in finding all unknown parameter in the direct signal model $B_C(t)$ by minimizing the discrepancy between the measured signal and the estimated one. A particle swarm optimization (PSO), is executed in the time domain, where the signal length and the calculation time is fixed to 5 seconds for real-time capabilities.

3. NUMERICAL RESULTS

In this section we show the cumulative distribution functions (CDF) relative to 1000 estimation of the respiration and heartbeat frequencies f_r and f_h. For each simulation, amplitudes and frequencies take random values with Gaussian distribution, within realistic ranges, while the phases take uniformly distributed random values. A good estimation of phases grants more robust results for the frequencies, as highlighted by the authors in [4]. The SNR is set here to 20 dB, a typical value in practical systems proposed in the literature. Different RBM are considered, by varying both their maximum amplitudes and time durations.

Figs. 2 shows the CDF in the presence of a RBM of maximum amplitude of 1 cm ((a) and (b)) and 2 cm ((c) and (d)), having different durations. Three cases have been considered: a short movement (1 s), an average movement (2 s), and a long movement (5 s), where the short and long definitions should be meant with respect to the total observation duration (5 s). The presence of a RBM does not prevent a reasonably accurate estimation of the frequencies, as long as its duration is not comparable with the observation duration.

In the most critical scenario, the Doppler radar could wait until the patient is again at rest and proceed with a new estimation. Data processing based on the patient medical history should be employed in this limited case in order to conclude about its medical conditions and decide how to proceed (e.g., temporarily using longer observation windows).

4. CONCLUSIONS

We have discussed the impact of RBMs on the contactless monitoring of vital signs through Doppler radar at 60 GHz. Real-time applications are specifically targeted, where the observation window is very short and potentially sensitive to irregular movements. However, a good robustness of the proposed estimation technique has been assessed. Data processing algorithms should be employed in the worst-case scenarios where the detection loses precision due to strong and long-lasting movements.

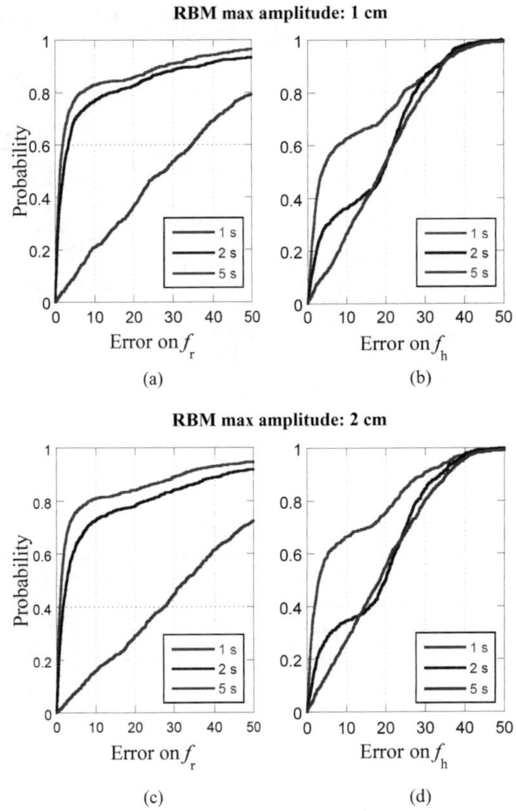

Figure 2: CDF obtained from the PSO optimization results, related to the frequencies f_h and f_r, in the presence of a RBM. (a) f_r with a RBM of 1 cm; (b) f_h with a RBM of 1 cm; (c) f_r with a RBM of 2 cm; (d) f_h with a RBM of 2 cm.

5. ACKNOWLEDGMENTS

The authors would like to thank Sorbonne Universités which has funded the EBiomed Chair and this work. This work was also performed within the Labex SMART supported by French state funds managed by the ANR within the Investissements d'Avenir programme under reference ANR-11-IDEX-0004-02.

6. REFERENCES

[1] P. A. C. Aguilar, J. Boudy, D. Istrate, B. Dorizzi, and J. C. Moura Mota. A Dynamic Evidential Network for Fall Detection. *IEEE Journal of Biomedical and Health Informatics*, 18(4):1103–1113, JUL 2014.

[2] C. Li and J. Lin. Optimal Carrier Frequency of Non-contact Vital Sign Detectors. In *IEEE Radio and Wireless Symp.*, pages 490–493, Long Beach, CA, Jan. 2007.

[3] T. Zhang, J. Sarrazin, G. Valerio, and D. Istrate. Non-Contact Estimation at 60 GHz for Human Vital Signs Monitoring Using a Robust Optimization Algorithm. In *2016 IEEE Int. Symp. Antennas Prop.* , Fajardo, Porto-Rico, June 2016.

[4] T. Zhang, J. Sarrazin, G. Valerio, and D. Istrate. Investigation on non-contact vital signs monitoring using Doppler radar at 5 GHz and 60 GHz. *IEEE Antennas Wireless Prop. Lett.*, submitted.

Antenna Radiation Efficiency Considerations in Body Area Networks

Julien Sarrazin
Guido Valerio
Solofo Razafimahatratra
Massimiliano Casaletti
Aziz Benlarbi-Delaï
L2E - Sorbonne Université
UPMC Univ Paris 06, UR2
F-75005, Paris, France
julien.sarrazin@upmc.fr

François Sarrazin
ESYCOM (EA 2552), UPEMLV,
ESIEE-Paris, CNAM,
F-77454 Marne-la-Vallée France
francois.sarrazin@u-pem.fr

Luca Petrillo
Philippe De Doncker
Wireless Communications Group
Université Libre de Bruxelles (ULB)
B-1050 Brussels, Belgium
lpetrill@ulb.ac.be

ABSTRACT
In this paper, we present a theoretical investigation on the radiation efficiency of small on-body antennas in the context of Body Area Networks. In particular, we show that operation at frequencies above 20 GHz experiences less human-tissue losses than below 6 GHz, and could therefore be a suitable candidate for more efficient off-body wireless communications.

Keywords
Body Area Networks (BAN); complex image method; millimeter-wave; dipole above multilayer half-space.

1. INTRODUCTION
Body area networks (BAN) are networks of sensors embedded on the human body in order to provide healthcare monitoring. A promising application of such networks lies in the "well-being" of the elderly. If BAN can provide a seamless way to monitor in real time the condition of people, it would be then possible to prevent rather than cure. To answer the needs of such long-term applications, BANs have to be completely autonomous in terms of energy while using small sensors (for the user to tolerate wearing them). Power consumption is therefore a critical issue. Sensors are supposed to communicate wirelessly, so a large amount of the consumed power is directly related to the radiofrequency hardware.

When sensors are embedded close to the human body surface, the radiated electromagnetic field strongly interacts with the user and experiences some losses that will ultimately heavily impact the system's autonomy. While the losses due to the propagation channel have been extensively investigated [1-3], it is more difficult to draw general comments related to the antenna radiation efficiency since among the studies in the literature, different types of antennas are used, and the heights between the antenna and the body varies a lot, thereby making comparison meaningless. Consequently, this paper addresses from a theoretical point of view the question of radiation efficiency when antennas are located close to the human body. The idea is to give some insights regarding the choice of operation frequency. For this purpose, a canonical structure, i.e. a vertical dipole, is used as a source located on the human body, which is modeled by a multilayer structure. Section 2 describes the geometry as well as the approach to define a radiation efficiency that is relevant in the BAN context. Section 3 introduces some simulation results and Section 4 provides a more general discussion on these results. The conclusion is drawn in section 5.

SAMPLE: Permission to make digital or hard copies of all or part of this work for personal or classroom use is granted without fee provided that copies are not made or distributed for profit or commercial advantage and that copies bear this notice and the full citation on the first page. To copy otherwise, or republish, to post on servers or to redistribute to lists, requires prior specific permission and/or a fee.
Conference'11, December 15–16, 2016, Turin, Italy.
DOI: http://dx.doi.org/10.1145/12345.67890

2. PROBLEM FORMULATION
The geometry considered in this paper is presented in Fig.1. The human body is modeled as a multilayer structure composed of skin, fat, and muscle. The thickness of the skin and the fat are h_{skin} = 1 mm and h_{fat} = 0.5 mm, respectively, while the muscle is considered infinite along the negative z-axis. The permittivity of the three layers is taken from [4] and varies with respect to the frequency. The vertical dipole is of length l, at a height h above the human skin. Its radius is kept constant throughout the paper at a = 0.25 mm.

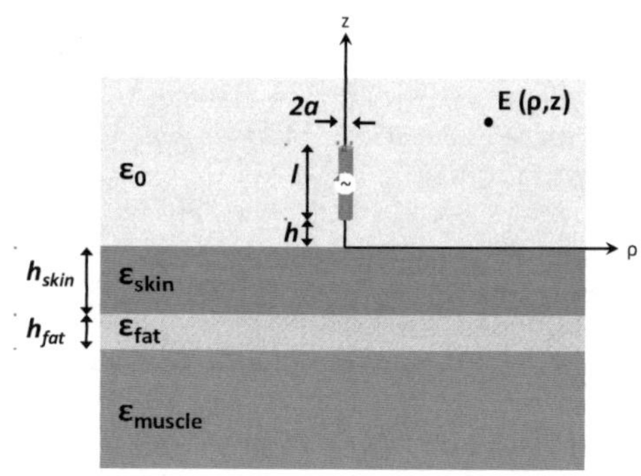

Figure 1. Geometry under investigation: vertical dipole over the human body

In order to theoretically address the issue of radiation efficiency in BAN, we first define the radiation efficiency as:

$$\eta = \frac{P_{rad}}{P_{in}}$$

where P_{in} is the real input power accepted by the dipole and P_{rad} is the radiated power in far field *in the upper half-space only* (the power radiated in the lower half-space is considered not to contribute to the BAN communications, and vanishes anyway in far-field because of the losses). The dipole is supposed to be perfectly matched and P_{in} = 1W for all frequencies of investigation. To do so, the following input current magnitude is applied at the dipole feeding access (located at $z = h + l/2$):

$$I_0 = \sqrt{\frac{2P_{in}}{R_{in}}}$$

where R_{in} is the real part of the dipole impedance Z_{in} above the multilayer structure. The dipole current I is considered sinusoidal:

$$I(z) = I_0 sin\, k_0 \left[\frac{l}{2} - \left|z - \left(\frac{l}{2} + h\right)\right|\right], \qquad h \leq z \leq l + h$$

where k_0 is the free space wave number. The input impedance Z_{in} is computed as in [5] using the complex image method in order to take into account the multilayer structure shown in Figure 1. P_{rad} is obtained by integrating the Poynting vector in the upper half space (i.e. $z > 0$ in Fig.1). To do so, the expression of the radiated electric far field is calculated using geometrical optics and is therefore the sum of a direct and a reflected ray.

3. OFF-BODY SIMULATION RESULTS

Simulations are performed and the obtained radiation efficiency η is given in Fig.2a with a dipole length $l = 10$ mm and in Fig.2b with $l = 1.6$ mm (which corresponds to a typical substrate thickness). In each figure, η is plotted with respect to frequency for different dipole height h values.

The efficiency largely varies with respect to the frequency but it is interesting that only at lower frequency (typically less than 6 GHz) does the efficiency increase proportionally to the dipole height h above the skin surface for both dipole length l values. This remark is also true in the 20-40 GHz range when $l = 10$ mm whereas when $l = 1.6$ mm, this trend is only noticeable for frequencies above 40 GHz. In the 6-20 GHz band when $l = 10$ mm, and in the 6-40 GHz when $l = 1.6$ mm, the behavior of η with respect to frequency is less predictable and it is therefore more difficult to draw general trends.

If the considered dipole is taken as a reference for vertically polarized antenna without ground plane, it appears that better radiation efficiency can be reached by operating at higher frequencies. This highlights the potential of millimeter-wave operation for off-body links.

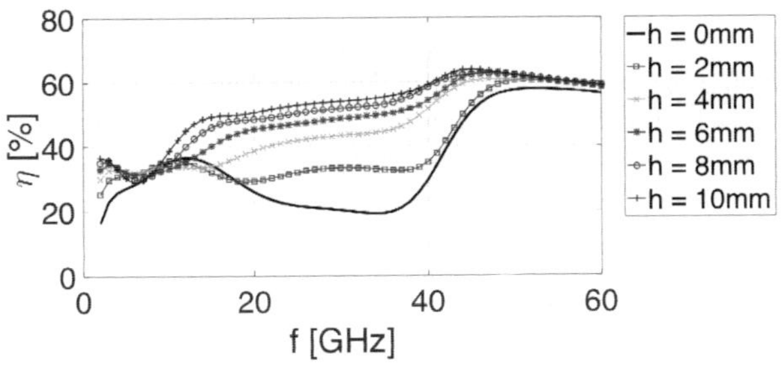

(a)

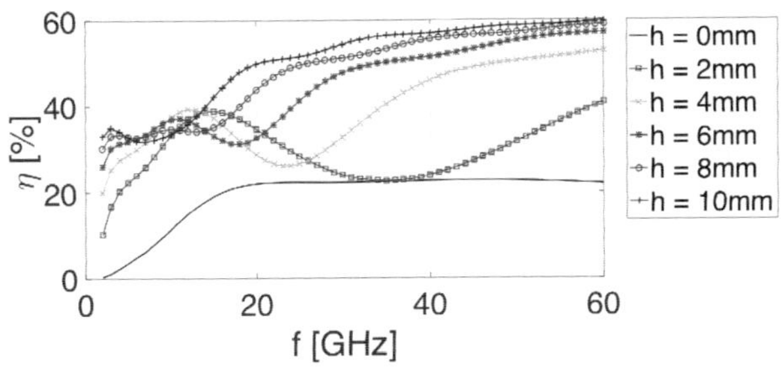

(b)

Figure 2. Radiation efficiency η for different dipole length (a) $l = 10$ mm, and (b) $l = 1.6$ mm

4. DISCUSSION

It is worth noticing that unlike in classic link budget that uses Friis formula, results with respect to frequency are given here while keeping a constant antenna size, as opposed to a constant antenna gain. We believe this is a fairer comparison for applications like BAN where the antenna has to be as small as possible. As seen in previous section 3, the fact that efficiency increases with frequency is attributed to two main phenomena. The first one is due to fact that the conductivity of the human tissues increases with frequency, thereby acting more and more as a ground plane as the frequency increases ($\sigma_{skin} = 36$ S/m at 60 GHz). Thus the power radiated from the dipole is more reflected at the skin interface (and less transmitted). The second effect is that the real part of the permittivity decreases with respect to frequency. So at low frequency, the human body permittivity being high, the electromagnetic field is much more concentrated in the lower half-space (i.e. the human body) than in the upper one.

5. CONCLUSION

Based on a theoretical approach, it has been shown that operation at frequencies as high as 20-60 GHz could be suitable in order to reach better radiation efficiency in off-body communications for BAN applications.

As perspectives of this work and in order to provide even more relevant guidelines for the choice of operation frequencies, horizontally polarized antennas will be investigated as well as the losses involved by impedance matching networks.

6. ACKNOWLEDGMENTS

This work was performed within the Labex SMART supported by French state funds managed by the ANR within the Investissements d'Avenir programme under reference ANR-11-IDEX-0004-02.

7. REFERENCES

[1] Petrillo, L., Mavridis, T., Sarrazin, J., Lautru, D., Benlarbi-Delaï, A., and De Doncker, P. 2014. Analytical Creeping Wave Model and Measurements for 60 GHz Body Area Networks. *IEEE Trans. on Antennas and Propagation.* 62, 8 (Aug. 2014), 4352-4356. DOI= 10.1109/TAP.2014.2324558

[2] Mavridis, T., Petrillo, L., Sarrazin, J., Lautru, D., Benlarbi-Delaï, A., and De Doncker, P. 2014. Creeping Wave Model of Diffraction of an Obliquely Incident Plane Wave by a Circular Cylinder at 60 GHz. *IEEE Trans. on Antennas and Propagation.* 62, 3 (March 2014), 1372-1377. DOI= 10.1109/TAP.2013.2296321

[3] Guraliuc, A. R., Zhadobov, M., Valerio, G., Sauleau, R. 2014. Enhancement of on-body propagation at 60 GHz using electro textiles. *IEEE Antennas and Wireless Propagation Letters.* 13 (2014), 603-606. DOI= 10.1109/LAWP.2014.2313019

[4] Andreuccetti, D., Fossi, R., and Petrucci, C. An Internet resource for the calculation of the dielectric properties of body tissues in the frequency range 10 Hz - 100 GHz. Website at http://niremf.ifac.cnr.it/tissprop/. IFAC-CNR, Florence (Italy), 1997. Based on data published by C.Gabriel et al. in 1996

[5] Shubair, R. M. and Chow, Y. L. 1993. A closed-form solution of vertical dipole antennas above a dielectric half-space. *IEEE Trans. on Antennas and Propagation.* 41, 12 (Dec. 1993), 1737-1741. DOI= 10.1109/8.273319

Smart Cane System: Direction guidance system for the blind using GS1 and EPCIS system

Invited Paper

Soonil. Lim
Samsung Electronics Co.
Maetan 3-dong, Yeongtong-gu, Suwon-si, Gyeonggi-do
Republic of Korea
sunding.lim@kaist.ac.kr

Hongkeun. Yu
KAIST
25, Nonhyeon-ro 28-gil, Gangnam-gu, Seoul
Republic of Korea
hongkunyoo@kaist.ac.kr

Sanha. Kang
KAIST
25, Nonhyeon-ro 28-gil, Gangnam-gu, Seoul
Republic of Korea
sanacor@kaist.ac.kr

Daeyoung Kim
KAIST
25, Nonhyeon-ro 28-gil, Gangnam-gu, Seoul
Republic of Korea
kimd@kaist.ac.kr

ABSTRACT

The Smart Cane System is developed to inform the location for people who are visually impaired. This system adopts GS1 and EPCIS to manage the surrounding information with the standard. The system suggests that the unique key could be collected from the Braille block via RFID and send to EPCIS server to notice the location. The Smart cane sends the key to the mobile application through Bluetooth. The EPCIS server communicates with the mobile application and manages GLN (Global Location Number) key for the location of the Braille block and GTIN (Global Trade Item Number) key for the registered blind. The mobile application receives the surrounding information of the Braille block where the blind is from the server. Using the GS1 key and EPCIS system ensures that the Smart Cane system can be used internationally.

CCS CONCEPTS

• **Computer systems organization** → Embedded and cyber-physical systems → **Embedded systems**; • **Networks** → Network Services

KEYWORDS

Internet of Things, Smart Cane, GS1, EPCIS, RFID

1 INTRODUCTION

According to the WHO report, 285 million people are estimated to be visually impaired worldwide: 39 million are blind and 246 have low vision in 2014 [1]. There are a lot of mobility assisting devices for the blind people, such as the Braille blocks, white cane, guide dogs [2]. Among these devices, the white cane is widely used to inform obstacles on the way. Also the cane helps to identify protruding blocks called "the Braille Block".

Although the white cane and the Braille block give directions whether to stop or go, it is not enough information to visit the new places. Additionally, the blind cannot recognize whether the information is provided by the Braille or not and hard to find where the Braille is located. Another issue is the Braille located outside is usually dirty and have hygiene problems. Therefore, we suggest the "Smart Cane System" providing detailed location information using existing the Braille block system. Combining the Braille blocks with RFID chips enables "Smart Cane" to receive location information [7,8]. This protocol has possibility to be expanded for global use with GS1 and EPCIS.

In this paper, we will introduce what technologies were implemented to "Smart Cane system" in Section 2. The architecture of this system and components are explained in Section 3. In the following Section 4, the implementation and demonstration of the system are clarified in detail. Finally, this paper will be end with a conclusion in Section 5.

2 RELATED WORK

To communicate between the Braille block and the Smart Cane, the wireless communication technology like RFID, Bluetooth, and NFC shall be used. Because the recognition range of NFC is too short, the blind who uses the Smart Cane may miss the Braille block. In the case of the Bluetooth, it needs continuous power supply, additional steps, and enough time for pairing between the Braille block and the Smart Cane. So, we think the RFID technology is suitable for the Smart Cane system.

2.1 RFID

RFID (Radio Frequency IDentification) is used to identify a unique ID for specific object [3]. In the Smart Cane system, RFID is installed in the Braille block and indicates its installed location. RFID can be used semi permanently and reuse repetitively. Smart Cane used by RFID reader can recognize the RFID tag at close range without direct contact in contrast with NFC.

The RFID Tags and readers communicate by given frequency. Given the type of the frequency, characteristics like recognition range can differ. If the frequency is low, the recognition distance is short. However, in contrast, if the frequency is high, the range becomes long and in relation the usage of electronic power and cost are increased [3,4].

The collected unique key of RFID by the Smart Cane is required to perform a query in the database on the server. It will be discussed in the chapter 3.4.

2.2 GS1 and EPCglobal

The GS1 (Global Standard 1) is international organization to help identify, capture and share information for supply and demand chains [5]. GS1 has opened offices in 112 countries and millions of corporations which are associated with GS1 are currently adopting this as a standard.

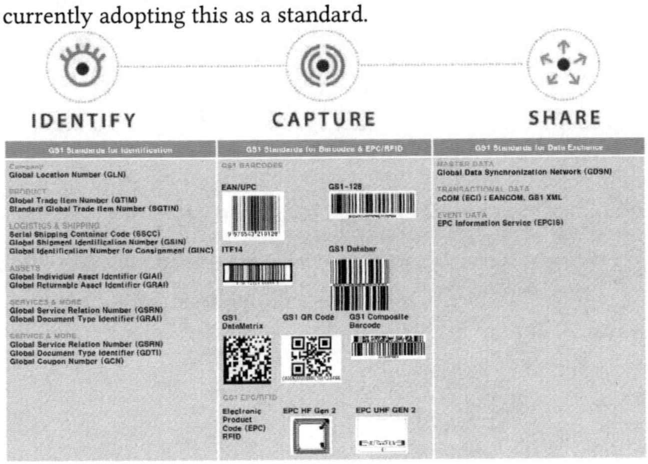

Figure 1: **GS1 Overview [5].**

As in Fig. 1, the GS1 standards show three part of its system - identifying, accurately capturing and automatically sharing information about products, locations, assets and more [5]. Identification defines unique identification codes. The GS1 provides 11 GS1 Identification keys for events and information, and the Smart Cane system adopts two keys as shown in the Table 1. Each Smart Cane has a unique number to identify the blind and their location. The GS1 Key for the Braille block represents where the block is located. The Smart Cane captures the GS1 Key of Braille Block and shares it to the server which has the database of the information of the user's surroundings.

The EPCglobal (Electronic Product Code global) is the system for the GS1 identification using RFID [6]. Through this system, the information of the products can be shared globally. The EPCglobal requires the standardization for identification key and exchange interface. The standardized data is captured and filtered, grouped by event capturing system like mobile application. Finally, the EPCIS-level events are transferred to EPCIS server and stored and shared. So, by applying the EPCglobal system, the Smart Cane system can be established for the global blind guidance standard. This can be used for the other field like local information system.

Table 1: **Two GS1 Identification Keys in the Smart Cane System**

ID Key		Used to Identify	Example
Global Trade Item Number	GTIN	Products and Services	Registered Smart Cane
Global Location Number	GLN	Parties and locations	Location of Braille Block

3 ARCHITECTURE

3.1 System Overview

The Smart Cane system is the blind guidance service. When the blind walks along the Braille block using the cane, they can get the voice information of their route like Fig. 2.

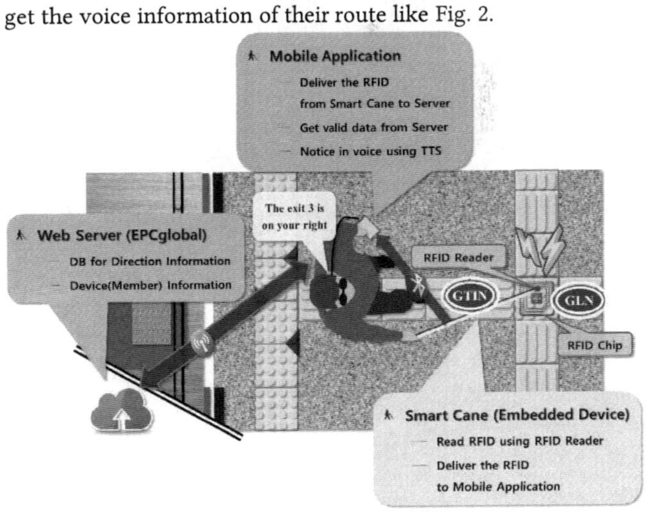

Figure 2: **The guide system for the blind using RFID and its components**

The Braille Block has its own key for the location at the installed RFID chip. The Smart Cane can capture the key of the Braille block using RFID reader and send to the blind's smartphone via Bluetooth technology. The smartphone will then send the key of the block and the cane to the server and receive the data of the surrounding. In doing so, smartphone application refines the data and notifies to the blind by voice.

As the GS1 system and RFID system, the Smart Cane consists of three parts as shown in the Fig. 2. The Braille Blocks are identified with unique RFID using GLN. The Smart Cane captures RFID and delivers it to the mobile application. The mobile application connects to server to get the valid information and shares it.

3.2 Modeling

The Smart Cane service captures the blind's behavioral events and we defined them as Table 2. The event type is ObjectEvent since it captures sensing data. Action is ADD because it accumulates the events. bizLocation ID is made out of block RFID and geo extension has the block location. bizStep is defined as collecting since our system collects the user tagging events. StickId and ActualLocation are extended features. It represents mobile ID (Android) and actual user location respectively.

Table 2. **Example of modelling user behaviour event**

EPCIS Event	Event Type	ObjectEvent
	Action	ADD
WHEN	EventTime	2015-12-09T15:16:35.880+09:00
WHAT	epcList	urn:epc:id:sgtin:8809421.862511.001
WHERE	bizLocation	urn:epc:id:sgln:8809421.862513.200
	geo extension	37.48442, 127.0340
WHY	bizStep	urn:epcglobal:cbv:bizstep:collecting
Extension	StickId	622669b92134af6e
	AcutalLocationLat	37.481907860365936,
	AcutalLocationLng	127.04296946525574

Our XSD is defined as above schema. Stick ID's type is restricted to integer. Each stick position's type (latitude, longitude) should be double since it represents Geo location information. Finally the mobile ID's type is string since it contains Android mobile ID. Following is the Example of a XSD for user behavior event.

```
<xs:schema xmlns="http://tempuri.org/XMLSchema1.xsd"
xmlns:matns="http://tempuri.org/XMLSchema1.xsd"
xmlns:xs="http://www.w3org/2001/XMLSchema"
id="XMLSchema1"
targetNamespace=http://tempuri.org/XMLSchema1.xsd
elementFormDefault="qualified">
  <xs:element name="StickId">
    <xs:simpleType>
      <xs:restriction base="xs:integer"/>
    </xs:simpleType>
  </xs:element>
  <xs:element name="StickPostionLat">
    <xs:simpleType>
      <xs:restriction base="xs:double"/>
    </xs:simpleType>
  </xs:element>
  <xs:element name="StickPositionLng">
    <xs:simpleType>
      <xs:restriction base="xs:double"/>
    </xs:simpleType>
  </xs:element>
  <xs:element name="MobileId">
    <xs:simpleType>
      <xs:restriction base="xs:string"/>
    </xs:simpleType>
  </xs:element>
</xs:schema>
```

In event capturing, first, the mobile fetches the Block RFID through Bluetooth communication. Then it captures the current location information with GPS sensor (android.location API) followed by getting an android ID. Finally it constructs an XML out of its data and sends it with Http POST method to EPCIS server through OkHttp library, which Square Inc. has developed. The source code is widely accessible.

4 IMPLEMENTATION & DEMONSTRATION

4.1 The Braille Block with RFID

Normally, the "Stop" Braille block is installed at the fork or used as a guide to warn. So, only the "Stop" Braille block is identified with a unique GLN key using RFID. This GLN key locates where the blind who touches at that Braille Block using the Smart Cane is. Also, the key is used to give useful information about what's around that Braille Block.

In this system, we choose LF 125 kHz with consideration for range and size. If the frequency is increased, the RFID chipset size is also bigger and expensive. On the contrary, if the frequency is decreased, the Smart Cane cannot recognize the RFID chipset installed in the Braille block.

4.2 Embedded Device: The Smart Cane

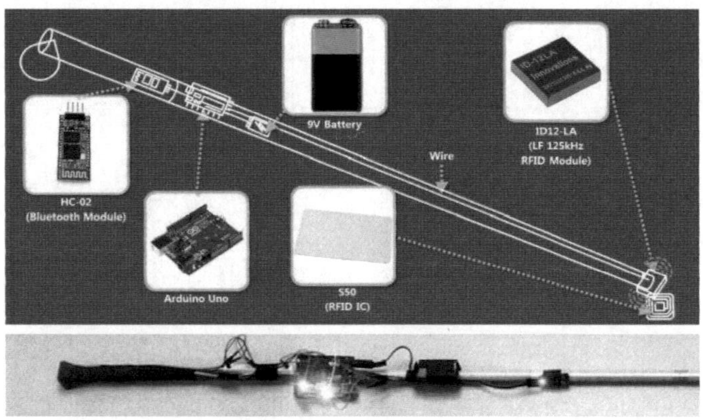

Figure 3: **The guide system for the blind using RFID and its components**

We make the Smart Cane using the Arduino with RFID reader and Bluetooth module. At the end of the cane that touches the ground, the RFID reader is installed, in which will then capture the key of the RFID chipset. When the cane get a new GLN key from the block, it delivers the key to the Mobile Application via Bluetooth. We chose the Arduino Uno for the embedded board because it's cost efficient and spends low power.

Each Smart Cane has its own GTIN key, which represents the unique ID of the blond. With this GTIN key, the Smart Cane system can trace the path of the specific blind.

4.3 Mobile Application

The mobile application pairs with the Smart Cane device using Bluetooth and registers the blind using GTIN key at the EPCIS server. The user of this mobile application is blind, so we make its UI simple in order to provide convenience for the user to handle the application. The mobile OS like iOS and Android has accessibility feature to help the blind using voice assistant, so that the blind can pair between the Smart Cane and the Mobile device easily.

When the Mobile Device receives the GLN key of the Braille block from the Smart Cane, it queries to server to get the local information represented by the key. The local information indicates what is around the blind. The Table 3 is the example of the local information based on the four cardinal points.

Table 3: **The ScInfo table's schema**

ID	UUID	N	E	S	W
PRI key	GLN Key	North side	East side	South side	West side

After the receiving the local information from server, the mobile application will get the information where the blind is headed using the magnetic sensor and the acceleration sensor in the mobile device. Using the walking direction which is gathered by magnetic sensor, mobile application calculates the direction information dynamically as in Fig. 4.

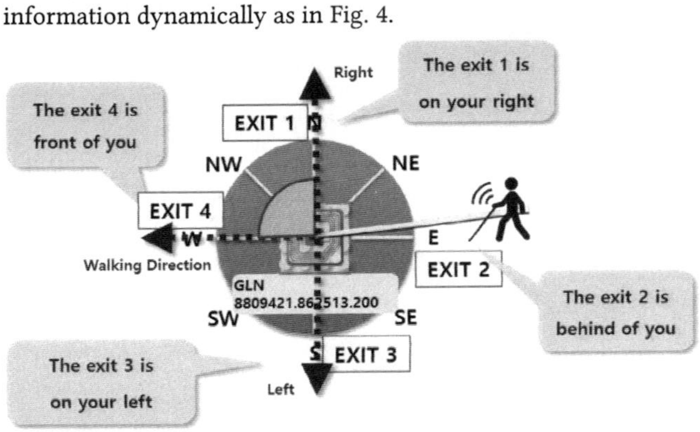

ID	UUID	N	E	S	W
01121321	8809421.862513.20 0	EXIT 1	Exit 2	Exit 3	Exit 4

Figure 4: **Calculating the direction information using GLN key and local information.**

Finally, the TTS(Text to Speech) system of the mobile OS, it notifies the direction information to the blind by voice.

Figure 5: **The mobile application of Smart Cane and execution the TTS service**

4.4 EPCIS Server

The EPCIS server stores the GLN and the local information like the Table 3 as the master data. It accumulate events like the when, where and which Braille is captured by the Smart Cane. It also records which Smart Cane has passed which specific Braille Block. When the Smart Cane is registered on the server, it would record as the transaction data.

Those data can access globally, so the blind can get the local information regardless of the country.

4.5 Demonstration

We decided to do a demonstration on the way inside the subway station. Because the Braille block is installed well and it's easy to clarify the direction. We decide 4 points and made Table 4 with information related to the exit. With this information, we tested to find the exit 4 from the faregate just bank on the TTS guide. The test movie is at https://youtu.be/uLoLjlXAKhk. (The TTS in the movie speaks in Korean.)

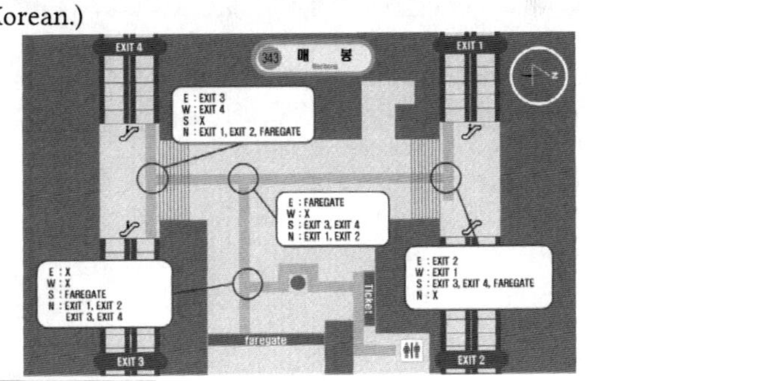

Figure 6. The Map for the demonstration (at Maebong Station, Seoul, South Korea)

Table 4. The partial database for the demonstration

ID	UUID (GLN)	N	E	S	W
0001	4567 1234 0001	EXIT1 EXIT2 EXIT3 EXIT4		FAREGATE	
0002	4567 1234 0002	EXIT1 EXIT2	FAREGATE	EXIT3 EXIT4	
0003	4567 1234 0003	EXIT1 EXIT2 FAREGATE	EXIT3		EXIT4
0004	4567 1234 0004		EXIT2	EXIT3 EXIT4 FAREGATE	EXIT1

5 CONCLUSION

From our field trial, the Smart Cane system is helpful to the blind in giving the information of direction. If we adopt and expand the system of ONS and EPCIS, the Smart Cane system can establish as the global standard for the blind. The local information is managed by the server of each country. When the blind travels to another country, they can get the information of the direction in the voice of their own language.

There are some parts to improve. It needs to receive feedback from the blind about using the Smart Cane system, and also how to make the device simple and easy to use. Most important point is the consideration of RFID system. The rate of recognition must be increased for actual situation.

The systems that notice the local information can be combined with navigation system. The Braille block which installed the RFID chip can connect the route for the destination that the blind person wants to go to. Managing the local information using GS1 and RFID system will become an inexhaustible resource.

REFERENCES

[1] WHO, 2014. Visual impairment and blindness, DOI: http://www.who.int/mediacentre/factsheets/fs282/en/

[2] World Blind Union, 2015. White Cane Information, DOI: http://www.worldblindunion.org/English/resources/Pages/White-Can-information.aspx

[3] H. Hamam, A.O. Dahmane, and B. Fennani, 2011. RFID overview. *In ICM 2011 Proceeding*. pp. 1–5.

[4] Wikipedia, Radio-frequency identification, DOI: https://en.wikipedia.org/wiki/Radio-frequency_identification

[5] GS1 Global Office, 2015. GS1 Annual Report 2014-2015, *GS1 Global Office* DOI: http://www.gs1.org/docs/annual_report/GS1_Annual_Report_2015.pdf

[6] J. Byun, and D. Kim, 2015. Oliot EPCIS: New EPC information service and challenges towards the Internet of Things, *2015 IEEE International Conference* on, pp.70–77.

[7] J. Chen, Z. Li, M. Dong, and X. Wang, 2010. Blind Path Identification System Design Base on RFID. *2010 International Conference on Electrical and Control Engineering*, 548–551.

[8] H. Fernandes, V. Filipe, P. Costa, and J. Barroso, 2014. Location based Services for the Blind Supported by RFID Technology. *Procedia Computer Science, 27(Dsai 2013)*, 2–8.

A Robust Remote Health Monitoring and Data Processing System for Rural Area with Limited Internet Access

Mohammad Pourhomayoun
California State University,
CS Dept., Los Angeles, CA
mpourho@calstatela.edu

Nabil Alshurafa
Northwestern University
Dept. Prev. Med., Chicago, IL
nabil@northwestern.edu

Foad Dabiri
WANDA Inc.
San Francisco, CA
foad@yourwanda.com

Kartik Yadav
UCLA
School of Nursing, Los Angeles, CA
kyadav@sonnet.ucla.edu

Costas Sideris
UCLA
CS Dept., Los Angeles, CA
costas@cs.ucla.edu

Li (Linda) Tseng
Google
San Francisco, CA
Linda.Tseng.0816@gmail.com

Hassan Ghasemzadeh
Washington State Univ.
EECS, Pullman, WA
hassan@eecs.wsu.edu

Adeline Nyamathi
UCLA
School of Nursing, Los Angeles, CA
anyamath@sonnet.ucla.edu

Majid Sarrafzadeh
UCLA
CS Dept., Los Angeles, CA
majid@cs.ucla.edu

ABSTRACT

Emerging technologies such as Body Sensor Networks (BSN) and Remote Health Monitoring Systems (RHMS) allow for collecting continuous data from patients, providing clinical interventions to improve patients' physical and mental health, and to prevent medically adverse events. Although RHMS have shown promises in reducing healthcare costs and improving quality of care, designing a robust, flexible and portable RHMS that can adequately handle technological and environmental restrictions such as data communication disruptions caused by low-quality infrastructure is by large an open problem.

In this paper we present an end-to-end robust RHMS including body area networks for monitoring and management of patients with HIV/AIDS. The proposed system includes an Android application to be installed on mobile devices to collect and preprocess data from patients, a wireless body area network to handle data communication and transmission, and a backend cloud-based server coupled with a NoSQL database and web-portal for data visualization and analysis.

The proposed system addresses a number of serious challenges in RHMS design including data transmission and synchronization in a body area network with poor network connection (e.g. in a rural area with poor or unavailable internet connection). The proposed system is fully implemented and deployed in a large research study involving 600 women living with HIV/AIDS in rural parts of India. The results demonstrate the effectiveness, reliability, robustness, and accuracy of the proposed RHMS.

CCS Concepts

• Social and professional topics→ Medical technologies→ Remote medicine • Networks→ Wireless access networks • Computer Systems organizations→ Embedded and cyber-physical systems→ Sensor networks

Keywords

mHealth, Remote Health Monitoring Systems (RHMS), Body Area Networks, Remote Health Management, AIDS.

1. INTRODUCTION

With rapid increase in healthcare expenditures, there is a growing need for alternative and innovative approaches for chronic disease monitoring and management, which can help early diagnosis and adverse event prevention. Innovative technologies such as Body Sensor Networks (BSN) and Remote Health Monitoring Systems (RHMS) allow for collecting continuous data from patients or any person with special needs, and provide an effective platform for information integration and retrieval, data analysis, and predictive analytics for health conditions. They also enable clinical interventions to improve patients' physical, physiological, and mental health, and to prevent medically adverse events from taking place.

Rapid advances in many technological domains including mobile systems, wireless communications, internet, and sensors has led to the development of effective RHMS that can collect various physiological information including vital signs and other medical conditions through wearable/implantable body sensors, body area sensors, or digital questionnaires [1]-[17]. RHMS and BSNs can reform the healthcare structure by increasing the efficiency of healthcare systems, expanding the reach of healthcare services to all segments of the population, and reducing the costs of chronic disease management.

Although RHMS have shown promises in reducing healthcare costs and improving quality of care, designing a robust, flexible and portable RHMS that can properly handle system restrictions such as data communication disruptions is yet an open problem. For example, most of existing RHMS have been developed based on the assumption that the RHMS always has access to a perfect internet, mobile, or landline connection. However, in many applications, specially for a portable RHMS in areas with poor internet connection, a robust and reliable system is needed to ensure reliable data collection and transmission with no damaged or missing data.

In this paper, we present an end-to-end, robust, portable, and distributed RHMS for monitoring of patients with HIV/AIDS. The case study focuses on Women Living with HIV/AIDS (WLHA) in rural India. This study is a collaborative effort between UCLA School of Nursing (Nyamathi, R01-MH098728-4), UCLA Computer Science department, University of California San Francisco (UCSF) School of Medicine, and All India Institute of Medical Sciences (AIIMS).

The rest of the paper is organized as follows: Section 2 describes the project motivations and specific aims, Section 3 provides the system architecture, methods, and the details of the proposed framework and components. In Section 3 we also talk about the challenges in data collection and transmission, and then provide technical details of the proposed approaches to mitigate these challenges. It also describes the details of the developed system including BSNs, frontend and backend, mobile app, webserver and web portal. Finally, Section 4 describes the results and conclusion.

2. MOTIVATION and SPECIFIC AIMS

This paper presents an end-to-end RHMS and BSN for monitoring of patients with AIDS. This study focuses on 600 WLHA residing in a rural area of India.

The Joint United Nations Program on HIV/AIDS reported that India has the third largest population of individuals living with HIV/AIDS in the world, with 1.7 to 2.6 million affected with HIV/AIDS [23]. Rural women living with HIV/AIDS (WLHA) in India face serious challenges in accessing and following treatment regimens, caring for family members, and maintaining positive mental health [19][20]. They experience ongoing barriers to HIV testing and treatment [19]. Furthermore, they are generally underweight and malnourished, with very low adherence to antiretroviral therapy (ART) [19][20]. The Indian Government designed a successful approach to address the health requirements of the rural population by training local social workers as ASHA (Accredited Social Health Activists) to help enhance the physical and mental health condition of rural WLHA [19][20].

The UCLA School of Nursing, in collaboration with UCSF, AIIMS, and Indian Council of Medical Research (ICMR) designed and implemented a novel three-year study (Nyamathi, R34-MH082662) focusing on rural WLHA in India, with the main goal of enhancing their adherence to antiretroviral therapy (ART) and improving their physical, mental, and psychological health. In this study, the intervention and support was delivered by rural village women trained as HIV-focused care providers (ASHAs) partnered with nurses. These ASHA support WLHA by providing care, mental and physical support, and assistance to WLHA by decreasing barriers to ART adherence. Findings from this pilot study revealed significant improvement in adherence to ART, depressive symptoms, internalized stigma and avoidant coping, as well as weight gain and increased lean body mass, among the ASHA-intervention women compared to those in usual care [19][21][22].

The subsequent five-year longitudinal study, initiated in 2013, utilizes a 2x2 factorial design, specifically, 1) ASHA support alone for WLHA, vs. 2) ASHA support for WLHA + nutrition (food-based) training, vs. 3) ASHA support for WLHA + food supplementation, vs. 4) ASHA support for WLHA + nutrition training + food supplementation, to test the effects of nutrition training and/or food supplementation on anthropometric parameters and immune status of the WLHA at 6-, 12- and 18-month follow-up.

This five-year study also aims to examine the effects of the intervention on ART adherence of WLHA at baseline and 6-, 12- and 18-month follow-up, changes in psychological health of the WLHA over 18 months, measured by improvement in CES-D and stigma scores, the effect of the intervention on nutritional adequacy of the WLHA over 18 months, measured by comparisons of vitamin, mineral and macronutrient intake, lipid normalization of WLHA (triglycerides and cholesterol), and anthropometric parameters and psychomotor development of the index children at 6-12-, and 18-month follow-up.

In this study, we designed and developed a RHMS to collect and transmit data from and to patients. The collected data includes physiological information, vital signs, demographics, contextual information, social and physical activity, psychological and mental health information,, medication adherence, and nutrition information. It also includes lab data such as blood and urine test results. The system wirelessly transmits the collected data to the backend cloud-based database. This data can be later visualized and analyzed by authorized experts through the system web portal. In next sections, we discuss the technical details of the system design and architecture.

3. METHODS

3.1 System Architecture

Figure 1 shows the overall architecture of the proposed system. In this study, we designed and developed an Android based application to be installed on tablet devices provided to the research staff, supervisor, project manager, data manager, and the administrator. The mobile app is responsible for collecting data from patients, preprocessing the collected data, visualizing the data, and transmitting it to a backend server. The mobile app has been designed to support two different languages: English and Telugu. By switching to the Telugu language setting, all questionnaire forms, as well as all app items, menu bars, and buttons will change into Telugu language.

After collecting patient's data, the app wirelessly and securely transmits this data to the backend cloud-based server through either WiFi or 4G internet connection. Several research staff carry the tablets to visit patients simultaneously and independently; therefore, it is very important to synchronize the tablets on a timely basis to have the updated status of all patients in all tablets to avoid data overwrite or repeated visits and interviews. Since the internet connection can be poor or unavailable in rural areas, where most of the patients are located, it is very challenging to transmit the data and synchronize the patients' status in real-time. In the next section, we discuss the details of the network and the best approaches to deal with internet connection problems.

We have designed and developed a webserver and web portal to visualize the results to authorized people, and allow them to analyze the data, extract information, statistics and graphs, edit or revise the data, and export/download it in various formats. In section 3.1.1, we discuss the system accessibility and security, and how the users with various levels of authority can access or control the database. Also, in section 3.2.3, we provide more details about the webserver design and capabilities. As shown in Figure 1, the results can be analyzed by authorized experts, who provide feedback, comments, or new prescriptions, or recommend for specific interventions as how to improve patients' physical, physiological, and mental health condition.

3.1.1 System Accessibility

The proposed system allows for defining various levels of access to the data and control over the system. The users including *patients, research staff, supervisors, selected research staff and selected research investigators* may have various levels of access to the system. Here is the defined accessibility protocol:

- *Patients* have the right to *refuse to respond* to a question for any reason (either if they don't like to answer, or they don't know the answer). "Don't know the answer" is usually a selectable option in multiple choice questions. The interviewer can also mark a question as "refuse to respond" if a patient refuses to answer the question, no matter what the reason is.
- *Research staff* are not allowed to skip a question (unless it is a "refuse to respond" case). They can only upload the questionnaire one time when completed. The interviewer cannot go back to a previous section if it has already been completed, however, she can save the questionnaire partially, and complete it later.
- *Supervisors* can revise the data on the mobile device only before uploading the questionnaire. For security purposes, the database will keep all revisions of the data including the changes that have been made on the device side.
- *Authorized Research Principal Investigator/Co-Investigators* have full access/control over the system database. For example, they can manually add new data samples, or they can view, export, or revise the previously collected data.
- *Other Research Staff* may have limited access to the system database after getting permission from the Research Principal Investigator/Co-investigators to only view/export the collected data.
- All users including research staff, supervisors, and authorized research staff need to enter their unique user/password to be able to use the system. The system will then identify the user, and give him/her the proper level of access.
- Any changes in the data through the app or web such as revise, edit, or addition will be recorded in the database along with the date/time of change, and the name or user account of the person who made the change. The system always allows to recover the revised data.

3.2 System Components

3.2.1 Android Application

In this study, we designed and developed an Android application that can be installed on tablet or mobile devices. The mobile app is responsible for collecting data from patients on a timely basis including baseline round, and 6-month, 12-month, and 18-month follow up rounds, as well as laboratory results. The app supports two different languages: English and Telugu. By switching to Telugu, all questionnaire forms, app items, menu bars, and buttons change from default English to Telugu language. The app is also responsible for preprocessing the collected data, making a wireless connection to the internet network to transmit the collected data to a backend server, and making sure that the intact and full data is received by the server. The details of data transmission and network configuration is provided in section 3.2.2.

A more complete list of items that can be collected by the app includes: physiological information, vital signs, demographics, contextual information, physical activity, adherence measurements, stigma survey, adherence survey, social activity survey, psychological and mental health survey, medication compliance, and nutrition information. The app also collects lab data including blood and urine test results. We have designed and implemented specific pages in the app to collect each one of the aforementioned items.

The app also performs data preprocessing and basic data analysis including generating automatic alerts based on the collected data, reporting the alerts to the administrators by sending automatic emails, calculating depression score as a metric to measure patient's mental health (particularly depression), and enabling/disabling/revising questions in survey forms based on patients' responses to previous questions.

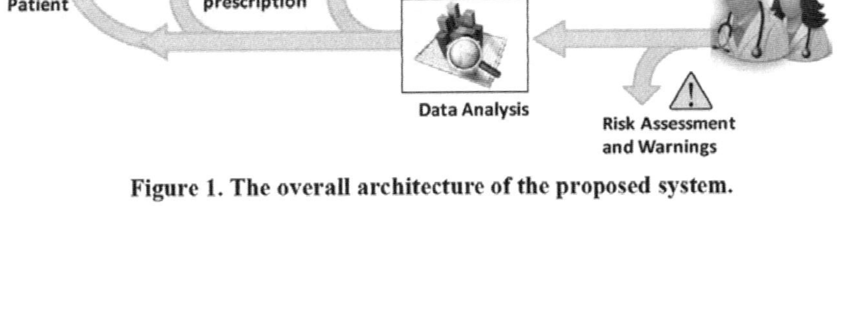

Figure 1. The overall architecture of the proposed system.

Figure 2 represents some sample pages of the android application: Figure 2-a shows the *patient list* page including the list of all patients along with brief status of each patient. Figure 2-b indicates the *profile page* of a specific patient that represents the details of previously collected data, and allows for starting, editing, or completing a new data collection procedure. Figures 2-c and 2-d show a sample *questionnaire* in *English* and *Telugu*. As shown in Figures 2-c and 2-d, we used a variety of icons and colors to indicate the status of a question in questionnaire forms. For example, *unanswered questions* are indicated with grey *U/A*, *refused to answer* items are indicated with red *R/A*, and regular *answered questions* are indicated with green *A* icons.

3.2.2 Body Area Network

The app may communicate (send or receive data) with the backend server for three main purposes: 1- To upload the collected data to the server; 2- To build a new user ID (add a new patient); 3- To synchronize the patients' status. As shown in Figure 1, the app can connect to the server wirelessly through either WiFi or 4G internet services. Since the internet connection can be poor or unavailable in many rural areas, where most of the patients are located, it is very important to design and utilize reliable protocols for data transmission.

Figure 3-a shows an ideal scenario to upload the collected data. In this scenario, each one of the devices will connect to the internet network directly to transmit the data wirelessly and simultaneously. However, in practice, we needed to design and employ a more robust data transmission procedure to deal with internet connection issues. In this approach, the app will test network connectivity and internet bandwidth/speed before any transaction. If the network does not satisfy the bandwidth/speed requirements (based on the amount of data that is ready to upload at the moment), then the app will just save the data on local memory of the device and mark it as un-uploaded data. In this case, the app will notify the user about internet connection problems. The system will keep checking the internet connection on a timely basis and re-attempt to upload the stored data as soon as a satisfying connection is established. Furthermore, we have designed an acknowledge-based method between the app and the server to assure intact and perfect data transmission.

In this project, a number of ASHA and research staff visit different patients simultaneously and independently. When a research staff visits a patient for the first time, she needs to make an account for the patient in the system. In this case, the app needs to have access to the database to avoid making duplicate user IDs. If a patient is already visited by a another research staff, the new staff member needs to know the status of previous visits (including baseline or follow up visits) and data collection procedure to avoid data overwrite or repeated data entry. In any case, whether it is the first visit, or it is a follow up visit, or even if it is a visit to continue an incomplete data collection procedure, all ASHA need to have access to the latest status of all patients. To this end, it is required to synchronize the devices (e.g. tablets) on a timely basis by transmitting any new changes with the status of patients.

Figure 3-b shows an ideal scenario for synchronizing, where the server checks the status of each device, and then transmits the latest updates to the device. Since the internet connection may be unavailable for some devices, a more reliable approach is to take advantage of possible inter-communication among devices (e.g. through Bluetooth), so that an outdated device can get the latest changes from a previously updated device, as soon as they happen to be within Bluetooth range of each other. Figure 3-c represents this new scenario, where one of the devices that has been previously synchronized, will be later used as an interface device to synchronize other devices. In this approach, a set of devices can communicate with each other to eventually find a previously updated device as a source of data, and broadcast the updates over the network to synchronize other devices.

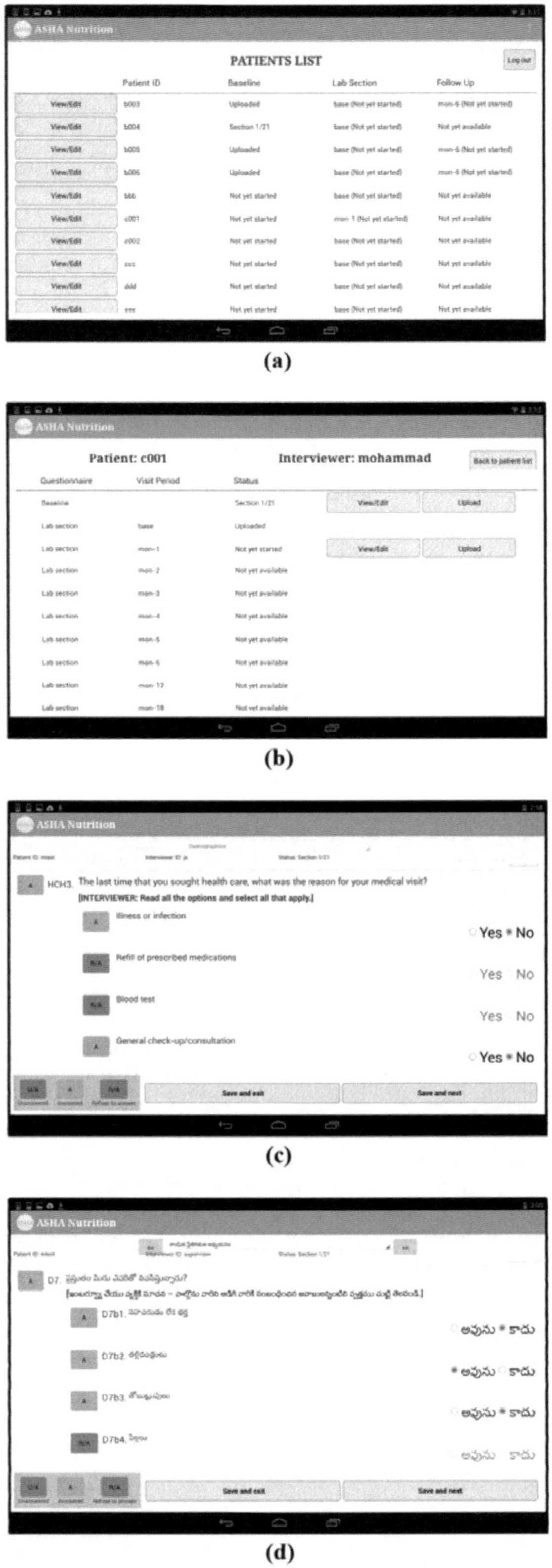

Figure 2. Sample pages from Android Application: a) Patient List page, b) Patient Profile Page, c) Questionnaire page in English, d) Questionnaire page in Telugu.

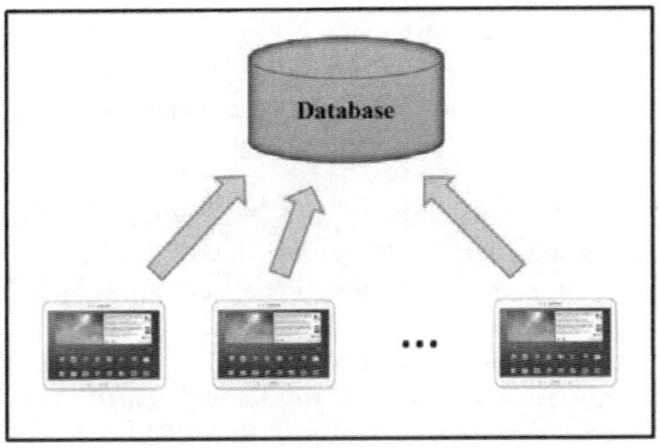

(a)

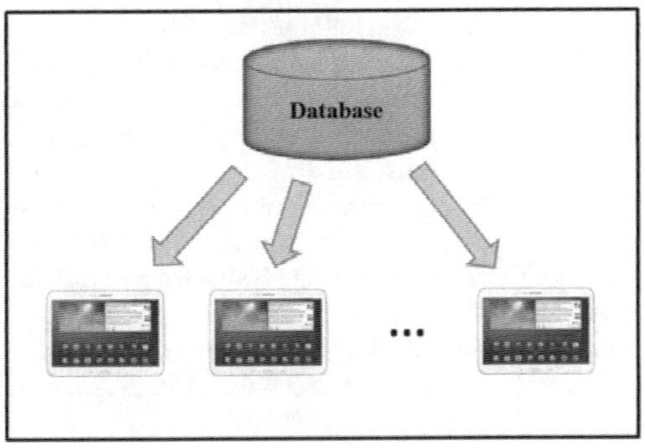

(b)

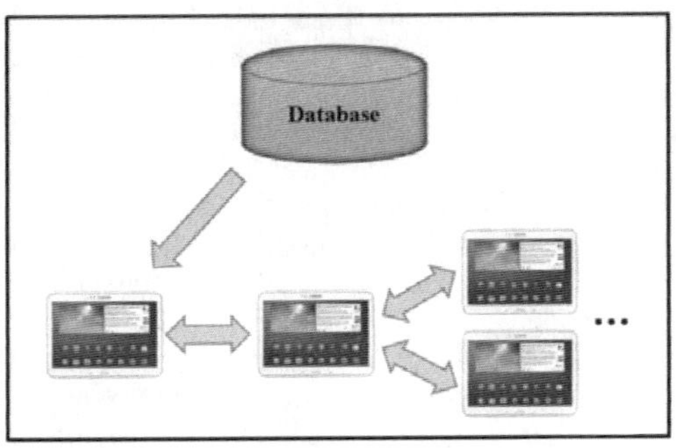

(c)

Figure 3. System network and data transmission: a) Wireless data transmission from app to server, b) Synchronization by transmitting data from the server to all devices (tablets), c) Device-to-device synchronization in the case of poor internet connection.

3.2.3 Webserver and Database

A cloud-based NoSQL database has been built to store and manage the data received from tablet devices. A webserver and web-portal have been designed and developed to visualize the results to authorized research staff, and allow them to analyze the data, extract statistics and graphs, edit or update the data, and export/download it in desired formats. As mentioned in section 3.1.1, various types of users can have various levels of access to the system to view, update, or control the database.

The authorized research staff and research investigators will analyze the results and extract useful information from the collected data. They can later provide feedback, comments, or prescriptions, or recommend specific interventions in order to improve patients' physical, physiological, and mental health.

Figure 4 shows some sample snapshots of the developed web portal. Figure 4-a represents the *patient list* page including the list of all patients along with their basic demographics. This page allows the users to export desired data and statistics for all patients together in a single list in various formats. This page also allows the user to enter the patient's profile page by clicking on a patient ID. Figure 4-b represents a sample *patient profile* page, where the users can have access to all collected data from each patient. This page also allows the authorized users to manually add new data samples, or revise the previously collected data. Any changes on the original data through the app or web such as revisions, edits, or additions will be recorded in the database along with the date/time of change, and the name/user-account of the person who made the change to ensure accountability. This page shows all different revisions of the data in case a data sample is edited or updated manually. Figure 4-c illustrates a sample *graph* that is generated by the web portal. The graphs and plots can be really informative and helpful in this study since they can indicate the process of health condition improvement or deterioration.

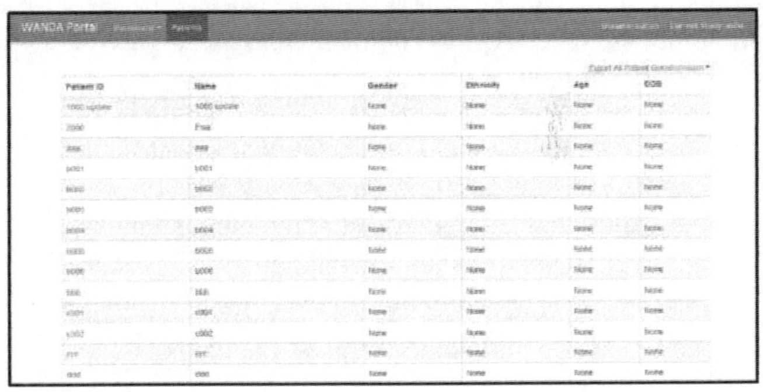

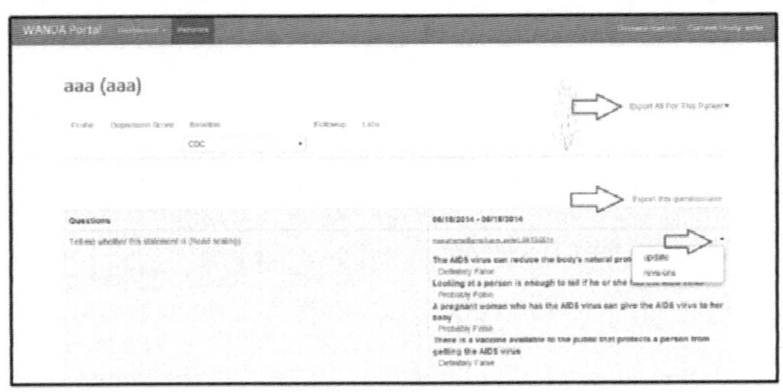

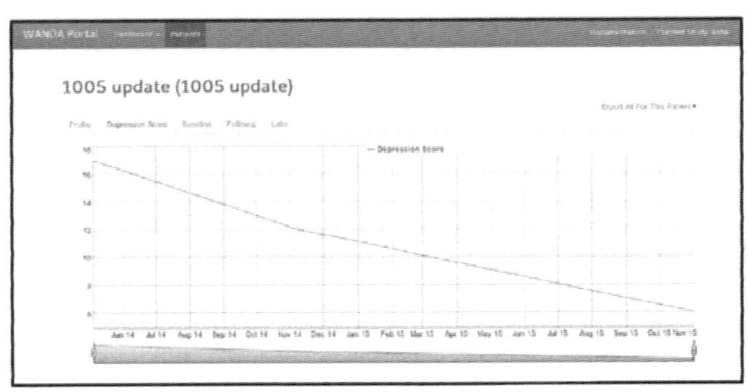

Figure 4. Sample pages from Web Portal: a) Patient List page, b) Patient Profile Page, c) Sample Graph plotted in web portal.

4. CONCLUSION

Although new technologies such as BSN and RHMS have shown promises in improving quality of care, designing a robust and reliable RHMS that can deal with system restrictions such as limited internet connection or intermittent communication problems is yet an open problem.

This paper presented an end-to-end, robust, portable, and distributed RHMS for monitoring and management of patients living with HIV/AIDS. The proposed system includes an Android application to manage data collection and preprocessing, a wireless BSN to handle data communication and transmission, and a backend cloud-based server along with NoSQL database and web-portal for data visualization and analysis. The mobile app is responsible for collecting timely data from patients including baseline, 6-month, 12-month, and 18-month follow up rounds, as well as laboratory results. The proposed system particularly addresses a number of serious challenges in RHMS including data transmission and synchronization under limited network connectivity (e.g. in rural areas with poor or unavailable internet connections). Various techniques have been proposed to deal with network connection problems to assure full and intact data transfer, minimize the system delay and latency, and maximize the quality and efficiency of data transmission.

The proposed system has been implemented and is being used in a large research study to monitor *600 WLHA* in rural parts of India. This study is a collaborative work between UCLA computer science department, UCLA School of Nursing, UCSF, and All India Institute of Medical Sciences (AIIMS).

The patients are split into 4 groups (150 patients in each group), and total 16 social workers are taking care of the patients (4 social workers per group). To date, the baseline data collection round has completed for 500 patients. The baseline round includes 426 data items (for each patient) collected and transmitted through the system. Also, the 6-month follow-up data collection round has been finished for 400 patients, the 12-month follow-up data collection round has completed for 300 patients, and the 18-month follow-up data collection round finished for 200 patients. The follow up rounds include 411 data items (for each patient) collected and transmitted through the system. Furthermore, the baseline lab data has been collected and transmitted through the app for 500 patients, as well as 1-month, 2-month, 3-month, 4-month, and 5-month lab data that has been collected and transmitted for 400 patients. The results prove the effectiveness, reliability, robustness, and accuracy of this system in satisfying clinician needs in collecting, transmitting, and managing the data, providing a powerful platform for data analysis.

The next step in this study is to include more wearable devices and pervasive sensors in patient's living space to monitor and track patient's physical activity, motions, and locations. Furthermore, we would like to add a backend Analytics Engine to analyze the collected data based on machine learning algorithms, and perform predictions about the study outcomes including patients' health conditions, adherence, and adverse events.

5. ACKNOWLEDGMENTS

The authors would like to thank WANDA Inc. (www.yourwanda.com) for valuable help and support.

This study was funded by the National Institute on Mental Health R01MH098728 on 07-23-2013 to Investigators AN, MK, SS.

6. REFERENCES

[1] M. Lan, N. Alshurafa, H. Ghasemzadeh and M. Sarrafzadeh, "WANDA: An End-to-End Remote Health Monitoring and Analytics System for Heart Failure Patients," Wireless Health Conf., 2012b.

[2] M. K. Suh, et al., "Dynamic Self-adaptive Remote Health Monitoring System for Diabetics," EMBC, 2012.

[3] M. K. Suh, et al., "A Remote Patient Monitoring System for Congestive Heart Failure," JOMS, June 2011a.

[4] N. Alshurafa, et al. "Anti-Cheating: Detecting Self-Inflicted and Impersonator Cheaters for Remote Health Monitoring Systems with Wearable Sensors," BSN 2014.

[5] M. K. Suh, et al., "WANDA B: Weight and Activity with Blood Pressure Monitoring System for Heart Failure Patients," in IEEE Workshop on IREHSS, 2010b.

[6] N. Alshurafa, et al. "Battery optimization in smartphones for remote health monitoring systems to enhance user adherence." Int. Conf. on PErvasive Technologies Related to Assistive Environments. 2014.

[7] N. Alshurafa, et al. "Improving Compliance in a Remote Health Monitoring System through Smartphone Battery Optimization". IEEE J Biomed Health Inform, 2014.

[8] S. I. Lee, H. Ghasemzadeh, B. J. Mortazavi, M. Lan, N. Alshurafa, M. Ong, M. Sarrafzadeh, Remote Health Monitoring Systems: What Impact Can Data Analytics Have on Cost?, in Wireless Health, 2013.

[9] M. Pourhomayoun, Z. Jin and M.L. Fowler, "Accurate Localization of In-Body Medical Implants Based on Spatial Sparsity," IEEE Trans. on Biomedical Engineering, 2013.

[10] M. Pourhomayoun, M. Fowler, Z. Jin, "A Novel Method for Medical Implant In-Body Localization," Int. Conf. of IEEE Engineering in Medicine&Biology Society (EMBC), 2012.

[11] M. Pourhomayoun, et. al., "Multiple Model Analytics for Adverse Event Prediction in Remote Health Monitoring Systems," IEEE EMBS Conference on Healthcare Innovation & Point-of-Care Technologies, 2014, pp. 106-110.

[12] M. Pourhomayoun, Z. Jin and M.L. Fowler, "Indoor Localization, Tracking and Fall Detection for Assistive Healthcare Based on Spatial Sparsity and Wireless Sensor Network," International Journal of Monitoring and Surveillance Technologies Research, 2013.

[13] K. Hung and Z. Yuan-Ting, Implementation of a WAP-based telemedicine system for patient monitoring, Information Technology in Biomedicine, IEEE Trans. on, 2003.

[14] W Wu, et al. "The smartcane system: an assistive device for geriatrics", Proceedings of the ICST 3rd international conference on Body area networks.

[15] T Massey, T Gao, M Welsh, JH Sharp, M Sarrafzadeh, "The design of a decentralized electronic triage system," AMIA annual symposium proceedings 2006, 544.

[16] T Gao, T Massey, M Sarrafzadeh, L Selavo, M Welsh, "Participatory user centered design techniques for a large scale ad-hoc health information system," Proceedings of the 1st ACM SIGMOBILE international workshop on Systems and networking support for healthcare and assisted living environments.

[17] R Jafari, F Dabiri, P Brisk, M Sarrafzadeh, "Adaptive and fault tolerant medical vest for life-critical medical monitoring," Proceedings of the 2005 ACM symposium on Applied computing, 272-279.

[18] A. G. Logan, et al., "Mobile Phone–Based Remote Patient Monitoring System for Management of Hypertension in Diabetic Patients," American Journal of Hypertention, 2007.

[19] Nyamathi A., et al., "ASHA-Life Intervention Perspectives Voiced by Rural Indian Women Living with AIDS," Health Care Women Int. 2016 Apr; 37(4): 412–425.
[20] Nyamathi A., et al. "Challenges experienced by rural women in India living with AIDS and implications for the delivery of HIV/AIDS care", HealthCare for Women Int. 2011; Apr; 32(4):300-13.
[21] Nyamathi, A., et al., Impact of a rural village women (ASHA) intervention on adherence to antiretroviral therapy in southern india. Nursing Research, 2012 Sep-Oct; 61(5):353-62.
[22] Nyamathi, A., Salem, B., Meyer, V., Ganguly, K., Sinha, S., Ramakrishnan, P., Impact of an ASHA intervention on depressive symptoms among rural women living with AIDS in India: Comparison of the ASHA life and usual care program AIDS Education & Prevention, 2012 Jun; 24(3):280-93.
[23] UNAIDS. AIDS info. 2014. Retrieved from http://www.unaids.org/en/dataanalysis/datatools/aidsinfo.

Mobility Management and Delay Cost Analysis in SDNized WLAN

Manzoor Ahmed Khan
DAI-Labor, Technische Universität
Berlin, Germany
manzoor-ahmed.khan@dai-labor.de

Patrick Engelhard
DAI-Labor, Technische Universität
Berlin, Germany
patrick.engelhard@dai-labor.de

Tobias Dörsch
GT ARC
Berlin, Germany
tobias.doersch@gt-arc.com

ABSTRACT

The paradigm shift in network control is envisioned as the next evolution milestone of mobile communications. A more flexible control of network technologies will be enabled by implementing the concept of Software Defined Networking (SDN). This dictates that amongst others users' mobility in mobile networks should also be managed by SDN controller. In this paper, we develop necessary tools and software modules to realize the SDNized WLAN. We then implement a distributed mobility management protocol and investigate its performance in terms of handover delays. The paper focuses on studying the delay sources and the impact of system dynamics (e.g., topology size and controller load) on different delay components. To carryout investigations in a more realistic environment, we develop a full scale SDN controlled WLAN testbed.

CCS CONCEPTS

•**Networks** → **Network performance modeling; Network experimentation;** *Network monitoring; Mobile networks;*

KEYWORDS

Software Defined Networking, Mobility Management

1 INTRODUCTION

Recent past has witnessed tremendous evolution of telecommunication networks, which is strongly driven by their positioning as main channel of delivery of most modern services. The principles of SDN does not only enable the centralized control of overall infrastructure but also transform the network to a programmable and flexible network, which can dynamically be shared by the diverse set of network services. However, the popular use of SDN is still confined to Data-center networks, where SDN nodes are interconnected by high speed lines. The problem domain in this case is restrained to optimizing the network behavior only. With SDN concepts blending in the mobile networks, the problem domain widens to include mobility management, which strains SDN's scalability issue even more. The challenges of traditional mobile networks came from the classical design of mobile network, which is hierarchical and mainly centrally controlled. The centralized gateway and backhauling of data consequence in high bandwidth requirements on the bit pipe and single point of failure. Such challenges were addressed by transiting to the flattened architecture. The evolution towards flattened architecture is described in [2], which highlights functional components in the flattened architectures of different network technologies and 3GPP efforts to address the user plane scalability problems.

The architectural evolution has a consistent impact on the way mobility management solutions are implemented. Mobile IP, which was primarily deployed in the hierarchical architecture kept evolving with numerous variants like [3]: HIMPv6, PMIPv6, FMIPv6, Dual Stack MIP, etc. The development of these variants strictly followed the device layer entities and applications requirements (e.g., bandwidth hungry users of 5G, densified networks, and IoT, etc.), which pushed the mobility management concept to a more distributed control approach. IETF just a few years back chartered a working group on Distributed Mobility Management (DMM). This group focuses on stipulating approaches to decompose control and data planes of traditional centrally controlled architecture. Amongst the main goals of DMM, the following were the main highlights: i) Mobility management mechanisms should be distributed and offered dynamically. ii) To reduce the signaling overhead, the mobility mechanisms should be dynamically activated / deactivated. iii) The group should rely on then current mobility management protocols e.g., MIPv6, HMIPv6, PMIPv6, etc.

Distributed mobility management concept may be applied to different segments of the network [3] e.g.; i) DMM in core - realized by distributing the mobility anchors topologically or geographically. ii) DMM in access network - realized by techniques similar to LIPA and SIPTO, which assist in by passing the core infrastructure. DMM allows to decouple the control and data planes, as opposed to classical mobility management approaches, where the control signaling and data pass through a centralized entity (mobility anchor). Hence, separating the data plane, which contributes much bigger portion of the load when compared with control traffic, we to great extent address the scalability issue of mobility anchor. By putting the control plane in centralized node, effective approaches for data plane steering and mobility management be realized. SDN on the other hand is characterized by the similar philosophy i.e., decoupling the control from data plane the SDN controller control the flows on forwarding entities. Owing to obvious complementary characteristics of these two paradigms, literature contributes with a number of proposals for implementing the DMM approaches on SDNized network e.g., [3, 5, 7, 9, 11]. Authors in [9] suggest to separate mobility functionalities of the PMIPv6 nodes and discuss two different possibilities of these functionalities in the SDN architecture i.e.; i) co-location of LMA and MAG at the controller level, ii)

LMA located in controller and MAG located in the access switch. A survey on mobility management approaches and their limitations is given in [3]. The authors also discuss potential implementation approaches of the mobility management protocol in SDNized network, which we believe provides a good overview / roadmap of mobility protocols implemented in SDNized controlled mobile networks. [5] highlights the suitability of DMM approaches for 5G networks and proposes the implementation of PMIPv6 in SDNized networks, where the MAG functionality is replaced by a gateway featuring mobility anchoring function and LMA functionality is implemented as control application at the controller level. Similar to (or inspired by) [5], the authors in [11] suggest a DMM solution based on SDN architecture. The authors investigate the handover delays of their contributed mobility management protocol. The implementation of HMIPv6, a variant of MIPv6 on SDNized network is discussed in [7].

Major chunk of the research literature approaches in general discuss the protocols on abstract level by avoiding the implementation details, few do not study the performance in terms of handover delays, whereas the others validate the performance on either emulation platform or numerically analyze them with a number of assumptions. We believe that given the fact that SDNized wireless networks are still in their infancy, deriving conclusions on the assumptions or high level modeling may not support the claims of optimality in mobility management or minimizing the handover delays. In this work, we implement a DMM protocol on a full scale SDNized WLAN testbed. We study the handover delay cost budge on granular level by decomposing it into more granular components and studying the impact of system dynamics over the delay components. This in turn helps understanding the contribution by each delay component to the overall handover delay cost budget. We believe that studying the impact of system dynamics on each delay component to a great extent helps in localizing major source of handover delays and hence the source of bottleneck(s).

2 DISTRIBUTED MOBILITY MANAGEMENT APPROACH IN SDNIZED WIRELESS NETWORKS

In this section, we elaborate on implementation of the PMIPv6 [1] inspired mobility management solution in the SDNized wireless networks. Before we discuss the proposed approach, let us briefly discuss the main objectives of carrying out the control communication between PMIPv6 nodes (i.e., Mobility Anchor Gateway (MAG) $\leftrightarrow$ Local Mobility Anchor (LMA)), which may broadly be categorized under the following two objectives: **O1** Mobile Node (MN) Tracking - the MAG should communicate MN's association and disassociation messages to LMA, the central control entity. **O2** Path configuration - for configuration of the network segments on the path between Correspondent Node (CN) and MN.

When it comes to implementing the PMIPv6 on the SDN network, the functionalities of MAG and LMAs may be positioned in different architectural levels e.g., MAG and LMA both encamped at controller level (depicted as configuration 2 in Figure 1) or positioning MAG in a SDN forwarding entity and implementing LMA as SDN native application (depicted as configuration 1 in Figure 1).

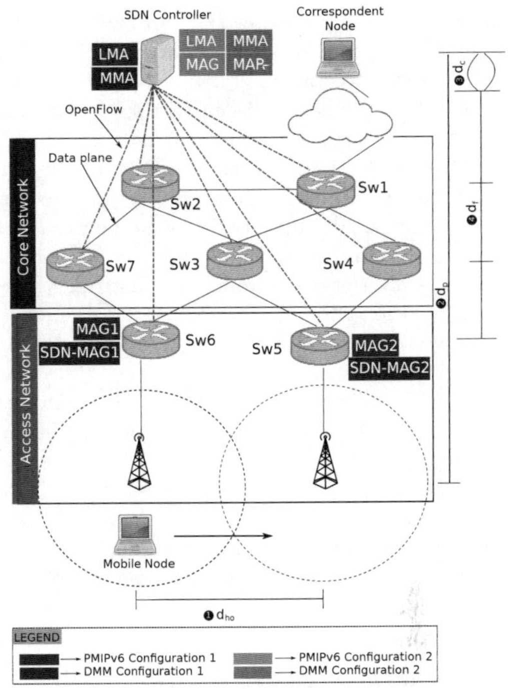

Figure 1: Potential Implementation Scenarios for DMM in SDNized Networks

Figure 1 presents the big picture, which depicts both the topology and protocol architecture.

The proposed architecture implements centralized control plane and distributes data plane. The centralized (SDN) controller implements major mobility management functionalities by Mobility Management Application (MMA) e.g., logic to handle the mobility triggers, path computation and crafting switches configuration logic to be deployed in the switches connecting MN and CN. The edge switch (which interfaces a number of APs on the downstream) acts as an anchor point, which also handles the signaling on behalf of MN. We term the edge switch as SDN-MAG hereafter owing to its adapted functionality for the proposed approach. It is now obvious that the first objective O1 is implemented in the edge switch and the objective O2 is implemented in controller (by MMA). Enabling the control communication between these two entities, we achieve distributed mobility management. Similar to the SDN concept, the controller implements de-facto protocol (OpenFlow) on the southbound to interface the edge switches. Hence, these entities talk the OpenFlow language to each other.

In the following, we provide the sequence and details of interactions carried out between entities for implementing the proposed mobility management approach. Since the call admission control is also implemented by the SDN controller, MN's call request should be extended to the controller over the access and core network entities. When SDN-MAG detects the MN's attachment to an AP interfaced to it, the SDN-MAG translates the MN attachment as the call admission trigger, and maps it to OpenFlow packet-in trigger. The trigger contains MN context information. Upon receiving the trigger, the controller then implements the call admission logic by registering and computing the flow rules for MN. The flow rules installed on the intermediate switches between MN & CN, which enables the inter-MN-CN communication.

Now if the MN detaches from its current point of attachment, the SDN-MAG translates this in disassociation event (which it receives from the radio part) into OF handover trigger. The trigger is propagated to the controller, which the controller handles by implementing the mobility management application. Upon association to the new point of attachment, the SDN-MAG translates and extend the association event to the controller. The controller computes the new path between CN and MN and crafts the configuration rules. These flow configuration rules are then forwarded through FlowMod messages to all intermediate switches on the new path. The FlowMod basically populates the flow tables of intermediate switches. It should be highlighted that as opposed to the classical implementation of PMIPv6, which uses IP-in-IP tunneling techniques between LMA and MAGs, in the proposed approach the data path is configured by the SDN controller i.e., upon receiving the handover trigger, the controller updates the flow table of intermediate switches toward the new point of attachment. Hence, packets are forwarded without IP tunnel.

3 DELAY COST BUDGET EVALUATION

In this section, we study the delay cost budge of proposed mobility management application in the SDNized WLAN. We know that mobile node will only receive the packets on the newly associated access point of attachment after the handover process is completed. An obvious definition of the mobility cost is; the time between transmission of the last IP packet through the old connection and the first packet through the new connection. Mobility cost budget may be defined in terms of different components, which is strongly influenced by the type of mobility management protocols used, network topology, and network technologies. We decompose the total handover delay cost budget into granular delay components and investigate the impact of different system dynamics (e.g., controller load, topology thickness, etc.) on the overall delay cost budge. Let $\mathcal{D}_t$ represent the total cost budget for mobility management approach, whose delay components are summarized in Table 1. Hence $\mathcal{D}_t$ is given by:

$$\mathcal{D}_t := d_e + d_{p,h}^{e\rightarrow c} + d_c + d_{f,h}^{c\rightarrow e} \tag{1}$$

4 IMPLEMENTATION OF SDNIZED WLAN

We implement the topology shown in Figure 2. We use commodity laptops connected with a simple hardware switch to create the topology. Mobility application is implemented as native application of OpenDaylight controller. By creating multiple virtual bridges on each physical machine, we are able to create topologies of variable complexity and sizes. To create the topology of variable sizes, we deployed a mix of virtual and physical bridges. To understand the implemented experimental configurations, assume that $\mathcal{L}_{g,o}$ represents topology length, where index g corresponds to two paths $\mathcal{A}$ and $\mathcal{B}$ and o represents the path size (i.e., small, medium, and long). Table 2 summarizes the extensions on each path and total number of hops for the three configurations.

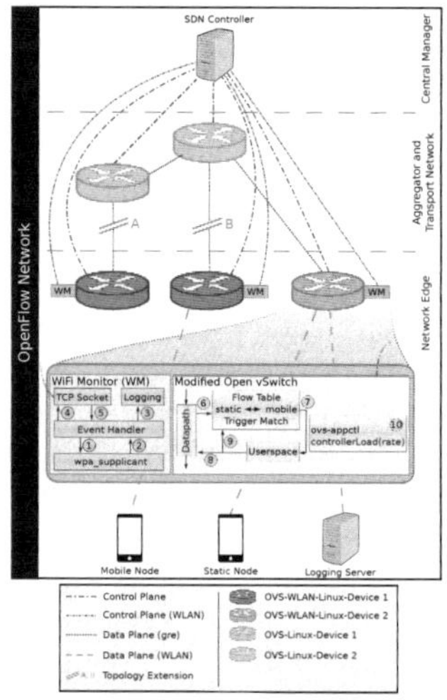

Figure 2: Experimental Setup

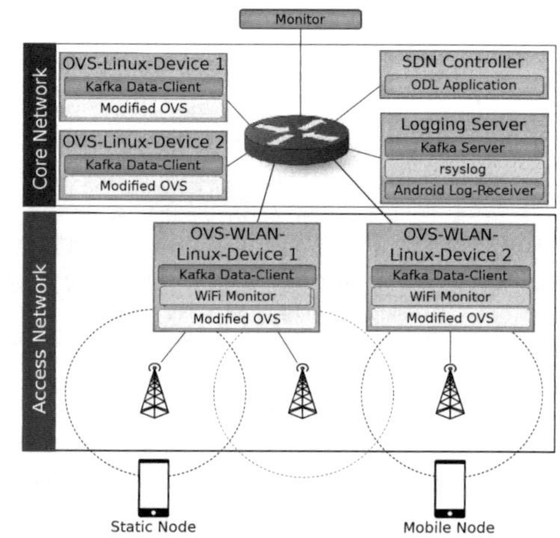

Figure 3: SDNized Wireless LAN - Device Overview

In the following, we briefly discuss our developed tools and software modules to realize the SDNized WLAN. Figure 3 pictorially presents these tools and modules, Table 4 summarizes the inter-tools and inter-entities interactions. Table 3 briefly discusses our developed tools and software modules to realize the SDNized WLAN.

5 DELAY COST BUDGET MEASUREMENT - THE TECHNICAL PERSPECTIVE

In this section, we discuss the technical details of approaches we implemented to capture the delay components mentioned in section 3. The delay cost budget defined by Equation 1 is extended in this section based on the lessons learned from the experiments we carried out in SDNized WLAN. This is to say that the intuitive delay cost budget that we modeled in Equation 1 or the ones presented in research literature with intuitive assumptions may not be realistic representatives of the delay cost budget of handover in the SDNized WLAN. Hence, our extended delay cost budget in

Component	Delay	Remarks
Link Establishment	d_e	Link establishment delay with edge switch (e) i.e., the time required by physical interface to establish new association.
Trigger Propagation	$d_{p,h}^{e \to c}$	MN's (dis/a)ssociation is translated at edge switch (e) and propagated over network hops (h) towards the controller (c).
Computation Delay	d_c	Having received the trigger event, the controller computes the rules to handle the event, which we represent with d_c
Route setup	$d_{f,h}^{c \to e}$	The new rules are transferred and implemented on the switches of newly computed paths.

Table 1: Table Summarizing Delay Components of Mobility Delay Cost Budget

Config-uration	Path	Extension	Hop Sum
Small	A	$\mathcal{L}_{S,A} = 0$	4
	B	$\mathcal{L}_{S,B} = 0$	3
Medium	A	$\mathcal{L}_{M,A} = 3$	7
	B	$\mathcal{L}_{M,B} = 5$	8
Large	A	$\mathcal{L}_{L,A} = 6$	10
	B	$\mathcal{L}_{L,B} = 15$	18

Table 2: Topology Overview - Hops

this section captures more realistic cost. Table 5 summarizes the extended set of delay components and their technical implementation details. Based on the delay components detailed in Table 5, we regenerate the Equation 1 in the following.

$$\mathcal{D}_{t,.} = \overbrace{d_{e,a} + d_{e,n}}^{d_e} + d_{p,h}^{e \to c} + \underbrace{\tilde{d_c} + \overline{d_c}}_{d_c} + d_{f,h}^{c \to h} + d_u$$

6 RESULTS AND ANALYSIS

We now evaluate the performance of implemented mobility management solution in authors developed validation framework in terms of delay cost budge. We study the impact of different system dynamics on various aforementioned delay components, of which the most prominent ones include: *i) Impact of topology size on the delay components* - Varying topology size is achieved by deploying virtual and physical bridges in the topology as discussed in section 4 and Table 2. *ii) Impact of control computation load on the delay components* - A brief description on generation of varying controller load is given in Table 3.

We start by analyzing the link establishment delay in Figure 4(a). It should be highlighted however, that this delay component is less relevant to SDN based handovers as it is mainly introduced by hardware and is in theory not affected by topology size or controller load. This assumption is supported by the graphs in Figure 4(a), in which the measured delay is constant and similar independant of topology size and controller load. For WLAN link layer establishment, we have on average experienced delays within the range of $300 - 400msec$.

In Figure 4(b), we study the impact of controller load and topology sizes on the propagation delay component. As obvious from the figure that the varying controller computation load does not impact the propagation delay. However, the change in topology size does have impact on the propagation delay. The propagation delay of the small configuration increased by 70-100% after 4 hops were introduced to the configuration. Similarly further increase of 40-50% is observed when 8 hops are introduced over the the medium configuration. This behavior may be explained by further details of the experiment setup. A very similar behavior is seen for the flow setup delay component, which we see in Figure 4(c). The flow modification messages are sent asynchronously by the controller over the physical network, which is why we expect an increase of this delay component in the larger logical network topology. As these messages are sent to each node on a separate connection, we expect this delay to be higher if there are more OpenFlow nodes in the network to be reconfigured. Since the controller is the node both sending messages and measuring the delay, we expect a minor impact of controller load on this component. This behavior is advocated by Figure 4(c), where the only impacting parameter is topology size.

The impact of computation delay is depicted in Figure 4(d). As the core network topology is, in most cases, static, routes through the core network can be cached by the controller. The controller builds the cache the first time it calculates a route through the network, which causes the first computation event of an experiment to be an order of magnitude larger than the following computation delays. As the size of the cache increases with increasing topology size and complexity, we expect to see an increase of this delay component when changing the OpenFlow network topology. The graph shows the computation delay without the initial calculation of the cache. We assume that the lookup-time is negligibly small. Hence, the increase of this delay component stems solely from the higher number of flows that have to be prepared if more nodes have to be reconfigured.

7 CONCLUSION

In this paper, we have implemented a distributed mobility management protocol in SDNized network. The performance of the proposed distributed mobility management is evaluated in terms of handover delays. We also studied the impact of controller load and topology thickness on the handover delay values. The experiments were carried out on a full scale SDNized WLAN testbed.

Component	Description
WiFi Monitor	To achieve efficient tracking of mobile hosts, we develop WiFi monitor tool using C++, which runs on linux system. For more please refer to [8]
Monitoring Tool	Keeps track of experiments states and detects anomalies by showing state of active switches. We used Apache Kafka messaging system. It comprises of three components: i) Kafka server - resides in our logging server. ii) Kafka data client - locally monitors switch state. iii) Monitor - contains kafka command client and user interface, where UI displays flow tables of switches.
ODL Application	Build on ODL version 1.4.2-Helium. The application uses the following ODL services: i) Monitoring - contains server to which the WiFi monitor instance is connected. ii) Routing - uses monitoring module to identify the APs associating the communicating hosts. It computes and installs the flows.
Android Application	Functions in two modes namely *Sender* and *Receiver*. The *Sender* sends *UDP_PKT*s to the *Receiver* at a specified rate. The *Receiver* stores a time-stamp, which determines, when a packet was received. After a given timeout, the *Sender* automatically changes to a different Access Point.
Load Generation	For this, we extended the functionality of OVS such that it causes a specified bridge to generate a dummy *PACKET_IN* at a specified rate.
SDN Debugger	For demonstration and debugging purposes, we implement a graphical user interface, which allows users to closely monitor the various components of the experiment. It offers a unified view of all events occurring during the experiment. Since we automate the execution of the experiment, we also implement a replay feature which reads log-files of all nodes recorded in the past as if they were generated in real-time. This enables us to track down odd behavior and errors which occurred during unsupervised experiment runs.

Table 3: Descriptions of components and software modules to realize the WLAN

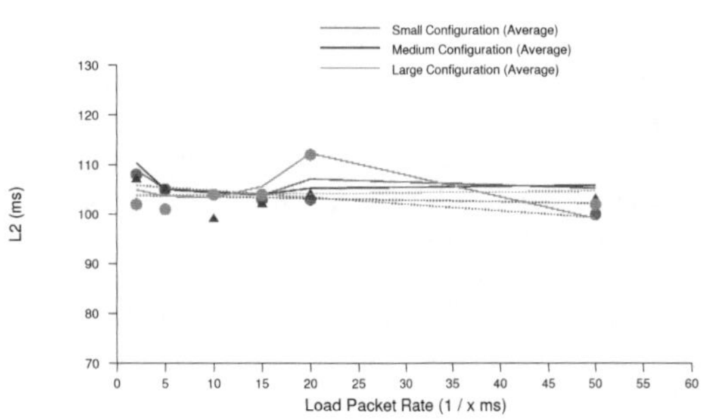

(a) Link Establishment Delay

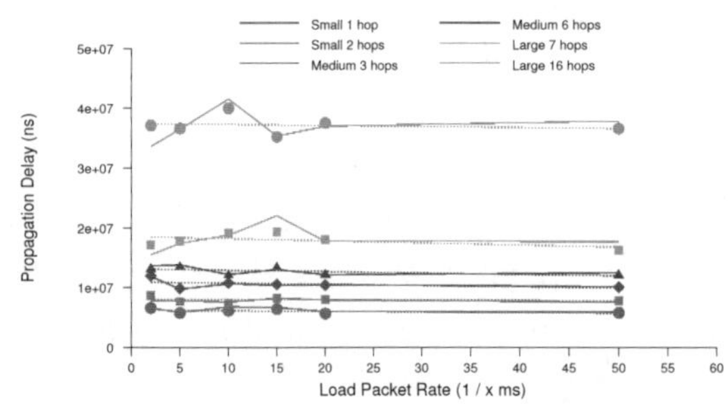

(b) Impact of controller load and topology size on propagation delay

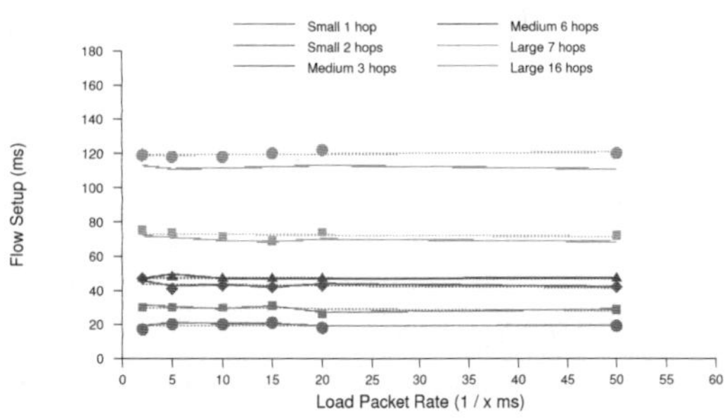

(c) Impact of controller load and topology size on flow setup delay

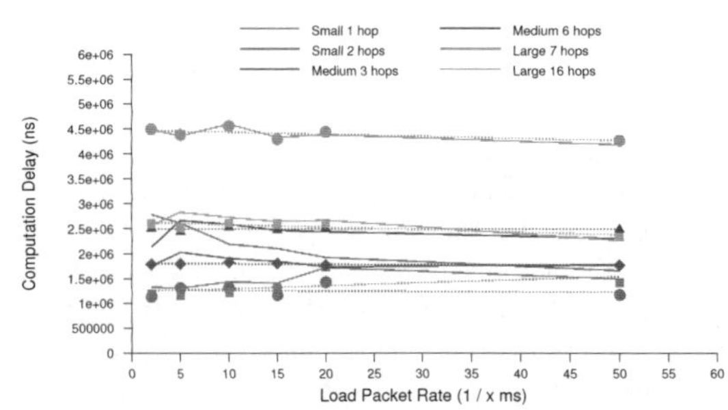

(d) Impact of controller load on the computation delay

Figure 4: Experiment results

Notation	Message-Type	Receiver	Sender	Answer	Notes
FMOD	OpenFlow *FLOW_MOD*	OVS	Controller	*FMOD_ACK*	-
PIN	OpenFlow *PACKET_IN*	Controller	OVS	-	Might cause *FMOD*
FMOD_ACK	OpenFlow *PACKET_IN*	Controller	OVS	-	Source MAC 00:00:00:00:00:00; Used for measurements
LOAD	OpenFlow *PACKET_IN*	Controller	OVS	*FMOD*	Source MAC 00:00:00:00:00:01; Loads the controller; *FMOD* executed on dummy OVS
L2_EVT	L2 (Dis-)Association Event	Controller	WiFi Monitor	*L2_EVT_ACK*	Informs controller about host connection
L2_EVT_ACK	Acknowledge of *L2_EVT*	WiFi Monitor	Controller	-	Used for measurements
UDP_PKT	Datagram Packet	Android Receiver	Android Sender	-	Contains running ID and send timestamp

Table 4: Control & Measurement Messages

Component	Sub-comp.	Notation	Remarks
Overall	Sending	$\mathcal{D}_{t,s}$	It is difference in send timestamps *s* between the last received *UDP_PKT* before a handover and first received *UDP_PKT* after a handover.
	Receiving	$\mathcal{D}_{t,r}$	In this we use the receive timestamps instead of the send timestamps.
Link Establishment	Re-association	$d_{e,a}$	For the measurement of the L2-Reassociation delay, all devices that run an instance of the WiFi-Monitor (i.e. every AP) are synchronized using the NTP protocol ([4, 6]) Every L2-Event is logged to Logging-Server. The difference in timestamps of an L2-Event-Pair (i.e. disconnect-event and corresponding connect-event) is considered to be the L2-Delay. Since NTP server is used for synchronization is within our local network, the difference of clocks of the APs *can maintain synchronization nominally within one millisecond* [10]. L2-Delay is fairly high (> $100ms$), thus the possible inaccuracy is acceptable for our purpose.
	Connectivity	$d_{e,n}$	As the sending operation is paused during a handover. After the L2-Handover is completed, the Android Application directly tries to continue sending. Time between time to continue sending and the first successfully sent packet is the L2-Connection delay.
Propagation	-	$d_{p,h}^{e\to c}$	It is the time consumed to propagate a (dis-)association event from the Access Point to the Controller. To measure propagation-Delay of an L2-Event, the WiFi-Monitor starts a timer directly before sending a *L2_EVT* message (connect/disconnect) to the ODL-application. The ODL-application answers with a *L2_EVT_ACK* on reception. The previously started timer is stopped as soon as the WiFi-Monitor receives the acknowledge from the controller. This gives us a round-trip-time which is then divided by two to obtain the Propagation-Delay.
Computation	Pre-computation	$\tilde{d_c}$	Time between the reception of a *PIN* on controller and the time when handling of this *PIN* starts. In ODL, each received packet contains a time-stamp defining when this packet was received, which we utilize to determine time passed between the reception and handling this packet.
	Main	$\overline{d_c}$	The time that expires while the controller calculates new flows. It is measured by starting a timer before calculating a route and stopping the timer, right before sending out the corresponding *FMODs*.
Flow Setup	-	$d_{f,h}^{c\to e}$	The time it takes to apply the previously calculated flow updates. Similar to propagation delay, we measure a round-trip-time by starting a timer on the controller, right before sending a *FMOD* command. We have implemented a functionality in OVS that each switch answers with a *FMOD_ACK* message immediately after the new flow was applied. The timer is stopped as the controller receives the *FMOD_ACK* message.
Unmeasured	-	d_u	The difference between C_A and the sum of all other components. E.g. the ARP resolution, that Android triggers after changing the Access Point.

Table 5: Table illustrating various delay components and their technical details in SDNized WLAN environment

Acknowledgment: This work was partially carried out in a project, iMoveFAN, a collaboration project under Huawei Innovation Research Program. Authors would like to thank Dr. Zoran Despotovic for his feedback and constructive comments.

REFERENCES

[1] Carlos Jesús Bernardos and Gramaglia. 2010. Network-based localized IP mobility management: Proxy mobile IPv6 and current trends in standardization. *JoWUA, Special issue: Advances in Wireless Mobile and Sensor Technologies)* 1, 2/3 (2010), 16–35.

[2] László Bokor, Zoltán Faigl, and Sándor Imre. 2011. *Flat Architectures: Towards Scalable Future Internet Mobility.* Springer Berlin Heidelberg, Berlin, Heidelberg, 35–50.

[3] H Anthony Chan, Hidetoshi Yokota, Jiang Xie, Pierrick Seite, and Dapeng Liu. 2011. Distributed and Dynamic Mobility Management in Mobile Internet: Current Approaches and Issues. *Journal of Communications* 6, 1 (feb 2011). DOI: http://dx.doi.org/10.4304/jcm.6.1.4-15

[4] H. Gerstung, C. Elliott, and B. Haberman. 2010. *Definitions of Managed Objects for Network Time Protocol Version 4 (NTPv4).* RFC 5907. RFC Editor.

[5] F. Giust, L. Cominardi, and C. J. Bernardos. 2015. Distributed mobility management for future 5G networks: overview and analysis of existing approaches. *IEEE Communications Magazine* 53, 1 (January 2015), 142–149. DOI: http://dx.doi.org/10.1109/MCOM.2015.7010527

[6] B Haberman and DL Mills. 2010. RFC 5906: Network Time Protocol version 4: Autokey specification. *Internet Engineering Task Force* (2010).

[7] S. F. Hasan. 2015. A discussion on software-defined handovers in Hierarchical MIPv6 networks. In *Industrial Electronics and Applications (ICIEA), 2015 IEEE 10th Conference on.* 140–144. DOI: http://dx.doi.org/10.1109/ICIEA.2015.7334099

[8] Manzoor Khan, Patrick Engelhard, and Tobias Dörsch. 2016. SDNizing the Wireless LAN - A Practical Approach. In *Proceedings of EUROSIM 2016.*

[9] S. M. Kim and H. Y. Choi. 2014. OpenFlow-based Proxy mobile IPv6 over software defined network (SDN). In *IEEE 11th CCNC.* 119–125. DOI: http://dx.doi.org/10.1109/CCNC.2014.6866558

[10] D. L. Mills. 1985. *Network Time Protocol (NTP).* RFC 958. RFC Editor. http://www.rfc-editor.org/rfc/rfc958.txt http://www.rfc-editor.org/rfc/rfc958.txt.

[11] Tien-Thinh Nguyen, Christian Bonnet, and Jérôme Härri. 2016. SDN-based distributed mobility management for 5G networks. In *WCNC 2016, IEEE Wireless Communications and Networking Conference, Track 3 - Mobile and Wireless Networks, 3-6 April 2016, Doha, Qatar.* Doha, QATAR. DOI: http://dx.doi.org/10.1109/WCNC.2016.7565106

Evaluating Human Activity-Based Ambient Lighting Displays for Effective Peripheral Communication

Kadian Davis
Eindhoven University of Technology
Eindhoven, The Netherlands
k.a.davis@tue.nl

Evans Owusu
Independent Researcher
Eindhoven, The Netherlands
Owboateng@gmail.com

Lucio Marcenaro
The University of Genova
Genova, Italy
lucio.marcenaro@unige.it

Loe Feijs
Eindhoven University of Technology
Eindhoven, The Netherlands
l.m.g.feijs@tue.nl

Carlo Regazzoni
The University of Genova
Genova, Italy
carlo.regazzoni@unige.it

Jun Hu
Eindhoven University of Technology
Eindhoven, The Netherlands
j.hu@tue.nl

Ambient Assisted Living (AAL) applications leverage pervasive sensing and ambient intelligence technologies to enable older people to live independently and to support their social inclusion and connectedness. Wearable sensors can be used to gather the elderly's activities of daily living (ADLs) data, thus enabling remote monitoring. Lately, ambient displays have been deployed to relay activity information in the periphery of the caregivers' attention in order to increase awareness of the activities of the elderly and to create a sense of connectedness. Moreover, there is accumulated evidence demonstrating the ability of ambient displays to influence and promote social connectedness between the elderly and their caregivers. In recent years, intelligent ambient lighting, a subclass of ambient displays, is emerging as an effective tool for conveying physical activity information. Existing literature suggests lighting encodings or configurations combining color, rate of change, position and brightness to communicate such information. Within AAL, there is little empirical evidence surrounding ambient lighting encodings that support this cause effectively. In this paper, we present an exploratory study investigating how potential caregivers perceive and interpret ambient lighting configurations for presenting activity information of the elderly. User preference, change noticeability and accuracy of the interpretation of three ambient lighting configurations were evaluated.

CCS Concepts

•Human-centered computing → Ubiquitous and mobile computing; •Ubiquitous and mobile computing → *Ambient Intelligence;*

Keywords

context awareness; ambient lighting displays; ambient assisted living; social connectedness

1. INTRODUCTION

Ambient intelligent solutions can have positive implications on improving the health and well-being of older adults [10]. A widely accepted definition of Ambient Intelligence (AmI), was introduced in 2001 by the ISTAG [9], an EU advisory group, to demonstrate a new approach to designing intelligent environments with a user-centric focus on improving the quality of life. An excerpt from the ISTAG mantra [9], describes an AmI world where, "People are surrounded by intelligent intuitive interfaces that are embedded in all kinds of objects and an environment that is capable of recognising and responding to the presence of different individuals in a seamless, unobtrusive and often invisible way." Within AmI environments, such as ambient assisted living (AAL), human activity recognition (HAR), i.e. the recognition and monitoring of activities of daily living (ADL) is a distinctive feature to support independent living among older adults. A common approach to HAR, includes the deployment of wearable sensors such as accelerometers and gyroscopes to support context awareness [26].

As we experience a new wave of AAL technologies, privacy and protection of personal information remains as one of the biggest challenges surrounding the continuous monitoring of people [3, 10]. Explicit presentation of users' activities such as "walking", "sleeping", "cooking" among others often cause users to express privacy concerns about their personal information. Pedersen and Sokoler in [24], proposed a "kind of shielding" of personal activity information through abstraction, exploiting features such as visual or auditory cues to provide "non-attentional demanding awareness".

Peripheral awareness is defined in [24] as, "our ability to maintain and constantly update a sense of our social and physical context." Ambient information systems, an application area of ambient intelligence, is grounded in the theories of peripheral awareness, whereby information is subtly portrayed in the periphery of the user's attention. This allows users to receive information in the background while performing other tasks in the foreground. In a digital era, people are often inundated with information, from emails to a variety of social media applications [20]. Ambient displays are part of the solution to reducing the amount of information mentally processed by providing an overview of the content. Moreover, ambient displays [16], capitalize on the principle of calm technology [28], as they transition effortlessly from the foreground to the background of the user's attention. Thus, a critical feature of ambient displays is their capability to be perceived at a quick glance, which triggers pre-attentive processing to reduce the user's cognitive load. Moreover, ambient displays should not distract users from performing their main tasks. In AAL environments, ambient displays hold promise as they can present information to users whenever and wherever needed, to support context awareness and to improve interpersonal relationships as demonstrated in [21].

Importantly, when designing ambient lighting displays the designer has to establish a context for decoding the information [22]. Specifically, in order to grasp the information received, the viewer has know the meaning of each lighting characteristic. In certain instances, users can understand intuitively or they can be explicitly told about the significance of the encoding [20, 22]. Occasionally, there are discrepancies between the designer's intention of the encoding and the viewers interpretation of the encoding. In reality, what matters most is what is understood by the viewer and not the designer's intention [22].

This paper builds on the proposal in [3, 4, 7] to present activity information using subtle ambient lighting displays to support social connectedness and context awareness between the elderly and their caregivers. Following this proposal, a smartphone activity recognition system was developed using the hybrid SVM-HMM model with an overall accuracy of 99.7% [5]. This model was used to classify six activity states namely, walking, walking upstairs, walking downstairs, standing, laying and sitting. To provide abstraction and privacy protection, the complexity of activity states was reduced to activity levels [6]. In this work, the six activity states have been discretized into three activity levels i.e. "resting", "passive" and "active". This abstraction of activity states into activity levels was based on user generated mappings. Users mapped activity states to levels based on their jobs and opinions of which activity states they considered to be active, passive or resting. As a continuation of the work in [5, 6], we seek to investigate how ambient lighting parameters can be exploited to encode activity information. What is lacking for designers are consistent design guidelines for encoding activity information within an AAL context.

In this paper, we focus on the design and evaluation of three lighting configurations taking into consideration position of the light source, frequency of light changes and lighting color properties (hue and brightness). Inspired by the work in [19], we designed a study where participants had to identify light changes and state their preferences for the lighting configurations. Matviienko et al. designed a study where participants had to map lighting patterns to a set of scenarios. However, our study was centered around an AAL context with the goal of finding the best lighting parameters for encoding the elderly's activity information. Based on the aforementioned requirements we evaluated:

- noticeability and accuracy of interpretations of the lighting configurations. We assume a glanceable ambient light, which gives clear information would be less distracting and easily move from the foreground to the background of attention.
- subjective attributes such as usefulness, suitability, intuitiveness, etc., towards the system. We hypothesize that the higher the subjective positive attitudes toward the ambient lighting configuration, the more the likely it will be adopted.
- user's perceptions on future system adoption and their recommendations for lighting parameters to encode activity information.

2. RELATED WORK

In an AAL setting, the integration of lighting, the Internet and sensors can realize systems that go beyond illumination. In particular, lighting through the Internet of Things (IOT), is capable of sensing and communicating vast amounts of data from the environment. Thus, light has huge potential for enabling context awareness and enhancing well-being. Also, the varying visual properties of light e.g., colour, brightness, saturation, position and frequency of changes discussed in [3, 20] make it ideal for encoding physical activity information. Within AAL, the rendering of activity information through ambient displays has demonstrated potential for strengthening connectivity between the elderly and their caregivers [21]. For instance, the SnowGlobe, an ambient lighting display was used to encode movement information in an AAL context, for creating interpersonal awareness between two remote persons. In this design, movement information was rendered using a measure of purple light and fluttering snowflakes. When communication was initiated by one person, the other person's snowgloble reflected a bright orange light accompanied by fluttering snowflakes. Similarly, the Casablanca Intentional Presence Lamp [13], conveyed presence information to two remote users using different images and colour. In another scenario, the Lumitouch [2] deployed ambient light for emotional communication. However, in these studies the information encoded was varied and as such was lacking in a consistent framework for encoding activity information especially for an AAL context.

Previous studies have exploited lighting features for conveying physical activity information using different encodings. For instance, ActivMON is a wrist-based ambient display, which uses coloured lighting to inform users about their activity levels [1]. In addition, a pulsing light is used to convey information about the activity levels of others. ActivMON uses a colour fade from red-to-green, where red shows no daily activity while green demonstrates that the user's daily activity goal is achieved. A fast pulsing light indicates high physical activity levels for other users while a slow pulsing light shows their inactivity. The HealthBar [17] is an ambient lighting display, deployed in working environments to counteract the effects of prolonged sitting. The HealthBar exploits a light tube placed at the user's desk, which fades from green-to-red. A fully charged HealthBar is initially set to green and gradually fades to red to prompt the user to take a break. If the break is not initiated, a pulsing light is used as a break reminder. In a similar way, ambient light was deployed through the Movelamp [11] to stimulate increased movement in office environments. Using a Philips Living Colours lamp, the Movelamp was positioned in the user's peripheral vision. It changed using a colour fade from green-to-red with increasing brightness. Green shows periods of physical activity while red displays no activity, the brightness was a medium to alert the user's attention [11]. The Pediluma ambient display, is a shoe accessory that uses one colour (green), with varying intensities to visualize the wearer's physical activity [15]. More physical activity is reflected with a brighter glow, encouraging users to increase their activity levels.

Overall, we observed that colour, brightness, position and a pulsing light are the four most common combination of lighting parameters to encode activity information. However, within an AAL context, a pulsing light would be more relevant to convey an emergency or crisis situation, which is not an intended goal of this research. As an aside, most of the earlier studies on ambient light displays encoding activity information have focussed primarily on how the receipt of the information influenced the users' activity levels. Quantitative evidence showing how people perceive the visual information received is largely left unexplored. As mentioned earlier, ambient displays are meant to trigger pre-attentive processing, an intuitive process often based on instinct, snap judgements and gut feelings as mentioned in [12]. As Gladwell argues, rapid cognition is not always correct, which in this case, can be harmful within an AAL setting. Consequently, opening up the problem space for researchers to explore whether the caregiver's perception of activity encodings at a glance, matches with the physical reality of the elder's activities.

A considerable amount of work has been published on design guidelines for the design [8, 25, 27] and assessment of ambient displays [16, 18]. These design guidelines and heuristics were used to set the initial requirements for our ambient lighting display. However, they were still too general and more specificity would better assist designers to tailor ambient lighting solutions to encode physical activity information. In an attempt to fill this gap, Matviienko et al. [19] derived a set of guidelines for encoding lighting parameters. Yet, these guidelines were not matching the intended outcome of our overall research i.e. not only to provide context awareness but also to enhance the social connectedness experience through the use of lighting parameters such as colour.

Therefore, the specific colour choice should not only convey activity information but also evoke a subtle sense of remote presence based on the elder's current activity level. In retrospect, the derived lighting patterns for presenting situations in [19], were not sufficient for both end-goals as the authors recommended different colours for status information classes showing presence and physical activity data. Consequently, driving the need for one colour scheme that could achieve both outcomes.

To fill this gap, we reviewed the literature on colour symbolism. Our findings showed varied interpretations on colour, which were heavily reliant on culture, age and situational context. For example, the authors in [23] demonstrated affective implications of lighting colour using colour emotion scales such as "passive" or "active". The more reddish the colour, yielded a more "active" colour emotion response by both elderly and younger adults while higher variations of blue were in most instances ranked as more passive by both user groups. Moreover, as demonstrated in [6], red was useful for showing high activity levels while simultaneously evoking an invigorating sense of presence, while blue was convenient for showing periods of low activity levels with a lesser degree of remote presence. These findings helped to set the stage for the design choice on the colour scheme.

3. METHODOLOGY

As we strive for more appropriate guidelines for encoding activity information to fit an AAL context, a controlled experiment was designed with two parts. Specifically, we focused on understanding how potential caregivers perceived and decoded lighting cues and examined their preferences for lighting parameters for encoding the elderly's physical activity information to provide context awareness and illicit feelings of social connectedness. A review of published work and a user-centered approach were adopted to design three lighting configurations.

3.1 Participants

Fourteen (14) participants were recruited from the University of Genova to take part in the experiment, which lasted 50 minutes per participant. The demographics were as follows: 64.3% were between 25−34, while 21.4% were between 18 − 24 and 14.3% were between 35 − 44 years. The sample was comprised of 85.7% males and 14.3% females, while 66.7% were students and 33.3% were employed. The sample was predominantly Italian (5 males and 1 female), followed by Pakistani (3 males), with small numbers of other nationalities such as Tunisian (1 male), Colombian (1 male), Iranian (1 male), Indian (1 female) and Lebanese (1 male). All participants had normal or corrected-to-normal visual acuity and were tested for colour vision deficits using the Ishihara color blindness test [14]. Participants were informed of the required procedure and signed their consent form.

3.2 Design

The primary goal of this experiment was to empirically assess the users' perspectives regarding the use of lighting parameters to convey activity information of an elderly person to a caregiver in order to support social connectedness and context awareness. Accordingly, the lighting parameters deployed must be glanceableable, non-distracting and aesthetically pleasing in order to evoke a subtle sense of presence. Based on existing literature and a cognitive walk-through with six prospective users to inspect their interpretations of lighting parameters (position, rate of change and color properties) on encoded activity information, we had three main findings:

- Ambient light must be glanceable, easily controlled (e.g., turned on or off, adjust the brightness levels etc.,) and should be positioned within the field of view of the users. As mentioned in [3], participants were more in favour of lighting applications that can be easily incorporated in their everyday routines. One recommendation of a light source that would readily fit this criterion, was a desk lamp.

- A pulsing light might be too distracting and fails to inconspicuously convey activity information.

- The most obvious properties of light (hue and brightness) should be varied smoothly to subtly convey activity information.

- Red was more favoured to represent a high activity level, green for an intermediate level and blue for resting.

As discussed earlier, a user can at any point in time be in one of three activity levels: active, passive or resting. Each activity level can be represented by one distinct lighting color property. Also, the amount of time a user stays in an activity level is another dimension that can be overtly relayed (represented by lighting color property) or covertly relayed (intuitively decerned by users). Based on these findings, three lighting configurations (X,Y,Z) were designed.

Configuration X can convey both changes in activity levels and also the temporal duration of stay in a particular level. Figure 1, shows configuration X, where red, green and

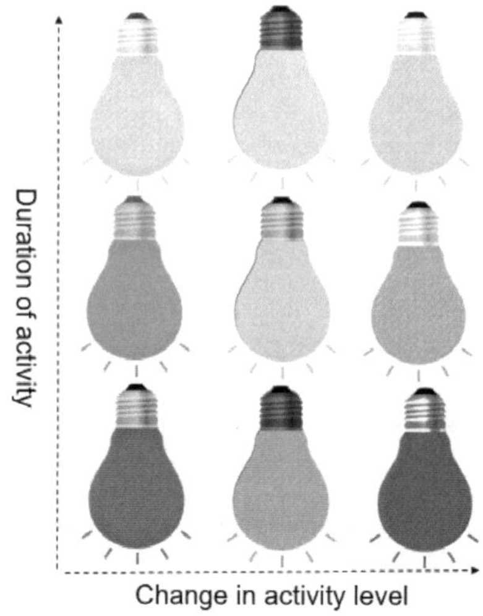

Figure 1: Lighting Configuration X

blue lights represent active, passive and resting levels respectively, while changes in light intensity depict how long a person has stayed in a specific activity level. From [6], our human activity detection model can detect a user's activity level every 1.28 seconds. Consequently, the minimum amount of time for the ambient lighting color change is 1.28 seconds. For this experiment, the brightness for an activity level was initially set to 33.3%, while activity levels lasting for more than 10 seconds and 20 seconds were set to 66.6% and 100% respectively.

Inspired by the Pediluma [15], configuration Y exploited changes in brightness of a single default green color to convey changes in activity levels. Temporal duration of activity levels was not overtly conveyed. Configuration Y is depicted in figure 2.

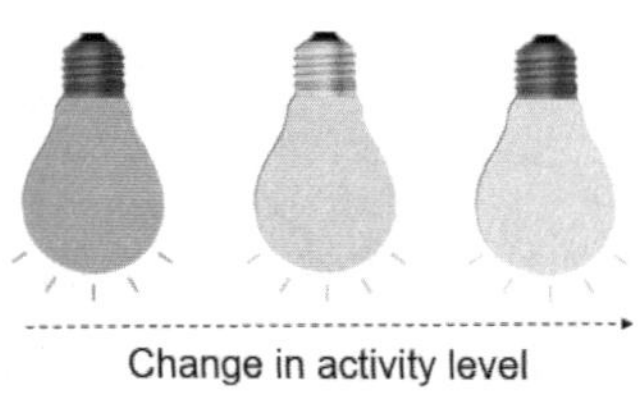

Figure 2: Lighting Configuration Y

To convey changes in activity levels, configuration Z employed changes in lighting color in the same manner as configuration X. Like configuration Y, the temporal duration of activity levels was not overtly represented. Figure 3, demonstrates lighting configuration Z.

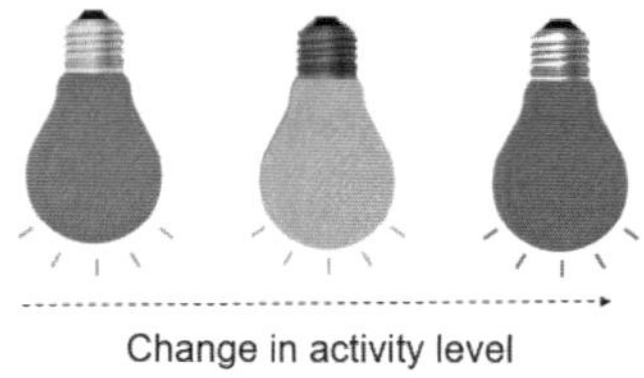

Figure 3: Lighting Configuration Z

3.3 Experiment setup and procedure

The experiment was carried out in a room, located at the University of Genova, with dimensions of 10.4 x 4.3 meters. The walls and ceiling were off-white and the floor consisted of marble tiles. The ambient light source was a desk lamp exploiting the Philips Hue, a connected lighting system that enables lighting color properties to be controlled over a network. The Philips Hue is furnished with a network bridge for connecting to the internet and provides an API for building custom applications to control the light over the network. A hand held tally counter was used by participants to monitor the changes in lighting color. The experiment was divided into two phases using a repeated measures design methodology. Figure 4, illustrates an example of a participant performing the experiment.

Figure 4: An example of a participant performing experiment

Phase one investigated how quickly participants processed the ambient information at a glance and examined the accuracy of recognition of the lighting changes. Notably, in this phase, participants were told that activity information was encoded through different lighting patterns without specifying the details of the mappings. A set of five practice trials were deployed to allow participants to familiarize themselves with the protocol and to clarify their misconceptions. Subsequently, they were given a total of three block trials with a randomized presentation of lighting configurations X, Y and Z with each block comprising of ten trials. The unified length of each trial was 30 seconds with each activity lasting a minimum of 1.28 seconds (i.e. the minimum detectable activity duration of the hybrid SVM-HMM HAR model). Participants were instructed to click the counter each time they noticed a change in light. Following the display of each lighting pattern, the participant had 30 seconds to respond to the questions concerning each trial. With respect to the accuracy of change noticeability, participants were to refer to the counter and respond how many times they noticed changes in the light. The total change count was the final number seen on the hand-held tally counter. Participants then selected the correct description of the presented configuration from a list of options. Additionally, participants were asked to report the summation of the number of distinct lighting configurations observed and describe their interpretations of what each configuration tried to convey.

In phase two, the significance of the lighting parameters and their mappings to activity levels (passive, active, resting) for each lighting configuration was explained. Subsequently, an activities of daily living (ADL) scenario of an elderly person was described to each participant, then he or she viewed the simulated activity information for lighting configurations X, Y and Z in a randomized order. After viewing each lighting configuration, participants performed a heuristic evaluation in terms of ten desirable features (usefulness, suitable abstraction, suitability, interest, perceptibility and distinctiveness, noticeability, intuitiveness, learning ease, distraction and aesthetics). Finally, participants ranked the lighting configurations from most to least preferred and provided their qualitative feedback.

4. RESULTS

Regarding the lighting color property, change noticeability and accuracy of interpretations, the root mean squared errors (RMSE) of the reported change counts and interpretations were calculated per participant for each configuration. Overall, three RMSE's per participant were obtained per configuration. Figure 5, displays a box plot of the errors.

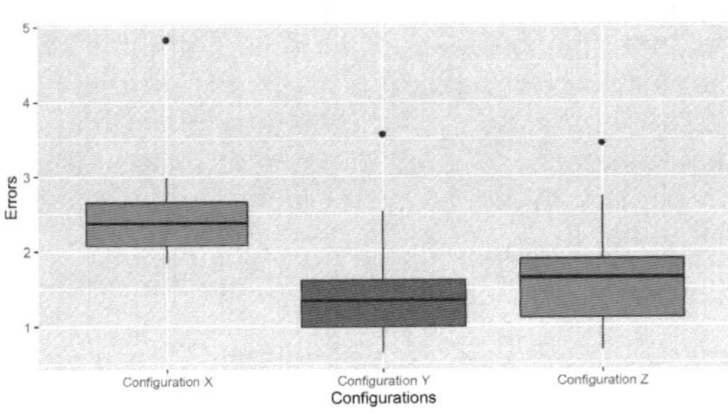

Figure 5: Boxplot of RMSEs of noticed changes and accuracy of interpretations

An analysis of variance (one-way ANOVA) of the RMSEs was calculated using the R Project for Statistical Computing. An F value of 7.6 with a p value of 0.00156 was obtained. This revealed a statistically significant reported mean error difference ($p < 0.05$) among the three configurations. A Tukey post-hoc (HSD) test was conducted to determine, which reported errors differed. Reported errors differed significantly between configurations X and Y ($p = 0.002$) and between X and Z ($p = 0.01$). However, there was no significant difference in reported errors between configurations Y and Z ($p = 0.78$). This suggests that configuration X was more susceptible to misinterpretations compared to configurations Y and Z.

With reference to the heuristic evaluation of the configurations, in terms of desirable features, the sum of positive and negative perceived attributes were computed for each configuration. For a desired attribute, "strongly agree" carried weight of 2, "agree" = 1, "neither agree nor agree" = 0, "disagree" = -1 and "strongly disagree" = -2 and the opposite for a non-desirable attribute. User responses are presented in figures 6, 7 and 8.

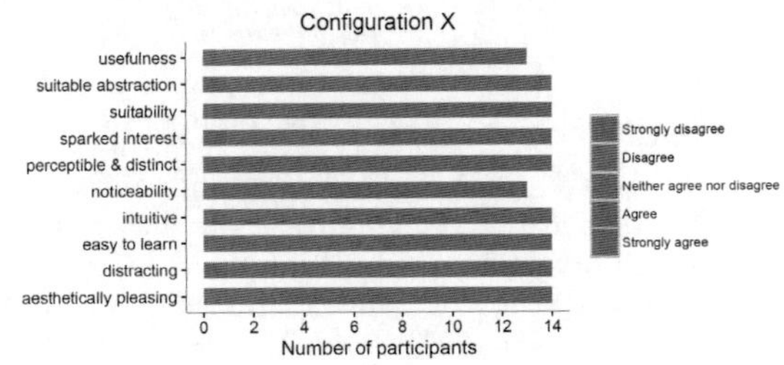

Figure 6: Heuristic evaluation of Configuration X

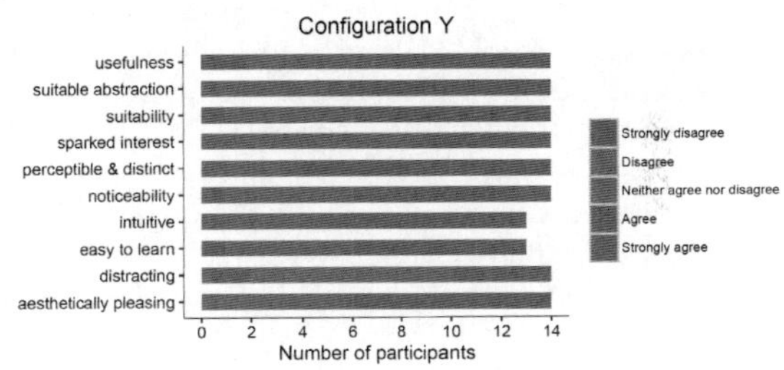

Figure 7: Heuristic evaluation of Configuration Y

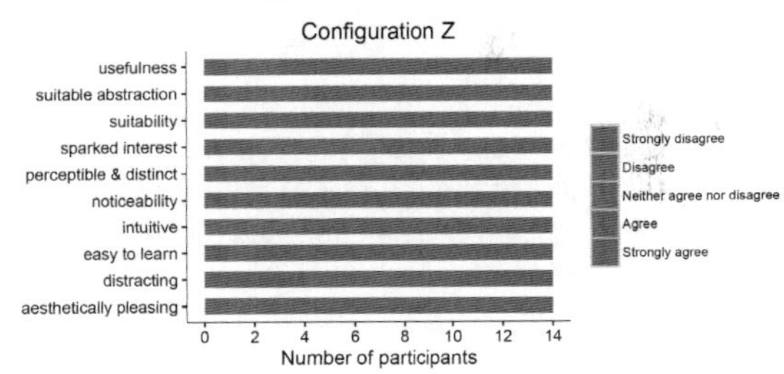

Figure 8: Heuristic evaluation of Configuration Z

The configurations received a sum of 82, 56 and 105 for X, Y and Z respectively. A one-way ANOVA revealed a statistically significant difference in the mean of perceived positive attributes with $F = 4.05$ and $p = 0.029$. A Tukey post-hoc (HSD) test revealed a statistically significant difference between only configuration Z and Y ($p = 0.022$). This shows that participants had more positive attitudes toward configuration Z compared to Y.

Finally, figure 9 shows the ranking of preferences of the configurations with a rank of 3 being the most preferred and 1 being the least preferred. A one-way ANOVA of the ranking revealed a statistically significant difference ($F = 23.93$ and $p = 1.65e-07$) between user preferences of the configurations. A Tukey post-hoc (HSD) test showed that participants preferred configuration Z to configuration Y ($p = 1.6e-06$) and configuration X to Y ($p = 1.6e-06$). The preference difference between configurations Z and X was not statistically significant.

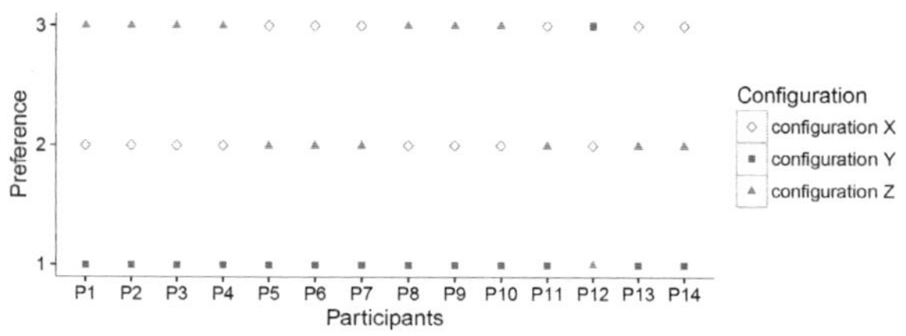

Figure 9: Scatter plot of user preference rank

5. DISCUSSION AND CONCLUSION

The aim of this study was to assess three different lighting configurations to derive the best lighting parameters for encoding activity information in an AAL context. Confirming our expectations, more errors were experienced with configuration X (three colours and three intensity levels), when compared to configurations Y and Z. Our participants confirmed in their reflection, that configuration X had too many changes i.e. both in hue and brightness, and consequently misidentification was a common occurrence with this configuration. Based on our observation of participants, changes in brightness were often misclassified as changes in colour.

There was no statistical significance for change noticeability for configurations Y and Z. Notably, participants in their qualitative assessment mentioned that configuration Y (one colour changing its brightness on three levels), was too subtle and confusing. They generally articulated that important notifications could be easily missed with this configuration. For example, one participant mentioned, "with one colour and three intensity levels, it is more difficult to notice the changes in intensity. Also, when both colour and intensity changed in configuration X, it was confusing." Moreover, with configuration Y, some participants mentioned that they were more engaged in thinking only about one type of activity, while configuration Z made them think about changes in activities while intuitively discerning the concept of time. We hypothesize that configuration Z (3 colours at the same intensity) had less errors due to its easily distinguishable properties such as lighting colour with constant brightness. Overall, the results suggest that a higher cognitive load was experienced with configuration X.

In retrospect, participants generally preferred configuration Z for encoding activity information. When the lighting configuration was shown the colour of the lights was red for active, green for passive and blue for resting. Participants generally indicated that the intuitive meaning of these colours were effortlessly mapped to activity levels.

With respect to suitability, participants articulated that lighting configuration Z, had specific lighting properties, which made it particularly suitable for encoding activity information. These include, it provided suitable abstraction of personal information and a clear mapping of activity information, its aesthetic quality, noticeability, intuitiveness, little distraction and ease of learning. However, with the introduction of ambient lighting systems in AAL environments, privacy was a major concern among our participants.

Building on the previous research on ambient displays, the recommendations and experiment results, we now present a few design guidelines for the encoding of activity information for an AAL context.

- Devise clear mappings for representing activity information with lighting. Brightness might not be appropriate as it often becomes confusing. However, if brightness is used, sudden changes in intensity should be avoided.
- Abstraction is necessary to ensure the privacy of personal information.
- Lighting changes should be intuitive and match the user's mental model of the other person's activities. Moreover, the lighting parameters used should create a dynamic understanding of the changes in the other person's environment.
- Designers should not overwhelm its users with too many changes of lighting parameters.
- The lighting source should be aesthetically pleasing and should be smoothly integrated into the user's environment.
- When choosing the colour, the effects of colour on affect should be considered. Red is suitable for high periods of activity, green for periods of relaxation and blue for resting periods. However, this can be based on personal taste, situational context and cultural diversity. The use of one colour with varying intensities to represent different activity levels might not be acceptable as changes could be frequently indistinguishable.
- Designers should consider the temporal nature of activity information and as such the duration of activities should be intuitively perceived by viewers. Moreover, it might be prudent to exploit light's parameters to show the history of an elder's activities in time.

In summary, the findings of our exploratory study provided insights into the perceptions of the lighting parameters to inform the design of an ambient lighting display to portray activity information for an AAL context. The study shows the relevance of lighting parameters such as colour to encode activity information for easy interpretation, minimal distraction and reduced mental effort. This could have implications for the design of future ambient lighting displays within an AAL context because of its great potential for increasing awareness and affective responses.

6. ACKNOWLEDGEMENTS

This work was supported in part by the Erasmus Mundus Joint Doctorate (EMJD) in Interactive and Cognitive Environments (ICE), which is funded by Erasmus Mundus under the FPA no. 2010-2012. Many thanks to the participants who took part in this experiment.

7. REFERENCES

[1] P. Burns, C. Lueg, and S. Berkovsky. Activmon: encouraging physical activity through ambient social awareness. In *CHI'12 Extended Abstracts on Human Factors in Computing Systems*, pages 2363–2368. ACM, 2012.

[2] A. Chang, B. Resner, B. Koerner, X. Wang, and H. Ishii. Lumitouch: an emotional communication device. In *CHI'01 extended abstracts on Human factors in computing systems*, pages 313–314. ACM, 2001.

[3] K. Davis, L. Feijs, J. Hu, L. Marcenaro, and C. Regazzoni. Improving awareness and social connectedness through the social hue: Insights and perspectives. In *Proceedings of the ITAP'16: International Symposium on Interactive Technology and Ageing populations*. ACM, In press, 2016.

[4] K. Davis, J. Hu, L. Feijs, and E. Owusu. Social hue: A subtle awareness system for connecting the elderly and their caregivers. In *Pervasive Computing and Communication Workshops (PerCom Workshops), 2015 IEEE International Conference on*, pages 178–183. IEEE, 2015.

[5] K. Davis, E. Owusu, V. Bastani, L. Marcenaro, J. Hu, C. Regazzoni, and L. Feijs. Activity recognition based on inertial sensors for ambient assisted living. In *2016 19th International Conference on Information Fusion (FUSION)*. IEEE, 2016.

[6] K. Davis, E. Owusu, J. Hu, L. Marcenaro, C. Regazzoni, and L. Feijs. Promoting social connectedness through human activity-based ambient displays. In *Proceedings of the ITAP'16: International Symposium on Interactive Technology and Ageing populations*. ACM, In press, 2016.

[7] K. Davis, E. Owusu, C. Regazzoni, L. Marcenaro, L. Feijs, and J. Hu. Perception of human activities a means to support connectedness between the elderly and their caregivers. In *Proceedings of the 1st International Conference on Information and Communication Technologies for Ageing Well and e-Health*, pages 194–199. SCITEPRESS, 2015.

[8] A. Dey, J. Mankoff, and A. K. Dey. From conception to design, a practical guide to designing ambient displays. 2003.

[9] K. Ducatel, M. Bogdanowicz, F. Scapolo, J. Leijten, and J.-C. Burgelman. Scenarios for ambient intelligence in 2010. *Office for official publications of the European Communities*, 2001.

[10] P. L. Emiliani and C. Stephanidis. Universal access to ambient intelligence environments: opportunities and challenges for people with disabilities. *IBM Systems Journal*, 44(3):605–619, 2005.

[11] J. Fortmann, T. C. Stratmann, S. Boll, B. Poppinga, and W. Heuten. Make me move at work! an ambient light display to increase physical activity. In *2013 7th International Conference on Pervasive Computing Technologies for Healthcare and Workshops*, pages 274–277. IEEE, 2013.

[12] M. Gladwell. *Blink: The power of thinking without thinking*. Back Bay Books, 2007.

[13] D. Hindus, S. D. Mainwaring, N. Leduc, A. E. Hagström, and O. Bayley. Casablanca: designing social communication devices for the home. In *Proceedings of the SIGCHI conference on Human factors in computing systems*, pages 325–332. ACM, 2001.

[14] S. Ishihara. *Test for colour-blindness*. Kanehara Tokyo, Japan, 1987.

[15] B. Y. Lim, A. Shick, C. Harrison, and S. E. Hudson. Pediluma: motivating physical activity through contextual information and social influence. In *Proceedings of the fifth international conference on Tangible, embedded, and embodied interaction*, pages 173–180. ACM, 2011.

[16] J. Mankoff, A. K. Dey, G. Hsieh, J. Kientz, S. Lederer, and M. Ames. Heuristic evaluation of ambient displays. In *Proceedings of the SIGCHI conference on Human factors in computing systems*, pages 169–176. ACM, 2003.

[17] V. Mateevitsi, K. Reda, J. Leigh, and A. Johnson. The health bar: a persuasive ambient display to improve the office worker's well being. In *Proceedings of the 5th Augmented Human International Conference*, page 21. ACM, 2014.

[18] T. Matthews, G. Hsieh, and J. Mankoff. Evaluating peripheral displays. In *Awareness Systems*, pages 447–472. Springer, 2009.

[19] A. Matviienko, V. Cobus, H. Müller, J. Fortmann, A. Löcken, S. Boll, M. Rauschenberger, J. Timmermann, C. Trappe, and W. Heuten. Deriving design guidelines for ambient light systems. In *Proceedings of the 14th International Conference on Mobile and Ubiquitous Multimedia*, pages 267–277. ACM, 2015.

[20] H. Müller, J. Fortmann, M. Pielot, T. Hesselmann, B. Poppinga, W. Heuten, N. Henze, and S. Boll. Ambix: Designing ambient light information displays. In *Proceedings of Designing Interactive Lighting workshop at DIS*. Citeseer, 2012.

[21] E. D. Mynatt, J. Rowan, S. Craighill, and A. Jacobs. Digital family portraits: supporting peace of mind for extended family members. In *Proceedings of the SIGCHI conference on Human factors in computing systems*, pages 333–340. ACM, 2001.

[22] D. Offenhuber and S. Seitinger. Over the rainbow: information design for low-resolution urban displays. In *Proceedings of the 2nd Media Architecture Biennale Conference: World Cities*, pages 40–47. ACM, 2014.

[23] L.-C. Ou, M. R. Luo, P.-L. Sun, N.-C. Hu, and H.-S. Chen. Age effects on colour emotion, preference, and harmony. *Color Research & Application*, 37(2):92–105, 2012.

[24] E. R. Pedersen and T. Sokoler. Aroma: abstract representation of presence supporting mutual awareness. In *Proceedings of the ACM SIGCHI Conference on Human factors in computing systems*, pages 51–58. ACM, 1997.

[25] Z. Pousman and J. Stasko. A taxonomy of ambient information systems: four patterns of design. In *Proceedings of the working conference on Advanced visual interfaces*, pages 67–74. ACM, 2006.

[26] P. Rashidi and A. Mihailidis. A survey on ambient-assisted living tools for older adults. *IEEE journal of biomedical and health informatics*, 17(3):579–590, 2013.

[27] M. Tomitsch, K. Kappel, A. Lehner, and T. Grechenig. Towards a taxonomy for ambient information systems. In *Ambient Information Systems*, 2007.

[28] M. Weiser and J. S. Brown. The coming age of calm technology. In *Beyond calculation*, pages 75–85. Springer, 1997.

Impedance Characteristics and Field Separation of Body Implanted Antennas

Qiong Wang
Chair for RF Engineering,
Communication Laboratory
Dresden University of Technology,
Dresden, Germany
+49 351 463-42387
qiong.wang@tu-dresden.de

Xiao Fang
Chair for RF Engineering,
Communication Laboratory
Dresden University of Technology,
Dresden, Germany
+49 351 463-42387
xiao.fang@tu-dresden.de

Dirk Plettemeier
Chair for RF Engineering,
Communication Laboratory
Dresden University of Technology,
Dresden, Germany
+49 351 463-33203
dirk.plettemeier@tu-dresden.de

ABSTRACT

In this paper, the input impedance characteristics variance and field region separation of the implanted antenna for body area communications are investigated. The input impedance of half wave dipole wire antenna inside the human body torso and vacuum are calculatedthrough HFSS simulation and theoretical formula. Moreover, impedance measurement results of previously proposed implanted antenna is shown in this paper. Compared with the free space/vacuum operating environment, biological tissue will dramatically shrink the input impedance and resonance frequency of the implanted antenna. On the other hand, far field separation characteristics inside biological tissue are investigated for three kinds of implanted antennas which are dielectric resonance antenna (DRA), helical antenna and discone antenna. The relationship between the receiving antenna aperture and far-field boundary are simulated. In words, this paper gives insights on the impedance variance and far field separation of the implanted antennas, which will provide reference for implanted antenna development, body area communication system design as well as antenna measurement and corresponding on-body antenna design.

CCS Concepts

• CCS → Hardware → Communication hardware, interfaces and storage → Wireless devices

• CCS → Human-centered computing → Ubiquitous and mobile computing → Ubiquitous and mobile devices → Personal digital assistants

Keywords

Implanted antenna; Impedance characteristics; Far-field boundary; Phase error.

1. INTRODUCTION

Body area communications have shown more and more important roles in supporting medical and health care services. Many promising applications have already been identified from the concept of wireless body area network (WBAN). For example, a few wireless communication solutions using radio frequency (RF) technologies have been used for a number of in-body medical sensing applications like implantable cardioverter defibrillators (ICDs), cortical implants, and wireless capsule endoscopes (WCEs). The ultra-wideband (UWB) spectrum of 3.1-10.6 GHz [1] is expected to be a promising RF solution to support wider channel bandwidths for novel applications like smart electronic pills or WCEs for therapeutic procedures in addition to diagnosis. WCE capsule can take pictures/videos and then transmit the real-time biological data from the inside of the gastrointestinal tract to exterior medical instruments. The current technical challenges for UWB implanted body area communications lies in the demands of deep implantation and larger bandwidth for higher-resolution video transmission. RF frontend antennas of the TX/RX system play a critical role in the high performance of the high frequency and larger bandwidth for deep implantation communication.

Antenna development for body area communications is highly subject to the surrounding operating medium, that is, the lossy biological body. In fact, wave propagation mechanisms as well as characteristics are significantly different from that in free space. For example, the dominant wave propagation mechanisms in radio frequencies for on-body transmission link could be surface waves or diffraction for LOS or NLOS links [2]. The wave propagation speed is slowed down inside the biological tissue compared to that in free space due to the high permittivity properties of the biological tissue and the corresponding wavelength will be therefore shortened. And the so-called "shortening effect/factor" is therefore often referred for the implanted antenna development [3]. Besides, wave propagation inside the biological body will endure a fast and severe decay due to the highly lossy and dispersive property of the biological tissue. Due to the specific propagation characteristics in biological tissue environment, antenna characteristics (such as input impedance, pattern, field region separation, beam width, polarization, side lobe level, gain, beam direction, radiation efficiency, etc) will not vary in the same manner as in free space/vacuum. Specific design guidance is highly advisable for antenna development for body area communications.

In this paper, we will mainly investigate the input impedance characteristics variance and field region separation of the implanted antenna for body area communications. The two antenna characteristics will be directly indicators of the surrounding medium alteration. Input impedance of the antenna will endure a dramatic change when it is submerged inside body tissue. The resonance performance will be thence changed. [4] has studied the submerged wire antenna performance in lossy environment, such as in the earth or sea. Field region separation investigation is of high importance for implanted body area communication system design, especially the corresponding wearable antenna design as well as antenna measurements. For example, for the WCEs, the implanted capsule transmitting antenna will define its own near/far field region which will influence the reaction with the on-body receiving antenna. Dimension/aperture of the on-body receiving antenna will also be subject to the field region separation of the capsule antenna.

2. Input impedance characteristics of body implanted antenna

Impedance matching is the first step in antenna development. If the antenna is barely and deeply submerged in a lossy medium (underground, submarines and biological tissue), the current decay on such an uninsulated antenna metal/wire is very rapid. In practice, an insulating layer/jacket is highly suggested. Regarding an implanted insulated wire as a coaxial transmission line with an infinite lossy outer conductor, where the surrounding lossy medium acts as the lossy outer conductor, [4] derives a theoretical model for this lossy coaxial line model. Based on the derived propagation constants for this lossy coaxial line, the input impedance and current distribution can be determined from standard transmission line theory.

In WCEs application, assuming a half wave dipole wire antenna operates inside the human body torso at 4GHz, i.e., around the center frequency of the UWB low band (3.4-4.8 GHz). Figure 1 shows the lossy transmission line model of the insulated dipole wire antenna inside human torso tissue. It consists of three layers: inner metal wire, insulating layer and surrounding biological tissue. The surrounding tissue layer acts as the lossy outer conductor of the transmission line model, with a certain dielectric permittivity. Table 1 gives the electromagnetic parameters of the insulated dipole model inside human torso tissue at around 4 GHz. The insulating layer will be kind of polyethylene and the torso tissue will have the averaged muscle dielectric properties. In this table, r is the propagation constant, δ is the skin depth and a_3 is the attenuation constant in the human torso tissue, a_0 and a_i are the outer and inner radii of the insulating layer.

The propagation constant of the implanted transmission line can be approximated as follows [4]:

$$r \approx r_2\left(1-\frac{\frac{j\pi}{4}+\ln\sqrt{2}(0.89)\,{}^{a_0}\!/_{\delta}}{\ln({}^{a_0}\!/_{a_i})}\right) \quad (1)$$

The approximation of the propagation constant of the lossy transmission line model depends on the restriction that the intrinsic propagation constant for the biological tissue is much greater than the transmission line propagation constant, that is, $r_3 >> r$. Besides, the approximation should be good if $a_0 < \delta/10$. Assume that the dipole is deeply implanted and with insulated end, the input impedance of the transmission line is

$$Z_{OC} = Z_0 \coth rl \quad (2)$$

where l is the length of the line section which is half length of dipole antenna and Z_0 is the characteristic impedance:

$$Z_0 \cong \left(\frac{\frac{1}{2\pi}\ln a_0}{a_i}\right)\frac{r}{j\omega\varepsilon_2} \quad (3)$$

For the biological torso tissue, the averaged dielectric properties are constant as shown in Table 1. The skin depth δ of the torso tissue at 4 GHz is derived as around 12mm. We choose an reasonable insulating jacket radius to be $a_0 = 0.1mm$ to satisfy the approximation limitation $a_0 < \delta/10$. Figure 2 shows the comparison of HFSS simulated and calculated impedance of an implanted half

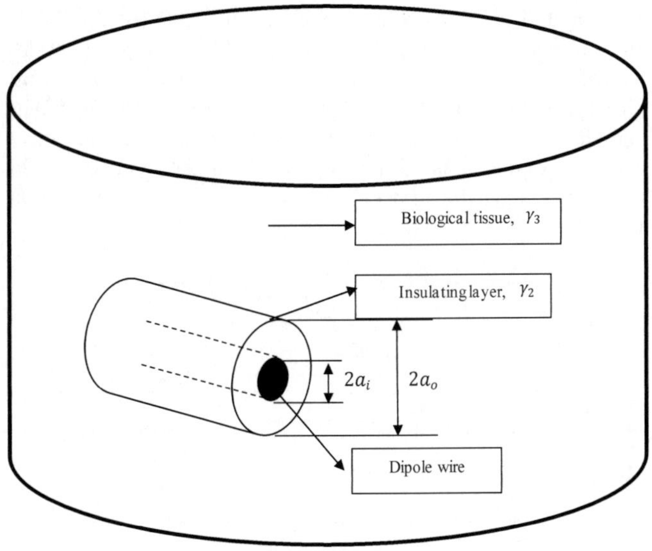

Figure 1. Lossy transmission line model of an insulated dipole inside human torso tissue

Table 1. Electromagnetic parameters of the implanted lossy transmission line model

	Insulating layer/jacket	Biological tissue (averaged body torso)
Propagation constant and related Parameters	$r_2 = \sqrt{-\omega^2\mu_2\varepsilon_2}$ $\mu_2 = \mu_0$ $\varepsilon_2 = \varepsilon_0\varepsilon_{2r}$ $\varepsilon_{2r} = 2.25$ (polyethylene)	$r_3 = \sqrt{-\omega^2\mu_3\varepsilon_3} = \alpha_3 + j\beta_3$ $\mu_3 = \mu_0$ $\varepsilon_3 = \varepsilon_0(\varepsilon_{3r} - j\frac{\sigma_3}{\omega\varepsilon_0})$ $\varepsilon_{3r} = 51.4$ $\sigma_3 = 3.2$ $\delta = \frac{1}{a_3}$ $a_3 = \omega\sqrt{\frac{\mu_3\varepsilon_0\varepsilon_{3r}}{2}\left[\sqrt{1+\left(\frac{\sigma}{\omega\varepsilon_0\varepsilon_{3r}}\right)^2}-1\right]}$

wave dipole wire antenna inside the human body torso around 4 GHz and a close agreement can be seen. In fact, the approximation calculation also has been validated based on comparison with measured dipole impedance [4]. Compared to the dipole input impedance in free space, it can be concluded that the resonance impedance of the implanted dipole antenna has been reduced (from 73 Ohm to around 40 Ohm) and the resonance frequency also shifts down (from 4 GHz to 1.2 GHz).

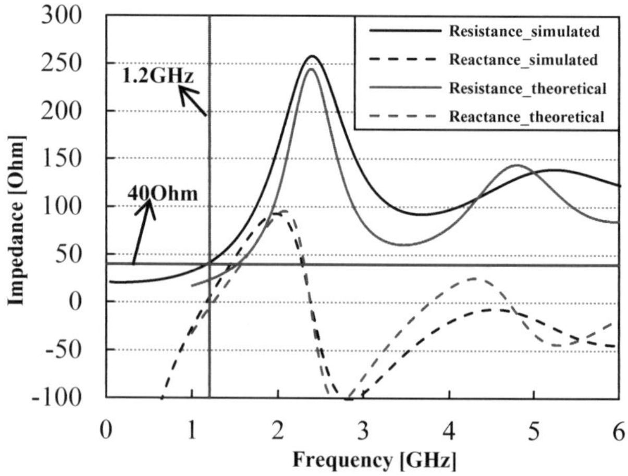

Figure 2. Comparison of simulated and theoretically calculated impedances for deeply implanted dipole with 0.1 mm polyethylene insulating jacket

In fact, input impedance of the free space antenna will endure a dramatic change when it is submerged inside body tissue. At first, we assume the body tissue is with no loss, i.e,. kind of ideal dielectric with certain high dielectric permittivity property. Figure 3 shows the simulated impedance variance of 4 GHz dipole in vacuum and when it is submerged in ideal dielectric. Both resistance and reactance parts show a sharp decline. The influence of the high permittivity property of the biological tissue lies in: reduce the overall input impedance, shift down the resonance frequency and the resonance impedance. Figure 4 further compares the impedance variance when the 4 GHz dipole is implanted in real biological torso tissue with polyethylene insulating jacket. Due to the influence of the insulating jacket, the impedance and resonance frequency shift-down becomes alleviative compared with that of directly implanted in ideal dielectric. In words, the influence of the insulating jacket lies in: increase the overall impedance, shift up the resonance frequency and the resonance impedance.

Meanwhile, in terms of the results in Figure 4, the overall input impedance has been largely decreased when the free space dipole antenna implanted inside biological tissue. In fact, in terms of dipole wire antenna, the implantation/submergence process will largely decrease the overall/resonance impedance as well as the resonance frequency. The intrinsic wave impedance of the operating medium shrinks a lot. In free space, the intrinsic impedance is $\eta = \sqrt{u_0/\varepsilon_0}$ while in biological tissue it changes to $\eta = \sqrt{\mu_0/\varepsilon_3} = \sqrt{\mu_0/(\varepsilon_0/\varepsilon_{3r} - j\sigma_3/(\omega\varepsilon_0))}$ which will be much smaller than the free space wave impedance. Input impedance of the dipole wire antenna is proportional to the wave impedance of the operating environment [5]. Therefore, decline of the overall input impedance as well as the resonance impedance can be expected. In fact, beside the impedance variance due to implantation/submergence, vicinity effect is also widely investigated, for example, ground effects of lossy electric conducting surface [5], where half space effect can be interpreted although it is not fully submerged/implanted.

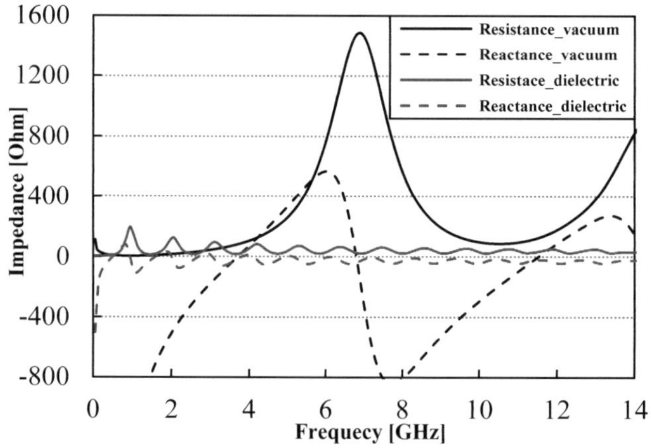

Figure 3. Comparison of the dipole impedance in vacuum and in ideal dielectric

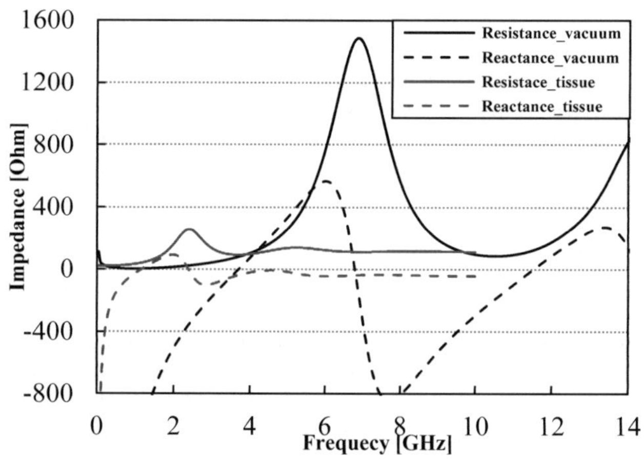

Figure 4. Comparison of the dipole impedance in vacuum and in biological tissue

Figure 5 compares the influence of three different insulating materials (air, Teflon, polyethylene) on the dipole resonant resistance and resonant frequency. The thicker the insulating thickness, the higher the resonant frequency and the resonant resistance. Teflon (with permittivity 2.1 and loss tangent 0.001) and polyethylene (with permittivity 2.25 and loss tangent 0.001) give almost the same performance. The high variance sensitivity comes from the fine wire radius a_i as well as the ratio of insulating thickness and wire radius (embodied in a_0/a_i). Besides, the resonant resistance and frequency with air insulating layer are higher than that with normal insulating dielectric layer like Teflon and polyethylene. That is due to the phase constant of air is smaller than that of Teflon and polyethylene. In fact, the phase constant of the whole implanted antenna is typically several times greater than that of the insulating layer which itself is greater than in free space. That is why the resonant lengths of implanted antennas are typically much smaller than in free space.

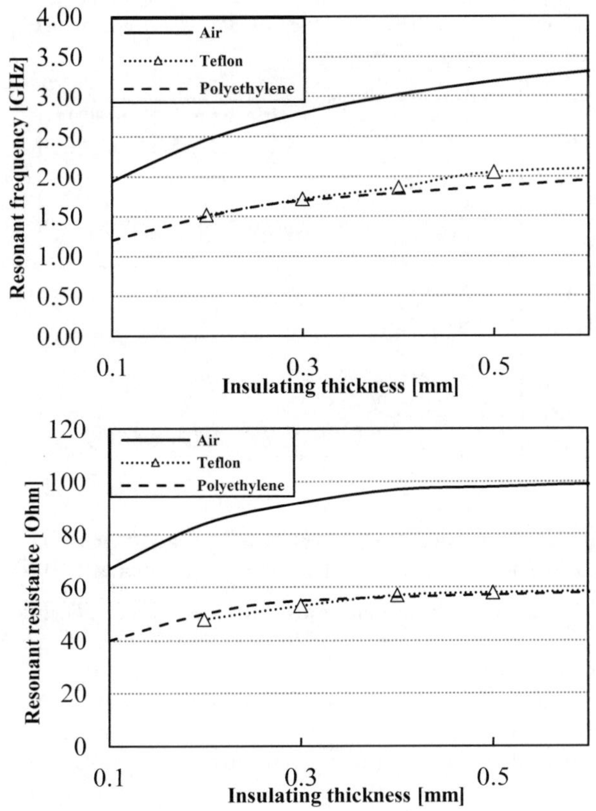

Figure 5. Implanted dipole resonance resistance andresonance frequency with different insulating materials (air, Teflon, polyethylene) and different insulating thickness.

Figure 6 shows the measured input impedance of the previously developed DRA antenna for WCE [3] in free space as well as inside body phantom. As expected, an overall/resonance impedance shrink phenomenon can be observed when it is implanted in phantom. Similar to wire antenna, the declined intrinsic wave impedance of the operating medium results in the declined antenna input impedance. In practice, antenna development for implanted antenna must take the input impedance variance as well as the shortening effect into account.

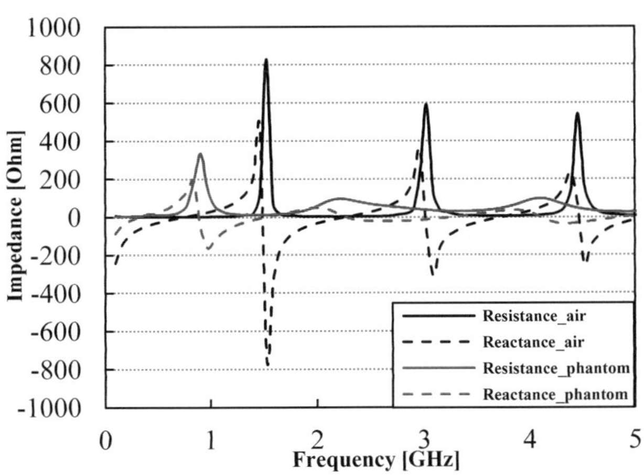

Figure 6. Measured impedance for DRA antenna in free space and inside body phantom

3. Field region separation of body implanted antenna

The space surrounding an antenna is usually subdivided into three regions: reactive near-field, radiating near-field (Fresnel) and far-field (Fraunhofer) regions [5]. The field region separation for implanted antenna is of importance especially when it comes to antenna measurements and corresponding wearable antenna development. The boundaries separating these regions are not unique, although various criteria have been established and are commonly used to identify the regions [5]. Many investigators have shown through numerous examples that a maximum total phase error of $\pi/8$ rad (22.5°) can be acceptable as a practical criterion for most practical antennas with overall length greater than a wavelength ($l > \lambda$). In spite of various criteria, a maximum total phase error of $\pi/8$ rad (22.5°) can be approximately used to identify the far-field region for implanted antennas.

In the WCE communications, the transmitting antenna is confined within possible region 10x10x5 inside the capsule (overall dimension around 11x22 mm). The implanted depths (from torso surface to the capsule) can range from 5 cm to 40 cm depending on the localization position of the capsule through the digestive tract especially the small intestine. The receiving wearable antenna can be expected on body torso surface with a relative large dimension where the antenna dimension/volume is not as demanding as the implanted capsule antenna. Strictly speaking, in terms of the WCE communications, the far-field region investigation of the implanted antenna should be combined with the aperture of the wearable receiving antenna.

In order to provide reference for the antenna measurement and the receiving antenna development, investigation on the relationship between the far-field boundary on receiving antenna aperture is of high importance for implanted body area communication system design. Figure 7 shows three different capsule antenna models operating in UWB low-band in HFSS: DRA antenna, helical antenna and discone antenna. The central operating frequency of them is around 4 GHz. The detailed descriptions of the three antennas can be found in [6]

The models of DRA antenna, discone antenna and helical antenna in HFSS are shown in Figure 7, their resonant frequencies are identical to 4GHz. These antennas are implanted in the tissue whose relative permittivity ε_r=51.4 and conductivity σ=3.3.

(a) DRA antenna (b) Discone antenna (c) Helical antenna

Figure 7. The HFSS models of DRA antenna, discone antenna and helical antenna

Figure 8 shows the rendering image of electrical phase of DRA antenna. The effective wavelength at 4 GHz in body torso (average relative permittivity ε_r=51.4 and conductivity σ=3.3) is around 10 mm. As shown in Figure 8, with the increasing of implanted distance and size of receiving antenna aperture, the arc of electrical phase become smaller, which means the phase difference distributing on the aperture of receiving antenna become smaller.

Figure 8. The phase distribution of DRA antenna simulated by HFSS

Figure 9 shows the simulated phase error of the implanted DRA antenna with variance of implanted depth r as well as receiving antenna aperture D. D/λ is the ratio of implanted depth. The effective wavelength and electrical characteristics of body torso is identical with Figure 8. The receiving antenna aperture D varies from 12mm to 40mm with spacing step 4mm. As shown in Figure 9, under the condition that receiving antenna aperture is 12mm (similar aperture as the implanted antenna), far-field boundary with phase error of $\pi/8$ rad (22.5°) is around 6.3λ. When the aperture becomes 16mm, far-field boundary becomes around 9λ. The deeper the antenna implanted, the smaller the phase error and it approaches zero when the observation point gets close to infinity. When the far-field boundary condition becomes larger than 20λ, the phase error in all the receiving antennas shown in Figure 8 can satisfy with the limitation of $\pi/8$. In the actual measurement, in order to satisfy operating at far-field region for the standard horn antenna whose aperture is 40mm, the implanted distance of DRA antenna should be set to be larger than 20λ.

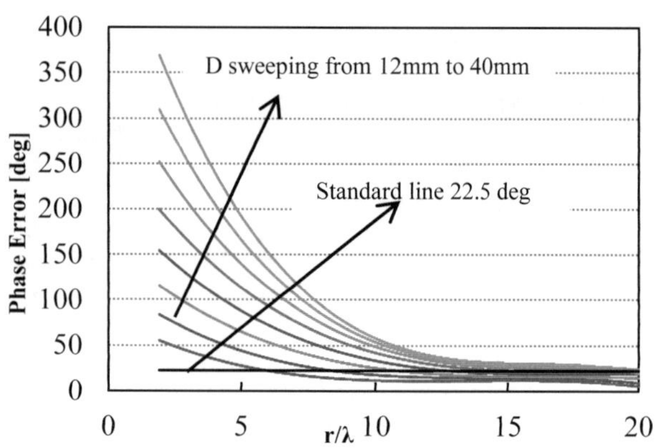

Figure 9. Relationship of phase error of DRA antenna and implanted depth with receiving antenna aperture D sweeping (effective wavelength λ around 10 mm at 4 GHz)

Figure 10 shows the phase error comparison using HFSS and CST respectively. The computational electromagnetic algorithm HFSS bases on is FEM which is a kind of frequency-domain algorithm. HFSS is beneficial to simulate some small electrical and complicated structures, and also it has great advantages in simulating antenna working at narrow bandwidth. In other way, the algorithm we used in CST is FIT which is a kind of time-domain algorithm for large space structures and antenna working at wide bandwidth. We compare the results in Figure 10, as expected, the curves got from HFSS is similar with that from CST. Due to the calculation domain of CST, we just compare the results which are limited in the domain whose size is less than 12λ.

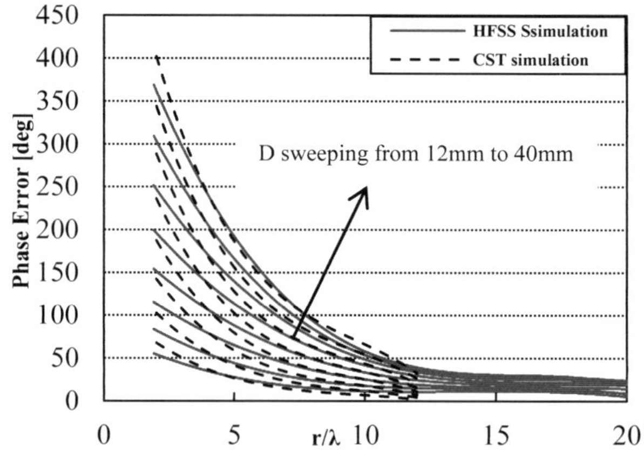

Figure 10. Simulated phase error of DRA antenna with HFSS and CST (effective wavelength λ around 10 mm at 4 GHz)

The simulation configuration of discone antenna is identical with DRA antenna: working frequency is 4GHz, efficient wavelength is 10mm, and receiving antenna aperture D varies from 12mm to 40mm with spacing step 4mm. The trend of phase error is similar with DRA antenna which also approaches to zero with increasing of implanted distance. When the implanted distance is larger than 40λ, the antennas whose aperture is less than 40mm can satisfy the limitation of phase error.

As we can see from Figure 11, phase error has raising trending after the implanted distance exceeds than 20λ. This is because that the fluctuation of phase becomes larger with the increasing of implanted distance due to the calculation error which is resulted from the limitation of calculation domain. The results shown in Figure 11 is fitted by polynomial fit technique, which means that large fluctuation result in large phase error. When the calculation domain is limited, the boundaries will influence the electrical field.

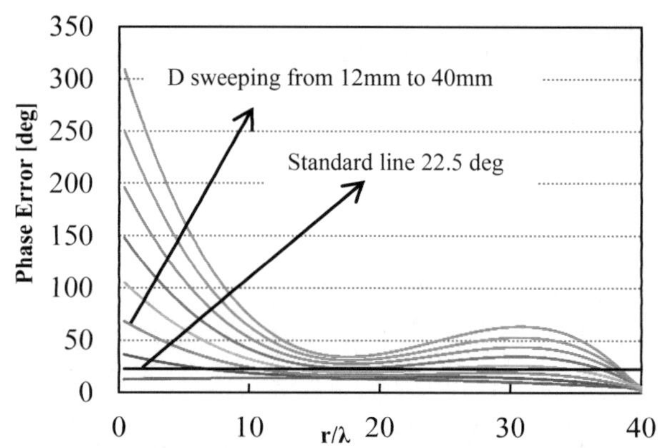

Figure 11. Relationship of phase error of discone antenna and implanted depth with receiving antenna aperture D sweeping (effective wavelength λ around 10 mm at 4 GHz)

For example, under the condition of limited height of calculation domain, the calculation error becomes larger with the increasing of length of the calculation domain. The comparison of original curves and polynomial fitted curves is shown in Figure 12. It is obvious that the fluctuation become large after the implanted distance is larger than 20λ.

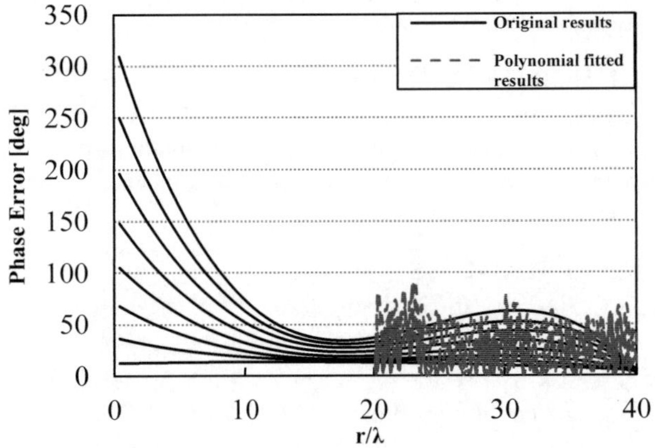

Figure 12. Comparison of original curves and polynomial fitted curves (effective wavelength λ around 10 mm at 4 GHz)

The far-field boundary of helical antenna is also simulated with configuration identical with DRA antenna and discone antenna, and the result is shown in Figure 13. Under the condition that size of receiving antenna aperture is from 12mm to 40mm, the far-field boundary starts from 2.5λ. Limited to the calculation domain, the phase distribution is confined in the region which is less than 15λ. The Figure 13 shows that if implanted distance is larger than 15λ, the receiving antenna whose aperture size is less than 24mm can satisfy the phase error requirement, which indicates that the implanted distance is at least larger than 15λ with the condition that size of receiving antenna aperture is larger than 24mm. Similar with the result shown in Figure 11, the phase error has a rising trending when implanted distance is more than 10λ. This is also because that limited calculation domain results in calculation error. Meanwhile, the negative phase error is the result of polynomial fitting.

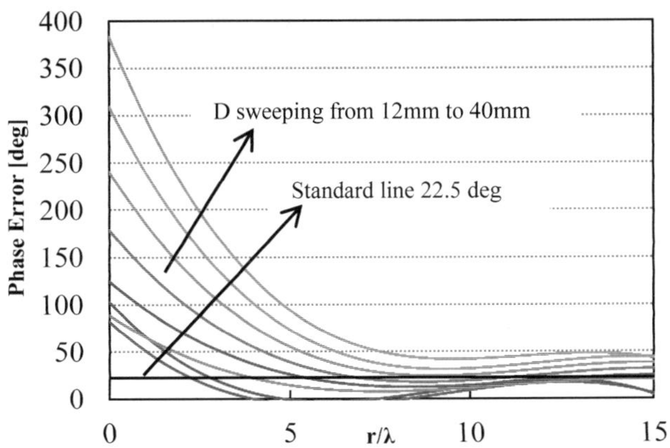

Figure 13 Relationship of phase error of helical antenna and implanted depth with receiving antenna aperture D sweeping (effective wavelength λ around 10 mm at 4 GHz)

The summarization is shown in Figure 14, which is the relationship of implanted depth with 22.5° phase error limitation and receiving antenna aperture for three kinds of antennas. As shown in Figure 14, the implanted distance increasing with the size of antenna aperture. Assuming the calculation domain with enough domain, the slop of the curves shown in Figure 14 approaches zero.

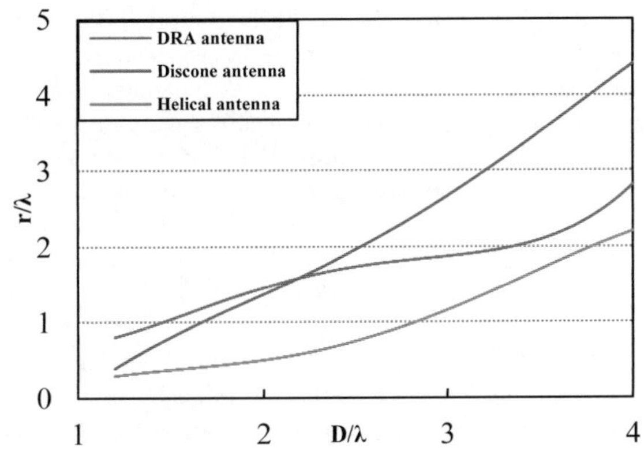

Figure 14. Relationship of implanted depth with 22.5 deg phase error limitation and receiving antenna aperture. (effective wavelength λ around 10 mm at 4 GHz)

The implanted antenna and receiving antenna are combined to calculate the wireless power transmission loss through the transmission line, which verifies the influence of implanted distance and size of antenna aperture for the transmission loss. The transmission-line mode is set operating at 3-5 GHz, center frequency at 4GHz. Discone antenna is used as the in-body transmitting antenna and Vivaldi antenna [6] is used as the on-body receiving antenna whose aperture dimension is around 40mm. Meanwhile, the implanted distance of in-body antenna is from 60mm to 85mm. The power transmission loss is simulated with different implanted distances. In order to figure out the real coupling ability of TX/RX antennas, the distance-dependent path loss is excluded from the overall transmission loss. The distance-dependent path loss can be calculated based on the path loss lognormal model [7]. Eqn.4 can calculate the path loss in human body [7]:

$$PL(d)_{dB} = PL(d_0) + 10nlog_{10}\left(\frac{d}{d_0}\right) + \sigma_s \qquad (4)$$

Where d_0 is the reference distance, n is the pass-loss exponent, and σ_s is the shadow fading, $PL(d_0) = 48.6$, n = 10.6, and $\sigma_s = 8.2$. Figure 15 shows the wireless power transmission loss excluding the distance-depended path loss. As the implanted distance increases in the range from 60mm to 85mm, coupling strong between in-body and on-body antenna become stronger.

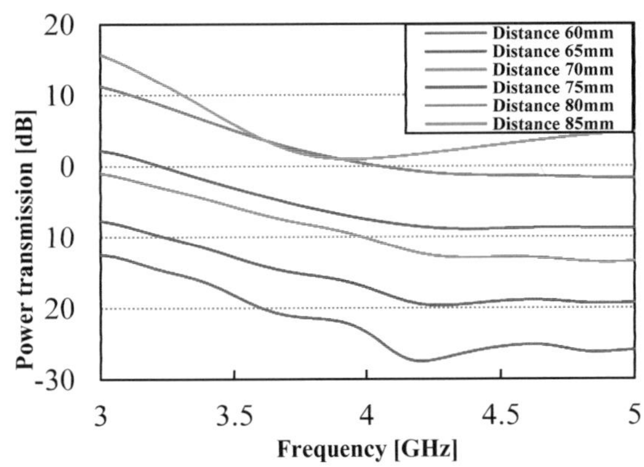

Figure 15. Wireless power transmission loss excluding distance depended path loss

From Figure 11, it is obvious that, under the condition that aperture size of receiving antenna is 40mm, phase error decreases with the growth of implanted distance. For receiving antenna operating at near field of implanted antenna, phase error distributed on the antenna aperture severely influences its ability to couple power from transmission antenna. In the process of designing on-body receiving antenna, it is of importance to sufficiently consider the implanted distance and the size of receiving antenna aperture to maximize the coupled power.

4. Conclusion

This paper analyzed the input impedance characteristics variance and field region separation of the implanted antenna for body area communications. The input impedance of half wave dipole wire antenna inside the human body torso and vacuum are calculated, separately with HFSS simulation and theoretical formula. It is obvious that input impedance of the antenna will endure a dramatic change when it is submerged inside body tissue and the resonance performance will be thence changed. And the influence of three types of insulating materials (air, Teflon, polyethylene) on the dipole resonant resistance and resonant frequency is also compared. The thicker the insulating thickness, the higher the resonant frequency and the resonant resistance. Meanwhile, the measured impedance of the previously developed DRA antenna in free space as well as inside phantom is shown. The reducing of impedance and shrinking of resonant frequency are observed from the results.

Three kinds of implanted antennas which are separately DRA antenna, helical antenna and discone antenna are investigated for their far-field boundaries satisfied $\pi/8$ rad phase error. For the constant size of antenna aperture, the trend of phase error approaches to zero with increasing of implanted distance. Phase error is also influenced by the size of aperture, which approaches zero more easier in smaller antenna aperture. Thus strictly speaking, the field separation investigation of the implanted antenna should be combined with the aperture of the receiving antenna.

The coupling ability is a significant factor evaluating the performance of receiving antenna, which is obviously influenced by phase error distributed in the antenna aperture. The field separation region calculation can be helpful reference to receiving wearable antenna development. Thus, in the process of designing on-body receiving antenna, it is of importance to sufficiently consider the implanted distance and the size of receiving antenna aperture to maximum the coupled power.

5. ACKNOWLEDGMENTS

This research is supported by "WiBEC" (Wireless In-Body Environment) project which has received funding from the European Union's Horizon 2020 research and innovation programme under grant agreement No. 675353.

6. REFERENCES

[1] FCC 2002. 02-48, Revision of Part 15 of the Commission's rules regarding ultra-wideband transmission systems.

[2] Zasowski T. , Meyer G. , Althaus F. 2006. UWB Signal Propagation at the Human Head, *IEEE Transaction On Microwave Theory And Techniques*, 54, 4 (April 2006), 1836-1845. DOI=http://doi.acm.org/10.1109/TMTT.2006.871989.

[3] Wang Q., Wolf K., and Plettemeier D. 2010. An UWB capsule endoscope antenna design for biomedical communications. In *3rd International Symposium on Applied Sciences in Biomedical and Communication Technologies* (Rome, Italy, November 07-10, 2010). ISABEL. DOI= http://doi.acm.org/10.1109/ISABEL.2010.5702832.

[4] Fenwick R. and Weeks W. 1963. Sumberged antenna characteristics. *IEEE Transactions on Antennas and Propagation*, 11, 3 (May 1963), 296-305, DOI=http://doi.acm.org/10.1109/TAP.1963.1138035.

[5] Balanis C. A. 2005. *Antenna Theory: Analysis and Design, 3nd Edition*, Wiley, New Jersey.

[6] Anzai D., Katsu K., Chavez-Santiago R., Wang Q., Plettemeier D., Wang J., Balasingham I. 2014. Experimental evaluation of implant UWB-IR transmission with living animal for body area networks. *IEEE Trans. Microwave Theory Tech.*, 62, 1 (Nov 2013),183–192, DOI=http://doi.acm.org/10.1109/TMTT.2013.2291542.

[7] Wang J., Wang Q. 2012. *Body Area Communication: Communication Systems, and EMC*, Wiley, USA, NJ.

Secure Monitoring of the Patients with Wandering Behaviour

Udaya Tupakula, Vijay Varadharajan, Kallol Karmakar
Advanced Cyber Security Research Centre
Faculty of Science, Macquarie University
Sydney, Australia
{udaya.tupakula, vijay.varadharajan}@mq.edu.au,
Kallol.Karmakar@students.mq.edu.au

ABSTRACT

Today there are several health care related problems such as dementia and cancer with no possible cure. Hence there is considerable interest in the medical sectors and constant encouragement from the governments to make use of the latest technological advancements for supporting such patients. Software Defined Networking(SDN) is a promising technological advancement in the networking world. In this paper we propose techniques for making use of the SDN, Wireless LAN and wearable devices for secure monitoring of the patients with wandering behaviour in hospital environments. Our model makes use of the global network knowledge available at the SDN controller to deal with the attacks in WLAN and provide priority for real time location monitoring of the patients. We will also present the prototype implementation of our model using ONOS SDN controller and OpenFlow Access Points.

CCS Concepts

•**Security and privacy** → **Usability in security and privacy;**

Keywords

Secure Healthcare, Dementia, Wandering, SDN, Security attacks, WLAN Localisation, SDN, OpenFlow

1. INTRODUCTION

Dementia [1, 9, 17, 4] causes degradation of mental ability to a level that can interfere with the tasks performed in daily life. There are different forms of dementia such as Alzheimer's, vascular dementia, Parkinson's disease dementia and mixed dementia. Although this is more common in aged people, there are cases where young people are infected with such disease. Currently there is no cure for some forms of dementia and the life span of the patients can range from 5-20 years depending on the seriousness of disease. Alzheimer's is one of the most common forms of dementia which is followed by vascular dementia which occurs after a stroke. Vascular dementia results due to blockage of major blood vessels in the brain and can severely impact the mental ability of the patient. Depending on the damage of the blood vessels the patient can have symptoms such as confusion, vision loss, wandering, trouble with speaking and understanding.

There are several challenges for the hospitals to deal with patients with specific requirements such as patients with vascular dementia. For example, vascular dementia patients who have been admitted to hospital after stroke for treatment can exhibit behaviour that is harmful for the patient and also violate policies of the hospital. In some cases, dementia patients can get into some locations that is harmful for them and will not be able to convey any information due to the conditions caused by the vascular dementia. In some cases, the vascular dementia patients can enter the room of other patients and violate their privacy. In some cases, the dementia patients can leave the hospital premises. For example, [14] reported a case of missing dementia patient from Anglican Care Nursing Home at Castle Hill, Sydney. Failure to detect such events is serious concern for hospital managements. Hence, even minor lack of attention from the nursing staff can lead to havoc or security breach in such environments. Although the nursing staff make sincere effort for taking care and monitoring of the patients, it is rare that a nursing staff is allocated to each patient. Hence there is a need for continuous location monitoring for some of the patients with specific requirements such as people with vascular dementia.

Currently there is considerable interest for making use of different heterogeneous technologies for healthcare applications. However, there are several challenges for making use of different technologies for healthcare applications. First there is a need to consider the specific requirements for the healthcare application. Then there is a need to consider the challenges with specific technologies used for the healthcare application. In particular, there is a need to ensure that the healthcare related services receive priority during events such as legitimate failures, congestion and attacks.

In this paper, we propose techniques for secure monitoring of dementia patients in hospital or elderly care environ-

ment. One of the aims of our work is to use technology for secure monitoring of vascular dementia patients from getting into locations that are harmful to the patient or detect if the behaviour of the patient violates the policies of the hospital, or even violates privacy policies of other patients. Our approach makes use of Software Defined Networks(SDN), Wireless LAN (WLAN) and wearable devices of the patients. Our approach incurs low cost since WLAN is widely deployed. However there are some challenges for making use of WLAN for monitoring dementia patients since it is primarily used for accessing Internet and the open nature of the communication is vulnerable to different types of security attacks. Hence we make use of SDN to solve some of these challenges and provide priority for the monitoring services. For example, since a SDN Controller has a global view of the network, devices in the network and traffic originating from the devices, it is able to differentiate between the traffic related to patient monitoring application and Internet browsing by the users. Hence in events such as congestion, the Controller can dynamically configure the OpenFlow Access Points(OF-APs) to provide priority to the patient monitoring traffic and drop/rate limit other traffic.
The paper is organised as follows. Section 2 gives a brief overview of the SDN technology and Section 3 presents some of the related work. In Section 4, we present our approach and operation of our model. Section 5 presents the implementation details and Section 6 concludes.

2. SDN OVERVIEW

SDN [11] enables programmable networks and simplifies the tasks of the network administrators for managing complex networks. The idea of SDN is based upon the separation of the control plane from the data plane. This separation results in the network switches becoming simpler forwarding devices with the control logic implemented in a logically centralized Controller. Also, it enables the design of new innovative network functions, protocols and applications. First, it is simpler and less error-prone to modify network policies through software, than via low-level device configurations. Second, a control program can automatically react to spurious changes of the network state and thus maintain up to date high-level policies in place. Third, the centralization of the control logic in the Controller with network wide knowledge simplifies the development of more sophisticated network functions.

Figure 1 shows an overview of the SDN architecture with different components in the control plane and data plane. The control plane consists of a logically centralised Controller (which can be distributed in practice) with native applications for the management and security (rarely considered by existing Controllers) of the devices in SDN network. Also there can be several 3rd party applications that can be hosted or accessing different services in the Controller. The interface between the Controller and the applications is called as the North Bound. The data plane consists of the networking devices and the interface between the Controller and the networking devices is called as the South Bound. OpenFlow [11] is one of the commonly used protocols for communication between the Controller and the networking devices. However different protocols such as sflow, and snmp are also supported for communication between the

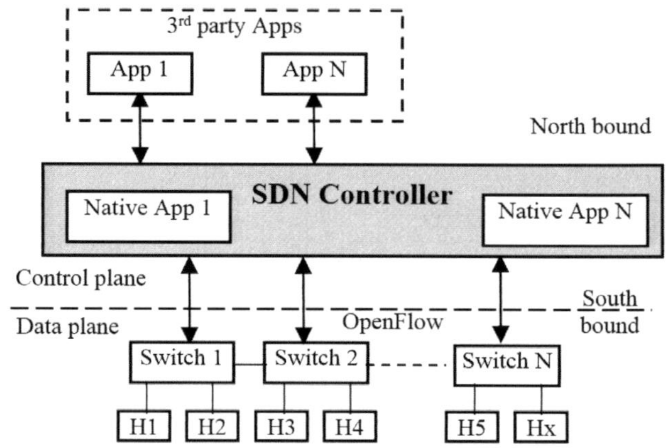

Figure 1: SDN Overview

Controller and the switches. In SDN terminology, a switch is used to represent any networking device that operates in Layers 2 to 7 in the OSI model.
The Controller manages the flow-entries in the flow tables of the switches through a secure channel (that exists in the switch itself). This management process might be done both reactively (in response to packets) as well as proactively. There are several SDN Controllers [22] available at present with different programming languages and environments. For example, NOX is based on C++ and Python programming languages; POX is based on Python; and Beacon and Floodlight are based on Java.
An OpenFlow compatible switch in the data plane contains three parts: i) A flow table, with an action linked with each flow entry, which tells the switch how to process the flow; ii) A secure channel that joins a switch to a remote control process (the Controller), allowing instructions and packets to be sent between a Controller and the switch using OpenFlow protocol; iii) The OpenFlow protocol, which provides an open and standard way for a Controller to interconnect with a switch. An entry in the flow table has three fields: a) a packet header that defines the flow; b) the action, which defines how the packets should be handled; c) counters, which keep track of the amount of packets per flow, and the time since the last packet matched the flow.
In traditional networks, when the network devices receive the traffic from the host, they make a decision depending on the route information available in the device (configured using CLI and/or captured from different network devices) and destination address of the traffic. In SDN, the OpenFlow switches are only used as dumb devices. When the switches receive a flow from a host, they simply forward the traffic as packet in messages to the Controller and rely on it to establish the communication path. Since the Controller has a global view of the network, it makes a dynamic decision on how to forward the traffic to the destination and configures corresponding flow rules on all the switches between the source and destination. Hence in this paper we make use of global network knowledge and per flow decision making of the SDN Controller to deal with the attacks and provide priority for the real time location tracking of the dementia patients.

3. RELATED WORK

In this section we present some of the related work in the areas of localisation techniques, attacks in WLAN and SDN security.

Different location tracking techniques [10, 3, 6, 25] have been proposed earlier. For example, GPS based tracking [10] techniques provide an accurate location estimation in the areas where there is a line-of-sight from the satellites to the tracked device. Hence it is mostly used in open environments. However it is not efficient for location tracking inside buildings due to signal blockage by walls and multipath effects. Techniques such as [3, 6, 25] can be used for indoor tracking but we need to consider the special requirements for dementia patients. For example, during the events such as congestion, there is a need to provide priority for the traffic related to patient monitoring. Also, there is a need to deal with the attacks originating in the wireless networks.

There are several prior works related to the attacks, analysis of the security protocols that have been proposed for secure communication in wireless networks and techniques to deal with the attacks in wireless networks. For example, Khan et al [15] considers different types of attacks that are possible in the WLAN, WiMax and WMAN technologies. The work specifically highlights the challenges to deal with the passive attacks and categorization of attacks at different layers of the protocol stack. Bellardo and Savage [7] have demonstrated how the attacker can perform different types of denial of service attacks such as deauthentication and disassociation attacks. He and Mitchell [13] also observed DoS vulnerabilities in 802.11i and the work in [21, 16] presents a detailed discussion on how the attacks can be implemented in practice. Liu and Yu [19] analyzed the authentication request flooding and association request flooding attacks and proposed to use MAC address filtering and traffic pattern filtering which enforces a limit on the maximum number of authentication or association requests from the mobile nodes. Furthermore, some techniques have been proposed to deal with the rogue access points in the wireless networks. Bahl et al [5] suggested dense deployment of sensors for monitoring the wireless networks for rouge access points. The technique makes use of the unused desktop resources in wired networks and USB based wireless adapters to minimize the deployment cost of the security sensors. The techniques proposed by Sheng et al [12] can be used to detect if mobile devices are connected to rouge access points. Since a wireless rogue access point can induce time delays between the communications, [12] detect the rouge access points by monitoring the changes in the round trip time when communicating with the local servers. Zeng et. al [27] proposed cookie based approach to deal with the denial of service attacks on the authentication mechanism during handover process. Xu et al [26] considered different types of jamming attacks and proposed dynamic changing of communication channels to deal with the attacks. Traynor et. al [24] used queue management techniques to deal with the saturation of the wireless links. Compared to these related work, our work addresses the specific requirements for secure healthcare applications particularly for dementia patients and makes use of SDN to deal with the attacks in WLAN.

There is some prior work related to security in SDN. Porras et al. [20] discussed the security challenges and the need for security enforcement kernel at the Controller. They proposed a role based enforcement of security policies and conflict resolution for NOX Controller. Li et al. [18] proposed to use multiple Controllers to deal with the case of failure or compromise of single Controller and each switch is managed by more than one Controller. To protect SDN from such kind of threats to the control plane, this technique assumes that majority of the Controllers are not compromised by the attacker and deals with the challenge of letting the Controllers continue operate correctly, even if some of them exhibit arbitrary, possibly malicious behavior. Shin et al. [23] proposed ROSEMARY to improve the resilience of the SDN Controller. Its design is based on sandboxing the network applications to prevent common failures of network applications from halting the SDN Controller operation. The main focus of our work is to make use of SDN to address some of the challenges related to secure and real time monitoring of the patients in hospital environment. Furthermore the proposed techniques [20, 18, 23] can complement our model for improving the security in SDN. For example, since the Controller has several 3rd party applications, role based access control can be enforced at the Controller in our model (similar to [20]) to deal with the malicious 3rd party applications and conflict resolution of the policies. Similarly multiple Controllers (such as [18]) or sandboxing of network applications in the Controller [23] can be used in our model to deal with the failure or compromise of the Controller.

4. OUR APPROACH

In this section we will first consider some of the requirements for our model. Then we will present the operation of our model and provide a discussion related to our model.

4.1 Requirements

- Although there is a need for continuous location monitoring of the dementia patients, note that there can be several other patients in hospitals that may not need such location tracking. So usage of sophisticated technologies for real time location monitoring of the patients can incur considerable cost for the deployment of the technology and also for training of the staff for the usage of the technology. Hence it is advantageous for making use of the widely deployed technologies such as WLAN.

- Tracking the location of the patients is possible on the wearable devices and from the network. Our design choice is to use network based tracking due to limited battery resources of the wearable devices and also due to the inability of the dementia patients. For example, providing location information on the wearable device may not be of much help for the dementia patients with loss of memory and/or visibility. Device based tracking will also result in the increase of the cost of the wearable device since it requires additional display mechanisms on the wearable device. Hence it is more useful for the nurses and hospital management to keep track of the dementia patients.

- The wearable devices are initially used to train our model for detecting the location of device to the required level of accuracy. As the number of samples used for training our model increase, the location detection accuracy of our model increases. Note that change in the layout of the building is somewhat a rare event, the training has to be performed only once to the required level of sensitivity. In case of changes to the building layout, the training data has to be updated to track the locations in the new layout.

- Patients with dementia can change their behavior. However this does not have any impact on our model since its operation is dependent only on the training using the wearable device.

- We assume that patient's information which is provided during admission is mapped to the wearable device ID and the devices are tagged to the patient. There is a need to ensure that the devices cannot be easily detached by the patients. Hence tracking the location of wearable device corresponds to the actual location of the patient.

- Each patient will be allocated a minimum of two wearable devices to ensure continuous tracking of the patients. For example, the wearable devices may have to be detached from the patients for recharging the battery. Hence there is a need for an additional device for continuous tracking of the patients.

4.2 Operation

As shown in the Figure 2, we consider a scenario where SDN is used for managing the WLAN. The WLAN is used for real time monitoring of the dementia patients and also for providing Internet services to other users (patients without dementia, guests and hospital staff). OF-APs are placed at different locations within the layout with overlapping range and there are some wireless sniffers (not shown) to capture the traffic in WLAN and monitoring different activities such as congestion of the medium, detection of rogue access points broadcasting unauthorized SSID, and traffic matching with attack signatures. We assume that the SDN Controller is a trusted entity within the domain and there are mechanisms for ensuring security and high availability of the Controller. For example, techniques such as [20, 18, 23] can be used for security and high availability of the Controller.

As shown in the Figure 2, we have developed a secure monitoring application for ONOS Controller for real time location tracking of the patients with wandering behaviour and deal with the attacks in WLAN. The monitoring application tracks the location of the patients and raises alarms to the hospital staff when the location of the dementia patient is violating the policies of the hospital or when the battery power in the wearable devices is falling below a threshold for recharging the devices. The monitoring application can be installed on any of the SDN Controllers with minimal modification. The application makes use of the global network information available at the SDN Controller and has additional sub components to provide priority to the traffic related to the patient monitoring and also deal with the attacks in WLAN. For example, the monitoring application makes use of information such as the global view of the network topology, devices in the network and traffic originating

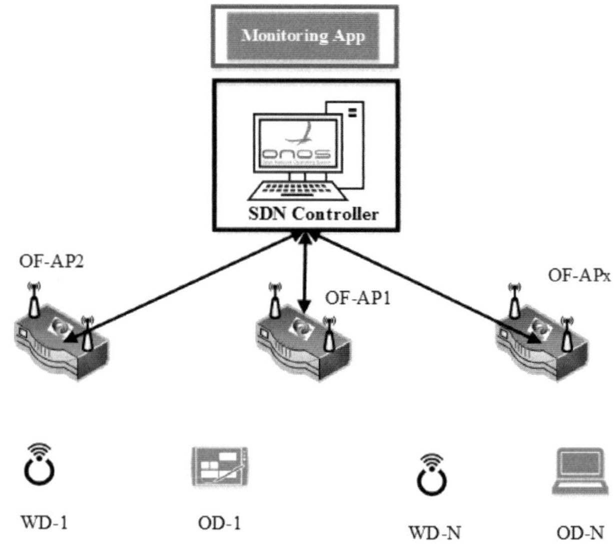

Figure 2: SDN Monitoring Scenario

from the devices to differentiate between the traffic related to patient monitoring application and Internet browsing by the users. Hence when there is congestion, the Controller can dynamically configure the OF-APs to provide priority to the patient monitoring traffic and drop/rate limit other traffic.

The wearable devices are configured to send updates to the monitoring application at regular intervals (3 seconds in the current implementation). Also the monitoring application configures the OF-APs to forward the updates from wearable devices with high priority. In the current model, the wearable devices are configured to convey only the information of the device ID, Received Signal Strength (RSS) from different OF-APs and battery level available in the device. The device ID enables to identify the patient, the RSS from different OF-APs enables to approximate the location of the wearable device by comparing with the fingerprints stored in the database and the battery level enables to determine if the wearable device has to be replaced with other device. The location of the patient is determined from the received signal strength from multiple OF-APs at the wearable device. The RSS is the measure of the signal power from the transmitting device to the receiving device. Since there are multiple OF-APs with overlapping range and the location of the OF-APs is fixed within the layout, it is possible to determine the location of wearable device from the RSS. In the training mode, the wearable devices are placed at different locations within the layout and the corresponding RSS from different OF-APs is used to relate the location of at the wearable device in the layout maps and stored in the database. In the online mode, the RSS from different OF-APs at the wearable devices of the patient are compared with the records in the database to approximate the location of patient.

The monitoring system has different sub components such as authentication, attack detection, database, and location tracking. Our current implementation makes use of shared secret and also supports 802.11i security. A detailed analysis of the 802.11i security can be found in [13]. Attack detection is based on signature matching, unauthorized SSID broadcast, and monitoring of the time delays between the transmitted and received signals. The signals transmitted from the wearable devices and OF-APs are time stamped just before transmission to discourage attacks. For example, the round trip time between the wearable devices and the OF-APs is used to detect man in the middle attacks. A detailed analysis on detecting such attacks can be found in [12]. If there is considerable delay between the signal transmitted by wearable device and signal received at the OF-AP then this can be considered to be suspicious. In such cases, our model raises alarms to the network administrator for physical monitoring of the location. Furthermore, if the sniffers detect any unauthorized SSID broadcasts, then RSS of the unauthorized SSID is also used to approximate the location of malicious devices. The database has information on the patients, wearable devices, building layout, signal to location mapping on the layout. The location monitor component makes use of the information stored in the database and the RSS for detecting the current location of the dementia patients. Our model makes use of the k-nearest neighbour algorithm to estimate the location of the patients. The k-NN algorithm computes the Euclidean distances in signal space between the online RSSs and stored RSSs in the database and then calculates the geometrical center of the k-nearest neighbours as the estimated location.

The room allocated to the patient is used as default location for the dementia patient. Mobility of the patient is detected by analysing the changes in the RSS between different OF-APs and the wearable devices. The monitoring application raises high priority alert if the location of dementia patients is found to be moving away from the default location. Hence the nurses and hospital management can track the current location of the patient and take necessary steps to transfer the patient to the default location.

4.3 Discussion

In this Section, we will provide some discussion related to our model.

- Legitimate failure of the devices: There is a possibility for the failure of the OF-APs and/or the wearable devices. Since the monitoring application has configured the OF-APs to forward the updates with high priority, all the OF-APs that are in the range of the wearable device transmission will forward the update to the monitoring application. To deal with the failure of the OF-AP, the Controller configures atleast two OF-APs to forward the traffic from wearable device to the monitoring application. Failure of the wearable devices will result in absence of the updates from the wearable device to the monitoring application at the expected interval. If the updates are not received for successive intervals, then an alert is raised to the staff with the last known location of the patient.

- Priority for patient monitoring traffic: The traffic related to patient monitoring is differentiated from other traffic based on the wearable device ID and is allocated high priority compared to other traffic. For example, the OF-APs are also used by other patients (without dementia) and guests of the patients for accessing Internet. Hence in the events such as attacks and congestion, the traffic related to tracking of the patients is given high priority in our model. Now let us consider the case where the OF-APs in critical location receives a request from a wearable device when they are unable to accept any new service requests from a wearable device. Since we assume an overlapping range of the OF-APs the Controller dynamically alters the existing traffic connections from other host machines to different OF-APs and provide priority to the traffic from wearable device. If there are no alternative OF-APs to transfer the traffic from other devices, then the services to other devices are rate limited or terminated to provide priority to the traffic from wearable devices.

- Attacks from other user devices: There is a possibility for attacks to be generated from other hosts that are making use of WLAN for accessing Internet. Hence all the traffic received at the OF-APs is monitored using the signature based detection engine. Furthermore, the sniffers capture all the traffic in the wireless medium and monitor for events such as congestion, unauthorized SSID broadcasts from rouge access points and also match the captured traffic with the known attacks signatures to detect if there is any ongoing attack. If any traffic from the other devices matches with the attack signature, then the monitoring application determines the OF-AP that is connected to the malicious host and dynamically configures the OF-AP to terminate the connections from the malicious host.

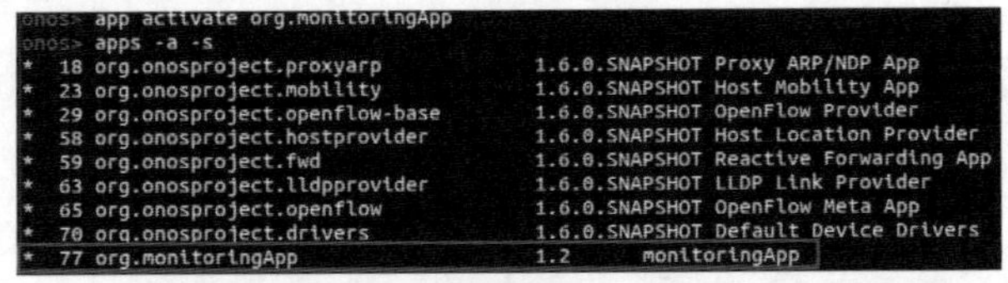

Figure 3: Monitoring Application for ONOS Controller

5. IMPLEMENTATION

We have implemented our model with ONOS Controller [8] and OpenFlow based access points as shown in Figure 2.

ONOS [8] adopts a distributed architecture for high availability and scale-out. The developers have used several modules such as switch manager, module management, link discovery and REST APIs from the Floodlight Controller. The data model in ONOS is implemented using Titan graph database, Cassandra key value store and the Blueprints graph API to expose network state to applications. The implementation of ONOS can be distributed across multiple servers and number of instances can be varied in accordance with the load. In distributed implementation, each server has a global view of the network but is responsible for managing subset of switches in the network. Hence any of the applications implemented on any instance of the Controller has access to the global view of the network. Applications read the global network view to make forwarding and policy deci-

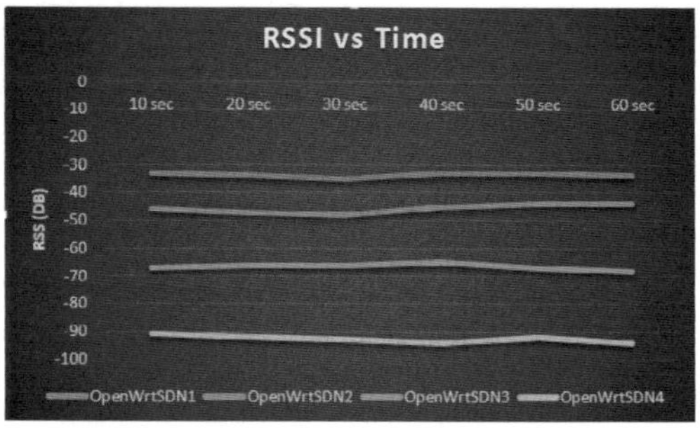

Figure 4: RSS vs Time

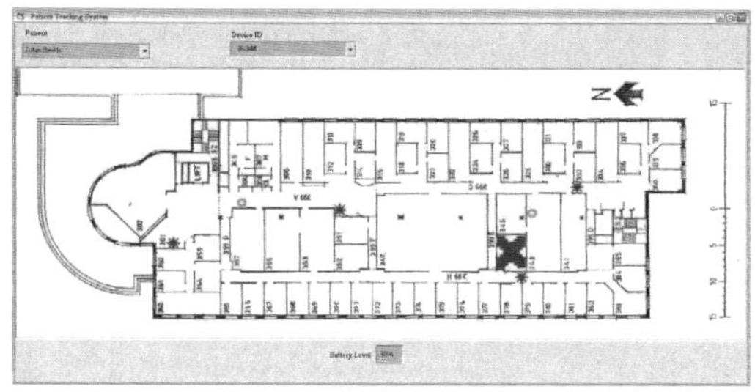

Figure 5: Patient Location

sions and write their policies to be enforced on the network view. Any changes in the policy are sent to the corresponding manager for enforcement of policies on the appropriate switches.

OpenFlow Wireless APs are not commercially available. For this reason, we have developed our own OpenFlow wireless AP using TP-link (TL-WR1043ND) wireless AP since they are low cost, easily available, and customizable. We have installed Open vSwitch to make the device compatible to OpenFlow 1.3. First we have replaced the old firmware of TL-WR1043ND with OpenWrt [2]. OpenWrt uses linux kernel (2.6) and was mainly used in embedded devices for instance ARM, Raspberry, some commercial and Customized APs for network traffic routing. Then installed and configured Open vSwitch to make the OpenWrt, OpenFlow enabled. This creates provision for connecting remote host wirelessly using OpenFlow.

Our prototype implementation makes use of a single ONOS Controller. As shown in Figure 3, we have developed monitoring application for ONOS for securing monitoring of the dementia patients. The security application have several sub-components for different purposes such as authentication, attacks detection, location detection and database components.

We have developed our own tracking device using Arduino uno, ESP8266 and a voltage regulator IC. The purpose of the device is to send the RSS value of nearby OF-APs to the connected Controller. We have used a 6000mAH 5volt battery to power the whole unit. This arrangement is extremely light weight and consumes less power (sufficient for powering the unit for more than one day). Arduino uno is a Micro-controller programmable interface that can be used for making small IoT units. ESP8266 is a very famous miniature WLAN chip which provides wireless capability to the Arduino. Since, ESP8266 (3.3V) works in a lower voltage than the Arduino, we have used a voltage regulator IC(1117). Arduino maintains a serial communication with ESP8266 and our chosen baud rate in this case is 9600. One of the I/O pin in Arduino is programmed to sense the battery level. Figure 4 shows a trace of RSS from different SDN AP in a particular time and from a particular tracking device.

We have implemented and tested our model in one of the university building on the third floor with sample hospital setup in some of the rooms. We have developed Arduino based wearable devices and also used Samsung mobile devices for tracking the patients. The green stars on the layout show the location of the OF-APs (OpenWrtSDNX). The OF-AP with the highest RSS is used as default OF-AP for providing access to the wireless devices and mobility of the users is detected by analysing the variations in the RSS. Also, the wearable devices are programmed to connect through specific OF-APs in their default location. In case where an OF-AP is not available or RSS falls below the threshold, the monitoring application assigns alternate OF-AP that can be used by the device. The RSS default value of -85 dBm threshold is used for changing the OF-APs for the wireless devices. The wireless devices are connected to the neighboring OF-APs if the signal strength is atleast 20 percent greater than the signal strength of the current OF-AP. Hence any operation from the wireless client devices that violate the configuration information raise an alert to the network administrator. In the case of congestion of specific OF-APs, the wearable devices are given high priority for connecting to the default OF-APs. Other client devices are redirected to the OF-APs with minimal load.

The RSS and location information are stored in XML database and this information is used to train our model. We have captured a minimum of 15 training samples for each room. Also, since the patients will be spending most of the time on their beds, a minimum of 5 training samples were taken at different locations on the bed such as corners of the bed, centre of the bed and remaining samples from different locations such as toilet, fridge and room entry. Then we have tested our model with minimum of 10 samples by placing the wearable device at different locations in the room. We have achieved accuracy of 2 feet for the cases where the patient location is on the bed and accuracy of 1 meter for different locations in the floor layout.

Figure 5 shows the interface that can be used by the hospital staff to track the location of specific patient. The stars represent the location of OF-APs and blue circles on the map represent the sniffers which promiscuously capture the traffic on the wireless medium and monitor for specific events such as traffic matching with attack signature, unauthorized SSID broadcasts from rouge access points and events such as congestion. Query can be issued on the patient name or using the device ID. The results show the current location of the patient and the battery levels in the wearable device of the patient. Our current model raises alarms for the following specific events: i) high alert to nursing staff when patient location found to be leaving the default location (allocated room), ii) high alerts with the current location of the patients to the nursing staff when the dementia patients enter into the rooms of other patients iii) high alert to the security staff when the patient is moving towards exit gate of the hospital, iv) medium alert to nursing staff when the battery level on the wearable device is at 20 percent and high alert when the battery level is 10 percent v) medium level alert to the network administrator during congestion and high alerts if traffic matching with attack signatures, vi) medium alert with the last known location of the patient to nurses when signals from wearable devices are not received for three successive intervals and vii) a high level alert with the last known location of the patient for nurses and security administrator if signals are not received for 5 successive intervals.

6. CONCLUSION

In this paper we have proposed techniques for making use of the SDN, WLAN and wearable devices of the patients for secure monitoring of the dementia patients in hospital environments. We discussed how SDN can help to resolve some of the challenges for real time monitoring of the patients and offers advantages for such critical applications. We have also presented a prototype implementation of our model using ONOS SDN Controller and OpenFlow access points.

7. REFERENCES

[1] http://www.alz.org/what-is-dementia.asp.

[2] Openwrt. https://openwrt.org/.

[3] A. Agiwal, P. Khandpur, and H. Saran. Locator: location estimation system for wireless lans. In *Proceedings of the 2nd ACM international workshop on Wireless mobile applications and services on WLAN hotspots*, pages 102–109. ACM, 2004.

[4] D. L. Algase, E. R. Beattie, and B. Therrien. Impact of cognitive impairment on wandering behavior. *Western Journal of Nursing Research*, 23(3):283–295, 2001.

[5] P. Bahl, R. Chandra, J. Padhye, L. Ravindranath, M. Singh, A. Wolman, and B. Zill. Enhancing the security of corporate wi-fi networks using dair. In *Proceedings of the 4th international conference on Mobile systems, applications and services*, pages 1–14. ACM, 2006.

[6] P. Bahl and V. N. Padmanabhan. Radar: An in-building rf-based user location and tracking system. In *INFOCOM 2000. Nineteenth Annual Joint Conference of the IEEE Computer and Communications Societies. Proceedings. IEEE*, volume 2, pages 775–784. Ieee, 2000.

[7] J. Bellardo and S. Savage. 802.11 denial-of-service attacks: Real vulnerabilities and practical solutions. In *USENIX security*, pages 15–28, 2003.

[8] P. Berde, M. Gerola, J. Hart, Y. Higuchi, M. Kobayashi, T. Koide, B. Lantz, B. O'Connor, P. Radoslavov, W. Snow, et al. Onos: towards an open, distributed sdn os. In *Proceedings of the third workshop on Hot topics in software defined networking*, pages 1–6. ACM, 2014.

[9] P. Dawson and D. W. Reid. Behavioral dimensions of patients at risk of wandering. *The Gerontologist*, 27(1):104–107, 1987.

[10] P. Enge and P. Misra. Special issue on global positioning system. *Proceedings of the IEEE*, 87(1):3–15, 1999.

[11] O. N. Foundation. Software-defined networking: The new norm for networks. https://www.opennetworking.org/images/stories/downloads/sdnresources/white-papers/wp-sdn-newnorm.pdf[Accessed12Dec.2015].

[12] H. Han, B. Sheng, C. C. Tan, Q. Li, and S. Lu. A timing-based scheme for rogue ap detection. *IEEE Transactions on parallel and distributed Systems*, 22(11):1912–1925, 2011.

[13] C. He and J. C. Mitchell. Security analysis and improvements for ieee 802.11 i. In *The 12th Annual Network and Distributed System Security Symposium (NDSS'05) Stanford University, Stanford*, pages 90–110. Citeseer, 2005.

[14] B. Jordan. Emergency services find lost dementia suffere. http://www.greatfete.com.au/media/NewsLocal-HillsShireTimes-13Aug2013-Page3.pdf, 2013.

[15] S. Khan, K.-K. Loo, T. Naeem, and M. A. Khan. Denial of service attacks and challenges in broadband wireless networks. *8; 7*, 2008.

[16] V. Kumkar, A. Tiwari, P. Tiwari, A. Gupta, and S. Shrawne. Vulnerabilities of wireless security protocols (wep and wpa2). *International Journal of Advanced Research in Computer Engineering & Technology (IJARCET)*, 1(2):34–38, 2012.

[17] C. K. Lai and D. G. Arthur. Wandering behaviour in people with dementia. *Journal of advanced nursing*, 44(2):173–182, 2003.

[18] H. Li, P. Li, S. Guo, and S. Yu. Byzantine-resilient secure software-defined networks with multiple controllers. In *2014 IEEE International Conference on Communications (ICC)*, pages 695–700. IEEE, 2014.

[19] C. Liu and J. Yu. A solution to wlan authentication and association dos attacks. *IAENG International Journal of Computer Science*, 34(1):31–36, 2007.

[20] P. Porras, S. Shin, V. Yegneswaran, M. Fong, M. Tyson, and G. Gu. A security enforcement kernel for openflow networks. In *Proceedings of the first workshop on Hot topics in software defined networks*, pages 121–126. ACM, 2012.

[21] R. H. Rahman, N. Nowsheen, M. A. Khan, and A. H. Khan. Wireless lan security: an in-depth study of the threats and vulnerabilities. *Asian Journal of Information Technology*, 6(4):441–446, 2007.

[22] A. Shalimov, D. Zuikov, D. Zimarina, V. Pashkov, and R. Smeliansky. Advanced study of sdn/openflow controllers. In *Proceedings of the 9th central & eastern european software engineering conference in russia*, page 1. ACM, 2013.

[23] S. Shin, Y. Song, T. Lee, S. Lee, J. Chung, P. Porras, V. Yegneswaran, J. Noh, and B. B. Kang. Rosemary: A robust, secure, and high-performance network operating system. In *Proceedings of the 2014 ACM SIGSAC conference on computer and communications security*, pages 78–89. ACM, 2014.

[24] P. Traynor, W. Enck, P. McDaniel, and T. La Porta. Mitigating attacks on open functionality in sms-capable cellular networks. *IEEE/ACM Transactions on Networking*, 17(1):40–53, 2009.

[25] Z. Xiang, S. Song, J. Chen, H. Wang, J. Huang, and X. Gao. A wireless lan-based indoor positioning technology. *IBM Journal of research and development*, 48(5.6):617–626, 2004.

[26] W. Xu, T. Wood, W. Trappe, and Y. Zhang. Channel surfing and spatial retreats: defenses against wireless denial of service. In *Proceedings of the 3rd ACM workshop on Wireless security*, pages 80–89. ACM, 2004.

[27] R. Zeng, C. Lin, H. Yang, Y. Wang, Y. Wang, and P. Ungsunan. A novel cookie-based ddos protection scheme and its performance analysis. In *2009 International Conference on Advanced Information Networking and Applications*, pages 861–867. IEEE, 2009.

Activity Level Assessment of Wheelchair Users Using Smart Cushion

Congcong Ma
School of Logistics Engineering
Wuhan University of Technology
Wuhan, P.R. China
macc@whut.edu.cn

Raffaele Gravina
Department of Informatics, Modeling, Electronics and Systems
University of Calabria
Rende, Italy
rgravina@dimes.unical.it

Wenfeng Li*
School of Logistics Engineering
Wuhan University of Technology
Wuhan, P.R. China
liwf@whut.edu.cn

Yu Zhang
School of Logistics Engineering
Wuhan University of Technology
Wuhan, P.R. China
sanli@whut.edu.cn

Qimeng Li
Department of Informatics, Modeling, Electronics and Systems
University of Calabria
Rende, Italy
liqimeng@msn.com

Giancarlo Fortino
Department of Informatics, Modeling, Electronics and Systems
University of Calabria
Rende, Italy
g.fortino@unical.it

ABSTRACT

A large majority of worldwide population, such as office workers and long journey vehicle drivers, spends lot of time everyday in sedentary activities. In this paper, we specifically focus on the assessment of different levels of wheelchair users' activity. The postures that wheelchair users assume during daily activities hide valuable information that can reveal their wellness and general health condition.

Aiming at mining such underlying information, we propose a hamming weight based algorithm to assess the activity level from sitting posture sequences. Using a smart cushion placed on the wheelchair, we can monitor users' postures. Postures sequence is transformed into binary value vector segments in order to reduce the computation load. The algorithm can detect three levels of activity (stationary, moderate or hyperactivity) with high accuracy. The proposed method could be embedded into several potential applications such as health estimation of sitting subjects, activity statistics, and detection of abnormal activities.

Keywords

Activity Level Assessment; Smart Cushion; Wheelchair Users; Posture Sequences; Hamming Weight

1. INTRODUCTION

In the context of Body Area Networks (BANs) [11], multi sensor fusion [18], wireless communication and embedded systems [13], many assist devices have been developed to enhance our daily lifestyle. As the elder population and the number of disabled persons is continuously raising, there is a strong need for better wheelchairs that are able to assist more independent life. As a consequence, several user-centric applications [20] such as smart home [8] and smart chair [26] are being developed.

People using wheelchairs spend long time in sitting posture and it is easier to incur in neck and back pain or pressure ulcer [1]. On the one hand, keeping the same posture for a long time is bad for health; on the other, very frequent posture transitions [17] might also represent evidence of discomfort. Posture transitions underly useful information. In this paper, we present an approach to monitor seating postures and assess users' activity level from posture sequences, so to provide users with reminders to correct posture adoption and therefore to minimize the health risk as well as to let caregivers take timely necessary interventions.

Our aim is to develop a fast, robust and highly accurate method for continuous activity level assessment. Specifically, the contributions of this paper are twofold. Firstly, we propose a hamming weight based algorithm to recognize three activity levels (i.e. stationary, moderate or hyperactivity); secondly, to reduce computational load, we propose to transform the posture sequences to binary value vector segments.

The reminder of the paper is organized as follows: Section 2 introduces the pressure sensing technology and knowledge discovery from postures; Section 3 describes in detail the proposed method and system design; Section 4 discusses experiments and obtained results. Finally, in Section 5 some conclusions and future works are drawn.

2. RELATED WORK

Posture/activity recognition and abnormalities detection

have been hot topics in many research areas, such as pervasive and mobile computing, context-aware computing, and ambient assisted living. As pressure sensor based smart cushion is unobtrusive, several related works adopted it to recognize physical activity [12], to measure comfort and wellness [2], posture and fatigue [23] of users sitting on normal chairs and wheelchairs. In the following paragraph, we introduce the related works of pressure sensing based posture recognition and discovery from posture analysis.

2.1 Pressure sensing for posture recognition

Tan et al. [32] used a commercially available pressure distribution sensor called body pressure measurement system (BPMS). Using principal components analysis to analyze pressure distribution map as a gray scale image, sitting posture classification was successfully achieved. Meyer et al. [27] presented their own capacitive textile pressure sensor array cushion to measure pressure distribution of the human body. They used a Naive Bayes classifier to identify 16 different sitting postures on the chair, with similar results to Tan. Multu et al. [29] proposed a robust low-cost non-intrusive seat; compared to the commercially-available Tekscan ConforMat system (2048 sensors) used in [32, 27], they managed to reduce the number of sensors, and an optimal sensor deployment with 19 pressure sensors was adopted to recognize sitting postures. Xu et al. [34] presented a textile-based sensing system called Smart Cushion to recognize the sitting postures of human being. Binary pressure distribution data were collected and the data model could be interpreted to binary representation of a gray scale image. They used dynamic time warping to analyze the pressure distributions and recognize postures. Kamiya et al. [21] used a 8×8 pressure sensor matrix embedded in a cushion of a chair to identify sitting postures. They used a radial basis function with default SVM to classify the postures. Fard et al. [9] presented a system that involves a 8×8 pressure sensor matrix for continuous monitoring of surface pressure. Pressure map was generated to recognize different postures with the aim of preventing pressure ulcer using a MATLAB application.

In contrast with using e-textile sensor arrays, recent research focused on using fewer, independent sensors. Benocci et al. [5] proposed a method using 5 pressure sensors and k-Nearest Neighbor (kNN) was used to classify 6 different postures. Bao et al. [3] also used 5 pressure sensors to recognize the sitting posture on wheelchairs, using density-based clustering methods to establish the evaluation model. Barba et al. [4] used 16 pressure sensors and an Arduino board to develop an on-line posture recognition system to monitor users' affective states, such as boredom, attention and nervousness, during learning scenarios. Min et al. [28] proposed a real-time sitting posture monitoring system based on measuring pressure distribution of the human body sitting on the chair. A decision tree is used to recognize 5 sitting postures; when the user deviates from the correct posture, an alarm function is activated. Our former research [24] used 3 pressure sensors (two on the seat and one on the backrest) to detect user's postures sittin on a smart wheelchair. Six different postures were recognized and experimental results showed high classification accuracy.

Posture recognition is important, but how we can uncover valuable knowledge from postures is probably yet more relevant. In the following, we discuss the state-of-the-art on knowledge discovery from postures.

2.2 Knowledge discovery from postures

Chica et al. [7] focused on the movement intentions of patients restricted to a medical bed, developing a recognition system using pressure map sequences to monitor even slight movements. Artificial neural networks were used to analyze the pressure map in real time. Cheng et al. [6] investigated on user activity detected from simple pressure sensors mounted under the legs of a chair. Results showed that it is possible to detect not only different postures, but also subtle hand and head related actions like typing and nodding. Fu et al. [14] proposed a robust, low-cost, sensor based system that is capable of recognizing sitting postures and activities. Eight force sensing resistors (FSRs) were placed on chair backrest and seat, and a Hidden Markov Model approach was used to establish the activity model from sitting posture sequences. Kumar et al. [22] have designed Care-Chair with just 4 pressure sensors on the backrest of a chair. Equipped with intelligent data analytics, their system can classify 19 kinds of complex user sedentary activities and it can also detect user functional activities and emotion based activities. Furugori et al. [15] used seated posture information to detect mental fatigue. It was found that changes in the center of mass represented the change of driver's posture, so authors claimed it is a good index to fatigue estimation.

In the following, we briefly present our sitting posture recognition method and we propose a hamming weight based algorithm to detect the activity level. Compared with former research, we transform the posture sequence to binary vector, with significant computation load reduction.

3. METHOD

3.1 Static sitting posture recognition

With respect to our former research [24, 25], we propose an improvement of the sensors deployment on the cushion. In order to better fit individual weight and anatomic differences, our new sensing device contains 6 pressure sensors (4 pressure sensors placed on the seat and 2 other pressure sensors placed on the backrest), as shown in Figure 1.

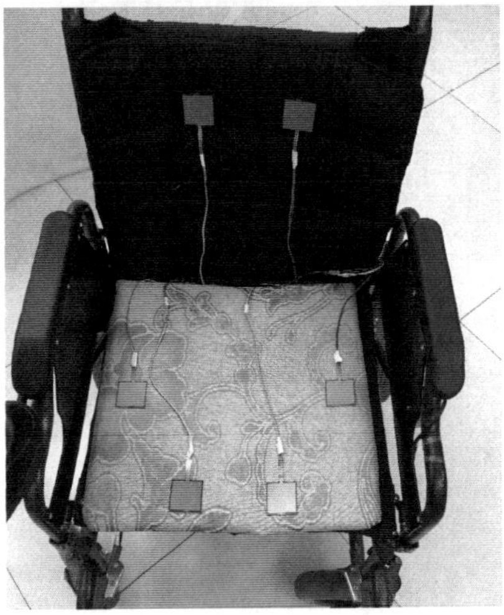

Figure 1: Cushion based wheelchair system.

Using the cushion based wheelchair system, we are able to recognize 5 different sitting postures [24] (Proper Sitting

(PS), Lean Left (LL), Lean Right (LR), Lean Forward (LF) and Lean Backward (LB)). Instance vectors are generated from the pressure sensors signals. In particular, raw data are acquired by the Arduino-based processing module at a sampling frequency of $2Hz$, so to reduce energy consumption. As demonstrated in our previous research, the aforementioned postures can be efficiently recognized with a J48 decision tree [30]. This classification algorithm is also easy to be implemented on embedded devices such as our Arduino platform. At time t, the posture can be represented as $P(t)$.

3.2 Activity level assessment

Kumar [22] defined several kinds of sedentary activities such as static activities, movement based activities, user functional activities and user emotion based activities. In [33], the authors proposed a method to detect three levels of activities (high-level, middle-level, and low-level intensity) using acceleration signal.

It has been reported that moderate exercise can reduce the risk of metabolic syndrome and better improve the health condition of the sedentary individuals [16].

Under this perspective, in this work we are not interested in the specific activities performed by wheelchair users, while we need to consider the activity level/intensity, as summarized in Table 1. The table also reports examples of activities that can fall under a specific activity level performed by the wheelchair users, defined as follows:

- Stationary Activity (sit still for a long time),
- Moderate Activity, and
- Hyperactivity (posture transition frequently in a short period)

Table 1: Categorization of different activity levels of wheelchair users

Activity Level	Description	Examples
Stationary	User is static sitting for a long time.	Napping, Reading, Watching TV
Moderate	User performs common daily life activities.	Reading, Watching TV, Desk working, Conversation, Doing exercise
Hyperactivity	User is excited, nervous or uncomfortable.	Watching TV, Conversation, Doing exercise, Feeling nervous, Uncomfortable

As described in Table 1, some activities can belong to different levels. To exemplify, if the user is watching a TV documentary, he/she might behave stationary, while if the user is watching a football match of his/her favorite team, he/she might behave hyperactivity.

Using the postures recognized in Section 3.1, we propose a novel algorithm to assess wheelchair user' activity level. In the following, we describe the posture sequence representation and our hamming weight based algorithm activity assessment method.

Let be the posture transition represented as Hi. We assume the initial state of H_0 is 1. Then, if two consecutive postures in the sequence change, we mark Hi as 1, otherwise we mark it as 0, as depicted in the code below.

```
if P(i) = P(i-1)
        Hi = 0
else
        Hi = 1
```

Thus, this process converts the posture sequence into a binary vector that is used for further processing. There are two advantages of transforming posture sequence to binary values: firstly, it can clearly indicate posture transitions and, secondly, it can reduce computation load.

Hamming weight is used in several disciplines including digital signal processing, image and data processing, encoding and error correction, cryptography, combinatorial search, and DNA computing [31]. The Hamming weight $\omega(A)$ of a binary vector A is the number of one bits in the vector. The flow chart of the algorithm is shown in Figure 2.

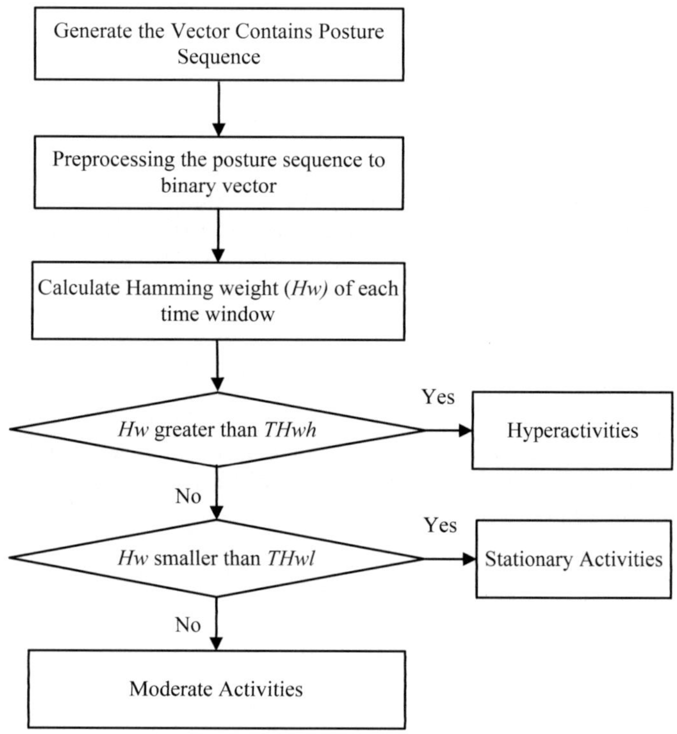

Figure 2: Algorithm of activity assessment.

The algorithm consists of the following three steps:

1. Posture sequence vector is generated. We detect the postures using the method described in Section 3.1, then we generate a vector containing postures represented as: $Pt = \{P1, P2, P3, P4, P5, P6, \ldots Pn\}$.
2. Sequence vector is transformed into binary vector representation. The complete posture sequence is transformed in terms of binary transition series as: $Ht = \{H1, H2, H3, H4, H5, H6, \ldots Hn\}$.
3. Decision making is executed. We calculate *hamming*

weight (Hw) of each frame, then wheelchair users' activity level is assessed using the Algorithm 1.

Based on preliminary tests performed in lab settings, a fixed time window of 1 minute is used to distinguish between different levels of activity. We performed experiments with time windows varying from 5s to 30s and we observed little changes of the activity levels. So we choose a longer time frame. Empirical tests showed little difference between 30s and 60s time windows, but 1 minute window can better capture peculiarities of hyperactivities.

One minute time frame contains 120 posture samples (remind that postures are recognized at $2Hz$ rate). We calculate the Hw of each frame. We defined two thresholds, $THwl$ and $THwh$, that are determined by the data we collected during our experiments. Using the two thresholds, we can determine if an activity belongs to stationary, moderate or hyperactivity.

Algorithm 1 Activity level assessment

```
Require: Ht (posture vector)
  if Hw > THwh then
    Return Hyperactivity
  else if Hw < THwl then
    Return Stationary Activity
  else
    Return Moderate Activity
  end if
```

3.3 System Design

The architecture of the proposed system is depicted in Figure 3.

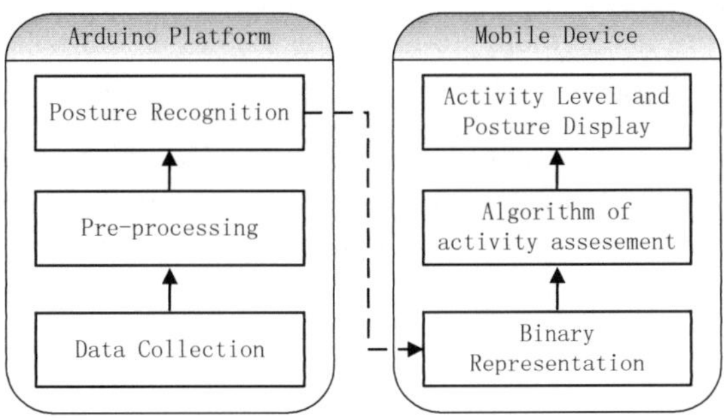

Figure 3: Architecture of the proposed system.

It is composed of two main parts:

- a wheelchair equipped with Arduino-based smart cushion to detect the postures,
- a mobile device (e.g. smartphone) to assess the activity level and give a friendly interface to interact with wheelchair users and to alert caregivers in case of abnormal states.

The data sensing module is equipped with pressure sensors produced by Interlink Electronics. As force is applied on the sensing areas, the resistance value of the pressure sensor will be correspondingly altered. As it is thin and flexible, it is suitable to be embedded into the chair textile or foam filling.

The data processing module is an Arduino DUE board. It features low energy consumption, high sampling rate and high processing speed, so it can be effectively used for sensor data acquisition and industrial automation.

The Arduino DUE has 12 analog inputs, allowing for a uniform distribution of sensors in the seat and the back of the cushion. The electrical diagram of the system is shown in Figure 4.

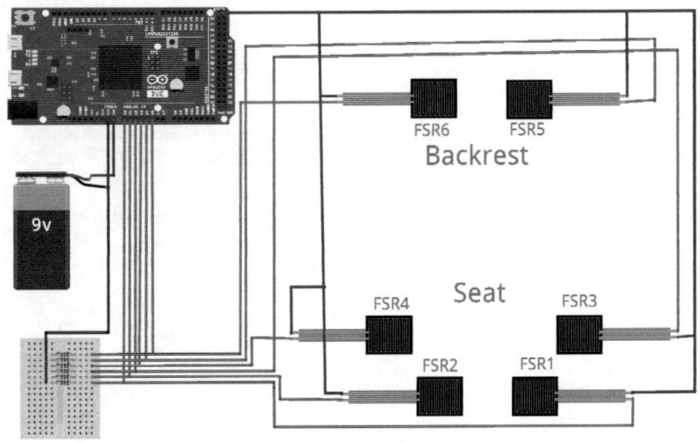

Figure 4: Circuit of the system.

Sensors data is collected and processed; then, posture recognition results are sent to the smartphone through wireless communication. We used Bluetooth technology as it is widely supported in the field of smart mobile devices.

4. EXPERIMENTS AND RESULTS

In this section, we describe the initial experimental testing of our system which aims at providing reminders - and alarms, when necessary - to users and caregivers. To maintain good health condition, long-term wheelchair users should avoid to keep the same posture for long time; conversely, hyperactivity on the wheelchair can be also the symptom of abnormal events that worth to be put to caregivers' attention.

4.1 Experiments

We recruited eight subjects that participated in this study: 5 males and 3 females (hereafter called S1 to S8), with age in the range of [22, 36] and BMI (Body Mass Index) in the range of [16, 34], in order to cover different body types such as thin, fit and fat. Experiments were conducted during two weeks. All the participants were informed of the purpose and procedure of the study and, after signing an informed consent, they filled a form including questions on gender, ethnicity, age, height, and weight.

During the experiment, they were free to choose the time period for the test session and they were asked to perform common activities on wheelchair among (1) Napping, (2) Reading a book, (3) Watching TV, (4) Working at a computer, (5) Having a conversation, (6) Doing physical exercise such as lifting a dumbbell. On average, experiment sessions lasted about 2 hours and each participant had to perform 6 sessions in the two weeks. All the experiment sessions have been video recorded so to manually label the samples of each performed activity with one of the three defined levels. It is worth noting that during the experiments we occasionally observed frequent posture transitions that, by inspecting the

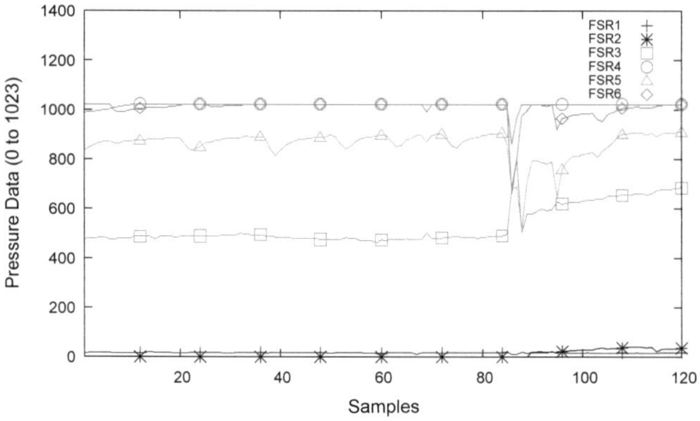

(a) Pressure sensor data of napping activity.

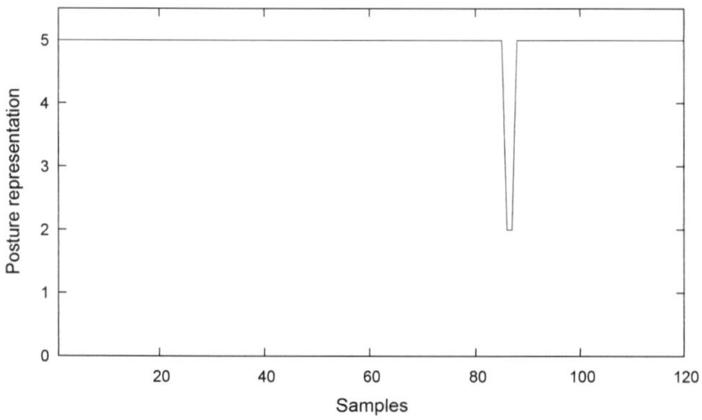

(b) Posture sequence of napping activity.

Figure 5: Data samples and posture sequence of napping activity.

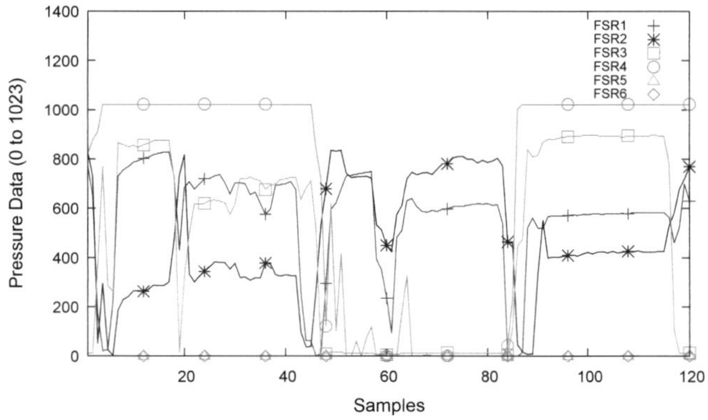

(a) Pressure sensor data during desk working.

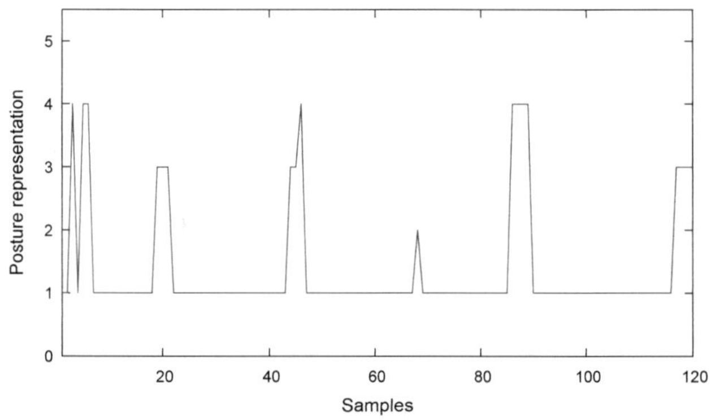

(b) Posture sequence during desk working.

Figure 6: Data samples and posture sequence during desk working.

video records, were found to be caused by short term excitement and discomfort (e.g. (i) S3 was watching a soccer match of the team he supports, (ii) S7 had a lively argument with another person, (iii) S8 was uncomfortable because not used to the provided wheelchair).

4.2 Results

To provide an exemplification, we show pressure sensor data and posture sequences corresponding to napping activity in Figure 5. Sensor data are obtained from each of the analog inputs of the Arduino DUE. For graphical clarity, we used 1, 2, 3, 4, 5 in the figures to represent Proper Sitting (PS), Lean Right (LR), Lean Left (LL), Lean Forward (LF) and Lean Backward (LB), respectively. As it can be noted in Figure 5, the pressure sensor data rarely changes and the posture only changes a little. The most common posture is LB (5) and occasionally changes to LR (2). By inspecting the video record, we found that the wheelchair user was napping slightly leaning against the right armrest. To provide another example, in Figure 6, we show plots corresponding to desk working (which belongs to moderate activity). As we can see, the most common posture is PS (1). In addition, in Figure 7 we show plots corresponding to a physical exercise activity (lifting the dumbbell with the left hand). As we can see, the most common postures are PS (1) and LL (3). Intuitively, when the wheelchair user is doing exercises, postures change more frequently.

With the data collected during the experiments (see Section 4.1) we generated a training set, then hamming weight of each one minute time window was calculated. Results are summarized in Table 2. The table shows that the napping activity has the lowest value while hyperactivities definitely lead to the highest hamming weight value.

As it can be noted in Table 2, there is a gap between two levels (e.g. max Hw value for stationary activity is 4 while min Hw value for moderate activity is 13). To address this issue, we propose to determine the $THwl$ and $THwh$ thresholds with the following formulas:

$$THwl = \frac{TH_{max}(Stationary) + TH_{min}(Moderate)}{2}$$

$$THwh = \frac{TH_{max}(Moderate) + TH_{min}(Hyperactivity)}{2}$$

Therefore, $THwl$ and $THwh$ are set as follows:

$$THwl = 8.5$$

$$THwh = 30$$

An initial performance evaluation has been carried out. In particular, we asked the eight participants to behave normally in their living space, without any restriction, for multiple sessions of 2 hours in which we also took video recordings. Collected data has been used to generate an independent test set.

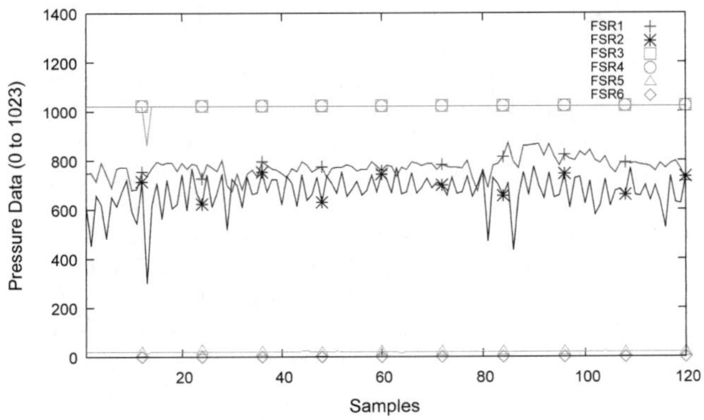

(a) Pressure sensor data during physical exercise.

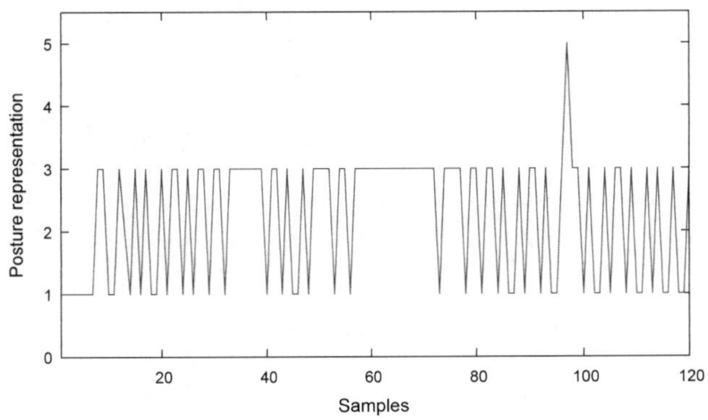

(b) Posture sequence during physical exercise.

Figure 7: Data samples and posture sequence during physical exercise (lift the dumbbell with left hand).

Table 2: Hamming weight of each activity level

Activity level	Min	Max
Stationary Activity	2	4
Moderate Activity	13	28
Hyperactivity	32	66

From these preliminary results, we obtained activity assessment precision of 100%, 96.6%, 93.7% for stationary, moderate, and hyperactivity, respectively. Specifically, we run the algorithm on the test set and we compared its output against our ground truth, which is the activity level labels that were manually annotated from the video recordings.

When wheelchair users are napping, or they are concentrated in reading or watching TV, they rarely change postures; we can indeed detect the stationary level very precisely. Sometimes, however, while the subjects e.g. watch TV (such as a football match) or have lively conversations, there might move the upper limb vigorously; in this case, even if we labeled the corresponding level as hyperactivity, our system has (erroneously) classified it as moderate. Conversely, in some cases, moderate activities have been recognized as stationary when they involve more upper limb movements rather than trunk or total body movements.

5. CONCLUSION

Stationary activity assessment of wheelchair users is an important factor in the evaluation of general health status and early prediction or prevention of severe pathologies such as pressure ulcers. In this paper, we proposed an efficient algorithm for fast and robust wheelchair users' activity level classification that is based on posture sequences analysis. It is suitable for monitoring the wheelchair users anywhere, anytime in mobility as it can be easily implemented with low-cost embedded devices.

Future works will be devoted to improve our Wheelchair Assist System so to provide remote real-time monitoring and 24/7 data access of mobility-impaired individuals to the caregivers. We are also investigating the integration of physiological sensor data [19, 10] to get more comprehensive health information. Furthermore, we will include the monitoring of upper limb movements using inertial wearable sensors to provide total body activity analysis and of waist movements to provide a quantitative metric of activity level. Finally, we plan to improve the accuracy of the method, specifically to recognize abnormal hyperactivities for the detection of user physical and mental discomfort.

6. ACKNOWLEDGMENTS

The research is financially supported by China-Italy S&T Cooperation project "Smart Personal Mobility Systems for Human Disabilities in Future Smart Cities" (China-side Project ID: 2015DFG12210, Italy-side Project ID CN13MO7).

7. REFERENCES

[1] D. E. Arias, E. J. Pino, P. Aqueveque, and D. W. Curtis. Unobtrusive support system for prevention of dangerous health conditions in wheelchair users. *Mobile Information Systems*, 2016:1–14, 2016.

[2] B. Arnrich, C. Setz, R. La Marca, G. Tröster, and U. Ehlert. What does your chair know about your stress level? *IEEE Transactions on Information Technology in Biomedicine*, 14(2):207–214, 2010.

[3] J. Bao, W. Li, J. Li, Y. Ge, and C. Bao. Sitting Posture Recognition based on data fusion on pressure cushion. *TELKOMNIKA Indonesian Journal of Electrical Engineering*, 11:1769–1775, 2013.

[4] R. Barba, Á. P. d. Madrid, and J. G. Boticario. Development of an inexpensive sensor network for recognition of sitting posture. *International Journal of Distributed Sensor Networks*, 2015:161, 2015.

[5] M. Benocci, E. Farella, and L. Benini. A context-aware smart seat. In *2011 4th IEEE International Workshop on Advances in Sensors and Interfaces (IWASI)*, pages 104–109, 2011.

[6] J. Cheng, B. Zhou, M. Sundholm, and P. Lukowicz. Smart chair: What can simple pressure sensors under the chairs legs tell us about user activity. In *UBICOMM13: The Seventh International Conference on Mobile Ubiquitous Computing, Systems, Services and Technologies*, pages 81–84, 2013.

[7] M. Chica, P. Campoy, M. A. Pérez, T. Rodríguez, R. Rodríguez, and Ó. Valdemoros. Real-time recognition of patient intentions from sequences of pressure maps using artificial neural networks. *Computers in biology and medicine*, 42(4):364–375, 2012.

[8] F. Cicirelli, G. Fortino, A. Giordano, A. Guerrieri, G. Spezzano, and A. Vinci. On the design of smart homes: A framework for activity recognition in home environment. *Journal of medical systems*, 40(9):200, 2016.

[9] F. Fard, S. Moghimi, and R. Lotfi. Evaluating Pressure Ulcer Development in Wheelchair-Bound Population Using Sitting Posture Identification. *Engineering*, 5:132–136, 2013.

[10] G. Fortino and V. Giampa. Ppg-based methods for non invasive and continuous blood pressure measurement: an overview and development issues in body sensor networks. In *IEEE International Workshop on Medical Measurements and Applications Proceedings (MeMeA)*, pages 10–13, 2010.

[11] G. Fortino, R. Giannantonio, R. Gravina, P. Kuryloski, and R. Jafari. Enabling Effective Programming and Flexible Management of Efficient Body Sensor Network Applications. *IEEE Trans. on Human-Machine Systems*, 43(1):115–133, 2013.

[12] G. Fortino, R. Gravina, W. Li, and C. Ma. Using Cloud-assisted Body Area Networks to Track People Physical Activity in Mobility. In *Proc. of the 10th Int. Conf. on Body Area Networks*, pages 85–91, 2015.

[13] G. Fortino, A. Guerrieri, F. Bellifemine, and R. Giannantonio. Platform-independent development of collaborative wireless body sensor network applications: Spine2. In *IEEE International Conference on Systems, Man and Cybernetics, SMC 2009*, pages 3144–3150, 2009.

[14] T. Fu and A. Macleod. Intellichair: An approach for activity detection and prediction via posture analysis. In *International Conference on Intelligent Environments*, pages 211–213. IEEE, 2014.

[15] S. Furugori, N. Yoshizawa, C. Iname, and Y. Miura. Measurement of driver's fatigue based on driver's postural change. In *SICE Annual Conference*, pages 264–269, 2003.

[16] K. Furusawa, F. Tajima, Y. Umezu, M. Ueta, M. Ide, T. Mizushima, and H. Ogata. Activation of natural killer cell function in recreational athletes with paraplegia during a wheelchair half-marathon race. *Archives of physical medicine and rehabilitation*, 84(5):706–711, 2003.

[17] R. Ganea, A. Paraschiv-lonescu, and K. Aminian. Detection and classification of postural transitions in real-world conditions. *IEEE Transactions on Neural Systems and Rehabilitation Engineering*, 20(5):688–696, 2012.

[18] R. Gravina, P. Alinia, H. Ghasemzadeh, and G. Fortino. Multi-sensor fusion in body sensor networks: State-of-the-art and research challenges. *Information Fusion*, 35:68–80, 2017.

[19] R. Gravina and G. Fortino. Automatic methods for the detection of accelerative cardiac defense response. *IEEE Transactions on Affective Computing*, 7(3):286–298, 2016.

[20] R. Gravina, C. Ma, P. Pace, G. Aloi, W. Russo, W. Li, and G. Fortino. Cloud-based activity-aaservice cyberphysical framework for human activity monitoring in mobility. *Future Generation Computer Systems*, Available online 22 September 2016, DOI: 10.1016/j.future.2016.09.006.

[21] K. Kamiya, M. Kudo, H. Nonaka, and J. Toyama. Sitting posture analysis by pressure sensors. In *Proc. of the 19th Int. Conf. on Pattern Recognition (ICPR2008)*, pages 1–4, 2008.

[22] R. Kumar, A. Bayliff, D. De, A. Evans, S. K. Das, and M. Makos. Care-chair: Sedentary activities and behavior assessment with smart sensing on chair backrest. In *2016 IEEE International Conference on Smart Computing*, pages 1–8. IEEE, 2016.

[23] C. Ma, W. Li, J. Cao, S. Wang, and L. Wu. A fatigue detect system based on activity recognition. In *International Conference on Internet and Distributed Computing Systems*, pages 303–311. Springer, 2014.

[24] C. Ma, W. Li, R. Gravina, and G. Fortino. Activity recognition and monitoring for smart wheelchair users. In *Proceedings of the 2016 IEEE Computer Supported Cooperative Work in Design*, pages 664–669, 2016.

[25] C. Ma, W. Li, R. Gravina, and G. Fortino. Cloud-based wheelchair assist system for mobility impaired individuals. In *Proc. of the 9th Int. Conf. on Internet and Distributed Computing Systems*, pages 107–118, 2016.

[26] L. Martins, R. Lucena, J. Belo, R. Almeida, C. Quaresma, A. Jesus, and P. Vieira. Intelligent chair sensor–classification and correction of sitting posture. In *XIII Mediterranean Conference on Medical and Biological Engineering and Computing*, pages 1489–1492. Springer, 2014.

[27] J. Meyer, B. Arnrich, J. Schumm, and G. Troster. Design and modeling of a textile pressure sensor for sitting posture classification. *IEEE Sensors Journal*, 10(8):1391–1398, 2010.

[28] S. Min. System for monitoring sitting posture in real-time using pressure sensors, 2016. US Patent 20,160,113,583.

[29] B. Mutlu, A. Krause, J. Forlizzi, C. Guestrin, and J. Hodgins. Robust, low-cost, non-intrusive sensing and recognition of seated postures. In *Proceedings of the 20th annual ACM symposium on User interface software and technology*, pages 149–158. ACM, 2007.

[30] T. Patil and S. Sherekar. Performance analysis of naive bayes and j48 classification algorithm for data classification. *International Journal of Computer Science and Applications*, 6(2):256–261, 2013.

[31] V. Sklyarov and I. Skliarova. Digital hamming weight and distance analyzers for binary vectors and matrices. *International Journal of Innovative Computing, Information and Control*, 9(12):4825–4849, 2013.

[32] H. Z. Tan, L. A. Slivovsky, and A. Pentland. A sensing chair using pressure distribution sensors. *IEEE/ASME Transactions On Mechatronics*, 6(3):261–268, 2001.

[33] Y. Tanimoto, K. Nanba, K. Furusawa, H. Yamamoto, A. Tokuhiro, and H. Ukida. Measurement of wheelchair users' activity level for developing a small device. In *2015 IEEE International Instrumentation and Measurement Technology Conference (I2MTC) Proceedings*, pages 1348–1352. IEEE, 2015.

[34] W. Xu, M. Huang, N. Amini, L. He, and M. Sarrafzadeh. eCushion: A Textile Pressure Sensor Array Design and Calibration for Sitting Posture Analysis. *IEEE Sensors Journal*, 13:3926–3934, 2013.

Study of oxide coated Mg-based bio-substrate for therapeutic purpose

Éva Fazakas
Bay Zoltán Nonprofit Ltd.
for Applied Research
Budapest, Hungary
+36-30-4150004
eva.fazakas@bayzoltan.hu

Ildiko Peter
Department of Applied
Science and Technology
Politecnico di Torino - Italy
+39 011 090 4670
ildiko.peter@polito.it

ABSTRACT

Porous modified Mg foam surface with functional properties is proposed as a platform for local drug release at the target. In particular, MgO coatings were prepared on the magnesium foams surfaces by an anodic electrodeposition process in concentrated 10M KOH solution followed by heat treatment in air. The corrosion behavior of the MgO-coated samples was evaluated by electrochemical measurements and immersion tests in 0.9 % NaCl solution. The experimental results show that the MgO-coated Mg foams show higher stability and lower corrosion rate, and thus enabled to improve the corrosion resistance, whereas the bare Mg foams suffered from severely localized corrosion attack.

CCS Concepts

• Applied computing → Physical sciences and engineering → Chemistry• Information systems → Information retrieval, interfaces and storage → Specialized information retrieval→ Chemical and biochemical retrieval.

Keywords

Metallic bio-materials, Mg-based implants, surface modification, human body

1. INTRODUCTION

Over the past few decades, a remarkable progress in the development of biomaterials occurred [1]-[4]. Medical implantation offers successfully solutions to unhealthy or damaged bones. Metallic biomaterials, i.e. stainless steel, Ti and its alloys, Co-based alloys have been widely used for such purpose. Because of their excellent combination of high mechanical strength and fracture toughness, good corrosion resistance their use offers some advantages over ceramics or polymeric materials. In case of permanent implants, some obstacles are present. Firstly, they cause stress shielding deriving by a different mechanical mismatch between their elastic modulus (above 100 GPa) and the adjacent bone (under 50 GPa). In such circumstances, the metallic implant-bone interface deteriorates and the regular bone healing and the following re-formation of healthy tissues can be compromised. On the other hand, even permanent biometals have to be removed from the body after a definite period through one more clinical intervention, causing less freedom and comfort for human being.

Over the years, biodegradable implants have extensively attracted the attention and a great progress in their design route and technology have been arises. Mg and its alloys, as biodegradable implants, can degrade naturally in the biological surroundings through corrosion and they have significant benefits over Fe-based or Zn-based ones. Mg alloy foams are definitely expected to be particularly advantageous due to low density of their metal matrix, which is approximately two thirds that of aluminum and due to their good mechanical properties. Mg alloys possess a density of about 1.7–2.0 g cm^{-3} that is close to that of natural bones (1.8–2.1 g cm^{-3}), the compressive strength and tensile strength are much higher than those of biodegradable polymers. Compared to Ti alloys (110–117 GPa), stainless steels (189–205 GPa), and Co-Cr alloys (230 GPa), the elastic modulus of Mg alloys (41–45 GPa) is the most closest one to that of natural bones. According to [4], Mg implants stimulate the formation of new bone. Mg^{2+} is the fourth most abundant cation in the human body and half of the total physical Mg is present in the bone tissue; additionally, it is key element in many human metabolic reactions, it is a cofactor in many enzymes and a crucial element of the ribosomal machinery that translates the genetic information encoded by mRNA into polypeptide structures [2]–[8]. Early clinical investigations and recent in vivo and in vitro studies have evidenced that Mg-based implants have good biocompatibility [9]–[11] and can encourage the development of a hard callous at fracture sites [9], [11].

However, Mg and its alloys are predisposed to corrosion: in particular in wet environment, principally related to the low electrode potential exhibited by Mg (-2.37 V) and it is sacrificial to all other engineering metals. Therefore, the principal weakness of their limited use is related to their low corrosion resistance. Two key factors contribute to the poor corrosion resistance of Mg alloys: (i) the presence of secondary phases or impurities and (ii) the formation of quasi-passive hydroxide layer on their surface, which is not as stable as those developed on Al or on stainless steel.

Corrosion is a surface effect, and the environment in which the material is situated has an important role in determining the level to which the corrosion occurs. In the presence of any chlorides with concentrations above 30 mmol/l, the developed hydroxide will evolve toward the production of magnesium chloride ($MgCl_2$) rather than magnesium hydroxide [12]. It was found that $Mg(OH)_2$ has protective action on the implant at pH>11.5, but the corrosion is accelerated when pH< 11.5. The pH of the human body fluid is about 7.4 or less, then the protective film dissolves and the surface of the metallic implant is unprotected and exposed always to the hazardous effect of Cl^- ions. When the environment is a biological fluid, with chloride concentrations of about 150 mmol/l, generally, surface pitting corrosion takes place [13]. Consequently, the Mg-based implants lose the basic mechanical integrity earlier than the necessary time for a fully reestablishment of the tissue.

For these reasons, over the years, many efforts have been dedicated to control the corrosion rate of Mg and Mg-based alloys and to improve their corrosion resistance. There are several ways to do this: (i) via alloying [5], [14], (ii) employing of composites [15], [13] or (iii) adopting an adequate surface treatment, i.e. protective coating on Mg and Mg-based alloys. [16], [17]. When alloying procedures have been adopted, special attention has to be observed in order to avoid elements which are harmful for the body, i.e. neurons [18], osteoblasts [19] or can be associated to Alzheimer disease [16]. Surface modification of Mg and Mg-based alloys constitutes an interesting task, because the corrosion rate is low in the early stage of the corrosion and thanks to the presence of the modified surface layer, the possibility to return to the normal value has been created. Such a degradation pattern is appropriate because the loss of strength of the implant would reflect the strengthening of the therapeutic [20].

In this research paper, MgO coating is proposed on Mg foams surface by a costless electrodeposition method. The results pointed out that the coated Mg foams show higher stability and lower corrosion rate, compared to the bare Mg foams, which suffer from severely localized corrosion attack, and also when compared to Mg-based alloys. Additionally, the porous surface can constitute a useful bio-network able to host some medicine allowing their local pre-programmed release at the target, promoting the repair of the bone and of the neighboring tissues.

2. EXPERIMENTAL

Samples of 10mm×10mm×10mm were cut from Mg metal or Mg metal foam (Mg, Mg-5% foam, Mg-10% foam, Mg-20% foam). The samples were used as working electrodes (anode), while a Pt plate was used as the counter electrode (cathode). Mg foam samples were prepared by melt foaming process. Prior to the electrochemical experiments, the samples were polished with alumina powder of 0.05 mm size, rinsed with distilled water, cleaned in ethanol in an ultrasonic bath and dried under an air pressure stream. Electrochemical measurements were performed on Zahner IM6 electrochemical workstation with a three-electrode system comprising the as-cleaned magnesium alloy slice as working electrode with an exposed geometric area of $6cm^2$, a platinum wire as auxiliary electrode, and a saturated calomel electrode (SCE) as reference electrode.

The MgO coatings on Mg samples were produced by anodic electrodeposition in 10 M KOH alkaline solution at constant potential of 1.0V (SCE) for 2 h, and subsequent annealing treatment at 450 °C for 8 h in air. All treated samples are ultrasonically cleaned in deionized water and dried before further characterization.

In order to evaluate the corrosion protection behaviors, electrochemical measurements and immersion tests were carried out in a 0.9 % NaCl isotonic solution. Immersion tests were carried out in accordance with ASTMG31-72 [9] (the ratio of surface area to solution volume was 100 ml). The pH value of the solution was recorded during the immersion tests (Thermo Fisher Scientific pH meter, Orion). Samples were removed after 1 days of immersion, rinsed with distilled water and dried at room temperature. Potentiodynamic polarization curves were acquired at a scanning rate of 10 mV/s in 100 ml 0.9% NaCl isotonic solution. For the microstructural characterization of the samples Keyence VH-Z250R optical microscope was used.

3. RESULTS AND DISCUSSION

Prior to anodic electrodeposition, a linear potential sweep was carried out to check the anodic oxidation process of magnesium alloy in an alkaline solution. Fig. 1 shows the anodic polarization curve of the Mg and Mg-foams electrodes in 10 M KOH solution at a scan rate of 10 mV s−1. As could be observed, the anodic oxidation curve in 10M KOH solution shows that the Mg foams experienced four processes, which are active dissolution, passivation, secondary oxidation and transpassive processes, which is in good agreement with [8]. The first step was ascribed to the anodic dissolution of magnesium leading to the formation of Mg^{2+} [9[, [10]:

$$Mg \rightarrow Mg^{2+} + 2e^-$$

Therefore, when the potential applied was more positive than the open circuit potential (Eocp), the Mg and Mg foams behaved active dissolution and the anodic oxidation product of magnesium is Mg^{2+}. When the concentration of Mg^{2+} on the electrode surface reached its saturation, deposited $Mg(OH)_2$ was formed on the electrode surface, which thickened with anodization time and progressively hindered the oxidation rate, and thus magnesium became passivated. Accordingly, the reaction for the anodic oxidation of magnesium in the passive region was the direct oxidation of magnesium to magnesium hydroxide, in which the hydroxyl passed through the film from solution to the surface of magnesium:

$$Mg + 2OH^- \rightarrow Mg(OH)_2 + 2e^-$$

The oxidation of magnesium in the secondary oxidation region is confirmed to form MgO [21].

$$Mg + H_2O \rightarrow MgO + 2H^+ + 2e^-$$

The trans-passive process was ascribed to oxygen evolution, which was confirmed by the observation of a large amount of bubbles on the Mg electrode surface. Consequently, when potential was controlled at oxidation region in 10M KOH solution for anodic oxidation of Mg and Mg foams, the formation of MgO coating was anticipated, on the other hand when the potential was controlled in passivation region, $Mg(OH)_2$ coating was produced, which could be converted into MgO by following calcination treatment in air at 450 °C, 8h [9], [21]. The corrosion resistance of the oxidized samples (MgO coating modified Mg and Mg foams) was determined in 0.9 % NaCl isotonic solution using potentiodynamic polarization tests as shown in Fig. 1. The corrosion potential (E_{corr}) and corrosion current density (j_{corr}) were derived directly from the polarization curves by Tafel region extrapolation (Tab. 1). In general, the cathodic polarization curve is attributed to hydrogen evolution reaction, due to the reduction of water, while the anodic polarization curve is associated with the dissolution of Mg, leading to the formation of Mg^{2+} [21], [22-24].

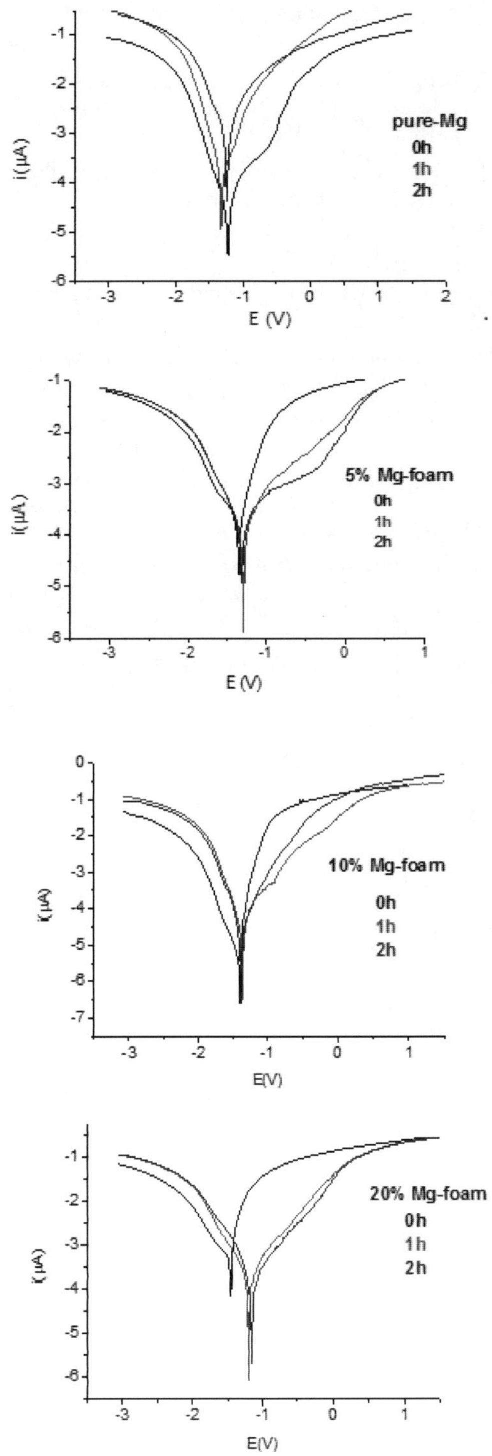

Figure 1. Potenciodynamic polarization curves of the pure Mg, 5% Mg-foam, 10% Mg-foam ad 20% Mg-foam samples in 0.9% NaCl solution.

Analysis of the polarization curves pointed out that the MgO-coated 20% Mg foam reveal weaker corrosion susceptibility than MgO-coated pure Mg, 5% Mg foam and 10% Mg foams and also compared to Mg based alloys too [20].

Table. 1: Corrosion parameters of pure-Mg and Mg foams modified by MgO coatings in 0.9% NaCl solution.

Samples	time (h)	E_{corr} (V)	j_{corr} ($\mu A/cm^2$)
pure-Mg	0	-1.24	1.62
	1	-1.16	1.19
	2	-1.32	1.15
5% Mg-foam	0	-1.63	1.34
	1	-1.22	1.67
	2	-1.24	1.76
10% Mg-foam	0	-1.66	1.54
	1	-1.36	1.51
	2	-1.38	1.27
20% Mg-foam	0	-1.8	1.09
	1	-1.03	1.33
	2	-1.1	1.4

Moreover, the pure-Mg with MgO coatings exhibits a corrosion potential at -1.24 V(SCE), the 20% Mg foam sample with MgO coatings shows a corrosion potential at -1.8 V(SCE), which is negatively shifted about 560 mV(SCE). Additionally, in the case of 20% Mg foam the corrosion potential after 2h was changed significantly, while in the case of pure-Mg almost the same demonstrating once again the higher corrosion tendency of this samples compared to the coated ones. Based on the polarization test results one can claim that MgO coating film could provide an adequate protection to the magnesium alloys in 0.9% NaCl corrosive mediums. Immersion behavior of MgO-coated Mg and Mg foams in 0.9% NaCl shows the variation of the pH value from 8.8 to 10.6 before and after immersion test respectively. When the bare pure-Mg and Mg foams substrate is immersed in NaCl solution, loose and porous $Mg(OH)_2$ formed quickly on samples surface. With increasing anodic potential during polarization, corrosive (Cl-) would be rapidly transferred trough the outer porous layer and reached the inner Mg matrix, which then resulted increasing polarization current. At the same time, thy chloride ions can transform $Mg(OH)_2$ to more soluble $MgCl_2$. Therefore, the pure-Mg showed rapid corrosion rate than the 20% Mg foam. In the case of 20% Mg foam the precipitation product, as ion, was less than the pure-Mg. Fig. 2 reports the surface morphology of the MgO coated samples before and after immersion test in 0.9% NaCl. The evolution of the microstructure confirm the highest corrosion tendency of the pure and MgO coated Mg sample (Fig.2a, b) compared to the MgO coated foam samples (Fig.2c-d).

). The surface, which does not present a compact protective oxide layer will undergo quickly to a localized corrosion attack.

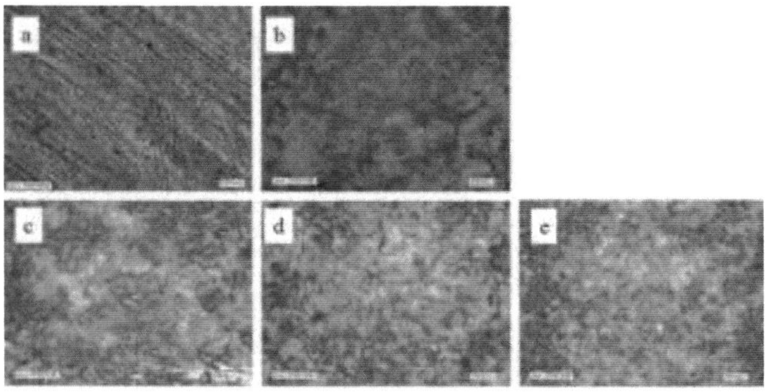

Figure 2. Surface morphology of the MgO coated samples: a) pure-Mg before and (b), (c), (d) after immersion test in 0.9% NaCl solution of 5% Mg-foam, 10% Mg-foam ad 20% Mg-foam respectively.

4. CONCLUSIONS

In this paper, MgO coatings were prepared on pure magnesium and magnesium foams surfaces by a low cost anodic electrodeposition process. The deposition was carried out in concentrated 10M KOH solution followed by heat treatment in air. The corrosion behavior of the MgO-coated samples was evaluated by electrochemical measurements and immersion tests in 0.9 % NaCl solution. The research carried out revealed that the MgO-coated Mg foams present higher stability and lower corrosion rate, leading to improve the corrosion resistance of such samples, while the un-modified Mg foams suffered from harshly localized corrosion attack. Additionally, the oxide layer protected Mg foam samples can be used as loading system for encapsulation of some medicine, which can be locally released contributing to the healing of the bone and eventually of the adjacent tissues.

5. REFERENCES

[1] M.P. Staiger, A.M. Pietaka, J. Huadmaia, G. Dias, Magnesium and its alloys as orthopedic biomaterials: a review, Biomaterials 27 (2006) 1728.

[2] J.H. Nordlien, S. Ono, N. Masuko, K. Nisancioglu, A TEM investigation of naturally formed oxide films on pure magnesium, Corros. Sci. 39 (1997) 1397.

[3] F. Stippich, E. Vera, G.K. Wolf, G. Berg, Chr. Friedrich, Enhanced corrosion protection of magnesium oxide coatings on magnesium deposited by ion beam-assisted evaporation, Surf. Coat. Technol. 103–104 (1998) 29–35.

[4] I. Peter, M. Rosso, "Study of Ti-enriched CoCrMo alloy for dental application", IEEE Access, The Journal for rapid open access publishing, Vol.3, 2015, pp. 73-80, doi 0.1109/ACCESS.2015.2398312.

[5] Frank Witte, Jens Fischer, Jens Nellesen, Horst-Artur Crostack, Volker Kaese, Alexander Pisch, Felix Beckmann, Henning Windhagen, In vitro and in vivo corrosion measurements of magnesium alloys Biomaterials 27 (2006) 1013–1018 doi:10.1016/j.biomaterials.2005.07.037

[6] N.-C. Quach, P.J. Uggowitzer, P. Schmutz, Corrosion behaviour of an Mg–Y–RE alloy used in biomedical applications studied by electrochemical techniques, C.R. Chimie 11 (2008) 1043–1054.

[7] X.N. Gu, W. Zheng, Y. Cheng, Y.F. Zheng, A study on alkaline heat-treated Mg– Ca alloy for the control of the biocorrosion rate, Acta Biomater. 5 (2009) 2790.

[8] G.L. Song, Control of biodegradation of biocompatable magnesium alloys, Corros. Sci. 49 (2007) 1696–1701.

[9] ASTM-G31-72: standard practice for laboratory immersion corrosion testing of metals. In: Annual book of ASTM standards[S], American Society for Testing and Materials, Philadelphia, PA, 2004.

[10] K. Latha, W.Z. Li, H.V. Charles, M.L. Roger, D.Z. Wang, Synthesis characterization and optical properties of Mg(OH)2 micro-/nanostructure and its conversion to MgO, Ceram. Int. 35 (2009) 3355–3364.

[11] R. Hahn, J.G. Brunner, J. Kunze, P. Schmuki, S. Virtanen, A novel approach for the formation of Mg(OH)2/MgO nanowhiskers on magnesium: Rapid anodization in chloride containing solutions, Electrochem. Commun. 10(2008) 288–292.

[12] Saw BA. Corrosion Resistance of Magnesium Alloys. ASM Handbook. 2003;13

[13] Song G. Control of Biodegradation and Biocompatible Magnesium Alloys. Corrosion Science. 2007;49:1696–1701

[14] F.Witte, V.Kaese, H. Haferkamp et al., "In vivo corrosion of four magnesium alloys and the associated bone response," Biomaterials, vol. 26, no. 17, pp. 3557–3563, 2005.

[15] F. Witte, F. Feyerabend, P. Maier et al., "Biodegradable magnesium-hydroxyapatite metal matrix composites," Biomaterials, vol. 28, no. 13, pp. 2163–2174, 2007

[16] A. Shypylenko, A.V. Pshyk, B. Grześkowiak, K. Medjanik, B. Peplinska, K. Oyoshi, A. Pogrebnjak, S. Jurga, E. Coy Effect of ion implantation on the physical and mechanical properties of Ti-Si-N multifunctional coatings for biomedical applications Materials & Design, Volume 110, 15 November 2016, Pages 821-829 http://dx.doi.org/10.1016/j.matdes.2016.08.050

[17] Ruben Kotoka, Nana Kwame Yamoah, Kwadwo Mensah-Darkwa, Timothy Moses, Dhananjay Kumar Electrochemical corrosion behavior of silver doped tricalcium phosphate coatings on magnesium for biomedical Surface and Coatings Technology, Volume 292, 25 April 2016, Pages 99-109 http://dx.doi.org/10.1016/j.surfcoat.2016.03.017

[18] S. S. A. El-Rahman, "Neuropathology of aluminum toxicity in rats (glutamate and GABA impairment)," Pharmacological Research, vol. 47, no. 3, pp. 189–194, 2003.

[19] C.H. Ku, D. P. Pioletti, M. Browne, and P. J. Gregson, "Effect of different Ti-6Al-4V surface treatments on osteoblasts behaviour," Biomaterials, vol. 23, no. 6, pp. 1447–1454, 2002.

[20] W S Pietrzak, D Sarver, M Verstynen Bioresorbable implants--practical considerations, Bone 1996 Jul;19(1 Suppl):109S-119S

[21] W.C. Jian, W.G. Xing, H.F. Peng, M.P. Li, J.D. Wen, Effect of heat treatment oncorrosion and electrochemical behavior of Mg-3Nd–0.2Zn–0.4Zr (wt%) alloy, Electrochim. Acta 52 (2007) 3160–3167.

[22] Zhiming Shi, Ming Liu, Andrej Atrens Measurement of the corrosion rate of magnesium alloys using Tafel extrapolation Corrosion Science 52 (2010) 579–588 doi:10.1016/j.corsci.2009.10.016

[23] V. Loscrì, A.M. Vegni, and G. Fortino, "On the Interaction between a Nanoparticulate System and the Human Body in Body Area Nanonetworks," Micromachines 2015, 6(9), 1213-1235; doi: 10.3390/mi6091213
[24] V. Loscrì, and A.M. Vegni, "On the Affection of the Human Immune System on a Nanoparticulate Nanomedicine System" in Proc. of 9th Intl. Conf. on Body Area Networks (BODYNETS 2014), September 29-October 1, 2014 London, Great Britain

Performance Analysis of IEEE 802.15.6 MAC Protocol in WBAN with Energy Harvesting Nodes

Fan Yun
cloudfan@mail.ustc.edu.cn

Bin Liu
flowice@ustc.edu.cn

Lei Zou
zoulei@mail.ustc.edu.cn

Key Laboratory of Electromagnetic Space Information, Chinese Academy of Sciences
School of Information Science and Technology
University of Science and Technology of China

Chang Wen Chen
Dept. of Computer Science & Engineering,
State University of New York,
University at Buffalo,
chencw@buffalo.edu

ABSTRACT

Wireless Body Area Network (WBAN) have been widely used in many fields. With the development of energy harvesting technologies, applying energy harvesting (EH) nodes to WBAN becomes more practical. In this paper, a Discrete-Time Markov Chain (DTMC) model is built to analyze the IEEE 802.15.6 Medium Access Control (MAC) protocol under saturation condition in the WBAN with energy harvesting devices. The long term performance including throughput and energy consumption is then derived based on the statistical characteristics of the analytical model. The simulation results demonstrate the accuracy of the analytical model. A conclusion has been drawn from the results that a better energy harvesting state will make the system perform better, and the influence of the energy harvesting state will be different for different priority nodes.

CCS Concepts

•**Networks** → **Network performance analysis;** *Network performance modeling;* Network simulations;

Keywords

IEEE 802.15.6; Energy Harvesting; Markov Chain; MAC Protocol; Wireless Body Area Network

1. INTRODUCTION

With the development of the emerging Wireless Body Area Network (WBAN) technology, a solid foundation has been laid for pervasive healthcare monitoring system. W-BAN has drawn increased attentions from healthcare community and engineering industry, due to its ability to improve health care efficiency and service quality of Electronic Health (eHealth) [7]. The WBAN usually contains one coordinator and several power-constraint sensor nodes in, on, or around human body, and physiological signals are collected by the sensor nodes and then transmitted to the coordinator for further analysis and observation [8]. However, the battery capacity of these sensor nodes is very limited, even replacing batteries periodically is not always available.

Fortunately, energy harvesting technology, which exploits supercapacitors to collect energy from ambient sources, such as electromagnetic source, solar source [11], has become an essential technology for low-power WBAN to prolong the system lifetime. Recently, energy harvesting technology has been adopted in many healthcare applications, especially for those where battery replacement is difficult or even impossible. Although energy from harvesting nodes is limited and stochastic, energy harvesting network can still work continuously via advanced technologies [6].

IEEE 802.15.6 task group (TG6) has published the IEEE 802.15.6 standard [1] to support the highly reliable and low-power wireless communication in WBAN. Quality of Service (QoS), extremely low power and high data rate are the main aims of IEEE 802.15.6 standard, and the MAC protocol is the key section of the standard. To better analyze the performance of IEEE 802.15.6 MAC protocol, an analytical Markov Chain model has been constructed by many researchers to model the process of CSMA/CA-based MAC protocol as the state transition. Analyses under saturated condition, i.e., always having data to send, and unsaturated condition in an ideal channel have been carried out in [10] and [4], respectively. It was shown in [10] that as the length of payload increases, the reliability of a node decreases, while the throughput increases. As the number of nodes in the network increases, the energy efficiency and throughput tends to decrease [4]. The different access phase employed on system degrades the throughput performance of IEEE 802.15.6 network under unsaturated condition in ideal channels [5]. However, none of the above analyses involved energy harvesting technologies. In [12], an analytical model for IEEE 802.11 network with energy harvesting devices was proposed, but the analysis for IEEE 802.11 standard cannot be directly applied to IEEE 802.15.6 standard due to the difference in MAC protocol design.

In this paper, we propose a Markov Chain analytical model for IEEE 802.15.6 MAC protocol in the WBAN with energy harvesting nodes. As the average energy harvesting rate is usually very small such that the harvested energy is not enough for the nodes with common data arrival rate to transmit their data in real time, here we assume the nodes

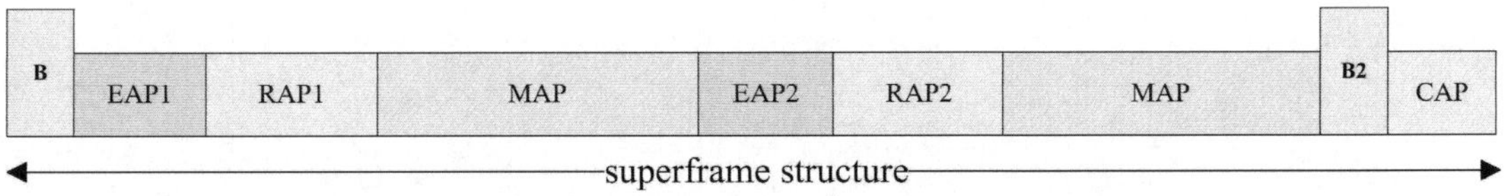

Figure 1 Structure of superframe for beacon mode [1].

in the WBAN are under saturation condition, i.e., the nodes always have data to send. Our contributions can be summarized as follows: 1) A four-dimensional DTMC model is built to analyze the system performance. Both MAC property and energy harvesting property are involved in the model. From what we know, it is the first time to build the analytical model for IEEE 802.15.6 MAC protocol in the WBAN with energy harvesting devices. 2) The long term performance including throughput and energy consumption is derived based on the statistical characteristics of the analytical model.

The rest of the paper is organized as follows. In Section 2, we give a brief introduction of IEEE 802.15.6 Standard, and present the MAC specification. The analytical models including energy harvesting model and Markov Chain model are described in Section 3. Numerical results are presented in section 4. Conclusions are drawn in Section 5.

Table 1 UP and Contention Windows (CW) of data [1].

UP	Traffic designation	CW
0	Background (BK)	[16,64]
1	Best effort (BE)	[16,32]
2	Excellent effort (EE)	[8,32]
3	Video (VI)	[8,16]
4	Voice (VO)	[4,16]
5	Medical data and network control	[4,8]
6	High-priority medical data and network control	[2,8]
7	Emergency and medical implant event report	[1,4]

2. IEEE 802.15.6 STANDARD

IEEE 802.15.6 Standard specifies short-range (human body range) wireless communications in WBAN [1]. To provide diverse service for various data, especially for emergency data, the standard defines different User Priorities (UPs) to ensure the QoS of data transmission in the proximity of human body.

2.1 An overview of IEEE 802.15.6 MAC protocol

IEEE 802.15.6 specifies three operation modes in MAC protocol and beacon mode with superframes is generally used. In the mode, the transmission period in WBAN is divided into multiple equal-length superframes starting with a beacon frame. Each superframe is comprised of seven phases which are Exclusive Access Phase 1 (EAP1), Random Access Phase 1 (RAP1), Managed Access Phase (MAP), Exclusive Access Phase 2 (EAP2), Random Access Phase 2 (RAP2), Managed Access Phase (MAP), and Contention Access Phase (CAP) [1]. Structure of the superframe is illustrated in Figure. 1. EAP can only be accessed by highest priority exclusively. If the length of CAP is greater than zero, B2 frame should be transmitted firstly as a flag after MAP. In addition, resources are usually allocated through polling mechanism in MAP. And nodes in EAP, RAP or CAP access the channel by contention. Contention mechanism in these access phases is either CSMA/CA or slotted ALOHA. In this paper, we focus on the performance analysis of CSMA/CA mechanism in IEEE 802.15.6 Standard. Thus, our analysis is based on beacon mode with superframes in which random access phase exists.

2.1.1 CSMA/CA mechanism

IEEE 802.15.6 Standard defines eight User Priorities (UPs) according to traffic designation, as shown in Table 1. Nodes transmit data with different user priorities and may access channel using CSMA/CA mechanism. A node in CSMA/CA mechanism maintains a backoff counter depending on W_k, which is the window value of backoff counter in UP_k. The value of backoff counter is set to a random integer ranging from 1 to W_k. The value of W_k changes with the number of retries r and can be formulated as follows,

$$W_k(r) = \begin{cases} CW_{k,min} & r = 0 \\ W_k(r-1) & r = odd, r \leq m \\ \min\{CW_{k,max}, 2W_k(r-1)\} & r = even, r \leq m \end{cases} \quad (1)$$

where k is the UP of data processed by nodes. Besides, $CW_{k,min}$ and $CW_{k,max}$ are the minimum and maximum value of CW in priority k. And m is the maximum number of retries.

Backoff counter of a node is locked or unlocked under several conditions. Backoff counter is locked in the following situations: 1) System resets the backoff counter or the counter decreases to zero. 2) Channel is occupied by other nodes when the node is listening. 3) The current time is not in RAP, CAP or EAP. 4) The current time is inside the period of RAP, CAP or EAP, but the length between the current time and the end of the phase is too short to send a frame. On the other hand, the backoff counter is unlocked when the channel has been idle for a Short Interframe Space (SIFS) period. At the same time, there is plenty of time for completing frame transmission until the end of the phase. In fact, nodes transmit packet when the value of backoff counter decreases to zero. If the packet is sent successfully, the value of r returns to zero. Otherwise, r is increased by one. However, value of r will never exceed m.

3. ANALYTICAL MODEL AND PERFORMANCE ANALYSIS

In this section, we first describe the energy harvesting model for sensor nodes and then develop a DTMC model for the CSMA/CA-based MAC protocol of IEEE 802.15.6 Standard in the EH-based WBAN. Based on the analysis of the DTMC model, we derive the close form formulations for the system performance of the WBAN with energy harvest-

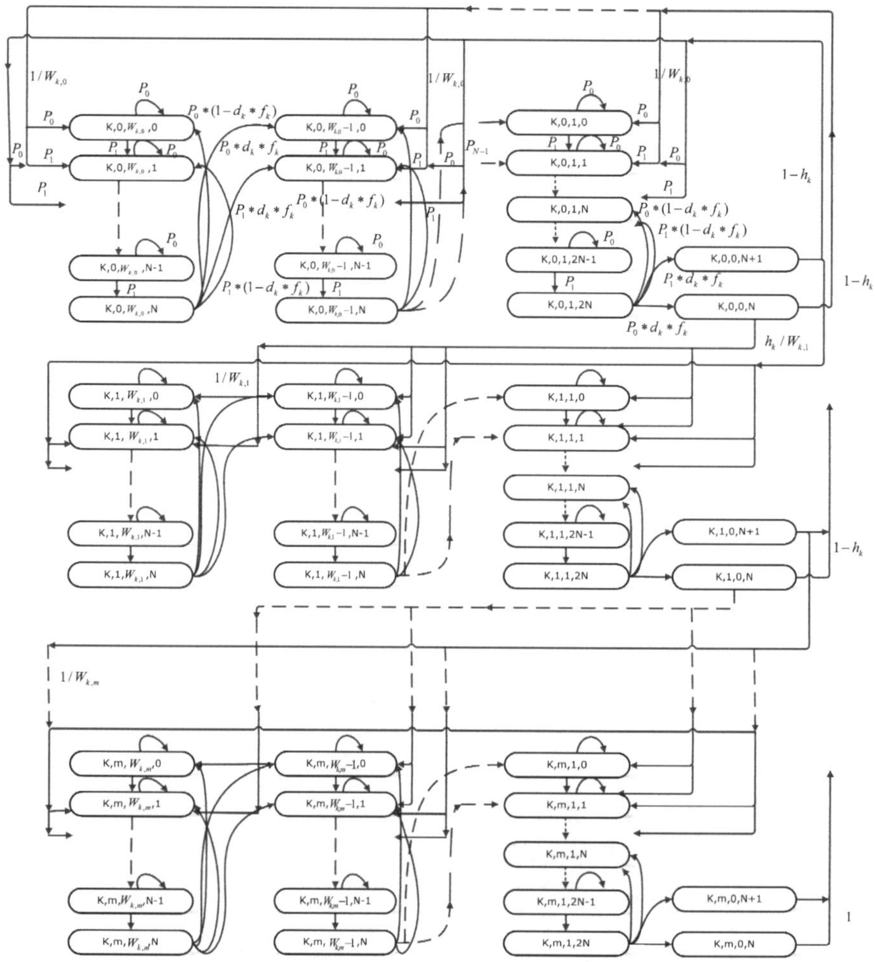

Figure 2 State transition diagram of DTMC model.

ing nodes. Here we assume that the WBAN is in saturation condition.

3.1 Energy harvesting model

Here we adopt a Poisson Distributed energy harvesting model for each node [2], i.e., the amount of energy arriving at the energy buffer of each node follows a Poisson Distribution. Here the energy buffer of each node is assumed to be unlimited. To simplify the analysis, we further transfer the EH model from the Poisson process to a Bernoulli process [12]. In this model, energy arriving at the buffer is packetized into some units and E_{unit} is used to denote the amount of one unit energy. If the quantity of energy arrival in a time slot exceed E_{unit}, we ignore the residual energy and regard the arrival energy as one unit. Otherwise, we regard the arrival energy as zero. Furthermore, it is assumed that when a node is sensing the channel or transmitting a packet, it can be charged simultaneously. Therefore, the energy model can be expressed as follows,

$$E(t) = \begin{cases} E(t-1) & P_1 \\ E(t)+1 & P_0 = 1 - P_1 \end{cases} \tag{2}$$

where t is the index of time slot and $E(t)$ is the state of the energy buffer.

3.2 Discrete-Time Markov Chain model

A Discrete-Time Markov Chain (DTMC) model is used to describe the process of CSMA/CA MAC protocol of IEEE 802.15.6 Standard. As stated in [3] that the power consumption in Clear Channel Assessment (CCA) period is approximately equivalent to the power consumption of transmission. Therefore, the energy consumption of channel sensing and packet transmission can assumed to be an equal value E_{th} and is denoted as N energy units. The DTMC model for CSMA/CA MAC protocol is then depicted in Figure. 2. Notations used in this model analysis are defined in Table 2.

The contention process in the MAC protocol is modeled as different state transition. Some identical state transition probabilities in Figure. 2 are omitted [4]. System states in the model are all observed at the end of each time slot. Every state is a tuple with four elements, which is denoted by $\{k, i(t), j(t), q(t)\}$. The first element denotes the user priority and the second element denotes the number of retries. The third element is the value of backoff counter. The last one is state of energy buffer q. When q reaches to N, it will be immediately used up by the node for CCA or transmitting if backoff counter greater than one. However, when the backoff counter decreases to one, the node will send the packet immediately in next state where the backoff counter equals to zero, so there need more energy in this state, i.e., $2N$ units of energy for both listening and transmission. The transition probability from state A to state B is denoted

Table 2 Notation Definitions.

Notations	Definitions
k	user priority k, $k \in (0, ..., 7)$
i	number of retries, $i \in (0, ..., m)$
j	value of backoff counter, $j \in (0, ..., W_{k,i})$
q	energy quantity of energy buffer, $q \in (0, ..., 2N)$
m	maximum number of retries
d_k	probability of the idle channel
n_k	number of nodes in UP_k
n	number of nodes in WBAN
h_k	collision probability after frame transmitting
τ_k	transmission probability for the node in UP_k
f_k	probability of leaving sufficient time for frame transmission
$b_{k,i,j,q}$	steady-state probability in certain state
P_0	probability that no energy arrives in a slot
P_1	probability that one unit energy arrives in a slot
N	energy needed in CCA or transmission in units
$W_{i,k}$	window value of backoff counter in the ith retry of UP_k

by $P(A|B)$ and the probabilities of some important state transitions in DTMC are given as follows,

$$P(k,i,j,q|k,i,j,q) = P_0,$$

$$j \geq 2, q \leq N-1 \ or \ j = 1, q \neq 2N$$

$$P(k,i,j,q+1|k,i,j,q) = P_1,$$

$$j \geq 2, q \leq N-1 \ or \ j = 1, q \neq 2N$$

$$P(k,i,j,q|k,i-1,0,N) = P_q h_k / W_{k,i},$$

$$i \neq 0, j \neq 0, q \in (0,1)$$

$$P(k,i,j,q|k,i-1,0,N+1) = P_{q-1} h_k / W_{k,i},$$

$$i \neq 0, j \neq 0, q \in (1,2)$$

$$P(k,0,j,q|k,i,0,N) = P_q (1-h_k) / W_{k,0},$$

$$i \neq m, j \neq 0, q \in (0,1)$$

$$P(k,0,j,q|k,i,0,N+1) = P_{q-1} (1-h_k) / W_{k,0},$$

$$i \neq m, j \neq 0, q \in (1,2)$$

$$P(k,0,j,q|k,m,0,N) = P_q / W_{k,0}, j \neq 0, q \in (0,1)$$

$$P(k,0,j,q|k,m,0,N+1) = P_{q-1} / W_{k,0}, j \neq 0, q \in (1,2)$$

$$P(k,i,j-1,q|k,i,j,N) = P_q (d_k f_k), j \geq 2, q \in (0,1)$$

$$P(k,i,j,q|k,i,j,N) = P_q (1 - d_k f_k), j \geq 2, q \in (0,1)$$

$$P(k,i,0,q|k,i,1,2N) = P_{q-N} (d_k f_k), q \in (N, N+1)$$

$$P(k,i,1,q|k,i,1,2N) = P_{q-N} (1 - d_k f_k), q \in (N, N+1)$$

Based on the above transition probabilities, we could obtain the steady-state probabilities of DTMC using property that sum of all steady-state probabilities is equal to one,

$$\sum_{i=0}^{m} \sum_{q=N}^{N+1} b_{k,i,0,q} + \sum_{i=0}^{m} \sum_{q=N}^{2N} b_{k,i,1,q}$$
$$+ \sum_{i=0}^{m} \sum_{j=2}^{W_{k,i}} b_{k,i,j,N} + \sum_{q=0}^{N-1} \sum_{i=0}^{m} \sum_{j=1}^{W_{k,i}} b_{k,i,j,q} = 1$$

The probability of packet transmission τ_k and the probability of CCA $P_{cca,k}$ can then be respectively calculated by

$$\tau_k = \sum_{i=0}^{m} \sum_{q=N}^{N+1} b_{k,i,0,q}$$
$$= \frac{d_k f_k P_1}{N \left[d_k f_k \sum_{i=0}^{m} h_k{}^i + \sum_{i=0}^{m} \frac{(W_{k,i}+1)}{2} h_k{}^i \right]} \sum_{i=0}^{m} h_k{}^i$$

$$P_{cca,k} = \frac{P_1 \sum_{i=0}^{m} \frac{(W_{k,i}+1)}{2} h_k{}^i}{N \left[d_k f_k \sum_{i=0}^{m} h_k{}^i + \sum_{i=0}^{m} \frac{(W_{k,i}+1)}{2} h_k{}^i \right]}$$

where the collision probability after transmitting h_k and the probability of the idle channel d_k are formulated as follows,

$$h_k = 1 - (1-\tau_k)^{n_k - 1} \prod_{i \neq k, i=0}^{7} (1-\tau_i)^{n_i}$$

$$d_k = (1-\tau_k)^{n_k - 1} \prod_{i \neq k, i=0}^{7} (1-\tau_i)^{n_i}$$

The corresponding transmission probability P_{tr}, the probability of successful transmission of one node in UP_k $P_{su,k}$, and the probability of successful transmission in the WBAN P_{su} can then be derived as follows respectively,

$$P_{tr} = 1 - \prod_{i=0}^{7} (1-\tau_i)^{n_i} \quad (3)$$

$$P_{su,k} = \tau_k d_k f_k = \tau_k f_k (1-\tau_k)^{n_k - 1} \prod_{i \neq k, i=0}^{7} (1-\tau_i)^{n_i} \quad (4)$$

$$P_{su} = \sum_{i=0}^{7} C_{n_i}^{1} P_{su,i} = \sum_{i=0}^{7} n_i \tau_i d_i f_i \quad (5)$$

3.3 Throughput

In this work, we assume that a failed transmission can only be caused by collision. The throughput S_k is defined as bits of packet transmitted successfully per second in UP_k and is formulated as

$$S_k = \frac{P_{su,k} L_p}{(1-P_{tr})\, t_{idle} + P_{tr} P_{su} t_{su} + P_{tr} (1-P_{su})\, t_{col}} \quad (6)$$

where t_{idle} is the time duration of no transmission and L_p is the average packet length in bits. t_{su} and t_{col} are used to represent the time duration for successful transmission and collision, respectively,

$$t_{su} = t_{packet} + t_{ACK} + t_{SIFS} \quad (7)$$

$$t_{col} = t_{packet} + t_{ACKtimeout} \quad (8)$$

where t_{packet} and t_{ACK} are the time periods to transmit a data packet and an ACK packet, respectively. t_{SIFS} is the time duration of SIFS. $t_{ACKtimeout}$ is the ACK timeout.

Table 3 Values of simulation parameters.

Simulation parameters	Values
Symbol Rate	$187.5ksps$
Slot length	$376\mu s$
Average packet length	$114bits$
Data rate	$303.6kbps$
SIFS	$75\mu s$
P_{TX}	$401\mu W$
P_{RX}	$405\mu W$
P_{CCA}	$405\mu W$

3.4 Energy consumption

Due to the much smaller energy consumption in sleep mode than channel listening or data transmission [3], we ignore energy consumption in sleep mode in which CCA and transmission are not performed. Energy consumption per unit time of a node with UP_k is denoted as

$$E_k = \frac{P_{su,k}E_{su,k} + (\tau_k - P_{su,k})\,E_{col,k} + P_{cca,k}E_{cca,k}}{(1-P_{tr})\,t_{idle} + P_{tr}P_{su}t_{su} + P_{tr}\,(1-P_{su})\,t_{col}} \quad (9)$$

where $E_{su,k}$ is the energy consumption for successful transmission, which is comprised of energy consumption of packet transmission and ACK reception. $E_{col,k}$ is the energy consumption for a failed transmission. $E_{cca,k}$ is the energy consumption in CCA.

$$E_{su,k} = t_{packet}P_{TX} + t_{ACK}P_{RX} \quad (10)$$

$$E_{col,k} = t_{packet}P_{TX} \quad (11)$$

$$E_{cca,k} = t_{cca}P_{CCA} \quad (12)$$

where P_{TX} and P_{RX} are the power consumption of transmission and receiving, respectively, P_{CCA} is the power consumption of CCA, and t_{cca} represents the time duration for CCA.

4. NUMERICAL RESULTS

In this section, some simulation results are obtained to demonstrate the effectiveness of the proposed analytical model for IEEE 802.15.6 MAC protocol. Here we only focus on the random access mechanism in IEEE 802.15.6, thus the manage access phases are left out in each superframe [1]. Parameters used in the simulations are summarized in Table 3. Although eight UPs are defined in IEEE 802.15.6 standard, we only use four UPs, i.e., UP_0, UP_2, UP_4, UP_6 in the simulations as four UPs are enough for performance analysis in WBAN [9]. The number of energy units required for packet transmission N can be determined in terms of different harvesting technologies [11] and here we alter it in some simulations to see its effect for system performance.

In Figure. 3, by fixing $P_1 = 0.6$ and $N = 25$, the performance curves are plotted for different user priorities as n varies. As shown in Figure. 3a and Figure. 3b, the transmission probability and the throughput decrease monotonically as n increases. It is due to the fact that more collisions happen if there are more number of nodes involved in the WBAN, which results in lower transmission probability and throughput. We could also find that higher priority nodes tend to achieve higher throughput since they access channel more frequently. As shown in Figure. 3c, the power consumption of different UPs increase as n increases since there are more nodes consuming energy. Although the lower priority nodes have higher power consumption, the difference of power consumption among different UPs is very small. It is because that lower UP nodes have larger CW and they need to sense channel more frequently, and the higher UP nodes transmit packet more often. The power required in CCA and transmission is equally considerable.

In Figure. 4, we test the impact of N and P_1 to the system performance. As shown in Figure. 4a, by setting $P_1 = 0.6$ and $N = 1000$, the probability of packet transmission almost remains unchanged with increasing n, which indicates that the number of nodes almost has no impact on throughput. This is because a large N implies a long energy-waiting period for transmission or CCA, and thus low packet transmission probability. Therefore, increasing n in the WBAN does not result in more collision, and certainly has little impact on system throughput. By setting $n = 12$ and $P_1 = 0.6$, the influence of varying N to the system performance is shown in Figure. 4b, where the packet transmission probability decreases as N increases due to the longer energy-waiting period. We can also find that the gap of packet transmission probability between each UP becomes smaller as N increases. It is because higher UP nodes have larger probability to transmit and thus need more energy. Therefore, a weak energy harvesting ability affects their performance more.

Figure. 4c plots the packet transmission probability versus the energy arrival probability with $n = 12$ and $N = 25$. We can find that, as P_1 increases, the probability of packet transmission also increases. With higher energy arrival rate, nodes recharge more quickly and sense channel more frequently. Consequently, the access probability of nodes tends to increase. Furthermore, the higher priority nodes achieve higher increasing rate compared to the nodes with lower priority. The result can be explained as follows. Despite the smaller CW of the higher priority nodes, if the higher priority nodes lack of energy, they are not able to sense the channel or transmit the packet. Thus, the performance of the higher priority nodes approach to that of the lower priority nodes for small energy arrival rate. However, if there are more energy arriving to the nodes, the superiority of higher priority nodes would reveal and they will achieve more opportunities to transmit packets.

5. CONCLUSIONS

In this paper, we develop a DTMC model for IEEE 802.15.6 MAC protocol in the WBAN with energy harvesting nodes. The long term performance of the WBAN in terms of throughput and energy consumption is analyzed. The effectiveness of the analytical model is demonstrated by the simulation results. This work is the first step to evaluate the performance of IEEE 802.15.6 MAC protocol in the WBAN with energy harvesting nodes. In the future work, we will consider a more practical energy arrival model. We will also consider the unsaturated case, i.e., the packets are arrived in each node based on some data arrival model, e.g., Poission arrival model.

6. ACKNOWLEDGMENTS

This work is supported by the National Natural Science Foundation of China (Grant No. 61202406).

7. REFERENCES

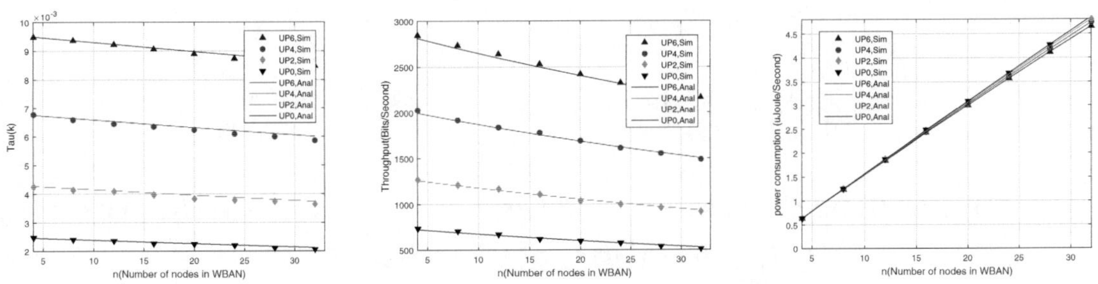

(a) **(b)** **(c)**

Figure 3 System performance curves for different user priorities

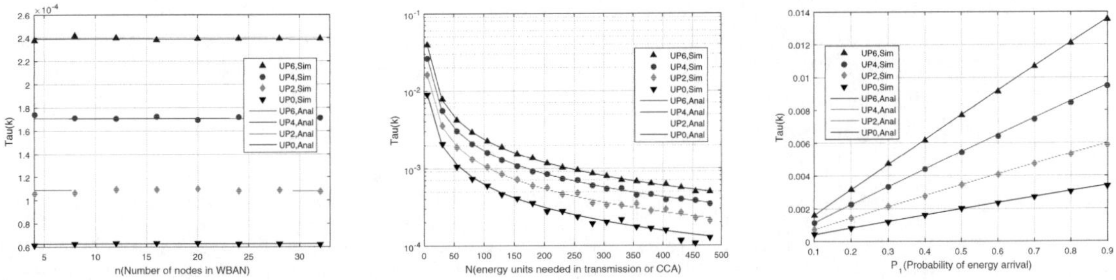

(a) **(b)** **(c)**

Figure 4 Packet transmission probabilities for different parameters.

[1] A. Astrin et al. Ieee standard for local and metropolitan area networks part 15.6: Wireless body area networks: Ieee std 802.15.6-2012. *The document is available at IEEE Xplore*, 2012.

[2] Q. Bai, J. Nossek, et al. Modulation optimization for energy harvesting transmitters with compound poisson energy arrivals. In *Signal Processing Advances in Wireless Communications (SPAWC), 2013 IEEE 14th Workshop on*, pages 764–768. IEEE, 2013.

[3] E. Casilari, J. M. Cano-García, and G. Campos-Garrido. Modeling of current consumption in 802.15. 4/zigbee sensor motes. *Sensors*, 10(6):5443–5468, 2010.

[4] B. H. Jung, R. U. Akbar, and D. K. Sung. Throughput, energy consumption, and energy efficiency of ieee 802.15. 6 body area network (ban) mac protocol. In *Personal Indoor and Mobile Radio Communications (PIMRC), 2012 IEEE 23rd International Symposium on*, pages 584–589. IEEE, 2012.

[5] P. Khan, N. Ullah, S. Ullah, and K. S. Kwak. Analytical modeling of ieee 802.15. 6 csma/ca protocol under different access periods. In *Communications and Information Technologies (ISCIT), 2014 14th International Symposium on*, pages 151–155. IEEE, 2014.

[6] A. Liberale, E. Dallago, and A. L. Barnabei. Energy harvesting system for wireless body sensor nodes. In *Biomedical Circuits and Systems Conference (BioCAS), 2014 IEEE*, pages 416–419. IEEE, 2014.

[7] B. Liu, S. Yu, and C. W. Chen. Optimal resource allocation in energy harvesting-powered body sensor networks. In *Future Information and Communication Technologies for Ubiquitous HealthCare (Ubi-HealthTech), 2015 2nd International Symposium on*, pages 1–5. IEEE, 2015.

[8] S. Movassaghi, M. Abolhasan, J. Lipman, D. Smith, and A. Jamalipour. Wireless body area networks: A survey. *Communications Surveys & Tutorials, IEEE*, 16(3):1658–1686, 2014.

[9] S. Rashwand, J. Misic, and V. Misic. Analysis of csma/ca mechanism of ieee 802.15.6 under non-saturation regime. *IEEE Transactions on Parallel and Distributed Systems*, PP(99):1–1, 2015.

[10] S. Sarkar, S. Misra, C. Chakraborty, and M. S. Obaidat. Analysis of reliability and throughput under saturation condition of ieee 802.15. 6 csma/ca for wireless body area networks. In *Global Communications Conference (GLOBECOM), 2014 IEEE*, pages 2405–2410. IEEE, 2014.

[11] W. K. Seah, Z. A. Eu, and H.-P. Tan. Wireless sensor networks powered by ambient energy harvesting (wsn-heap)-survey and challenges. In *Wireless Communication, Vehicular Technology, Information Theory and Aerospace & Electronic Systems Technology, 2009. Wireless VITAE 2009. 1st International Conference on*, pages 1–5. IEEE, 2009.

[12] G. Yang, G.-Y. Lin, and H.-Y. Wei. Markov chain performance model for ieee 802.11 devices with energy harvesting source. In *Global Communications Conference (GLOBECOM), 2012 IEEE*, pages 5212–5217. IEEE, 2012.

Direct and Indirect Access in Machine Type Communications: An Analytical Approach
Invited Paper

Panagiotis Sarigiannidis
Department of Informatics and Telecommunications Engineering University of Western Macedonia
Kozani, Greece 50100
psarigiannidis@uowm.gr

Dimitrios Pliatsios
Department of Informatics and Telecommunications Engineering, University of Western Macedonia
Kozani, Greece 50100
dpliatsios@uowm.gr

ABSTRACT

Machine-to-machine (M2M) communications have emerged as a cost-effective, flexible and efficient solution of facilitating the penetration of independent 'things' and machines in local networks and systems. The latest releases of long-term evolution (LTE) such as LTE-Advanced (LTE-A) are being transformed to support the migration of M2M devices to end terminals. 3GPP supports the definition of technical requirements and functional specifications that allows the adapting of existing technologies to support machine type communications (MTC) and the optimization of the design of advanced standards (e.g., LTE-A) for efficient data delivery. According to ETSI M2M architecture three types of MTC access methods are supported, the direct access, the gateway access and the coordinator access. An MTC can access an evolved NodeB (eNB) with or without relay nodes. Hence coverage and connectivity issues appear on designing and deploying MTC architectures. This work is focused on studying and analyzing the probability of having at least k machine devices connected in modern cellular network, where the deployed M2M devices are directly or indirectly connected to the eNB node. The provided analytic framework is verified by simulation results that indicate suitable deployment conditions in specific MTC scenarios.

CCS CONCEPTS

•Networks → Wireless access points, base stations and infrastructure; Network structure; Network range; Intermediate nodes; End nodes;

KEYWORDS

Coverage, Deployment, M2M, LTE, Relay

1 INTRODUCTION

Communication technologies have been evolving rapidly and the pace of change is only increasing. One of the most compelling trends is machine-to-machine (M2M) communications. M2M communications or machine type communications (MTC) are defined as the data communication between independent, machine-based devices without the need for human interaction. The number of those devices is growing exponentially, putting unprecedented load on cellular infrastructure [3], [4]. MTC involve data communication without or with limited human intervention among various devices, ranging from computers and smart sensors to mobile devices and vehicles. M2M devices demonstrate very high density, low bandwidth, small payload and uplink dominant traffic [6]. Long-term evolution (LTE) and LTE-Advanced (LTE-A) constitute promising solution for M2M communications infrastructure because of their longevity, cost-effectiveness and scalability. With the widespread introduction of LTE the migration of MTC devices to LTE is under development. In particular higher-layer system requirements should be addressed for facilitating the data delivery through LTE-A cellular systems. In this context intriguing challenges are emerged such as connectivity and coverage issues [7].

This work investigates coverage and capacity capabilities of direct and indirect access methods to the evolved NodeB (eNB). An analytical framework is provided in terms of full coverage and outage that provides the probability of ensuring a number of machine devices connection by having either them directly to the eNB or indirectly through relay machine gateways. Various topologies are considered, such as square, rectangular and disk areas so as to acquire the potential capabilities of MTC architecture. The provided analytical equations are validated through simulation results.

The remainder of the paper is organized as follows. Section 2 introduces the main features of MTC field. A detailed description of the provided analytical framework is included in Section 3. Section 4 presents the obtained results. Finally, conclusions are given in Section 5.

2 BACKGROUND

M2M devices access the network through wired or wireless links. Wired access methods can be a combination of different technologies such as cable, various digital subscriber line technologies (xDS L) and optical fiber. Wireless access methods can be short range, such as wireless local area network (WLAN), ZigBee and IEEE 802.15.4 or cellular such as global system for mobile communications (GSM), general packet radio service (GPRS), 3G standards,

LTE-A, and worldwide interoperability for microwave access (Wi MAX). Although wired solutions provide reliability, high data-rates, short delays and security, they may not be appropriate for M2M communications due to cost ineffectiveness, lack of mobility and low scalability. On the contrary, wireless cellular solutions offer excellent coverage, good security, mobility support, and ready-to-use infrastructure.

Considering the low-power budget of the M2M devices, coverage becomes a key challenge for a wide-area deployment. Coverage using Category-1 device has been studied in [1], with the maximum coupling loss (MCL) being 140.7 dB and 146.7 dB, for frequency division duplexing (FDD) and time division duplexing (TDD) respectively. Release 13 extends the MCL to 155.7 dB, providing thus increased coverage area as well as supporting devices in locations with high penetration loss. To achieve that, the following coverage improvements concepts are considered [1]:

- Repetition or subframe bundling: Longer transmission time allows more energy to be accumulated at the receiver, thus improving the strength of the desired signals.
- Power boosting: with power boosting more power can be used by the eNB on downlink transmissions to M2M user equipment (UE). For a given level of power boosting concentrates more power into a reduced bandwidth at the eNB or UE.
- Relaxing the current specification requirements, such as delay tolerance.
- Frequency hopping across wideband system to provide frequency diversity gain to narrowband UEs.
- Small cells: an operator may extend the coverage of current cells by deploying small cells such as pico- or femtocells, relays and repeaters etc.

System deployment scenarios may include urban and suburban macro-cell deployment [4]. Indicatively, For urban macro-cell scenario, the inter-site distance (i.e., the distance between one eNB site to another) is 500 meters, while for suburban macro-cell it is 1732 meters.

3 COVERAGE ANALYSIS

3.1 System Model

A two dimensional, flat field is considered without obstacles. The field is defined as the M2M deployment area. A high degree of spatial randomness may be presented when user and machine terminals are deployed [2]. Hence, in this work we assume a number of N stationary M2M devices that are randomly and independently deployed in the M2M deployment area. It is assumed that all these devices have been deployed in this field by prior arrangement. The M2M deployment area covers an area of E quadratic metric units.

3.2 Direct Access

MTC is feasible in direct access with an eNB in cellular networks without any intermediate device [7]. This type of connection is similar to that of a regular UE. An eNB is considered within the deployment area with a transmission range of R. For simplicity reasons we consider that the eNB is placed in such a location so as its coverage area is fully included within the deployment area.

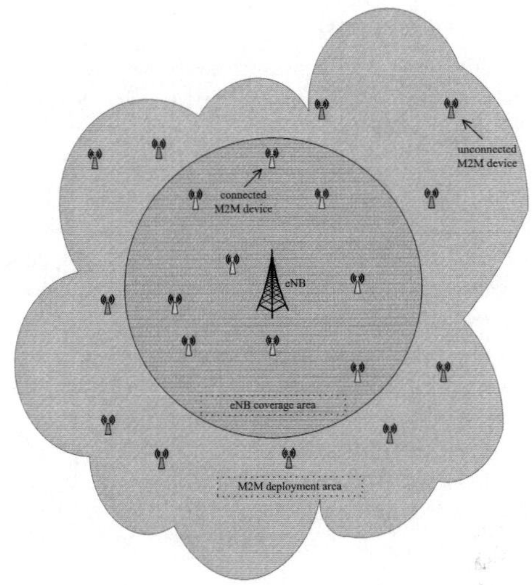

Figure 1: The M2M deployment area.

Figure 1 shows the deployment area where the eNB is placed. The transmission coverage of the eNB is defined as E_e:

$$E_e = \pi \cdot R^2 \tag{1}$$

Obviously the access probability for each machine to be connected with the eNB, denoted by p_d, is $p_d = \frac{E_e}{E} = \frac{\pi \cdot R^2}{E}$. Given that all machines have been randomly and independently deployed in the M2M deployment area and all machines are identical in terms of wireless interface and communication range, the probability of having i out of N machines that establish communication with the eNB follows a binomial distribution:

$$Pr(X = i) = \binom{N}{i} p_d^i (1 - p_d)^{N-i} \tag{2}$$

Accordingly, the probability of having all machines connected is $p_N = p^N$. Similarly, the probability of a total outage of all machines becomes $p_0 = (1 - p_d)^N$.

Once we have computed the access probability (p_d) we can derive the probability of at least k machine devices are connected to the eNB. This probability is denoted by p_k^d and it is calculated as follows:

$$\begin{aligned} p_k^d &= Pr(X \geq k) \\ &= 1 - Pr\{X = 0\} - Pr\{X = 1\} - \ldots - Pr\{X = k - 1\} \\ &= 1 - (1 - p_d)^N - \binom{N}{1} p_d (1 - p_d)^{N-1} \\ &- \ldots - \binom{N}{k-1} p_d^{k-1} (1 - p_d)^{N-k+1} \end{aligned} \tag{3}$$

Eq. (3) expresses the probability of having a minimum number of k machine devices connected to the eNB subject to the number of the machines (N), the range of the eNB (R) and the deployment area (E).

3.3 Relay Access

Apart from direct access a machine device may use a relay station to reach the eNB. Relay nodes provide coverage extension and throughput enhancement by forwarding an enhanced version of the received signal from devices to base station [5]. Coverage holes can be resolved by deploying additional infrastructural relays across the M2M network, e.g., M2M gateways. Assume that a number of M relay nodes are additional deployed in the M2M deployment area in a random way. We assume that the deployment of the relay nodes takes place in a way that no overlapping occurs between the relay nodes and the between the eNB and the relay nodes. In addition it is considered that eNB and relay nodes communicate each other using optical fiber connections. Hence, eNB concentrates the baseband signals from several relay nodes to a server platform for centralized signal processing [5]. Given that the communication range of each relay node is L, the transmission coverage becomes:

$$E_r = \pi \cdot R^2 + M \cdot \pi \cdot L^2 = \pi \cdot (R^2 + M \cdot L^2) \quad (4)$$

Thus, the access probability, denoted by p_r, is now defined as $p_r = \frac{E_r}{E} = \frac{\pi \cdot (R^2 + M \cdot L^2)}{E}$. Accordingly, the probability of at least k machines are connected either directly or indirectly to the eNB is transformed as follows:

$$\begin{aligned} p_k^r &= Pr(X \geq k) \\ &= 1 - Pr\{X = 0\} - Pr\{X = 1\} - \ldots - Pr\{X = k-1\} \\ &= 1 - (1 - p_r)^N - \binom{N}{1} p_r (1 - p_r)^{N-1} \\ &- \ldots - \binom{N}{k-1} p_r^{k-1} (1 - p_r)^{N-k+1} \end{aligned} \quad (5)$$

3.4 Special Cases

In this subsection a set of special topologies are investigated. It is likely the deployment area to have a predefined, common shape. We consider three common shapes: a) a square, b) a rectangle and c) a disk. Figure 2 illustrates the a square deployment M2M area. The eNB is placed in the center, or in any place that the supported coverage is fully included within the deployment area. Assuming that the square area has a side of q then the probability of having at least k machine devices connected becomes:

$$\begin{aligned} &Pr(X \geq k) = \\ &= 1 - (1 - \frac{\pi(R^2 + M \cdot L^2)}{q^2})^N \\ &- \binom{N}{1} \frac{\pi(R^2 + M \cdot L^2)}{q^2} (1 - \frac{\pi(R^2 + M \cdot L^2)}{q^2})^{N-1} \\ &- \ldots \\ &- \binom{N}{k-1} (\frac{\pi(R^2 + M \cdot L^2)}{q^2})^{k-1} (1 - (\frac{\pi(R^2 + M \cdot L^2)}{q^2}))^{N-k+1} \end{aligned} \quad (6)$$

A rectangular M2M deployment area covers an area of $u \cdot y$, where u and y are the length of the two sides. Figure 3 depicts

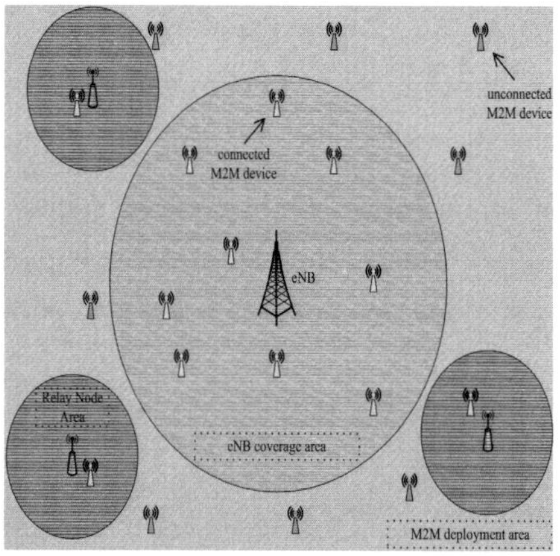

Figure 2: A square shaped M2M deployment area with three relay nodes.

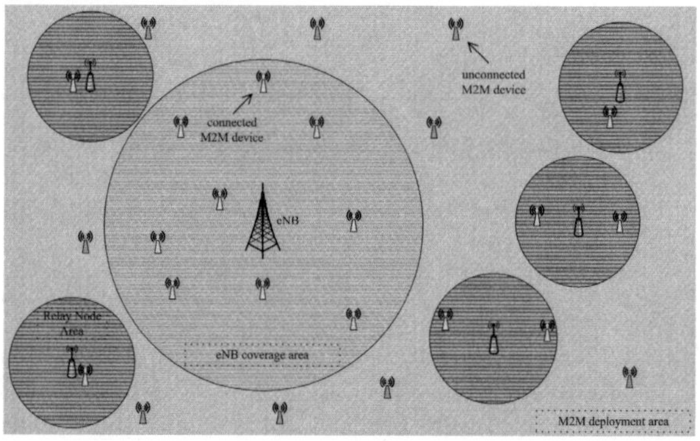

Figure 3: A rectangular shaped M2M deployment area with five relay nodes.

a rectangular deployment area. The at least k probability is now formed as:

$$\begin{aligned} &Pr(X \geq k) = \\ &= 1 - (1 - \frac{\pi(R^2 + M \cdot L^2)}{uy})^N \\ &- \binom{N}{1} \frac{\pi(R^2 + M \cdot L^2)}{uy} (1 - \frac{\pi(R^2 + M \cdot L^2)}{uy})^{N-1} \\ &- \ldots \\ &- \binom{N}{k-1} (\frac{\pi(R^2 + M \cdot L^2)}{uy})^{k-1} (1 - (\frac{\pi(R^2 + M \cdot L^2)}{uy}))^{N-k+1} \end{aligned} \quad (7)$$

Lastly, a disk shaped deployment area is drawn in Figure 4. When the deployment area is shaped as a disk with radius h, the at least k probability becomes:

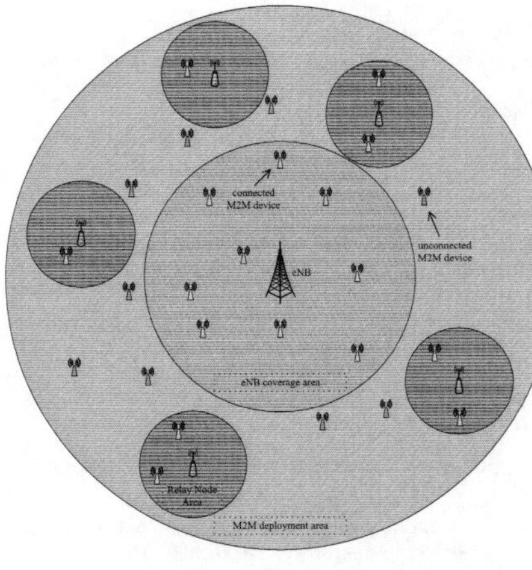

Figure 4: A disk shaped M2M deployment area with five relay nodes.

$$
\begin{aligned}
Pr(X \geq k) &= \\
&= 1 - (1 - \frac{R^2 + M \cdot L^2}{h^2})^N \\
&- \binom{N}{1} \frac{R^2 + M \cdot L^2}{h^2} (1 - \frac{R^2 + M \cdot L^2}{h^2})^{N-1} \\
&- \dots \\
&- \binom{N}{k-1} (\frac{R^2 + M \cdot L^2}{h^2})^{k-1} (1 - (\frac{R^2 + M \cdot L^2}{h^2}))^{N-k+1}
\end{aligned} \tag{8}
$$

4 VERIFICATION AND DISCUSSION

4.1 Environment

The verification environment was based on the LTE Systems toolbox in Matlab. An eNB and multiple machine devices were considered in the direct access method while an eNB, several relay machine gateways and multiple machines devices were assumed in the indirect approach. Three M2M deployment areas were considered: a) a square area of 3000 m × 3000 m (default values), a rectangular area of 3000 m × 6000 m (default values) and c) a disk area of $\pi \times 3000$ m × 3000 m. The eNB has a coverage range of 1732 m. Each relay gateway has a coverage range of 100 m.

The at least k machine devices probability is explored when a) the number of k changes and b) the M2M deployment area alters.

4.2 Machine Density Impact

First, the impact of the machine devices density is investigated. The number of k changes from 50 to 200 while the M2M deployment area remains stable. Figure 5 and Figure 6 depict the probability of having at least k machine devices connected in the eNB directly and indirectly respectively. The best performance is observed in the case of the square case since it the M2M deployment area is the lesser between the evaluated cases. The square case guarantees the connectivity of at least 150 out of 300 machine devices with probability 1. Then the probability diminishes and is

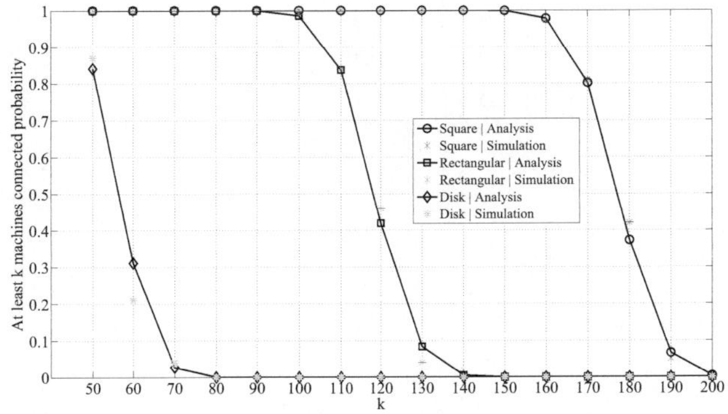

Figure 5: At least k connected machine devices probability. The deployment area includes the eNB only.

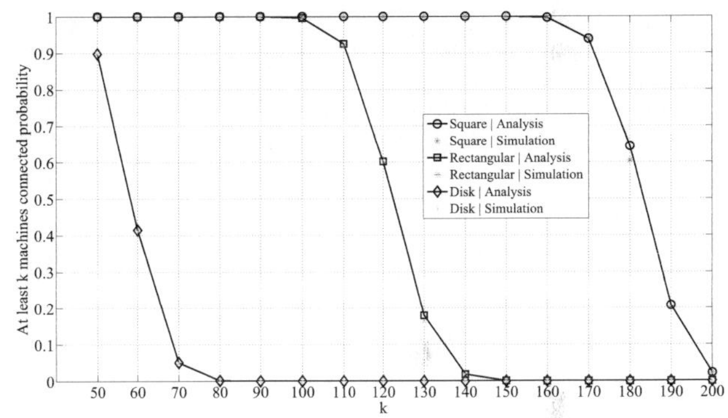

Figure 6: At least k connected machine devices probability. The deployment area includes the eNB and 10 relay nodes.

getting almost zero when the number of devices becomes 200. By observing Figure 6, we can infer that the presence of the 10 relay nodes increases the number of guaranteed machine devices from 150 to 160. In addition the probability diminishes less sharply than in Figure 5. In the rectangular case a number of 90 machine devices are guaranteed when a directly connection is applied. This number is getting larger in the indirect architecture, reaching almost 100 devices. Lastly, teh disk architecture presents the lowest performance since the M2M deployment are is even larger compared to the first two cases. The number of guaranteed machine devices is less than 50 (it is about 30 devices). The impact of the additional relay nodes is minimum since the probability of at least k machine devices is still low. Obviously additional relay nodes are needed to address the coverage gap of the disk architecture.

4.3 Deployment Area Impact

Second, the impact of the deployment area is examined. Figure 7 and Figure 8 illustrate the probability of having at least k machine devices connected in the eNB directly and indirectly respectively. The number of k is fixed and equal to 100. When the area is $24 \cdot 10^6$ m^2 the probability is almost 1, meaning that at least 100 machine devices are ensured. The probability is enhanced when a number of

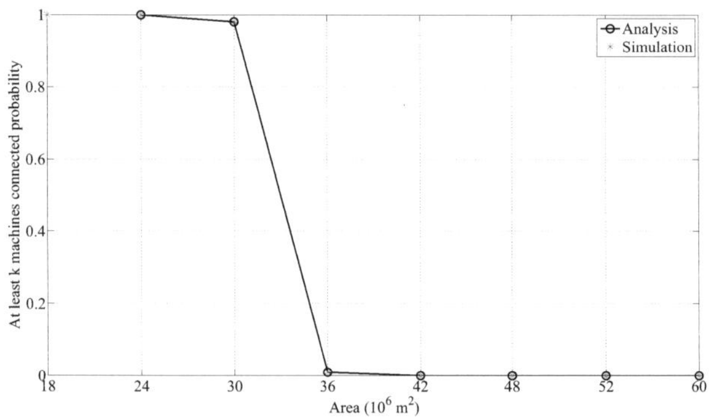

Figure 7: A disk shaped M2M deployment area with five relay nodes.

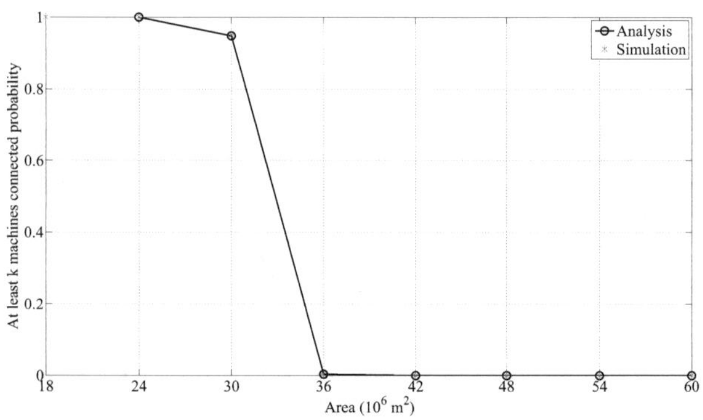

Figure 8: A disk shaped M2M deployment area with five relay nodes.

10 additional relay nodes increase the connectivity coverage of the M2M architecture. According to Figure 8 this number of machines devices are almost guaranteed when the area increases to $24 \cdot 10^6$ m^2.

5 CONCLUSIONS

An analytical framework for studying the coverage capabilities in MTC was presented in this paper. Both direct and indirect access methods were investigated. In addition three shapes of architecture were considered including square, rectangular and disk. The study was focused on the connectivity guarantees of different architectures in terms of connecting at least k machine devices with the eNB. The analytical framework was verified by simulation results that highlight specific remarks given different topologies.

REFERENCES

[1] 3GPP 2013. *Study on provision of low-cost Machine-Type Communications (MTC) User Equipments(UEs) based on LTE.* 3GPP. v.12.0.0.

[2] S. Andreev, A. Pyattaev, K. Johnsson, O. Galinina, and Y. Koucheryavy. 2014. Cellular traffic offloading onto network-assisted device-to-device connections. *IEEE Communications Magazine* 52, 4 (April 2014), 20–31. DOI: http://dx.doi.org/10.1109/MCOM.2014.6807943

[3] M. Chen, J. Wan, S. Gonzalez, X. Liao, and V. C. M. Leung. 2014. A Survey of Recent Developments in Home M2M Networks. *IEEE Communications Surveys Tutorials* 16, 1 (First 2014), 98–114. DOI: http://dx.doi.org/10.1109/SURV.2013.110113.00249

[4] R. Ratasuk, A. Prasad, Z. Li, A. Ghosh, and M. A. Uusitalo. 2015. Recent advancements in M2M communications in 4G networks and evolution towards 5G. In *Intelligence in Next Generation Networks (ICIN), 2015 18th International Conference on.* 52–57. DOI: http://dx.doi.org/10.1109/ICIN.2015.7073806

[5] S. P. Yeh, S. Talwar, G. Wu, N. Himayat, and K. Johnsson. 2011. Capacity and coverage enhancement in heterogeneous networks. *IEEE Wireless Communications* 18, 3 (June 2011), 32–38. DOI: http://dx.doi.org/10.1109/MWC.2011.5876498

[6] K. Zheng, F. Hu, W. Wang, W. Xiang, and M. Dohler. 2012. Radio resource allocation in LTE-advanced cellular networks with M2M communications. *IEEE Communications Magazine* 50, 7 (July 2012), 184–192. DOI: http://dx.doi.org/10.1109/MCOM.2012.6231296

[7] K. Zheng, S. Ou, J. Alonso-Zarate, M. Dohler, F. Liu, and H. Zhu. 2014. Challenges of massive access in highly dense LTE-advanced networks with machine-to-machine communications. *IEEE Wireless Communications* 21, 3 (June 2014), 12–18. DOI: http://dx.doi.org/10.1109/MWC.2014.6845044

Optimum Thermoelectric Energy Harvesting for Wearable System Applications

Rashid Abdulla Alshehhi, Md Shamsul Arefin, Taiyang Wu, and Mehmet Rasit Yuce
Department of Electrical and Computer Systems Engineering
Monash University, Melbourne, VIC-3800, Australia.
raals2@student.monash.edu, {md.arefin, taiyang.wu, Mehmet.yuce}@monash.edu

ABSTRACT

The limitations in wearable devices are the battery size, weight, and its limited life time. By placing thermoelectric generator (TEG) on human body, wearable devices with micro-power operations can be powered continuously. In this paper, a thermoelectric energy harvesting technique is presented to power a micro-power wearable watch. The output voltage of TEGs is required to be higher than a certain voltage level (e.g. 28.5mV) for efficient operations. The required input and output voltages of the TEG are maintained during different activities, environmental conditions, and load conditions. The experimental result shows an output voltage of 5 V at open circuit, and 4.15V when it produces output power of 86.8μW at optimum load resistance of 200 kΩ. Experimental results are also extended for hybrid energy harvesting using both TEG and solar which provides fast and efficient energy harvesting both indoor and outdoor.

Keywords

Human Power; Energy Harvesting; Wearable; Thermoelectric.

1. INTRODUCTION

Energy harvesting techniques, which are small power generators, are becoming popular to be integrated with self-powered wearable devices. The energy harvesting techniques, such as mechanical vibration, solar or electromagnetic energy, and heat flow, are used for self-powered wearable devices. Though the energy from heat flow is relatively lower than other techniques, wearable devices powered by thermoelectric energy are particularly useful for elderly and mobility impaired people [1].

The thermoelectric generator (TEG) is based on Seebeck effect which produces voltage depending on temperature differences between each side of p-type and n-type semiconductors. Although the human body can continuously generate about 100W of heat energy on average, TEG placed on human body can convert only 0.2-0.4% of heat energy into electricity due to high thermal and contact resistances [2, 3]. Some efforts have been made to design and fabricate for higher output power of TEG and improved thermal and contact conductance [3-8]. The performance of TEG is also explored for wearable applications, such as electrocardiography, electroencephalogram, and pulse oximeter, which require lower power compared to the power generated by TEG [2, 8-11]. Considerable efforts have also been made to design better radiators with lower contact resistance to improve heat flow as well as output power per unit area.

The open circuit voltage generated by TEG (V_{TEG_OC}), as shown in (1), is directly proportional to the temperature difference (ΔT), the number of thermoelectric element (N), and the material of the thermoelectric element or Seebeck Coefficient (S).

$$V_{TEG\_OC} = \mathrm{N} \times S \times \Delta T \qquad (1)$$

The maximum power produced by TEG (P_{load}) can be achieved by matching the internal resistance of the TEG, R_{TEG} with load resistance, R_L. The maximum power produced by wearable TEG is recorded in [11] to be 1.65mW for ΔT of 13.1°C during running outdoor condition.

This paper investigates an energy harvesting technique using TEG to achieve higher output voltage and power under different activities, environmental conditions, and load conditions. The performance of this technique with a boost converter circuit is also verified for charging up a super-capacitor as well as a wearable watch. The operating time and efficiency of the TEG is improved by adopting a hybrid TEG and solar cell for ultra-low power wearable devices.

2. THERMAL ENERGY HARVESTER

2.1 Design of TEG

Two commercial TEGs, Tellurex (TXL-287-03Z) and ZP9104, having dimensions of 6.2x6.2cm and 4x4cm, and internal resistances (RTEG) of 8.3Ω and 1.5Ω, respectively, are chosen for the experiments. The TEG comes with ceramic plates mounted on both sides, as shown on Fig. 1(a). The TEG is placed on human forearm, and thus heat is applied on one side. On the other side of the TEG, a heatsink is attached to maximize the temperature difference. A flat aluminum 2mm thickness heatsink is placed on TXL-287-03Z (big TEG), and a 6.2mm thick pinned aluminum heatsink is placed on ZP9104 (small TEG).

2.2 Characterization of TEG

By connecting both TEGs directly to a resistive load under outdoor and indoor conditions, as shown in Fig. 1(b), the maximum power generated by both TEGs is measured using $P_{load} = (V_{TEG\_OC})^2 \times R_L/(R_L + R_{TEG})^2$, where V_{TEG_OC} is measured by averaging 1-hour of voltage data at ambient temperature of 17°C. The energy

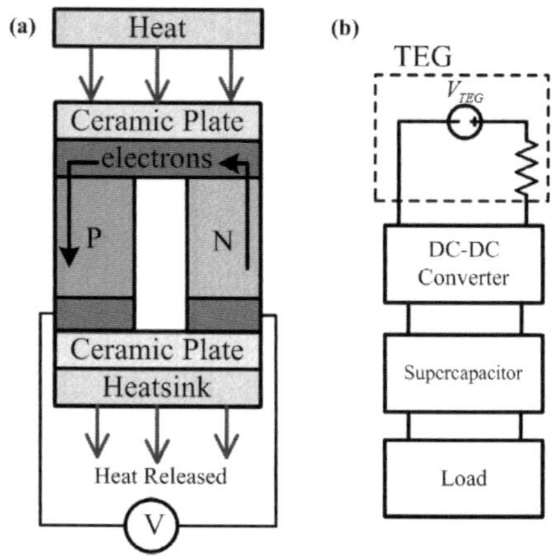

Figure 1. (a) Structure of a thermoelectric generator (TEG). (b) Block diagram of the energy harvesting system using TEG.

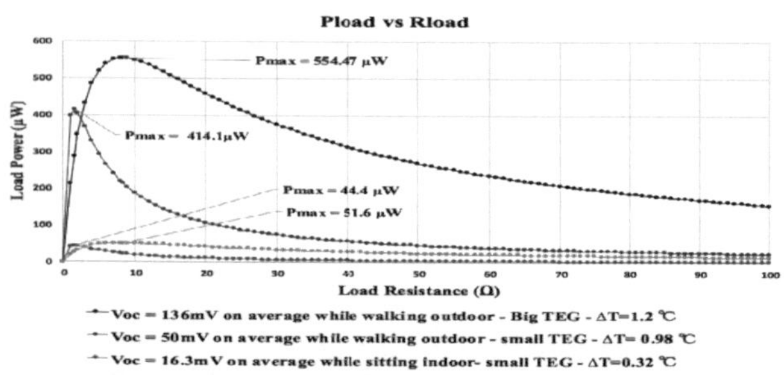

Figure 2. Load power of 6.2x6.2cm Big TEG and 4x4cm Small TEG under different activities, environmental conditions, and load conditions.

harvesting system uses a DC-DC boost converter circuit to deliver power to a supercapacitor and a load. The output voltage of the DC-DC boost converter (LTC3109) can provide a constant output voltage of 4.97 V if the input voltage is higher than 28.5mV. Therefore, the TEGs are optimized to provide higher output voltage under different activities, environmental conditions, and load conditions.

The output power calculated at different load resistances for both TEGs with heatsinks are shown in Fig. 2. For big TEG with flat heatsink at matching load, the maximum output power of 554.47 μW, which corresponds to power density of 14.42 μW/cm^2, is achieved under walking outdoor condition with V_{TEG_OC} of 136 mV and ΔT of 1.20° C. While walking outdoor condition yields higher output power, sitting indoor condition produces a maximum output power of 51.6 μW with V_{TEG_OC} of 41.4 mV and ΔT of 0.36° C. For small TEG with pinned heatsink at matching load, the maximum output power of 414.10 μW is achieved under walking outdoor condition with V_{TEG_OC} of 50 mV and ΔT of 0.98° C. Under sitting indoor condition, this TEG produces output power of 44.40 μW with V_{TEG_OC} of 16.3 mV and ΔT of 0.32° C. The internal resistances of the big and small TEG are 8.3Ω and 1.5Ω, respectively.

Though both TEGs produces enough power for ultra-low power wearable devices, it is required to provide a regulated and higher voltage for varying open circuit voltage output obtained from TEGs. A DC-DC boost converter (LTC3109) is used, as shown in Fig. 1(b), which can provide a constant output voltage of 4.97 V for more than 28.5 mV of input voltage from TEGs. The input voltage of the boost converter generated by both TEGs and the output voltage of the boost converter under different activities and environmental conditions are shown in Fig. 3. From the figure, walking outdoor and walking indoor conditions yield a stable output voltage from boost converter as both TEGs produces voltage higher than 28.5 mV due to higher temperature gradient from higher induced and natural convection of air. Since sitting outdoor condition is only influenced by natural air convection, the big TEG produces output voltages around 28.5 mV, which in turn yields fluctuating output voltage from boost converter. Due to smaller area of small TEG, the temperature difference as well as output voltage from TEG is smaller than big TEG under sitting outdoor condition. Both TEGs cannot produce enough voltage to produce a stable output voltage from boost converter under sitting indoor condition due to very limited natural air convection.

The average output power for both big and small TEGs, which are measured under walking outdoor condition with load resistance of 200 kΩ connected at the output of boost converter, are 86.8 μW and 66.5 μW, respectively. Though the output power from boost converter under sitting indoor and outdoor is lower, a supercapacitor can be used, as shown in Fig. 1, to store the energy.

A supercapacitor (ELNA 47mF, ESR = 120Ω, 5.5V) is used to store energy from the output voltage of boost converter while walking outdoor. The rate of voltage change during charging phase is 41.5 mV/minute using big TEG, as shown in Fig. 4. For small TEG, the rate of voltage change during charging phase is 39.3mV/minute. The current through the capacitor for big TEG and small TEG is 32.43μA and 29.61μA, respectively.

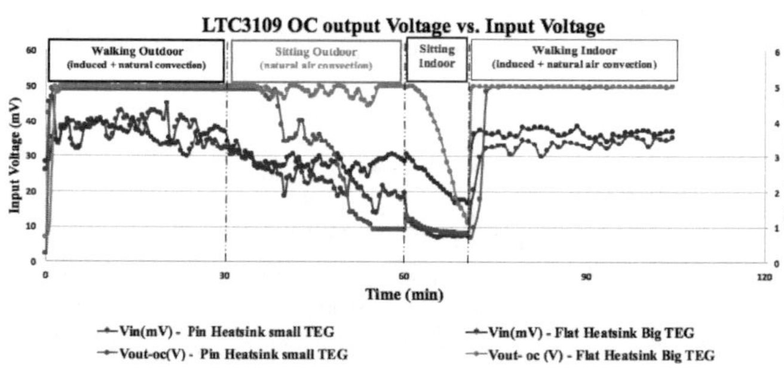

Figure 3. The input voltage of the boost converter generated by both TEGs and the output voltage of the boost converter under different activities and environmental conditions.

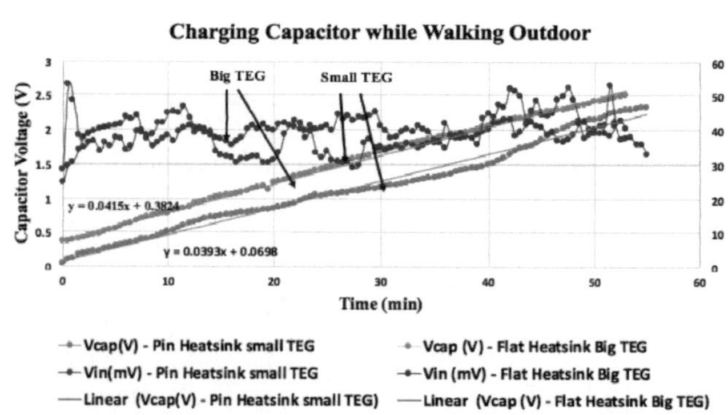

Figure 4. Charging characteristics of a 47mF supercapacitor for both big and small TEG.

2.3 Wearable Watch with TEG

A Casio watch (W-59-1VQES), which is used as a load for the circuit, is powered using the small TEG with pinned heatsink and the boost converter with output voltage regulated at 3V. Figure 5 shows the experimental setup to deliver power to a watch from TEG. The load current and the voltage has been recorded when walking outdoor and indoor, and sitting indoor. The load voltage and power of the watch during walking outdoor, sitting indoor, and walking indoor conditions are shown in Fig. 6. The watch remains operational as long as the load voltage (blue line) is above 1V or the power (orange line) is above 1.5μW. Under sitting indoor condition, the TEG can deliver power to the watch for 6 minutes. Under walking indoor or outdoor conditions, the TEG can deliver power to the watch.

To increase the duration of operating time under sitting condition, a capacitor is also connected in parallel with the watch. The output voltages of TEG and load with supercapacitor during walking outdoor, sitting indoor, and walking indoor conditions are shown in Fig. 7. This configuration can extend the operating time considerably for low-power wearable devices.

3. HYBRID THERMAL AND SOLAR ENERGY HARVESTER

3.1 Design of Hybrid TEG and Solar

To further extend the operating time, a hybrid TEG and solar cell is designed, as shown in Fig. 8. In this circuit configuration, the small TEG with pinned heatsink and a flexible solar cell is used. The Schottky diodes are used to control the power flow from TEG and solar cell to either capacitor or load. When solar cell is producing higher power than TEG under sunny outdoor condition,

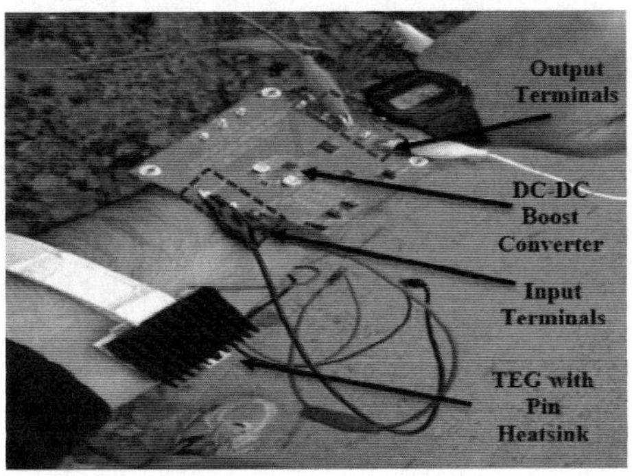

Figure 5. Experimental setup to power on a watch using TEG.

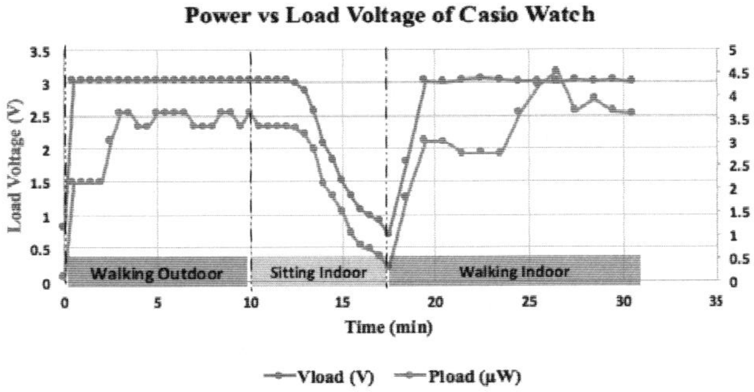

Figure 6. Load voltage and power of a watch during walking outdoor, sitting indoor, and walking indoor conditions.

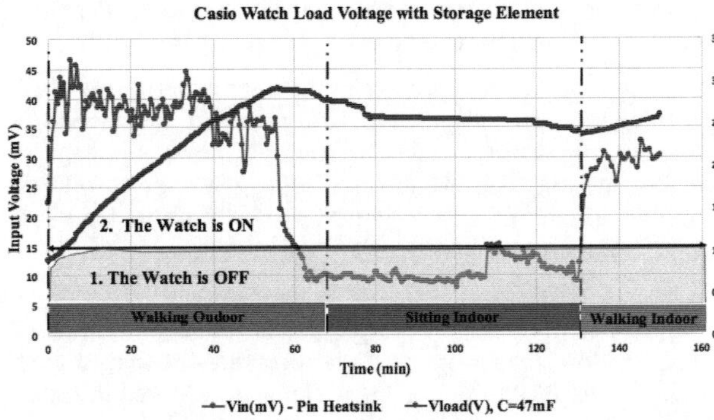

Figure 7. The output voltage of TEG and load with supercapacitor during walking outdoor, sitting indoor, and walking indoor conditions.

solar cell can deliver power to the load, R_{Load} while TEG can store energy in capacitor C_1. During dark or cloudy condition, TEG or stored energy from C_1 can deliver power to the load while solar cell can store energy in capacitor C_2. In this process, the energy harvested from thermal and solar can be used for low-power wearable devices. Figure 9 shows the experimental setup of hybrid TEG and flexible solar cell for efficient power management. The values of C_1, R_{Load}, and C_2 used during the experiments are 47mF, 200kΩ , and 1F, respectively.

3.2 Experimental Results

The output voltages at five nodes of hybrid energy harvester of TEG and solar cell circuit in Fig. 8 under different activities and environmental conditions are shown in Fig. 10. During walking outdoor under the shade (or dark) condition, output voltages at node A and B (V_A and V_B on TEG side) are increasing while output voltages at node D and E (V_D and V_E on solar side) remains constant. Since the output voltage at node B is higher than node D, the load voltage at node C follows the TEG side. Therefore, TEG

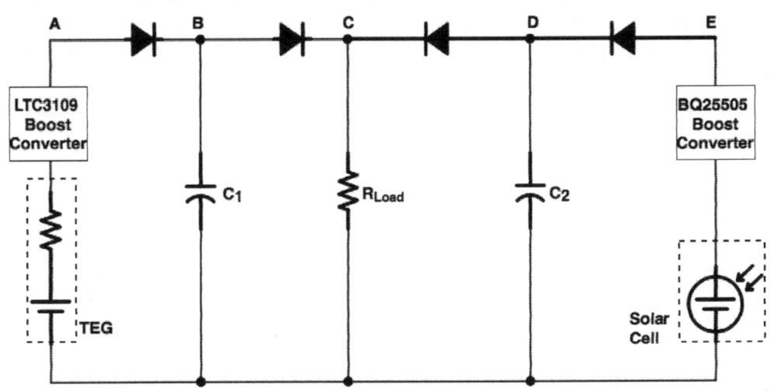

Figure 8. The hybrid energy harvester of TEG and solar cell.

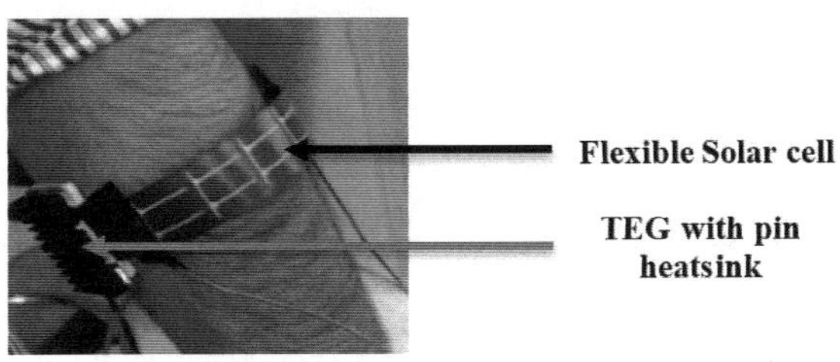

Figure 9. Experimental setup of hybrid TEG and solar cell.

delivers power to the load and C_1 and solar cell is storing energy in C_2 during walking outdoor conditions.

During sitting outdoor in partially cloudy environment, solar cell produces higher power compared to TEG which in turn increases output voltage from solar cell significantly. When output voltage at node D is higher than node B, the load voltage at node C follows the solar side. Therefore, solar cell delivers power to the load and C_2 and TEG is storing energy in C_1 during sitting outdoor in partially cloudy conditions.

During sitting indoor condition, the load voltage at node C continues to follow voltage at node D or solar side due to its higher voltage than node B. At this condition, the energy stored in C1 at node B can deliver power to load if the voltage at node D becomes lower. Therefore, the hybrid TEG and solar cell can improve the operating time for low-power wearable devices.

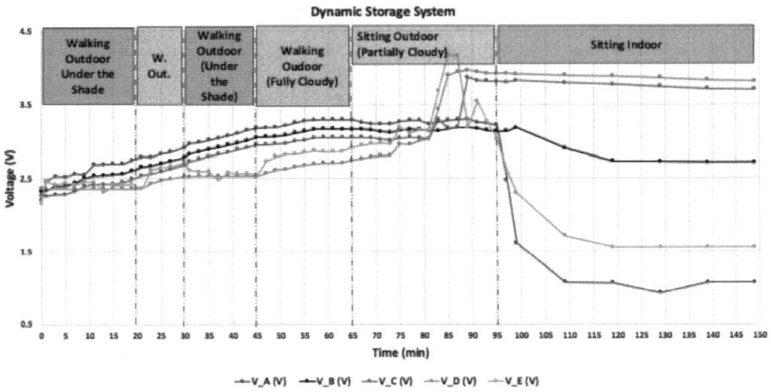

Figure 10. The output voltage at 5 nodes of hybrid energy harvester of TEG and solar cell circuit in Fig. 8 under different activities and environmental conditions.

4. PERFORMANCE SUMMARY

A performance comparison of the energy harvesting technique using TEG with previous wearable TEGs in the literature is shown in Table 1. The big TEG (without boost converter) placed on human forearm is capable of producing 554.47 μW with power density of 14.42 μW/cm^2 which is higher than that in [10]. The maximum power density is 25.9 μW/cm^2 using the small TEG (without boost converter) which is higher than the power densities in [8-10]. Though the maximum power density of 120 μW/cm^2 is reported in [3], the use of a fan with adjustable speed for forced air convection can consume higher power. In this work, the measurements are performed for natural and induced air convection.

5. CONCLUSION

An energy harvesting system consisting of thermoelectric generator and boost converter is designed. The experimental results also validate the applicability of this system for ultra-low power wearable devices. The operating time of the system is improved by connecting a supercapacitor in parallel with the load. A hybrid thermal and solar cell system is explored to further improve the operating time of the system which is suitable to deliver power to wearable devices under different activities, environmental conditions, and load conditions.

6. ACKNOWLEDGMENT

M. R. Yuce's work is supported by Australian Research Council Future Fellowships Grant FT130100430.

7. REFERENCES

[1] Leonov, V., *Wearable Monitoring Systems: Energy Harvesting for Self-Powered Wearable Devices*, Springer US, 27-49, 2011.

Table 1: State-of-the- Art of wearable thermoelectric generator.

Reference	This Work		This Work		[3]	[8]	[10]	[9]
Year	2016		2016		2016	2016	2014	2012
TEG Name	ZP9104 (small TEG)		TXL-287-03Z (big TEG)		Custom TEG	TEG with PDMS	G230–0313	wearable wristband
R_{TEG}	1.5 Ω		8.3 Ω		9 Ω	1.8Ω	7.6 Ω	10 Ω
Walking Outdoor Average Power or Power Density	414.10 μW or 25.9 μW/ cm^2		554.47 μW or 14.42 μW/ cm^2		120 μW/ cm^2 at 0.9 m/s of air speed	20 μW/ cm^2	20μW or 2.2μW/cm^2	280μW or 25μW/cm^2
Sitting Indoor Average Power or Power Density	44.40 μW or 2.8 μW/ cm^2		51.60 μW or 1.34 μW/ cm^2		20 μW/ cm^2 with no air flow	6 μW/ cm^2	-	-
TEG Location	Forearm		Forearm		Wrist	Forearm	Wrist	Forearm
Ambient Temp.	Indoor	Outdoor	Indoor	Outdoor	27°C	-	22°C	-
	22.5°C	17°C	22.5°C	17°C				
ΔT	0.32°C	0.98°C	0.36°C	1.20°C	<1°C	2.0°C	0.5°C	3.5°C
Heatsink Type	Pin Radiator		Plane Aluminum		Pin Radiator	Copper	Aluminum block	Checker-board

[2] Leonov, V., Vullers, J.M., *Wearable electronics self-powered by using human body heat: state of the art and the perspective*, Renewable Sustainable Energy, 1(6), 1-14, 2009.

[3] Suarez, F., Nozariasbmarz, A., Vashaee, D., and Mehmet C., *Designing thermoelectric generators for self-powered wearable electronics.* Energy & Environmental Science, 9(6), 2099-2113, 2016.

[4] Bahk, J., Fang, H., Yazawa, K., and Shakoun, A., *Flexible thermoelectric materials and device optimization for wearable energy harvesting,* Journal of Materials Chemistry C, 3(40), 10362-10374, 2015.

[5] Kossyvakis, D.N., Vassiliadis, S.G., Vossou, E.E., Potirakis, S.M., and Hristoforou E.V., *Computational Analysis of a Thermoelectric Generator for Waste-Heat Harvesting in Wearable Systems*, Electronic Materials, 45 (6), 2957-2966, 2016.

[6] Yang, P., Liu, K., Chen, Q., Mo, X., Xhou, Y., Li, S., Fenf, G., and Zhou, J., *Wearable Thermocells Based on Gel Electrolytes for the Utilization of Body Heat,* Angew. Chem. Int. Ed, 128(39), 12050-12053, 2016.

[7] Dziurdzia, P., Brzozowski, I., Bratek, P., Gelmuda, W., and Kos, A., *Estimation and harvesting of human heat power for wearable electronic devices,* 39th International Microelectronics and Packaging IMAPS, (Poland , 2015), IOP Publishing, 1-8.

[8] Hyland, M., Hunter, H., Liu, J., Veety, E., and Vashaee, D., *Wearable thermoelectric generators for human body heat harvesting,* Applied Energy, 182, 518-524, 2016.

[9] Settaluri, K., *Body Powered Thermoelectric Systems*, MIT, 2012.

[10] Wahbah, M., and Alhawari, M., *Characterization of Human Body-Based Thermal and Vibration Energy Harvesting for Wearable Devices.* IEEE Journal on emerging and selected topics in circuits and systems, 4 (3), 354-363. 2014.

[11] Voss, T., Subbian, V., and Beyette, F., *Feasibility of Energy Harvesting Techniques for Wearable Medical Devices,* 36th Annual International Conference of the IEEE Engineering in Medicine and Biology Society, 626-629. 2014.

A Hybrid Localization Algorithm for Wearable Safety Devices

Orlando Tovar Ordoñez
tovarordonez@ismb.it

Francesco Sottile
sottile@ismb.it

Emil Kallias
kallias@ismb.it

Claudio Pastrone
pastrone@ismb.it

Istituto Superiore Mario Boella, PerT Research Area
10138 Via P. C. Boggio, 61
Turin, Italy

ABSTRACT

Occupational safety and health (OSH) in industrial environments is gathering increasing attention in the era of Industry 4.0. In this context, location based services (LBS) can be adopted to support workers' safety in hazardous industrial environments. However, the provision of accurate location service in these harsh environments still faces big challenges.

To address these challenges, this paper presents a robust hybrid localization algorithm that combines ultra-wideband (UWB) based ranging measurements and inertial measurement unit (IMU) data. The algorithm has been implemented on a proprietary wearable platform and its performance has been evaluated in an indoor environment. The experimental results show that the proposed hybrid algorithm outperforms a non-hybrid, UWB-based, $Position-Velocity$ (PV) extended Kalman filter (EKF), which has been chosen as benchmark, in terms of both location accuracy and availability. Thanks to a modular approach, the proposed solution also leads to a lower computation processing compared to other hybrid solutions.

Keywords

Radio-based localization, UWB, IMU, wearable technology, Kalman filter, Industry 4.0.

1. INTRODUCTION

In the era of Industry 4.0 [12], the application of cyber physical systems (CPS) and, in general, the adoption of information and communication technology (ICT) are playing an important role as these contribute to the transformation of traditional working environments in a way that are both more productive and appealing for workers.

Another important aspect of Industry 4.0 is the workplace safety that has been triggering the adoption of innovative ICT solutions mainly based on wearable devices. For example, wearable technology can be used by workers in order to prevent their access to dangerous areas, such as regions of the shop floor in which there is a presence of high heat or toxic gas or other types of hazards. To this purpose, radio frequency (RF) positioning systems can be employed in order to alert workers approaching these dangerous areas. It is remarked that global navigation satellite systems (GNSS) cannot be used for these applications as the satellite signal is obstructed in indoor environments.

Many proposed indoor positioning systems are based on the ultra-wideband (UWB) radio technology as it provides accurate ranging measurements with a precision proportional to the signal bandwidth and independent from the environment [5]. In addition, the UWB technology is low cost, provides lower power consumption, in comparison to other radio technologies, and it is robust against interference and fading. Typically, in office scenarios, the UWB positioning error is in the order of centimetres. However, the performance of UWB-based localization systems is heavily affected in industrial environments due to high amount of metal surfaces, electrical motors, soldering robots, etc. [11]. In order to be more robust, location systems based only on inertial measurement unit (IMU) have been proposed [3][8]. The related position accuracy depends on the sensor quality and the ability to estimate its orientation in a robust way [2]. In addition, these location systems are infrastructure independent as they do not need the deployment of *anchor* nodes and provide good short-term accuracy, but lack in long-term stability due to biased measurements [6].

This paper, presents a hybrid localization system for industrial environments combining UWB-based ranging measurements and IMU data. In particular, the localization system uses a two-cascade Bayesian algorithm for a robust position estimation taking into account drifting problem of IMU sensors. In addition, the localization algorithm estimates the sensors's orientation (named *attitude*) and detect/remove ranging measurements outliers.

This paper is structured as follows: section 2 presents the related works. Section 3 presents the overview of the hybrid localization system as well as the application scenario. Section 4 shows a designed UWB-based wearable device for the hybrid algorithm implementation. Section 5 describes the designed hybrid localization algorithm. Section 6 exposes the experimental results and section 7 concludes this work.

Permission to make digital or hard copies of all or part of this work for personal or classroom use is granted without fee provided that copies are not made or distributed for profit or commercial advantage and that copies bear this notice and the full citation on the first page. Copyrights for components of this work owned by others than ACM must be honored. Abstracting with credit is permitted. To copy otherwise, or republish, to post on servers or to redistribute to lists, requires prior specific permission and/or a fee. Request permissions from permissions@acm.org.

2. RELATED WORKS

Some localization approaches have been proposed in the literature with the aim to enhance their performance in harsh industrial environments. The authors in [9] presented a method to reduce the self-interference of radio-based ranging measurements in order to enhance the accuracy of the estimated position. Other authors have focussed on inertial navigation systems proposing pedestrian dead reckoning localization [3][8]. In order to estimate sensor's orientation in a robust way, mechanisms for bias estimation and *attitude* error compensation have been developed; either by taking assumptions on the movement of persons or introducing additional sensors [6] such as a magnetometer for the heading computation. However, the magnetic field might be highly disturbed in industrial environments making the bias and *attitude* error correction challenging. The authors in [10] presented an effective and adaptive IMU/Magnetometer based filter for an *attitude* and heading reference system (AHRS). The experiments in [10] proved that the proposed method can improve the orientation estimation performance of low-cost IMU sensors. Also the authors in [2] presented a comparison of several state-of-the-art AHRS algorithms proposing an approach to improve their behaviour in industrial environments. Special emphasis has been given to the effects of magnetic perturbations. The experimental results showed that the proposed approach is highly recommended for a better orientation estimation performance in challenging environments.

Furthermore, many authors have proposed hybrid solutions combining different technologies. In [6] a localization system was presented fusing both received signal strength (RSS) ranging measurements and IMU measurements. The system was tested in an industrial environment providing an accuracy of 2 meters [6]. Notwithstanding RSS/IMU fusions are widely used, the localization accuracy is low. UWB/IMU fusions have recently received more attention, since they can achieve good position accuracy even at low update rates of ranging measurements, *e.g.* 1 Hz [4]. The authors in [4] presented a low-cost system for accurate localization in challenging environments that fuses UWB/IMU measurements. The system was tested both in outdoor and indoor environments. It was shown that the hybrid system can maintain a sub-meter accuracy of localization with an UWB update rate reduced from 10 Hz to 0.2 Hz.

The contribution of this paper is a hybrid localization algorithm that has been designed adopting a modular approach. In particular, the algorithm distributes the processing effort in a two-cascade extended Kalman filter (EKF). The first EKF implements the AHRS presented in [10] for the *attitude* estimation. In addition, here the approaches described in [2] are used to improve the performance of the AHRS in industrial environments. The second EKF implements a proposed $Position-Velocity-Acceleration$ (PVA) model to perform the localization. As a result, it is possible to perform reliable pedestrian localization in industrial environments by means of wearable devices and thus support the workers' safety.

3. OVERVIEW OF THE HYBRID LOCALIZATION SYSTEM

Figure 1 presents the overall architecture of the localization system. It consists of an UWB-based indoor positioning system, able to estimate the location of workers on the basis of a prototype UWB-based wearable device. The system is composed of the UWB-based wearable device, presented in more detail in section 4, (named *tag*), UWB fixed nodes (named *anchors*), and an UWB gateway (GW). The *tag* periodically communicates with the *anchors* performing time-of-arrival (ToA)-based ranging measurements [5]. These measurements along with the position of the *anchors* and the inertial measurements collected from the *tag*'s IMU, are processed by the localization algorithm implemented in the wearable device to estimate the worker's position. As soon as the estimated position is available, the *tag* sends it to the GW interacting with a computer which collects the estimated data. Figure 1 shows an example of application scenario related to occupational safety. In this scenario, in order to guarantee the safety, the PC implements an application that provides alerts based on a geo-fencing logics service by using a classical point-in-polygon algorithm: given a set of predefined forbidden/dangerous areas at the shop floor and the estimated workers' position, the geo-fencing application detects wether they are inside these areas, and generates an alarm if necessary.

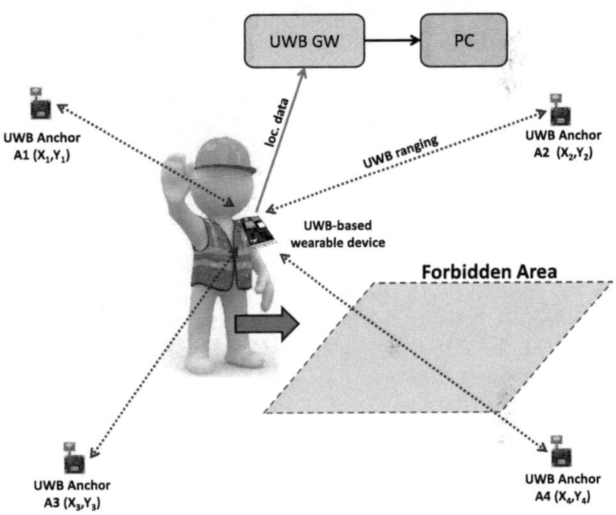

Figure 1: Overall architecture of the localization system.

4. OVERVIEW OF THE UWB-BASED WEARABLE DEVICE

This section presents the hardware (HW) features of the UWB-based wearable prototype, showed Figure 2, that has been used as a *tag* to test the localization algorithm. The size of the prototype is 46 mm x 29 mm.

The STM32F411 ARM Cortex F4 Microprocessor from ST Microelectronics[1] has been selected as the main processing unit. The wearable integrates two different wireless technologies that can be used for communication: a UWB radio module, which is mainly used for localization and small payload communication; and a Bluetooth Low Energy (BLE) module that can be used to transmit information to smartphones and other devices, *e.g.* tablets. In addition, an IMU sensor has been integrated to enable the hybrid localization.

[1]http://www.st.com

Figure 2: UWB-based wearable platform.

The UWB radio module is based on the DWM1000[2] component which is compliant with the IEEE802.15.4a standard [7]. It allows distance measurements between two devices with an accuracy of up to 10 cm in LoS. Under ideal circumstances this chip will be able to measure distances up to 300 m. The module uses centre frequencies of 3495.4, 3993.6, 4492.8 or 6489.6 MHz respectively and operates at bandwidths of 499.2 or 900 MHz. In addition, the ranging can be performed at data rates of 110 kbps, 850 kbps or 6.8 Mbps.

The BLE module is based on the SPBTLE-RF[3] component which is compliant with the second generation BlueNRG-MS chip[4] and provides a low power solution. This module operates as a radio receiver that also implements most of the Bluetooth 4.1 stack.

Finally, the IMU sensor is based on the MPU9250[5] device which includes a 3-axis gyroscope, 3-axis accelerometer and 3-axis magnetometer in one package.

Furthermore, the prototype also incorporates a USB port, LEDs and free GPIO pins and provides means for adding additional sensors in the future.

5. HYBRID LOCALIZATION ALGORITHM

Figure 3 presents the architecture of the localization algorithm. In particular, there are two main blocks involved in the localization: *Attitude estimator*, presented in section 5.1, and *Location estimator*, presented in section 5.2. The *Attitude estimator* provides orientation information as well as bias tracking for the gyroscope measurements. The *Location estimator* tracks the position and velocity of the target, and the bias of the accelerometer taking as input both the *attitude* and UWB-based range measurements. Since the readings of the sensors (*i.e.* UWB/Inertial/Magnetic measurements) have different update rates, the *attitude* and the localization modules can be executed at different intervals of time; thus, this helps distributing the processing efforts. Moreover, the disturbances that affect the performance of the hybrid algorithm are managed by the *Correction control* block and the outliers filter. The *Correction control* block performs analysis of the IMU measurements. This block is described in section 5.1. The outliers filter processes the ranging measurements and rejects ranging distances. In particular, ranging measurement with respect to an *anchor* can be rejected when the difference between the current estimated distance and the previous one, divided by the time step, is larger than the defined maximum walking speed of a person.

[2]http://www.decawave.com/products/dwm1000-module

[3]http://www.st.com/en/wireless-connectivity/spbtle-rf.html

[4]http://www.st.com/en/wireless-connectivity/bluenrg.html

[5]https://www.invensense.com/products/motion-tracking/9-axis/mpu-9250/

5.1 Attitude estimator

This block uses routines to compute and correct the sensor's *attitude* and the bias of gyroscope measurements by means of: the *Orientation computation*, the *EKF attitude error estimator* and the *Attitude correction* components inside the AHRS block.

The *Orientation computation* uses gyroscope measurements to update the *tag*'s *attitude* by using a Padè approximation [4]. The *attitude* is expressed as the direction-cosine-matrix (DCM) from body (b)-frame to navigation (n)-frame. Since the drift in gyroscope measurements increase in time, an error into the updated *attitude* will increases each time the Padè approximation is performed. Thus a method for tracking the bias and the *attitude* error has to be adopted. To this aim, the AHRS algorithm presented in [10] has been adopted and implemented by the *EKF attitude error estimator* component. This EKF estimates the *attitude* error expressed in Euler angles and the bias of the gyroscope measurements by means of accelerometer/magnetometer measurements in b-frame. The main characteristic of this component is the effective adaptability to set the EKF parameters according to the dynamic scale sensed by the accelerometers. The *Attitude correction* component adjusts the updated *attitude* by means of the tracked errors as in [8].

In general, AHRS algorithms are only able to track the previously mentioned errors in a reliable way under ideal conditions, *i.e.* no significant acceleration and magnetic disturbances. Thus the submodules in the *Correction control* block (*i.e.* SP/ZA/MD detectors) [3] have been fostered to detect the right time to track those errors. Then, the proper time to enable the AHRS block is when no magnetic disturbances are presented (established by the magnetic disturbances (MD) detector), and when there are static periods or zero acceleration instants (determinated by the static periods (SP) detector and the zero acceleration(ZA) detector, respectively).

5.2 Location estimator

This block implements an EKF that uses a PVA model to represent the dynamics of the system. The location of the worker is computed here in two steps: the EKF *predict phase* and the EKF *update phase*. The *predict phase* uses the estimated *attitude* presented in section 5.1, the accelerometer measurements and the dynamic equations to provide the *a priori* location information. The *update phase* uses the UWB-based ranging measurements to update and correct the predicted position by the previous phase as well as to track the bias of the accelerometer. In case the *anchor* connectivity is limited, the *update phase* cannot be implemented. However, *a priori* location information estimated in the *predict phase* can be used to provide accurate position estimation but over a short-period of time. This short-period depends on the bias of the accelerometer readings, since this affects the performance of the predicted positions.

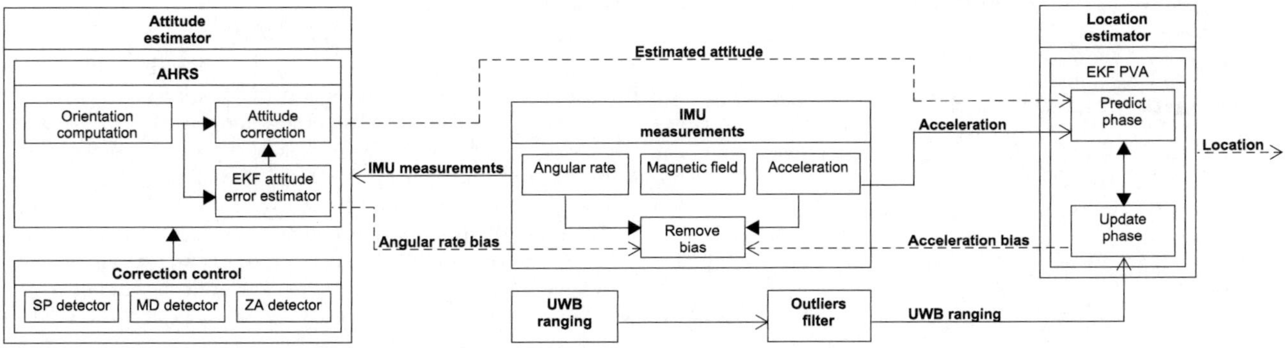

Figure 3: Block Scheme of the Hybrid Localization Algorithm.

5.2.1 EKF PVA Implementation

The EKF performance depends heavily on how well the systems dynamics and measurements, including their statistical characterization, are modelled; therefore, a properly definition of the state model that describes the system dynamics is relevant. This section focuses on the design and development of a low-complexity tracking algorithm in a low dynamics scenario, *i.e.*, localization workers in industrial environments. As mentioned, the dynamics of the system follow a PVA model. The state vector ($\boldsymbol{x}$) in Eq. 1 expresses the position, velocity and acceleration bias expressed in NED (North-East-Down) coordinates.

$$\boldsymbol{x} = [\boldsymbol{p}, \boldsymbol{v}, \delta\boldsymbol{a}]^T, \tag{1}$$

where, $\boldsymbol{p}$ and $\boldsymbol{v}$ are position and velocity vectors, respectively, expressed as $\boldsymbol{p} = [p_n, p_e, p_d]$ and $\boldsymbol{v} = [v_n, v_e, v_d]$, and $\delta\boldsymbol{a}$ is the acceleration bias defined as $\delta\boldsymbol{a} = [\delta a_n, \delta a_e, \delta a_d]$. Where the bias $\delta\boldsymbol{a}$ is the difference between the measured acceleration ($\tilde{\boldsymbol{a}}^n$) and the true acceleration ($\boldsymbol{a}^n$) both in the n-frame as $\delta\boldsymbol{a}^n = \tilde{\boldsymbol{a}}^n - \boldsymbol{a}^n$. In addition, $\tilde{\boldsymbol{a}}^n$ is computed by rotating the accelerometer measurements from b-frame to n-frame by means of the DCM obtained from the *Attitude estimator* (see section 5.1) as $\tilde{\boldsymbol{a}}^n = C_b^n \times \tilde{\boldsymbol{a}}^b$. Where C_b^n is the DCM from b-frame to n-frame.

The equations that describe the dynamics of the system are the following:

$$\boldsymbol{p}_k^n = \boldsymbol{p}_{k-1}^n + \boldsymbol{v}_{k-1}^n \Delta t_k + \boldsymbol{a}_k^n \Delta t_k^2/2, \tag{2}$$

$$\boldsymbol{v}_k^n = \boldsymbol{v}_{k-1}^n + \boldsymbol{a}_k^n \Delta t_k, \tag{3}$$

$$\boldsymbol{a}_k^n = \boldsymbol{a}_k^n, \tag{4}$$

where, Δt_k is the time elapsed between the previous estimation time t_{k-1} and the current estimation time t_k. The measured acceleration in n-frame is considered as an input to the system.

The *predict phase* and the *update phase* are further described in the following.

Predict phase

The discrete EKF state of a dynamic system is modelled by the following discrete time state equation [1].

$$\begin{aligned} \boldsymbol{x}_k &= f(\boldsymbol{x}_{k-1}, \boldsymbol{\mu}_k) + \boldsymbol{w}_k, \\ \boldsymbol{w}_k &\sim \mathcal{N}(\boldsymbol{0}, Q_k), \end{aligned} \tag{5}$$

where $\boldsymbol{x}_k$ is the state vector at time k, f is the state transition function which evolves the previous *a posteriori* state vector $\boldsymbol{x}_{k-1}$ and the input $\boldsymbol{\mu}_k$ to the system. The random process noise vector $\boldsymbol{w}_k$ is modelled as an independent random variable with zero mean and covariance matrix Q_k. The process noise vector takes into account the non-linearity and perturbations of the system.

The prediction of the state vector is estimated as follows:

$$\hat{\boldsymbol{x}}_{k|k-1} = f(\hat{\boldsymbol{x}}_{k-1|k-1}, \boldsymbol{\mu}_k) = F_k \hat{\boldsymbol{x}}_{k-1|k-1} + B_k \boldsymbol{\mu}_k, \tag{6}$$

where $F_k = \frac{\delta f}{\delta x}|_{\hat{\boldsymbol{x}}_{k-1|k-1}}$ is the Jacobian matrix of the state transition function f and B_k relates the input $\boldsymbol{\mu}_k$ with the dynamics of the system.

$$F_k = \begin{bmatrix} I_3 & \Delta t_k I_3 & -C_{bk}^n \Delta t_k^2 I_3/2 \\ 0_3 & I_3 & -C_{bk}^n \Delta t_k I_3 \\ 0_3 & 0_3 & I_3 \end{bmatrix}, \tag{7}$$

$$B_k = \begin{bmatrix} \Delta t_k^2 I_3/2 \\ \Delta t_k I_3 \\ 0_3 \end{bmatrix}, \tag{8}$$

where I_3 is a 3x3 identity matrix and 0_3 is a 3x3 matrix with all 0 entries.

The covariance $P_{k|k-1}$ associated to $\hat{\boldsymbol{x}}_{k|k-1}$ is also evaluated from the previous *a posteriori* $P_{k-1|k-1}$ and the process noise covariance matrix Q_k.

$$\boldsymbol{P}_{k|k-1} = F_k P_{k-1|k-1} F_k^T + Q_k, \tag{9}$$

$$Q_k = \begin{bmatrix} \Delta t_k^2 I_3/2 \\ \Delta t_k I_3 \\ I_3 \end{bmatrix} \begin{bmatrix} \sigma_{\breve{a}_1}^2 & 0 & 0 \\ 0 & \sigma_{\breve{a}_2}^2 & 0 \\ 0 & 0 & \sigma_{\breve{a}_3}^2 \end{bmatrix} \begin{bmatrix} \Delta t_k^2 I_3/2 \\ \Delta t_k I_3 \\ I_3 \end{bmatrix}^T, \tag{10}$$

where $\breve{a}_1^2, \breve{a}_2^2$ and $\breve{a}_3^2$ are the variances of an independent random accelerations that allow to track the different forces that could temporally affect target's dynamics (*e.g.*, friction) [1].

Update phase

This phase occurs at time k, when an observation vector $\boldsymbol{z}_k$ becomes available. This vector is modelled as follows [1]:

$$\begin{aligned} \boldsymbol{z}_k &= h(\boldsymbol{x}_k) + v_k, \\ \boldsymbol{v}_k &\sim \mathcal{N}(\boldsymbol{0}, R_k), \end{aligned} \tag{11}$$

where $\boldsymbol{z}_k$ is the measurements vector at time k, h is the observation function, which estimates the expected measurements at the state $\boldsymbol{x}_k$ and $\boldsymbol{v}_k$ is the random observation noise vector assumed to be normally distributed with zero mean and covariance matrix R_k.

The observations are modelled on the basis of the classical position and distance models [1]. The UWB-ranging measurements represent the observation vector $\boldsymbol{z}$ defined as the distances between the UWB-based wearable device and L connected *anchor* nodes. Note that L can change along the time.

$$\boldsymbol{z} = \left[\begin{array}{ccc} \tilde{d}_{\text{ref}_1} & \cdots & \tilde{d}_{\text{ref}_L} \end{array} \right]^T, \tag{12}$$

where a generic distance $\tilde{d}_{\text{ref}_l}$, where $l \in [1, L]$, is the estimated UWB ranging measurement. The measured distance can be modeled as:

$$\tilde{d}_{\text{ref}_l} = d_{\text{ref}_l} + \eta, \tag{13}$$

where η is the observation error and d_{ref_l} is the true ranging measurement defined as:

$$d_{\text{ref}_l} = \text{dist}\left(\boldsymbol{p}, \boldsymbol{p}_{\text{ref}_l}\right) = \sqrt{\sum_{i=1}^{3} \left(p_i - p_{i,\text{ref}_l}\right)^2}. \tag{14}$$

Typically the observation errors are modelled as uncorrelated white Gaussian noises so the covariance matrix R_k depends on the variance of the measurements $\sigma^2_{d_{\text{ref}_l}}$, $l \in [1, L]$:

$$R_k = \text{diag}\left(\begin{array}{ccc} \sigma^2_{d_{\text{ref}_1},k} & \cdots & \sigma^2_{d_{\text{ref}_L},k} \end{array} \right). \tag{15}$$

Consequently, the observation function h is defined as the distances between the position component of the state vector and the reference nodes:

$$h\left(\boldsymbol{x}_k\right) = \begin{bmatrix} \text{dist}\left(\boldsymbol{p}_k, \boldsymbol{p}_{\text{ref}_1}\right) \\ \vdots \\ \text{dist}\left(\boldsymbol{p}_k, \boldsymbol{p}_{\text{ref}_L}\right) \end{bmatrix} \tag{16}$$

since $h\left(\boldsymbol{x}_k\right)$ is non-linear, the Jacobian matrix H needs to be computed around the *a priori* state $\boldsymbol{x}_{k|k-1}$:

$$H_k = [H_k^{\text{aux}} | \mathbf{0}_{L,6}], \tag{17}$$

where H_k^{aux} is defined as:

$$H_k^{\text{aux}} = \begin{bmatrix} \frac{p_{1,k|k-1} - p_{1,\text{ref}_1}}{\text{dist}\left(\boldsymbol{p}_{k|k-1}, \boldsymbol{p}_{\text{ref}_1}\right)} & \frac{p_{2,k|k-1} - p_{2,\text{ref}_1}}{\text{dist}\left(\boldsymbol{p}_{k|k-1}, \boldsymbol{p}_{\text{ref}_1}\right)} & \frac{p_{3,k|k-1} - p_{3,\text{ref}_1}}{\text{dist}\left(\boldsymbol{p}_{k|k-1}, \boldsymbol{p}_{\text{ref}_1}\right)} \\ \vdots & \vdots & \vdots \\ \frac{p_{1,k|k-1} - p_{1,\text{ref}_L}}{\text{dist}\left(\boldsymbol{p}_{k|k-1}, \boldsymbol{p}_{\text{ref}_L}\right)} & \frac{p_{2,k|k-1} - p_{2,\text{ref}_L}}{\text{dist}\left(\boldsymbol{p}_{k|k-1}, \boldsymbol{p}_{\text{ref}_L}\right)} & \frac{p_{3,k|k-1} - p_{3,\text{ref}_L}}{\text{dist}\left(\boldsymbol{p}_{k|k-1}, \boldsymbol{p}_{\text{ref}_L}\right)} \end{bmatrix},$$

and $\mathbf{0}_{L,6}$ is a Lx6 matrix with all 0 entries.

The *a posteriori* state estimate $\hat{\boldsymbol{x}}_{k|k}$ and the corresponding covariance matrix $\hat{P}_{k|k}$ are estimated by correcting the *a priori* state estimate $\hat{\boldsymbol{x}}_{k|k-1}$ and the *a priori* state covariance matrix $\hat{P}_{k|k-1}$ with the following equations.

$$\hat{\boldsymbol{x}}_{k|k} = \hat{\boldsymbol{x}}_{k|k-1} + K_k \tilde{\boldsymbol{y}}_k, \tag{18}$$

$$P_{k|k} = \left(I_9 - K_k H_k\right) P_{k|k-1}, \tag{19}$$

where $\tilde{\boldsymbol{y}}_k$ is the innovation vector and K_k is the optimal Kalman gain defined as:

$$\tilde{\boldsymbol{y}}_k = \boldsymbol{z}_k - h\left(\hat{\boldsymbol{x}}_{k|k-1}\right), \tag{20}$$

$$K_k = P_{k|k-1} H_k^T S_k^{-1}, \tag{21}$$

where S_k is the covariance matrix computed as the expected measurement estimation error due to the *a priori* state error covariance plus the observation errors R_k.

$$S_k = H_k P_{k|k-1} H_k^T + R_k. \tag{22}$$

6. EXPERIMENTAL RESULTS

To evaluate the performance of the hybrid localization algorithm, an experimental campaign with dynamic conditions has been performed. Four UWB *anchor* nodes have been deployed in an indoor office area of 12 m × 9 m as depicted in Figure 4. The UWB-based wearable device (presented in section 4) has been used as *tag* worn by a person (named *the subject*), on the waist, at a height of 1.11 m performing ranging measurements with respect to all four *anchors* every 0.333 s. Accelerometer and gyroscope sensors have been sampled every 0.05 s while the magnetometer sensor every 0.1 s. The selected coordinates system is NED, which is the same used by the IMU/Magnetometer sensors.

During the experiment, the *subject* moved around the office in a moderate and steady way. In order to acquire the true position of the target along the time, the path followed by the *subject* has been marked with a metric tape attached to the floor. Besides, a laser has been used pointing down to the metric tape, which indicates the exact position of the UWB antenna. In addition, a camera has been used to register the laser point on the floor coinciding with the exact position of the *tag*. After that, the positions estimated by the algorithm have been compared with the exact ones taken, from the camera at the same time stamps, to calculate the accuracy. All raw data have been logged via USB on a PC and used to evaluate the performance off-line. Doing so, it has been possible to analyze our proposed algorithm and compare it with an UWB-only algorithm based on an EKF [1] using the PV model.

First of all, the logged raw data have been processed in order to set the correct parameters into the localization algorithms (*i.e.*, hybrid, PV EKF). For instance, the statistics for the ranging error were: average 0.37 m, standard deviation 0.21 m. Then the average value, which coincides with the bias, has been used to correct all range measurements. The settings for the UWB communication were: channel 2 (3993.6 MHz) at a bandwidth of 499.2 MHz and a data rate of 110 kbps. In order to use the ZA and SP detectors, presented in section 5.1, the magnitude of the accelerometer and gyroscope readings have been sampled in static conditions and then averaged providing 1.002 g and 0.0019 rad/sec, respectively. The error of the IMU measurements have been modeled according to the data sheet specifications.

Since the experiment has been carried out in an indoor environment, magnetic disturbances might be expected, thus affecting the performance of the *Attitude estimator*. It is clear then, that the performance of the hybrid localization strongly depends on the *Attitude estimator* efficiency.

Figure 4 shows the positions estimated by the proposed hybrid algorithm (described in section 5) and the UWB-only approach using the PV EKF [1]. In addition, the figure shows the true path and the locations of the *anchors*. Since the experiment has been performed at a constant height, the final location error has been analysed in 2D. The localization frequency has been set to 3 Hz for both algorithms (corresponding to the ranging measurement frequency). Localization at higher frequencies is not of interest for this experiment since the application is focused on pedestrian localization. It is worth mentioning that the hybrid algorithm would also be able to track the position at two higher frequencies, 10 Hz and 20 Hz corresponding to the sample frequency of the magnetometer and gyroscope, respectively.

The calculated RMS of the localization error is 0.23 m for

the hybrid algorithm and 0.4 m for the PV EKF algorithm, while the availability is 100% and 63.7%, respectively. The position availability for the PV EKF depends directly on the number of collected ranging measurements from *anchors*. Instead, for the hybrid algorithm there are no constraints regarding the *anchor* connectivity. As mentioned in section 5.2, the *Location estimator* can provide an estimated position in two moments; during the *predict phase* in absence of ranging, and *update phase* when ranging is available. However, the position provided by the *predict phase* can be used only for a short period of time because the bias correction for the accelerometer, which is part of the *update phase*, is not executed. Thus, apart from the accuracy, another advantage of the hybrid algorithm is the increased availability in harsh environments. This advantage could be exploited to reduce the number of *anchors* while meeting a desired level of performance. Additionally, the registered average ranging availability with four *anchors* was 74.1%. Note that a ranging measurement is considered available when both *tag* and *anchor* are able to exchange messages. The maximum range strongly depends on the environment. Typically, it is approximately 249 m in LoS and 27 m in NLoS.

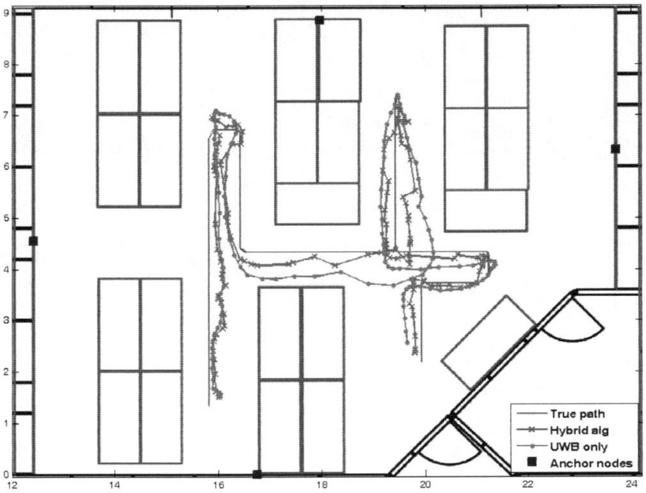

Figure 4: Plot of the location estimation.

7. CONCLUSION

This paper proposed a hybrid localization algorithm, combining UWB-based ranging measurements and IMU data, able to work in harsh industrial environments for pedestrian localization. This work has been motivated by the occupational safety scenario that is of great interest in the era of Industry 4.0. In order to improve the localization performance, the proposed hybrid algorithm has been based on the adoption of several existing filter techniques and disturbance measurement detectors that provide a reliable asset estimation. The estimation of the orientation is an input to the proposed hybrid PVA EKF block. The hybrid algorithm has been further improved by integrating a filter that removes ranging measurements outliers. To evaluate the localization performance in an indoor environment, the designed hybrid algorithm has been implemented in a proprietary wearable platform. This wearable device has also allowed the storage of the raw data into a PC for further off-line analysis.

The PV EKF algorithm [1], which is based only on UWB raging measurements, has been chosen as benchmark. Taking as input the collected experimental data, the proposed hybrid algorithm has provided a localization RMS error of 0.23 m and availability of 100%, outperforming the PV EKF algorithm, which has shows a localization error of 0.45 m and availability of 63.7%.

The main advantages of the proposed algorithm with respect to the PV EKF were: improved location accuracy, improved availability, accurate *attitude* estimation and the possibility to use higher localization update rates. The improved location availability could be used to reduce the number of *anchors* required while meeting a required level of performance; thus saving deployment costs and hardware maintenance. In addition, the modular approach adopted in the hybrid algorithm implementation led to a reduction of computational processing in comparison with other hybrid implementations [4]. In fact, the processing cost is saved because the matrixes are smaller.

8. ACKNOWLEDGMENTS

This work was partially supported by the European H2020 project SatisFactory, under contract no: 636302.

9. REFERENCES

[1] M. A. Caceres, F. Sottile, and M. A. Spirito. Adaptive location tracking by kalman filter in wireless sensor networks. In *2009 IEEE International Conference on Wireless and Mobile Computing, Networking and Communications*, pages 123–128, Oct 2009.

[2] E. M. Diaz, F. de Ponte Müller, A. R. Jiménez, and F. Zampella. Evaluation of ahrs algorithms for inertial personal localization in industrial environments. In *2015 IEEE International Conference on Industrial Technology (ICIT)*, pages 3412–3417, March 2015.

[3] E. M. Diaz, A. L. M. Gonzalez, and F. de Ponte Müller. Standalone inertial pocket navigation system. In *2014 IEEE/ION Position, Location and Navigation Symposium - PLANS 2014*, pages 241–251, May 2014.

[4] T. Gaedeke, M. Johnson, M. Hedley, and W. Stork. Fusion of wireless ranging and inertial sensors for precise and scalable indoor localization. In *2014 IEEE International Conference on Communications Workshops (ICC)*, pages 138–143, June 2014.

[5] S. Gezici, Z. Tian, G. B. Biannakis, H. Kobayashi, A. F. Molisch, V. Poor, Z. Sahinoglu, S. Gezici, Z. Tian, G. B. Giannakis, H. Kobayashi, A. F. Molisch, H. V. Poor, and Z. Sahinoglu. Localization via ultra-wideband radios. In *IEEE Signal Processing Magazine*, pages 70–84, 2005.

[6] F. Hartmann, T. Gaedeke, P. Leibold, L. Niestoruk, and W. Stork. Navigation for occupational safety in harsh industrial environments. In *Smart Objects, Systems and Technologies (Smart SysTech), 2014 European Conference on*, pages 1–8, July 2014.

[7] IEEE. IEEE 802.15.4-2015 - IEEE Standard for Low-Rate Wireless Networks. 2015.

[8] A. R. Jiménez, F. Seco, J. C. Prieto, and J. Guevara. Indoor pedestrian navigation using an ins/ekf framework for yaw drift reduction and a foot-mounted imu. In *Positioning Navigation and Communication*

(WPNC), 2010 7th Workshop on, pages 135–143, March 2010.

[9] A. Lewandowski and C. Wietfeld. A comprehensive approach for optimizing toa-localization in harsh industrial environments. In *Position Location and Navigation Symposium (PLANS), 2010 IEEE/ION*, pages 516–525, May 2010.

[10] W. Li and J. Wang. Effective adaptive kalman filter for mems-imu/magnetometers integrated attitude and heading reference systems. *Journal of Navigation*, 66(1):99–113, 007 2012.

[11] D. Lucke, E. Westkamper, M. Eissele, T. Ertl, and O. Siemoneit. Privacy-preserving self-localization techniques in next generation manufacturing an interdisciplinary view on the vision and implementation of smart factories. In *Control, Automation, Robotics and Vision, 2008. ICARCV 2008. 10th International Conference on*, pages 1183–1188, Dec 2008.

[12] K. Zhou, T. Liu, and L. Zhou. Industry 4.0: Towards future industrial opportunities and challenges. In *Fuzzy Systems and Knowledge Discovery (FSKD), 2015 12th International Conference on*, pages 2147–2152, Aug 2015.

Design and Calibration of A 60-GHz Personal Exposimeter for Exposure Assessment in Specular and Diffuse Environments

Reza Aminzadeh[1]*, Arno Thielens[1], Abdou Khadir Fall[2], Haolin Li[1], Carole Leduc[3], Maxim Zhadobov[3], Guy Torfs[1], Johan Bauwelinck[1], Luc Martens[1] and Wout Joseph[1]

*[1]Department of Information Technology, Ghent University/iMinds, Technologiepark-Zwijnaarde 15, B-9052 Ghent, Belgium
reza.aminzadeh@intec.ugent.be

[2]Institute of Electronics and Telecommunications of Rennes (IETR), INSA, UMR CNRS 6164, University of Rennes 1, 35708 Rennes, France

[3]Institute of Electronics and Telecommunications of Rennes (IETR), UMR CNRS 6164, University of Rennes 1, 35042 Rennes, France

ABSTRACT

For the first time, a personal exposimeter (PE) for 60 GHz radiation measurements is presented. The PE is designed based on numerical simulations, on-phantom and on-body calibration measurements under specular and diffuse exposure to determine the antenna aperture and measurement uncertainty of the PE. A 95% prediction interval of 6.6 dB is obtained for the PE's response using a combination of three nodes with different polarizations. The response of the PE is in the range of 0.7 to 1.2 for specular and diffuse fields.

CCS Concepts

•**Computer systems organization** → **Sensor networks;** •**Hardware** → *Sensor applications and deployments; Wireless devices;*

Keywords

Personal exposimeter; Calibration; Specular; Diffuse; Mm-waves; Exposure

1. INTRODUCTION

Recent developments in 60-GHz communication systems have heightened the need for assessing potential health effects of mm-waves [1]. Research on biological effects of mm-waves is necessary to ensure safety of mm-wave systems and to update the related safety standards. Before being commercialized, any wireless device should comply with international guidelines, such as those issued by the International Commission on Non-Ionizing Radiation Protection (ICNIRP) [2]. The incident power density (IPD) is used as a dosimetric quantity at 60-GHz [2].

Previous dosimetric studies in the 60 GHz band are not yet widely established on a real human subject [1,3]. Therefore, assessment of human exposure to mm-wave systems in real life scenarios is necessary.

A large number of studies, for example [4–6], have investigated everyday life IPD measurements using personal exposimeters (PEMs) for frequencies lower than 6 GHz. PEMs measure the total electric fields near the body instead of the actual incident fields, and are consequently faced with large measurement uncertainties [7].

People spend most of their time indoor and are exposed to EM radiation continuously. According to the room electromagnetics' theory [8], the total power in an indoor environment is composed of specular and diffuse multipath components (DMC), which result from coherent and non-coherent reflections (multiple sets of diffracted waves), respectively.

In this paper, for the first time, a prototype of wearable 60-GHz on-body personal exposimeter (PE) is presented for specular and diffuse fields exposure. The PE consists of three receiving nodes (antennas) to measure the IPD in realistic indoor environments, and is calibrated in anechoic conditions using a real human subject and in a mm-wave reverberation chamber (RC) on a skin-equivalent phantom. The measurement uncertainty of the proposed prototype of PE is assessed in terms of numerical simulations and calibration measurements.

2. MATERIALS AND METHODS

First, the design of the PE which is based on numerical simulations at 60 GHz, is described in Section 2.1. Next, the on-body calibrations on a real human subject (in ane-

*Corrosponding author.

choic conditions) and on two skin-equivalent phantoms (in anechoic conditions and in an RC) are described in Section 2.2. The processing of the measurements is described in Section 2.2.3.

2.1 numerical modeling

Figure 1 illustrates the proposed numerical model of a PE. The finite-difference time-domain (FDTD) simulation platform, Sim4Life [9], is used to determine the distribution of the on-body received power on the antenna. A homogeneous skin model ($200 \times 200 \times 10$ mm^3) is used during simulations to emulate the human body. The dielectric properties of this model are taken from dry skin at 60 GHz [10]. The antenna used for modeling (see Figure 1) is a microstrip-fed antenna array, operating in the 60-GHz band [11].

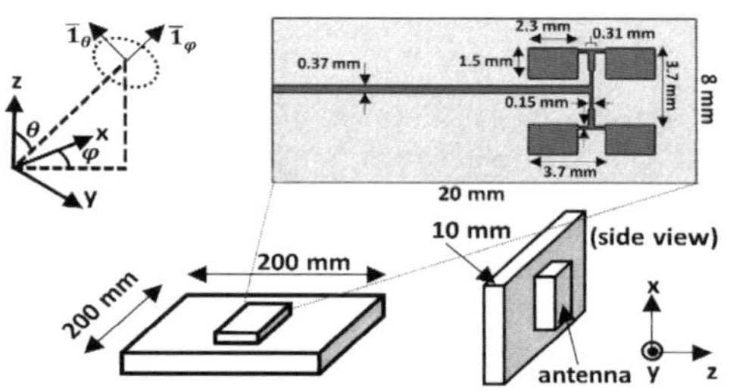

Figure 1: The proposed model for numerical simulations. Schematic representation of a single node (antenna) at 5.6 mm from the skin used for simulations and measurements [11].

Simulations are performed for the antenna in free space and near the skin model (5.6 mm due to the geometry of connector) to determine the response of the antenna. The response (R) of the antenna is studied as the ratio of the median received power on-body (P_r^{body}) to the median received power in free space (P_r^{free}):

$$R = \frac{P_r^{body}}{P_r^{free}} \tag{1}$$

The received power on an antenna can be determined from its aperture [12]:

$$P_r(\varphi, \theta) = AA(\varphi, \theta) \times S_{inc} \tag{2}$$

where AA and S_{inc} are the on-body antenna aperture and incident power density, respectively. In order to calculate the on-body aperture of the antenna $AA(\varphi, \theta)$, the directive gain of the antenna $D(\varphi, \theta)$ is extracted for azimuth angle (φ) and polar angle (θ) from numerical simulations as:

$$AA(\varphi, \theta) = \eta_{rad}(1 - |S_{11}|^2) D(\varphi, \theta) \frac{\lambda^2}{4\pi} \tag{3}$$

where η_{rad} is the radiation efficiency, $|S_{11}|^2$ is the antenna's power reflection coefficient, and λ is the wavelength. $AA(\varphi, \theta)$ can be determined for two orthogonal polarizations on the incident electric fields: θ and φ, which are the polarizations parallel to the unity vectors $\overline{1}_\theta$ and $\overline{1}_\phi$.

For the specular fields, a realistic far-field exposure scenario in the 60-GHz band for an indoor environment (IEEE 802.11 standard [13]) is considered to determine the response of the simulated on-body antenna. A Gaussian distribution with a cross polarization ratio of 20 dB is assumed for the indoor exposure scenario [13]. The phase (α) of plane waves is assumed to have a uniform distribution in the range of $0 < \psi < 2\pi$. For θ and φ, samples are drawn from their distributions [13].

For diffuse fields α, φ, θ and ψ are all assumed to have a uniform distribution [8].

2.2 calibration measurement setup

The calibration measurements are performed in anechoic conditions for specular fields (Section 2.2.1) and in a reverberation chamber for diffuse fields (Section 2.2.2).

2.2.1 on-body calibration: specular fields

Figure 2 demonstrates the measurement setup (at 60 GHz) for on-body calibration in specular fields. A standard gain horn antenna (19 dBi) is used as transmitter (TX) and is mounted on a rotation stage (see right hand side of Figure 2). The receiver (RX)-the same antenna used in simulations-is placed in the far field of the TX. An Agilent PNA-X N5247A network analyzer delivers a constant power (6 dBm) to the TX and measures the received on-body power on the RX. Two orthogonal polarizations of TX (to account for any realistic polarization) and RX (due to the asymmetric shape of RX) are studied.

First, the free-space incident power density S_{inc}^{free} is calculated using the Friis formula [12] and then is averaged over 20 cm^2 of the studied area [2].

Second, the RX is placed horizontally on a skin-equivalent phantom (30% gelatin, 70% water) following the instructions of [14]. The received power on the RX is calculated from the measured power gain ($|S_{21}|^2$) for five azimuth angles (φ): -20°to 23°.

Third, the above step is repeated for two polarizations of TX and RX by placing the RX on the forearm of a male subject.

In the fourth step, three locations are selected for the RX on the subject's forearm and the received power is measured on each RX. Next, the best combination of three antennas on the forearm is determined based on the 50% prediction interval (PI_{50}) of the measurements (see Figure 3).

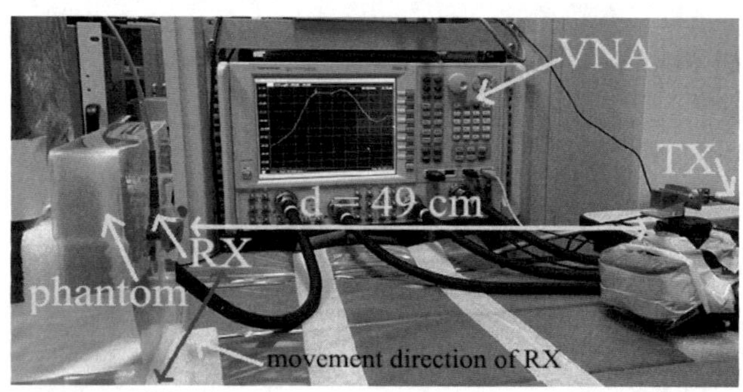

Figure 2: Measurement setup in anechoic conditions at 60 GHz.

2.2.2 on-body calibration: diffuse fields

Figure 4 shows the measurement setup in the reverberation chamber at 60 GHz. An RC with $0.58 \times 0.592 \times 0.595$ m^3 dimensions is used. A Wiltron 360 VNA is used to feed a rectangular WR-15 waveguide as the source (TX) and to

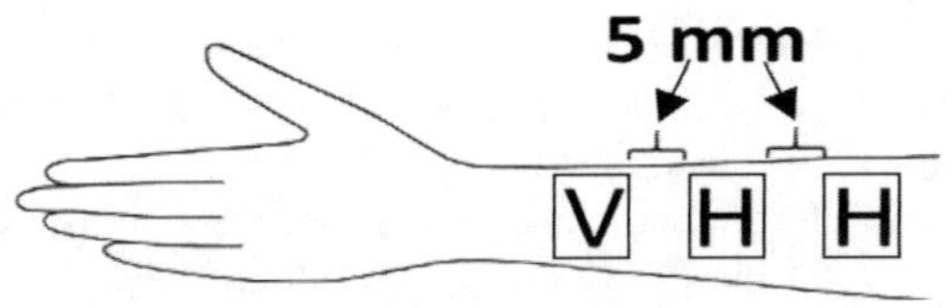

Figure 3: The optimized orientation of the antennas on the subject's forearm determined from the on-body calibration measurements (not to scale).

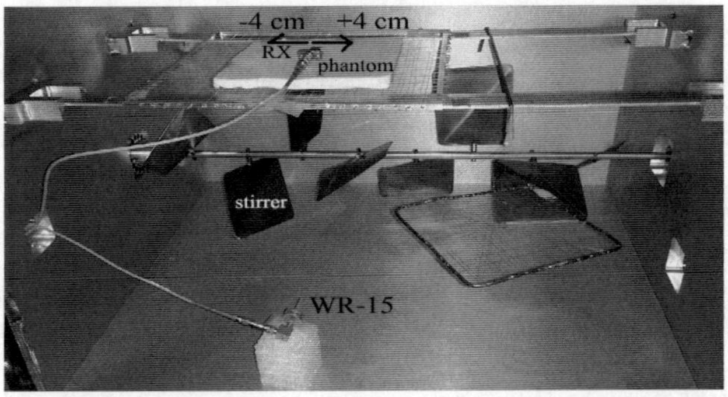

Figure 4: Measurement setup in RC at 60 GHz. Three locations of RX is indicated on top of the phantom. (± is used to indicate right and left.)

measure the scattering parameters of RX for 100 positions of the stirrer during a full rotation. A semi-solid phantom is used to emulate the dielectric properties of human skin at 60 GHz [15].

Firstly, scattering parameters are measured in free space in the RC. For the antenna on body, the lossy phantom can load the chamber during calibration measurements and thus will change the power density values inside the chamber [16]. Therefore, the phantom is placed far away from the RX during the free space measurements.

Secondly, the RX is placed on the center of the phantom and the scattering parameters are measured on three locations of RX on the phantom (see Figure 4; center and 4 cm from center on the right and the left).

The antenna aperture is calculated from the Q-factor [17]. Therefore, following equations(1) and (2), the response (the ratio of antenna aperture) for diffuse fields R_{RC} is defined as:

$$R_{RC} = \frac{AA_{phantom}}{AA_{free-space}} = \frac{\langle |S_{21,ph}|^2 - |\langle S_{21,ph}\rangle|^2\rangle}{\langle |S_{21,fr}|^2 - |\langle S_{21,fr}\rangle|^2\rangle} \quad (4)$$

where $S_{21,ph}$ and $S_{21,fr}$ are S-parameters for the RX on the phantom and the RX in free space (phantom at a far distance from the RX), respectively. The notation $\langle\rangle$ stands for an average over the stirrer's positions.

2.2.3 *Process measurements in a real environment*

During the measurements in the real environment a power ($P_{r,i}^{meas}$) is recorded on each antenna i. This received power can be used to determine the incident power density (S_{inc}):

$$S_{inc} = \frac{P_{r,i}^{meas}}{AA_i} \quad (5)$$

where AA_i (m^2) is the effective median on-body antenna aperture obtained from calibration measurements. For specular fields, $AA_i(\varphi,\psi)$ values are determined for any realistic polarization (as the the sum of two orthogonal polarizations) [18]:

$$AA_i(\varphi,\psi) = \frac{P_{r,i}^{body,H}(\varphi)}{S_{inc}^{free,H}} cos^2(\psi) + \frac{P_{r,i}^{body,V}(\varphi)}{S_{inc}^{free,V}} sin^2(\psi) \quad (6)$$

The free-space power density $S_{inc}^{free,H/V}$ for the same input power is obtained from the first step of calibration measurements. A Gaussian distribution that is applicable for indoor 60 GHz communications is used for specular fields [13]. For diffuse fields a uniform distribution is used [8]. During the calibration measurements the powers $P_{r,i}^{body,H/V}(\varphi)$ are registered for five angles (φ). These antenna apertures AA_i are determined for a realistic polarization ψ. Next, 1000 ψ-samples are generated for every measured power value and this is repeated during 1000 iterations. Calculating AA_i, for every pair of (φ,ψ), results in a distribution of AA_i for every antenna i.

For diffuse fields, R_{RC} values are used in equation (5) to calculate the incident power density on body.

3. RESULTS AND DISCUSSION

3.1 specular fields

Fig. 5 shows the distribution of the on-body antenna aperture obtained from calibration measurements for both H and V polarizations of the TX and RX. The measured antenna aperture for the horizontally (H) oriented RX on-body and on the skin equivalent phantom are also in good agreement (difference is only 8.3% for the median values). These data are in good agreement with the antenna aperture determined from simulations (difference of 17.7% for the median values). The median antenna aperture AA_i is 0.1 mm^2 (horizontal orientation of RX) on phantom, 0.092 mm^2 (horizontal RX) on body, 0.077 mm^2 (horizontal RX) for simulations and 23×10^{-3} mm^2 (vertical RX) on body. Thus, the results suggest that the absorbed energy for the body (horizontal RX) is higher than the phantom, which leads to a lower received power on the antenna on body and thus a lower AA value for the body with respect to the phantom.

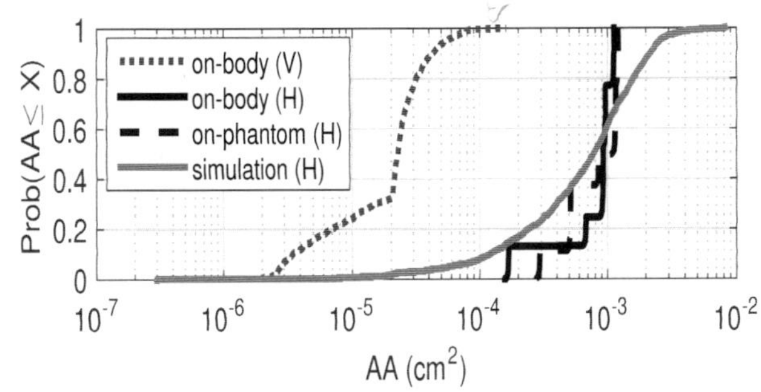

Figure 5: Distribution of the on-body antenna aperture: calibration measurements vs. simulations.

The response is determined using (1) and is equal to 0.8 (-0.96 dB), 0.75 (-1.25 dB) and 0.72 (-1.4 dB) for one-antenna calibration measurements on body, measurements on the phantom and for simulations on the phantom, respectively. This indicates underestimation of the incident electric fields with respect to free space values. This conclusion is also obtained for exposure assessment at frequencies $\leq$6 GHz [6,7].

3.2 diffuse fields

Figure 6 shows the ratio of AA (response) for diffuse fields. At 60 GHz the R_{RC} is equal to 1.2 which is higher than the calculated response for specular fields (0.75 for the phantom at 60 GHz). The value of R_{RC} changes in the range of 1-1.2 and is reduced to about 0.9 with increasing the frequency. The simulated response for the diffuse exposure is obtained as 0.96 at 60 GHz and is 22.2% different from the measured value at the same frequency.

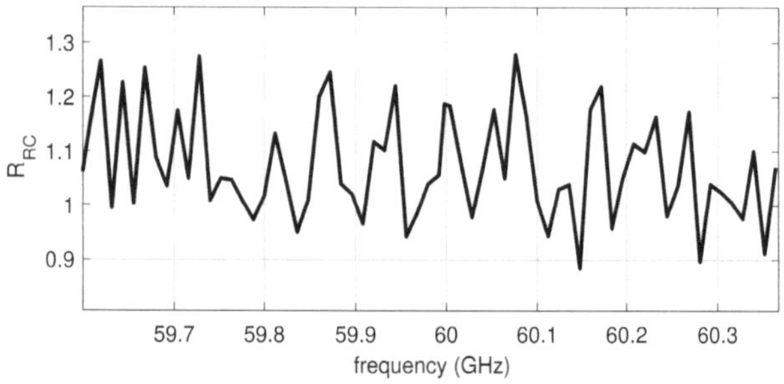

Figure 6: Ratio of antenna aperture in RC.

3.3 multi-node design of antennas

Fig. 7 compares the PI_{50} and PI_{95} of the angular averaged response (R_{meas}) of the PE consisting of 1, 2 and 3 antennas for the specular fields, according to the best combination of three antennas on the subject's forearm. The value of PI_{50} is reduced from 4.4 dB to 3.6 dB and 1.3 dB for three, two and one antenna, respectively. Thus an improvement of 3.1 dB is obtained for three antennas vs. one antenna. Our proposed exposimeter has an improved PI_{50} of 16.6 dB (1 antenna) and 19.7 dB (3 antennas) compared to the PI_{50} of commercial PEMs (up to 21 dB) at lower frequencies [7]. Also the PI_{95} value is reduced from 15.4 dB (1 antenna) to 6.6 dB (2 and 3 antennas), which is an 8.8 dB improvement.

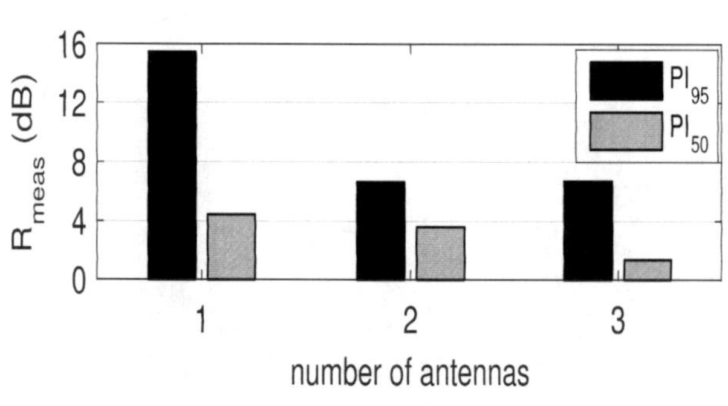

Figure 7: Angular averaged response with smallest 50% and 95% prediction intervals obtained from on-body calibration measurements.

4. CONCLUSION

A personal exposimeter is proposed using a limited number of wearable antennas in the 60 GHz band. Using a combination of multiple nodes, the proposed exposimeter showed good accuracy. An improvement of 3-9 dB is obtained for three antennas compared to a single antenna experiment. The proposed prototype is the first 60 GHz PE and to the authors' best knowledge no data are available in the literature. Future work will consist of developing the PE for an improved wearability and multiple nodes over the user's body as well as a real measurement campaign in the 60 GHz band.

5. ACKNOWLEDGMENTS

This work was supported by the Research Foundation - Flanders (FWO-V) under grant agreement No G027714N.

6. REFERENCES

[1] T. Wu, T.S. Rappaport, and C.M. Collins. Safe for generations to come: Considerations of safety for millimeter waves in wireless communications. *IEEE Microw. Mag.*, 16(2):65–84, March 2015.

[2] International Commission on Non-ionizing Radiation Protection (ICNIRP). Guidelines for limiting exposure to time-varying electric, magnetic, and electromagnetic fields (up to 300 GHz). *Health Phys.*, 74(4):494–522, 1998.

[3] M. Zhadobov, R. Sauleau, R. Augustine, C. Le Quément, Y. Le Dréan, and D. Thouroude. Near-field dosimetry for in vitro exposure of human cells at 60 GHz. *Bioelectromagnetics*, 33(1):55–64, 2012.

[4] J.F. Bolte and T. Eikelboom. Personal radiofrequency electromagnetic field measurements in the netherlands: Exposure level and variability for everyday activities, times of day and types of area. *Environment International*, 48:133 – 142, 2012.

[5] A. Thielens, S. Agneessens, L. Verloock, E. Tanghe, H. Rogier, L. Martens, and W. Joseph. On-body calibration and processing for a combination of two radio-frequency personal exposimeters. *Radiat Prot Dosimetry*, 163(1):58–69, 2015.

[6] R. Aminzadeh, A. Thielens, A. Bamba, L. Kone, D.P. Gaillot, M. Lienard, L. Martens, and W. Joseph. On-body calibration and measurements using personal radiofrequency exposimeters in indoor diffuse and specular environments. *Bioelectromagnetics*, 37(5):298–309, 2016.

[7] J.F. Bolte, G. van der Zande, and J. Kamer. Calibration and uncertainties in personal exposure measurements of radiofrequency electromagnetic fields. *Bioelectromagnetics*, 32(8):652–663, 2011.

[8] J. B. Andersen, J. O. Nielsen, G. F. Pedersen, G. Bauch, and J. M. Herdin. Room electromagnetics. *IEEE Antennas and Propagation Magazine*, 49(2):27–33, April 2007.

[9] Speag. *Sim4Life Reference Manual*, 2016. http://www.zurichmedtech.com/sim4life/.

[10] S. Gabriel, R.W. Lau, and C. Gabriel. The dielectric properties of biological tissues: III. parametric models for the dielectric spectrum of tissues. *Phys. Med. Biol.*, 41, 1996.

[11] N. Chahat, M. Zhadobov, L. Le Coq, S.I. Alekseev, and R. Sauleau. Characterization of the interactions between a 60-GHz antenna and the human body in an off-body scenario. *IEEE Trans. Antennas Propag.*, 60(12):5958–5965, Dec 2012.

[12] C. A. Balanis. *Antenna Theory: Analysis and Design.* Wiley-Interscience, 3 edition, 2005.

[13] A. Maltsev, V. Erceg, E. Perahia, Ch. Hansen, R. Maslennikov, A. Lomayev, A. Sevastyanov, A. Khoryaev, G. Morozov, M. Jacob, S. Priebe, Th. Kürner, Sh. Kato, H. Sawada, K. Sato, and H. Harada. Channel models for 60 GHz WLAN Systems. Technical Report IEEE 802.11-09/0334r8, IEEE, May 2010.

[14] R. Aminzadeh, M. Saviz, and A.A. Shishegar. Theoretical and experimental broadband tissue-equivalent phantoms at microwave and millimetre-wave frequencies. *Electronics Letters*, 50(8):618–620, April 2014.

[15] N. Chahat, M. Zhadobov, and R. Sauleau. Broadband tissue-equivalent phantom for ban applications at millimeter waves. *IEEE Trans. Microw. Theory Techn.*, 60(7):2259–2266, July 2012.

[16] A. K. Fall, P. Besnier, C. Lemoine, M. Zhadobov, and R. Sauleau. Experimental dosimetry in a mode-stirred reverberation chamber in the 60-GHz band. *IEEE Transactions on Electromagnetic Compatibility*, 58(4):981–992, Aug 2016.

[17] Philippe Besnier, Christophe Lemoine, and Jerome Sol. Various estimations of composite q-factor with antennas in a reverberation chamber. In *2015 IEEE International Symposium on Electromagnetic Compatibility (EMC)*, pages 1223–1227. IEEE, 2015.

[18] A. Thielens, S. Agneessens, H. De Clercq, J. Lecoutere, L. Verloock, E. Tanghe, S. Aerts, R. Puers, H. Rogier, L. Martens, and W. Joseph. On-body calibration and measurements using a personal, distributed exposimeter for wireless fidelity. *Health Phys.*, 108(4):407–418, 2015.

Why Do We Need a Remote Health Monitoring System? A Study on Predictive Analytics for Heart Failure Patients

Mohammad Pourhomayoun
California State University,
Los Angeles
CA, 90032
mpourho@calstatela.edu

Nabil Alshurafa
Northwestern University
Northwestern Univ., Chicago
IL, 60611
nabil@northwestern.edu

Foad Dabiri
WANDA Inc.
WANDA Inc., San Francisco
CA, 94104
foad@yourwanda.com

Ehsan Ardestani
WANDA Inc.
WANDA Inc., San Francisco
CA, 94104
ehsan@yourwanda.com

Ahsan Samiee
WANDA Inc.
WANDA Inc., San Francisco
CA, 94104
ahsan@yourwanda.com

Hassan Ghasemzadeh
School of EECS
Washington State University
Pullman, WA, 99164-2752
hassan@eecs.wsu.edu

Majid Sarrafzadeh
UCLA, Computer Science Dept.
UCLA, Los Angeles
CA, 90095
majid@cs.ucla.edu

ABSTRACT

Body area networks and remote health monitoring systems allow for collecting physiological data from patients, and provide a platform to utilize analytics algorithms to predict medical conditions. This paper presents an effective predictive analytic approach for hospital readmission prediction for patients with Congestive Heart Failure (CHF) and based on the physiological data collected in last days of hospital stay. We examine the proposed algorithm on the Electronic Health Records (EHR) of UCLA Hospital containing over 10 million clinical measurements collected from approximately 10,000 patients hospitalized at the UCLA Medical Center. The results show that it is possible to predict medically adverse events (e.g. hospital readmissions) for CHF patients if we have access to recent physiological measurements. This study suggests that a remote health monitoring system can provide an effective platform to reduce readmission rates by early prediction of readmissions based on freshly collected data, and then applying appropriate early clinical interventions to prevent the readmission.

Keywords

mHealth, Remote Health Monitoring Systems (RHMS), Predictive Analytics, Cognitive Heart Failure (CHF).

1. INTRODUCTION and MOTIVATION

As the number of elderly people has grown rather quickly over the past few decades, it is essential to seek alternative and innovative ways to provide affordable healthcare to the aging population [1]. A compelling solution is to enable pervasive healthcare for the elderly or patients with chronic disease in order to shift healthcare services from hospital settings to a remote and home-based scenarios [1]-[8]. Furthermore, the increasing cost of chronic disease management necessitates to utilize effective data analytics techniques, which can help early diagnosis, health condition prediction, and medically adverse event prevention (e.g., hospital readmissions, emergency visits, heart attack, and death) [3][5][6].

As of October 2012, the US government stared the Hospital Readmission Reduction Program, which levies punishment on hospitals with high readmission rates [5]. Congestive Heart Failure (CHF) is one of the leading causes of hospitalizations in the US. Statistics show that 20% to 30% of CHF patients are readmitted to hospitals within 30 days after discharge [5][9][10]. The increasing cost of re-hospitalization demonstrates the necessity of developing effective predictive techniques, which can forecast readmission in advance, and allow for appropriate intervention at early stage to prevent re-hospitalization.

In this paper, we investigate the possibility of predicting hospital readmission based on the physiological measurements collected in the last couple of days of stay in the hospital before discharge. In particular, we focus on CHF patients admitted to the UCLA Medical Center.

2. METHODS

2.1 Data

In this paper, we use the Electronic Health Records (EHR) of UCLA Hospital containing over 10 million clinical measurements collected from about 10,000 patients hospitalized at the UCLA Ronald Reagan Medical Center. The data contains of various contextual and physiological parameters such as vital sign information, demographics, laboratory results, and other physiological measurements.

In this study, we focus on CHF patients admitted to the hospital. We use the physiological measurements collected in the hospital in the last three days before discharge. In particular, we use systolic and diastolic blood pressure, heart rate, oxygen saturation SO2, respiration rate, body temperature, and weight, along with age, gender, and race as the main parameters to predict hospital readmission. Some of this measurements have been collected on daily basis (such as weight). However, some of these metrics have been collected multiple times a day. For example, blood pressure and heart rate have been measured every 15 minutes. In case multiple measurements, we calculate and use mean value as the daily average of each metric.

2.2 Predictive Analytics Algorithm

The first step in predictive analytics is to preprocess the data and extract the most informative features. Statistical and morphological parameters are the most common features used for data analytics. In this study, we derived total 90 features for each data sample (in this context, a data sample refers to a patient admission). The statistical features include mean, median, rms, minimum, maximum, variance, first/last sample, maximum fluctuation, standard deviation, and skewness of the set of measurements collected in the last 3 days of hospital stay.

We have to note that only a small portion of these 90 extracted features will be eventually used in the classification stage. In this study, after applying supervised feature selection, only the best 15 features are selected. Then, for the sake of reducing the redundancy and avoiding overfitting, we applied another layer of unsupervised dimensionality reduction, and selected only 8 features for the classification stage.

After feature selection stage, the best set of features will be used in classification stage to build a prediction model. In this research, we tried various classification algorithms such as SVM, Random Forest, BayesNet, and Logistic Regression. According to our results, SVM classifier provided fast and the most accurate prediction results for our dataset. We use Monte-Carlo algorithm with 500 runs to make sure that the results are not random or biased. In each round, we randomly split the dataset into training and testing sets (with no overlap), the training set is used to train a new classifier model, and the testing set is used to examine the classifier. In each round, we calculate the Area Under Curve (AUC) of Receiver Operating Characteristic (ROC) to evaluate the accuracy of the classifier. The average of all 500 AUCs (derived from 500 runs) will be used to represent overall accuracy and the ability of the system to correctly classify the outcomes and predict hospital readmissions.

3. RESULTS

Figure1 shows the results of readmission prediction for CHF patients based on the physiological measurements collected in the last three days of stay in the hospital (last three days before discharge). We examined the results for prediction within various time windows (e.g. prediction within 7 days after discharge, within 8 days, ...). For each time window, we ran a Monte-Carlo algorithm with 500 runs.
The results show that the prediction accuracy degrades severely by extending the prediction time window from one-week to one-month. Predictions beyond one month are only a little better than random guess.

4. CONCLUSION

This paper presented an end-to-end predictive analytic algorithm to predict hospital readmission based on the physiological measurements collected in the last three days of stay in hospital. The results show that it is possible to predict the readmissions happening after discharge based on the physiological data collected before discharge. However, the prediction accuracy degrades rapidly when prediction window extends from one week to one month. For example, the AUC is about 0.63 for CHF readmission prediction within the first week. However, the AUC degrades to 0.57 for prediction within the first two weeks, and 0.55 for prediction within the first month (which is only slightly better than random guess). This results suggest that it is possible to accurately predict the hospital readmissions for CHF patients if we have access to recent physiological measurements. One effective approach to this end is to employ Remote Health Monitoring Systems (RHMS), which allow for collecting continuous data from patients, providing a platform to utilize analytics algorithms to predict medical conditions, and applying clinical interventions to prevent medically adverse events such as hospital readmissions, emergency visits, heart attack, or death. Remote health monitoring can revolutionize the healthcare system by increasing the efficiency of medical services, expanding the reach of healthcare services to every part of the population, and reducing the costs of chronic disease managements.

In summary, this study suggests that RHMS can provide an effective platform to reduce readmission rates by early prediction of readmission based on freshly collected data, and then applying effective early intervention to prevent the readmission.

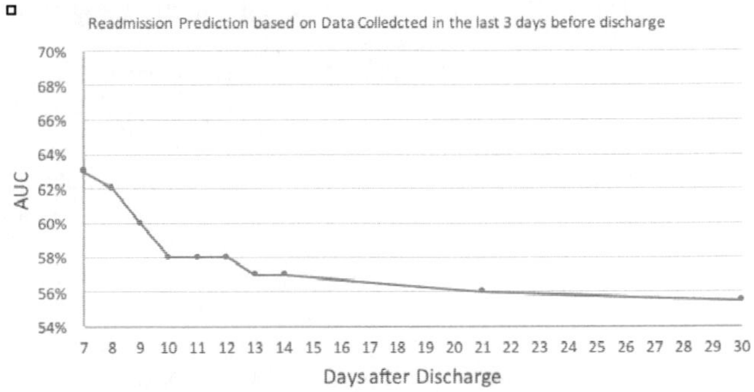

Figure 1. Readmission prediction based on the data collected in the last three days of stay at hospital.

5. ACKNOWLEDGMENTS

The authors would like to appreciate WANDA Inc. (www.yourwanda.com) for valuable help and support. The authors would like to thank the Ronald Reagan UCLA Medical Center, and David Geffen School of Medicine at UCLA.

6. REFERENCES

[1] M. Pourhomayoun, et al. "Context-Aware Data Analytics for Activity Recognition," International Conf. on Data Analytics, DATA ANALYTICS 2015, July 19 - 24, 2015, France.

[2] M. Lan, et. al., "WANDA: An End-to-End Remote Health Monitoring and Analytics System for Heart Failure Patients," Wireless Health Conf., 2012b.

[3] M. K. Suh, et al., "A Remote Patient Monitoring System for Congestive Heart Failure," JOMS, June 2011a.

[4] N. Alshurafa, et al. "Improving Compliance in a Remote Health Monitoring System through Smartphone Battery Optimization". IEEE J Biomed Health Inform, 2014.

[5] S. I. Lee, et. al., Remote Health Monitoring Systems: What Impact Can Data Analytics Have on Cost? in Wireless Health, 2013.

[6] M. Pourhomayoun, et. al., "Multiple Model Analytics for Adverse Event Prediction in Remote Health Monitoring Systems," IEEE EMBS Conference on Healthcare Innovation & Point-of-Care Technologies, 2014, pp. 106-110.

[7] K. Hung and Z. Yuan-Ting, Implementation of a WAP-based telemedicine system for patient monitoring, Information Technology in Biomedicine, IEEE Trans. on, 2003.

[8] A. G. Logan, et al., "Mobile Phone–Based Remote Patient Monitoring System for Management of Hypertension in Diabetic Patients," American Journa of Hypertention, 2007.

[9] J. S. Ross, et. al., "Recent national trends in readmission rates after heart failure hospitalization," Circulation: Heart Failure, vol. 3, pp. 97-103, 2010.

[10] S. F. Jencks, M. V. Williams, and E. A. Coleman, "Rehospitalizations among patients in the Medicare fee-for-service program," New England Journal of Medicine, 2009.

Fitness Trackers and Wearable Devices: How to Prevent Inference Risks?

Ilaria Torre
ilaria.torre@unige.it

Frosina Koceva
frosina.koceva@gmail.com

Odnan Ref Sanchez
odnan.sanchez@tnt-lab.unige.it

Giovanni Adorni
giovanni.adorni@unige.it

Department of Computer Science, Bioengineering, Robotics and Systems Engineering (DIBRIS)
Genoa, Italy

ABSTRACT

Wearable and personal devices are becoming more and more part of people's everyday lives. These devices produce enormous amount of personal data which are handled by third parties as authorized by the user. However, such third parties may be able to infer sensitive information using the collected personal information. In this paper we present a case study based on fitness trackers and we sketch our model for privacy management and inference prevention. For this study, we built a Bayesian Network and used it to compute the risk of inferring unknown data. Using the simulated case we show the feasibility of inferring some private data from a set of personal data available to a third party as authorized by the user (i.e., sensor data and profiling data provided by the user while registering for the service). This paper provides a step towards the open issues of privacy and security management in the field of ubiquitous devices.

CCS Concepts

•**Security and privacy** → Human and societal aspects of security and privacy - Privacy protection;

Keywords

User support service; Privacy management; User attribute inference; Wearable devices; Fitness tracker, Internet of Things, Personal data manager

1. INTRODUCTION

As the advent of Internet of Things (IoT) has come, an estimate of 16.3 billion devices has already been connected to the network as of 2015 and the market is expected to steadily increase and reach 26.3 billion devices by the year 2020 [8]. Reaching an estimated compound annual growth rate of 49%, IoT in the field of health and wellness (e.g., health trackers, medicine dispensers, wellness devices, etc.) is anticipated to achieve the fastest growth in the IoT market [8]. This tremendous increase of personal devices is able to exponentially increase an individual's personal data that will be processed and shared among third parties.

Today, wearable devices such as fitness trackers (provided for example by Fitbit, Jawbone, Apple, Garmin, etc.) have caught the attention of many users due to their promise of improving their active and healthy lifestyle. Fitbit trackers [12], for example, are able to monitor the individual's steps, sailed distances, calories burned, active minutes, hourly activity and stationary time. This tracker also reminds the user to move and tracks her/his sleeping habits. All these are possible due to its numerous sensors (i.e., GPS, 3-axis accelerometers, 3-axis gyroscope, digital compass, optical heart rate monitor, altimeter, ambient light sensor, vibration motor, etc.) built in the tracker. Fitbit users can also share their activities on social networks and challenge their friends in a competition which further encourages them to be active. In this study, we focus on evaluating fintess trackers, as a working example.

One of the major state-of-the-art issues of IoT concerns the security and privacy of users. In the past years, several approaches and solutions have been proposed to improve the user security and privacy by preventing unauthorized access of data generated by IoT devices. However, recent articles [15] [27] report about privacy breaches coming from the supposedly trusted third parties which are granted by the user's permission. A relevant risk is that third parties may be able to derive personal and sensitive information of the users by processing (e.g., through data mining techniques, machine learning algorithms, predictive filtering, etc.) the collected user information.

The use of personal data managers (PDM) is emerging as one of the ways to manage and control heterogeneous personal devices. These tools are conceived as a gateway to all third parties trying to access sensor data of a specific user. They can be located in a user's device, computer or in a personal cloud (e.g., InPUT Project [16]). They typically include security features, however, current PDMs are mostly focused on data minimization, authorization and authentication control, which do not prevent inference derivation.

In this respect, we proposed a model to extend PDMs [28] [29] in order to secure the user from undesired inference derivation of sensitive information. Basically it defines an

Permission to make digital or hard copies of all or part of this work for personal or classroom use is granted without fee provided that copies are not made or distributed for profit or commercial advantage and that copies bear this notice and the full citation on the first page. Copyrights for components of this work owned by others than ACM must be honored. Abstracting with credit is permitted. To copy otherwise, or republish, to post on servers or to redistribute to lists, requires prior specific permission and/or a fee. Request permissions from permissions@acm.org.
BODYNETS 2016 December 15–16, Turin, Italy

Adaptive Inference Discovery Service (AID-S), designed to be integrated in a PDM in order to manage information prevention. It is aimed to compute the inference risk measured as the probability to infer new data from a set of shared data. This information can be used to take further actions such as alerting the user or transforming personal data items before they are shared. State-of-the-art solutions and techniques are also integrated in the approach.

In this paper, we briefly present our model and then we describe an instance of it focused on preventing inferences when using fitness wearable devices such as Fitbit and the other trackers mentioned above. In this implementation, we use Bayesian Networks for computing the inference risk.

The remainder of the paper is structured as follows. Section 2 presents the background and related works. Section 3 sketches the model based on our framework and Section 4 evaluates the case of fitness trackers using a Bayesian Networks for computing the inference probability. Finally, Section 5 concludes the paper with possible future works.

2. RELATED WORKS

In this section, first we present an overview of approaches to manage personal/sensed data shared among third parties. Then, we mention the state-of-the-art related works concerning inference risks when using wearable IoT devices.

Privacy management

Privacy concerns have given rise to new proposals for empowering users with control over their data. Several projects are being carried out to develop platforms which allow users to control their personal data and the policies to make them available to third parties. PDMs belong to such solutions [30, 34, 7]. These platforms typically require users to specify what they want to hide from or share with a third-party application. Access is allowed only if the corresponding permission is granted by the user. However, regulating the access of one's data cannot deny the possible disclosure through inference. Inference attacks are based on the integration and correlation of known data about an individual which leads to the discovery of private data. The inference is done by linking sensitive information to the knowledge that may be available to a third party as a background knowledge, common sense or domain-specific knowledge [23]. In this respect, a framework that is similar to our model is ipShield [6]. As in our approach, it monitors the inference risks, but, it is limited only to the sensors on the phone.

Several techniques can be found in the literature to address inference attacks. Most of them concern anonymization and transformation [2]. However, such techniques cannot be always deployed. For example, [26] analyze physiological signals from wearable devices. They show that several inferences can be derived (e.g. detecting variation of heartbeat, respiratory disorders) but they explain that, in these cases, defensive techniques that are based on data transformation and obfuscation may be critical since they can compromise diagnostic services. For instance, the interbeat interval in ECG is typically between 300ms to 2,000ms [9] and it should not loose accuracy. In this case, only approaches that preserve the accuracy and the characteristic of the signal are appropriate.

Personal data leakage from a singular data source

The popularity of wearable devices, fitness devices and health care monitoring systems has increased the detail level, volume, collection, exchange and sharing of personal user data among applications. While on the one hand there are various health and wellness benefits, the disadvantage is that the shared data is raising privacy concerns. For instance, the results of [19] indicate that keystroke inference attacks using typing-induced motion data captured by smartwatch gesture classification using accelerometer and gyroscope data is highly effective. Furthermore, physiological data shared for healthcare studies can also be used to infer addictions like smoking or drinking [11]. For instance, by using custom hardware and analyzing the data from wrist-worn sensors, it has been shown how to successfully classify smoking gestures [22], eating gestures [10] or smoking cessation [25]. Motion sensor data from smart phones held in hand has been shown to provide enough information to impersonate a stylus [1] and a mouse [33]. From data sensed by activity trackers, [32] examine whether a predefined event, e.g., walking from office to a nearby coffee shop, can be identified from among many other routine inference of sensitive human behavior events. Through real-world experiments, they found that pedometer readings that are captured even at a coarse granularity, such as one minute, enable the accurate inference of events such as grocery shopping, walking to coffee shop, visiting gym, etc.

Personal data leakage from aggregated data of different sources

Even though singular data could appear harmless and non-sensitive, assembling each one with other data from different sources can result in a so-called global inference attack and global inference chains [13]. This risk, based on the correlation and aggregation of data from heterogeneous sources and even from self-generated content, is often not grasped by users. In our previous work [4, 5] on inference attacks in social systems, we analyzed the inadequacy of permission-based protection for users that accorded their permission to a subset of data. The experimental study showed the possibility for an adversary to aggregate user data discovered from various sources into a more complete profile, and infer further data that the user had not shared. Moreover, we found that the risk of information leakage in online social networks is directly correlated with the number of shared personal data and with the number of user profiles owned by the user over time and then forgotten. This risk can be applied also to user data that are collected from IoT devices and shared, suggesting that the higher the number of devices owned by the user and running background applications (e.g., smart home gadgets, fitness appliances, etc.), the higher the risk that a huge amount of historical personal data are collected with associated risks of information leakage.

For instance, Fitbit provides users with the possibility of sharing their fitness statistics on Tweeter, i.e. #fitstats tweets are created together with a link to the user's Fitbit dashboard. Based on the correlation of the tweeter profile public data with Fitbit dashboard public data a possible de-anonymization attack and behavior inference could be performed. Furthermore, the user's average step counts are shared by default unless user opts-out, thus a user's behavior can be easily inferred as described by [32].

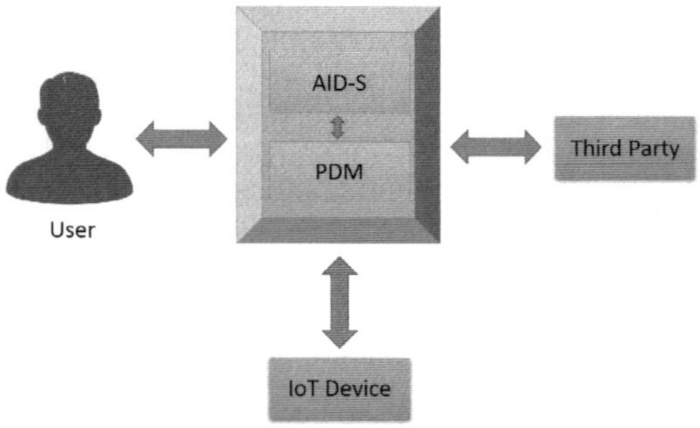

Figure 1: General overview of our proposed model.

3. INTERACTION MODEL

This section describes the model we defined to prevent the risk of personal data disclosure through inference attacks. Figure 1 shows the general overview of our model which is in accordance with the framework described in in [29].

As shown in Figure 1, the <PDM + AID-S> function block acts as a gateway among a user, an IoT personal device and a third party. The interaction among these entities is controlled by the <PDM + AID-S> function block which ensures that i) the user is made aware about privacy risks related to her/his privacy settings ii) a common privacy agreement is defined among them. PDMs can be placed in the user phone, laptop, or in personal clouds [16] and AID-S works as a service requested by the PDM to accomplish reasoning tasks which may be integrated in the PDMs or being asked as a separate cloud service.

3.1 Interaction Workflow

This part describes briefly the workflow of the system which is derived from the previous work in [29]. The interaction workflow consists of 4 phases, namely, Statement Declaration, Inference Check, Recommendation and Negotiation. The flow starts as soon as a third party requires for the first time to access a set of personal data to provide its services to the user.

3.1.1 Statement Declaration

To start, a Statement is sent to the PDM by the third party. Formally, a Statement is a declaration wherein the third party specifies the list of data items it requires and processes, their quality, granularity, and which of them will be shared with other applications. A detailed example of a Statement is provided by My Data Store PDM [30].

When the PDM receives this Statement, it examines it and compares it with the user privacy settings that are already stored in the user profile. The related steps depend on how a PDM operates as in [30, 34, 7]. After the PDM approves that a Statement is compliant with the user privacy settings, it sends a request to AID-S for an inference check.

3.1.2 Inference Check

This phase is aimed to measure the risk that a third party is able to infer sensitive information by processing the collected data gathered from the list of data stated in the Statement. An ideal representation of inference probabilities based on correlations among user features is defined in the inference matrix below.

DEFINITION 1. *We define an inference matrix, $I_{j,k}$, as the set of all the probabilities that a user attribute can be inferred given the combination of data stated in the Statement.*

$$I_{j,k} = \begin{pmatrix} P(a_1|c_1) & \cdots & P(a_1|c_k) \\ \vdots & \ddots & \vdots \\ P(a_j|c_1) & \cdots & P(a_j|c_k) \end{pmatrix} \quad (1)$$

where:

- a_j: *is the* j^{th} *user data that could be inferred*
- c_k: *is the* k^{th} *combination of user data*
- *D: user data set,* $a_j \in D$ $(1 \leq j \leq |D|)$
- $P\{D\}$: *power set of D,* $c_k \in P\{D\}$ $(1 \leq k \leq |P\{D\}|)$
- $P(a_j|c_k) \in [0,1]$

AID-S refers to this matrix when a request is issued from the PDM to check if there is a risk of possible inference. The key is to find combinations of data listed in the Statement that are highly correlated with other non-shared personal data, since this results in high probability to infer such data. However, the real risk for user privacy depends also on the user perception about the possible disclosure of such data. Some individuals could rate a_j as a sensitive data while others could be less worried about its disclosure. The user perception about possible disclosure is expressed in the user profile (with her/his privacy settings). Thus, in case $P(a_j|c_k)$ reaches more than the set threshold for a_j disclosure, this information is sent to the PDM for managing recommendation to the user (see the next phase).

Notice that the probabilities in the matrix can be computed according to several algorithms (e.g., data mining techniques, machine learning algorithms, predictive filtering, etc.) on proper data sets, and/or by exploiting correlations and conditional probabilities that are already available in the literature. In this study, we exploit the correlations found in other works, referenced in Table 1.

From the description above, it is clear that the Inference Check is carried out by using Statement data only (i.e., metadata). This means that AID-S does not store and process personal user data, but only their description. This enables AID-S to be easily integrated into many PDM platforms with no need to be trusted by the users it itself as a new third-party application.

3.1.3 Recommendation

When it is over a given threshold, the inference risk is relayed by the PDM to the user. As stated above, this threshold specifies users preferences of sharing a data item. Privacy settings are stored in a user profile. They can be configured by the users on the PDM (as for example in [6]) or estimated by the PDM from a set of user-configured data items [20]. Recommendation techniques notify about risks and provide suggestions about personal data that should not be shared with the third party in order to lower the probability of inferring a_j.

3.1.4 Negotiation

In this phase, the third-party Statement can either be refused or accepted entirely/partially by the user, depending on the recommendation provided by the PDM about the privacy settings. The negotiation among the user, the third party and the <PDM + AID-S> goes on until a satisfying

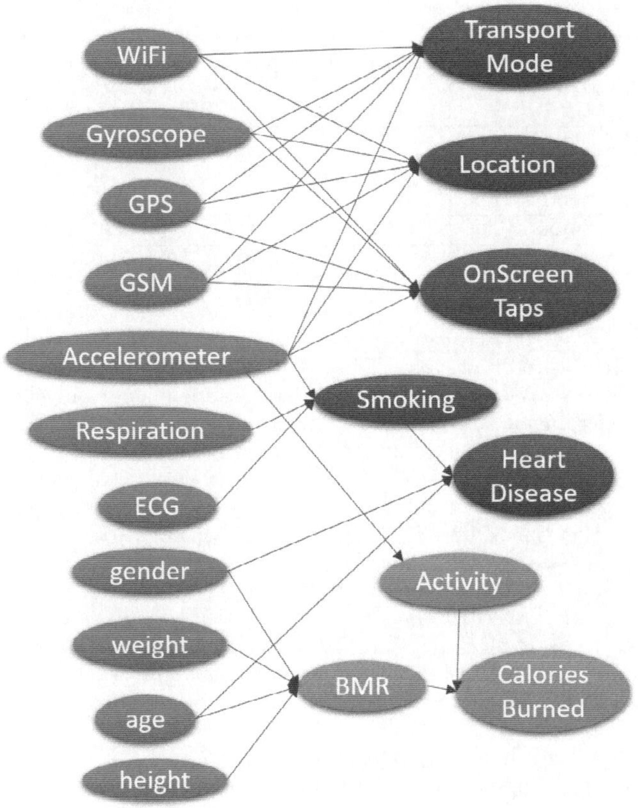

Figure 2: An example of a Bayesian Network graphical model in the case of fitness wearable devices.

trade-off between both preserving *privacy* and the *utility* of the third-party service is gained.

4. A CASE EXAMPLE WITH FITNESS DEVICES

In this section we present a case example from fitness devices. By simulating sensed and shared data from common fitness trackers (e.g., Fitbit, Jawbone and Bioharness), we computed the inference probability of a set of unknown personal data.

To compute the inference probability (inference risk), we built a Bayesian network (i.e., a graphical probabilistic model which represents dependencies among nodes) as shown in Figure 2. Then, we simulated the availability of some data (i.e. evidences in parent nodes) and through propagation, we obtained the posterior probability of child nodes.

Parent nodes on the left side of Figure 2 (green nodes) represent personal user data (i.e., sensor data and user attributes) required in the hypothetical third-party Statement (e.g., Fitbit, Jawbone and Bioharness Statements). Arcs represent dependencies among these nodes and the child nodes on the right (blue and grey nodes). *BMR*, *Activity*, and *Calories Burned* (grey nodes) are user attributes which are computed by the third party as part of its service (to be exact, the grey nodes in the figure are from Fitbit) and are not considered for inference computation since they are computed by Fitbit and this is known by the users in this particular example.

4.1 Bayesian network initialization

Bayesian Networks represent a set of variables and their conditional dependencies via a directed acyclic graph. They are built on the Bayes theorem. With reference to Matrix $I(x,y)$, Bayesian Network is used as follows:

$$P(a_j|c_i) = \frac{P(c_i|a_j) \cdot P(a_J)}{P(c_i)} \qquad (2)$$

where:

- a_j: is one of the inferable child nodes (blue nodes)
- $c_i = \{b_1, b_2, ..., b_l\}$: is a combination of parent nodes b (combination of green nodes), with l: the number of incoming arcs from c_i to a_j
- $a, b \in D$

4.1.1 Prior Probabilities

As stated, the objective of the network in this study is to compute the probability that a third party may infer a_j (blue node) if it knows $c_i = \{b_1, b_2, ..., b_l\}$ (green nodes). To initialize the network, the prior probability that the third party knows each b_i is necessary. It represents the chance for the third party to know b_i. In our scenario, which assumes that the third party has no knowledge about the user when the flow starts, the prior probability $P(b_i)$ depends on the willingness of the user to release this data. $P(b_i)$ values ranges from 0 to 1 in increasing order proportional to the user's willingness to share this information. That is, $P(b_i) = 1$ means that the user is 100% willing to share this information, $P(b_i) = 0$ means the user never wants to share this information, and between these values are the user's perception towards the uncertainty on her/his willingness.

Accordingly, the prior probabilities can be computed starting from the privacy settings in the user profile managed and stored by PDM. We call this measure "*disclosure Propensity Index*" (PI). It is computed similarly to [6] with a mixed user and system-driven approach:

i) *User-driven*: since it exploits the privacy settings provided by the user for predefined categories of personal data (specific for each PDM),

ii) *System-driven*: since computations are performed to estimate PI from the privacy settings in the user profile. In fact, personal data that have to be rated by the user have generally a granularity lower than the nodes in the Bayesian Network (in order to be user friendly).

Thus, for PI computation, a mapping schema is exploited first to associate user profile privacy settings to the network nodes. Then, privacy settings in the user profile are converted into PI values normalized to [0 1]. PI values of profile items that correspond to parent green nodes can be directly used as prior probability P(b_i). For b_i nodes that do not have a computed PI value, prior probability can be estimated using PI values of their children in the network by performing a weighted average as described in the following equation:

$$P(b_i) = \frac{1}{n}\sum_{j=1}^{n} w_j PI(a_j) \qquad (3)$$

where:

- $PI(a_j)$: is PI computed for node a_j

- w_j: is the weight that represents the strength of the correlation between b_i and a_j; $w_j \in [0, 1]$
- n: is the number of the child nodes of b_i.

For instance, if a user has a computed PI for his *Location* information in Figure 2, this value should be inherited by *Accelerometer*, *WiFi*, *Gyroscope*, *GPS* and *GSM*. However, if there is also a PI value for *Transport mode*, which is as well inherited from *Accelerometer*, *WiFi*, *Gyroscope*, *GPS*, *GSM*, the prior probability of the GPS, for example, is given by the weighted average of *Location* PI and *Transport mode* PI.

4.1.2 Conditional probabilities

In addition to prior probability, Bayesian Networks require input conditional probabilities on child nodes in order to be initialized. In this study we considered the following child nodes whose correlations with parent nodes have been reported in the literature (references in Table 1): *Transport Mode*, *Location*, *On-Screen Taps*, *Smoking*, and *Heart Disease* (blue nodes in Figure 2). We have normalized these correlations and have used them to specify the conditional probabilities of the child nodes.

Bayesian networks showed to be very robust to missing data and thus are useful when the knowledge about some nodes is not precise, as in our case [17].

Below, we provide brief descriptions of the child nodes and of the correlations used to specify the conditional probabilities. In the table we report only the highest correlation value among the set of personal data combinations in Figure 2.

Transport mode: identifies whether the user is being stationary, walking, running, biking or using motorized transport [24]. Using a Hidden Markov Model classifier, the researchers were able to identify the transport mode with at least 93.6% of accuracy using GPS and Accelerometer. They also provided the inference accuracy based on the combinations of further sensors: *GSM*, *WiFi* and *Gyroscope*. The classifier was designed to work on mobile phone and thus, there are different sensing modalities on which combination and classification accuracy could increase with respect of the basic modality represented by *GPS* and *Accelerometer*.

Location: identifies where the user is (e.g., hospital, home, office, etc.). It may be inferred by different combinations of sensors with different accuracy [3, 18, 21]. The highest accuracy is obtained by using the accelerometer information, with 200m radius of accuracy by using a trajectory inference model [14].

Smoking: detects if the user is a smoker or not. It is detected with a gesture recognition algorithm by processing data from wristband detecting arm trajectory with an accuracy of 95.7% [22]. This user attribute has also been inferred by exploiting *ECG*, *respiration* and *accelerometer* data with different accuracy values [26].

Heart Disease: (or, specifically, prediction of stroke) has been studied in relation to several factors - age, systolic blood pressure, use of antihypertensive therapy, diabetes mellitus, cigarette smoking, prior cardiovascular disease, atrial fibrillation, left ventricular hypertrophy by electrocardiogram - and identified with different correlation coefficients [31]. For this study, we use only *Smoking*, *gender*, *age* as the parent nodes since these are available in the fitness trackers.

Activity: can be automatically detected by the tracker, which is set or manually logged by the user after the activity. It can be calculated from, at least, the three-axis

Table 1: Simulation: PI estimation for a given user, inference probability, References in the literature.

Inferred Attributes	PI	Inference Probability	**Cond. Prob. References**
Transport mode	0.9	95%	[24]
Location	0.3	97%	[3, 18, 21]
On-Screen Taps	0.4	80%	[3, 18, 21]
Smoking	0.3	90%	[26, 22]
Heart Disease	0.1	68%	[31]

accelerometer that provides motion patterns and the energy expenditure of activity expressed by Metabolic Equivalents (METs). We assume that the parent node should only be accelerometer since it is not crucial in this example and the major focus is on the inference of the blue nodes.

Basal Metabolical Rate (BMR): the value is calculated by the third-party using its equations. For example, Fitbit uses the Mifflin-St Jeor equation, which involves age, height, weight and gender [12].

Calories Burned: is estimated by the BMR, activity tracker and activity record manually.

For *BMR*, *Activity*, and *Calories Burned* (shown in gray nodes), we assume a 100% inference probability since they can always be computed by Fitbit given the required parent nodes.

It is worth noting that the significance of correlations among nodes and the related probability levels depend on the sample size used in each specific study that we used as references. For initializing our network, when the literature did not provide enough details, we estimated this value with the available data.

4.2 Inference computation

The computation of the posterior probabilities are defined in this subsection. The main steps from the user settings to the inference computation are briefly explained below.

4.2.1 User Privacy Settings

User Privacy settings are managed by the PDMs. However, the task of privacy preferences and threshold estimations are managed by AID-S.

In this case study, we assume that the PDM has acquired the user preference settings and then shares them with AID-S as needed for inference computation. For example, PDM provides AID-S with the following user privacy settings. User Setting $=[Transport\ Mode = 4.5$, $Location = 1.5$, $On - Screen\ Taps = 2$, $Smoking = 1.5$, $Heart\ Disease = 0.5]$ in a 0 to 5 range.

4.2.2 PI Computation

AID-S computes the PI values as described in Section 4.1.1. In this example, the network nodes in AID-S are the same as the PDM user setting and thus AID-S simply normalizes the data $\in [0\ 1]$. In other cases some mappings are required as mentioned above. The obtained values will be the PI for the blue nodes as indicated in Table 1. To estimate the prior probabilities of the green nodes based on blue nodes, Eq. 3 is used with an assumption of equal weights.

4.2.3 Belief Propagation

Once the Bayesian Network is initialized, it can be used to estimate the inference risks for a given set of evidences. In our example, evidences correspond to the personal data required by the third party in the Statement. In other terms, data that are available with certainty=1 are named evidences. Thus, we have an evidence when $P(b_i) = 1$. Given some evidences, the Bayesian Network operates by propagating beliefs throughout the network.

For example, simulating the case of a Statement which requires the user to share all data of parent green nodes except two nodes, e.g., GSM and $WiFi$, we have ($P(b_i) = 1$) for all the required data. The result of the simulation shows that all the child nodes have updated probabilities which represent the risk that the third party may infer them, exploiting the correlations among the requested data. The inference probabilities that are returned in this example are shown in Table 1.

One of the advantages of using Bayesian networks is that they optimally works when an inferred node is used to condition another inferred node. For example, given that the third party knows data sensed from ECG, respiratory sensor and accelerometer, it has 0.9 probability to infer whether the user is a smoker or not (i.e., P(smoking=true|ECG=true, respiratory=true, accelerometer=true) = 0.9). Afterwards, given the further evidence about age and gender combined with the smoking probability, it allows a third party to compute the inference probability of heart diseases.

Several algorithms are available to compute inference measures for limited subsets of the Inference Matrix. A working example is from [32], which computes the probability of inferring the user behavior (e.g., walking, running, etc.) and the user's typical paths (e.g., going to coffee shop, grocery, outdoors, etc.) only by exploiting the steps per minute computed from a fitness IoT pedometer. It has been reported that as their threshold value, ϵ - denoting the Euclidian distance between the two time-series (sense sequence, query sequence), varies, it could infer the user behavior with at least 50% accuracy, thus, $P(a|c_k) = 0.50$.

The evaluation of the mSieve system [26] and its model-based substitution scheme, by using 660 hours of ECG, respiration, location and accelerometer data collected over multiple user studies with over 43 participants, demonstrates that sensitive behavioral inferences, such as onset of stress, smoking, and cocaine use, can be protected while still retaining meaningful utility ($\geq$ 85% accuracy when privacy sensitivity is high and $\geq$ 90% on average) of the shared physiological signals in terms of their use for tracking heart rate, breathing irregularities, and detecting conversation episodes.

Other examples are provided in [20]. This patent estimates the information entropy of a non-shared data item and utilizes the information entropy to compute inference probability.

5. CONCLUSION AND FUTURE WORKS

Today, having a set of heterogeneous IoT devices for each individual justifies the need for a PDM. Though current designs of PDMs are able to protect data from unauthorized third parties, they are still not sufficient enough to prevent the risk of inference of private information from the permitted data collection of authorized third parties.

The high risk of inferring sensitive information using wearable sensors has been discussed in various works. This paper uses an innovative model based on our framework for inference prevention based on handling privacy statements between the user and a third party. Specifically, this paper describes an Adaptive Inference Discovery Service (AID-S) for the particular example in the domain of fitness devices, as an extension to PDMs in order to assure that private information will not be inferred given the combination of information released to fitness third parties.

We focused in particular on fitness devices, which are gaining popularity in the field of IoT. To implement the reasoner, we used a Bayesian Network, initialized with prior probabilities and conditional probabilities, for parent and child nodes, respectively. Thus, we were able to simulate the posterior probabilities which represent the measure of the risk that a third party may infer a private data item given the set of shared data. This paper aims to show that the leakage of private information from trusted third parties becomes pervasive with the rise of personal IoT devices.

As for future work, we intend to extend the model on different domains, also with other reasoning methods. Concerning the current implementation, next steps are the optimization of weights, w_i and PIs computation from the user profile. We also intend that this paper will be an eye opener for researchers who operate in this field.

6. REFERENCES

[1] S. Agrawal, I. Constandache, S. Gaonkar, R. Roy Choudhury, K. Caves, and F. DeRuyter. Using mobile phones to write in air. In *Proceedings of the 9th international conference on Mobile systems, applications, and services*, pages 15–28. ACM, 2011.

[2] S. H. Ahmadinejad, P. W. Fong, and R. Safavi-Naini. Privacy and utility of inference control mechanisms for social computing applications. In *Proceedings of the 11th ACM on Asia Conference on Computer and Communications Security*, pages 829–840. ACM, 2016.

[3] N. Brouwers and M. Woehrle. Detecting dwelling in urban environments using gps, wifi, and geolocation measurements. In *Workshop on Sensing Applications on Mobile Phones (PhoneSense)*, pages 1–5. Citeseer, 2011.

[4] F. Carmagnola, F. Osborne, and I. Torre. Escaping the big brother: An empirical study on factors influencing identification and information leakage on the web. *Journal of Information Science*, 40(2):180–197, 2014.

[5] F. Carmagnola, F. Osborne, and I. Torre. User data discovery and aggregation: the cs-udd algorithm. *Information Sciences*, 270:41–72, 2014.

[6] S. Chakraborty, C. Shen, K. R. Raghavan, Y. Shoukry, M. Millar, and M. Srivastava. ipshield: a framework for enforcing context-aware privacy. In *11th USENIX Symposium on Networked Systems Design and Implementation (NSDI 14)*, pages 143–156, 2014.

[7] A. Chaudhry, J. Crowcroft, H. Howard, A. Madhavapeddy, R. Mortier, H. Haddadi, and D. McAuley. Personal data: thinking inside the box. In *Proceedings of The Fifth Decennial Aarhus Conference on Critical Alternatives*, pages 29–32. Aarhus University Press, 2015.

[8] Cisco Systems, Inc. The Zettabyte Era – Trends and Analysis. Technical report, Cisco, 2016.

[9] G. D. Clifford, F. Azuaje, and P. McSharry. *Advanced methods and tools for ECG data analysis.* Artech House, Inc., 2006.

[10] Y. Dong, A. Hoover, J. Scisco, and E. Muth. A new

method for measuring meal intake in humans via automated wrist motion tracking. *Applied psychophysiology and biofeedback*, 37(3):205–215, 2012.

[11] E. Ertin, N. Stohs, S. Kumar, A. Raij, M. al'Absi, and S. Shah. Autosense: unobtrusively wearable sensor suite for inferring the onset, causality, and consequences of stress in the field. In *Proceedings of the 9th ACM Conference on Embedded Networked Sensor Systems*, pages 274–287. ACM, 2011.

[12] Fitbit. Fitbit Store, 2016. Last accessed: 25-10-2016.

[13] G. Friedland, G. Maier, R. Sommer, and N. Weaver. Sherlock holmes' evil twin: on the impact of global inference for online privacy. In *Proceedings of the 2011 workshop on New security paradigms workshop*, pages 105–114. ACM, 2011.

[14] J. Han, E. Owusu, L. T. Nguyen, A. Perrig, and J. Zhang. Accomplice: Location inference using accelerometers on smartphones. In *2012 Fourth International Conference on Communication Systems and Networks (COMSNETS 2012)*, pages 1–9. IEEE, 2012.

[15] A. Hilts, C. Parsons, and J. Knockel. Every Step You Fake: A Comparative Analysis of Fitness Tracker Privacy and Security. Technical report, Citizen Lab, University of Toronto, 2016.

[16] Input Consortium. In-Network Programmability for next-generation personal cloUd service supporT, 2015. Last accessed: 12-10-2016.

[17] K. Iqbal, X.-C. Yin, H.-W. Hao, Q. M. Ilyas, and H. Ali. An overview of bayesian network applications in uncertain domains. *International Journal of Computer Theory and Engineering*, 7(6):416, 2015.

[18] D. H. Kim, Y. Kim, D. Estrin, and M. B. Srivastava. Sensloc: sensing everyday places and paths using less energy. In *Proceedings of the 8th ACM Conference on Embedded Networked Sensor Systems*, pages 43–56. ACM, 2010.

[19] A. Maiti, M. Jadliwala, J. He, and I. Bilogrevic. (smart) watch your taps: side-channel keystroke inference attacks using smartwatches. In *Proceedings of the 2015 ACM International Symposium on Wearable Computers*, pages 27–30. ACM, 2015.

[20] S. G. Motahari and Q. Jones. System and method for protecting user privacy using social inference protection techniques, Aug. 6 2013. US Patent 8,504,481.

[21] S. Nirjon, R. F. Dickerson, P. Asare, Q. Li, D. Hong, J. A. Stankovic, P. Hu, G. Shen, and X. Jiang. Auditeur: a mobile-cloud service platform for acoustic event detection on smartphones. In *Proceeding of the 11th annual international conference on Mobile systems, applications, and services*, pages 403–416. ACM, 2013.

[22] A. Parate, M.-C. Chiu, C. Chadowitz, D. Ganesan, and E. Kalogerakis. Risq: Recognizing smoking gestures with inertial sensors on a wristband. In *Proceedings of the 12th annual international conference on Mobile systems, applications, and services*, pages 149–161. ACM, 2014.

[23] M. Prakash and G. Singaravel. An analysis of privacy risks and design principles for developing countermeasures in privacy preserving sensitive data publishing. *Journal of Theoretical & Applied Information Technology*, 62(1), 2014.

[24] S. Reddy, M. Mun, J. Burke, D. Estrin, M. Hansen, and M. Srivastava. Using mobile phones to determine transportation modes. *ACM Transactions on Sensor Networks (TOSN)*, 6(2):13, 2010.

[25] N. Saleheen, A. A. Ali, S. M. Hossain, H. Sarker, S. Chatterjee, B. Marlin, E. Ertin, M. al'Absi, and S. Kumar. puffmarker: A multi-sensor approach for pinpointing the timing of first lapse in smoking cessation. In *Proceedings of the 2015 ACM International Joint Conference on Pervasive and Ubiquitous Computing*, UbiComp '15, pages 999–1010, New York, NY, USA, 2015. ACM.

[26] N. Saleheen, S. Chakraborty, N. Ali, M. M. Rahman, S. M. Hossain, R. Bari, E. Buder, M. Srivastava, and S. Kumar. msieve: differential behavioral privacy in time series of mobile sensor data. In *Proceedings of the 2016 ACM International Joint Conference on Pervasive and Ubiquitous Computing*, pages 706–717. ACM, 2016.

[27] The Guardian. Samsung's voice-recording smart TVs breach privacy law, campaigners claim, 2015. Last accessed: 12-10-2016.

[28] I. Torre, G. Adorni, F. Koceva, and O. R. Sanchez. Preventing disclosure of personal data in iot networks. In *Proceedings of the IEEE 12th International Conference on Signal-Image Technology &Internet-Based Systems*, pages 389–396, 2016.

[29] I. Torre, F. Koceva, O. R. Sanchez, and G. Adorni. A framework for personal data protection in the iot. In *Proceedings of the 11th International Conference for Internet Technology and Secured Transactions*, 2016.

[30] M. Vescovi, C. Moiso, M. Pasolli, L. Cordin, and F. Antonelli. Building an eco-system of trusted services via user control and transparency on personal data. In *IFIP International Conference on Trust Management*, pages 240–250. Springer, 2015.

[31] P. A. Wolf, R. B. D'Agostino, A. J. Belanger, and W. B. Kannel. Probability of stroke: a risk profile from the framingham study. *Stroke*, 22(3):312–318, 1991.

[32] T. Yan, Y. Lu, and N. Zhang. Privacy disclosure from wearable devices. In *Proceedings of the 2015 Workshop on Privacy-Aware Mobile Computing*, pages 13–18. ACM, 2015.

[33] S. Yun, Y.-C. Chen, and L. Qiu. Turning a mobile device into a mouse in the air. In *Proceedings of the 13th Annual International Conference on Mobile Systems, Applications, and Services*, pages 15–29. ACM, 2015.

[34] G. Zyskind, O. Nathan, et al. Decentralizing privacy: Using blockchain to protect personal data. In *Security and Privacy Workshops (SPW), 2015 IEEE*, pages 180–184. IEEE, 2015.

Food Watch: Detecting and Characterizing Eating Episodes through Feeding Gestures

Shibo Zhang
Preventive Medicine Dept.
Northwestern, Chicago
shibo.zhang@northwestern.edu

Rawan Alharbi
Preventive Medicine Dept.
Northwestern, Chicago
rawan.alharbi@northwestern.edu

William Stogin
Preventive Medicine Dept.
Northwestern, Chicago
wstogin@northwestern.edu

Mohamad Pourhomayun
Computer Science Dept.
CSULA, Los Angeles
mpourho@calstatela.edu

Bonnie Spring
Preventive Medicine Dept.
Northwestern, Chicago
bspring@northwestern.edu

Nabil Alshurafa
Preventive Medicine Dept.
Northwestern, Chicago
nabil@northwestern.edu

ABSTRACT

Obesity, caused primarily by overeating, is a preventable chronic disease yielding staggering healthcare costs. To detect overeating passively, a machine learning framework was designed to detect and accurately count the number of feeding gestures during an eating episode to characterize each eating episode with a feeding gesture count. With the ubiquitous nature of wrist-worn sensors, existing literature has focused on detecting eating-related gestures and eating episodes that are at least five minutes long. In this paper, our objective is to show the potential of commercial smartwatches to be used in detection of eating episodes with short durations confounded by other activities of daily living in order to truly capture all eating episodes in the field. The effect of time-series segmentation and sensing configurations on the accuracy of detecting and characterizing feeding gestures is then analyzed. Finally, the effects of personalized and generalized machine learning models in predicting feeding gestures are compared. Results demonstrate the large within-subject variability of eating, where a generalized user-independent model yields a 75.7% average F-measure, whereas a personalized user-dependent model yields a 85.7% average F-measure. This shows the effects of personalized clustering on feeding gesture count, resulting in a root mean square error of 8.4.

CCS Concepts

•Computing methodologies → Machine learning; •Applied computing → Consumer health;

Keywords

Wrist-worn sensors, wearables, hand-to-mouth gestures, overeating, inertial sensors

1. INTRODUCTION

Eating is essential to human life, but overeating relative to need is not. Unfortunately, once bad eating habits are formed, they become challenging to overcome. People overeat for many reasons, such as loss of control [14], impulsivity due to cues [16], or heightened emotional state as a result of stress [15] or negative affect [8], or even positive affect [6]. Being able to passively detect overeating in real time will enable researchers to understand the antecedents and causes of overeating.

Prior to detecting overeating, researchers have been focused on detecting eating compared to other confounding activities of daily living. However, many of the developed eating detection systems are challenging for participants to adhere to throughout the day, requiring multiple on-body sensors [4] or specialized neck-worn [1], ear-based [3, 5], or chest-based sensors [23]. Moreover, the efficacy of these systems to detect eating in a variety of real-life settings is yet to be validated.

Prior research on eating using commercial wearable products has focused primarily on detecting the act of eating [24], but fall short of characterizing eating episodes to enable behavioral scientists to properly understand the causal determinants of problematic eating behaviors. Due to the ubiquitous nature and acceptability of wrist-worn sensors [12], they provide a viable solution to seamlessly and objectively detecting eating episodes. Gathering this data will empower nutrition researchers to develop improved systems of dietary recall, and enable behavioral scientists to test timely interventions to successfully understand and prevent problematic eating.

Prior literature has begun examining eating episodes in the wild through feeding gestures [24] and counting of bites [9]. However, much of the eating episodes involve participants sitting and continuously eating, uninterrupted by the realities of daily life. While these systems prove to work well in lab settings, they are unable to consistently and accurately detect short eating episodes, let alone characterize them with accurate counts of feeding gestures. In this paper, these efforts are further expanded upon by analyzing more realistic eating episodes, where participants make phone calls, walk around to answer the door, type on their laptops, and converse with people in a room.

Objectively detecting physical activity through passive sensing of wearable sensors has been researched extensively [17]. It is currently feasible, within reasonable error, and using passive sensing from wearable sensors, to detect bouts and minutes of sedentary, moderate, and vigorous physical activity, and ultimately classify a subset of activities of daily living. The problem of passively sensing and characterizing eating episodes, however, is yet to manifest in behavioral interventions. This paper attempts to address important practical challenges in deploying such a system.

2. RELATED WORKS

The widespread availability of embedded wearable accelerome-

Permission to make digital or hard copies of all or part of this work for personal or classroom use is granted without fee provided that copies are not made or distributed for profit or commercial advantage and that copies bear this notice and the full citation on the first page. Copyrights for components of this work owned by others than ACM must be honored. Abstracting with credit is permitted. To copy otherwise, or republish, to post on servers or to redistribute to lists, requires prior specific permission and/or a fee. Request permissions from permissions@acm.org.

Figure 1: A participant wearing two Microsoft Band 2's (one on each wrist) prepared to begin eating.

ters and gyroscopes has enabled a new area of research to detect eating passively through on-body inertial sensors. The focus of this research effort is on detecting and characterizing eating through feeding gestures.

The problem of identifying hand-to-mouth gestures has also been studied to detect smoking activities in order to predict smoking relapse [21, 22]. PuffMarker successfully detects the timing of a relapse using multiple sensors, where detecting hand-to-mouth gestures and hand orientation (using roll and pitch angles) are part of the smoking lapse system [21]. RisQ also leverages multiple inertial measurement units (IMUs) placed on a person's body together with 3D animation to detect hand-to-mouth gestures, and while the focus of these systems is primarily smoking, their systems have shown preliminary success in detecting feeding gestures [19].

Dong et al. shows correlation between bites and caloric intake and measure intake via automated tracking of wrist motion [10, 11]. Some of their limitations include requiring the user to turn the device on and off, and they focus primarily on detecting the start and end of an eating episode throughout the day, as opposed to characterizing a given eating episode.

Thomaz et al. present a framework for detecting eating episodes using wrist-worn accelerometer data [24] and density-based spatial clustering of applications with noise (DBSCAN) to identify eating episodes throughout the day. Assumed in the study under primary consideration in this paper are that the beginning and end of an eating episode are defined, interspersed with activities of daily living, and this study takes the next step of accurately characterizing the eating episode through feeding gestures. The loop is thus closed on the practical aspects of deploying an eating gesture system, providing insight into the impact of slow, fine-grained and fast coarse-grained segmentation, and report on using both personalized and generalized classification models and their impact on counting the number of feeding gestures.

The following are the contributions of this effort: 1) Showing the correlation and association of feeding gestures and eating duration with caloric intake; 2) Presenting accuracy of counting feeding gestures; 3) The impact of the non-dominant hand, sensor, and feature combinations on detecting hand-to-mouth gestures; 4) The benefits of a personalized compared to a generalized machine learning model using clustering techniques on detecting feeding gestures; and 5) Characterizing eating episodes, interspersed with confounding activities, by accurately detecting and counting feeding gestures. In the following sections our system and results are described in more detail.

3. DATA COLLECTION

3.1 Eating Study

Participants in an in-lab experiment were requested to wear one wrist-worn sensor on each hand (Microsoft Band 2s), while following an eating and activity protocol. Fifteen participants were recruited, 7 male and 8 female. The mean age of the participants was 31.5 years (ranging from 21 - 63 years, std=12.6). Two participants were left-handed. The participants were scheduled to come into the lab on two separate occasions, once for breakfast and another for lunch. Tables 1 and 2 provide descriptions of the tasks performed during each meal.

		Breakfast	
Activity	*Object*	*Task Method*	*Calories*
Eating	Fruit Cup	Fork	60
Non-Eating	Glasses	Wear & adjust	-
Eating	Pancake	Fork & Knife	100
Non-Eating	Conversation	Talk naturally	-
Drinking	Water	Hands	0
Non-Eating	Phone	Call	-
Eating	Yogurt	Spoon	140
Drinking	Tea	Hands	0

Table 1: Activities and food consumed during breakfast.

		Lunch	
Activity	*Object*	*Task Method*	*Calories*
Eating	Sandwich	Hands	340
Non-Eating	Keyboard	Type	-
Eating	Soup	Spoon	230
Non-Eating	Walk	Walk naturally	-
Drinking	Sparkling Water	Hands	0
Eating	Chips	Hands	150

Table 2: Activities and food consumed during lunch.

Participants were asked to perform activities that involved eating using different methods, both using utensils (fork and knife, fork alone, and spoon alone) and eating with their hands. Intermittently they were asked to perform other activities such as: have a conversation, make a phone call, put on and off a pair of sun glasses, walk around the room, and type on the keyboard. The participants were requested to focus on eating, unless they felt discomfort, and in the event that a participant was full, they were given the opportunity to take a break and continue after the break. If they could not eat more food, the remaining food was weighed to estimate the amount of food consumed during the meal.

The entire session was recorded using a camera to annotate the activities and serve as ground truth for our models. Different colored stickers were placed on the chin, hands, and throat of the participants to aid in annotating the video. Figure 1 shows a participant wearing the sensors.

3.2 Video Labeling

A Logitech C615 HD webcam camera was placed on the side of the non-dominant hand in order to see the plate, both hands, and the participants face. We used Chronoviz [13] to label data. Although in this paper we focus on detecting primarily feeding gestures, the variety of our labels includes eating, drinking, non-eating, food-to-mouth (F-M), bite, back-to-rest (B-R), chewing duration, and swallows. Figure 2 illustrates the system used to annotate the recorded data with time-synchronized ground truth labels.

3.3 Devices and System

An Android application was designed to act as an information gateway to the wrist bands and our backend database. The data is stored in an sql-lite relational database, and can both be transmitted to a back-end or accessed directly from the smartphone through local storage. The application allows researchers to specify several parameters, including participant ID, study ID, device name, and the option to turn on a combination of sensors (accelerometer, gy-

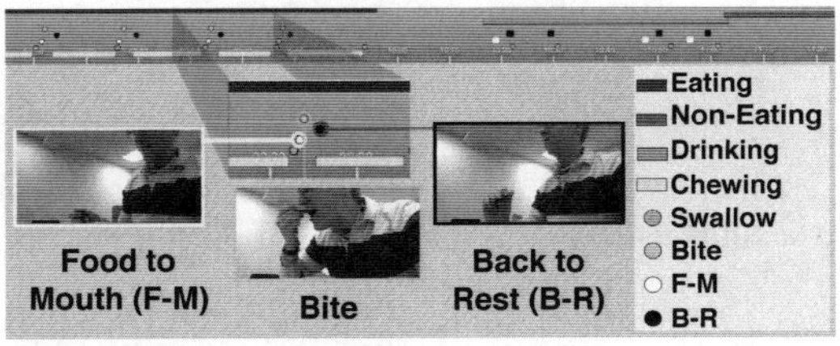

Figure 2: Labeling data using Chronoviz to enable the detection of feeding gestures.

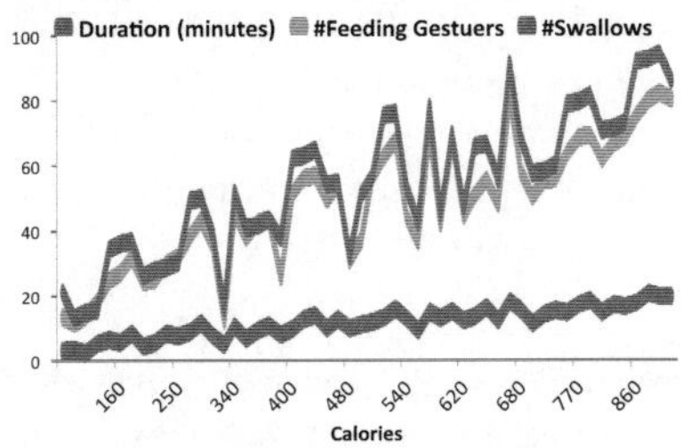

Figure 3: Relationship between Calories and feeding gestures, swallows, and eating duration for 54 foods consumed.

roscope, heart-rate, skin temperature, etc.) and their corresponding sample rates. The local database makes it possible to readily upload the data to a back end where the data is analyzed for in-the-wild studies.

One essential challenge was streaming data disconnecting from the Microsoft Band 2. As a result, a heart beat was added to the Android application that checks intended sensor connectivity every one minute, and reestablishes connectivity if necessary.

3.4 Features and Calories

While passive sensing cannot currently capture caloric overeating, determining how and when people eat still conveys information about increased caloric consumption. Despite the fact that a single bite of food can vary drastically in kilocalorie content, it is consistently true that the more someone puts into their mouth, the more kilocalories they are consuming. Figure 3 shows the average of hand-to-mouth gestures, swallows, and eating duration based on an average of all 15 participants, showing 54 combinations of foods (from Table 1 and 2). While the trend of the number of feeding gestures in a meal combination does dip around 340 kilocalories (that specific meal included the sandwich which did not require as many feeding gestures as other meals), the general trend is the number of feeding gestures linearly increasing with kilocalories. The Pearson product-moment is used to examine the association between kilocalories and each of number of feeding gestures, number of swallows, and eating duration (in minutes).

A significant association between Calories and each of feeding gestures ($r = .86, P < .0001$), swallows ($r = .87, P < .0001$), and eating duration ($r = .91, P < .0001$) was found.

4. MODEL DEVELOPMENT

In order to build a model that will be used to detect an intended outcome, data quality and reliability must be assessed and improved. Figure 4 presents this study's approach to developing a model that detects and characterizes moments of eating through feeding gestures, including algorithms that perform data preprocessing, segmentation, and classification, in order to build personalized and generalized models to count feeding gestures.

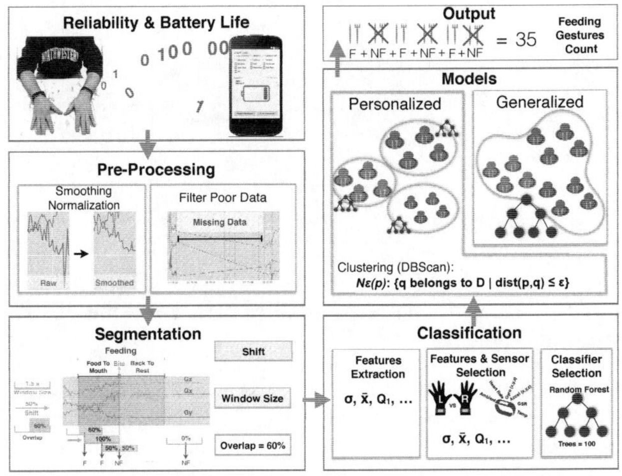

Figure 4: Framework for building a model that detects feeding gestures.

4.1 Data Preprocessing

Prior to processing the data, we analyze its reliability to ensure correct sample rate and negligible missing data. Tri-axial accelerometer and gyroscope data is collected at a sampling rate of 31Hz (or 31 samples per second, on average), a setting offered by the Microsoft Band 2.

The first step is to remove poor data from the training models. For one participant about 23 seconds of data was lost and excluded from our model training. The second step of data preprocessing is to ensure that the inertial signals' intended measurements were captured, primarily by smoothing to reduce noise and normalization. The premise of smoothing data is that one is measuring a variable that is both slowly varying and corrupted by random noise. Consequently replacing each data point with an average of surrounding points reduces the level of noise, while hopefully not biasing the values. To smooth the gyroscope and accelerometer data a rolling mean (*pandas.rolling_mean*) with a window size of 100 points (approximately 3 seconds, which we empirically set) is applied. Then the data is normalized to unit norm which can improve the accuracy of results when quantifying the similarity of signals across samples.

4.2 Segmentation

A feeding gesture is defined through two subfeeding moments: food-to-mouth, and back-to-rest. Figure 5 provides an illustration of each part of a gyroscope signal during a feeding gesture. Prior to processing values for three variables are set: 1) *window_size*; 2) overlap threshold (*overlap*); and 3) sliding window shift (*shift*). When processing the data a fixed time subdivision of the data is continuously analyzed in order to decide if it is a feeding gesture or not. *Window_size* is the fixed time subdivision of the signal (1.5 seconds in Figure 5), and the *shift* represents how fast the window is being slid; a 50% shift is shown in Figure 5, where the greater the percentage the faster the window is slid and the less overlap there is between consecutive data samples. The *overlap* is the threshold of overlap between the window and the true feeding gesture label that determines whether the segment is labeled as a feeding gesture or not.

When processing the data, however, as shown in Figure 5 a window is identified as a feeding gesture (as a 'F' in Figure 5) only if the window overlaps with the food-to-mouth segment or the back-to-rest segment more than the overlap threshold. For example, in Figure 5, since the overlap threshold is set to 60%, segment 3 will be

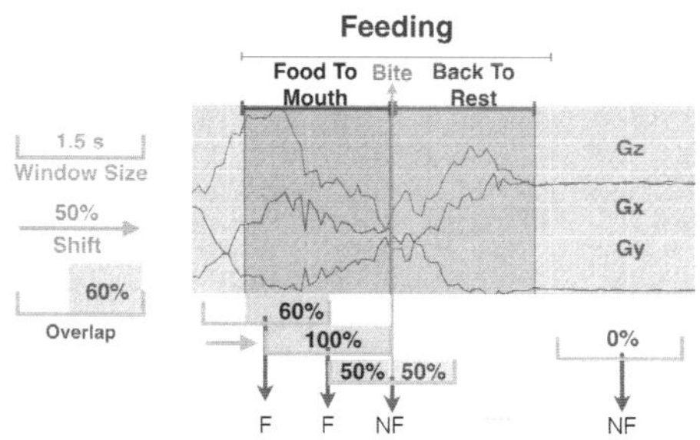

Figure 5: Segmentation process of Gyro data with window size, overlap and shift.

characterized as a non-feeding gesture. As a result, it will identify the bite section as a non-feeding gesture. This is important because some people spend a longer time biting, which might impede the detection of feeding gestures. Dynamic Time Warping (DTW) may be able to account for this problem [18] in detecting similarity between signals that vary in time.

4.3 Feature Extraction

Following data preprocessing of the raw signal, it is important to determine what features to collect on the raw signal that will be predictive of one's outcome. Due to the high variability across signals that represent the same activity, and to ensure that the system is capable of running in real-time, 11 statistical features are extracted on fixed time subdivisions of the data that are known to be useful in detecting activity [2] and eating [24], including: mean, median, max, min, standard deviation, kurtosis, interquartile range, quartile 1, quartile 3, skewness, and root mean square (RMS). Running each statistical feature on each axis of the inertial sensors generates 132 features, creating samples with 132 dimensions in the $\mathbb{R}^{132}$ feature space.

4.4 Fine-tuning Signal Processing Parameters

A subsequent step to preprocessing is fine-tuning the signal processing parameters. It is important to test whether a slow-moving fine-grained (small window size, small shift, and high overlap) or fast-moving coarse (large window size, large shift, and low overlap) segmentation of the data provides improvements in the analysis of feeding gestures. While several prior efforts in detecting feeding gestures overlook this important step, this can drastically impact the results of classification and can provide insight into the detection of feeding gestures. We tested window sizes ranging from 1 to 2.5 seconds, sliding window shifts from 30% to 70%, and signal overlap thresholds from 50% to 80%.

In order to test the performance of each signal processing parameter, data was used from the 13 right-handed participants and each participant's data was balanced into equal feeding and non-feeding gestures (total of 520 samples). Random Forest (with number of trees n=100) was used to build predictive models from the training set prior to testing [7].

Each parameter setting was tested using 10-fold Cross Validation (CV) and Leave One Subject Out Cross Validation (LOSOCV). To ensure stability 10-fold CV was run ten times using a different random seed and average results.

4.5 Selecting the Best Feature Subset

After identifying the optimal signal processing parameters, the dimensionality of the problem space is further reduced in order to identify the primary predictive features. To ensure there is no bias, feature selection is performed on a different dataset than the one

	Precision	Recall	F-measure
Avg	0.859	0.858	0.857
Std	0.041	0.042	0.042

Table 3: Results of the 67/33 train/test split on data of breakfast and lunch combined.

used to train the predictive models in order to prevent over-fitting of the training data, and then select the top six features. A filter-based chi-squared statistical method is used for feature selection to assign a score to each feature with respect to the outcome.

4.6 Selecting the Optimal Classifier

Once the optimal feature subset and signal processing algorithms are identified, a varied set of classification algorithms is tested in order to ensure selection of the optimal classifier. The tested algorithms include Logistic Regression (LogisticReg), AdaBoostClassifier (AdaBoost), C4.5 Decision Trees (DecisionTree), Gaussian Naive Bayes (GaussianNB), Linear Support Vector Classifier (LinearSVC), and Random Forest (RF) with n=100 trees. Both LOSOCV and 10-fold CV (averaged 10 times) were tested. The variability across the different runs was also calculated to ensure that not only was the classifier with the highest F-measure (harmonic mean of precision and recall) selected, but the one with the lowest variability (i.e. highest consistency) across the runs. This is essential to show the consistency of the classifiers when tested on different subjects or a different test set.

4.7 Personalization

It was desirable to test the effect of personalized models on the accuracy of detecting feeding gestures, compared to generalized models. As a result the breakfast and lunch were combined and a 67/33 split was performed between training and testing data. The results of a purely personalized model are tested on each participant and F-measure, precision, and recall are reported.

4.8 Clustering to Detect Feeding Gestures

When detecting feeding gestures, it is important to perform post-processing of the data, in order to cluster feeding gestures. Since there is overlap between window sizes, and because some feeding gestures are longer than others, it is important to identify small clusters of feeding gestures, and filter any isolated feeding gestures. Density-based spatial clustering of applications with noise (DBSCAN) is applied to group together the samples that are close together (high density), while marking as outliers the points that are lower density. A range of values is tested for the two parameters used by the DBSCAN algorithm: 1) ε is used to create an neighborhood of points to assess whether a cluster is worthy of being formed (a range from 2-4 is tested), and 2) *minPts* is used to calculate the minimum number of points required to form a dense region (a range from 1-3 is tested).

5. RESULTS

5.1 Fine-tuning Signal Processing Parameters

The average feeding gesture in the training set used was about 2.8 seconds. However, when looking purely at the LOSOCV (Figure 6) the results seem like there are several optimal parameter combinations (the blue regions have the highest F-measure). However, a very important feature in analyzing performance is variability across the different runs. Thus the optimal results from 10-fold CV (Figure 7) and LOSOCV are combined, and then the results that exhibited

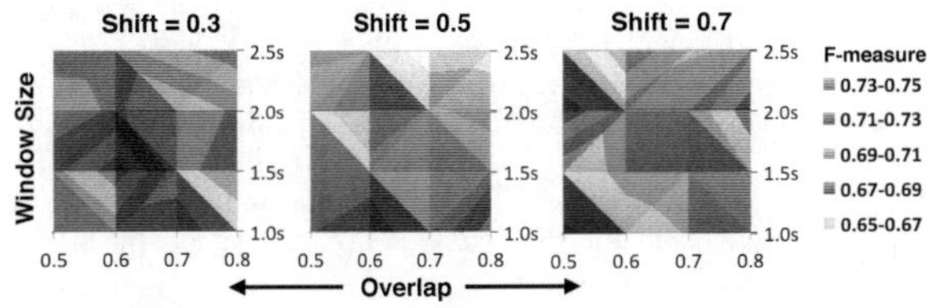

Figure 6: LOSOCV results varying signal processing parameters.

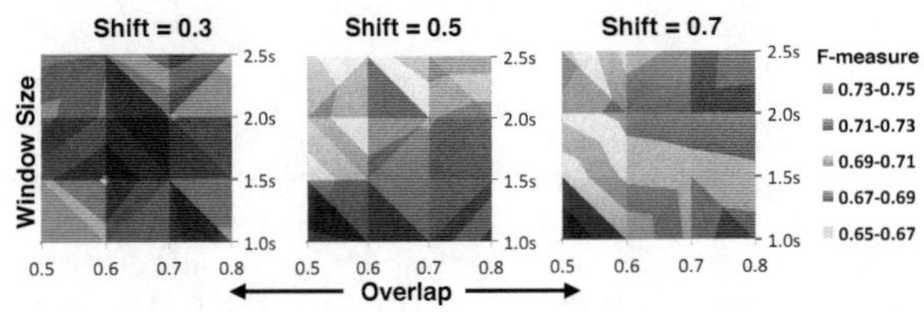

Figure 7: 10FCV results varying signal processing parameters.

the lowest variability, or highest consistency in performance across the test set, are selected.

Two parameters were discovered to yield optimal results (both high F-measure and low variability). One combination represents a slow fine-grained approach (window size = 1.0sec, overlap = 0.8, and shift = 0.3) and resulted in LOSOCV F-measure = 0.746 and variance = 0.008, and the other is more of a fast, coarse-grained approach (window size = 1.5 sec, overlap = 0.7, and shift = 0.5) and resulted in LOSOCV F-measure = 0.732, and variance = 0.02. The slow, fine-grained approach identified feeding gestures with the following pattern "FFNFF" or "FFNNFF," where the bite in the middle of the gesture was captured as a non-feeding gesture moment (N), and the food-to-mouth and back-to-rest were detected as feeding gestures (F).

5.2 Optimal Feature Subset

The top six features (*Gx_qurt*1, *Gx_mean*, *Gz_irq*, *Gx_stdev*, and *Gx_min*) that were selected involved the gyroscope z- and x-axes, which correspond to the pitch and roll, respectively. Figure 5 shows the gyroscope data (the rise in G_x and drop in G_z prior to the bite) of the individual eating yogurt with a spoon.

5.3 Selecting the Optimal Classifier

It was decided to test the predictive power of multiple classification algorithms to assess which classifier will outperform the other in detecting feeding gestures using the subset of features. The performance using LOSOCV was compared. It was found that while the AdaBoost classifier outperforms other classifiers in LOSOCV with an F-measure of 75.7%, the Random Forest Classifier outperforms all algorithms in 10-fold CV with an F-measure of 75.2% and produces a comparable F-measure of 75.3% in LOSOCV (See Figure 8). The interesting factor arises in the fact that LOSOCV often outperforms 10-fold CV (averaged 10 times), which shows that the within-subject variability may be so high that even when the training data contains test-subject data, it remains challenging to predict feeding gestures.

5.4 Personalization

As a result of the large within-subject variability experienced within each subject, the logical next step was seen as building models based purely on each participant's data. This experiment would show the results of an individual exhaustively trained in an in-lab setting.

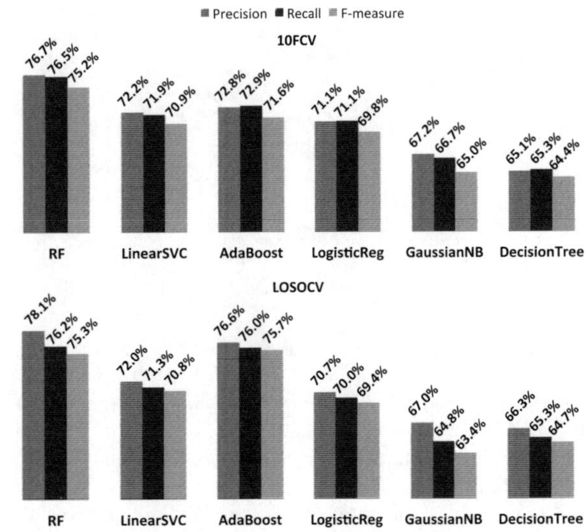

Figure 8: Optimal classifier selection.

We see that the results of a 67/33 split of train/test data yields high recall and F-measure as shown in Table 3. Subject 8 seems the most consistent in her eating pattern, and subject 14 seems to exhibit the most variability in feeding gestures.

5.5 Clustering to Count Feeding Gestures

Without clustering we realized that our classification model would overestimate the number of feeding gestures. This could be a result of the overlap in the sliding window. As a result we felt that applying clustering algorithms would improve our feeding gesture count. By testing a range of ε and *minPts* values, however, we achieved poor feeding gesture count for a generalized model (RMSE = 30.2).

As a result, we tested a more personalized cluster model setting for each individual, where the model was trained on lunch data and tested on breakfast. The results for counting feeding gestures are presented in Figure 9, and show an RMSE of 8.43.

6. DISCUSSION

The results show promise in the potential to detect feeding gestures using wrist-worn sensors (the Microsoft Band 2). Challenges do exist with streaming multiple sensor data, but by adding a heart beat to reestablish connectivity a high reliability of data is ensured. While feeding gestures may not provide the granularity of caloric intake required to assess weight loss, it can provide an indicator of overeating, which can potentially be a trigger for intervention.

The results of this study show that statistical features surrounding gyroscope data are most informative, and further support prior research surrounding the effectiveness of pitch and roll in predicting feeding gestures [21, 10]. We also show that optimizing time-series segmentation parameters can provide further insight in improving the accuracy of feeding gestures. However, the effect of fine- and coarse-grained data analysis is shown to yield similar results. Nonetheless, personalizing segmentation parameters for each individual can still optimize the detection of feeding gestures.

The system studied shows promise in detecting feeding gestures despite several confounding factors that include talking on the phone, walking and playing with glasses. Thomaz et al. [24] show promise in designing a generalized eating detection algorithm that detects eating at a coarse level over 60-minute window sizes with an F-measure of 76.1%, however, being able to provide generalized fine-grained characterization of an eating episode remains a challenge.

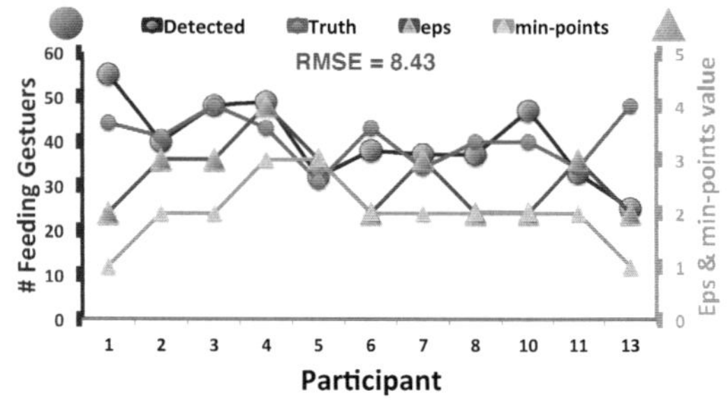

Figure 9: DBSCAN personalized clustering results.

This effort shows that within-subject variability is large and that testing a personalized model to detect feeding gestures for one individual over long periods of time will be a strong contribution to the study of eating habits and behavior.

The ultimate goal of this research is to predict problematic eating episodes. Prior to prediction, we are developing features that characterize these eating episodes in an attempt to predict them. Rahman et al. have started analyzing "about-to-eat" moments in order to trigger a just-in-time eating intervention, and attempt to estimate the time until the next eating event [20]. We hope to further expand on this effort and not only predict eating moments, but also predict problematic eating episodes.

7. CONCLUSION AND FUTURE WORK

These findings show the challenge and potential of detecting feeding gestures in a confounded eating setting. The results of a generalized and personalized model to detect feeding gestures is reported on in detail and show a significant correlation between caloric intake and feeding gestures (r=0.86). Also shown is that given the large within-subject variability in eating, a personalized machine learning and density-based clustering model can characterize eating episodes with feeding gestures with an RMSE of 8.4. To further assess our models, future testing assess whether the models used in this study will hold with participants in the wild. Future work will test different clustering methods, as well as the effect of different methods of coding feeding gestures. Moreover, combining wrist-worn sensors with other sensing modalities, such as neck-worn or ear-based sensors, has the potential to increase the accuracy of characterizing eating episodes.

8. ADDITIONAL AUTHORS

Additional authors: Angela F. Pfammatter (Northwestern University, email: angela@northwestern.edu).

9. REFERENCES

[1] N. Alshurafa, H. Kalantarian, M. Pourhomayoun, S. Sarin, J. Liu, Jason, and M. Sarrafzadeh. Non-invasive monitoring of eating behavior using spectrogram analysis in a wearable necklace. In *Healthcare Innovation Conference (HIC), 2014 IEEE*, pages 71–74, Oct 2014.

[2] N. Alshurafa, W. Xu, J. J. Liu, M.-C. Huang, B. Mortazavi, M. Sarrafzadeh, and C. Roberts. Robust human intensity-varying activity recognition using stochastic approximation in wearable sensors. In *2013 IEEE International Conference on Body Sensor Networks*, pages 1–6, May 2013.

[3] O. Amft, M. Stäger, P. Lukowicz, and G. Tröster. *Analysis of Chewing Sounds for Dietary Monitoring*, pages 56–72. UbiComp'05. Springer-Verlag, Berlin, Heidelberg, 2005.

[4] O. Amft and G. Träster. On-body sensing solutions for automatic dietary monitoring. *IEEE Pervasive Computing*, 8(2):62–70, 2009.

[5] A. Bedri, A. Verlekar, E. Thomaz, V. Avva, and T. Starner. A wearable system for detecting eating activities with proximity sensors in the outer ear. In *Proc. of the 2015 ACM Int. Symposium on Wearable Computers*, ISWC '15, pages 91–92, New York, NY, USA, 2015. ACM.

[6] P. Bongers, A. Jansen, R. Havermans, A. Roefs, and C. Nederkoorn. Happy eating: The underestimated role of overeating in a positive mood. *Appetite*, 67:74–80, 2013.

[7] L. Breiman. Random forests. *Machine Learning*, 45(1):5–32, 2001.

[8] J. Cools, D. E. Schotte, and R. J. McNally. Emotional arousal and overeating in restrained eaters. 101(2):348–351, 1992.

[9] Y. Dong, A. Hoover, and E. Muth. A device for detecting and counting bites of food taken by a person during eating. In *Proc. of the 2009 IEEE Int. Conf. on Bioinformatics and Biomedicine*, pages 265–268. IEEE, 2009.

[10] Y. Dong, A. Hoover, J. Scisco, and E. R. Muth. A new method for measuring meal intake in humans via automated wrist motion tracking. *Applied Psychophysiology and Biofeedback*, 37(3):205–215, Sep 2012.

[11] Y. Dong, J. Scisco, M. Wilson, E. R. Muth, and A. Hoover. Detecting periods of eating during free-living by tracking wrist motion. *IEEE Journal of Biomedical Health Informatics*, 18(4):1253–1260, Jul 2014.

[12] J. M. Fisher, N. Y. Hammerla, L. Rochester, P. Andras, and R. W. Walker. Body-Worn Sensors in Parkinson's Disease: Evaluating Their Acceptability to Patients. *Telemed J E Health*, 22(1):63–69, Jan 2016.

[13] A. Fouse, N. Weibel, E. Hutchins, and J. D. Hollan. Chronoviz: A system for supporting navigation of time-coded data. In *CHI '11 Extended Abstracts on Human Factors in Computing Systems*, CHI EA '11, pages 299–304, New York, NY, USA, 2011. ACM.

[14] A. B. Goldschmidt, M. Jones, J. L. Manwaring, K. H. Luce, M. I. Osborne, D. Cunning, K. L. Taylor, A. C. Doyle, D. E. Wilfley, and C. B. Taylor. The clinical significance of loss of control over eating in overweight adolescents. *International Journal of Eating Disorders*, 41(2):153–158, 2008.

[15] C. G. Greeno and R. R. Wing. Stress-induced eating. 115(3):444–464, 1994.

[16] C. Herman and J. Polivy. External cues in the control of food intake in humans: The sensory-normative distinction. *Physiology and Behavior*, 94(5):722–728, 2008.

[17] O. D. Lara and M. A. Labrador. A survey on human activity recognition using wearable sensors. *Communications Surveys & Tutorials, IEEE*, 15(3):1192–1209, 2013.

[18] M. Müller. Dynamic time warping. *Information retrieval for music and motion*, pages 69–84, 2007.

[19] A. Parate, M.-C. Chiu, C. Chadowitz, D. Ganesan, and E. Kalogerakis. Risq: Recognizing smoking gestures with inertial sensors on a wristband. In *Proc. of the 12th Annual Int. Conf. on Mobile Systems, Applications, and Services*, MobiSys '14, pages 149–161, New York, NY, USA, 2014. ACM.

[20] T. Rahman, M. Czerwinski, R. Gilad-Bachrach, and P. Johns. Predicting "about-to-eat" moments for just-in-time eating intervention. In *Proc. of the 6th Int. Conf. on Digital Health Conference*, DH '16, pages 141–150, New York, NY, USA, 2016. ACM.

[21] N. Saleheen, A. A. Ali, S. M. Hossain, H. Sarker, S. Chatterjee, B. Marlin, E. Ertin, M. al'Absi, and S. Kumar. puffmarker: A multi-sensor approach for pinpointing the timing of first lapse in smoking cessation. In *Proc. of the 2015 ACM Int. Joint Conf. on Pervasive and Ubiquitous Computing*, UbiComp '15, pages 999–1010, New York, NY, USA, 2015. ACM.

[22] E. Sazanov, P. Lopez-Meyer, and T. Stephen. A wearable sensor system for monitoring cigarette smoking. *Journal of Studies on Alcohol and Drugs*, 74(6):956–964, Nov 2013.

[23] M. Sun, L. E. Burke, Z.-H. Mao, Y. Chen, H.-C. Chen, Y. Bai, Y. Li, C. Li, and W. Jia. ebutton: A wearable computer for health monitoring and personal assistance. In *Proc. of the 51st Annual Design Automation Conf.*, DAC '14, pages 16:1–16:6. ACM, 2014.

[24] E. Thomaz, I. Essa, and G. D. Abowd. A practical approach for recognizing eating moments with wrist-mounted inertial sensing. In *Proc. of the 2015 ACM Int. Joint Conf. on Pervasive and Ubiquitous Computing*, UbiComp '15, pages 1029–1040, New York, NY, USA, 2015. ACM.

SWAN-Lake: Opportunistic Distributed Sensing for Android Smartphones

Nicolae Vladimir Bozdog
Vrije Universiteit Amsterdam
Amsterdam, The Netherlands
n.v.bozdog@vu.nl

Roshan Bharath Das
Vrije Universiteit Amsterdam
Amsterdam, The Netherlands
r.bharathdas@vu.nl

Aart van Halteren
Vrije Universiteit Amsterdam
Amsterdam, The Netherlands
a.t.van.halteren@vu.nl

Henri Bal
Vrije Universiteit Amsterdam
Amsterdam, The Netherlands
h.e.bal@vu.nl

ABSTRACT

Today, smart devices like mobile phones and fitness trackers have many sensors. Formatting, combining and querying sensor data from such devices can be a challenging and cumbersome task. In this paper we introduce SWAN-Lake, a distributed mobile framework that provides structured access to sensor data. SWAN-Lake provides access to local sensors as well as access to sensors of nearby devices. Here, we take a distributed approach by using device-to-device communication for exchanging sensor data between smartphones. We evaluate the performance and resource utilization using different sensing scenarios for our SWAN-Lake Android implementation. As a result, we show that our framework is energy efficient and performs well under high load.

CCS CONCEPTS

•Human-centered computing →Ubiquitous and mobile computing systems and tools; Smartphones;

KEYWORDS

Distributed sensing, ad-hoc data sharing, device-to-device communication, mobile computing, Internet of Things, Android

1 INTRODUCTION

The Internet of Things starts to become a reality. New mobile devices emerge, starting from fitness trackers to high-end smartphones. All these devices have in common the ability to sense the environment by means of a large variety of sensors. While fitness trackers are equipped with only few sensors that are required for tracking a particular activity, smartphones have plenty of sensors that allow them to perform complex activities. The simplest smartphone sensing applications use only one sensor to provide very specific functionality. For example, Shazam uses the microphone to identify a song being played and Pedometer uses the accelerometer to count the steps. While these applications are able to detect simple activities like walking or listening to music, they are not aware of the complete context of the user (e.g., walking in the park, while listening to music). To detect more complex scenarios, applications like Tasker [13], Trigger [14] and IFTTT [6] combine information from *many* sensors and from the internet to trigger user defined actions based on context. Still the ability of these applications to identify the context is limited by the given onboard sensors of the smartphone.

In this paper we investigate the possibility of sharing sensor data between nearby smartphones in order to enhance their sensing capabilities in the context of the Internet of Things. For example, a context-aware application could determine the waiting time at a bus stop, traffic light or supermarket by checking how long the phones of the people around have been staying still. To support this and other scenarios, we propose a framework for sharing sensor data between smartphones. Our framework, called SWAN-Lake, extends the work from [8] by adding support for building context-aware applications that not only use the sensors available on the smartphone, but also the sensors from nearby devices. SWAN-Lake exposes a simple API to developers and makes use of an intuitive language for defining context expressions. More specifically, our contributions are as follows:

- We introduce SWAN-Lake, which extends the SWAN framework [8] by adding support for sharing sensor data between close-by smartphones. In SWAN-Lake, we implement mechanisms for detection of nearby smartphones and sharing of sensor data with them over Bluetooth and WiFi links.
- We extend SWAN-song [11], the high-level language for defining context expressions in SWAN, in order to support sharing of sensor data between co-located devices.
- We evaluate SWAN-Lake under different sensing scenarios that use up to 7 remote sensors. Our measurements focus on the performance of the framework, energy efficiency and tolerance to failures.

The remaining of the paper is structured as follows: section 2 describes previous work that our research is based upon, the architecture of SWAN-Lake is explained in section 3 followed by evaluation results in section 4, section 5 presents a concise literature review, and section 6 concludes the paper.

2 BACKGROUND

In this section we describe briefly the SWAN framework [8], which we base our work upon. SWAN (Sensing With Android Nodes) is a framework for easily building context-aware applications for smartphones. SWAN acts as a middleware between applications and sensors. It focuses on helping application developers by providing a high-level abstraction for accessing the sensors. It also eliminates redundancy caused by multiple sensor-based applications running in parallel by providing a centralized solution for collecting and storing sensor data locally.

Multiple applications can interact with SWAN using its domain specific language called SWAN-song. The application registers a SWAN-song expression to SWAN, which evaluates the expression and sends back the result. As an example, the following expression gets the current light intensity:

```
self@light:lux{MAX,1000ms}
```

where `self` is the *location identifier* of the device, `light` is the sensor name, `lux` is the value path, `MAX` represents the history reduction mode and `1000ms` represents the history window. The expression computes the maximum among the values generated by the light sensor in the last 1000 milliseconds.

SWAN's architecture comprises all the components depicted in Fig. 1 except the Proximity Manager, which we introduce in SWAN-Lake. Applications can register SWAN-song expressions using the SWAN API. On registering an expression, the Expression Evaluation Engine invokes the Sensor Library in order to query the sensors used in expressions.

SWAN also supports sharing of sensed data with other devices. For this, it uses the Google Cloud Messaging (GCM) service to register context expressions remotely for evaluation. This method adds much overhead when the devices that are connecting are in proximity, in which case more efficient technologies like Bluetooth or WiFi Direct can be used. In the remaining of the paper we address this issue, by extending SWAN to support efficient collaborative sensing between co-located devices.

3 SWAN-LAKE FRAMEWORK

The main motivation behind SWAN-Lake is to create a tool that simplifies the development of context-aware applications by adding support for real-time sharing of sensor data with nearby smartphones.

3.1 Architecture

SWAN-Lake's architecture is shown in Fig. 1. There are two main changes compared to the original architecture of SWAN. First, we implement the Proximity Manager, which handles all the exchanges of sensor data with remote devices. Second, we enhance SWAN-song to allow registration of remote context expressions by using the *NEARBY* keyword as specifier for the location where the expression should be evaluated.

3.1.1 Remote expressions in SWAN-song. In SWAN-Lake, we extend the semantics of the *location identifier* from SWAN-song

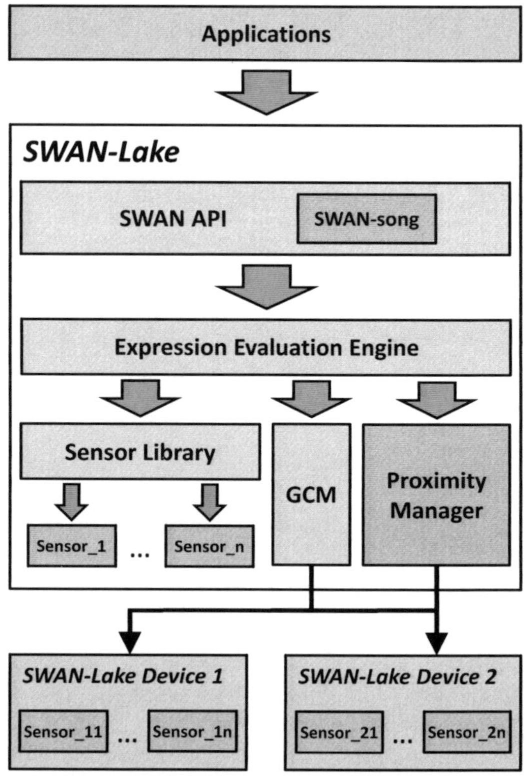

Figure 1: Architecture of SWAN-Lake

(see section 2) by allowing it to take as values a Bluetooth ID or the *NEARBY* keyword, like below:

```
bluetooth_ID@light:lux{MAX,1000ms}
NEARBY@light:lux{MAX,1000ms}
```

If a Bluetooth ID is used, then the Proximity Manager looks around for a device having that ID and, if found, it registers the expression to the remote device. Then, the remote device evaluates the expression and sends back the result.

If the *NEARBY* keyword is used, then the expression is sent to *all* nearby devices for evaluation (we will detail later how SWAN-Lake discovers nearby devices). Upon receiving the expression, all nearby devices register it in their instances of SWAN-Lake and, whenever the result of the expression changes, it is sent back to the device that issued the expression. This process continues until either the expression is unregistered by the device that issued it, or the latter moves out of range.

3.1.2 The Proximity Manager. The Proximity Manager (Fig. 2) handles the registration of remote context expressions, discovery of the nearby SWAN-Lake enabled devices and exchange of sensor data with them. The communication with the rest of the SWAN-Lake components is done through the Expression Evaluation Engine, to which it exposes an API with two methods:

```
registerExpression(exprId, exprBody, deviceId);
unRegisterExpression(exprId);
```

The first method is used to register a context expression written in the SWAN-song language with one device, if `deviceId` is a

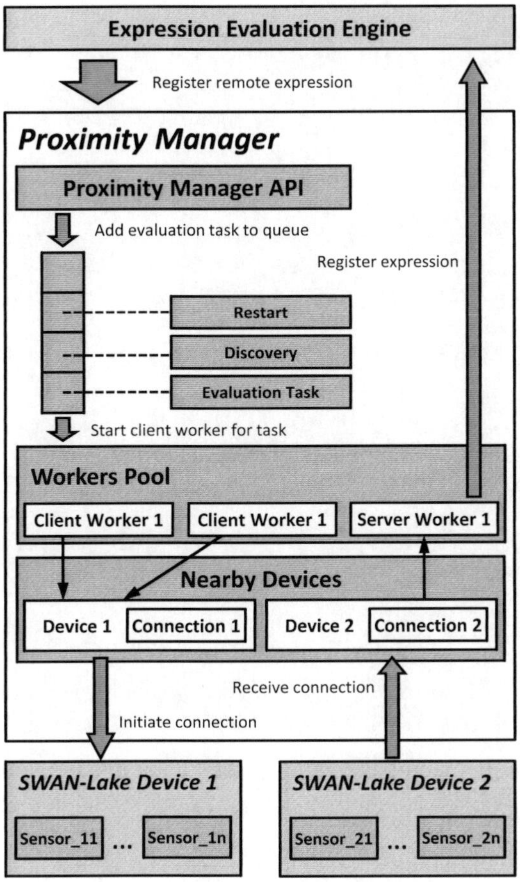

Figure 2: The Proximity Manager

Bluetooth device ID, or with all nearby devices, if `deviceId` is set to *NEARBY*. The other two parameters denote an unique ID for the expression (`exprId`) and the expression body (`exprBody`), which is the part after @ in the example we gave earlier. If an expression is registered with a specific Bluetooth device, a new *evaluation task* is created for that device and introduced in the processing queue. Otherwise, if the expression is registered with all nearby devices, a new task is created for each device detected in proximity and added to the queue.

The purpose of the processing queue is to synchronize different types of tasks that cannot happen at the same time. Besides evaluation tasks, whose purpose is to register expressions to other devices, there are also *restart tasks* that restart the Bluetooth adapter in case of failures and *discovery tasks*, which trigger a Bluetooth discovery session of the close-by devices. Each time a new device is found, it is added in the *Nearby Devices* list. To differentiate between SWAN-Lake devices and other Bluetooth devices, our framework alters the Bluetooth ID of the smartphone by appending "swan" at the end of it followed by a unique ID. These three types of tasks cannot happen in parallel because evaluation tasks imply the opening of Bluetooth connections, which cannot happen while the adapter is restarting or discovering. Also, we do not want to restart the adapter while discovery is taking place. While restart tasks are scheduled only in the presence of failures, discovery tasks are scheduled periodically, with a frequency depending on how loaded the Proximity Manager is.

3.2 Operation Modes

SWAN-Lake supports two operation modes: *opportunistic* and *connected.* While the opportunistic mode is suitable for large loosely connected groups of devices (e.g., random people in a supermarket exchanging data about waiting times at checkout queues), the connected mode is better for small groups of devices that are strongly connected (e.g., people in a house playing a multiplayer game). Below we explain how they work.

3.2.1 Opportunistic mode. When working in opportunistic mode, a SWAN-Lake enabled smartphone should be able to share data efficiently with surrounding devices regardless of their number or their mobility. This is difficult to attain, given that Bluetooth supports at most 7 concurrent connections. To overcome this, we close connections with remote devices as soon as the sharing of sensor data ends to make room for other connections. Also, to reduce the overhead of opening and closing connections, we group requests for the same remote device on the same connection.

Another limitation of Bluetooth that we discovered in our tests is that if two Android smartphones try to connect to each other at the same time, the connection attempts might block indefinitely. Since this is very likely to happen when operating in *opportunistic mode*, we fixed this issue by alternating connections between each pair of devices in a group.

3.2.2 Connected mode. When running in connected mode, SWAN-Lake enabled smartphones are supposed to efficiently stream sensor data over long lived connections that are less affected by churn. To support this scenario, we implement a mechanism for caching connections in SWAN-Lake. Connection caching is done by keeping connections open even if no worker thread is using them, as opposed to the opportunistic mode, where unused connections are closed. This way, if a new context expression is registered, a cached connection can be used immediately without having to wait for a new connection to be established.

4 EVALUATION

We implemented SWAN-Lake as a library for Android. In our implementation we used Bluetooth for communication between nearby smartphones when operating in *opportunistic mode* and both Bluetooth and WiFi for the *connected mode.* In the experiments with WiFi we connected all phones to a local area network. We also considered WiFi Direct [4] and Bluetooth Low Energy (BLE) as alternatives, but were hindered by various limitations. In the case of WiFi Direct, the main problem is that it requires *manual* pairing between devices, while in the case of BLE only high-end smartphones have the capability of advertising their presence. Therefore, we currently use standard Bluetooth, which is supported by most smartphones and does not require manual pairing [1].

[1]Although standard Bluetooth is mostly used by manually pairing devices, the Bluetooth Android API also offers the option to connect smartphones without pairing them first.

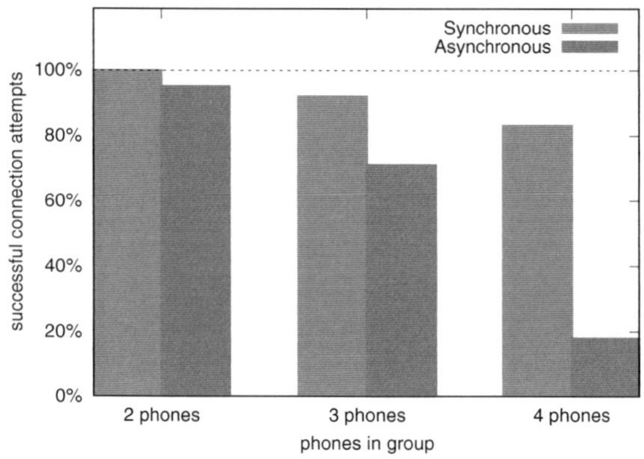

Figure 3: Success rate of connection attempts

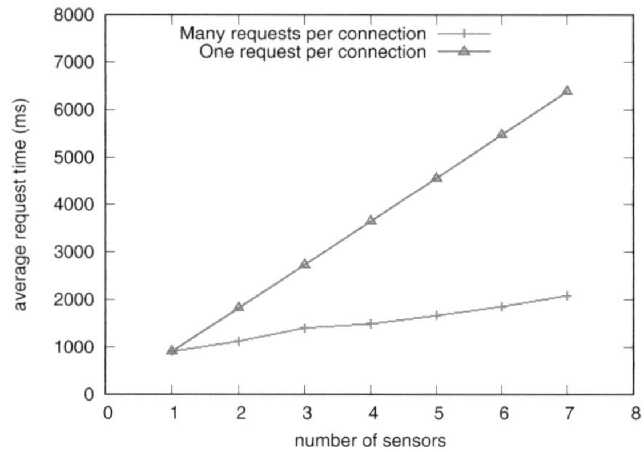

Figure 4: Average total time spent per request

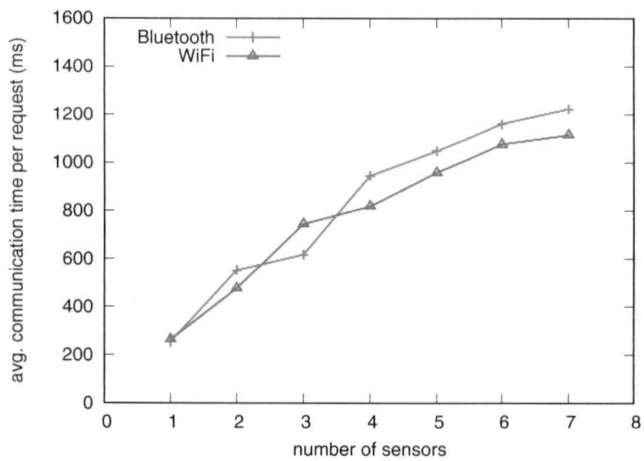

Figure 5: Average communication time spent per request

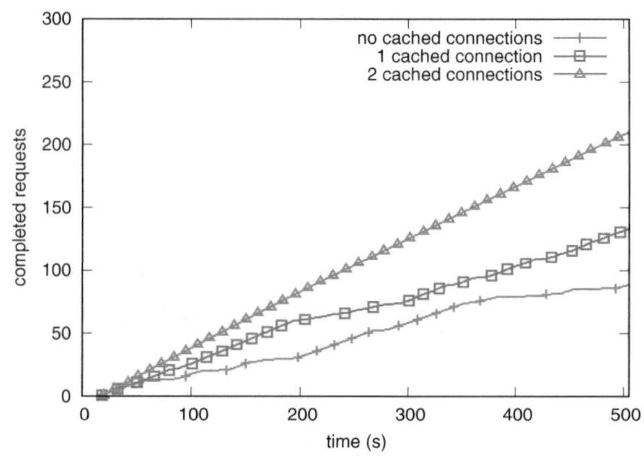

Figure 6: Number of completed requests for different numbers of cached connections

We used 4 phones in our measurements: Huawei Nexus 6P, LG Nexus 5 and two Motorola Moto G 4G. We ran experiments with 2, 3 or 4 phones. In every experiment, each phone requests data from N remote sensors on all the other phones in the group, where N ranges between 1 and 7. The requests are done by registering *NEARBY* expressions (see section 3.1.1) in a round-robin fashion to all phones in the group with a sample interval of one second between them. In all experiments we kept the screens of the phones on, except for those that measured the energy consumption. We used the following sensors in the tests: light sensor, accelerometer, gyroscope, magnetometer, battery level sensor, proximity and microphone. All these sensors are present in all the test phones.

4.1 Performance

4.1.1 Connection attempts. We start by looking at the number of successful connection attempts during 5 minutes experiments (Fig. 3) with groups of 2, 3 and 4 phones. In these experiments, each phone attempts to connect to the other phones in the group in a round-robin fashion (as needed by the *NEARBY* construct). If a connection fails, the initiator moves to the next phone in the group. We note here that SWAN-Lake handles connection failures gracefully, so they will not crash the system or slow down other tasks. The percentage of successful connection attempts is computed out of the total number of connection attempts to all phones in the group for the whole duration of the experiment. We explained in section 3.2 that alternating connections between Android smartphones can increase the chances of connection attempts to be successful. Therefore, in this experiment we compare the cases when connections between devices are alternating (synchronous) or not (asynchronous). As can be seen, the percentage of successful attempts drops steeply with the number of collaborating phones when connections do not alternate. When the optimization is used, the rate of failed attempts is reduced with up to 65%. Still, the failure rate is not reduced to 0 even with the optimized version, most likely due to interference.

4.1.2 Processing time. In SWAN-Lake we minimize the request processing time by grouping requests for many sensors on the same connection (see section 3.2). Hence, in Fig. 4 we compare the average request processing times achieved by the optimized version against those obtained if each request was made on a separate connection. We estimate the latter by multiplying the average processing time for one sensor with the number of sensors used. In

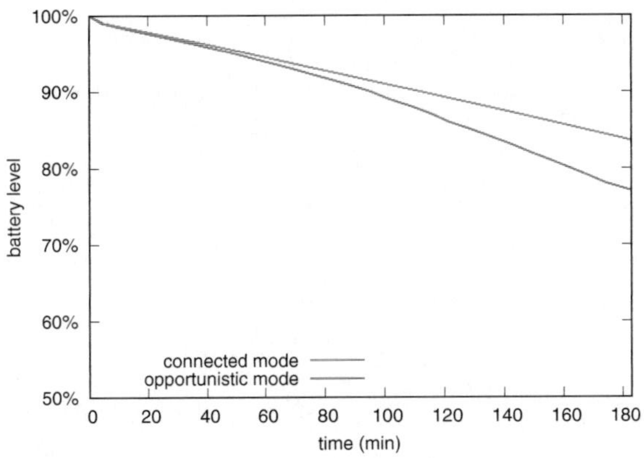

Figure 7: Battery usage for the two operation modes

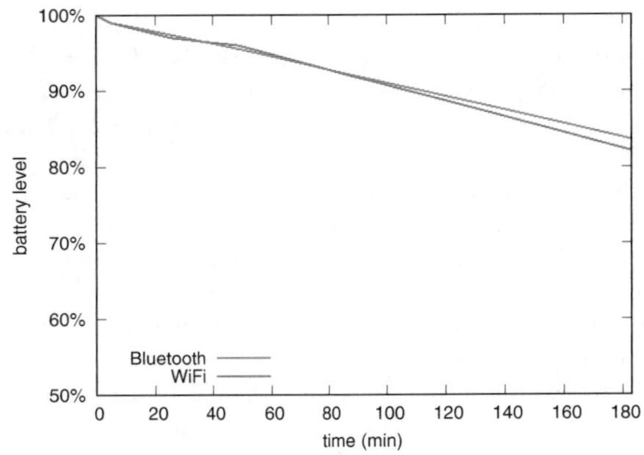

Figure 8: Battery usage for Bluetooth and WiFi in connected mode

this experiment we had a group of 3 phones collaborating in opportunistic mode. As we can see, the optimized version is performing much better regardless of the number of sensors used.

4.1.3 Communication time. In the next experiment we study how Bluetooth and WiFi work for a group of 3 phones exchanging sensor data in *connected mode* (Fig. 5). The results show that with both techniques our framework performs reasonably well, with a small advantage for WiFi when more than 3 sensors are queried. Each additional sensor adds approximately 160 ms for Bluetooth and 140 ms for WiFi, which are close to the communication overhead when operating in opportunistic mode. Therefore, we can conclude that the latency of the communication protocol influences the performance of the framework.

4.1.4 Cached connections. SWAN-Lake uses cached connections in order to reduce communication time (see section 3.2). In the next experiment we keep the same setup as in the previous one and analyze how the number of successful requests in a fixed time interval is affected by the number of cached connections (Fig. 6). As we can see, for every point in time, the number of requests completed by that moment increases with the number of cached connections.

4.2 Resource Usage

In this section we examine several scenarios that highlight the resource utilization of SWAN-Lake. All the experiments presented in this section were done under stress conditions, therefore the results presented here represent an upper limit of the SWAN-Lake's resource utilization.

We start by looking at the energy consumption of our framework when operating in opportunistic and connected modes (Fig. 7). In this experiment we let 2 phones exchange sensor data over Bluetooth continuously for 3 hours. All the 7 available sensors were used. As the figure shows, there is a clear difference in favor of running the framework in connected mode. This is expected, as in opportunistic mode the two phones keep connecting and disconnecting from each other for each request, which causes the Bluetooth adapters of the phones to consume more energy.

Next, let us see which of Bluetooth and WiFi performs better when operating in connected mode. As Fig. 8 shows, at first sight they are both almost equally good, with Bluetooth saving 2% of the battery. However, for the 3 hours of the experiment there were only 2686 requests completed over WiFi compared to 2844 requests completed over Bluetooth. We determined that this behavior was due to the fact that the WiFi adapter goes into a low-power state if the screen is inactive, as opposed to the Bluetooth adapter, which operates at full potential all the time.

Finally, we looked at the CPU load and memory usage. In our tests the CPU load did not exceed 11% and the memory usage did not go beyond 20 MB regardless of the number of queried sensors. These values are normal given the high number of sensors used and the high frequency of the readings. The Mosden sensing framework [12], which is the closest work related to ours, uses up to 20% of the CPU and 23 MB of memory in similar usage conditions.

5 RELATED WORK

Mosden [7, 12] is a platform that enables collaborative processing of sensor data. It extends GSN [1], a middleware for processing sensor data in the cloud, by adapting it to run on resource constrained mobile devices. Mosden and SWAN-Lake are similar, as they both follow a distributed architecture in which mobile devices can perform sensing tasks collaboratively. Unlike SWAN-Lake, Mosden does not allow for sharing of sensor data with anonymous nearby devices.

Sharing of mobile data over D2D links has already been proven useful for context computation offloading [3] and group activity recognition [2]. Also, emerging protocols like Zigbee [9] or Z-Wave [5] offer new opportunities for applications relying on ad-hoc sharing of data.

When it comes to commercial solutions, most of them are focused on storing and analyzing data collected by the Internet of Things [10]. To our knowledge, the only commercial tool for collaboratively sensing in proximity is Google Nearby, which uses a combination of short range communication techniques and cloud services to connect Android smartphones with nearby services.

6 CONCLUSIONS

In this paper we introduced and evaluated SWAN-Lake, a framework for building collaborative mobile sensing applications. Our framework leverages sharing of sensor data within groups of colocated devices in order to improve the accuracy of context detection in smartphone applications. We tested SWAN-Lake under various sensing scenarios on a small group of devices. Our measurements showed that our framework performs well under stress conditions and has low resource consumption.

As future work, we intend to make SWAN-Lake more customizable in terms of privacy, by extending SWAN-song to support various privacy directives. These directives should give users control about which other phones to trust or not (based on contact lists, location, etc.). Also, different privacy settings could be used for sensitive sensors (e.g., the user's heartbeat level) and less sensitive ones (e.g., ambient noise). To prevent the interception of sensitive data by third-parties, we consider encrypting sensor data that is being shared. Finally, we plan to study the performance of our framework for groups of phones with high mobility. To this end, we aim to incorporate SWAN-Lake in a crowdsensing application and test it during an event with a large number of participants.

ACKNOWLEDGEMENTS

This publication was supported by the Dutch national program COMMIT/. We thank Marc Makkes for his comments that greatly improved the manuscript. We are also grateful to the anonymous reviewers for their useful insights.

REFERENCES

[1] Karl Aberer, Manfred Hauswirth, and Ali Salehi. 2007. Infrastructure for data processing in large-scale interconnected sensor networks. In *2007 Int. Conf. on Mobile Data Management*. IEEE, 198–205.

[2] Amin B Abkenar, Seng W Loke, Wenny Rahayu, and Arkady Zaslavsky. 2016. Energy Considerations for Continuous Group Activity Recognition Using Mobile Devices: The Case of GroupSense. In *2016 IEEE 30th International Conference on Advanced Information Networking and Applications (AINA)*. IEEE, 479–486.

[3] Khaled Alanezi, Xinyang Zhou, Lijun Chen, and Shivakant Mishra. 2015. Panorama: A Framework to Support Collaborative Context Monitoring on Co-located Mobile Devices. In *Int. Conf. on Mobile Computing, Applications, and Services*. Springer, 143–160.

[4] Daniel Camps-Mur, Andres Garcia-Saavedra, and Pablo Serrano. 2013. Device-to-device communications with Wi-Fi Direct: overview and experimentation. *IEEE wireless communications* 20, 3 (2013), 96–104.

[5] Carles Gomez and Josep Paradells. 2010. Wireless home automation networks: A survey of architectures and technologies. *IEEE Communications Magazine* 48, 6 (2010), 92–101.

[6] IFTTT. 2016. https://ifttt.com. (2016). Accessed: 2016-11-16.

[7] Prem Prakash Jayaraman, Charith Perera, Dimitrios Georgakopoulos, and Arkady Zaslavsky. 2013. Efficient opportunistic sensing using mobile collaborative platform mosden. In *Collaborative Computing: Networking, Applications and Worksharing, 2013 9th Int. Conf. on*. IEEE, 77–86.

[8] Roelof Kemp. 2014. *Programming Frameworks for Distributed Smartphone Computing*. Ph.D. Dissertation. Vrije Universiteit, Amsterdam.

[9] Patrick Kinney and others. 2003. Zigbee technology: Wireless control that simply works. In *Communications design conference*, Vol. 2. 1–7.

[10] Julien Mineraud, Oleksiy Mazhelis, Xiang Su, and Sasu Tarkoma. 2015. Contemporary Internet of Things platforms. *arXiv preprint arXiv:1501.07438* (2015).

[11] Nicholas Palmer, Roelof Kemp, Thilo Kielmann, and Henri Bal. 2012. SWAN-song: a flexible context expression language for smartphones. In *Proceedings of the Third International Workshop on Sensing Applications on Mobile Phones*. ACM, 12.

[12] Charith Perera, Prem Prakash Jayaraman, Arkady Zaslavsky, Peter Christen, and Dimitrios Georgakopoulos. 2014. Mosden: An internet of things middleware for resource constrained mobile devices. In *2014 47th Hawaii International Conference on System Sciences*. IEEE, 1053–1062.

[13] Tasker. 2016. http://tasker.dinglisch.net. (2016). Accessed: 2016-11-16.

[14] Trigger. 2016. http://gettrigger.com. (2016). Accessed: 2016-11-16.

SmartNecklace: Designing a Wearable Multi-sensor System for Smart Eating Detection

Eli Cohen
Northwestern University
Chicago, IL 60611
ecohen@u.northwestern.edu

William Stogin
Northwestern University
Chicago, IL 60611
wstogin@u.northwestern.edu

Haik Kalantarian
UCLA
Los Angeles, CA 90095
kalantarian@ucla.edu

Angela F. Pfammatter
Northwestern University
Chicago, IL 60611
angela@northwestern.edu

Bonnie Spring
Northwestern University
Chicago, IL 60611
bspring@northwestern.edu

Nabil Alshurafa
Northwestern University
Chicago, IL 60611
nabil@northwestern.edu

ABSTRACT

Characterizing eating behaviors to inform and prevent obesity requires nutritionists, behaviorists and interventionists to disrupt subjects' routine with questionnaires and unfamiliar eating environments. Such a disruption may be necessary as a means of self-reflection, however, prevents researchers from capturing problematic eating behaviors in a free-living environment. An automated system alleviates many of these disruptions; however, success in automating sensing of eating habits has proven to be a challenge due to high within-subject variability in people's eating habits. Given a positive correlation between eating duration and caloric intake, along with the fact that many problematic eaters spend time alone, this paper presents a passive sensing system designed with the following three goals: detecting eating episodes through data analytics of passive sensors, detecting time spent alone while eating, and designing a passive sensing system that people will adhere to wearing in the field, without disrupting regular activity or behavior. A real-time coarse multi-layered classification approach is proposed to detect challenging eating episodes with confounding factors using data from piezoelectric, audio, and inertial sensors. The system was tested on 7 participants with 14 eating episodes, resulting in an 80.8%, and 91.3% average F-measure for detection of eating and alone time, respectively. Additionally, results of a survey highlights the importance of user-customization to increase adherence to neck-worn sensors.

CCS Concepts

•Applied computing → Consumer health; Health informatics; •Hardware → Wireless devices;

Permission to make digital or hard copies of all or part of this work for personal or classroom use is granted without fee provided that copies are not made or distributed for profit or commercial advantage and that copies bear this notice and the full citation on the first page. Copyrights for components of this work owned by others than ACM must be honored. Abstracting with credit is permitted. To copy otherwise, or republish, to post on servers or to redistribute to lists, requires prior specific permission and/or a fee. Request permissions from permissions@acm.org.

Keywords

wearables, passive sensing, eating detection, alone, piezoelectric sensor, audio, accelerometer, wireless

1. INTRODUCTION

The American Medical Association now considers obesity a disease that increases the risk of other chronic diseases [1]. A major contributing factor to obesity is excess caloric intake, the imbalance between calories consumed and calories burned. Steps toward automated ingestion detection are being made to detect eating episodes in hopes of defining problematic eating, identifying its antecedents and ultimately predicting and preventing problematic eating episodes and habits. In the 21st century, the traditional family sit-down dinner setting is rapidly giving way to people eating alone while performing other activities, such as making/accepting phone calls, watching television, or responding to email on a laptop. It has been observed that people who exhibit problematic eating may show patterns of long meals and time alone [7]. In this study participants exhibited a significant linear correlation (Figure 1) between eating duration and caloric intake. Steps toward automated ingestion detection are being made in hopes of defining problematic eating and ultimately predicting and preventing problematic eating episodes.

When people eat, the skin surrounding the neck vibrates and moves in unique ways as a result of chewing and activity within the mouth, and during swallowing, food is moved through the pharynx and into the esophagus, during which the larynx rises to guard food from going into our lungs [9]. In this work a customized (using a 3-D printed casing) neck-worn sensor system is presented and shown in Figure 2 to detect such unique motion to identify eating episodes in company and alone.

In prior work [2], spectrogram-based features were used to detect swallows from a piezoelectric vibration sensor around the neck. One of the major challenges was removing artifacts due to non-eating motion (activity such as walking) and audio (conversation and talking); this design attempts to solve these problems (see Figure 2). The neck-worn device comprises a tri-axial accelerometer to remove motion artifacts, a microphone to remove talking and conversation effects and to determine whether or not the participant is alone, and a piezoelectric vibration sensor to detect neck-motion.

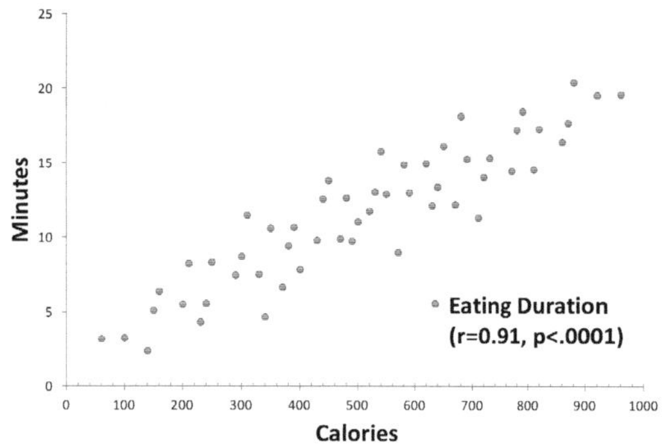

Figure 1: Correlation between eating duration and Calories

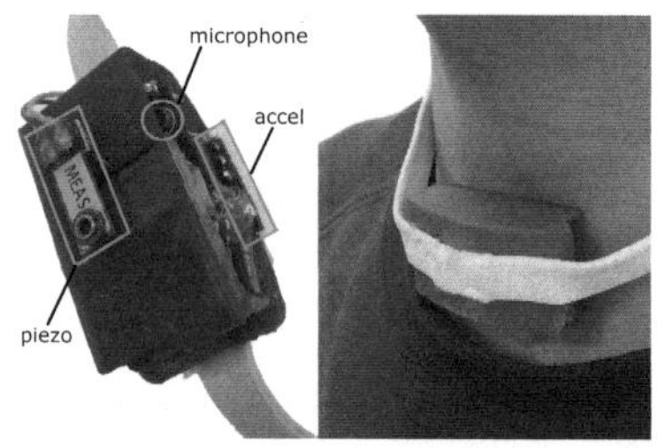

Figure 2: A microcontroller, inside a customizeable 3D-printed case, streams sensor data via Bluetooth

2. RELATED WORKS

Traditional diet assessment methods such as diaries, ecological momentary assessments (EMAs), and interviewer-assisted recalls have been used retrospectively to assess eating via self-report [8], but these self-reported methods often suffer from fatigue, non-adherence, social desirability bias, and recall failure [14]. To overcome these issues, research groups around the world have been focusing on developing automated methods to observe ingestive behavior in free living populations.

Many researchers have resorted to using audio [15, 3, 5] as the sensing mechanism, mounted either in the ear or on the throat to detect sounds produced by chewing and swallowing. Others have employed strain gauges [16], and piezoelectric [10, 2] and inertial [4] sensors to detect the unique motions made by the neck during eating sessions. Researchers have also assessed the feasibility of using proximity sensors in or around the ear to identify chews by the deformation of ear canal walls [6], or camera-based configurations to capture food through imaging [13].

This study aims to build on this related work with the following contributions:

- A neck-worn sensor system to detect activity, eating, and time alone.
- A personalized and generalized multi-layer classification model to detect eating episodes.
- A survey presenting the acceptability of personalized wearable devices.

3. EXPERIMENTAL SETUP

3.1 Sensor System

This system was designed to best emulate conditions in the wild. To reduce all obstacles for the user, the system is powered by a 250mAh lithium coin cell for extended battery life, and it transmits data wirelessly to a companion Android application. Additionally, the size of the device was carefully taken into account during the design process, so as to reduce obstruction of normal eating habits and decrease conspicuousness and discomfort caused by the device. To gather features for our multi-layer classifier, a microphone and piezoelectric sensor were integrated into a custom PCB board. The piezoelectric sensor was mounted with the end opposite the terminals resting just above the sternum, such that the unique motions of the neck while swallowing could be captured. The microphone was directly embedded into the board and the audio signal pre-processed with an on-board amplifying circuit before being recorded and transmitted. The tri-axial accelerometer embedded in the 3D-printed case outputs the orientation and acceleration in the x, y, and z directions, using a serial protocol instead of an analog voltage to communicate with a Bluetooth Low-Energy (BLE)-enabled RFduino microncontroller.

Data was collected by establishing a BLE connection with the mobile app and sampling the analog (piezo, audio) and digital (inertial) values at 100Hz, before transmitting and logging the data in CSV format to the smartphone's local storage. The system was tested for battery life and lasted more than 24 hours while streaming data, far longer than a standard smartphone's battery life; this prevents disruption in the most common charging cycle for users of mobile phones, which is to charge the devices overnight.

3.2 Eating Study

Seven participants (3 male and 4 female, with a mean age of 33 years) of varying BMIs were recruited to be the subjects of the in-lab study. Each participant attended two meal sessions on separate days, the first being a lunch session, and the second a breakfast session. In each session, the neck-worn device was placed around their necks, and they were instructed to follow a standardized protocol. The classification of the activities into Alone/Not Alone and Eating/Non-Eating are shown in Table 1. For the breakfast session participants drank tea and water and ate a cup of fruit, pancakes, and yogurt, interspersed with activities where they wore and adjusted their glasses, made a phone call, and had a conversation with someone in the room. During the lunch session they drank sparkling water and ate a sandwich, soup, and chips, and for non-eating activities typed on a keyboard and got up for a two-minute walk.

The entire meal was recorded using a Logitech C615 HD webcam, and the subjects were allowed to eat their fill. The caloric intake for each food item was known in advance based on food labels and was weighed after each meal to approximate caloric intake. Ground truth was labeled as eating (E), not-eating (NE), activity (A), not-activity (NA), alone (A) and not-alone (NA) time segments using Chronoviz [11]. Eating is defined as the time spent consuming food. When the participant speaks with someone, or when someone else is speaking with them, we identify that time as a not-alone segment. Finally, activity is defined by whether or not the participant is walking.

	Eating	Not Eating
Alone	Tea Water Fruit Pancakes Yogurt Sparkling Water Sandwich Soup Chips	Adjusted glasses Typing Walk
Not Alone		Phone call Conversation

Table 1: Classification of each activity into Alone/Not Alone and Eating/Non-Eating.

4. METHODS

4.1 Analysis

Prior to performing any machine learning analysis, a Savitzky-Golay convolution filter is applied to smooth each signal, and the data is normalized within each sensor to remove scale and translation effects (we subtract the signal by its mean and divide by standard deviation).

Samples are generated using a fixed-time subdivision of the data using a sliding window of 5, 10, and 30 seconds, with a 50% sliding window shift and a 60% overlap threshold; if greater than 60% of the window overlaps with ground truth of a certain class, then the whole window is labeled as that class.

Several statistical features shown in Table 2 are extracted from the windows generating a total of 70 features. Correlation based Feature Subset (CFS) selection was then applied to all features to select the optimal features. CFS determines the information gain of each subset of attributes by calculating the predictive power of each feature, subtracting its degree of redundancy [12]. Features that were highly correlated with the class label but have low inter-correlation were selected.

The following classifiers were chosen because they are known to be beneficial in detecting eating and talking and result in both generative and discriminative models: kNN, BayesNet, Random Forest (n=100 trees), C4.5 Decision Tree (DT), Logistic Regression(LR), and Adaptive Boosting (Adaboost).

Type	Feature
Average	Mean Median Root Mean Square
Quartiles	1st and 3rd Quartile Interquartile Range
Shape of distribution	Skew Kurtosis Standard Deviation
Extremes	Minimum Maximum Zero-crossing Rate

Table 2: Statistical features gathered from each sensor, for each window.

Because people can perform several types of activities at the same time, like walking, talking and eating, a multi-layer classification scheme (Figure 3) is tested to avoid the problem of non-eating activities interfering with eating detection. Activity is first filtered through RF1, then a separate eating/non-eating classifier (RF2) is applied when the participants are inactive, and an alone/not-alone detection classifier (RF3) is run independent of whether the subject is active or not. Since physical activity detection is shown to be reliable in detecting when participants are active vs. inactive, results focus on eating (RF2) and alone or not (RF3).

4.2 Evaluation

The classification algorithms were evaluated against ground truth from the recorded video of the subjects using Leave One Subject Out Cross Validation (LOSOCV), and a user-dependent model, where for each participant, the algorithms were trained on data from the lunch session and tested on data from the breakfast session. The metrics used include precision (positive predictive value), recall (sensitivity), and F-measure, which is the harmonic mean of precision and recall.

5. RESULTS

The results for testing multiple window sizes to detect eating and alone time are provided in Table 3. Based on these results, the window size of 30 seconds was selected for analysis.

Window (sec)	Eating (F-measure)	Alone (F-measure)
5	78.6%	63%
10	78%	58%
30	78.3%	75%

Table 3: LOSOCV Random Forest results for varying window sizes.

5.1 User-Independent Model

The results for the various user-independent classifiers used for alone/not-alone are shown in Figure 5 and for eating/not-eating are shown in Figure 4. The optimal classifier for detecting eating was the Random Forest (n=100 trees), yielding a 78.3% average F-measure, while Naive Bayes provided optimal results for detecting alone time, with a 77.7% average F-measure.

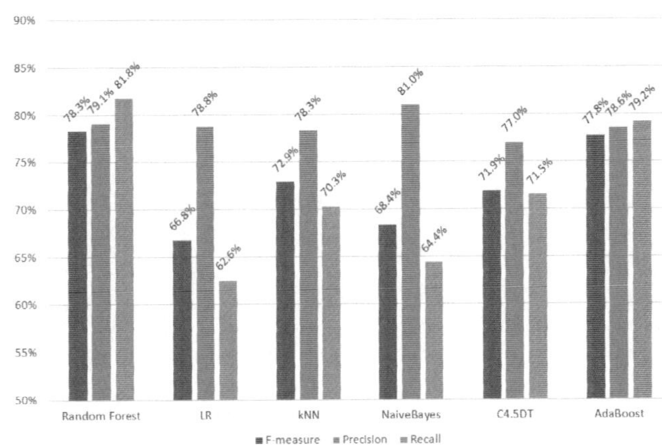

Figure 4: LOSOCV (User-independent) Results for Eating/Not Eating.

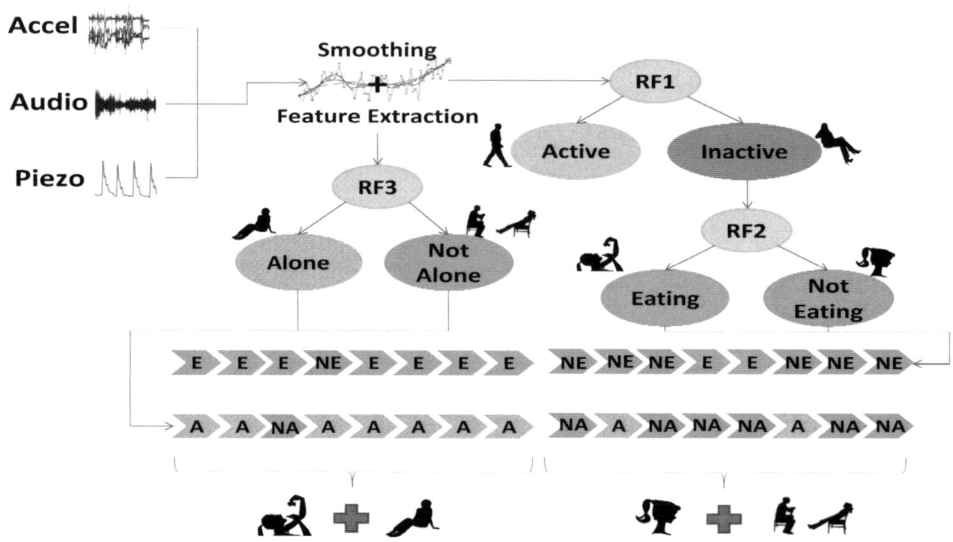

Figure 3: A multi-layer framework for detecting eating and alone time.

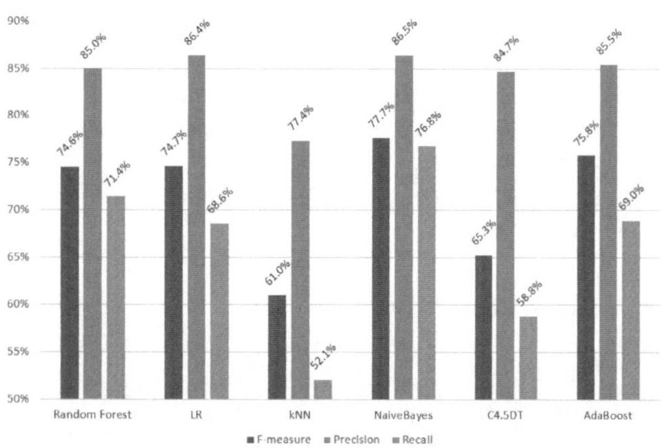

Figure 5: LOSOCV (User-independent) Results for Alone/Not Alone.

Random Forest	Eating	Alone
F-measure	80.8%	91.3%
Precision	79%	93.8%
Recall	86.5%	90.2%

Table 4: User-dependent Model Results

5.2 User-Dependent Model

The user-dependent model was developed by training on lunch and testing on breakfast. The optimal window size was 30 seconds, resulting in an optimal average F-measure of 80.8% and 91.3% for both eating and alone-time detection respectively using the Random Forest (n=100 trees) classifier.

5.3 Survey and Wearability

Unlike a smartphone or a smart watch, a neck-worn device

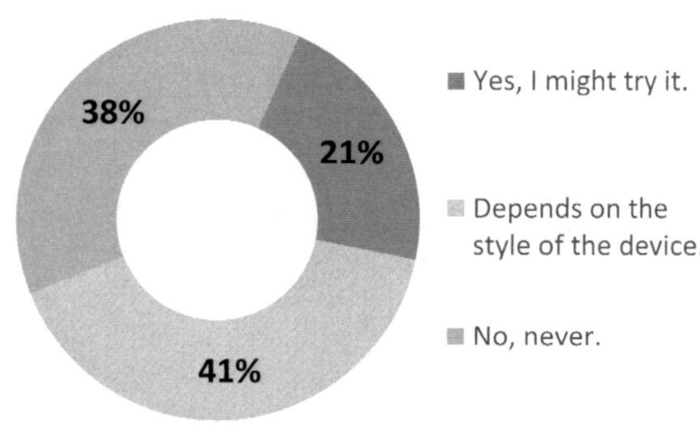

Figure 6: University students' responses to a survey about desirability of the neck-worn device

will be extremely visible with almost any outfit. Therefore, one that will be simultaneously attractive as well as relatively inconspicuous has the greatest appeal for potential users, and will be the most usable in the wild.

To gauge the general desirability of the device, 93 college undergraduate and graduate students were asked to answer a short 5-minute survey about the device. The survey included two simple yes-or-no questions: whether or not they would be willing to wear such a device during daily activity, and whether their willingness to do so would be affected by a one-time user customization of the device.

While the number of answers in favor of wearing and using the device regularly was relatively low at 21.5%, this amount reached 62.5% upon offering the possibility for a one-time user customization of the device. This agrees with existing trends, as user customization and personalization of technology-based products is rapidly becoming mainstream. For example, Motorola allows users to combine different materials and colors, and even add custom engravings before purchasing a smartphone, and Apple allows purchasers of an Apple Watch to choose their preferred casing size and material, as well as the material and color of the watch band.

6. CONCLUSION

A neck-worn passive sensing system was designed to gather data from multiple sensors with the ultimate goal of detecting periods of eating and alone-time, and a secondary goal of developing a low-distraction, inconspicuous device that users could adhere to in the wild. This system performed well when using a generalized model, trained across all subjects, to detect eating and alone-time with average F-measures of 78.3% and 77.7%, respectively.

The system actually improved when using a personalized model, trained and evaluated within a single subject, with an average F-measure of 80.8% and 91.3% in detecting eating and alone-time respectively. The potential for such a system to aid in detecting and characterizing problematic episodes can prove to be reliable if participants feel the device can be customized or fashionable, and as a result future efforts will look into enabling 3D-printing customization of the neck-worn sensor. In the future, this system will be evaluated across obese and overweight subjects, with a diverse range of activities, in a free-living environment.

7. REFERENCES

[1] D. B. Allison, M. Downey, R. L. Atkinson, C. J. Billington, G. A. Bray, R. H. Eckel, E. A. Finkelstein, M. D. Jensen, and A. Tremblay. Obesity as a disease: a white paper on evidence and arguments commissioned by the Council of the Obesity Society. *Obesity (Silver Spring)*, 16:1161–1177, 2008.

[2] N. Alshurafa, H. Kalantarian, M. Pourhomayoun, S. Sarin, J. J. Liu, and M. Sarrafzadeh. Non-invasive monitoring of eating behavior using spectrogram analysis in a wearable necklace. In *Healthcare Innovation Conference (HIC), 2014 IEEE*, pages 71–74, Oct 2014.

[3] O. Amft, M. Kusserow, and G. Troster. Bite Weight Prediction From Acoustic Recognition of Chewing. *IEEE Transactions on Biomedical Engineering*, 56(6):1663–1672, June 2009.

[4] O. Amft and G. Tr. On-body sensing solutions for automatic dietary monitoring. *IEEE Pervasive Computing*, 8(2):62–70, 2009.

[5] O. Amft and G. Troster. Methods for detection and classification of normal swallowing from muscle activation and sound. In *2006 Pervasive Health Conference and Workshops*, pages 1–10. IEEE, 2006.

[6] A. Bedri, A. Verlekar, E. Thomaz, V. Avva, and T. Starner. A wearable system for detecting eating activities with proximity sensors in the outer ear. In *Proceedings of the 2015 ACM International Symposium on Wearable Computers*. ACM, ACM, 2015.

[7] C. M. Bulik, K. A. Brownley, and J. R. Shapiro. Diagnosis and management of binge eating disorder. *World Psychiatry*, 6(3):142–148, Oct 2007.

[8] M. C. Carter, V. J. Burley, C. Nykjaer, and J. E. Cade. Adherence to a smartphone application for weight loss compared to website and paper diary: pilot randomized controlled trial. *J. Med. Internet Res.*, 15:e32, 2013.

[9] B. Essenfeld. Respiratory system. *The Gale Encyclopedia of Science*, 2004.

[10] M. Farooq and E. Sazonov. Comparative testing of piezoelectric and printed strain sensors in characterization of chewing. In *2015 37th Annual International Conference of the IEEE Engineering in Medicine and Biology Society (EMBC)*, pages 7538–7541, Aug. 2015.

[11] A. Fouse, N. Weibel, E. Hutchins, and J. D. Hollan. Chronoviz: a system for supporting navigation of time-coded data. In *CHI'11 Extended Abstracts on Human Factors in Computing Systems*, pages 299–304. ACM, 2011.

[12] M. A. Hall and L. A. Smith. Feature selection for machine learning: Comparing a correlation-based filter approach to the wrapper. In *Proceedings of the Twelfth International Florida Artificial Intelligence Research Society Conference*, pages 235–239, 1999.

[13] C. K. Martin, T. Nicklas, B. Gunturk, J. B. Correa, H. R. Allen, and C. Champagne. Measuring food intake with digital photography. *J Hum Nutr Diet*, 2014.

[14] S. Passler and W. Fischer. Acoustical method for objective food intake monitoring using a wearable sensor system. In *2011 5th International Conference on Pervasive Computing Technologies for Healthcare (PervasiveHealth)*, pages 266–269, May 2011.

[15] T. Rahman, A. T. Adams, M. Zhang, E. Cherry, B. Zhou, H. Peng, and T. Choudhury. Bodybeat: A mobile system for sensing non-speech body sounds. In *Proceedings of the 12th Annual International Conference on Mobile Systems, Applications, and Services*, pages 2–13, 2014.

[16] E. Sazonov, S. Schuckers, P. Lopez-Meyer, O. Makeyev, N. Sazonova, E. L. Melanson, and M. Neuman. Non-invasive monitoring of chewing and swallowing for objective quantification of ingestive behavior. *Physiol Meas*, 29(5):525–541, May 2008.

AUTHOR INDEX

AUTHOR INDEX